SIXTH EDITION

Theories of Counseling and Psychotherapy

A Multicultural Perspective

Allen E. Ivey
University of Massachusetts, Amherst
University of South Florida, Tampa

Michael D'Andrea
University of Hawai'i, Manoa

Mary Bradford Ivey
University of South Florida, Tampa
Microtraining Associates, Inc.

Lynn Simek-Morgan
Chamiade University, Honolulu, Hawai'i

PEARSON

Boston • New York • San Francisco
Mexico City • Montreal • Toronto • London • Madrid • Munich • Paris
Hong Kong • Singapore • Tokyo • Cape Town • Sydney

Executive Editor: Virginia Lanigan
Editorial Assistant: Matthew Buchholz
Senior Development Editor: Mary Kriener
Senior Marketing Manager: Kris Ellis-Levy
Production Editor: Gregory Erb
Editorial Production Service: Trinity Publishers Services
Composition Buyer: Linda Cox
Manufacturing Buyer: Linda Morris
Electronic Composition: Omegatype Typography, Inc.
Interior Design: Joyce Weston
Cover Designer: Linda Knowles

For related titles and support materials, visit our online catalog
at www.ablongman.com.

Between the time website information is gathered and then published, it is not unusual for
some sites to have closed. Also, the transcription of URLs can result in typographical
errors. The publisher would appreciate notification where these errors occur so that they
may be corrected in subsequent editions.

Library of Congress Cataloging-in-Publication Data

Theories of counseling and psychotherapy : a multicultural perspective / Allen E. Ivey . . .
[et al.].—6th ed.
    p.   cm.
  Includes bibliographical references (p.   ).
  ISBN 0-205-48225-2
  1. Psychotherapy. 2. Counseling. I. Ivey, Allen E.

  RC465.5.T474 2006
  616.89'14—dc22

2006050692

Printed in the United States of America

10 9 8 7 6 5 4 3 2 1 RRD-VA 10 09 08 07 06

Brief Contents

Contents

Chapter 8: Rational-Emotive Behavioral Therapy and Reality Therapy

Part Three: The Fourth Force in Counseling and Therapy: Multicultural and Feminist Perspectives   319

Chapter 13: Developmental Counseling and Therapy: Integrative Theory and Practice   402

Chapter 14: Family Counseling and Therapy: Theoretical Foundations and Issues of Practice   429

by Sandra Rigazio-DiGilio, University of Connecticut, Storrs

Chapter 15: Identifying Your Own Integrated Approach to Counseling and Therapy

Special Features Contents

Preface

We are very excited about this newly revised edition of *Theories of Counseling and Psychotherapy: A Multicultural Perspective.* Our mission in writing this book has always been to provide future counselors and therapists with a solid foundation in the theoretical concepts of the major theories of counseling and psychotherapy; to enable them to take these theories directly into counseling and clinical practice; to assist them in examining present-day counseling and therapy from a practical culture-centered perspective while simultaneously respecting traditional individual approaches to the field; and to start them on a journey toward skillful practice. While the sixth edition offers thorough insight into many of the theories discussed in the last edition, we are particularly excited to introduce students to new movements in the field that are having a significant impact on counseling and psychotherapy. This edition continues to bring **Multicultural Counseling and Therapy** to the table as a distinct approach to integrating theory and practice and incorporates new thinking throughout, including feminist theory and social justice perspectives. Positive psychology/wellness perspectives are also introduced.

In addition, a major aim of *Theories of Counseling Psychotherapy: A Multicultural Perspective,* 6th edition, is to help students effectively link counseling and psychotherapy theories to practice. Theories and techniques abound, but the basic issue remains: How can we as counselors make a difference with our clients and use theory wisely? As in previous editions, our commitment to help students move beyond an intellectual understanding of the various skills needed to work effectively, respectfully, and ethically with clients is reflected in the numerous competency-building activities contained in each of the chapters.

To this end, you also will find in each chapter a new Professional Development Extension feature deliberately aimed at stimulating students' thinking about their professional opportunities. Our own work as mental health professionals has made us keenly aware of the many ways that various counseling and therapy theories can be used outside of the traditional one-on-one therapeutic helping process. We hope that this new dimension of the text will extend your thinking about their options.

How This Book Is Organized

The inclusion of this new information has led to a number of significant changes in the organization of this sixth edition.

Part One, The Foundations of Counseling and Therapy: Past and Present Trends

Part One introduces the three major theoretical forces that have shaped the fields of counseling and psychology during the 20th century, as well as new paradigms that are presently reshaping the mental health profession. Chapter 1 (Charting the Theoretical Changes in Counseling and Psychology) presents an overview of the psychodynamic, cognitive-behavioral, and existential-humanistic theories of counseling and therapy while also introducing the multicultural-feminist-social justice and the positive psychology/wellness counseling movements in the field. Chapter 2 (The Multicultural-Feminist-Social Justice Movement) provides a detailed discussion of the multicultural-feminist-social justice movement and also introduces concepts and intervention strategies related to this fourth theoretical force, which are infused throughout the book.

Chapter 3 (Positive Psychology and Wellness Counseling) discusses the emergence of the positive psychology/wellness counseling movement in counseling and psychology. The rise of this influential movement greatly extends thinking about the many ways in which counselors and therapists can foster psychological wellness and human development by advocating for a holistic approach to healthy living in the 21st century.

Chapter 4 (Using Microskills in Counseling and Therapy: Foundations of the Intentional Interview) describes the specific skills that mental health professionals need to acquire to work effectively and respectfully with clients from diverse groups and backgrounds, regardless of the theoretical orientation they ultimately choose to implement in their professional practices. The microskills framework presented in Chapter 4 encourages a better understanding of many of the practical skills needed to conduct effective counseling and therapy sessions with clients.

Part Two, The First, Second, and Third Forces in Counseling and Psychotherapy

Part Two focuses on the three major theoretical forces that have traditionally shaped the field of counseling and psychology. Chapters 5 (The Psychodynamic Tradition: Theoretical Constructs and Practical Applications) and 6 (Adlerian and Jungian Counseling and Therapy) discuss the first major theoretical force that shaped the mental health professions during the 20th century by detailing the emergence of psychodynamic counseling and therapy theories. The discussion includes examining the impact of Sigmund Freud's psychoanalytic therapeutic approach on the evolution of the mental health professions, discussing how John Bowlby and Mary Ainsworth's attachment theory extends Freud's thinking of unconscious defense mechanisms, and describing the significance of the contributions of Alfred Adler and Carl Jung.

Chapters 7 (Cognitive-Behavioral Counseling and Therapy) and 8 (Rational-Emotive Behavioral Therapy and Reality Therapy) explore the evolution of cognitive-behavioral therapy, the second major theoretical force. These chapters explore the early influence of behavioral theorists on the beginnings of the cognitive movement to the contemporary works of cognitive-behavioral therapists.

Chapters 9 and 10 focus on the third major theoretical force that has significantly impacted the fields of counseling and psychology over the past several decades; the existential-humanistic force. Chapter 9 (The Existential-Humanistic Tradition) looks at Carl Rogers's important contributions to this important theoretical force; Chapter 10 (Logotherapy and Gestalt Counseling) explores the work of Viktor Frankl (logotherapy) and Fritz Perls (Gestalt counseling).

Part Three, The Fourth Force in Counseling and Therapy: Multicultural and Feminist Perspectives

Part Three explores some of the challenges that counselors and therapists face when working with individuals from diverse groups and backgrounds. Chapter 11 (Feminist Counseling and Therapy), written by Judy Daniels of the University of Hawai'i, Manoa, describes counseling and therapy from a feminist perspective. Chapter 12 (Multicultural Counseling and Therapy) provides new insights into many of the factors that are important to keep in mind when working with persons from diverse cultural, ethnic, and racial groups.

Many of the theoretical concepts presented in all of the preceding chapters are synthesized in Allen and Mary Ivey's developmental counseling and therapy (DCT) framework, which is described in Chapter 13 (Developmental Counseling and Therapy: Integrative Theory and Practice). The updated information outlined in this chapter is intentionally designed to assist students in effectively integrating many of the concepts that relate to the major theoretical forces presented earlier in this book.

Chapter 14 (Family Counseling and Therapy: Theoretical Foundations and Issues of Practice), by Sandra Rigazio-DiGilio of the University of Connecticut, Storrs, offers a breadth of information about family counseling and therapy theories and outlines some of the essential skills that are necessary to work effectively and respectfully with families from diverse groups and backgrounds.

Chapter 15 (Identifying Your Own Integrated Approach to Counseling and Therapy) assists students in developing their own unique approach to counseling and therapy by helping them integrate the information contained the preceding chapters.

New to This Edition

In addition to a reorganization and complete update of theoretical discussions throughout the book, the sixth edition of *Theories of Counseling and Psychotherapy: A Multicultural Perspective* contains a number of new features and discussions that reflect the needs of the field of counseling and psychotherapy.

- A new chapter, Chapter 2, **The Multicultural-Feminist-Social Justice Movement,** expands the discussion of multicultural counseling to emphasize the commonalities that multicultural, feminist, and social justice counseling theorists, practitioners, and advocates share. This expanded discussion reflects a more accurate and comprehensive understanding of human development over the past three and a half decades.

- Chapter 3, **Positive Psychology and Wellness Counseling,** extends students' thinking about the new roles and services provided by counselors and therapists that foster the physical and psychological well-being of their clients, including the expressed need to implement holistic helping approaches.

- A new chapter, Chapter 6, **Adlerian and Jungian Counseling and Therapy,** explores the contributions of Adler and Jung to psychotherapy and counseling.

- A new chapter, Chapter 8, **Rational-Emotive-Behavioral Therapy and Reality Therapy,** explores these approaches.

- A new chapter, Chapter 11, **Feminist Counseling and Therapy,** authored by Judy Daniels, examines counseling and therapy from a feminist perspective and offers many practical ideas when working with female clients.

- New **Professional Development Extension** features in every chapter expand students' perspectives for applying their knowledge, training, and skills in real-world settings. This new feature is deliberately aimed at stimulating thinking about the tremendous potential all of the theoretical forces have for use in other aspects of the work counselors and therapists are commonly called upon to do.

Additional Features and Learning Aids

Included in the sixth edition of *Theories of Counseling and Psychotherapy: A Multicultural Perspective* are various features and learning aids to help students prepare for a career in the helping field.

A review of critical microskills necessary to master theoretical approaches rapidly and effectively is incorporated in general discussions as well as in **Competency-Building Activity** features in every chapter, which offer prospective counselors multiple opportunities to develop and practice these practical and necessary skills.

Research Exhibit features appear in various chapters, emphasizing the authors' belief in the importance of research informing counseling and clinical practice. These features highlight new and significant findings within the field and offer contemporary perspectives on traditional approaches.

At the end of each chapter, **Summaries** highlight the core concepts discussed within the chapters and help the reader synthesize the information. In addition, a **Multimedia Resources for This Chapter** section highlights relevant material on the Companion Website and the MyHelpingLab site that can expand the reader's knowledge beyond the text.

Supplements

A **Companion Website** (www.ablongman.com/Ivey6e) includes a number of learning aids, including video clips that demonstrate how key concepts associated with various theoretical models can be used in multicultural counseling and therapy sessions. These video clips are intentionally designed to help the reader get a clearer picture as to how the various theories presented in this book are used in multicultural counseling role-plays.

MyHelpingLab (www.myhelpinglab.com) brings practice to life for counseling and psychotherapy students through video clips, case studies, study tools, and licensing/career preparation information. (Note to instructors: MyHelpingLab can only be accessed using a special code available for your students as a value-pack option. Speak with your Allyn and Bacon representative to order and go to **www.myhelpinglab.com** to register.) Resources on MHL include:

- Video Lab: An extensive selection of video clips of internationally recognized therapists working with real clients touching on a variety of theoretical approaches, therapeutic skills, and client issues.

- Interactive Case Archive: A collection of professional cases, easily accessed by topic and subject area, that allow for observation and analysis of client-practitioner interactions.

- Flashcards: An interactive study tool that reinforces basic concepts and key words used in your course of study.

- Research Navigator: Pearson's Research Navigator is the easiest way to start a research assignment or research paper.

- Licensing Center: Explore a collection of links to state and national organizations that enables you to quickly and easily access resources helpful in meeting licensing requirements.

- Career Explorations: These online, in-depth video interviews with counselors, family therapists, social workers, and human service professionals educate students about various career paths and professions and their challenges and rewards. Quiz questions can be used to stimulate classroom discussions and may also be assigned as homework.

- PowerPoint™ Presentation: Ideal for lecture presentations or student handouts, the PowerPoint™ presentation created for this text provides dozens of ready-to-use graphic and text images (available online at the Allyn & Bacon Instructor Resource Center at ablongman.com/irc).

An **Instructor's Resource Manual with Test Items** contains helpful instructional resources that correlate to chapter concepts, as well as test items for assessing your students' understanding.

Acknowledgments

As we stated earlier, we are very excited about the ways in which we have maintained our commitment to offer a textbook that infuses multicultural counseling considerations throughout all of the theories discussed in this new edition. Many of the changes that have been incorporated come from suggestions offered by students, faculty members, and other colleagues in the field.

We would like to extend a special thank you to our colleagues who have contributed to this edition and to editions in the past. For this edition, Dr. Judy Daniels provided a wonderful and insightful chapter on feminist counseling (Chapter 11), which we feel broadens the reach of this book even further. Dr. Daniels, a professor in the Department of Counselor Education at the University of Hawai'i, is a past recipient of the prestigious Gilbert and Kathleen Wrenn Award for a Humanitarian and Caring Person from the American Counseling Association. She received her doctorate from Vanderbilt University. Dr. Sandra Rigazio-DiGilio, University of Connecticut, Storrs, reprised her involvement for this edition with her revision of Chapter 14 (Family Counseling and Therapy: Theoretical Foundations and Issues of Practice). Dr. Rigazio-DiGilio is a professor in marriage and family therapy and holds a joint appointment in the university's Department of Psychiatry. A very heartfelt thank you to both of these contributors for their valuable contributions to this edition.

Contributors to past editions include: Harold Cheatham, Clemson University; Paul Pederson, University of Hawai'i; Lynn Simek-Morgan, Chamiade University; and Derald Wing Sue, Columbia University.

We are particularly grateful for the numerous comments and suggestions that were made by the persons who reviewed drafts of this revised edition. With much appreciation we want to extend our aloha to Amir Abbassi, Texas A&M University, Commerce; Timothy Atchison, West Texas A&M University; Andrew V. Beale, Virginia Commonwealth; Greg Berg, San Jose State University; Seth Brown, University of Northern Iowa; Claire Sham Choy, California State University, Fresno; Maryanne Conway, Missouri Baptist University; Lisa Cromer, University of Northern Colorado; Lisa Dillon, Oklahoma State University, Oklahoma City; Meredyth G. Fellows, West Chester University of Pennsylvania; Larry Golden, University of Texas at San Antonio; Barbara Herlihy, University of New Orleans; Mary A. Hermann, Mississippi State University; Nicole Hill, Idaho State University; Sharon Horne, University of Memphis; Ken Hughey, Kansas State University; Ron Jacques, Brigham Young University, Idaho; Kristi Kanel, California State University, Fullerton; Mary Margaret Livingston, Louisiana Tech University; Eugene R. Moan, Northern Arizona University; Charles Pemberton, University of Louisville; Scott Safford, Oregon State University; and Carla Strassle, York College of Pennsylvania.

A special word of thanks is extended to our "professional family" at Allyn and Bacon: Executive Editor Virginia Lanigan and Senior Development Editor Mary Kriener have been wonderful in supporting us through the long months of preparing this new version of our textbook and for challenging us to think in new ways about the manner in which we could best present our thinking about the theories of counseling and therapy that are contained in this final product. Their commitment and long hours of work on this project are sincerely appreciated. Production Editor Greg Erb has demonstrated patience and professionalism throughout this process. And Evelyn and John Ward of Trinity Publishers Services have been, as always, delightful to work with. We genuinely believe that there could be no better or more helpful editing and production team.

Because we embrace the importance of being lifelong learners, we invite you to share any reactions you might have about the ideas, competency-building activities, and video clips that are presented in this edition and the newly developed Companion Website that accompanies it.

About the Authors

Allen E. Ivey received his counseling doctorate from Harvard University. He is Distinguished University Professor (Emeritus) at the University of Massachusetts, Amherst; Courtesy Professor, Counselor Education, University of South Florida, Tampa; and president of Microtraining Associates, an educational publishing firm. A past president and Fellow of the Division of Counseling Psychology of the American Psychological Association, Dr. Ivey is a Diplomate of the American Board of Professional Psychology. He is also a Fellow of APA's Society for the Study of Ethnic and Minority Psychology and the Asian American Psychological Association. Awards throughout his career include the International Award from the Division of Counseling and Psychotherapy of the Portuguese Psychological Association for his new writings on developmental counseling and therapy; the Professional Development Award from the American Counseling Association; and recognition as a "Distinguished Elder" for lifetime contributions to multicultural psychology at the National Multicultural Summit and Conference. Allen is the author or coauthor of more than 30 books and 200 articles and chapters, translated into 18 languages. His recent work has focused on applying Developmental Counseling and Therapy to the analysis and treatment of severe psychological distress. With Mary, he continues to write and conduct workshops on counseling and spirituality.

Michael D'Andrea received his doctorate in human development counseling from Vanderbilt University in 1982. He is currently professor in the Department of Counselor Education at the University of Hawai'i, Manoa. In addition to his work as a university professor, Dr. D'Andrea serves as the executive director of the National Institute for Multicultural Competence. He has authored or coauthored more than one hundred journal articles, book chapters, books, and other scholarly works on a broad range of issues related to human development and multicultural counseling. Besides his contributions as executive director, professor, writer, and researcher, Dr. D'Andrea is well known for his political and social activism in the fields of counseling and psychology. His greatest source of life satisfaction comes from his partnership with Judy Daniels and his relationship with his son, Shawn D'Andrea, and his two daughters, Kara Shea Pitt-D'Andrea and Mahealani Daniels.

Mary Bradford Ivey received her doctorate at the University of Massachusetts, Amherst. She serves as vice president of Microtraining Associates and Courtesy Professor, Counselor Education, University of South Florida, Tampa. She is a former school counselor in the Amherst schools and has served as visiting professor at the University of Massachusetts, Amherst; University of Hawai'i, Manoa; and Flinders University, South Australia. She is a nationally certified counselor (NCC) and a licensed mental health counselor (LMHC). Mary received national recognition when her elementary counseling program was named one of the ten best in the nation. She is one of the first 15 honored Fellows of the American Counseling Association and a recipient of the American Counseling Association's O'Hana Award for her work in multicultural counseling in the schools. She has presented workshops and keynote lectures with Allen throughout the world and is known for her work in promoting and explaining development guidance and counseling. She has authored or coauthored 11 books, translated into multiple languages.

Lynn Simek-Morgan received her doctorate from the University of Massachusetts, Amherst. She is director of Special Services at the Battenkill Valley Supervisory Union in Arlington, Vermont. She also is adjunct associate professor at Goddard College. Dr. Simek-Morgan has been a director of counseling services at three universities, most recently at Florida International University, Miami. She has taught at five universities in the departments of psychology, education, sociology, health, and communication skills and in family and community medicine at the University of Massachusetts Medical Center. A certified secondary teacher in three states, she serves on the research review committee of three professional journals. She has authored and coauthored several texts and many research articles.

The Foundations of Counseling and Therapy: Past and Present Trends

The first part of this book is aimed at achieving three goals. First, it will assist you in becoming more knowledgeable of the three major theoretical forces that have historically dominated the fields of counseling and psychology. To achieve this goal, an overview of the psychodynamic (first force), cognitive-behavioral (second force), and existential-humanistic (third force) perspectives of counseling and therapy are presented in Chapter 1. A much more detailed description of each of these traditional helping perspectives is provided later, in Chapters 5 through 10.

The second goal of Part One is to help you gain a greater understanding of two new theoretical models that are having a tremendous impact in the mental health professions at the present time. This includes what we refer to as the multicultural-feminist-social justice counseling framework and the newly emerging positive psychology/ wellness counseling paradigm. Although many of the concepts associated with these two new conceptual frameworks are infused throughout this book, we think your knowledge of these important theoretical forces will be particularly heightened after you have read the information presented in Chapters 2 and 3. Your ability to begin to use many of the concepts that underlie the multicultural-feminist-social justice counseling framework and the positive psychology/wellness counseling framework will be greatly enhanced as a result of completing the competency-building activites that are included in both of these chapters.

The third goal of this part of the book is to provide an opportunity for you to read about and practice a broad range of counseling and therapy skills that will be useful regardless of the theoretical perspective(s) that you decide to use in your work. The description of the microcounseling skills model and the presentation of the numerous competency-building activities presented in Chapter 4 will help you develop a number of concrete skills that you will need to effectively implement all of the counseling and therapy theories described in this textbook.

We genuinely hope that the information presented in Part One will provide a foundation that you can build on as you read the rest of this book and develop your own helping style as a result of other experiences you encounter in your professional training program and/or work settings. Best wishes as you continue your journey in becoming an effective mental health professional!

chapter 1

Charting the Theoretical Changes in Counseling and Psychology

chapter goals

This chapter is designed to:

1. Increase your knowledge of the important theoretical perspectives that have dominated the fields of counseling and psychology over the past one hundred years.

2. Broaden your understanding of many of the current changes that are occurring in the fields of counseling and psychology.

3. Introduce you to the concepts of "multiple perspectives," "postmodernism," and "relativity" and discuss how they relate to the complex world of counseling and therapy in the 21st century.

4. Present an overview of some of the ways that the three traditional theoretical forces (e.g., the psychodynamic, cognitive-behavioral, and existential-humanistic forces) can be used in practical counseling and therapy situations today.

5. Discusss the relevance of spirituality and religion for counseling and psychotherapy.

6. Heighten your understanding of the term *scientific practitioner* as it relates to the work counselors and psychologists do in the field.

7. Emphasize the importance of ethics in professional practice.

8. Increase your awareness of some of the ways that psychodynamic, cognitive-behavioral, and existential-humanistic concepts are commonly used by many people in the general public as well as by mental health professionals who provide consultation, training, and support services with teachers, parents, and graduate students.

Introduction

The fields of counseling and psychology have undergone many changes over the past one hundred years. These changes have been largely stimulated by the development of new theoretical forces that have greatly impacted the way mental health professionals view their role in helping people realize untapped aspects of their human potential. By using different theories of counseling and therapy in this way, mental health professionals have been able to help countless numbers of people develop more effective, satisfying, and productive ways of living (Wampold, Lichenberg, & Waehler, 2002).

The emergence of new theories in the fields of counseling and psychology is exciting in that it leads mental health professionals to gain a broader understanding of the many factors that influence human development. The rise of new theoretical perspectives also helps to foster the ongoing evolution of the mental health professions by enabling practitioners to become more cognizant of the different variables that contribute to their clients' problems. By gaining new insights into the complex and multidimensional nature of human development and becoming more knowledgeable of the genesis of people's problems, counselors and psychologists are better positioned to assist their clients in learning new ways to lead more effective and personally satisfying lives.

The mental health professions continue to undergo changes at the present time. These changes are altering the way counselors and psychologists have traditionally thought about the purpose and purview of their role and function in this country's health care system. To gain a good understanding as to what these changes are and why they are occurring in the mental health professions at the current time, it is important to be cognizant of the following areas.

First, it is essential to be well versed in the strengths and limitations of the three traditional theoretical forces that have shaped the fields of counseling and psychology over the past one hundred years. This includes having a critical understanding of the **psychodynamic** (first force), **cognitive-behavioral** (second force), and **existential-humanistic** (third force) theories of counseling and therapy.

Second, it is important to be cognizant of the current socio-political-cultural changes that are rapidly occurring in the United States and the implications that these changes have for the mental health professions. It is particularly important to be aware of the rapid cultural-racial transformation of the demography of the United States and the need for mental health practitioners to acquire new professional competencies that will enable them to work more effectively, ethically, and respectfully with persons from diverse groups and backgrounds in our contemporary society.

Third, counselors and psychologists will increasingly be challenged to learn about and implement concepts that are associated with two newly emerging theoretical perspectives that are dramatically impacting the mental health professions at the present time. This includes acquiring new knowledge about the **multicultural-feminist-social justice counseling movement** and the emergence of a more recent theoretical perspective that is referred to as **positive psychology/wellness counseling.**

The richness of the three traditional theoretical forces (the psychodynamic, cognitive-behavioral, and existential-humanistic forces) and the newly emerging multicultural-feminist-social justice and positive psychology/wellness counseling orientations offer tremendous potential in helping mental health practitioners face the challenges of a rapidly changing world. These multiple helping perspectives represent unique ways of viewing human development, mental health, counseling, and psychotherapy. These different helping perspectives are described in general terms in the following sections of this chapter and in much more detail in the chapters that follow this one.

Before going further with this discussion, we want to underscore the importance, beauty, and power of operating from multiple perspectives in our professional and personal lives. For this reason we have taken time in the following section to briefly explore what we mean by "operating from multiple perspectives" and discuss the importance of adapting a multiple perspective orientation in our personal and professional lives.

Multiple Perspectives

Our Stories about Reality Depend on Our Perspective

We are all in the same world, but each of us makes different sense of what we see and experience. This important premise underscores one of the central challenges counselors and psychologists face when working with their clients. That is, to gain an accurate understanding of the different ways clients construct meaning in their lives, the challenges and problems they face, and the sources of strength that help sustain them through times of heightened stress.

Historically, mental health professionals have used Western therapeutic theories to guide their thinking about the different problems clients present in clinical settings. This has generally involved the use of a host of psychodynamic, existential-humanistic, and cognitive-behavioral counseling theories and techniques in professional practice. Although these three traditional theoretical forces are described in much greater depth later in this book, it is important to note that the use of any one of these theoretical orientations significantly influences the way counselors make sense of their clients' problems and the strategies therapists use to address their clients' concerns in counseling and therapy.

Some counselors and psychologists spend a great deal of time and energy arguing over what they believe to be the "best" counseling theory to use when working with clients. Over time, mental health practitioners have increasingly come to realize that there are many ways to help people deal with the challenges, concerns, and problems that characterize their lives. This realization has led most practitioners to embrace an "eclectic" approach to counseling and therapy (Rigazio-DiGilio, 2001). Consequently, rather than becoming locked into one particular counseling or psychotherapeutic theory, there is a growing tendency for mental health professionals to be flexible and open-minded as they utilize ideas and strategies that are associated with different helping models.

The importance of maintaining this sort of flexible and open-minded attitude has been emphasized by numerous multicultural-feminist-social justice counseling theorists and researchers (Ponterotto, Casas, Suzuki, & Alexander, 2001; Toporek, Gerstein, Fouad, Roysircar, & Israel, 2006). These and other experts in the mental health professions (U.S. DHHS, 2001) point out that a rigid adherence to traditional Western counseling theories often results in ineffective (and, in some instances, even harmful) outcomes when used with persons in diverse client populations (D'Andrea, 2004a; Sue & Sue, 2003).

The emergence of the multicultural-feminist-social justice movement in the mental health professions has stimulated a greater awareness of the importance of considering the relative effectiveness and ineffectiveness of using traditional counseling theories among women and persons from other culturally diverse groups and backgrounds. In addition to the growing awareness of the ineffectiveness of using traditional Western helping theories with persons from diverse client populations, the fields of counseling and psychology are also being influenced by the rising popularity of what is referred to as a "postmodern perspective" (D'Andrea, 2000; RiGazio-DiGilio, 2001).

Although postmodernism is discussed in greater detail later in this chapter, it is important to point out here that this perspective complements the multicultural-feminist-social justice counseling theoretical force in that it emphasizes the need for counselors and psychologists to adapt a **multiple perspectives orientation** when working with their clients. When mental health practitioners incorporate such a perspective in their professional practices, they acknowledge that

- their clients' stories represent different ways of constructing meaning about their lives and the challenges they are experiencing
- the theories that practitioners have historically used in their work are embedded in a host of cultural biases, values, and beliefs about mental health that have much relevance for persons in the dominant cultural-racial group in the United States but do not necessarily match the worldviews, psychological strengths, and personal needs of many women and persons in other marginalized groups in our society
- the theories that have historically been used in the fields of counseling and psychology are relative and do not represent universal truths about psychological wellness and disorder
- there are numerous ways that one can go about helping people who are experiencing personal distress in their lives
- respectful, effective, and ethical counseling and therapy involve an understanding of the similarities and differences that exist in the counselor's and the client's worldview

And what do we the authors believe? We are committed to a world in which difference is celebrated rather than feared. In this process we have found that the traditional methods and theories of counseling and therapy offer useful perspectives on helping, but that they are also incomplete. In particular, we believe that the multicultural-feminist-social justice perspective has been missing in our field or, at best, given lip service. With all of this in mind, we have written this book to promote a more comprehesive approach to helping that incorporates new thinking while maintaing the best of the old worldviews about counseling and psychotherapy.

In this chapter, we provide an overview of the three traditional theoretical forces that have dominated the fields of counseling and psychology over the past one hundred years (e.g., the psychodynamic, existential-humanistic, and cognitive-behavioral theoretical forces). Additional chapters that follow in Part One will draw your attention to two new forces that are currently reshaping the mental health professions. This includes a discussion of the rise of the multicultural-feminist-social justice theoretical force (Chapter 2) and the emergence of the positive psychology/wellness counseling paradigm (Chapter 3).

One of the central purposes in providing an overview of the three traditional forces as well as the two newly emerging helping paradigms that are briefly mentioned above early in this textbook is to help you become aware of the multiple perspectives and worldviews that underlie the different counseling and psychotherapeutic frameworks that are commonly used in the field. As you read on, you will learn how the different worldviews associated with each theoretical force significantly affect (1) how counselors and psychologists think about their clients' strengths and problems and (2) the manner in which practitioners assist clients in learning more effective ways of dealing with the challenges and problems they experience in their lives.

The Importance of Understanding Our Clients' Worldviews

All counseling and therapy theories operate from the assumption that significant contact between the client and the counselor is possible. You, as a counselor or therapist, will be called on to demonstrate creativity and artistry in the way you observe and interact with your clients as they walk down life's path. If you can enter your clients' psychological worlds for a time and join them on their journey, you may find a new understanding and respect for how their constructions of the world are different from your own. Sometimes, simply validating your clients' alternative perceptions of reality may be all that is needed to facilitate a greater understanding of their view of the world.

Other clients may want to change direction, to find new perspectives and new ways of acting. In these cases, your task is more difficult because you will need to understand their ways of thinking and being, to share yourself and your own view of the world, and to work with them to seek new directions for the future.

To provide counseling and therapeutic services in a respectful and effective manner, mental health professionals need to be keenly aware of the ways in which their own worldview influences how they

- make sense of the challenges and problems their clients are experiencing
- strive to assist clients to find new ways to deal with their concerns so that their clients can learn to lead more satisfying and productive lives

Simply stated, **worldview** refers to the manner in which individuals construct meaning of the world. More specifically, worldview includes the various beliefs, values, and biases that one develops as a result of her or his historical-cultural-social conditioning.

Counselors and psychologists commonly experience changes in their own worldview as a result of participating in professional training programs. These training programs expose individuals to various psychological theories that reshape and expand students' thinking about mental health, psychological problems, and appropriate helping strategies. Upon graduating from their professional training programs, coun-selors and psychologists use their expanded views of these issues to guide the work they do with their clients (D'Andrea & Daniels, 2005). Because mental health practi-tioners and the clients they work with typically adhere to different worldviews, it is important to understand how such differences may impact the process of counseling and therapy.

The importance of considering how our own worldviews complement or conflict with our clients' constructions of the world cannot be understated, as this task rep-resents the most important aspect of respectful, effective, and ethical counseling and therapeutic practice. By taking time to thoughtfully reflect on these important con-siderations, we are better able to work effectively, ethically, and respectfully with persons from a broad range of cultural groups and backgrounds.

The three major theoretical forces that have historically shaped the development of the mental health professions (e.g., the psychodynamic, existential-humanistic, and cognitive-behavioral forces) as well as the two newly emerging helping paradigms (e.g., the multicultural-feminist-social justice and the positive psychology/wellness counseling frameworks) are all embedded in different worldviews. The following sections of this chapter provide a general overview of the three major theoretical perspectives that have dominated (and, to a large degree, continue to dominate) the way mental health professionals think about their role and purpose as professional helpers.

An Overview of the Three Traditional Theoretical Forces

The Psychodynamic Force

The genesis of psychodynamic theories can be traced to Sigmund Freud's psychoan-alytic worldview that emerged during the turn of the 20th century. Although his theory of human development profoundly affected the thinking of many persons in the mental health professions during that time, Freud's theoretical model has been greatly expanded with the passage of time. The evolution of the psychodynamic force has been fueled by the contributions of numerous persons who offer alternative conceptualizations of Freud's view of personality development.

The notable individuals who have extended Freud's original work include John Bowlby and Mary Ainsworth, whose attachment theory is discussed in greater detail in Chapter 5, as it extends our understanding of the relevance of many of Freud's psychoanalytic concepts when working with children, adolescents, and adults. Competency-Building Activity 5.1, which is included in the discussion of attachment theory, offers a way to use the psychodynamic principles associated with this model to foster your own professional development and self-understanding.

Many other persons have helped refine and build on Freud's original efforts to promote a psychodynamic perspective in the mental health professions. In particular, Alfred Adler's theory of individual psychology and Carl Jung's analytic theory of personality development (see Chapter 6) further expand our understanding of the impact that the psychodynamic force has had in the fields of counseling and psychology.

Despite the differences that are reflected in other theorists' efforts to build on Freud's original theoretical framework, there are a number of common characteristics that cross all psychodynamic counseling and therapy theories. This includes a belief in

- the role that unconscious factors play in a person's psychological development

- the use of defense mechanisms to cope with anxiety and stress

- the effect that past experiences have on people's present sense of mental health and personal well-being

The Cognitive-Behavioral Force

The primary intent of the cognitive-behavioral approach to counseling and therapy is to help clients (1) become more aware of their thoughts and feelings, (2) reframe their thinking about the challenges and problems they encounter in their lives, and (3) develop new behaviors that are deliberately aimed at helping people experience a greater level of personal satisfaction in their lives. Counselors who use a cognitive-behavioral theoretical approach in their work commonly utilize various life skills training techniques such as assertiveness and relaxation training as well as other psychoeducational interventions to help clients learn new ways of effectively coping with their unique life stressors.

The origins of cognitive-behavioral therapy (CBT) can be traced to the rise of the behaviorist movement in the United States during the middle of the 20th century. Largely fueled by the work of B. F. Skinner (1953), behaviorist counseling and therapy primarily focuses on assisting individuals to (1) extinguish behaviors that result in unsatisfying outcomes and (2) develop new behaviors to more effectively deal with life's challenges and problems. David Meichenbaum (1985, 1991) was of primary importance in helping move behavioral therapy to its present cognitive-behavioral orientation. Meichenbaum's cognitive-behavioral theory is described in much greater length in Chapter 7. In light of the important linkages that exist between the behaviorist movement and the emergence of cognitive-behavioral therapy, which has become the approach of choice for many mental health practitioners at the present time, we refer to the collective impact of these complementary helping perspectives as the cognitive-behavioral (CBT) force in this book.

Two additional contributors to the evolution of the cognitive-behavioral force are Albert Ellis and William Glasser. Albert Ellis is the founder of what is called rational-emotive behavior therapy (REBT), more recently referred to as rational-emotive-behavior-contextual therapy (REBCT) (Rigazio-DiGilio, Ellis, D'Andrea, Ivey, & Gutterman, 1999). Mental health practitioners who use an REBCT approach in their work assist clients in examining the irrational dimensions of their thinking. This is done to help clients become more aware of the ways in which such cognitions adversely impact their emotional development and their behavioral responses to various events that occur in their lives. An REBCT approach to counseling and therapy emphasizes that once clients become aware of the tremendous impact irrational or "faulty" thinking patterns have on their lives, they are better able to develop alternative behaviors that are grounded in new ways of thinking and feeling about themselves and the world in which they live (Ellis, 1995).

Another cognitive-behavioral theory that is widely used in the fields of counseling and psychology is William Glasser's reality therapy framework. Reality therapy asserts that clients primarily experience problems in life because they select ineffective behaviors that almost ensure their failure in and dissatisfaction with various dimensions of their lives. One of the distinguishing aspects of reality therapy relates to the concept of personal responsibility (Glasser, 1998). In short, reality therapy stresses that individuals are themselves responsible for deciding to enact behaviors that result in problematic outcomes or, alternatively, they can choose to act in ways that heighten their chances of leading more satisfying and productive lives. Both Glasser's and Ellis's cognitive-behavioral theories are presented in Chapter 8.

The Existential-Humanistic Force

The existential-humanistic perspective is distinguished from the other two traditional theoretical forces (e.g., the psychodynamic and cognitive-behavioral forces) in many ways. One aspect of this theoretical orientation is its emphasis on understanding the individual life experiences and the ways in which one constructs meaning of the world. Existential-humanistic-oriented practitioners place a high value on respecting the unique ways that clients develop their own worldviews. These practitioners make a conscious effort to assist their clients in learning new strategies that may be useful in dealing with the challenges of life. Practitioners do this by building on their clients' strengths and working to conscientiously respect clients' personal values, beliefs, and worldviews in counseling and therapy.

The existential-humanistic force has led to the development and implementation of a host of client-centered therapeutic approaches (Rogers, 1995) (Chapter 9), including the use of logotherapy (Frankl, 2000) and Gestalt counseling techniques (Perls, 1992a, b) (Chapter 10). All of these therapeutic strategies are intentionally aimed at helping clients realize new dimensions of their untapped human potential for wellness and mental health.

Although the three theoretical forces that have traditionally shaped the fields of counseling and psychology are only briefly described here, it is hoped that you are beginning to get a sense of some of the differences that fundamentally distinguish the psychodynamic, existential-humanistic, and cognitive-behavioral perspectives from one another. You will gain a much more detailed understanding of the many ways that these theoretical perspectives are different from each other as you continue to read this text and complete the competency-building activities provided in the ensuing chapters.

You will also gain an increased understanding of the many positive ways that clients can benefit from the use of these three traditional theoretical forces in counseling and psychotherapy as you read the chapters in Part Two of this book. In addition to understanding the potential benefits that can be derived from implementing these theoretical perspectives into your professional practices, it is equally important to be cognizant of a number of limitations associated with each of these forces.

Limitations of the Three Traditional Theoretical Forces

The three major theoretical forces briefly described above have significantly impacted the consciousness and practice of the majority of mental health professionals who work in the United States. Each force represents a distinct perspective of human development, mental health, and psychological disorder. Although these three major theoretical forces have many distinguishing characteristics, they are similar in a number of fundamental ways as well. These similarities include the manner in which each theoretical force

- dichotomizes aspects of a person's psychological development into discrete parts (e.g., the id, ego, and superego, from a psychodynamic perspective; irrational thoughts and ineffective behaviors, from a cognitive-behavioral perspective; and a hierarchy of needs, from an existential-humanistic perspective) (Parham, 2002)

- emerges from culturally and gender-biased views of psychological development, which amplify the importance of autonomy, independence, separateness, and individualism over interdependence, connectedness, and collectivity (Comstock, 2005; Pedersen, Draguns, Lonner, & Trimble, 2002)

- underemphasizes the role counselors and psychologists can play in promoting environmental-contextual changes that foster the mental health and well-being of persons from diverse groups and backgrounds (Lewis, Lewis, Daniels, & D'Andrea, 2003)

Newly Emerging Theoretical Forces and Constructs

Clearly, the numerous counseling and therapy theories that have evolved from these three broad theoretical forces are useful in alleviating the psychological pain and suffering that many persons experience in their lives (Gladding, 2000). However, it is also equally apparent that these theories are not as effective (and, in some instances, even harmful) when used with women and persons from culturally and racially diverse populations (Ballou & Brown, 2002; Pedersen et al., 2002). A growing dissatisfaction with the gender and cultural biases that characterize the three above-mentioned forces has catalyzed the emergence of two new theoretical perspectives: the multicultural-feminist-social justice movement and positive psychology/wellness counseling movement (Chapters 2 and 3).

Given the significant differences that exist among all five of these major theoretical frameworks, one of the important challenges that mental health practitioners and students currently enrolled in professional training programs face is how to deal with what may sometimes feel like overwhelming and contradictory views of counseling and therapy. In our own experiences as faculty members, we have frequently heard students talk about feeling "oversaturated" with all of the theories they are presented with in their professional training programs.

The following section acknowledges that these feelings are indeed understandable in light of our increasing knowledge of human development and the proliferation of counseling and therapy theories. Kenneth Gergen, a noted postmodern theorist, has written about the concept of the "saturated self" (Gergen, 1994, p. 112). We think this concept is useful to interject here, as it directly relates to the information overload that many people are experiencing in our society in general and in professional training programs in particular. Although the ideas presented by postmodern theorists like Gergen may not necessarily provide concrete solutions to the uncomfortable feelings that are commonly associated with the "saturated self," these theorists can offer helpful explanations for these feelings.

By providing a general discussion of some of the key concepts associated with postmodernism and their relationship to the multiple realities and worldviews reflected in the different counseling theories you will learn about in your career, we hope that you will come to recognize that the anxiety and/or frustration you may experience as a result of being presented with multiple helping perspectives are indeed normal reactions. By normalizing such feelings, we hope you will be better able to remain tolerant of the broad range of psychological realities inherent in the theoretical perspectives presented in this book and that ideally you will experience a sense of professional and personal growth in the process.

Postmodernism

Different Worldviews in Counseling and Therapy

Clearly, the multitude of theories that counselors and therapists have available to them makes choosing one particular helping approach difficult. The three traditional theoretical forces described above represent unique ways of conceptualizing clients' problems. Needless to say, the techniques and methods associated with each of these theoretical frameworks leads to very different treatment methodologies. Respecting the value of all of the helping approaches presented in this textbook underlies a postmodern view of counseling and therapy.

Postmodernism has a multiplicity of points of view at its center. The number of diverse perspectives that characterize the postmodern age in which we live can create a heightened sense of discomfort and confusion for individuals, who may experience information overload. Gergen's (1991, 1994) concept of the "saturated self" helps us understand why these feelings are increasingly manifested among people in the general public as well as individuals in professional counseling and psychological training programs.

Think about your own situation and the many forces and possibilities that challenge your thinking about your life at the present time. Family, friends, community, cultural change, conflict, recreation, the media, and work influences—all of these and other forces can result in a sense of "overchoice," leaving you feeling overstimulated, confused, and frequently just plain "stressed out."

One way to cope with the feelings associated with being overwhelmed by our complex modern world is to tell stories about our experiences. Telling stories that reflect how we have learned to make meaning of our life experiences helps our clients and ourselves understand and synthesize the past as well as gain a better sense of control over present life experiences. By engaging in this kind of personal storytelling, we may develop new views of the world that make possible a more integrated, meaningful future for each of us.

You may already be feeling a little overwhelmed with the information that has been provided thus far in this chapter. After all, we have introduced you to three of the major forces that have evolved over the past one hundred years in the fields of counseling and psychology and alluded to two new theoretical paradigms that are currently emerging in the mental health professions. Perhaps the general description of these theoretical forces is starting to make you think about the one that best fits your own personal helping style. You may also be starting to wonder how you will ever handle all of this information when working with clients.

Competency-Building Activity 1.1 is designed to help you effectively manage the thoughts and feelings you may be presently experiencing as a result of reading the information presented thus far in this textbook. It is hoped that the time and energy you take in completing the following competency-building activity will help you develop new self-understanding and self-management skills that will be useful in dealing with the additional knowledge you will acquire about counseling and psychotherapy theories as you continue reading this book.

To develop the sort of self-understanding that can be helpful in more effectively managing the new information that is presented in this text, Competency-Building Activity 1.1 encourages you to consider the personal biases and preferences you hold about counseling and therapy at this early stage in your professional development. In doing so, you are asked to take a few minutes to "tell your own story" about your personal theoretical preferences at this point in time. Additionally, it is also hoped that the following activity will help you avoid feeling oversaturated with the information that has been presented about the three traditional theoretical forces.

Linking Theory to Practice

As you proceed through this book, you will find additional competency-building activities that are aimed at stimulating your self-knowledge in other ways. Beyond helping you acquire new self-knowledge, we are also committed to providing opportunities that will help you develop a broad range of professional skills that underlie effective counseling and therapeutic practices, regardless of the theoretical orientation you ultimately choose to use in your work. This commitment underlies our

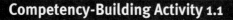

Competency-Building Activity 1.1

Gaining Insight into Your Theoretical Preferences

Each of us has personal preferences that relate to the type of counseling theory we are most comfortable implementing in our work. Many individuals are not conscious of these personal preferences and how they may influence their preferred style of helping at the early stage of their professional development. Competency-Building Activity 1.1 is designed to help you become more aware of some of your personal preferences as they relate to the type of helping approach you may be inclined to use at this stage of your own professional development.

While you will be encouraged to develop a clearer understanding of the five major theoretical forces in counseling and psychology described in this book, it may be useful to pause here to reflect on the ideas that have been presented up to this point to see how they fit your own personal preferences.

Instructions: It is helpful to complete this competency-building activity by working with a small group of persons (perhaps other students in your training program or other colleagues you work with). Someone should be designated to facilitate a group discussion in which all of the persons participating in this activity would be encouraged to respond to the following questions:

1. What made you decide to become a mental health professional?

2. When you think about counseling clients, how would you describe your preferred way of working with them?

3. Do you think you would prefer to focus on clients' thoughts (what they think about their situation), feelings (how they feel about their situation), or behaviors (what they actually do in various situations) when you are counseling people?

4. Do you think it is important to help clients explore their past history to see how it might impact their current situation, or do you prefer to keep the focus on what is going on right now in your clients' lives?

5. To what degree do you think you are inclined to focus on different cultural factors (including clients' religious/spiritual group identity, economic class background, sexual identity, ethnic/racial background, etc.) when working with clients in counseling and therapy?

6. What level of importance do you think you would presently direct to your clients' personal and collective strengths in fostering a greater level of psychological, physical, and spiritual wellness in your clients' lives?

7. Given what you have learned about the three traditional forces as well as the two new frameworks emerging in the mental health professions up to this point in time, which framework do you see best fitting your personal preferences and the work you will do as a mental health professional in the future?

8. Which theoretical force do you think will require more of an effort to understand and try out in the future?

After everyone in the group has had a chance to respond to these questions, the facilitator should take a few minutes to process any additional reactions any member of the group may have had in completing this competency-building activity. You may find it useful to talk about any new insights you gained about yourself as a result of completing this exercise.

Hopefully, you will experience some increased self-understanding after you have had a chance to tell your story in this kind of group setting. It is also hoped that you have gained some new insights into the counseling preferences you bring to the table at this point in time as well as acquired a better understanding of some of the therapeutic approaches to which you may need to devote greater time, attention, and effort in the future.

It is useful to write down your reactions to this group exercise once you have finished. Place this reaction paper in a file that represents the first of a number of written entries you will do as you complete other competency-building activities throughout the book. In this way you will begin to organize the sort of personal/professional development portfolio that will be helpful in assessing your own growth as you proceed through the rest of this textbook.

Competency-Building Activity 1.2

Expanding Your Thinking about Counseling and Therapy

Instructions: Consider the following scenario: A client comes to you for help and says, "My eight-year-old isn't doing well in school. It worries me. I never succeeded at school either. Actually, I hated school. My parents sometimes had to beat me to get me out of the door. But the same approach doesn't seem to work with my son. Now I'm told by the school counselor that I'm being abusive and that they are going to file a complaint with the local youth services. They said that my child might be taken away unless I change. I don't want to be here. What are you going to do to help me?"

It is important to note that the first two tasks that counselors and therapists are ethically bound to address when dealing with a client who has expressed the sort of concerns described above include (1) assessing the potential or actual abuse that exists for the client's child and (2) implementing strategies to protect the youngster if necessary. These issues represent both legal and ethical concerns that need to be at the forefront of the practitioner's thinking when counseling this particular client.

No matter what theory or worldview a therapist may choose to use with this client, protecting the client's child from harm is our first responsibility as mental health professionals. Thus, careful assessment of the degree to which this client might harm the youngster involved is essential so that appropriate action may be taken. In making this assessment, it is vital that you consider the accuracy of the story and the cultural attitudes that this client may hold regarding the discipline of children.

Let us assume that you have taken time to assess these issues with this client and have determined that the youngster may be at risk for future abuse but is presently safe. How would you proceed to respond to this client? What feelings and thoughts are going through your mind as you think about this client? Take a moment to think about your "gut" feelings as they relate to this situation and how you might respond to this person in counseling. Then take a blank sheet of paper and write down how you might respond to this client's comments, as described above.

Once you have written your response to this scenario, proceed to read the description of some of the ways that counselors might approach this situation if they were to implement one of the five theoretical orientations covered in this book. After you have read some of the ways that other therapists might respond to this client, take a few minutes to compare your own response to these other counseling strategies. Then, write down any additional things you now think you might say or focus on if you were to respond to this client.

On completing this competency-building activity, you should (1) gain additional insights into some of the present assumptions, preferences, and biases that underlie your current thinking about counseling and therapy and (2) become aware of some new and different ways of dealing with the problem this client presented that you may not have previously considered. When you have completed this exercise be sure to file your written reactions in your personal/professional portfolio.

belief in the importance of linking counseling and therapy theories with a clear understanding of the pragmatic skills and interventions that one can use to promote clients' mental health.

Competency-Building Activity 1.2 is designed to stimulate your thinking about some of the ways that counseling theories can be practically manifested in the way you might approach a client who presents the problem that is described above. As you read about this client's situation, compare how your approach to helping this client may be similar to or different from the ways in which other counselors might respond to the presenting problem if they were operating from any one of the five major theoretical forces that have been briefly discussed thus far in this chapter.

The Effect of Theoretical Orientation on Therapeutic Response

The following section provides a discussion of some of the ways that counselors and psychologists might use various aspects of the five theoretical orientations that are covered in this textbook when working with the client described in Competency-Building Activity 1.2. In addition to increasing your general understanding of these five theoretical forces, the following demonstrates how one might concretely implement these theories into real counseling and therapy situations.

The Psychodynamic Orientation. The psychodynamic orientation stresses that the past is often a prelude to the future. Research clearly indicates that those who abuse others often suffer from abusive childhoods themselves. A psychodynamic counselor believes that change will not be lasting unless clients have some sense of how their present actions relate to their past experience. Consequently, a possible response from a psychodynamic professional might be:

> You say you were beaten by your own parents, and now you find you are doing the same thing with your own child. It will take some time, but our goal is to find out how your past experiences are being reflected in your present behavior with your child. Let's start by you sharing some of your own thoughts and feelings about what happened to you during your childhood.

The Cognitive-Behavioral Orientation. The cognitive-behavioral worldview is more oriented to action and short-term treatment. Relaxation training, parent education, and stress management are some of the many techniques and strategies that might be used in this regard. The cognitive-behavioral counselor will focus on short-term observable change but will keep an eye to the future and work with the client for long-term maintenance of behavioral change. With this in mind, the cognitive-behavioral practitioner might respond to this client's presenting problems by stating the following:

> There's a lot happening in your life. We'll be doing different things in our counseling sessions that are aimed at helping you learn new ways to deal with the concerns you have expressed here today. What I think might be useful as a beginning step is to have us talk about how I might help you deal with your frustration at having to be here. Then we could get down to the hard work of seeing what you can do to gain a greater sense of self-control in general and in the way you relate to your child in particular. We'll be looking at some very practical things you can do to work more effectively with your son and, in the process, I hope to help you feel better about yourself as a parent. We'll start with some stress management techniques, move on to look at your own beliefs about parenting, and then see if we can come up with new ways of thinking and acting as a parent.

The Existential-Humanistic Orientation. The existential-humanistic worldview seeks to understand how the client makes sense of the world. Believing firmly in self-actualization, therapists using this theoretical orientation listen to their clients carefully as they embrace the notion that their clients will ultimately find their own positive direction in life. Thus, one response that an existential-humanistic therapist might use with the client who is described in Competency-Building Activity 1.2 might be the following:

> It sounds as if you are deeply troubled and angry about being here. At the same time, I hear that you desperately want to straighten things out. Am I hearing you accurately?

The Multicultural-Feminist-Social Justice Orientation. Practitioners who use a multicultural-feminist-social justice approach in counseling and therapy will freely integrate various aspects of the three theoretical orientations described above. Beyond integrating various approaches from these traditional theoretical worldviews, practitioners in this orientation distinguish themselves by the way they view individual clients within a family and sociocultural context. This means that one part of the therapeutic process is aimed at helping clients see how their difficulties may be related to societal issues concerning race, ethnicity, gender, and/or socioeconomic status issues.

The following might be one response that a practitioner operating from a multicultural-feminist-social justice orientation would present to this client:

> We'll need to look at this issue from three levels. First, I'd like to hear your story as you make sense of it. Then, I'd like to introduce some stress management techniques that may help you deal with the immediate problem. As part of this process, we'll be looking at how gender, race, and class may play a part in your situation. I'd particularly like to know about what the words "family" and "community" mean to you and to learn more about the nature of your connections with present support systems at this time in your life.

The multicultural-feminist-social justice worldview may require more than individual action. Because clients are seen as being a part of a larger social system in which past and present communities are important, counselors adopting this helping approach are likely to refer their clients to consciousness-raising groups to sustain and amplify the therapeutic gains that are achieved in individual counseling settings. These practitioners may also take time to explore ways in which their clients might realize new and untapped dimensions of their personal development by encouraging them to become involved in community action projects that are aimed at promoting various forms of social justice for parents who are experiencing similar stresses as this client (Daniels et al., 2000).

The Positive Psychology/Wellness Counseling Orientation. The newly emerging positive psychology/wellness counseling paradigm may be more accurately referred to as a "metatheory." A metatheory is a theory about theories; as such, this new paradigm integrates many key theoretical perspectives of all of the above-mentioned frameworks.

One of the central concepts that distinguishes this orientation from the others described above is the manner in which wellness counselors direct particular attention to clients' personal assets and resources. Thus, rather than focusing on a person's problems, this new paradigm "starts with a focus on wellness in the belief that clients grow best if we first attend to their strengths" (Ivey, Ivey, Myers, & Sweeney, 2005, p. 18).

Sweeney and Myers (2005) point out that a positive psychology/wellness counseling approach to mental health care involves a very different way of thinking about our role and function as counselors and psychologists. These experts further elaborate on this point by noting that "traditionally, counselors and therapists solve problems, remediate difficulties, and seek to alleviate pathology. A wellness approach attacks these same issues, but seeks to work with human health rather than human illness. Such an approach builds on client strengths and resources" (Sweeney & Myers, 2005, p. 40).

Consequently, a practitioner operating from a positive psychology/wellness counseling orientation might respond to the client in the following manner:

> You have many problems and concerns that I can see you want to deal with in our session today. We will certainly look at all of the issues you have mentioned in much more detail and work together to find new and more satisfying ways to deal with all of them. But before we try to do this, it is often important to take a minute to think about the personal strengths you have that get you through these stressful situations.
>
> I see a number of strengths that you seem to possess just by what you have said so far. For instance, you seem to care very much about your child. Your persistence and courage in coming here today, even though you are not sure that is exactly what you want to do, are other strengths I notice in you. And your fortitude in coping with the way your own parents treated you in your childhood seems to be another source of strength in yourself. I wonder if we could look at these personal strengths first and see how you might be able to use any or all of them to deal with the problems you have brought to my attention today. This might be a good way to start to think about what it would take to help you find healthier and more satisfying ways to deal with all of the challenges you face in your life.

As you can see from these different responses, there are many ways to approach a client's expressed concerns, depending on the practitioner's theoretical orientation. By taking an eclectic approach to counseling and therapy, one that includes multiple aspects of the different theoretical orientations presented in this book, mental health practitioners are able to increase their effectiveness among clients from diverse groups and backgrounds. An important area for consideration in using an eclectic approach when counseling persons from diverse groups and backgrounds involves the role of spirituality and religion in the helping process.

Spirituality and Religion

Historically, psychotherapy and counseling have directed minimal attention to issues of spirituality and religion. Yet, as we encounter the complexity of the multicultural, postmodern world in which we are situated, it is becoming increasingly apparent that more and more clients are seeking the feeling of wholeness that spirituality and religion make possible. Van Pelt (1993, 1995), a physician and a logotherapy practitioner, argues that issues of faith and spirituality arise from the very core of human experience, whether physical or psychological.

As stated earlier, human beings are storytellers. It is interesting to note, however, that the narratives people use to talk about the way they construct meaning of life commonly extend beyond their immediate individual interests and problems. Frequently, clients will include issues that directly relate to their religious and spiritual beliefs, concerns, and awareness when they tell their personal stories in counseling and psychotherapy (Fukuyama & Sevig, 1999). Religious or spiritual awareness is seen by Van Pelt as central to individual, family, and community well-being. Unless we touch on that core in counseling and psychotherapy, she argues, we are missing the most essential part of our humanity.

Vontress (1995c) underscores the importance of spiritual considerations in counseling from an existential-humanistic perspective (Chapter 9). In doing so he points out that:

> People cannot be segmented into parts, as if the pieces are somehow unrelated to the whole. My research in West Africa has convinced me that the spiritual dimension of human beings impacts the physical, psychological, and social aspects of living. Human beings need the respect, direction, love, and affection of parents, elders, departed ones, and spiritual figures. (pp. 1–2)

While Vontress's existential-humanistic position regarding spirituality is elaborated later, it is important to note here that the authors of this textbook have found that many students in the counseling and psychology courses we have taught, as well as many of the clients these students work with in their practicum and internship settings, openly express the importance of spirituality and religious issues in their own lives. Surveys of our classes constantly reveal that 60 percent or more of students openly say that these issues are important to them and a source of personal strength as well.

As individuals get in touch with multicultural experiences, they often find that spirituality is closely related. For example, the emphasis on individual decision making in much of Western psychotherapy and counseling can be related to the Judeo-Christian tradition. Yet many would argue that individuals make decisions best when they consider their spiritual foundations.

The connection of the individual to one's community in the Afrocentric orientation is reflected in a spirituality of relationship. This being-in-relationship orientation—as found in Islamic, Buddhist, Earth-centered, Native American Indian, and other forms of religion and spirituality—is increasingly becoming a recognized part of psychotherapy thanks to the continuing efforts of many feminist and multicultural advocates in the mental health professions. As you carefully listen to the narratives that many of your clients express when they tell their personal stories in counseling and therapy, you are likely to hear them talk about various strengths and concerns that can be linked to their relationship with themselves, other people whom they encounter in their lives, and the world at large.

Issues related to the expression of personal narratives and storytelling are important concepts that are infused in different ways throughout this book. Eventually, you will tell your own story of counseling and psychotherapy and share it with your

---

Competency-Building Activity 1.3

The Community Genogram

One of the things you can do to begin to acquire the skills necessary to effectively use the community genogram in counseling and therapy is to complete your own genogram. Later, you may want to try to use this activity with another student or colleague who would agree to complete a community genogram following your directions. For now, the time you spend completing your own community genogram should help you become clearer about the types of practical skills that are required to use this counseling strategy in practice as well as increase your appreciation of the various persons and groups that have played key roles in your own development.

Instructions:

Develop a Visual Representation of Your Community

1. Consider a large piece of paper as representing your broad culture and community. You should select the community in which you were primarily raised, but any other community, past or present, may be used.

2. Place yourself or the client in that community, either at the center or another appropriate place on the paper. Represent yourself or the client by a circle, a star, or other significant symbol.

3. Place your own or the client's family or families on the paper, again represented by the symbol most relevant. The family can be nuclear or extended or both.

4. Place the important and most influential groups on the community genogram, again representing them by circles or other visual symbols. School, family, neighborhood, and spiritual groups are most often selected. For teens, the peer group is often particularly important. For adults, work groups and other special groups tend to become more central.

5. Connect the groups to the individual, perhaps drawing heavier lines to indicate the most influential groups.

Search for Images and Narratives of Strengths

Although many individual difficulties and problems arise in a family, community, and cultural context, the community genogram focuses on strengths. Ivey (1995b) comments on this important point by stating that:

> The community genogram provides a frame of reference to help the client see her- or himself-in-context. The client is asked to generate narratives of key stories from the community where he or she grew up. If relevant, key stories from the present living community may also be important. The emphasis is on positive stories from the community and positive images. The community genogram is kept and posted on newsprint during the entire series of counseling interviews. (pp. 1–2)

In its first stages, the community genogram focuses on positive stories and images. The importance of this cannot be overstated. If this positive approach has been used first, clients will have a foundation for exploring more difficult and troublesome areas of their lives later in the therapeutic

continued on next page

clients. As you work through this book, consider the role that spirituality and religion may play in your own professional practices.

Throughout this book, a number of exercises are included to help you learn about some of the practical approaches counselors and therapists can use to deal with issues related to religion and spirituality in counseling and psychotherapy. One such exercise is the community genogram presented in Competency-Building Exercise 1.3. This community genogram has three primary goals:

Competency-Building Activity 1.3, continued

endeavor. In addition, the counselor or therapist will have a good foundation that will help in understanding the positive interconnections clients have with their communities, families, and cultural backgrounds.

In following this procedure, counselors and therapists are also able to effectively assess their clients' positive resources, which can be drawn on in times of heightened stress. The following process can be useful in helping your clients (or yourself) think about the ways positive resources can be utilized in the following manner.

Step 1: *Focus on one single community group or your (or your client's) family.* You (or the client) may want to start with a negative story or image, but do not work with the negative until positive strengths are solidly in mind first.

Step 2: *Develop a visual, auditory, or kinesthetic image that represents an important positive experience of the group or family image generated from Step 1.* Allow the image to build in your mind and note the positive feelings that occur with the image. If you allow yourself or your client to fully experience this positive image, you may experience tears and/or other strong bodily feelings. These anchored bodily experiences represent positive strengths that can be drawn on to help you and your clients deal with difficult issues raised in therapy and in life.

Step 3: *Tell the story of the image.* If it is your story, you may want to write it down in journal form. If you are drawing out the story from a client, listen sensitively.

Step 4: *Develop at least two more positive images from different groups within the community.* It is useful to have a positive family image, spiritual image, and cultural image. Again, many persons who do a community genogram will want to focus on negative issues and past experiences. When this starts to happen, respectfully encourage a refocusing on positive images, strengths, and resources.

Step 5: *Summarize the positive images in your own words and reflect on them.* Encourage clients to summarize their learning, thoughts, and feelings in doing this activity in their own words. As you or your client think back, what occurs? Record the responses, for these can be drawn on in later therapy sessions or in one's daily life.

Although the word *images* is used in this competency-building activity, some clients will find it easier to represent their experiences in terms of auditory (sounds), kinesthetic (tactile sensation), or olfactory (smell and taste) events. Thus, using the community genogram requires you as a counselor or therapist to be sensitive and creative in working with clients' individual cultural, ethnic, and perceptual style differences.

Write a brief summary of your own reactions to doing this competency-building activity. This summary should include reflections of some of the thoughts and feelings you had in completing this exercise as well as any comments you might want to make about the skills you used in doing this activity with another person. When you have completed this reaction paper, be sure to file it in the personal/professional portfolio you are developing as you continue to work through this book.

1. to generate a narrative story of the client in community context

2. to help the client generate an understanding of how we all develop in community

3. to use visual, auditory, or kinesthetic images as sources of strength. These images of strengths can be called on later in the counseling and therapy interview as positive resources to help clients cope with life's difficulties.

This exercise will help you understand the cultural background of your client, for it is through family and community that we learn our cultural framework. Many clients will have had difficult life experiences in their communities. They may be tempted to first focus on the negative as they develop their awareness and present stories of how they have grown and lived in a community setting. Although you will need to attend to negative stories, focus first on clients' positive strengths.

When the community genogram is used in professional practice, therapists and counselors often find that clients routinely refer to different persons and groups that have profoundly impacted their own spiritual and religious development. By encouraging clients to continue to talk about the impact these persons and groups have on their lives, it becomes apparent that these experiences represent important sources of psychological meaning and strength for many of the individuals.

Taking time to learn about these sources of strength and support using the community genogram at the early stages of the helping process provides a practical means by which counselors and psychologists can assist clients in better understanding how they might rely on these personal assets when they face difficult challenges and problems in their lives. We hope that you will learn new ways to assist your own clients in thinking in more expansive ways about their personal and collective strengths as a result of completing Competency-Building Activity 1.3.

The Scientist-Practitioner

The increasing attention that mental health professionals are directing to issues related to spirituality, religion, and community factors in counseling and therapy is a favorable perspective. The cultural transformation of the demography of the United States and the high value that many persons from culturally and racially diverse groups place on spirituality, religion, and community connectedness require such a perspective.

As noted earlier, increasing numbers of mental health professionals are becoming aware of the various ways that individuals in diverse client populations connect spiritual, religious, and community concepts to their thinking about mental health and psychological well-being. However, it is important to note that the fields of counseling and psychology will also continue to draw heavily on the concept of the scientist-practitioner.

The scientist-practitioner is a helping professional who (1) draws on research for more effective practice and (2) uses information from clinical work to generate new research questions and plans. You personally may not be a researcher. However, it is ethically important that you familiarize yourself and continually update your knowledge about the scientific findings that are related to whatever theoretical orientation and worldview you eventually choose to use in your professional practice. The information presented in Research Exhibit 1.1 is aimed at increasing your knowledge of numerous research findings that report on the effectiveness of individual counseling and psychotherapy.

Counselors and psychologists are ethically bound to commit themselves to an ongoing process of professional development. The Professional Development Extension explores some of the ways you can extend your use of counseling and therapy approaches in your professional practice. After graduating from your professional training program, you as a mental health practitioner will commit time and energy to learn about innovations in the field and strive to develop new competencies that enable you to increase your level of effectiveness throughout your career. The scientist-practitioner model provides a useful means of fostering your ongoing professional development, as it encourages counselors and psychologists to

- keep updated on recent research findings and theoretical advancements that are published in the field

- formulate hypotheses that are rooted in their expanding knowledge of relevant theoretical and research contributions when working with their clients

- test their clinical hypotheses by using various counseling and psychological strategies with persons who are experiencing various challenges in their lives

- evaluate the impact of testing such hypotheses in counseling and psychotherapeutic settings

Research Exhibit 1.1

Summary of Counseling and Psychotherapy Outcome Research

Studying the extensive data on the effectiveness of psychotherapy, Hans J. Eysenck let loose a bombshell on the therapeutic profession in 1952. On reviewing numerous counseling and psychotherapy outcome studies at that time, Eysenck summarized his findings by pointing out that:

In general, certain conclusions are possible from these data. They fail to prove that psychotherapy, Freudian or otherwise, facilitates the recovery of neurotic patients. They show that roughly two-thirds of a group of neurotic patients will recover or improve to a marked extent within about two years of the onset of their illness, whether they are treated by

means of psychotherapy or not. This figure appears to be remarkably stable from one investigation to another, regardless of type of patient treated, standard of recovery employed, or method of therapy used (cited in Eysenck, 1966, pp. 29–30).

Eysenck's claims and research methodology have been ably and sharply rebutted in numerous professional publications since he drew these conclusions. Most of the criticisms that have been directed at Eysenck's original work relate to a number of serious flaws noted in the internal and external validity of his research.

A host of researchers have since published numerous articles that report on findings

continued

Research Exhibit 1.1

related to the effectiveness of psychotherapy. These include several publications in a 1996 special issue of the *American Psychologist* (the main journal of the American Psychological Association) and, more recently, in Beutler's (2000) compelling report on an extensive multi-year study that he and his colleagues conducted in this area. These and other research findings confirm Rosenthal's (1990) statement that, in terms of trying to promote positive outcomes when using various counseling and therapeutic approaches with clients, "we are doing considerably better than we may have thought we were doing" (p. 776). Additional support for the effectiveness of counseling and psychotherapy includes the following recent research findings:

- Lambert and Bergin (1994) reviewed the extensive literature on the effectiveness of psychotherapy and concluded that research in this area "is not only statistically significant, but also clinically meaningful. Psychotherapy facilitates the remission of symptoms. It not only speeds up the natural healing process but also often provides additional coping strategies and methods for dealing with future problems The effects of therapy tend to be lasting" (pp. 80–81).

- The bulk of research that has been done since Eysenck's questionable work in this area suggests that psychotherapy (as practiced in controlled situations) is generally effective, although questions remain as to the specificity of the types of positive effects that researchers have found in their investigations and their generalizability to other clinical settings (Hollon, 1996).

- Barlow (1996) states that "there are now a number of studies with high internal validity demonstrating the efficacy of psychotherapeutic procedures as compared with other alternative

helping strategies for a variety of problems" (p. 1056).

- In a 1995 survey conducted by *Consumer Reports* of more than 4,000 persons who indicated that they had sought professional help for various mental health concerns, 54 percent reported that it had helped "a great deal," and 90 percent reported that it had helped "at least somewhat."

- Beutler's (2000) extensive review of outcome studies and his own research in this area have led him to confirm several therapeutic principles that, when implemented in psychotherapy, promote positive changes in clients who experience mental health problems. Some of Beutler's key research findings include the following therapeutic principles:

1. Therapeutic change is greatest when the therapist is skillful and provides trust, acceptance, acknowledgment, collaboration, and respect for the patient within an environment that both supports risk and provides maximal safety.

2. Therapeutic change is most likely to occur when the relative balance of interventions favors the use of either skill-building and symptom-removal procedures with externalizing patients or insight- and relationship-focused interventions with internalizing patients.

3. Therapeutic change is greatest when the directiveness of the intervention inversely corresponds to the patient's current level of resistance.

4. Therapeutic change is greatest when a patient is stimulated to emotional arousal in a safe environment until problematic responses diminish or extinguish (Beutler, 2000, p. 1005).

By using the scientist-practitioner model in this way, counselors and psychologists are able to enhance their own professional effectiveness and support constructive changes in the field.

There are three avenues to major change and growth in the field: (1) new theoretical orientations, such as family therapy, developmental counseling, and multicultural-feminist-social justice helping theories; (2) research; and (3) clinical discoveries made through direct practice. All three methods are critical for effective practice, useful theory building, and meaningful research.

Currently, the field is moving toward a greater level of accountability. As used here, the term *accountability* includes (1) efforts to support the theoretical approach one uses in professional practice with research findings that demonstrate its effectiveness and (2) contracting with clients to evaluate the specific results that ensue from counseling and psychotherapy. With accountability as a goal, the scientist-practitioner model becomes of central importance in the work mental health practitioners do.

Professional Ethics and the Helping Process

Effective professional practice is not only scientific but also ethical. There are many reasons why it is important for mental health practitioners to be knowledgeable of the ethical codes that are codified by the professional groups of which they are a part. One of the primary reasons why it is important to do so involves our awareness that when individuals come for counseling or psychotherapy, they are vulnerable and open to destructive action by practitioners who are not committed to provide services in an ethical manner. Professional helping organizations such as the American Association of Marriage and Family Therapy (AAMFT), the American Counseling Association (ACA), the American Psychological Association (APA), and the National Association of Social Workers (NASW) have codified detailed ethical guidelines that their members are urged to follow in their work.

The bulk of ethical responsibility lies with you, the professional helper. While it is important to take the time to carefully review all of the ethical guidelines that have been developed by the professional group you are a part of, the core of our ethical responsibility is to *do nothing that will harm the client or society*. The following is a list of some fundamental ethical guidelines that cut across all of the mental health professions:

1. *Maintain confidentiality.* Counseling and psychotherapy depend on trust between counselor and client. You as the therapist are in a powerful position in the counseling and therapy relationship; the more trust you build, the more power you have in your relationship with your clients. This book asks you to practice many basic strategies of counseling and therapy in a confidential and ethical

Professional Development Extension

Expanding the Use of Traditional Counseling and Psychotherapy Approaches in Your Professional Practices

Contemporary society continues to be affected significantly by the three major theoretical forces that have emerged in the fields of counseling and psychology over the past one hundred years. Various aspects of these forces permeate many dimensions of our daily lives. For example, many people have come to accept such psychodynamic concepts as unconscious drives and unresolved conflicts as well as their impact on the way we interact with different persons. General agreement also exists in the lay public regarding the ways in which such defense mechanisms as denial, projection, repression, and regression are commonly used when people experience heightened anxieties and stressors in their lives (Freud, 1982).

In a similar way, the cognitive-behavioral force has been generally accepted, as reflected by the existence of many self-help books, groups, and organizations. It can be argued that the rise of the self-help movement in the United States is largely attributed to the growing acceptance of one basic cognitive-behavioral premise—namely, that people can change their feelings and behaviors by intentionally altering the thought processes they have been conditioned to adopt by being socialized into the various historical/environmental/cultural settings of which they are a part (Ellis, 1971, 1983).

A number of constructs linked to the existential-humanistic force have also been accepted by many people. This is commonly manifested in the emphasis that many in our contemporary society place on the notion of personal responsibility and the importance of thoughtfully making choices that increase the probability that individuals can lead meaningful, satisfying, and productive lives despite the adverse situations they may face (Frankl, 1959).

As you continue your journey of becoming a mental health professional, you will inevitably encounter colleagues in the field who hold strong preferences for one or more of these theoretical forces. You are also likely to come across other individuals in the field who have a strong aversion to different aspects of one or more of these helping orientations. Although you will ultimately decide which theoretical principles fit you best, based on your own personal values, biases, and preferences, you need to be aware of how these traditional theoretical forces can be useful when providing a broad range of professional services beyond the counseling and psychotherapeutic setting.

For instance, when providing consultation and training services among parents and teachers, various aspects of the psychodynamic force have been found to be helpful in broadening the sensitivity and understanding of children's behavior in classroom and family settings. In parent and teacher effectiveness training services, teachers and parents commonly are interested in learning how they might deal more effectively with children who unconsciously use different defense mechanisms to cope with the various anxieties they encounter in their lives.

Stress management programs, particularly with individuals in business settings and with student athletes (Wallace, D'Andrea, & Daniels, 2001), have gained popularity and reflect some of the many ways in which cognitive-behavioral principles can be applied in society. Other cognitive-behavioral techniques can be helpful in assisting these persons to realize new dimensions of their professional and athletic performance. Such techniques involve helping these individuals learn new ways to more effectively implement a broad range of cognitive-behavioral techniques—including, but not limited to, goal setting, positive self-talk, visualization, guided imagery training, and muscle relaxation training—to realize new and untapped dimensions of their human potential.

Throughout this book, you will be introduced to various ways in which you can use the skills and principles of the various theories explored here to extend your professional outreach. Each of the Professional Development Extensions offers suggestions for your own personal and professional growth.

manner. It is essential that you maintain the confidence of your clients. If you are a student, you do not have legal confidentiality, and your clients should be made aware of this. Confidentiality is designed to protect clients (not counselors), and only the courts, in the final analysis, can provide a guarantee of confidentiality.

2. *Recognize your limitations.* It is vital that you maintain an egalitarian atmosphere with your clients, classmates, or coworkers. Share beforehand with them the task you wish to work through. Inform them that they are free to stop the process at any time when completing any of the competency-building activities included in this textbook. Do not use the exercises included in this book as a place to delve into the life of another person.

3. *Seek consultation.* As you practice the competency-building activities presented throughout this text, remain in consultation with your professor, workshop leader, mentor, or coworker. Counseling and psychotherapy are often very private. It is important that you obtain supervision and/or consultation when doing these competency-building activities. You may also find it helpful to discuss your own growth as a helper with others after you have completed the competency-building activities in this book. At the same time, be very careful in discussing what you have learned about your clients with others.

4. *Treat the client as you would like to be treated.* Put yourself in the place of the client. Every person deserves to be treated with respect, dignity, kindness, and honesty.

5. *Be aware of individual and cultural differences.* This point will be repeatedly stressed throughout this text. It should be noted, however, that an emphasis on cultural issues can sometimes lead to stereotyping an individual. At the same time, an overemphasis on individuality may obscure multicultural issues.

6. *Review ethical standards constantly.* Read and reread professional ethical codes as you encounter new ideas in this text. The following organizations and the websites include the the ethical codes and guidelines that have been developed and endorsed by various professional mental health associations in the United States.

- The American Association for Marriage and Family Therapy (AAMFT)
  http://www.aamft.org/resources/lrmplan/ethics/ethicscode2001.asp

- The American Counseling Association (ACA)
  http://www.counseling.org/

- The American Psychological Association (APA)
  http://www.apa.org/

- The National Association of Social Workers (NASW)
  http://www.socialworkers.org/pubs/codenew/code.asp

Summary

This introductory chapter provides an overview of the three traditional theoretical forces that have shaped the mental health professions over the past one hundred years and describes two newly emerging paradigms that are having a tremendous effect in the fields of counseling and psychology at the present time. In this chapter, we have highlighted some of the unique aspects of the different worldviews that are reflected in all five of these important forces. Although you will gain a much more detailed understanding of each of these theoretical perspectives as you continue to work through this book, we hope that this chapter has helped to stimulate a greater awareness of some of the basic elements that comprise the psychodynamic, cognitive-behavioral, existential-humanistic, multicultural-feminist-social justice, and positive psychology/wellness counseling approaches to counseling and therapy.

Chapters 2 and 3 are designed to further expand your awareness of recent changes that are occurring in the mental health professionals, which are being specifically spurred by the impact of the multicultural-feminist-social justice (Chapter 2) and the positive psychology/wellness counseling (Chapter 3) movements. Although in the next two chapters your attention will be directed to the important changes that these two new theoretical orientations are having in the mental health professions, we want to conclude Chapter 1 by highlighting how the three traditional theoretical forces are regularly used outside of counseling and therapy situations.

Beyond increasing your understanding of some of the ways that these three traditional theoretical forces can be used in counseling and therapy, the Professional Development Extension on page 26 demonstrates how many of the ideas and helping strategies that are embedded in these theories can be used in other settings as well.

Multimedia Resources for This Chapter

The following online resource offers video and other resources of particular relevance to this chapter of your text.

Companion Website

Go to www.ablongman.com/Ivey6e to view the following video clip:

- Video clip 1.1 demonstrates how one therapist deals with the issue of spirituality in a multicultural counseling situation. Review this video clip and compare the manner in which this therapist approaches the issue of spirituality with the way you might do so with clients you will work with in the future.

chapter 2

The Multicultural-Feminist-Social Justice Movement

---

chapter goals

The chapter is designed to:

1. Increase your understanding of the sociopolitical changes occurring in contemporary society and their impact on the mental health professions.

2. Provide you with a broad and inclusive way of thinking about "multiculturalism," "multicultural counseling and therapy," and "multicultural competence."

3. Help you become more knowledgeable of the ways in which the multicultural-feminist-social justice movement is transforming the mental health professions.

4. Assist you in assessing your current level of multicultural competence.

5. Encourage you to integrate traditional theories of counseling and psychotherapy with concepts that are embedded in the growing multicultural-feminist-social justice counseling movement.

6. Stimulate new thinking about how you can use the concepts presented in this chapter to expand your effectiveness as a mental health professional.

Introduction

The sociopolitical changes occurring in our society are largely being fueled by the unprecedented cultural/racial transformation of the demography of the United States. The nature of this demographic transformation is reflected in the fact that, while the United States has historically been comprised of a majority of persons who come from White, Western European, English-speaking, and Christian backgrounds, it is rapidly becoming a country in which most of its residents will come from non-White, non-European, non-English-speaking, and increasingly non-Christian backgrounds (D'Andrea & Daniels, 2001a). Mental health practitioners need to be knowledgeable of these demographic changes, as they have significant implications for the work they do within the context of a culturally diverse 21st-century society.

The landmark report by the U.S. Surgeon General entitled, "Mental Health: Culture, Race, and Ethnicity" (U.S. DHHS, 2001) highlights numerous implications for counselors and psychologists of the rapidly changing demography of the United States. Two of the many important points made in this report are stressed below, as they have particular relevance both for the work of counselors and psychologists as well as for the topics presented in this book.

First, the Surgeon General's report encourages mental health professionals to rethink the efficacy of using traditional theories of counseling and therapy with persons from diverse populations. This is important, as traditional counseling and psychotherapeutic theories are often not only ineffective but also potentially harmful when used with women and culturally diverse clients (Brabeck, 1999; D'Andrea, 2004a). The chances of producing ineffective and even harmful psychological outcomes with these individuals is heightened when practitioners fail to direct attention to the impact that a client's environment has on her or his psychological well-being. Equally important, practitioners often do not consider the unique ways in which women and culturally diverse persons construct meaning of mental health, psychological stress, and appropriate helping strategies (Ponterotto, Casas, Suzuki, & Alexander, 2001; Sue & Sue, 2003).

Second, the Surgeon General's report underscores the need for practitioners to acquire new competencies and embrace a broad range of professional roles if they are to become a more viable and relevant part of this country's mental health care system (U.S. DHHS, 2001). Social justice counseling advocates have stressed that mental health practitioners can be more effective in addressing the needs of larger numbers of persons from diverse groups and backgrounds when they embrace a multifaceted role of educator, consultant, advocate, and organizational change agent as well as counselor and therapist (Ballou & Brown, 2002; Lewis, Lewis, Daniels, & D'Andrea, 2003).

The cultural/racial transformation of our citizenry, the growing awareness of the ineffectiveness of traditional counseling and psychotherapeutic approaches to meet the needs of diverse people in society, and the growing interest in the multiple roles practitioners can play in promoting wellness and preventing mental health problems all reveal that a major paradigm shift in delivery of services is needed in a culturally diverse 21st century. Among these changes is a growing recognition that mental health professionals must acquire new competencies if they are to work effectively, respectfully, and ethically in an increasingly pluralistic society.

Although slow in coming, gradual awareness of this major paradigm shift has resulted in a number of important institutional changes in our professional associations. Multicultural counseling competencies have been endorsed by the American Counseling Association (Arredondo et al., 1996; Sue, Arredondo, & McDavis, 1992). In addition, this professional organization has also approved social justice advocacy competencies (Lewis, Arnold, House, & Toporek, 2003). Furthermore, *Guidelines on Multicultural Education, Training, Research, Practice, and Organizational Change for Psychologists* has been approved by the American Psychological Association (APA, 2003). These organizational changes are transforming the way many counselors and psychologists think about their roles as mental health professionals. The challenge is how best to serve the needs of larger numbers of persons from diverse client populations in the future (Ivey et al., 2005).

The Rise of the Multicultural-Feminist-Social Justice Force in Counseling and Psychology

Despite the fact that traditional methods are often ineffective and may even produce adverse outcomes, traditional theoretical systems and strategies continue to dominate how many mental health practitioners approach their work. Relatively little attention has been given to adapting these systems to meet the needs of culturally diverse populations in the past. Women, persons of color, and other oppressed groups suffer from these limitations. Many clients from White Western European background also can experience harm, because most counseling and therapy fail to consider their contextual and social history. Thus, the multicultural-feminist-social justice movement is liberating to the White majority just as it is for other populations.

The rise of the multicultural-feminist-social justice movement in the fields of counseling and psychology was in direct response to the perpetuation of various gender-biased and ethnocentric constructs that are embedded in the traditional theoretical forces—namely the psychodynamic (first force), behavioral/cognitive-behavioral (second force), and existential-humanistic (third force). The goal of this text is not to dismiss traditional theory and practice. Rather, the goal is to show how all can benefit from the coming paradigm shift to increase cultural and social awareness. Throughout the book, attention is given to identifying how existing methods can be broadened for the benefit of all.

The genesis of this movement can be traced to the latter part of the 1960s, when the United States was in the midst of a social-cultural revolution. During this time, increasing numbers of female and Black theorists and researchers provided a gender and racial critique of counseling and therapy (Reed, 1964; Vontress, 1969, 1971). They also presented alternative ways of thinking about mental health, psychological disorder, and helping strategies that were more responsive to the unique strengths and needs of women and persons of African descent (Bowman et al., 2001; D'Andrea, 2005b; Jackson, 1995).

The early multicultural-feminist-social justice counseling movement gained added momentum from other theorists and researchers, who directed attention to the unique psychological strengths, vulnerabilities, and challenges that persons of Asian, Latino/Latina, and Native American descent experience as a result of being subjected to various forms of racism and oppression. While different constituency groups contributed to the rise of the multicultural-feminist-social justice movement in the fields of counseling and psychology, several unifying issues bonded them together as a united front. These unifying issues included an awareness of:

- the strengths, vulnerabilities, and needs of persons from diverse ethnic-racial backgrounds (Sue & Sue, 2003)

- the failure of mental health professionals to meet the unique life challenges and problems that millions of persons from marginalized and devalued groups experience in our society (Jackson, 1995)

- the need to create a more comprehensive theoretical view of human development, counseling, and therapy that is more respectful of and responsive to the unique cultural/racial differences that underlie the psychological development of millions of people from diverse groups and backgrounds in our society (D'Andrea et al., 2001)

While multicultural-feminist-social justice counseling advocates have encountered (and, in many instances, continue to encounter) much resistance within the existing mental health establishment, this theoretical perspective is increasingly emerging as a new and accepted paradigm in the mental health professions (D'Andrea, Arredondo, & Daniels, 2005). More and more practitioners are coming to recognize how this new helping paradigm benefits mental health practitioners and their clients.

Among the chief benefits derived from this new theoretical paradigm shift is a more comprehensive and accurate understanding of the complexity of human development. Added to this is a greater knowledge of and sensitivity to the limitations and cultural biases that have dominated the fields of counseling and psychology over the past one hundred years. Practitioners demonstrate an increasing awareness of the need to develop and implement new professional competencies and roles that enable mental health practitioners to have a more positive and lasting impact on larger numbers of clients from diverse groups and backgrounds in our society (Lewis et al., 2003).

Advocates of feminist psychology have been particularly clear in stating the goals of feminist counseling and therapy. They point out that the essential goal of feminist psychology is to broaden mental health professionals' understanding of female development in ways that

- emphasize the linkages that exist between women's mental health and their fair, equitable, respectful, and just treatment in our society

- highlight the need for practitioners to ameliorate the barriers that undermine women's psychological well-being by promoting a social justice perspective in their work (Brown, 1995; Worell & Remer, 2003).

In comparison to their feminist counterparts, multicultural counseling advocates have been more ambiguous regarding the persons to be included within the rubric of the "culturally" different. This ambiguity causes some students and practitioners to ask who is included in the multicultural counseling movement and what are its goals.

The founders of the multicultural counseling movement primarily focused on the psychological needs of persons of color in the United States. However, in time, the exclusive focus on ethnic-racial issues was criticized by advocates of other oppressed groups (e.g., gays and lesbians, the disabled, religious minorities). While the controversy between promoting an exclusive focus (e.g., primarily ethnic/racial) or a more inclusive focus (e.g., including persons from a diverse range of oppressed "cultural" groups) continues to exist to some degree at the present time, most multicultural advocates have moved to embrace a broader and more inclusive definition of multiculturalism.

Respectful Counseling and Therapy

This book embraces an inclusive definition of multiculturalism to emphasize the importance of assessing the multidimensionality of human development, especially as it relates to the strengths and needs of clients from oppressed groups. The inclusive definition of multiculturalism is also used throughout this book to encourage you to think more broadly about your role as a multicultural-feminist-social justice advocate in the helping professions (Daniels et al., 2000).

The RESPECTFUL counseling framework is one way to increase your thinking about the expanded definition of multiculturalism. This framework can stimulate your appreciation of the multidimensional nature of human development, counseling, and psychotherapy as well as enhance your understanding of the various factors that counselors and psychologists need to consider when planning counseling and psychotherapeutic interventions that are aimed at promoting clients' mental health and sense of well-being.

The RESPECTFUL counseling framework (Cartwright & D'Andrea, 2004) stresses the importance of incorporating a comprehensive model of human diversity into the work mental health practitioners do. This new theoretical framework is comprised of ten factors that represent vital considerations in working effectively, respectfully, and ethically with persons from different cultural groups and backgrounds. It emphasizes the need to incorporate one's understanding of a broad range of "cultural" factors when providing psychological services among persons from diverse groups and backgrounds.

It is important to point out that the RESPECTFUL counseling model does not represent an exhaustive listing of all the factors that affect human development. Rather, the ten factors that comprise this framework have been selected because they are clearly known to affect clients' psychological development and sense of personal well-being in many important ways. The specific variables that the RESPECTFUL framework directs particular attention toward include a person's

Religious/spiritual identity
Economic class background
Sexual identity
Psychological maturity
Ethnic/racial identity
Chronological/developmental challenges
Traumatic experiences and other threats to one's well-being
Family identity and history
Unique physical characteristics
Location of residence and language differences

Not only do all of these factors influence the manner in which people learn to view themselves and others, but each factor frequently affects the way clients and mental health practitioners themselves construct meaning of the different strengths, challenges, and problems individuals present in counseling and psychotherapeutic settings.

Think of yourself in a RESPECTFUL manner. When you do, take time to note that regardless of your background, ethnicity, race, gender, or color, you are a multicultural person, defined by multiple social identities. Contrast the multiple identities of the RESPECTFUL framework with the all-too-often unidimensional perspective of traditional counseling and psychology.

Religious/Spiritual Identity

The first component in the RESPECTFUL model focuses on the manner in which individuals personally identify with established religions or hold beliefs about extraordinary experiences that go beyond the boundaries of traditional Western thought (D'Andrea & Daniels, 2001b). Kelly (1995) notes that the terms *religion* and *spirituality* are grounded in an affirmation of transcendental experiences that are typically manifested in religious forms extending beyond the boundaries of ordinary and tangible life experience. As used in the RESPECTFUL counseling framework, religion and spirituality refer to a person's belief in a reality that transcends physical nature and provides individuals with an "extra-ordinary" meaning of life in general and human existence in particular.

Because clients' religious/spiritual identity may play a vital role in the way they construct the meaning of life experiences, it is important that counselors and therapists take time to consider this issue early in the helping process. It is equally important that mental health practitioners take time to consider how their own religious/spiritual identity and beliefs may positively or negatively impact the work they do with clients who embrace different perspectives than their own.

Economic Class Background

Traditional theories of counseling and psychotherapy have largely been developed by middle-class individuals who directed little attention to the ways in which poverty impacts poor people's psychological development and sense of personal well-being. However, a person's attitudes, values, worldview, and behaviors are indeed all affected by his or her economic class standing, background, and identity (Liu, 2001). Given the influence that this aspect of clients' multidimensionality has on their development, practitioners need to be attentive to the ways in which socioeconomic issues, particularly poverty and financial challenges, contribute to their clients' identified strengths and expressed problems during counseling and psychotherapy.

In addition, some counselors and therapists may have developed inaccurate and negative views and prejudices about persons from economic backgrounds that are different from their own. Therefore, it is also important that mental health professionals evaluate their own class-based assumptions, biases, and stereotypes.

Sexual Identity

One of the most complex, though often understudied, aspects of human development involves the sexual identity development of all individuals, particularly those from diverse groups and backgrounds. As used in the RESPECTFUL counseling model,

sexual identity relates to a person's gender identity, gender roles, and sexual orientation. **Gender identity** relates specifically to an individual's subjective sense of what it means to be either male or female. A person's gender identity is clearly affected by the different roles men and women are expected to play within different cultural/ethnic/racial contexts, which influence his or her sexual identity.

A person's sexual identity is also influenced by his or her sexual orientation. Generally speaking, sexual orientation includes such concepts as bisexuality, heterosexuality, and homosexuality. In light of the negative stereotypes that have historically been associated with the term *homosexuality,* terms such as *gay male, gay,* and *lesbian* are considered more acceptable and respectful in describing this dimension of a person's sexual identity (D'Andrea & Daniels, 2001b). The tremendous impact that feminist theories are having in promoting a clearer understanding of the role that one's gender and sexual identity has in the helping process represents important contributions that are discussed in greater detail in Chapter 11.

Psychological Maturity

Counselors and therapists often work with clients who share common demographic characteristics (e.g., age, gender, socioeconomic history, etc.) and racial/ethnic background but who appear to be very different psychologically. In such instances, one client might be described as "more or less psychologically mature" than another. "Immature" clients might be described as "demonstrating limited impulse control in social interactions" or "having a low capacity for self-awareness." More mature clients might be characterized as "being able to discuss problems with much insight," "being highly self-aware," or "having developed a much broader range of interpersonal and perspective-taking skills" than other clients.

Cognitive-developmental theories view psychological development as a process in which individuals move from simple to more complex ways of thinking about themselves and their life experiences. This movement can be traced along a set of invariant, hierarchical stages that reflect qualitatively different ways of thinking, feeling, and acting in the world (Sprinthall, Peace, & Kennington, 2001).

By assessing clients' levels of psychological maturity, counselors and therapists are better positioned to design more effective interventions that respectfully meet their clients' unique psychological strengths and needs. It is also important that counselors and therapists take time to reflect on their own level of psychological development, as the therapeutic process can easily be undermined when practitioners are matched with persons who are functioning at a higher level of psychological maturity than practitioners are themselves. Particular attention to these developmental considerations and their relevance for counseling and therapy are more fully discussed in Chapter 13.

Ethnic/Racial Identity

Clearly, tremendous psychological differences exist among persons who come from the same ethnic/racial groups in our society. This variation is commonly referred to as **within-group differences**. Given the within-group variation that is manifested among persons from the same ethnic/racial groups, it is important that counselors and therapists develop the knowledge and skills necessary to accurately assess these important differences and to respond to them in effective and respectful ways. It is also very important that counselors and therapists understand how their ethnic/racial experiences have affected their own psychological development, the way they construct meaning of the world, and the types of biases they have acquired toward others in the process.

Results from the 2000 census underscore the transformational changes that are occurring in the ethnic/racial makeup of the United States. Mental health practitioners increasingly realize that it is not possible to work effectively and ethically within the context of a pluralistic society without acquiring an awareness of a broad range of issues related to human diversity in general and individuals' group-referenced identities in particular.

Chronological Developmental Challenges

In the RESPECTFUL counseling model, **chronological challenges** represent age-related developmental changes and characteristics normally associated with infancy, childhood, adolescence, and adulthood. The normal age-related developmental changes that people predictably manifest from infancy through adulthood include physical growth (e.g., bodily changes and the sequencing of motor skills), the emergence of different cognitive competencies (e.g., the development of perceptual, language, learning, memory, and thinking skills), and the manifestation over time of a variety of psychosocial skills (e.g., the ability to manage one's emotions and the demonstration of more effective interpersonal competencies) (Dacey & Travers, 2004).

Human development researchers have greatly helped counselors and therapists refine their thinking about the unique challenges clients face at different points across the life span. Practically speaking, this knowledge enables practitioners to work more effectively with persons who face difficult chronological challenges by implementing age-appropriate intervention strategies in counseling and therapy.

These considerations also allow practitioners to be mindful of the unique challenges they are likely to encounter when significant chronological differences exist between themselves and their clients. For example, young practitioners are likely to encounter major challenges in gaining a high level of trust, respect, and professional legitimacy when working with some clients who are much older than themselves (D'Andrea & Daniels, 2001b). On the other hand, a young client might consider an older, more mature practitioner to be out of touch with the needs of young people. Ultimately, a common bond has to be found and a connection forged when these aspects of the RESPECTFUL model are manifested in counseling/therapy.

Trauma and Other Threats to One's Well-Being

Trauma and threats to one's well-being are included in the RESPECTFUL counseling model to emphasize the complex ways in which stressful situations put people at risk of psychological danger and harm. Such harm typically occurs when the stressors individuals experience exceed their ability to cope in constructive and effective ways. An individual's personal resources (coping skills, self-esteem, social support, and the personal power derived from one's cultural group) may be overtaxed when one is subjected to ongoing environmental stressors. Persons who experience stressors for extended periods of time are commonly referred to as being "vulnerable" or "at risk" (Lewis et al., 2003).

Counselors and therapists are frequently called on to work with persons in various vulnerable, at-risk groups including poor, homeless, and unemployed people; adults and children in families undergoing divorce; pregnant teenagers; individuals with HIV or AIDS; persons with cancer; and individuals who are victimized by various forms of ageism, racism, sexism, and other forms of cultural oppression. Heightened, prolonged, and historical stressors often result in more severe and adverse psychological outcomes for many persons from oppressed groups in contemporary society (Salzman, 2001).

To be effective in their work, counselors and therapists need to be able to accurately assess the different ways that environmental and historic stressors contribute to the trauma in the lives of clients. In particular, practitioners need to be knowledgeable of the ways in which intergenerational trauma may contribute to the adverse psychological problems that many persons from various cultural/racial groups experience in their lives.

Duran and Duran (1995) write extensively about the adverse impact of this sort of trauma, referring to it as an intergenerational "soul wound." This wounding significantly contributes to the complex psychological and spiritual problems that many Native American Indians experience today. This "soul wound" effect is also thought to adversely impact the lives of many others in our nation, including people of African descent, women, children, and gay/lesbian/bisexual/transgendered persons who have been subjected to various forms of abuse and violence in their lives (Lewis et al., 2003).

With this knowledge in mind, mental health professionals are better able to develop and implement helping strategies that are deliberately aimed at addressing the negative psychological and spiritual ramifications of such complex forms of trauma. It is also important for mental health practitioners to consider how various life stressors and traumatic events may have a lasting impact on their own psychological development, as such experiences can influence the way mental health professionals work with their clients.

Family Background and History

The rapid cultural diversification of the United States includes an increasing number of families that are very different from the traditional notion of "family" that many counselors and therapists have historically used as a standard for determining "normal family life" and "healthy family functioning." The different types of families (e.g., single-female-headed families, blended families, extended families, families headed by gay and lesbian parents) that counselors and therapists increasingly encounter in their work challenge these practitioners to reassess the traditional concept of the nuclear family, which has been used as a standard against which all types of other families have been compared.

Counselors and therapists will increasingly be pressed to understand the unique strengths that clients derive from different family systems and to implement strategies that effectively foster the healthy development of these diverse familial units. In addition to learning about the personal strengths that individuals derive from diverse family systems, mental health practitioners are encouraged to assess the biases and assumptions they may have developed about family life as a result of their own familial history and experiences. If left unexamined, these biases and assumptions may adversely impact the counseling and therapeutic relationship that mental health practitioners have with clients who come from families that are very different from their own. These and other issues related to family counseling and psychotherapy are explored in greater detail in Chapter 14.

Unique Physical Characteristics

The RESPECTFUL counseling framework emphasizes the importance of being sensitive to the ways in which our society's idealized images of physical beauty negatively impact the psychological development of many persons whose physical nature does not fit the narrow view of beauty that is fostered in our contemporary culture. When working with clients whose unique physical characteristics may be a source of stress and dissatisfaction, it is important for counselors and therapists to reflect on the ways in which the idealized myth of physical beauty may have resulted in internalized negative views and stereotypes.

As a practitioner, you need to be able to help your clients understand the ways in which being socialized into a society that adheres to myopic views of beauty contributes to irrational thinking about their own sense of self-worth (Worrell & Remer, 2003). In particular, practitioners need to be sensitive to and knowledgeable of issues experienced by people with various physical disabilities. To respectfully assist these clients, practitioners are encouraged to help these persons identify and build on the unique personal strengths that they bring to counseling and psychotherapy (Cartwright & D'Andrea, 2004).

Location of Residence and Language Differences

The location of one's residence refers to the geographic region and setting where one resides. For example, D'Andrea and Daniels (2001b) identify five major geographic regions in the United States—the Northeast, Southeast, Midwest, Southwest, and Northwest—that differ in terms of climate patterns and geological terrain. These areas also are distinguished by the types of persons who reside there and the types of occupations and industry commonly available to workers in these locations.

When mental health practitioners work with persons from geographical regions or residential settings that are different from their own, they need to be open to understanding how geographic influences may have affected their clients' development and perspectives. They also need to be aware of the possible stereotypes and biases they may have developed about such individuals and regions.

This is particularly important when working with persons who use a different dialect or language in interpersonal interactions. As is the case with the other components of the RESPECTFUL counseling model, this self-assessment by practitioners is important, because any such stereotypes and biases may lead to inaccurate assumptions and clinical interpretations within the helping setting.

As a "multidimensional" being who is affected by the various factors that make up the RESPECTFUL counseling model, it is vital that you become aware of any assumptions, stereotypes, and biases you may have about clients who are different from yourself in terms of all of the dimensions of the RESPECTFUL framework. Completing Competency-Building Activity 2.1 will help you become more aware of your own multidimensional nature and to gain insights into some of the generalized assumptions and biases you may have developed about persons from other groups and backgrounds as a result of your own social-cultural conditioning. As you think about the clients you are working with or are likely to

Competency-Building Activity 2.1

Using the RESPECTFUL Counseling Model to Foster Personal and Professional Development

Instructions: Take a few minutes to reflect on the ways in which each factor that comprises this theoretical framework impacts your own life. In doing so, it is helpful to write a short description of yourself as it relates to each component of this model in the space provided or on a separate piece of paper. Then briefly state how your understanding of these components and their impact on your development may affect the work you do with clients from different groups and backgrounds you are likely to work with in the future. Think about some of the generalized assumptions and biases you may have developed about persons from other groups and backgrounds as a result of your own social-cultural conditioning. Be sure to record your reactions to this exercise in your personal-professional portfolio.

R—

E—

S—

P—

E—

C—

T—

F—

U—

L—

We wish you good luck on your RESPECTFUL journey toward your own integrative model of counseling and psychotherapy.

Source: M. D'Andrea and J. Daniels, RESPECTFUL counseling and development (2005). Training materials developed in the Department of Counselor Education at the University of Hawaii, Honolulu. Reprinted by permission.

work with in the future, it is useful to reflect on the RESPECTFUL model and consider the impact that issues of diversity may have in the here and now of every interview you have with your clients.

Professional Ethics and Multicultural Competence

If counseling and psychotherapy is provided effectively, it necessarily follows that it be done in a respectful manner. Respectful counseling demands sensitivity to and acknowledgment of the various ways in which contextual and cultural factors impact the development of both you and your clients. These considerations also have a profound impact on the ethical dimensions of your professional practices as well.

At a major conference on the future of professional psychology held more than three decades ago, Korman (1973) made the following statement about the ethical underpinnings of professional practices as they relate to the work mental health practitioners do with persons from culturally diverse groups and backgrounds:

> The provision of professional services to persons of culturally diverse backgrounds by persons not competent in understanding and providing professional services to such groups shall be considered unethical; it shall be equally unethical to deny such persons professional services because the present staff is inadequately prepared; it shall be the obligation of all service agencies to employ competent persons or to provide continuing education for the present staff to meet the service needs of the culturally diverse population it serves. (p. 105)

Despite the clarity of this statement, the fields of counseling and psychology have moved very slowly to implement these recommendations. Since the time of Korman's (1973) statement, numerous others have voiced similar concerns (Daniels et al., 2002; Pedersen Carey, 2003). These individuals have emphasized that the continued use of psychological assumptions and practices that have been developed within the majority cultural context and implemented among clients from different cultures without empirical support for doing so represents a serious ethical issue that continues to exist in the mental health professions (Daniels et al., 2002; LaFromboise, Foster, & James, 1996; Pedersen & Marsella, 1982).

The American Counseling Association (2005) focuses on diversity as a central ethical issue in the Preamble to their Code of Ethics:

> The American Counseling Association is an educational, scientific, and professional organization whose members work in a variety of settings and serve in multiple capacities. ACA members are dedicated to the enhancement of human development throughout the life-span. Association members recognize diversity and embrace a cross-cultural approach in support of the worth, dignity, potential, and uniqueness of each individual within their social and cultural contexts.

It is clear that counselors and therapists are ethically bound to consider their clients within the context of cultural uniqueness. The RESPECTFUL model provides a good beginning outline of issues that need to be considered in this regard. But how can you actually implement a culturally respectful style of counseling and therapy?

The Association for Multicultural Counseling and Development (AMCD) formulated and operationalized a set of 31 competencies that represent minimal standards for cultural competence in the counseling profession (Sue, Arredondo, & McDavis, 1992; Arredondo et al., 1996). This original list was later expanded to 34 competencies to give full attention to multicultural organizational and social justice competencies as well (Sue et al., 1998). Collectively, these competencies and the APA multicultural guidelines represent important advancements in counselors' and psychotherapists' understanding of what constitutes ethical and effective counseling and psychological practices from a multicultural-feminist-social justice perspective. A listing of all 34 of these competencies is presented in Table 2.1

Multicultural counseling advocates have done much to help clarify the meaning of the term **multicultural competence** as it relates to the need for new ethical considerations to be institutionalized in the mental health professions (Arrendondo et al., 1996; Parham, 2002; Sue et al., 1998). These advocates emphasize that practitioners need to keep in mind three overarching goals that underlie effective and ethical counseling practices with culturally diverse persons.

1. *Counselors' awareness of their own cultural values and beliefs.* To experience a genuine sense of empathic understanding for persons from different backgrounds, it is essential that you become increasingly aware of your own social-cultural conditioning in general and the various assumptions, preferences, values, and biases that accompany this conditioning in particular. Competency-Building Activity 2.1 is intentionally designed to have you thoughtfully explore your own cultural multidimensionality. Other competency-building exercises in this book aim to help you in this process further.

2. *Counselors' awareness of their clients' worldviews.* Mental health professionals can work toward achieving this broad competency goal by making a commitment to read about and learn from individuals in culturally diverse groups with whom they work. It is particularly important for you to become knowledgeable of the worldviews and family experiences of persons from culturally diverse groups and to complement your increasing understanding of these areas with a genuine desire to learn more about the ways that these and other cultural factors impact your own psychological development as well. Reading needs to be supplemented by getting out into the community and attending multicultural events. Best of all, developing solid friendships with people different from you is an excellent way to realize new and untapped dimensions of your cultural competence.

Table 2.1

Multicultural Competencies and Standards

GOAL: Increasing Counselor Awareness of Own Assumptions, Values, and Biases

Awareness Competencies

Culturally competent counselors are:

1. Sensitive to their own cultural heritage and to valuing and respecting differences.
2. Aware of how their own cultural background and experiences, attitudes, and values and biases influence psychological processes.
3. Able to recognize the limits of their competencies and expertise.
4. Comfortable with differences that exist between themselves and clients in terms of race, ethnicity, culture, and beliefs.

Knowledge Competencies

Culturally competent counselors:

5. Have specific knowledge about their own racial and cultural heritage and how it personally and professionally affects their definitions and biases of normality/abnormality and the process of counseling.
6. Possess knowledge and understanding about how oppression, racism, discrimination, and stereotyping affect them personally and in their work. This allows them to acknowledge their own racist attitudes, beliefs, and feelings. Although this standard applies to all groups, it may mean that White counselors need to strive to understand how they directly or indirectly benefit from individual, institutional, and cultural racism.
7. Know about their social impact on others. They are knowledgeable about communication style differences, how their style may clash or facilitate the counseling process with minority clients, and how to anticipate the impact it may have on others.

Skill Competencies

Culturally competent counselors:

8. Seek out educational, consultative, and training experiences to enrich their understanding and effectiveness in working with culturally different populations. Being able to recognize the limits of their competencies, they:
   - Seek consultation.
   - Seek further training or education.
   - Refer out to more qualified individuals or resources.
   - Engage in a combination of these.
9. Constantly seek to understand themselves as racial/cultural beings and actively seek to develop a nonracist identity.

GOAL: Understanding the Worldview of Culturally Different Clients

Awareness Competencies

Culturally competent counselors are:

1. Aware of their negative emotional reactions toward other racial and ethnic groups that may prove detrimental to their clients in counseling and therapy. They are able to contrast their own beliefs and attitudes with those of their culturally different clients in a nonjudgmental fashion.

continued on next page

Table 2.1, continued

2. Aware of their stereotypes and preconceived notions that they may hold toward other racial and ethnic groups.

Knowledge Competencies

Culturally competent counselors:

3. Possess specific knowledge and information about the particular group they are working with. They are aware of the life experiences, cultural heritage, and historical background of their culturally different clients. This particular competency is strongly linked to the racial/ethnic/minority development models available in the literature.
4. Understand how race, culture, and ethnicity may affect personality formation, vocational choices, manifestation of psychological disorders, help-seeking behaviors, and the appropriateness or inappropriateness of counseling approaches.
5. Know about sociopolitical influences that impinge on the life of racial and ethnic minorities. Immigration issues, poverty, racism, stereotyping, and powerlessness all leave major scars that may influence the counseling process.

Skill Competencies

Culturally competent counselors:

6. Should familiarize themselves with relevant research and the latest findings regarding mental health and mental health disorders of various ethnic and racial groups.
7. Become actively involved with minority individuals outside the counseling setting (via community events, social and political functions, celebrations, friendships, neighborhood groups, and so forth) so that their perspective of minorities is more than an academic or professional helping exercise.

GOAL: Developing Appropriate Intervention Strategies and Techniques

Awareness Competencies

Culturally competent counselors:

1. Respect clients' religious and/or spiritual beliefs and values about physical and mental functioning.
2. Respect indigenous helping practices and minority community intrinsic help-giving networks.
3. Value bilingualism and do not view another language as an impediment to counseling (monolingualism may be the culprit).

Knowledge Competencies

Culturally competent counselors:

4. Have a clear and explicit knowledge and understanding of the generic characteristics of counseling and therapy (culture bound, class bound, and monolingual) and how they clash with the cultural values of various minority groups.
5. Are aware of institutional barriers that prevent minorities from using mental health services.
6. Know of the potential bias that is embedded in assessment instruments and use procedures and interpret findings by keeping in mind the cultural and linguistic characteristics of their clients.
7. Have knowledge of minority family structures, hierarchies, values, and beliefs. They are knowledgeable about the community characteristics and resources as well as the client's family.

continued on next page

Table 2.1, continued

8. Are aware of relevant discriminatory practices at the societal and community levels that may negatively affect the psychological welfare of the population being served.
9. Are knowledgeable of numerous models of minority and majority identity development and understand how these models relate to the counseling relationship and the therapeutic process. (New competency added by Sue et al. in 1998.)

Skill Competencies

Culturally competent counselors:

10. Engage in a variety of verbal and nonverbal helping responses. They are able to send and receive both verbal and nonverbal messages accurately and appropriately. They are not tied to only one method or approach to helping but recognize that helping styles and approaches may be culture bound. When they sense that their helping style is limited and potentially inappropriate, they can anticipate and ameliorate its negative impact.
11. Exercise institutional intervention skills on behalf of their clients. They can determine whether a "problem" stems from racism or bias in others (e.g., the concept of healthy paranoia) so that clients do not inappropriately blame themselves.
12. Seek consultation with traditional healers or religious and spiritual leaders and practitioners in the treatment of culturally different clients when appropriate.
13. Take responsibility for interacting in the language requested by the client. A serious problem arises when the linguistic skills of the counselor do not match the language of the client. If this is the case, counselors should seek a translator with cultural knowledge or refer to a knowledgeable and competent bilingual counselor.
14. Have training and expertise in the use of traditional assessment and testing instruments. They not only understand the technical aspects of the instruments but also are aware of the cultural limitations. This allows them to use test instruments for the welfare of clients from diverse cultural, racial, and ethnic groups.
15. Attend to as well as work to eliminate biases, prejudices, and discriminatory practices. They should be cognizant of sociopolitical contexts in conducting evaluations and providing interventions and should develop sensitivity to issues of oppression, sexism, and racism.
16. Take responsibility in educating their clients to the processes of psychological intervention such as the goals and expectations in counseling and therapy, the client's legal rights, and the counselor's helping orientation.
17. Tailor their relationship-building strategies, intervention plans, and referral considerations to the particular stage of their clients' cultural/racial identity development, while taking into account his or her own level of identity development as well. (New competency added by Sue et al. in 1998.)
18. Engage in psychoeducational or systems intervention roles in addition to their clinical role. Although the conventional clinical role is valuable, other roles, such as the consultant, advocate, adviser, teacher, facilitator of indigenous healing, and so on, may prove more culturally appropriate. (New competency added by Sue et al. in 1998.)

Sources: Adapted from D. W. Sue, P. Arredondo, & R. J. McDavis. (1992). Multicultural counseling competencies and standards: A call to the profession. *Journal of Counseling and Development*, 70, 477–486; and D. W. Sue et al. (1998). *Multicultural counseling competencies: Individual and organizational development*. Thousand Oaks, CA: Sage. Used with permission.

3. *Culturally appropriate intervention strategies.* Throughout this book a variety of interventions are offered for persons of differing cultural backgrounds and perspectives. In addition, as the multicultural-feminist-social justice counseling movement continually develops new ideas and practices, counselors and therapists have a responsibility to seek out and adapt appropriate new strategies for all clients

One of the important ethical standards in counseling and psychology involves the importance of knowing your professional limitations. From a multicultural perspective, this requires mental health practitioners to thoughtfully reflect on their limitations as they relate to their current level of multicultural counseling competence. Competency-Building Activity 2.2 encourages you to think more in depth about your own level of multicultural competence and offers practical suggestions for increasing your professional competence in this important area.

Completing the following activity will help you gain a clearer understanding of some of your strengths and weaknesses in this aspect of your professional development. In doing so, you will be able to intentionally engage in learning activities in your professional training program that will enhance those dimensions of your multicultural counseling awareness, knowledge, and/or skill areas that were rated low in this activity. The Professional Development Extension identifies some of the ways that the theoretical concepts presented in this chapter can be used in interventions in your professional practice.

Summary

This chapter provides an overview of the rise of the multicultural-feminist-social justice movement in the fields of counseling and psychology. It directs particular attention to some of the controversies associated with this newly emerging theoretical force in the mental health professions. One of the major controversies discussed relates to the manner in which the term *multiculturalism* is defined.

Embracing a broad and inclusive definition of this term encourages mental health practitioners to understand the multidimensional nature of their clients as well as their own development. The RESPECTFUL counseling framework is presented to stimulate a practical understanding of some of the important variables that affect our clients' and our own development as cultural beings.

In an effort to help you develop a greater understanding of the various factors that affect your personal and professional development, specific attention is directed to 10 "cultural" factors known to have a tremendous impact on the ways individuals construct meaning of the world, life experiences, and the types of problems and challenges people encounter in their lives. Many of the concepts presented in Chapter 3 complement the different views of mental health and personal well-being that have been put forth by multicultural counseling theorists and researchers.

Competency-Building Activity 2.2

Assessing Your Own Multicultural Competence

This competency-building activity encourages you to reflect on your professional development using the multicultural counseling competencies that are outlined in Table 2.1 as a guide for self-assessment.

Instructions: Read down the items presented below and rate your level of competence on a scale of 1 to 3 in the space provided next to each item. A score of 1 indicates a "poor" level of competence in that area; a score of 2 indicates an "average" or moderate level of competence in that area ; and a score of 3 indicates "high" competence in that area.

This activity uses an expanded definition of the term *multicultural*—one that reflects the RESPECTFUL counseling model. Thus, it is important to rate your awareness, knowledge, and skills on the items across a broad range of culturally diverse persons (e.g., individuals who operate from different spiritual/religious, economic class, sexual, psychological, ethnic/racial, chronological, family identities, geographic identities and backgrounds).

Multicultural Self-Assessment Survey

1. Rate yourself in terms of your awareness and knowledge of your own cultural heritage.

    _____

2. Rate your awareness of the ways in which your own cultural background, experiences, values, and biases influence your current thinking and feeling. _____

3. Rate your ability to recognize the limits of your own cultural competence and expertise.

    _____

4. Rate your level of comfort with differences that exist between yourself and people from diverse cultural groups and backgrounds. (Remember, this includes individuals who have developed a spiritual/religious, economic class, sexual, psychological, ethnic/racial, chronological, family , and/or geographic identity that is different than your own.) _____

5. Rate your knowledge of the ways in which clients' racial and cultural heritage affect their psychological development, their notions about normality/abnormality, and the counseling process. _____

6. Rate your overall understanding of the ways in which oppression, racism, discrimination, and stereotyping affect the lives of clients who come from devalued groups in our society. _____

7. Rate your knowledge of the communication style differences that persons from culturally diverse groups use to express themselves and the impact these differences might have in counseling and psychotherapy. _____

8. Rate your overall motivation to seek out educational, consultative, and training experiences that are intended to enrich your effectiveness when working with persons from culturally different populations. _____

9. Rate your ability to identify ways you may unintentionally help perpetuate various forms of racism and cultural oppression in your work as a mental health professional. _____

10. Rate your ability to remain nonjudgmental when working with persons from culturally and racially different groups who express beliefs and attitudes that are very different from your own. _____

11. Rate your awareness of the preconceived notions you hold about persons who come from cultural groups and backgrounds that are different from your own. _____

12. Rate your overall knowledge of the various cultural/racial identity development theories that have emerged in the fields of counseling and psychology over the past 35 years. _____

13. Rate your understanding of the ways in which cultural and racial factors affect personality formation, vocational choices, the manifestation of psychological disorders, help-seeking behavior, and the appropriateness or inappropriateness of counseling approaches. _____

continued on next page

Competency-Building Activity 2.2, continued

14. Rate your overall understanding of the sociopolitical influences that impinge on the life of culturally and racially underserved people in the United States. _____

15. Rate your knowledge of the relevant research and the latest findings regarding the psychological challenges persons from diverse cultural groups commonly experience in their lives. _____

16. Rate how actively involved you are with persons from diverse cultural/racial groups outside the counseling setting (via community events, social and political functions, celebrations, friendships, neighborhood groups, and so forth). _____

17. Rate your knowledge of the diverse religious and/or spiritual beliefs about physical and mental functioning that clients from different groups are likely to manifest in counseling and therapy. _____

18. Rate your level of awareness of the indigenous helping practices and unique help-giving networks that characterize persons from diverse cultural/racial groups in our society. _____

19. Rate the degree to which you value bilingualism and do not view another language as an impediment to counseling and therapy. _____

20. Rate your understanding of the ways in which the culture-bound, class-bound, and monolingual characteristics of counseling and therapy may clash with the cultural values and behavior styles of persons from diverse groups and backgrounds. _____

21. Rate your understanding of the institutional barriers that prevent culturally different persons from using mental health services in the United States. _____

22. Rate your knowledge of the cultural biases that exist in the assessment instruments and the interpretations of psychological evaluation procedures that are used among culturally, racially, and linguistically diverse clients. _____

23. Rate your knowledge of different family structures, hierarchies, values, and beliefs that characterize the lives of persons who come from diverse cultural/racial groups. _____

24. Rate your understanding of the various forms of oppression that continue to adversely affect the psychological welfare of clients from culturally diverse populations. _____

25. Rate your knowledge of the various ways that cultural/racial identity development theories can be effectively, respectfully, and ethically used in counseling and psychotherapy. _____

26. Rate your ability to use a variety of verbal and nonverbal helping responses that are intentionally designed to effectively and respectfully acknowledge the different communication styles of persons from culturally and racially diverse groups. _____

27. Rate your ability to effectively exercise institutional intervention strategies and skills that are deliberately aimed at promoting more respectful and just environmental conditions where culturally diverse clients live, learn, work, and develop. _____

28. Rate how open you are to consulting with traditional healers and religious/spiritual leaders within the different cultural/racial groups that you are likely to serve as a mental health professional. _____

29. Rate your ability to interact in the language that is requested by the culturally diverse clients you work with as a mental health professional. _____

30. Rate your ability to use psychological assessment tools and evaluation procedures that serve the well-being of clients from diverse cultural, racial, and ethnic groups you are likely to work with in the future. _____

31. Rate your ability to reduce the cultural biases, prejudices, and discriminatory practices that continue to be perpetuated in

continued on next page

Competency-Building Activity 2.2, continued

the assessment and evaluation strategies counselors and psychologists continue to use in their work. _____

32. Rate your ability to educate culturally diverse clients about the goals, expectations, and ethical issues related to counseling and therapy. _____

33. Rate your ability to tailor your relationship-building strategies, intervention plans, and referral considerations to your clients' stage of cultural/racial identity development. _____

34. Rate your ability to develop and implement systems change interventions (i.e., organizational development strategies, community-building services, etc.) in addition to providing traditional counseling and therapy

services for clients in diverse cultural populations. _____

Now look back and identify the items on which you scored yourself highest. Keep these strengths in mind, as you may be able to use these areas of multicultural competence to help you develop other areas that need improvement.

Then look over your lowest scores and identify two or three competencies you hope to strengthen. Record these items in your personal/professional portfolio. When you have completed working through this book, refer back to your responses to this competency-building activity to see if you would rate yourself any differently on the items on which you scored lowest. Be sure to record your reactions to this exercise in your personal-professional portfolio.

Multimedia Resources for This Chapter

The following online resource offers video and other resources of particular relevance to this chapter of your text.

Companion Website

Go to www.ablongman.com/Ivey6e to view the following video clip:

- Video clip 2.1 demonstrates how some professional competencies might be manifested in a counseling session involving a White male therapist working with a female client of African descent. Identify the competencies listed in Table 2.1 that this counselor exhibits when working with the client.

MyHelpingLab

myhelpinglab

If a MyHelpingLab passcode was included with your textbook and you have activated your passcode:

- go to http://www.ablongman.com/myhelpinglab
- enter the "Counseling" area of the site by clicking on that tab
- select "Video Lab" from the toolbar to the left of the page
- select "MyHelpingLab Videos by Theoretical Approach"
- select the "Culture-Sensitive" module to view various video clips of a therapist using this approach with a client

Professional Development Extension

Using Multicultural Theory in Consultation and Training Interventions

As demographic changes continue to unfold in the United States, you will be challenged to increase your awareness and knowledge of the multicultural-feminist-social justice counseling perspective. You also will need to embrace new professional roles that will enable you to positively impact the lives of more persons from diverse groups and backgrounds than counselors and therapists have worked with in the past. These new roles may include working as a consultant, psychoeducator, life skills trainer, organizational development specialist, client advocate, community organizer, coalition builder, social change agent, and professional development trainer, to name a few. Each role will offer you opportunities to use the various theories and skills associated with the multicultural-feminist-social justice orientation to enhance your consultation and professional training efforts and also to serve as your clients' advocate in different situations. Becoming skilled in assessing clients' development on the 10 dimensions that comprise the RESPECTFUL framework is an important step in the process. The following case demonstrates the knowledge that can be gained about a client that will inform your work

Manuel is a 38-year-old physically disabled client who came to counseling for assistance with a career change. Early in the first session, the counselor used the RESPECTFUL counseling model to get to know Manuel better. What follows is a summary of Manuel's responses to questions based on the 10 components of the RESPECTFUL model:

Religious/spiritual identity
Client: Like most Latinos, I am a Christian, and I believe that God has a purpose in everything that happens. After my accident, I was very depressed for several months. But now I believe God has a purpose for this, and I have to find out what that is.

Economic class identity
Client: I am middle class. While I could always use more money to get the things I want, I think I am doing OK. But I need to look to my future and how I can get the training I need to move into a new career.

Sexual identity
Client: Before the accident I was a very active and strong guy. I was divorced eight years ago and dated a number of women that I really liked. But the accident changed all that. It's not easy to put the pieces back together.

Psychological maturity
Client: Before the accident I didn't think too much about psychological things. But after that, I have had to deal with being depressed, and I found new strengths I didn't know I had. I also recognize there are other areas I have to work on. You could say the accident helped me to get more mature in these ways.

Ethnic/cultural identity
Client: As I said before, being a Latino, I have a strong belief in God and why He allows things to happen to people. I also come from a very large family that is very supportive. I get a lot of strength from my family.

Chronological challenges
Client: One of the best things about being 38 years old is that I have had a chance to learn from my past. I have a long life in front of me, and I think my biggest challenge is to become a good teacher so I can have a positive impact on younger people.

Threats to personal well-being
Client: I really want to become a teacher and know I have the ability to do it. I guess the biggest threat to me getting there is worrying about how other people might see me and not give me a chance to become a teacher.

Family history
Client: I have learned to persevere through hard times from my parents. They had it rough when I was younger. They had to go through a lot of discrimination because of the racism around us. But they persisted through all the hard times.

continued on next page

Unique physical characteristics

Client: I know I have this disability, but that does not mean I'm a sick or helpless. It makes me mad when other folks look at disabled people as being helpless. I know I have to move on and make a life for myself and hopefully have a positive impact on young people along the way.

Location of residence and language issues

Client: I am a city guy and can relate to urban kids because I know what it means to be a part of the street culture. I also speak Spanish, and that helps me connect with a lot of Latino people in ways that many other people can't. So you see, I have a lot of things going for me even though I had this accident. I think you may have a better picture about who I am, and I enjoyed talking about these things. So where do we go from here?

The case of Manuel demonstrates how, by using the RESPECTFUL model early in the counseling process, the counselor was able to identify strengths and concerns that Manuel brought to the session that may not have surfaced until later in counseling, if at all. From a multicultural perspective, client advocacy requires becoming aware of and knowledgeable about your clients' and your own cultural worldviews, values, preferences, and biases and acquiring the skills that are necessary to advocate for the rights and well-being of your clients in ways that are respectful of and consistent with their cultural worldviews, strengths, and needs. There are many directions one could go in working with Manuel. Having gained the information provided above, what might you do next with this client?

Chapter 3

Positive Psychology and Wellness Counseling

Introduction

Counseling and psychotherapy were developed to help people cope with life's problems. Given this, clients tend to be described in terms of what is wrong rather than what is right. Of course, we as therapists help clients overcome their problems. Assisting them in gaining a thorough understanding of life challenges and problems is vital for effective counseling and therapy. But continual emphasis on problems can sometimes lead clients to a downward cycle in which they find themselves focusing more on the negatives of their lives while downplaying their positive potential for change.

People grow and solve their problems when they focus on what they can do rather than what they cannot do. This is a basic tenet of brief counseling and therapy, which is discussed in more detail later in this chapter. This positive psychological approach to helping has been around for some time. Carl Rogers (1961) spoke of the importance of communicating positive regard in counseling and psychotherapy sessions. Leona Tyler, one of the first female presidents of the American Psychological Association, introduced what she termed "minimal change therapy" (1961). Tyler's approach was to find the strengths in the client and then build on these strengths toward client satisfaction and action. Ivey and Gluckstern (1974) developed the positive asset search as a concrete helping strategy that leads therapists to focus on client resources.

Over the years, the fields of counseling and psychology have stressed the importance of focusing on positive aspects of the client. In contrast, more medically oriented clinical psychology and psychiatry have given this area less emphasis.

The concept of **positive psychology** has become highly influential in recent years. Clinical psychologist Martin Seligman (2000b) first introduced this term to the mental health professions in the following way: "Modern psychology has been co-opted by the disease model. We've become too preoccupied with repairing damage when our focus should be on building strength and resilience, especially in children" (p. 4).

Seligman criticizes the helping fields as having become too focused on individualism, with insufficient attention given to connection. In critiquing the role individualism plays in our thinking about counseling and therapy, Seligman emphasizes the importance of moving to an "I-we balance" in promoting mental health. This theoretical perspective stresses that counseling and therapy need to explore resources of the client, both in the client and in the client's immediate environment, with the intent of facilitating healthy human development. To do this, counselors and psychologists are increasingly being encouraged to examine the interconnections and relationships that clients have within their world context and to determine how these relationships impact clients' lives.

There is an extensive literature, research, and instrumentation built on the positive psychology framework (Peterson & Seligman, 2004; Snyder & Lopez, 2001). However, the positive psychology/wellness counseling model has given relatively little attention to multicultural and social contextual issues, despite its growing popularity in the mental health professions (D'Andrea, 2005b).

Although the work of Seligman and other positive psychology/wellness counseling advocates is presently gaining increasing attention, it is important to point out that a similar helping paradigm was introduced in the counseling profession in the mid 1980s (Witmer, 1985; Sweeney & Witmer, 1991). More recently, Sweeney and Myers (2005) use the term *wellness counseling* to capture the essence of this paradigm.

The Wellness Model

Sweeney and Myers present a comprehensive, empirically tested, life-span model that describes the dynamic nature of human growth and personal health. Using the general theory of wellness counseling as a guide, Myers and Sweeney (2005b) derived an evidence-based model based on more than 15 years of research that validates many of the theoretical concepts that underlie healthy human development. What makes Sweeney and Myers's wellness counseling model particularly relevant are their recommendations and strategies for using specific counseling and psychotherapy approaches to optimize wellness and healthy development among clients from diverse groups and backgrounds who are seen by mental health practitioners.

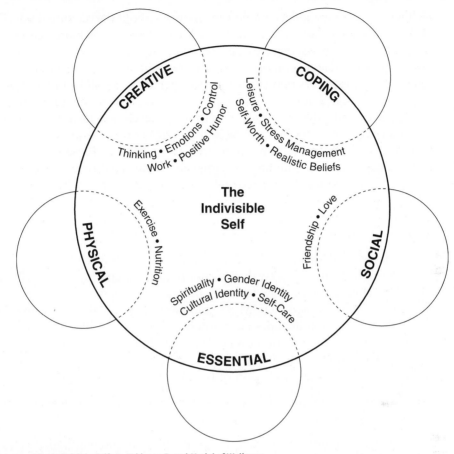

Figure 3.1 The Indivisible Self: An Evidence-Based Model of Wellness

Source: J. E. Myers & T. J. Sweeney (2005). Counseling for wellness: Theory, research, and practice. Alexandria, VA: American Counseling Association. Reprinted with permission.

An overview of Sweeney and Myers's wellness model is presented in Figure 3.1. This model is, first of all, contextual in that the authors point out that our clients come to us from a family and neighborhood and that they are deeply affected by societal institutions and even by world events and politics. Sweeney and Myers point out that even the client's view of time is an essential aspect of the helping context. Their model is highly integrative in that it emphasizes the need for people to learn ways of effectively addressing and balancing several dimensions of wellness to realize their highest level of health and well-being. Sweeney and Myers's use of the term *the indivisible self* highlights the importance of viewing wellness as a comprehensive and integrative process of human growth and development.

Myers and Sweeney's (2005b) research reveals five major components of **the indivisible self,** a self that is connected with a person's life context and environment in multiple ways. The components of the IS-Wel model may be assessed using the Five Factor Wellness Inventory (Myers & Sweeney, 2005b). In this way, their wellness counseling model complements notions about the **relational self** (Comstock, 2005) and the **self-in-relation** (Miller & Stiver, 1997), which are central considerations of feminist counseling theories (Chapter 11).

The five interlacing components of Myers and Sweeney's theoretical framework have several subfactors that contribute to a person's overall health and sense of personal well-being. Counselors who use a positive psychology/wellness counseling approach identify the strengths clients have developed in any of these wellness components early in the counseling and therapy process. If we start counseling and therapy from a positive frame of reference, we can use these strengths to resolve many client issues. The internal strengths that clients have already developed, not just the external theories and practices of the therapist, are what produce positive changes in clients' lives.

The Essential Self

The first aspect of Sweeney and Myers's wellness model is referred to as the essential self. Research findings suggest that the essential self is comprised of three subfactors, including concern with care for self, others, and transcendent issues (Myers & Sweeney, 2005b). According to Myers and Sweeney's (2005b) counseling framework, a wellness orientation includes attention to spiritual and self-care matters as well as an awareness of and pride in one's gender (including sexual orientation) and cultural identity. The word *caring* might best sum up the essence of this aspect of wellness. What follows is a brief discussion of the importance of spirituality, gender identity, cultural identity, and self-care as they relate to Sweeny and Myers's notion of the essential self.

Spirituality. As noted in Chapter 1, the fields of counseling and psychology have historically avoided dealing with issues related to spirituality. In fact, the field of psychology has been described by some as a secular religion. However, spirituality is a vital part of existence for many individuals, with 95 percent of the people in the United States stating a belief in God (Miller & Thoresen, 2003).

The ability of mental health practitioners to work with spiritual and religious issues is an expected and important part of professional practice. Research evidence suggests that persons who have a spiritual orientation tend to also have better health (Powell, Shahabit, & Thoresen, 2003). Given the importance of this area, spirituality as a therapeutic dimension is explored in several other parts of this book.

Gender Identity. Being aware and proud of one's gender and sexual orientation are critical dimensions of wellness (D'Andrea, 2005a). It can be argued that the feminist and gay liberation movements have done more for women and gay/lesbian/bisexual/transgendered people than all of the work counselors and therapists have done over the years (Reicherzer, 2005).

Men also benefit from increasing awareness of gender identity issues. As awareness increases, men consider what it means to be a male and how certain aspects of male privilege are maintained in our contemporary society at the expense of many women's psychological, economic, and social development and well-being. These and other gender-related issues are explored in greater detail in Chapter 11.

Cultural Identity. The Sweeney and Myers wellness model was very early in recognizing multicultural issues as foundational to good mental health. Becoming aware of oneself as a cultural being is increasingly recognized as a critical dimension of human development and personal well-being (Parham, 2002).

As a precursor to Sweeney and Myers's work, the Black awareness movement of the 1960s was an important impetus for promoting cultural identity issues in the mental health professions. African-American thought and action in this area has also influenced the development of other identity frameworks and has served as a model for women, gays, and lesbians as they seek pride in their special identities as well (Sue & Sue, 2003).

Cultural identity development theory is stressed in more detail in Chapter 12, where the multicultural counseling and therapy (MCT) framework is explored. It is important to recognize that cultural identity, on both a conscious and unconscious level, is a critical dimension of our sense of psychological well-being.

Clients come to counseling and therapy with multiple cultural identities. For example, the client may be male, White, gay, Catholic, and of Polish descent. Changes in any one of these identity dimensions over the course of one's life will affect an individual's overall cultural identity and sense of personal wellness. Some aspects of cultural identity (such as those listed in the RESPECTFUL counseling and development framework in Chapter 2) may be more salient than others when clients seek help in counseling and therapy.

Self-Care. This wellness dimension may be contrasted with self-neglect, where clients fail to take care of themselves adequately. Emotional health and wellness are facilitated when the person develops safety and prevention habits, including maintaining cleanliness, wearing safety belts, seeking adequate dental and medical care, avoiding harmful substances, and realizing the need for a safe environment for healthy development. A clear sign of emotional distress is the absence of caring for oneself.

The Coping Self

Self-caring is not enough in itself to achieve an optimal state of positive psychology and personal wellness. We also need to be able to effectively cope with the multiple stressors that are inherent to our environment. Sweeney and Myers identified four key subfactors associated with this aspect of the indivisible self.

Realistic Beliefs. Each day, we are overwhelmed with data and information about the world. As described in Chapter 1, all of this data and information can become stressful and even overwhelming. However, by taking a realistic view, these stressors can be reframed as unique challenges and opportunities that can help us realize new and untapped aspects of our personal development, health, and wellness.

Many people develop irrational and cynical beliefs about themselves, others, and the world, often in response to the magnitude of life stressors, the bombardment of information, and the rapid changes that characterize our technological society (Hawkins, 2002). The development of such beliefs is antithetical to the notions of wellness and positive psychology.

Those who face things as they are are better able to take responsibility for their actions and do something about their situation. This is especially true if a sense of hopefulness and optimism is embedded in the individual's personal psychology. Albert Ellis talks extensively about these issues in his rational-emotive-behavioral-contextual therapy (REBCT) model, which is discussed in Chapter 8.

It is important to note that irrational beliefs are often manifested by statements that emphasize what a person and others "should" or "ought" to be doing in life. It is particularly important to avoid the trap of perfectionism and the many "shoulds" and "oughts" that go with these unrealistic and irrational beliefs. Examining your own and your clients' irrational beliefs is an important aspect of positive psychology and wellness counseling.

Stress Management. Even if we have realistic beliefs, life does not always give us what we want and deserve. Former president Jimmy Carter once noted that "life is not fair." Everyone experiences stressors that are associated with unfair life experiences. Those who do not handle such stressors well suffer not only psychosocial difficulties, but physical problems as well. A wellness helping approach involves assisting clients in learning new and more effective ways to deal with these types of stress.

Cognitive-behavioral counseling theories (Chapters 7 and 8) are particularly well suited to help clients learn new coping strategies that foster more effective, satisfying, and productive lifestyles. Competency-Building Activity 3.1 describes a sample of a stress management program that we have found to be very effective to use when working with students and clients from a broad range of backgrounds in counseling and therapy. It is provided here to assist you in acquiring some of the skills that are necessary in promoting a positive psychology/wellness counseling approach in your work.

Self-Worth. This dimension of the coping self is often described as a positive self-concept or one's level of self-esteem. Feeling good about oneself is clearly an aspect of the healthy person. While extensive theorizing about these concepts has been done by many persons in the fields of counseling and psychology, it is useful to remember that simply accepting yourself for who you are is the most basic aspect of a sense of self-worth. While all theories, in one way or another, involve issues of self-worth, existential-humanistic counselors and therapists direct particular time and energy in dealing with these issues. The work of Carl Rogers, Victor Frankl, and Fritz Perls are central in this regard (Chapters 9 and 10).

Leisure. The United States is a country of workaholics. People's vacations in the United States are among the shortest in length of any industrialized country. This is

Competency-Building Activity 3.1

Developing Your Own Stress Management Program

You may use any of a large number of positive psychology/wellness strategies in individual counseling and therapy to help clients deal with stress. For example, you might teach a lonely or shy person the microskills of listening and then use assertiveness training to help this individual become more socially effective. You can teach relaxation training or desensitization to clients experiencing fears about different situations that occur in their lives. Developing and implementing stress management programs are yet another useful way that counselors and psychologists can foster clients' overall sense of wellness.

Instructions: To experience the power of stress management programming, get together a small group of three or more individuals with similar issues and spend at least one hour teaching them some of the basic principles of stress management. A model stress management group includes, but need not be restricted to, the following:

Step 1. *Establishing rapport and relating program goals to your group's special needs.* Usually, there is a special topic or need that the group members share with one another. For example, your group might be comprised of teenagers, graduate students, adult children of alcoholics, women dealing with job stress, or an in-patient group whose members are experiencing more serious mental health difficulties. At the initial stage of your meeting with the group, use your counseling skills to build a sense of trust and confidentiality among the individuals who agree to participate.

As you continue to build trust with the persons participating in this activity, take time to explain the overall goal of this intervention (e.g., to assist the participants in learning new strategies to more effectively deal with stressors that occur in their lives). After doing so, take time to find out what the participants hope to get out of their involvement in this process and how they think it may help them better deal with their own unique life stressors. It would be useful to modify your agenda to meet the unique needs and wishes of the group members as they explain what their personal hopes are in this regard.

Step 2. *Providing cognitive instruction that explains the origins of stress and how stress impacts people.* In an effort to build a collaborative working atmosphere with the persons participating in this activity, it is important to draw out the nature of specific stressors that the persons in the group commonly experience in their lives. Encouraging the participants to engage in storytelling and personal sharing will draw your group together and help define common stressors that the group members are experiencing.

You can also provide a brief talk on the nature of stress and explain what it does to the body and mind. An analysis of the antecedents, behaviors, and consequences of stress can be especially helpful. In addition, you may want to brainstorm ways in which the many stressful events we face affect our daily lives. This list may include various stressors associated with commuting to work, conflicts that may occur with our supervisors, family arguments, loss of a job, medical issues, or the neighbor's dog barking when we are trying to sleep.

Step 3. *Stress management training.* Select your own favorite stress management techniques for this role-play session. Review your own special skills and experience, and make your first try at stress management training from what you know best. Usually, stress management programs include some form of relaxation training, meditation, yoga, personal sharing of coping mechanisms, listening skills training, and/or assertiveness training. Be sure not to overplan for this initial group meeting, and be sure your program is not rushed and stressful in itself.

continued on next page

Competency-Building Activity 3.1, continued

Step 4. *Homework.* Introducing the concept of relapse prevention and reviewing practical relapse prevention techniques the group members might find useful when dealing with future stressors are important considerations to include in your stress management program. It is also important to keep in mind that, unless your trainees are encouraged to "take home" what they have learned,

the benefits they may have gained from participating in this intervention are likely to be quickly forgotten. Follow up with your workshop participants a week later to see how effective your program was in helping them deal more effectively with their life stressors.

Be sure to record your reactions to this exercise in your personal-professional portfolio.

unfortunate, since a balanced approach to life is essential if one is to work effectively and live pleasurably. Leisure, recreation, sports, and just having time for personal relaxation are all a part of a healthy person's world.

Leisure counseling is not a topic covered with any degree of thoroughness in most counseling and psychology training programs. Despite a lack of formal training in this area, practitioners can nonetheless help many clients that make positive changes and resolve personal issues by just helping them find a way to have time for fun in their daily lives. Someone who is constantly tense and does not experience much fun in life is usually not fun for others to be with. Consequently, issues related to one's leisure time are frequently tied to the overall quality of wellness that characterizes one's social self.

The Social Self

Another important aspect of the indivisible self model is one's ability to relate to the world in a socially connected manner. Two major components—friendship and love—comprise this aspect.

Friendship. Positive psychology and wellness researchers have reported that the type of interpersonal connections people have with others is directly related to their overall health status (Snyder & Lopez, 2001). People with friends and broad social networks tend to not only be happier, but also to live longer and survive illnesses more effectively than individuals with limited social support and few friends (Myers, Sweeney, & Witmer, 2000). A holistic assessment of clients' wellness includes an evaluation of their personal connections with others, the quality of their friendships, and the extent to which they are a part of an interdependent social support network.

Love. Given the important role that love plays in a person's overall wellness, there is an unfortunate lack of attention to this topic by professional training programs and clinical practices. In spite of the lack of attention directed to this important human factor, love is a central dimension of positive psychology and wellness (Fisher, 2004).

In discussing different aspects of love, Myers and Sweeney (2005a) note that:

> Characteristics of healthy love relationships include the ability to be intimate, trusting, and self-disclosing with another person and the ability to receive as well as express affection with significant others. The life task of love also necessitates having a family or a family-like support system which has the following nine characteristics: shared coping and problem-solving skills, commitment to the family, good and frequent communication, encouragement of individuals, regular expression of appreciation, shared religious/spiritual values, social connectedness, clear roles, and shared interests, values, and significant time together. (p. 54)

Taking time to assist clients in assessing how love is manifested in various ways in their lives is an important component of wellness counseling. It is equally important to examine the areas in which the client would like to experience a greater level of love and then to help the client develop realistic strategies for realizing this aspect of wellness.

The Creative Self

This area of self speaks to the thoughts and emotions individuals experience when they intentionally strive to realize their creative potential. Besides the unique thoughts and feelings we experience in creative activity, operating from the creative domain also requires the ability to control what occurs around us as we direct our psychological energy into our acts of creativity.

A positive sense of humor and satisfaction from work completed comprises what Sweeney and Myers (2005) refer to as the creative self. The healthy person is able to intentionally create new ideas and ways of dealing with the world and oneself that result in satisfying and productive outcomes. The creative self thus involves the aspects of thinking, emotions, positive humor, control, and work.

Thinking. The thinking self is both analytical and creative. This human capacity enables people to solve problems and meet personal challenges that occur in their lives. Cognitive-behavioral therapy (Chapters 7 and 8) is associated with examining how a person's thoughts impact one's behavior, although all therapies work to assist clients in creating new meaning in their lives. Multicultural counseling and therapy (MCT) (Chapter 12) is based in creativity through its emphasis on reframing and finding new and more culturally respectful ways of considering the issues and challenges clients from diverse groups and backgrounds bring to the helping process.

Emotions. Being in touch with what one "really feels" in the moment is a foundation of positive mental health. The healthy person is one who is able to experience a broad array of emotions. The existential-humanistic theories described in Chapters 9 and 10 are particularly concerned with this area of wellness, although all theories attend to clients' emotions in varying degrees.

Positive Humor. There is growing evidence that a person's thoughts, moods, emotions, and belief systems have a fundamental impact on one's overall sense of wellness and physical health (Chunn, 2002). Increasingly, researchers are turning their attention to the role that humor plays in stimulating wellness and a positive psychology. A good summary of the results of numerous studies in this area can be found on the following website: **Holisticonline.com.** What follows is a brief overview of some of the conclusions that have been drawn from studies done on the impact of humor and laughter in people's lives that are contained on this website:

> Humor is a universal language. It's a contagious emotion and a natural diversion. It brings other people in and breaks down barriers. Best of all, it is free and has no known side reactions.
>
> Laughter is infectious. Hospitals around the country are incorporating formal and informal laughter therapy programs into their therapeutic regimens. In countries such as India, laughing clubs—in which participants gather in the early morning for the sole purpose of laughing—are becoming as popular as Rotary Clubs in the United States. Laughing is found to lower blood pressure, reduce stress hormones, increase muscle flexion, and boost immune function by raising levels of infection-fighting T-cells, disease-fighting proteins called gamma-interferon, and B-cells, which produce disease-destroying antibodies. Laughter also triggers the release of endorphins, the body's natural painkillers, and produces a general sense of well-being.

From a counseling perspective, it is important to know that there is increasing empirical evidence to suggest to clients that if what they are doing doesn't work, try laughing. All of us experience stressful situations in our lives. Sometimes, these situations may appear impossible to overcome. In these situations we may feel that all we have left to do is laugh or cry. Positive humor releases us to be more creative and certainly helps our physical health. Despite the importance of humor in promoting personal wellness, it is seldom stressed in counseling and therapy.

Control. Another aspect of the creative self relates to the degree of control people feel that they have in their lives. Sweeney and Myers (2005) point out that "the results of numerous studies indicate that people experience positive outcomes when they perceive themselves as having an impact on what happens to them and negative outcomes (e.g., depression) when they perceive a lack of control. Perceived control is associated with emotional well-being, successful coping with stress, better physical health, and better mental health over the lifespan" (p. 56).

Work. A healthy work and career life enables one to achieve economic success. Our vocation gives our life meaning and direction. It not only fills our time, but meaningful work fulfills our psychological lives in many positive ways as well.

Work is a way to contribute to a greater good and to be recognized in the world. At the same time, we need to recognize that groups such as the working poor may not always enjoy the privileges of the middle or upper class and thus may experience work in very different ways. Finding meaning and value in our own work and helping our clients find similar meaning can be a key to the sort of personal satisfaction that fosters wellness.

The Physical Self

The mind only works well if it exists in a sound body. This simple truth underscores the need for counselors and therapists to be aware of principles of nutrition and exercise and the ways in which these dimensions of the physical self are manifested in our clients' lives. As counselors and therapists, we need to model self-care in the way we treat our bodies.

The most effective therapy for some clients is through building self-respect—the sort of self-respect that directs attention to the ways in which clients work to develop and maintain a healthy physical self. When the body moves in flexible and healthy ways, the mind is also likely to move in flexible and healthy ways.

Nutrition. Eating properly is not just following the recipe for eating in the latest diet fad. On the contrary, we all need to be aware that a healthy diet is essential to our overall wellness. In thinking about this area of health, counselors and psychologists need to be mindful of the long-term complications of being overweight and understand that obesity is now identified as one of the leading causes of death in the United States (Chunn, 2002). Being overweight and out of shape also undermines many people's sense of self-esteem, emotional wellness, and most of the other dimensions listed in the wellness paradigm.

The twin partners in becoming overweight are lack of regular exercise and a poor diet. Whether one chooses a low-carb, low-fat, or grapefruit diet, a sense of self and direction is needed for healthy eating. Part of developing a better sense of oneself is appropriate nutrition. It is time that counselors and therapists increased their awareness of this important dimension of health and intentionally incorporate it into their counseling practices.

Exercise. Stretching and exercise are essential components of wellness and are especially important in old age. Failure to routinely exercise throughout one's life diminishes a person's ability to realize optimal health and well-being. Physical exercise is a vital part of wellness no matter what one's age. Witness the vast increase in child obesity that has occurred in our nation over the past few decades.

We recommend strongly that you ask your clients about their physical health and help them think about and implement new behavioral strategies that will lead to better nutrition and exercise for their bodies. Such counseling strategies can lead to many positive outcomes for clients. For example, depression is less likely to persist when one is actively involved in regular physical exercise (Lark & Richards, 2000). Numerous researchers and theorists also support the exploration of exercise in wellness counseling settings through encouraging clients to consider participating in other alternative health programs, including yoga and meditation training (Lewis et al., 2003).

Taking a Contextual and Personal Approach to Wellness Counseling

The wellness counseling approach that we advocate does not just focus on individual clients, but considers the multiple contexts that affect people's lives across the life span. Because the positive psychology/wellness counseling paradigm is truly a holistic approach to human development, the outcomes that result from this helping framework are manifested in a series of choices made one at a time, on a day-to-day basis as clients strive to realize new and untapped dimensions of their health and wellness. The effects of these life choices are cumulative and holistic, in the sense that change in one area of a person's life affects changes in other areas of one's development for good or for worse.

Poor choices about exercise and nutrition, for example, ultimately affect other aspects of a person's well-being, including one's mood, thinking, and coping capacities. Likewise, living in an oppressive environment can thwart people's growth and health over time, just as encouragement can help individuals transcend physical or other challenges that occur in their lives.

The best way to understand the wellness approach is not just to read about it, but also to participate and experience the ideas associated with this new theoretical movement personally by implementing wellness concepts into your own life. Although formal wellness assessment instruments are available for clinical and research purposes (Myers & Sweeney, 2005a), it would be most useful to conduct an informal wellness self-assessment of your own present level of positive psychology and wellness following the guidelines in Competency-Building Activity 3.2. In doing so, you will gain a better understanding of many of the concepts presented and gain new competencies that will enable you to work more effectively when using a positive psychology/wellness approach in your work.

After you have applied the ideas presented in the activity to yourself, try them out with a friend, family member, or classmate. In doing so you will be better prepared to help clients assess their own wellness potential in your professional practice in the future.

It is helpful to begin your career thinking through the implications of the wellness approach for your own personal life and professional practice. Some counselors and therapists have entered the field to work on their own problems. Others spend endless time searching through various theories to label what is wrong with their clients. Counselors and therapists can be more effective and their clients better served if practitioners spend more time identifying their clients' and their own strengths and strive to build on these personal assets in ways that lead to more satisfying and productive human outcomes.

Competency-Building Activity 3.2

Assessing Personal Wellness

Instructions: The self exists in multiple contexts, all of which affect an individual's development and sense of personal well-being. Review the description of the indivisible self model and the related concepts presented in Figure 3.1. Then describe and assess your own level of wellness by using the questions/guidelines included for each of the following dimensions:

The Contextual Self

As Myers and Sweeney (2005a) assert, we are selves-in-relation to multiple contexts in our lives. With this in mind, please describe on a separate piece of paper some of the significant social contexts or environmental systems within which you have developed that can be included in your personal/professional portfolio. Another way of thinking about this issue is to ask yourself the following question: How are you connected to the world? The following guidelines can further assist you with this part of the wellness self-assessment process:

1. Think of your family, your neighborhood, and your community. How has your life been affected by these environmental systems? What strengths and resources have come to you from interacting in these social contexts?

2. Institutions around us affect our being in many ways as well. What strengths might you have gained from your education, religion, government, and business/work settings?

3. Each of us is born into a global environment. How has politics, the broad culture, specific global events, the environment, and the mass media affected your personal development? Can you identify resources that have come to you through the larger world around you?

4. Change is both inevitable and a factor of time. Are you a purposeful and positive person, or are you less positive and more resigned to the impact that life circumstances have on your development? Do you tend to view change as an opportunity for growth or a problem to be dealt with?

5. Draw a lifeline (i.e., a line that represents the time of your birth to the present time). Identify significant events and influences in your development on this timeline. Who, what, how, and when may be important considerations to keep in mind when completing this part of your self-assessment.

6. Next, look to the future. Continue your lifeline with significant persons, experiences, and events you expect or plan to encounter or experience at a later time. If possible, invite a partner to help you explore the significance of these moments on your present and projected development. Do you see patterns in your development? Are your choices moving you to higher levels of wellness? If not, how might you change toward making deliberate choices for wellness? If not now, when?

The Indivisible Self

The five major areas of the healthy self and their subcomponents are listed below. Please rate yourself on a 10-point scale on each of the following wellness dimensions. In addition, take time to anchor each rating with a positive story or event from your life. The purpose of the anchor is to remind you and your client of specific resources and strengths that can be used to facilitate a greater level of wellness in your clients' and your own future. Regardless of your rating, think of one story or event in this area that provides you with a positive asset, resource, or strength. Briefly describe this story or event and the personal asset, resource, or strength associated with it.

continued on next page

Competency-Building Activity 3.2, continued

The Essential Self

1. Spirituality: Low   High
                        1 2 3 4 5 6 7 8 9 10

    Spirituality Anchor:

2. Gender Identity: Low   High
                        1 2 3 4 5 6 7 8 9 10

    Gender Anchor:

3. Cultural Identity: Low   High
                        1 2 3 4 5 6 7 8 9 10

    Cultural Identity Anchor:

4. Self-Care: Low   High
                        1 2 3 4 5 6 7 8 9 10

    Self-Care Anchor:

The Coping Self

1. Realistic Beliefs: Low   High
                        1 2 3 4 5 6 7 8 9 10

    Realistic Beliefs Anchor:

2. Stress Management: Low   High
                        1 2 3 4 5 6 7 8 9 10

    Stress Management Anchor:

3. Self-Worth: Low   High
                        1 2 3 4 5 6 7 8 9 10

    Self-Worth Anchor:

4. Leisure: Low   High
                        1 2 3 4 5 6 7 8 9 10

    Leisure Anchor:

The Social Self

1. Friendship: Low   High
                        1 2 3 4 5 6 7 8 9 10

    Friendship Anchor:

2. Love: Low   High
                        1 2 3 4 5 6 7 8 9 10

    Love Anchor:

The Creative Self

1. Thinking Self: Low   High
                        1 2 3 4 5 6 7 8 9 10

    Thinking Anchor:

2. Emotions: Low   High
                        1 2 3 4 5 6 7 8 9 10

    Emotions Anchor:

3. Self-Control: Low   High
                        1 2 3 4 5 6 7 8 9 10

    Self-Control Anchor:

4. Positive Humor: Low   High
                        1 2 3 4 5 6 7 8 9 10

    Positive Humor Anchor:

5. Work: Low   High
                        1 2 3 4 5 6 7 8 9 10

    Work Anchor:

The Physical Self

1. Nutrition: Low   High
                        1 2 3 4 5 6 7 8 9 10

    Nutrition Anchor:

2. Self-Care in Exercise: Low   High
                        1 2 3 4 5 6 7 8 9 10

    Self-Care Anchor:

Increasingly, research findings are pointing out that using positive psychology and wellness strategies in counseling and therapy are helpful in fostering healthy human development (Snyder & Lopez, 2001). Take time in every interview to identify your clients' positive assets and strengths. This deliberate focusing on clients' strengths is not part of most counseling theories; it is particularly manifested in Frankl's logotherapy (Chapter 10) and the integrative developmental counseling and therapy (DCT) model that is presented in Chapter 13.

It is possible to work from a positive psychology/wellness counseling framework in all the theories you will encounter in this textbook. Recommendations for doing so are included throughout the ensuing chapters. Another important reason for emphasizing wellness counseling issues is that the general public is increasingly demanding greater accountability of the positive outcomes that mental health care professionals purportedly facilitate in the services they offer.

Brief Therapy and Wellness Counseling

We live in an age that emphasizes accountability and concrete results. Many mental health professionals working in community agencies, private practice, schools, and business and industry are increasingly asked to shorten their time with clients and provide clear evidence of counseling effectiveness. One answer to this trend for greater professional accountability and effective service delivery is the rising popularity of brief counseling and therapy interventions (Berg, 1994; Sklare 2005).

Brief counseling seeks to find strengths in the client, gives minimal attention to problem definition, and helps clients find immediate and workable solutions to the unique challenges they face in their lives. In these ways, it is a good complement to the positive psychology and wellness counseling paradigm that is emerging in the mental health professions.

Brief therapy (one to ten sessions) is not a cure-all but rather a specific way of providing clients with useful approaches to deal with particular concerns and problems. By learning practical approaches to concrete stressors that occur in their lives, individuals can resolve other problems they may encounter.

Brief counseling and therapy is less useful with clients who have issues concerning the meaning of life or are interested in examining how various aspects of their personal history continue to impact their current thoughts, feelings, and behaviors. Individuals with these goals are likely to be better served by existential-humanistic or psychodynamic-oriented counselors and therapists.

Clients suffering from severe depression may benefit from some of the short-term solutions offered in brief counseling, but cognitive-behavioral (Chapters 7 and 8) and integrative developmental counseling and therapy (Chapter 13) methods may be of more benefit for these clients. However, all models of counseling and therapy can be potentially enhanced by brief therapy helping approaches if these are used appropriately.

Brief counseling and therapy methods can be useful with culturally diverse clients, because of its direct emphasis on problem solution, minimal analysis of the problem, and a positive approach to helping. However, brief therapists can err if they move too fast and fail to consider how cultural factors may be relevant for the unique contextual challenges their clients experience. Such failure can be compounded when practitioners do not take time to assist culturally different clients identify their individual and collective strengths and to help them explore how these personal assets can be used to address their unique life issues, challenges, and problems.

In brief counseling and therapy, it is important to effectively build positive rapport and trust with all clients who participate in this helping modality, especially with those who are culturally different from ourselves. For example, Australian Aboriginals tend to respond well to an approach to counseling and therapy that places emphasis and value on building positive rapport and trust with the practitioner. Positive therapeutic outcomes are possible when practitioners use Western counseling theories with persons in this cultural group but only if sufficient time and attention is devoted to building a solid relationship between the therapist and the client. The therapist can participate in the helping process in ways that involve sharing of personal life experiences and expression of personal thoughts, beliefs, and feelings about the counseling process early in the brief counseling process.

Native American Indians also place a high value on this sort of interpersonal connection with the therapist and need to establish a high level of trust before they are comfortable discussing personal issues in counseling and therapy settings. Many Native American Indians also have different notions about time and its relevance for brief counseling and therapy interventions. Given the different worldview of this cultural group, it is important to understand the psychology of Native American clients before using a brief counseling and therapy approach.

LaFromboise (1996a) comments on these concepts from an indigenous Native American perspective, pointing out:

> The Native American Indian idea of time is quite different—elongated and more subtle. It's important that you be there when you are needed rather than relying on artificial boundaries. The time for termination in counseling needs to be extended. In a sense, your being as a person will be tested more completely than was taught in any counseling degree program. There is a tendency to prefer open directive approaches to helping. The reflective, client-centered approach is often viewed with suspicion.
>
> Working with Native American Indians is a wonderful opportunity for counselors and therapists to learn what community means and what it means by waiting for the right time and working within the client's frame of reference. This is a real test of discipline—a chance to be a true friend when you are really needed. You'll also learn humility. (p.5)

Social constructivists point out that cultural factors will impact the meaning of time, the problem-oriented versus positive psychological approach to helping, and the practitioner's understanding of what a "solution" means to clients from diverse groups and backgrounds (D'Andrea, 2000; Sexton & Griffin, 1997). Given the relevance of these cultural considerations for brief counseling and therapy, it is useful to routinely think about the various ways that these issues will emerge in your professional training experiences (e.g., when participating in role-plays) and in professional situations where you will use brief counseling strategies with your clients (e.g., in your practicum and internship courses).

Competency-Building Activity 3.3 presents an overview of the specifics of brief counseling and therapy. As you proceed with this competency-building activity, please be mindful of what was stated above about cultural considerations and the importance of taking time to build a positive and trusting relationship with clients who come from diverse cultural backgrounds.

Keep in mind that brief counseling theorists constantly emphasize the importance of helping clients identify their strengths early in the therapeutic process. Thus, this competency-building activity starts with positive images and stories from the client's family and community genogram. Feminist and multicultural theorists hold that we can find our greatest strengths by exploring who we are as selves-in-relation. This can effectively be done by taking time to reflect on our family and community networks as sources of strength when searching for solutions to our own and our clients' problems.

Efforts to build positive rapport are often accorded less time in brief counseling settings. However, as has been stated earlier, the effective use of relationship-building skills is vital in any successful therapeutic encounter, for without a caring and empathic understanding, the chances of finding solutions with our clients are greatly reduced.

Brief counseling and solution-oriented experts like Guterman (1996) and Sklare (2004) stress that practitioners need to structure the initial client interview in such a way as to encourage a search for solutions. These theorists also suggest that a positive attitude on the part of the counselor is essential in communicating that something can be done to help.

Consequently, during the first few minutes of the first stage of the counseling process, the counselor needs to emphasize that something can indeed be done, both in the short and longer term, to make a positive difference in the client's life. With some clients, a brief wellness assessment (see Competency-Building Activity 3.2) may be a good way to establish a positive relationship. In doing so, you will be better able to learn about your clients' strengths. This will enable you to help clients in ensuing counseling sessions by encouraging them to think of some of the ways they might use their personal assets to more effectively deal with their problems.

Although the basic listening sequence remains important, brief therapy holds that most counselors and therapists spend too much time listening to problems and issues. Therefore, the second stage—gathering data about the problem and identifying clients' personal assets—should be brief and to the point. While the client's feelings are noted and reacted to sensitively, brief counseling is more focused on concrete and specific behaviors and actions that clients can take to realize more satisfying and productive lives. As part of this action approach, the search for clients' strengths are stressed repeatedly in the therapeutic encounter.

Competency-Building Activity 3.3

Brief Counseling and Therapy

Instructions: The following structured exercise may be used with a volunteer or real client. You should photocopy the following set of instructions and share them with your client beforehand so that the client knows specifically what is going to happen and why. This sharing of interview plans, seeking of the client's reactions to this therapeutic technique, and willingness to adjust the brief counseling approach based on the client's feedback moves you toward what social constructionist and postmodern theorists refer to as "coconstructing" the helping process (Sexton & Griffin, 1997). D'Andrea (2005a) refers to this approach to counseling and therapy as an intentional effort to "democratize the helping process."

After you have shared this set of instructions with your client and taken time to respond to her or his feedback regarding this action plan, you can proceed by implementing the following steps. Keep in mind that this activity may take an hour or longer to complete. You may wish to have a second session with your client if either or both of you think that would be beneficial. Recall that brief counseling therapy is considered anything less than ten sessions.

Brief Therapy Process

Stage 1. Building Rapport and Structure

Spend some time making the client comfortable in your own way. Share the interview plan in writing and talk about what is to happen. "What would you like to have happen today?" is a suggested opening question. This opening implies that something is indeed going to happen. Usually the client will express a concern or issue. Be sure to listen carefully to what the client has to say in response to this question before moving to the second stage of this exercise.

Stage 2. Gathering Data and Identifying Assets

Community Genogram. Tell the client that before you go further, you'd like to learn more about his or her background and strengths. Then proceed to develop a community genogram with your client. (Refer to Competency-Building Activity 1.2 in Chapter 1 as a guide in completing this part of this exercise.)

Try to limit the development of the community genogram to 15 minutes as a beginning step with your client. Make it clear that you want to avoid negative stories about her or his background at this time and that you will focus only on strengths derived from her or his community and family. Later in this session or in following sessions, you can focus on other issues that may arise as a result of helping the client develop the community genogram.

It is particularly important to generate two to three positive family and community images when completing this part of the competency-building activity. In doing so, be sure to help the client locate some of the feelings that are associated with these images in specific parts of the body. These are resources and strengths that can be discussed in greater detail later in this exercise.

Listening to the Client's Concern. Briefly return to the original concern and help the client draw out the issue or task to work on in more detail in this session. Even at this early stage of the helping process, it is useful to ask questions that focus on positive aspects of the client's personal strengths as well as other resources and sources of support that are available from her or his family or community. We have found the following questions particularly helpful in keeping clients focused on their personal strengths and familial/community resources when using this brief counseling approach in our work: (1) "Are things any better now?" (2) "What's keeping it from getting worse?" (3) "Are there any good things you observe in the situation?"

After you have helped identify some of the client's strengths and other sources of support,

continued on next page

you are ready to have the client clarify the specific concern or issue to work on. This part of the helping process involves encouraging the client to share a "narrative" about a particular situation to be changed. Part of this process is making sure that the concern is presented in a specific, concrete fashion and that clearly observable behaviors are identified. If thoughts or emotions are the issue, being clear and specific about these components of the client's narrative are equally important to explore.

Positive Asset Search. As you explore the client's issue or concern in greater detail, be sure to continue to use the strengths-based approach described above. This is done by referring to the specific personal assets (e.g., various strengths and other sources of support) that were identified when completing the community genogram with the client. Some questions that you may find useful in reminding clients of the various strengths and sources of support they can rely on when dealing with the concerns they bring to counseling and therapy include the following: (1) "What are you already doing right now to deal with this concern?" (2) "What personal strengths and assets did you talk about as we completed your community genogram that may be helpful in dealing with this concern right now?"

Stage 3. Determining Outcomes

The basic question of the third stage of brief counseling and therapy is "What is your goal?" You may want to introduce this central question even in the first phase of rapport building. Your task as counselor or therapist is to help clarify, specify, and concretize clients' goals. If the problem or issue is complex and multifaceted, work only on a part of the issue. This avoids having the client get frustrated by trying to do too many things at once to change the situation. Without clear-cut directions and goals, brief counseling will not succeed. It may be helpful to write down with your client the specific achievable goal(s) the two of you have defined.

After goal setting, the major focus of your session will be on how to achieve those goals. Use the client's own words and language in establishing and clarifying the goals for brief counseling. If the client's first language is other than English, have the client write the goals in that language as well.

Stage 4. Generating Alternative Solutions

The final stage of brief counseling and therapy involves generating alternative solutions and transferring the learning that occurs in counseling and therapy to the specific situation the client is dealing with. This requires you to assist clients in brainstorming possibilities that meet their goals.

The process of brainstorming a range of alternative strategies clients might use to deal with the issues they bring to counseling requires a good deal of creativity from you and your clients. Essentially, your joint task is to create new solutions to old issues and to encourage your clients to act on these solutions—ideally in the near future.

Both you and your client should feel free to refer to the following brainstorming list, especially during your first attempts at brief counseling and therapy.

Brainstorming Suggestions. Some examples of questions that may be useful in facilitating effective brainstorming at this stage of brief counseling and therapy include the following:

1. Tell me about times when the problem is absent or less strong.

   - What is happening when the problem is not going on?
   - What about when the problem doesn't seem to be as strong at other times?

2. Tell me about the exceptions to the problem.

   - When does the problem not happen?
   - What is different about those times?
   - How do you get to that more positive result?
   - What did you do (they do) to get a more satisfactory ending?

continued on next page

Competency-Building Activity 3.3, continued

3. Tell me about other ways to consider this problem.

   • What do you do for fun? (This question can break a mind-set and may provide surprising answers.)

   • What could be funny about this issue? (Using humor and surprise in a culturally sensitive fashion may be exceptionally helpful.)

   • How does your family and culture relate to these issues?

   • What supports or answers do your family and culture provide?

Family and Multicultural Issues

Referring to the results of the community genogram, which you completed earlier with your client, often provides new ideas, positive assets, and support at this stage of the brief counseling and therapy process. The following questions can be based on the completed genogram:

• Drawing on your image of your family that you talked about when completing the community genogram, you repeatedly mentioned the positive influence of the elders in your family. How do you think the elders in your family would look at this issue?

• Imagine the elders are standing at your side. What would they say to you right now in terms of the situation you are dealing with?

• Your community (or group) has many strengths. Where would you go for support with some of these issues?

Taking It Home

Aim constantly for the generalization and transferability of the new ideas and resolutions that are generated at this stage of brief counseling to the specific issues of the client. The more specific you and the client can get in formulating joint solutions to the situation, the more likely it is that benefit will result from the counseling session. You may want to write a contract for action in both English and your client's own language (if it is different). As part of the brainstorming and transfer-of-learning process, the following questions may be helpful:

• How will your life be different after you have implemented the plans we have talked about today?

• Who will be the first to notice change when you implement these action plans?

• What is that person likely to say to you when you implement these action plans?

• How will you respond to this person?

• What would you like to happen after you implement these action plans?

• How can we make that happen?

Rehearsal and role-playing, using the concepts of assertiveness training (see Chapter 7), are useful here. The specificity and immediacy of these techniques are helpful, because assertiveness training in itself is a form of brief therapy. Do not hesitate to add other theories and strategies according to the needs of your clients when using brief counseling and therapy with them. Relapse prevention (an important cognitive-behavioral strategy that is also described in Chapter 7) may be very useful at this point to ensure ongoing generalization and effective transfer of learning to the specific situation(s) the client presents in brief counseling and therapy.

Follow-Up

Use the telephone or e-mail to follow up and provide support for your client. Encourage your clients to call in and tell you how things are going. Remind your clients that they can contact you later for another session to work on a different part of the issue if they choose to do so.

   Be sure to record your reactions to this exercise in your personal-professional portfolio.

"What do you want to have happen?" is the question that highlights the essence of the third stage of the five-stage interview structure. In brief counseling, goal setting is the centerpiece of effective intervention. Competency-Building Activity 3.3 provides several specific strategies for setting goals and determining outcomes with clients.

Stages 4 and 5 of the five-stage structure are often combined into one stage in brief therapy and solution-oriented counseling. As each solution is brainstormed in the helping context, the therapist immediately focuses on how the client could take the problem resolution into the real world of daily life.

Transfer of the client's learning is particularly important in brief counseling, as practitioners are keenly aware that resolving issues in a limited number of sessions does not completely remake the client. This approach to therapy does not seek "cures" or personality transformation. Rather, brief counseling often asks clients to think about counseling and therapy sessions as similar to stopping for gas at a service station. This attitude might be expressed as follows: "All of us have problems and face unique challenges from time to time. We've worked on this issue over three sessions, and you've achieved some real progress. But new issues will present themselves again in the future. Think of me and our counseling center as a place to come back to when new concerns arise. It may be six weeks or six months or six years, but I look forward to seeing you again when you'd like to explore what is happening in your life at some future time."

The idea that "there is no lifelong cure" is a useful concept to promote in all counseling and therapy endeavors. All of us face issues constantly, and long-term therapy may help us find meaning or gain a better understanding of our developmental history. But even with the best long-term therapy, specific issues (e.g., divorce, death, living with a serious illness, etc.) may lead a client back to therapy again and again.

Brief counseling and therapy offers a useful model to be implemented in conjunction with other traditional helping methods. At times we need to examine life in depth, but often many clients will do well by implementing specific strategies that are intentionally designed to ameliorate short-term problems and promote a greater sense of personal competence, empowerment, and satisfaction in the process.

Limitations and Practical Implications of Brief Therapy and Positive Psychology/Wellness Counseling

Brief counseling and therapy has increased in use and popularity in recent years. As a result of its growing popularity in the mental health professions, brief therapy is close to the stage where it could be recognized as a major theory in itself. The positive strengths-based emphasis, clear practice strategies, and results orientation of this therapeutic modality are all applicable in many clinical settings.

It is possible, of course, to be too positive and ignore or minimize real client issues in the process. Consequently, it is important to balance a positive psychology/wellness counseling approach to helping with sensitivity and understanding of the real-life problems that many clients experience in their daily lives.

Professional Development Extension

Using the Sweeney and Myers Wellness Model in Sports Counseling

Many of the positive psychology/wellness counseling concepts used in individual therapeutic settings also can be helpful in other professional and personal situations. One particular area of professional mental health practice that provides a natural fit in incorporating the positive psychology/wellness counseling paradigm involves the services that counselors and therapists might provide for student athletes. Numerous positive psychology/wellness counseling concepts have been found to be effective in fostering the psychological development and personal well-being of top athletes (Wallace, D'Andrea, & Daniels, 2001). The following case describes how two sports counselors used the Sweeney and Myers wellness model to help a client realize new and untapped dimensions of his total wellness:

> Phil, a gifted 19-year-old college athlete at a large university, set up an appointment with two sports counselors who provide various services to student athletes, including wellness counseling. Phil indicated an interest in getting an assessment of his own level of personal wellness. During the first meeting, the sport counselors used the Sweeney and Myers (2005) model to explain the five major areas of the healthy self. This involved talking about the essential self, coping self, social self, creative self, and physical self, and their subcomponents. The counselors pointed out that by assessing these areas and their subcomponents, individuals can identify the strongest aspects of their health and wellness as well as areas in need of improvement. After describing this wellness model, Phil was asked to complete a personal wellness assessment like the one in Competency-Building Activity 3.2.

> Upon completing this form, Phil noted that he scored highest in the physical and social wellness areas, lower on the creative and essential self, and lowest on the coping self. The sports counselors explained that they could help Phil learn new coping skills and strategies that would help him improve his low score in this area. This

included helping him learn how to use meditation, visualization, and muscle relaxation skills as well as new problem-solving and time management strategies. Phil responded positively to working on all of these coping strategies, and an action plan was agreed upon for the next four weeks.

> The counselors began the next counseling session by talking about different meditation, visualization, and muscle relaxation techniques and how they might help Phil cope more effectively with some of his life stressors. The counselors described how to do these activities, and then Phil practiced doing short meditation, visualization, and muscle relaxation exercises during the meeting. Before ending that session, the sports counselors had Phil commit to using various combinations of these techniques at different times of the day on his own before the next session (e.g., using meditation or visualization in the morning, muscle relaxation or meditation in the afternoon, and visualization or meditation in the evening).

> During the next two sessions, the counselors helped Phil explore new problem-solving strategies and time management techniques. They also helped him identify specific ways that he could implement these strategies and techniques to deal with the unique demands of being a college athlete.

> The final session was used to assist Phil in reflecting on all of the new coping skills he had learned in the preceding weeks. At this point, all three discussed whether any additional wellness counseling would be useful or if they had successfully accomplished the goals Phil had in mind.

> Upon completing the wellness counseling, Phil reported that he found the entire experience to be very positive and empowering, as he found himself coping better with many of the stressors he was experiencing at that time.

The strengths-based approach that characterizes the positive psychology/wellness counseling intervention can be helpful when working with coaches as well as athletes. Helping coaches and student athletes identify and build on individual academic and athletic strengths can create a positive psychology among the entire team. This, in turn, fosters the development of a positive "family spirit among the players and coaches" (Wallace et al., 2001, p. 99).

The case of Phil describes only a few of the many ways that counselors and psychologists can use the Sweeney and Myers personal wellness model to promote healthy human development. Although the counseling approaches used with Phil would have to be modified when working with persons of different ages and diverse groups and backgrounds, the comprehensive nature of the Sweeney and Myers framework makes it useful to implement when working with a broad range of clients.

Another limitation associated with the positive psychology/wellness counseling movement relates to the infrequency with which multicultural and feminist counseling theorists are credited for their contributions to the positive psychology knowledge base (Seligman, 2002b; Snyder & Lopez, 2001). Two possible explanations have been offered to explain this omission. First, it is hypothesized that the proponents of the current positive psychology/wellness counseling movement may simply not be aware of the many multicultural publications that detail a positive psychology viewpoint from the perspective of people in marginalized, devalued, and oppressed groups in our society (Sue, Ivey, & Pedersen, 1996; Ponterotto, Casas, Suzuki, & Alexander, 2001). Second, it has been asserted that the proponents of the positive psychology/wellness counseling theoretical paradigm may be aware of the earlier contributions but may not have given credit where credit is due (D'Andrea, 2005a). Regardless of the reason for the omissions, the failure of positive psychology/wellness counseling theorists to acknowledge the ways in which previously published multicultural theories describe a positive approach to mental health and spiritual well-being limits our understanding of the tremendous potential of this paradigm in fostering the healthy development of persons in culturally diverse groups.

Another important limitation to recognize, of course, is that not all clients will benefit from short-term work. There are many long-term clients in need of ongoing professional assistance. Moreover, not all clients will find the rapid-fire strategies of brief therapy appropriate to their cultural perspective. As noted above, brief counseling practitioners may need to spend more time in relationship building than has been previously stated by the advocates of brief counseling and therapy.

Proponents of brief therapy may need to listen in more detail to the difficulties that are brought to counseling before their clients are willing to respond to short-term methods that may be beneficial. Despite these limitations, brief therapy concepts are important and can be integrated as part of other theoretical approaches to help clients work through critical issues in their lives.

The positive psychology/wellness paradigm can be utilized in a number of settings. The Professional Development Extension discusses some of the ways that the positive psychology/wellness counseling approach can be used in other aspects of professional practice.

Summary

This chapter is aimed at increasing your understanding of what we refer to as the "fifth force" in counseling and psychology—the positive psychology/wellness approach to counseling/therapy. Having read the information presented above and completed the competency-building activities included in this chapter, you should be well on your way to gaining a foundational understanding of the positive psychology/wellness counseling paradigm that is emerging in the mental health professions.

Although positive psychology/wellness advocates often overemphasize an individualistic approach, we have stressed the importance of operating from an expansive understanding of human development when using the concepts and helping strategies associated with this theoretical perspective in your professional practice. In doing so, we have emphasized the importance of being ever mindful of the contextual and cultural factors that influence our clients' development when using a positive psychology/wellness counseling approach in our work.

This chapter has also provided an overview of the rudiments of brief counseling and therapy. The general public's increasing demand for health care providers to become more accountable for the services they provide is leading many counselors and therapists to be increasingly aware of the need to operate in as efficacious a manner as possible when working with clients who are interested in learning new ways to lead more satisfying and productive lives. By combining many of the theoretical concepts that underlie the positive psychology/wellness counseling movement with the brief counseling strategies described in this chapter, counselors and psychologists will be better positioned to meet the demands for high-quality and efficient mental health care services in the future.

Your ability to implement many of the ideas described in the first three chapters will be greatly enhanced as you work through Chapter 4, which details the microskills framework that Allen and Mary Ivey have developed and implemented for more than 30 years. Connecting the theoretical concepts with your expanding skill base will help you develop personal and professional empowerment.

Multimedia Resources for This Chapter

The following online resource offers video and other resources of particular relevance to this chapter of the text.

Companion Website

Go to **www.ablongman.com/Ivey6e** to view the following video clip:

- Video clip 3.1 highlights one way that a White male therapist and a Black female client explore some of the positive aspects of the client's spirituality and cultural identity as they relate to her coping with the problem of "invisibility" that she discusses in this therapy session. Note how these components of the positive psychology/wellness counseling paradigm can be included into the therapeutic process.

chapter 4

Using Microskills in Counseling and Therapy: Foundations of the Intentional Interview

chapter goals

This chapter is designed to:

1. Introduce you to the notions of professional intentionality and intentional competence.
2. Stimulate your thinking about multicultural intentionality.
3. Discuss the importance of understanding, developing, and effectively communicating an empathic attitude in counseling and therapy.
4. Describe the basic microskills that are used in all counseling and therapy theoretical orientations.
5. Examine the implications of using microskills in multicultural counseling and therapy settings.
6. Present a basic five-stage interview structure that can be used in all theoretical approaches.
7. Increase your thinking about some of the ways you can use the concepts presented in this chapter to expand your effectiveness as a mental health professional.

Introduction

Throughout this book, you will encounter the richness of psychodynamic thought, the thoroughly researched and effective cognitive-behavioral tradition, and the ever popular existential-humanistic theories of Carl Rogers, Clement Vontress, and Fritz Perls. All of these systems are challenged and enriched by multicultural counseling and therapy (MCT) and the positive psychology/wellness counseling framework that was discussed in Chapter 3. Together, they represent the major theoretical forces of our field.

In the past, students in counseling and psychology have been encouraged to identify their "theory of choice." This resulted in many practitioners deciding to become thoroughly committed to a single helping approach. Committing to a single theory does have value in the sense that no one can fully master the numerous counseling and therapeutic theories that have proliferated in the mental health professions. But in selecting a single theoretical approach, one misses out on the potential useful strategies and techniques available in other theories.

It is safe to say that most practitioners find selecting aspects of different theories a more satisfactory approach to the challenges they face in their work. But this approach brings problems as well. The "mix and match" approach can result in scattered counseling and therapy practices, which may lead to confusion for both you and the client over the content, process, and purpose of the helping process.

Although you will ultimately select an approach to counseling and therapy that complements your own preferences, values, and biases, it is important to use a systematic, eclectic helping approach in your professional work (D'Andrea & Daniels, 2001c). Such an approach to counseling and therapy draws on multiple theories in ways that complement your clients' psychological development, cultural identity, and other historical-contextual considerations that are of unique relevance for each person you serve.

Regardless of the theoretical approach you decide to use in your professional practice, it will be necessary to acquire a set of skills that are foundational to all the theoretical approaches described in this book. By acquiring a broad range of interviewing skills and developing an understanding of the major theoretical forces that underlie most of the counseling and therapy done in the United States, you will be well positioned to implement helping strategies that reflect a heightened sense of intentionality.

Professional Intentionality and Intentional Competence

Few persons would be happy with a counselor or therapist who operates haphazardly by making statements or asking questions that lack thoughtful purpose. Because such an approach to counseling is likely to lead to ineffective and perhaps even harmful outcomes, it could be viewed as a violation of the fundamental ethical principle to "do no harm" to one's clients. To work more effectively and ethically, practitioners are encouraged to demonstrate the sort of professional intentionality that is rooted in a sound and comprehensive understanding of counseling and therapy theories and accompanied by a broad range of influencing skills deliberately implemented to foster positive psychological outcomes.

Intentionality is a goal of effective counseling and therapy that has two dimensions. First, from the practitioner's perspective, intentional counseling involves selecting a theoretical approach and using various skills in a deliberate and purposeful manner. The deliberate and purposeful manner in which one selects a given theoretical approach and various counseling skills depends on a host of cultural factors, many of which are outlined in the RESPECTFUL counseling model (see Chapter 2).

Second, rather than trying to find a single correct response to clients' issues, intentional counseling is aimed at assisting individuals to look at their life situation in a new light with an increased sense of hopefulness and direction. Ivey and Ivey (2007) explain this dimension of intentionality in the following manner:

Intentionality is acting with a sense of capability and deciding from among a range of alternative actions. The intentional individual has more than one action, thought, or behavior to choose from in responding to changing life situations. The intentional individual can generate alternatives in a given situation and approach a problem from different vantage points, using a variety of skills and personal qualities, adapting styles to suit different individuals and cultures. (p. 17)

Multicultural Intentionality

Intentional living and helping occur in a cultural context. Cultural expertise and intentionality imply three major abilities:

1. *The ability to generate a maximum number of thoughts, words, and behaviors to communicate with self and others within a given culture.*

Common to people who come to counseling for assistance on personal issues is a sense of personal immobility—the inability to act intentionally and resolve problems, of feeling fixed in one place. Immobility is described differently in several of the helping theories that are explored later in this book. For example, psychodynamic theorists (Chapters 5 and 6) discuss polarities and unconscious conflicts; Rogerian therapists (Chapter 9) talk about discrepancies between the ideal and real self; Gestalt therapists (Chapter 10) talk about splits and impasses.

A therapist oriented toward multicultural-feminist-social justice issues might examine the person's historical, cultural, gender, and social contexts, giving special attention to the different modes of being that exist among diverse cultural groups. A family therapist might work with the entire family in the belief that the "identified patient" is in some way enacting family wishes.

These are only a few of a myriad of therapeutic approaches that can be used effectively to free clients so they can generate new behaviors and be more fully functioning. The underlying purpose or overall goal of all counseling and therapy is to increase clients' response capacity and their ability to generate or create new behaviors and thoughts.

2. *The ability to generate the thoughts, words, and behaviors necessary to communicate with a variety of diverse groups and individuals. Both clients and counselors need to communicate within their own culture and learn to understand and effectively interact with persons from other cultures as well.*

Several research studies have shown that 50 percent of racial minority individuals do not return for a second counseling interview (Sue & Sue, 2003). Most counseling theories in use in North America are rooted in European-American middle-class culture. However, what is appropriate behavior for a European-American may be unsuitable for persons from diverse cultural, racial, and ethnic groups. For example, the expression of emotion necessary in client-centered and psychodynamic therapy may be totally inappropriate for some Asian-Americans and Native Americans (as well as many European-Americans from diverse ethnic backgrounds). Thus, not only the goal but also the process, style, and techniques of traditional helping theories may be inappropriate and alienating for those of diverse cultures.

Fortunately, most theories and helping approaches stress the importance of evaluating the appropriateness of the therapeutic method used for a particular client. Practitioners must be ever mindful that it is their ethical responsibility to reflect, analyze, and choose appropriate responses and techniques when working with persons from diverse client populations. A therapist who is skilled and knowledgeable in many theories has a strong basis for multicultural intentionality.

As you complete the competency-building activities in every chapter, think about the ways in which you can implement multicultural intentionality in your own work. It is vital to do so, because, as mounting evidence suggests, a client's culture, religious background, socioeconomic status, age, and gender can be as important as the unique personality of the client and the problem that is being presented. The multicultural counseling video clips contained on the Companion Website for this book may be useful for seeing and hearing what a therapist's approach looks and sounds like when implementing multicultural intentionality in the therapeutic process with a client who is different from the practitioner in terms of gender and racial background.

3. *The ability to formulate plans, act on many possibilities existing in a culture, and reflect on these actions.*

"Unfreezing" individuals so that they are able to generate new behaviors is a vital aspect of counseling and therapy, but just generating new ways of responding and acting creatively is not enough. At some point, individuals must become committed to ongoing actions and decide to routinely implement alternative ways of responding to life situations in an effort to lead more satisfying and productive lives. However, not all counseling and psychotherapeutic theories have a clear commitment to action as a goal in the helping process.

Cognitive-behavioral approaches to counseling do place a particular emphasis on action. Clear, observable goals are developed, accompanied by follow-up and evaluation plans. The cognitive-behavioral therapist often assigns specific "homework" assignments so that the ideas generated in therapy sessions can be taken home and practiced outside the counseling setting. Most approaches to psychotherapy are not this specific, but all therapeutic approaches encourage clients to look at their life plans, the results of their actions, and new ways to lead more satisfying and productive lives.

Although these three goals cross most counseling and therapy approaches that are used in the mental health professions, this book emphasizes the importance of being ever mindful of addressing cultural factors when promoting any therapeutic goal, whether that goal is explicitly or implicitly stated in counseling and therapy. This is one of the most important and challenging ethical responsibilities practitioners face in their work.

The treatment of eating disorders, such as bulimia and anorexia, is an example of the difficulty in establishing culturally appropriate goals. Generally, these are problems women commonly experience in North American culture, although male eating disorders are on the rise. Although thinness is valued in the North American culture, it is not a universally shared value across all cultural groups. Thus, in helping clients with eating disorders generate a more positive body image and accept their weight, the counselor often works against imperatives of the dominant cultural view of body image in the United States.

Cultural awareness and consciousness-raising strategies often need to be included in the treatment of bulimia and anorexia. Such awareness should include addressing the fact that some cultures consider heaviness desirable and view thinness as less attractive. The therapist must be aware that what is considered successful adjustment and adaptation in one culture can create serious problems in another.

Middle-class European-Americans, for example, are considered socially adjusted if they have accumulated private wealth. Although they may distribute some portion of their material possessions to family members, friends, or charities, the societal value is on individuals keeping their material wealth. In South Pacific Fiji, the societal custom is that individuals give away forever any material possession a friend or family member requests. The Native American practice of the *potlatch* ceremony is another example of a cultural tradition in which wealth is given to others. These examples highlight how in some cultures individuals may gain status and prestige by sharing rather than acquiring material wealth for themselves.

The concept of mental health is also relative, depending on one's cultural perspective and conditioning (Ivey, Pedersen, & Ivey, 2001). Despite the complex and relative nature of the meaning of this construct, there are a number of counseling and psychotherapeutic skills that can be applied across client groups to foster the mental health and personal and collective well-being of clients from diverse populations.

This chapter addresses some foundational skills that are an inherent part of all counseling and therapy approaches. The skills are drawn from the microskills framework developed by Allen and Mary Ivey (2007) and supported by research. Developing a solid background in the microskills model will provide you with the basics to implement all the theories presented in this book. You also will be better positioned to intentionally draw on a number of skills that increase the probability of promoting positive outcomes in counseling and therapy if you effectively use these skills in appropriate and culturally responsive ways in the helping process.

Although it is vital to develop a broad range of skills that will enable you to work intentionally to foster positive outcomes in counseling and therapy, mental health practitioners must also possess an attitude that makes counseling and therapy work for their clients. This is often referred to as the **empathic attitude** (Ivey, D'Andrea, Ivey, & Simek-Morgan, 2002). Much has been written about empathy and the potential to stimulate restorative, healing, and empowering outcomes when counselors communicate an empathic attitude throughout the helping process (Chung & Bemak, 2002; Johnson & Jacob, 2000; Rogers, 1961).

Individual, Family, and Cultural Empathy

Empathy is often described as seeing the world through another's eyes, hearing as another might hear, and feeling and experiencing another's internal world. Native American Indians call this "walking in another's moccasins." Empathy does not, however, involve mixing your thoughts and feelings with those of your client. Although the empathic attitude requires that you accept the client's being, as a therapist and counselor you need to remain true to yourself and your own beliefs.

Empathy is most often considered an individual issue, but it also rests on an understanding and acceptance of the other person's total life experience. Family and culture deeply intertwine in clients' lives. Really entering the worlds of others requires you to understand not only the concrete individual in front of you, but also how family and culture affect their very being.

This chapter first focuses on traditional concepts of empathic understanding. Then it examines multicultural factors that affect the way individuals construct their worlds, considers family issues, and presents some central multicultural dimensions to be considered in developing a genuine empathic understanding and relationship in the helping interview.

Defining Empathy: The Facilitative Conditions

In 1957 Carl Rogers produced a landmark paper entitled "The Necessary and Sufficient Conditions of Therapeutic Personality Change." This article made a strong case that empathy and related constructs are all that are needed to produce positive changes in a client. To help another person grow, Rogers said, requires an integrated congruent relationship with the client, the expression of unconditional positive regard for the client, and the communication of empathy from the counselor to the client. According to Rogers, "no other conditions are necessary" (p. 27).

The influence of this article has continually expanded, and its tenets are now principles of faith for those who primarily operate from the existential-humanistic orientation (see Chapters 9 and 10). Moreover, cognitive-behavioral, psychodynamic, and most other orientations to counseling and therapy now accept the importance of empathy. Empathy and the accompanying empathic conditions, such as respect, warmth, and genuineness, are foundational to most helping theories.

Rogers offers the following definition of empathy:

> This is not laying trips on people. You only listen and say back the other person's comments, step by step, just as that person seems to have it at that moment. You never mix into it any of your own ideas, never lay on the other person anything that person didn't express. To show that you understand exactly, making a sentence or two which gets exactly at the personal meaning this person wanted to put across. This might be in your own words, usually, but use that person's own words for the touchy main things. (Gendlin & Hendricks, 1978, p. 120)

Competency-Building Activity 4.1

Acceptance as the Foundation of Empathy

Instructions: Acceptance may be described as the foundation of empathy. How would you define and experience acceptance? The following exercise may be helpful in answering this question:

Recall a time when you felt accepted by someone else just as you are or were. Re-create the situation in your mind. What is happening and what are you seeing? What is being said? What are your thoughts and feelings that go with the image? Focus on your body. Can you locate a specific place in your body for your feelings? If you are not as comfortable with visual images, use words, poetry, sounds, scents and odors, or bodily feelings.

Counseling and therapy ask you to accept clients as they are. It is easy to feel acceptance toward a small child suffering from an emotional hurt or toward a survivor of spousal abuse. However, it is far less easy to feel accepting of the bully on the playground or the perpetrator of family violence. The following exercise can help you explore your ability to be accepting:

How do you imagine yourself if you were to work with a bully or an abuser? Take time to let this image arise. What do you see and hear? Most important, what do you feel? Can you locate that feeling in a specific place in your own body?

The feelings you experience in your own body may be the best indicator of your degree of acceptance and ability to be empathic. Most counselors have difficulty when working with those who hurt others. Yet the bully, the abuser, and the rapist need empathy and acceptance as much as the child, adolescent, or adult who has survived the attack. That is not to say, however, that one should use empathic understanding as a way to excuse the behavior of the perpetrator. This is the challenge of empathy. We need not accept the behavior, but at some level we must accept the person.

Be sure to record your reactions to this exercise in your personal-professional portfolio.

Source: This exercise was derived from the work of Gladys Lam of Hong Kong Polytechnic.

This definition takes empathy beyond an attitude. Rogers suggests specific actions and skills of the empathic attitude that the counselor or therapist can use in the helping interview to communicate genuine and respectful understanding of the client. Besides describing several of these actions and skills, Competency-Building Activity 4.1 offers you an opportunity to examine your own life experience with empathy.

Positive Regard and the Positive Asset Search

Positive regard is part of the empathic attitude and is aptly demonstrated by Rogers, whose positive attitude and hope for his clients have become legendary. Positive regard means that you as a therapist are able to recognize values and strengths in your clients, even when your client holds widely different attitudes from yours. Positive regard is a concept basic to all counseling and therapy theory. If you as therapist cannot believe there is something positive and valuable in the client, there is little hope for client change.

Leona Tyler, in her classic counseling text (1961), presents a concrete explanation of the importance of positive regard:

The initial stages of therapy include a process that might be called *exploration of resources*. The counselor pays little attention to personality weaknesses. [He or she] is most persistent in trying to locate ways of coping with anxiety and stress, already existing resources that may be enlarged and strengthened once their existence is recognized.

In essence, positive regard asks you to look at clients affirmatively, expecting that they have potential resources. By positively identifying clients' strengths, together you and your client can build a foundation for a working future. Tyler calls this "minimum change therapy," which is based on the assumption that if you can identify strengths or resources in the client and if you support these resources over time, they will grow and become more central to the client's life.

Positive regard is an attitude that can be fostered through some very specific actions of counselors and therapists. The following areas concerning client strengths are emphasized by different theorists in varying ways:

- resource development (Carkhuff, 1969)
- encouragement and strength assessment (Dinkmeyer & Dinkmeyer, 1995)
- exceptions to the problem in solution-oriented therapy (O'Hanlon & Weiner-Davis, 1989)
- resources, strengths, and the positive asset search (Ivey, Pedersen, & Ivey, 2001)

The positive asset search is a technique for building positive regard with clients and is explored in Competency-Building Activity 4.2.

Positive regard asks that we find positives in the worldviews and attitudes of those who are different from us. The Mexican-American counselor working with a European-American client has a responsibility to find positive meanings in the client's life experience. Similarly, the European-American counselor faces the same challenge with a Mexican-American client. The counselor must learn to respect, understand, and be able to work with different clients.

Seligman and Csikszentmihalyi (2000) have taken the notion of positive regard to another level of thinking by presenting a convincing argument that relates to the need to develop and implement a "positive psychology" in the mental health professions. After describing the limitations of using traditional counseling and psychotherapeutic approaches, which direct an inordinate amount of attention to clients' personal deficits and problems, Seligman and Csikszentmihalyi suggest that the fields of counseling and psychology would do well to reaffirm their commitment to promoting "mental health" and a "positive psychology" (p. 5). By demonstrating an increased focus and a heightened regard for their clients' personal strengths and assets, counselors and psychologists are better able to nurture the sort of "hope, wisdom, creativity, future mindedness, courage, spirituality, responsibility, and perseverance" (Seligman & Csikszentmihalyi, 2000, p. 5) that underlie high levels of mental health and psychological well-being. To effectively do this, practitioners must be able to demonstrate respect and warmth for their clients in the process of communicating a genuine sense of empathy and positive regard for them.

Competency-Building Activity 4.2

The Positive Asset Search: Building Empathy on Strengths

The tendency in counseling and therapy is to focus too much on clients' problems and concerns. If you give some attention early in the interview to positive strengths, clients will feel empowered and better able to cope with the negatives in their lives.

Instructions: To assist you in developing the skills that are necesaary to effectively conduct a positive asset search with your clients, ask a volunteer to work through the following brief exercise with you and proceed by following the instructions presented below.

Step 1. *Mention that counseling and therapy too often focus solely on the negative aspects of clients' lives.* To counter this tendency, you wish to begin your session with a strength assessment, and you will need the client's help to do so in this process.

Step 2. *Discuss with the client possible areas of strengths in her or his present-day life or the past.* These positive resources may include many things, but important among them are (a) present and past successes the client has enjoyed, (b) supportive family members or friends, (c) spirituality, (d) love of nature, (e) success in sports, and (f) important cultural or personal hero figures. As part of the client's history, specifically search out times when the client felt stronger and was doing well—that is, times that were exceptions to the current problem. These positives may provide ideas for full or partial solutions to many current client issues.

Step 3. *Draw out from the client a personal narrative or story that concretizes the positive strengths.* As you listen to the story, note how the client's body may shift to a less tense position. Reinforce that bodily experience by focusing for a moment on how the client feels when discussing a positive resource. Comment that this resource may be drawn on in the future, both in counseling and in daily life.

Step 4. *Draw on this positive story and the bodily sensations that go with it.* Do this as appropriate during later contacts when the client seems stressed.

It is important to think about the client when you are intentionally planning on doing a positive asset search. Clients typically come in to talk with counselors and therapists about their problems and difficulties. All this talk often "decenters" clients from a feeling of competency. To ground clients and "center" them, spend time on their positive strengths. Clients grow and develop from strengths that are already present as well as from the new ideas counseling and therapy can provide (Johnson & Jacob, 2000).

Be sure to record your reactions to this exercise in your personal-professional portfolio.

Respect and Warmth

An impassive counselor or therapist can appear professional and competent, but underlying the façade of professionalism may be an unconscious hostility toward and dislike of the client. The intentional counselor likes and respects other people and communicates these feelings to them.

Respect is close to positive regard and can be communicated verbally through the language of respect. Virtually all of the comments concerning positive regard and exploration of clients' positive assets communicate respect for another person. Enhancing statements might include such comments as "You express your opinion well" and "Good insight."

Respect is also communicated nonverbally through individually and culturally appropriate eye contact and body language. The concept of respectfully entering the other person's world has profound implications for family work and multicultural relationships. Multicultural empathy requires that we respect worldviews different than our own. As we seek to understand those who have different ethnic/racial, religious, or gender experiences from our own, we will find ourselves in a lifelong learning process.

It is important to remember that you do not have to support or respect a client's behavior to respect the client. It is especially important to sort out negative behaviors in counseling and therapy. At times, these behaviors must be forcefully stopped. Those individuals traditionally identified as antisocial and borderline offer a particular challenge to your ability to be respectful of them. However, most clients so categorized have histories of extremely severe child abuse and/or multiple traumas. Thus, these are the very clients who most need your positive regard and respect.

It is possible to respect another person's point of view but still lack the critical dimension of personal warmth. Together, however, respect and warmth present a powerful combination. The warmth of a counselor's response to clients is an important factor underlying an empathic relationship. But what is warmth?

Warmth may be defined as an emotional attitude toward the client expressed through nonverbal means. Vocal tone, posture, gestures, and facial expression are how the counselor's warmth and support are communicated to the client. Smiling has been found to be the best single predictor of warmth ratings in an interview.

Delineating warmth, respect, and positive regard as separate categories is perhaps not really possible. Yet it is difficult to imagine a counselor expressing positive feedback, respect, and positive regard to a client in a cold, distant fashion. A lack of warmth can negate the positive message. The communication of warmth through smiling, vocal tone, and other nonverbal means adds power and conviction to counselor comments.

Concreteness

The idea of concreteness is a vital dimension for effective counseling and therapy (Carkhuff, 1969). Counselors and therapists tend to think in an abstract, formal operational manner and thus often fail to work concretely with their clients. Piagetian scholars note that children operate primarily in a concrete manner and that approximately 25 percent of the adult U.S. population fails to reach full formal operations (Ivey, 1986). Many clients will give very concrete, linear descriptions of their experiences. If you tend toward abstractness and formal operations, you may lose contact with these clients. They, in turn, may be put off by your emphasis on abstract patterns and representations of experience.

Developmental counseling and therapy (DCT) gives special attention to clients' styles of making meaning and operational orientation (Ivey, 1986, 1991a; Ivey, Pedersen, & Ivey, 2001). In Chapter 13, operational orientations (such as formal, concrete, and so on) are discussed in more detail, as is DCT. DCT stresses the importance of the counselor's willingness to enter clients' concrete worlds and listen in detail to their stories. At a later point, you may be able to help them see patterns and discuss their issues more abstractly, but concreteness and a willingness to work with specific situations are critical counselor skills, especially in the early stages of counseling and therapy.

There are two main issues related to concreteness. The first, as just noted, is your willingness to be concrete with concrete operational clients. Later, after listening to their stories, you can help them see patterns of acting and responding.

The second is to help overly abstract clients become more concrete and in touch with what actually happens and the need for specific action to resolve issues. Abstract operational clients at times may have difficulty taking concrete ideas into practice. The concept of concreteness is particularly helpful in working with these clients.

Some clients come to therapy with vague, ambiguous complaints. A task of the intentional therapist is to help the client clarify and understand these vague ideas and problems. Effective interviews tend to move from vague descriptions of global issues to highly concrete discussions of what happened or is happening in the client's daily life. Through interviewing "leads" that focus on concrete client experience, the helper can move the discussion from generalization to a clear understanding of what actually happened. Becoming empathic and understanding is easier when you understand specific facts of clients' lives. Generally, most clients will welcome concreteness, as "objective facts" are less susceptible to distortions. Furthermore, specificity and concreteness will provide a solid base for client and therapist problem solving.

The search for concreteness underlies many, perhaps even most, helping interviews. Clients often lack full understanding and will tend to label situations incorrectly. Some clients use very abstract language and may talk in generalities. If you ask these clients for an example of a specific situation, they will often become more concrete. Asking clients the open-ended question "Could you give me a specific example?" can help them organize their thinking and become less abstract.

Sometimes an emotional experience may be too intense for immediate discussion of concrete specifics. In cases of rape and abuse, it may be wise to delay the search for concreteness. North Americans, in general, tend to prefer discussing concrete specifics of a problem, but this approach can put off many Europeans, Asians, or Native Americans whose cultures may be oriented toward a more subtle approach to helping.

Immediacy

Immediacy means that you move toward a more present-tense helping orientation and focus on the here-and-now experience of the interview by asking clients such questions as "What's going on with you, right now?" or "What are you feeling/experiencing at this moment?"

Egan (1994) describes "self-involving statements" in which you as the counselor share your own reactions with the client. For example, you might share your feelings with a client who refuses to return to a violent home situation in this way: "I'm glad you're taking your own direction and having faith in yourself. I'm impressed with your strength." Such statements tell clients where you are in relationship with them. At the same time, the primary focus in such statements is on the client rather than the therapist.

Egan also explores here-and-now immediacy in the counselor-client relationship. In the following example, the client and counselor talk directly about what is happening between them:

Counselor: I'd like to stop a moment and take a look at what's happening right now between you and me.

Agnes: I'm not sure what you mean.

Counselor: Well, our conversation today started out quite lively, and now it seems rather subdued to me. I've noticed that the muscles in my shoulders have become tense and I feel a little flushed. I sense something's up that way when I feel I might have said something wrong. [*Note how the counselor uses awareness of his own body to facilitate communication.*]

Agnes: What could that have been?

Counselor: Agnes, is it just me, or do you also feel that things are a bit strained between us right now?

Agnes: Well, a little.

Counselor: Last month you discussed how you control your friends with your emotions. This gets you what you want, but the price you pay can be too high. Now all of a sudden you've gone a bit quiet, and I've been asking myself what I might have done wrong. To be truthful, I'm feeling a bit controlled too. What's your perspective on all this? (pp. 226–227)

The use of here-and-now immediacy in examining the client-counselor relationship can be very powerful and enlightening. At the same time, it obviously can be overdone and thus needs to be used sparingly, with care and a sense of ethics.

Congruence, Genuineness, and Authenticity

Rogers (1957) has stated that the person who conducts a therapeutic or counseling interview should be authentic and real. His views on genuineness have become central to many in the field. It is important that you be yourself, "freely and deeply the opposite of presenting a facade either knowingly or unknowingly" (p. 97). Rogers asks you to allow yourself to experience yourself as a full, authentic human being. The helping experience at its best is core to the meaning of being a person. Who you are in the session as a person will have a deep impact on the client.

It is difficult to fault such a statement, as it is clear that openness and honesty on your part are central to your effectiveness as a counselor. There are times, however, when complete openness and spontaneity of expression may be damaging to the client. This point was forcefully made in a study of encounter group casualties by Lieberman, Yalom, and Miles (1972). They found that "open, authentic" group leaders produced more emotional casualties than did more conservative counselors, who developed relationships with group members more slowly and naturally.

There are two types of authenticity to consider. The first is authenticity to yourself. Being authentic, truthful, and open may be a laudable stance, but your client may not be ready for such behavior. A more important type of authenticity rests in having a genuine, congruent relationship with your client. This means taking into account where your clients "are at," listening to them, and opening an empathic dialogue.

The following exchange illustrates some issues related to genuineness:

Client: Yes, I can't decide what to do about the baby or the abortion until I know where I stand with Ronnie. He used to treat me nice, especially when we were first dating. He came over and fixed my car and my stereo; he liked to run errands for me. Now if I ask him anything, he makes a big hassle out of it.

Helper: At this moment, I can sense some confusion. Let me check this out with you. When someone is nice to me, I get to trust them and I feel comfortable. But then if they let me down, I get low and lost and really confused. Is my experience at all like yours?

Client: I guess I have felt like that. I know I blame him for getting me pregnant because he wouldn't do anything to prevent it. It makes me damn mad!

Helper: Right now, you really are angry with him.

The counselor shows genuineness in relationship to self through skillful self-disclosure and shares feelings and thoughts in a real and personal manner. Self-disclosure does not necessarily have to be specific and detailed; it can be relatively vague and nonconcrete.

Suppose the counselor was thinking of a past event concerning his or her parents. If that concrete event had been presented, the counselor would still be genuine in relation to self, but the introduction of an example so different from the client's immediate personal experience could disturb the counseling relationship. Genuine and appropriate self-disclosure, on the other hand, can produce increased genuineness on the part of the client. Intentional counselors tend to produce intentional clients.

Microskills: An Integrative Foundation for Counseling and Therapy

Counseling and psychotherapy rely on effective communication with the client. "Microskills are communication skill units of the interview that will help you interact more intentionally and effectively with a client. They provide specific alternatives for you to use with different types of clients. Microskills form the foundation of intentional interviewing" (Ivey & Ivey, 2007, p. 22). Communication skills are used in all theories of counseling and psychotherapy, but different theories use the skills in varying patterns and focus on different psychological issues in the helping process.

Figure 4.1 presents the various communication skills that comprise the microskills framework in visual form. Note that ethics, wellness, and multicultural understanding form the base of the microskills hierarchy before specific microskills are employed.

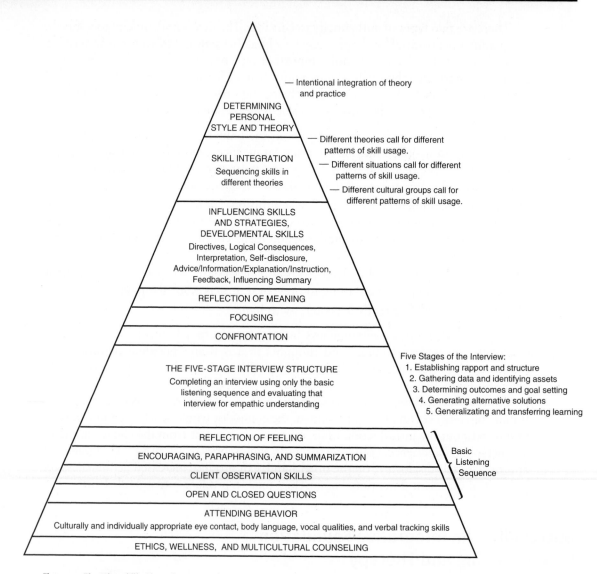

Figure 4.1 The Microskills Hierarchy
Note: The skill "reflection of meaning" is discussed in Chapter 9 in connection with the work of Viktor Frankl.
Source: The Microskills Hierarchy is copyrighted by Allen E. Ivey, 1982, 1995, 2001, and is presented here by permission.

Research Exhibit 4.1 (pp. 90–91) discusses the origins of the microskills framework and presents key findings from over 450 data-based studies of this model.

Attending Behavior: A Skill Used in All Theories

Regardless of the theory you choose to use in counseling or therapy, you should look at your clients and maintain natural eye contact when working with them. Further, your body should communicate interest in what the client has to say. It was once believed that counseling was solely a verbal occupation. However, with the advent of videotaping and the increased use of filming in interview training, it has become apparent that nonverbal communication plays an important role in effective interviewing, counseling, and therapy. Having stated this point, one could readily acknowledge that traditional psychoanalysis works from a different set of attending and listening expectations, as clients are often asked to lie down on a couch, while the therapist sits out of view of the individual during analysis.

Another basic aspect of attending behavior is vocal tone. Simply put, this skill involves asking yourself, "Does my voice communicate warmth and interest or boredom and lack of caring in the counseling session?" Even though you may be physically attending to a client, your voice often indicates the true quality of your willingness and interest in listening to what the client is saying.

Moreover, if you are to attend to someone, you must truly listen. Listening involves more than observable behaviors such as an interested body posture and appropriate facial expressions. Intentional therapists not only maintain these important nonverbal behaviors, but they also stay on the topic the client talks about and seldom interrupt or change topics abruptly during the therapeutic encounter.

Practitioners using different theoretical approaches to counseling and therapy will focus their attention in different ways. While most will try to have appropriate eye contact, body language, and vocal tone, what practitioners listen to and for will vary depending on their specific theoretical orientation. You also may find that clients tend to talk about what counselors and therapists like to listen to.

In the following exchange, note differences in **selective attention**. Selective attention refers to the tendency of counselors to listen selectively to what their clients are saying and to use their preferred theory as a screen to determine what is important and what may be of lesser interest.

Client: I went downtown this afternoon, and I really got anxious. Earlier that day, my boss "hit on" me. I just wanted to be alone. I even wanted to run when I saw a friend. I broke out in a sweat and felt I couldn't move. I don't know how I got through the afternoon, but somehow I survived.

Psychodynamic therapist (connecting the past with the present): It was a difficult afternoon for you. Would these feelings be similar to those you felt when your stepfather touched you?

Person-centered counselor (focusing on the client's emotions in the here and now): You appear anxious right now as you're talking to me.

Cognitive-behavioral therapist (searching for antecedents to the behavior and consequences in relation to the boss): I hear your anxiety. First, let's focus on what happened with your boss in more detail. What specifically did he say and do? . . . How did you react? . . . What happened afterward?

Counselor using a brief counseling approach (searching for positive resources and finding strengths in a problematic situation): I hear you say that you got through it and survived. What did you do that enabled you to make it through the day?

Research Exhibit 4.1

Research on Attending Behavior and Interviewing Microskills

Prior to approaches such as microskills, counseling and therapy were considered almost mystical, and the idea of systematic definition of interview behavior did not exist. Where does a basic construct such as attending behavior come from? In their study, Ivey and his colleagues (Ivey, Normington, Miller, Morrill, & Haase, 1968) sought to identify foundational, specific skills of helping. After months of study and experimentation led only to failure, a simple experiment, described below, laid the foundation for the microskills approach discussed in this chapter. (The original work on microskills occurred in a European-American context. The findings would have been different had multicultural issues been considered at that time.)

The basic breakthrough, which resulted in the concepts of attending behavior and microcounseling, occurred with one of our secretaries. The process consisted of five minutes of videotaping when she was interviewing a student volunteer. This was followed by a replay of the tape in which her behaviors, which reflected lapses of attending, were pointed out and direction given on how to increase identified attending behaviors.

She returned to reinterview the student and, after a moment of artificiality, began to respond in highly impactful ways. In fact, she performed like a highly skilled and experienced counselor. The change was not only dramatic, but, when we considered it was accomplished in only 20 minutes of training, almost shocking! We have seen less change of behavior in practicum students in an entire year.

When a hiatus was reached, the lack of training in counseling skills became apparent. The hiatus called for initiation of new areas, and the secretary did not follow one of our counseling traditions. If she had, she would have either waited for the client to respond (nondirective), initiated an expression of her own feeling state (recent client-centered), directed attention to early experience (analytic), presented a discriminative stimulus to elicit verbal responses that could be reinforced (learning theory), induced a trance state (hypnoanalysis), or brought out a Strong Vocational Interest Blank (vocational counseling).

In actuality, the secretary began to talk about an interesting experience in her own immediate past (standard social behavior). However, since

continued

Counselor with a multicultural-feminist-social justice orientation (any of the above responses would be possible, plus specific attention directed to the social context and the naming of the event as harassment or oppression): You made it through the day and that's good. But this is sexual harassment and cannot go on. Could you tell me more about what's been happening with him? This is the first time you've brought it up in therapy.

Whose is the "right" response? Each theorist takes a different approach. All use attending behavior, but each may differentially attend to this client's expressed concern. All responses can be useful in helping the client.

You will find that you listen to some topics and issues more than others and that you also prefer not discussing other topics. Clients will talk about what you selectively attend to. The first four counselor approaches in the example all focus on the individual, with minimal attention directed to the oppressive environment of

---

Research Exhibit 4.1

she still was attempting to engage in attending behaviors, this led rapidly to a new topic for the student, and the secretary again responded as would a highly skilled counselor.

As an indication of the relevance of attending and related constructs to behavior beyond the interview, our secretary entered the office on Monday and could not wait to tell us about attending to people over the weekend. She had developed an entirely new behavioral repertoire, which was reinforced by a new kind of excitement and involvement for her with other people. The impact even on her husband was apparent (Hackney, Ivey, & Oetting, 1970, p. 344).

This process of identification of researchable dimensions in counseling is cited in detail because it illustrates the sometimes whimsical nature of the research process in which discoveries are often made by chance rather than by choice. Since the original 1968 study on attending behavior, over 450 studies on the microskill of attending have been completed (Baker & Daniels, 1989; Baker, Daniels, & Greenley, 1990; Daniels, 2001; Daniels & Ivey, 2007). In Japan, Tamase conducted a wide-ranging series of

studies illustrating that microcounseling concepts work well in this culturally different country (Tamase, 1998; Tamase & Hirano, 1997; Tamase & Inui, 2000).

The following are some of the more important findings of microskills research:

1. Clients respond better and more positively, are more likely to verbalize at greater length, and indicate a greater willingness to return to attending counselors and therapists.

2. Experienced and sophisticated therapists and counselors seem to have good attending skills, whereas many beginning counselors score poorly on these dimensions.

3. Clients and therapists from varying cultures use microskills but in a different fashion than presented in the original Eurocentric framework.

4. Different counseling theories use microskills but focus on varying dimensions of client experience.

5. Training clients in microskills can be a useful part of a broader treatment program.

---

which the client is a part. When focusing on the individual, we tend to miss the cultural and contextual dimensions of the client's issues. The therapist with a multicultural-feminist-social justice orientation names the issue as oppression and thus immediately seeks to balance individual responsibility for the problem with what occurs in the real world.

Failing to consider the context of clients' issues is a major problem with traditional theoretical approaches to counseling and therapy. Multicultural-feminist-social justice counseling advocates emphatically point out that failure to attend to the contextual factors that underlie many of our clients' problems in the helping process is unethical and irresponsible. However, therapists of other orientations maintain that their only responsibility is to the client and that they are not social change agents.

The task of counselors of a multicultural-feminist-social justice orientation is to balance individual responsibility for the problem with environmental contingencies. It would, of course, be inappropriate to focus solely on the environment and forget that your client needs your attention as a hurting individual. This situation leads to the question: "How can we use traditional counseling and therapy theories in a culturally responsive and socially responsible manner?" You can begin to address this important question by focusing on using attending skills in counseling and therapy in ways that are respectful of cultural differences.

Attending and Cultural Differences. Attending behavior varies from culture to culture and from individual to individual (see Table 4.1). Data show clearly that individual differences among clients may be as important as cultural patterns. When reviewing such summaries of cultural patterns, do not assume that one pattern of attending (or influencing) is appropriate for every individual within a given cultural group.

Sue and Sue (2003) present a framework for culture-specific strategies in counseling and therapy. They cite research showing that many culturally and racially diverse clients terminate counseling earlier that do persons from White, European backgrounds. These multicultural experts suggest that more culturally sensitive and responsive approaches to helping would reduce the cultural/racial attrition gap that currently exists in these situations.

Derald Sue (1990) summarizes research findings in the professional literature that demonstrate the vital importance of including spatial, nonverbal, and related dimensions in the helping process. His findings are supported by a quote common among African-Americans: "If you really want to know what White folks are thinking or feeling, don't listen to what they say, but how they say it" (Sue, 1990, p. 427).

Attending Skills: The Basic Listening Sequence (BLS). Attending skills can be organized into a coherent and systematic framework called the **basic listening sequence (BLS)**. Table 4.2 identifies the specific microskills that underlie the BLS: open and closed questions, encouraging, paraphrasing, reflection of feeling, and summarization. These skills are intended to bring out clients' stories, concerns, and problems. The aim of the BLS is to discover how clients present their stories, with minimal intrusion on the part of the counselor or therapist.

All therapists and counselors use components of the BLS, since listening is crucial to learning about the uniqueness of the clients they are working with and the specific issues clients have brought to counseling. Some attending skills are particularly favored by different theoretical orientations. Although different helping theories may place a greater emphasis on particular listening strategies, all counseling and therapy approaches recognize the importance of learning about the client. If you intend to apply several theoretical orientations in helping clients, you will need (1) to acquire all the listening skills discussed in this chapter and (2) to develop the ability to listen differently, as each theory tends to focus on distinct issues and diverse helping methods.

Open and **closed questions** are seldom used in the person-centered orientation of Carl Rogers but are a main component of the increasingly employed brief counseling and therapy approach. Rogers has argued that questioning may represent an

Table 4.1

Nonverbal Attending Patterns in European–North American Culture Compared with Patterns of Other Cultures

Nonverbal Dimension	European–North American Pattern	Contrasting Example from Another Culture
Eye contact	When listening to a person, direct eye contact is appropriate. When talking, eye contact is often less frequent.	Some African-Americans may have patterns directly opposite and demonstrate more eye contact when talking and less when listening.
Body language	Slight forward trunk lean facing the person. Handshake a general sign of welcome.	Certain Eskimo and Inuit groups in the Arctic sit side by side when working on personal issues. A male giving a female a firm handshake may be seen as giving a sexual invitation.
Vocal tone and speech rate	A varied vocal tone is favored, with some emotionality shown. Speech rate is moderate.	Many Latina/o groups have a more extensive and expressive vocal tone and may consider European–North American styles unemotional and "flat."
Physical space	Conversation distance is ordinarily "arm's length" or more for comfort.	Common in Arab and Middle Eastern cultures is a six- to twelve-inch conversational distance, a point at which the European-American becomes uncomfortable.
Time	Highly structured, linear view of time. Generally "on time" for appointment.	Several South American countries operate on a "being" view of time and do not plan that specified, previously agreed-upon times for meetings will necessarily hold.

Note: It is critical to remember that individuals within a single cultural group vary extensively.

imposition on clients, in that it forces them to tell their stories from the questioner's point of view. However, brief therapists, cognitive-behavioral counselors (Chapters 7 and 8), and those who advocate integrative developmental counseling and therapy (DCT) (Chapter 13) rely on these questioning skills as central tools when working with clients. These counselors believe that carefully worded questions may enable clients to reveal their stories with more clarity and accuracy.

Table 4.2

The Basic Listening Sequence

Skill	Description	Function in Interview
Open questions	"What": facts "How": process or feelings "Why": reasons "Could": general picture	Brings out major data and facilitates conversation.
Closed questions	Usually begin with "do," "is," "are" and can be answered in a few words.	Quickly obtains specific data; closes off lengthy answers.
Encouraging	Repeating back to client a few of the client's main words.	Encourages detailed elaboration of specific words and their meanings.
Paraphrasing	Repeating back the essence of a client's words and thoughts using the client's own main words.	Acts as promoter for discussion; shows understanding; checks on clarity of counselor understanding.
Reflection of feeling	Selective attention to emotional content of interview.	Results in clarification of emotion underlying key facts; promotes discussion of feelings.
Summarization	Repeating back of client's facts and feelings (and reasons) to client in an organized form.	Clarifies where the interview has come to date; useful in beginning interview, periodically throughout session, and to close session.

Classical traditional psychoanalysts (Chapter 5) seldom use questions, while Adlerian therapists (Chapter 6) may use questions frequently. Regardless of one's theoretical orientation, it is generally agreed that questions used too early, too often, and too intrusively can be damaging to a therapeutic relationship, particularly if you are culturally different from your client. In such cases, self-disclosure and a more open stance on the counselor's part may be required.

The repetition of key words stated by the client and the use of other encouragers are used in all counseling and therapy approaches, even among the most classically trained practitioners, where therapist neutrality and objectivity are most fully stressed. The act of encouraging includes head nods, smiles, and other nonverbal behaviors that communicate interest, respect, and affirmation of what the client is saying. Psychoanalysts tend to use these behaviors cautiously, in an effort to maintain what they believe is therapeutic objectivity and neutrality.

Warmth, an important part of many helping approaches, is communicated most often by smiling and many of the other encouraging behaviors described above. The importance of warmth and encouragement was originally introduced in Roger's person-centered theory (Chapter 9). However, these qualities are not considered critical to effective relationship building in all theories of counseling and therapy. Approaches that support a natural, encouraging style include feminist therapy and multicultural counseling (Chapters 11 and 12).

Paraphrasing feeds back to clients the key points of what they have said, but in a distilled form. **Reflection of feeling** captures the emotional content of client expression. These two counseling skills will often appear together in therapeutic sessions. Carl Rogers's person-centered therapy brought the importance of these two listening skills to counseling and therapy several decades ago. These are important foundational skills, as clients need to know that their stories and feelings have been listened to fully and carefully. The more experiential and emotionally oriented counseling theories are, the more reflection of feeling will be an essential skill that counselors and therapists use in the helping process. In more fact- or thought-oriented theories, such as cognitive-behavioral therapy and rational-emotive-behavioral-contextual therapy (Chapter 8), practitioners will tend to use paraphrasing skills more often than reflection of feeling.

Summarization skills bring together paraphrasing and reflection of feeling but cover a longer time frame. Virtually all theories use the skill of summarization, as it helps bring the interview together into a more integrated whole. As a client presents a considerable amount of information in a session, it helps to periodically restate the main things that you have heard the client discuss using summarization. Again, therapists' use of summarization varies with their theoretical orientation. For example, the major focus of summarization for a psychodynamic therapist may be unconscious material, whereas a cognitive-behavioral therapist would likely focus on thoughts and behaviors expressed by the client. While all counseling and psychotherapy theories may direct some attention to clients' feelings, a person-centered therapist will tend to focus more on this area. The counselor with a multicultural-feminist-social justice orientation may do all of the above but may also summarize contextual and cultural data more frequently than counselors with other theoretical approaches.

For all these skills, it is important to take into account multicultural and gender issues. Men tend to ask more questions than women (and they also tend to interrupt more often). In groups, you may notice that it is often the men who raise their hands first and speak most often. Women tend to use the techniques of paraphrasing and reflection of feelings more often than men. If you are working with a client who is culturally different from yourself (e.g., different in terms of a client's ethnicity/race, gender, sexual orientation, etc.), questions should be used sparingly until trust is developed. Although it is vital that you draw out the key facts and the specific feelings that underlie clients' constructions of their situation, the basic listening sequence must be modified in the here and now of the interview.

Whether you are helping a client make a vocational decision, negotiate a divorce, or conduct a psychodynamic dream analysis, you will need to know the facts and how the client feels about those facts before moving forward with an analysis of

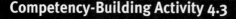

Competency-Building Activity 4.3

Using the Basic Listening Sequence (BLS) to Draw Out Client Stories

Regardless of whatever theory you select, it is important that you draw out client issues and stories as they tell them in their own way and minimize your influence on how clients present information about their stories. To effectively encourage clients to talk about their stories in this way, it is useful to ask yourself, "What are the key behaviors, thoughts, and feelings around those stories?" and to use this fundamental question as a guide in your interview with clients.

Instructions: This competency-building activity is aimed at helping you use the BLS in a role-play interview with another participant. Let the person who agrees to work with you in this activity know the purpose of this exercise and encourage her or him to think about a story to talk about in your

interview. Be sure to use only attending behavior and the basic listening sequence (described in the preceding section of this chapter) to bring the story out. Audiotape the session so you can examine and classify your listening skills after the role-play is finished. Videotape the session, if possible, so you can observe the nonverbal behaviors you exhibited in this role-play at a later time.

When you listen to the audiotape (or watch the videotape) of your interview, write your reactions to the following questions on a separate piece of paper to be included in your personal/professional development portfolio: (1) What do you notice about your listening style? (2) Did you tend to focus on certain dimensions of the client story rather than other dimensions? (3) Looking at multicultural issues, did you just focus on the individual, or were cultural/environmental factors discussed as well during your interview?

Be sure to record your reactions to this exercise in your personal-professional portfolio.

---

what the client can do to foster a greater sense of mental health and psychological well-being. The BLS and its accompanying microskills can be very useful when you employ the different therapeutic approaches discussed later in this book. Whether you are a cognitive-behavioral counselor (Chapter 7), a reality therapist (Chapter 8), or a family counselor (Chapter 14), the basic listening sequence provides you with a critical set of therapeutic tools that can promote positive counseling outcomes. Competency-Building Activity 4.3 will assist you in acquiring and refining some of the concrete techniques you can use to increase your listening effectiveness in counseling and psychotherapeutic situations.

Influencing Skills and Strategies

Clients can profit and grow even if you use only attending behavior and listening skills. However, a strict listening approach fails to take advantage of the many other possibilities that can be realized when a broader range of microskills is utilized in the helping process. The microskills system is comprised of an array of skills and strategies that can be useful in guiding clients to change their stories, thoughts, feelings, and behavior. Table 4.3 presents in summary form these key change strategies and skills.

Influencing skills are used much less frequently in all theoretical approaches than the attending and listening skills described above. It is important to use the BLS with

Table 4.3

Influencing Skills

Skill	Description	Function in Interview
Interpretation/reframing	Provides an alternative frame of reference from which the client may view a situation. May be drawn from a theory or from one's own personal observations. *Interpretation may be viewed as the core influencing skill.*	Attempts to provide the client with a new way to view the situation. The interpretation provides the client with a clear-cut alternative perception of "reality." This perception may enable a change of view that in turn may result in changes in thoughts, constructs, or behaviors.
Directive	Tells the client what action to take. May be a simple suggestion stated in command form or may be a sophisticated technique from a specific theory.	Clearly indicates to clients what action counselors or therapists wish them to take. The prediction with a directive is that the client will do what is suggested. Table 4.4 lists several specific directives drawn from different theories that will have differing anticipated results with clients.
Advice/information	Provides suggestions, instructional ideas, homework, advice on how to act, think, or behave.	Used sparingly, may provide client with new and useful information. Specific vocational information is an example of use of this skill.
Self-disclosure	The interviewer shares personal experience from the past or may share present reactions to the client.	Emphasizes counselor "I" statements. This skill is closely allied to feedback and may build trust and openness, leading to a more mutual relationship with the client.
Feedback	Provides clients with specific data on how they are seen by the counselor or by others.	Provides concrete data that may help clients realize how others perceive their behavior and thinking patterns, thus enabling an alternative self-perception.
Logical consequences	Shows client the logical outcome of thinking and behavior—if/then.	Provides an alternative frame of reference for the client. This skill helps clients anticipate the consequences or results of their actions.
Influencing summary	Summarizes counselor comments; most often used in combination with the attending summarization at or near the end of a session.	Clarifies what has happened in the interview and summarizes what the therapist has said. This skill is designed to help generalization from the interview to daily life.

greater frequency than influencing skills. Even the most directive of counselors and therapists must hear and understand the client's story before proceeding with influencing skills in the therapeutic endeavor.

Theories of helping vary more widely in their use of influencing skills than they do in listening skills. Even if used in limited ways in the counseling sessions, influencing skills, like interpretations and reframes, may result in extensive discussion, which will require the therapist to listen carefully before presenting still another influencing skill. The classic person-centered mode of counseling seeks to minimally influence client direction, while an active cognitive-behavioral counselor may use influencing skills extensively. Both helping approaches will still use attending and listening skills a great deal.

Interpretation and **reframing** are perhaps the central influencing skills, for in using these approaches, the counselor or therapist most directly seeks to help clients find new meaning in old stories and behaviors. Although microcounseling theory argues for clients finding their own meanings via the basic listening sequence, many people will benefit from assistance in developing new ways of thinking. Those who have experienced harassment—women, gay individuals, or persons with AIDS, for example—need to tell their stories, but they may also benefit from the therapist's ideas, interpretations, and reframes.

Furthermore, many people who are harassed frequently come to think that the problems they are encountering are "their fault." As many multicultural, feminist, and social justice counseling theorists and researchers note, this self-blaming often represents inaccurate and overgeneralized forms of self-depreciation that are embedded in internalized oppression (Helms & Cook, 1999; hooks, 2001b).

A basic reframe for helping clients see the social and contextual basis of their issues is to help them understand how sexism, discrimination, and/or internalized oppression are important factors that affect their sense of psychological well-being. Such observations are made from a multicultural counseling and therapy (MCT) frame of reference. Reframes from other theoretical approaches can also be helpful in uncovering the adverse impact that racism and sexism can have on clients' lives.

Psychodynamic theory may be useful in assisting clients to see how their personal histories and past experiences relate to their present stories. Cognitive-behavioral reframes will often help clients think more effectively about their stories and can provide action narratives for the future. The existential-humanistic reframe may help clients focus on their self-value. The point of reframing is to tell the story in a new way, one that is more functional and meaningful to the client.

These are not easy tasks to achieve in counseling and psychotherapy, especially when counselors and clients are culturally different. The difficulty in dealing with these issues in therapy is heightened when the counselor comes from the dominant cultural/racial group in the United States and the client comes from a group or culture that is oppressed in U.S. society.

All influencing skills are oriented in different ways toward the same objectives: finding new ways to think about old narratives and then assisting clients to act on this new knowledge in ways that promote more satisfying and productive

Table 4.4

Microskill Usage According to Theoretical Orientation

Microskill Category	First Force Psychodynamic Theory	Second Force Cognitive-Behavioral Theory	Third Force Existential-Humanistic Theory	Fourth Force Multicultural Theory
Focus	*Primarily on individual client.* The problem is understanding how past experience affects what occurs in the present. A major goal is understanding unconscious mental functioning.	*Primarily on individual client.* Clients are encouraged to explore how their cognitions (e.g., mental constructions) of the world are directly related to their personal problems and dissatisfaction in life.	*Primarily on individual client.* The problem will often be conceptualized as one of understanding one's own unique needs and wishes. A major goal is self-actualization.	*Balance between the individual, family, and multicultural issues.* The problem is thought of as developed in a context. A major goal is helping the client understand self in relation to context and taking action for self and others.
Listening skills	*Basic listening sequence used to draw out data relating to psychodynamic theory.* Questions and encouragers are especially important to facilitate exploration of unconscious processes.	*Listening skills are used to gain an understanding of how clients make meaning of their life experiences.* Openended questions are useful in probing the underlying beliefs that comprise clients' meaning-making systems and fuel their behavior.	*Central use of listening skills to facilitate client expression;* minimum use of questions. The therapist attempts to minimize influence on client constructions and meaning making. Major emphasis is on reflecting feelings.	*Basic listening sequence used to facilitate client understanding of self-in-system.* The therapist will tend to listen for family and contextual issues that affect client expression of self.
Influencing skills	*Interpretation is central skill.* In later stages of therapy, interpretations/ reframes may be the only skill used. There is little or no attempt to lead the client to behavioral action.	*Feedback, interpretation, and reframing skills are central to this theoretical approach to counseling and psychotherapy.* Confrontation techniques are commonly used as clients are supported and challenged to develop new cognitions that are used to alter past behavior patterns.	*Feedback and reflection of meaning most commonly used.* Interpretation and reframes are avoided. There is little or no attempt to lead the client to behavioral action.	*Varying use of the influencing skills depending on client's cultural context.* In general, there will be a greater emphasis on feedback and self-disclosure to build a more egalitarian relationship. Reframes will often focus on family and cultural issues. There may be an attempt to encourage the client to act on issues and to also consider action in the community and society as well.

personal outcomes. Later, as you read through this book, you will find that Rogerian person-centered counseling employs very few of these influencing skills. Cognitive-behavioral theory, however, uses an extensive array of influencing change strategies. As a professional counselor or therapist, you will want to find the balance and blend of listening and influencing you believe most appropriate for your own practice.

Focusing: Internal and External Attribution

The microskill of **focusing** is, at one level, quite simple. Where do you focus your attention when you talk to a client? Traditionally, counseling has focused on the client and the client's problem. A particular goal of training in the past was to help beginning practitioners focus on the client rather than the problem. We can focus our listening and influencing skills in many other directions as well. For instance, you may find it useful to focus on the client's family, significant others (friends, boss, etc.), or the cultural/environmental context in various therapy situations. In choosing specific areas of a client's life on which to focus therapeutic responses, the practitioner highlights what he or she believes are the primary attributes of the client's presenting problem.

Attribution is a central issue that counselors need to consider when using reframing and focusing skills. One aspect of this important issue may be reflected in the following questions: (1) Does the client see the problem or issue as one that he or she has to surmount? (2) Does it appear that the client accepts all or most of the responsibility for the presenting problem? Questions/statements made by clients who place responsibility for their difficulties internally—in their own body, mind, and/or behaviors—might be expressed in such statements as "What did I do wrong? Why did I do that? I'm at fault for all that is going on in my life."

On the other hand, external attribution may manifest itself by such statements as "It's not my fault. The system makes it impossible for me to succeed. I just can't deal with my problems because of my family history."

Historically, counseling theory has focused on internal attribution, with little attention directed to external, environmental factors. This results in insensitivity to contextually and environmentally based issues such as poverty, sexism, racism, and other forms of oppression that can contribute to clients' problems. The traditional rational-emotive behavioral counseling approach (Chapter 8) emphasizes that clients' thinking about things is more important than what actually happens outside the person. This way of conceptualizing the helping process has been employed for many years by traditional psychodynamic and existential-humanistic theorists as well.

While learning to think more positively and to control internal cognitions and feelings is important, the deep and lasting effects of external factors such as poverty, racism, sexism, and other forms of discrimination have been almost totally ignored by the fields of counseling and psychology. The liberation movements of African-Americans, women, and gay and lesbian persons have been founded on an awareness that "the system" may contribute in many significant ways to individuals' problems. The increasing acknowledgment of external environmental attributions as important contributing factors in clients' lives has, for many, had an invaluable mental health benefit. At the same time, it is important to also point out that external attribution can manifest as a lack of willingness to act on one's own behalf in the counseling context.

Often, a balanced approach to internal and external attribution may be most appropriate. Clients need to learn how to think about their issues in a social context, and counselors and therapists need to be willing to name and act against social oppression. But there is also a clear need for each client to be willing to take responsibility for his or her thinking, feelings, and behaviors. External attributions must be closely evaluated by counselors and clients working together to move clients away from excusing behavior and toward active construction of new meaning in their lives. All clients, even the most oppressed, have the capacity for internal growth and empowerment.

The empowerment of clients to act against oppressive systems is an important goal of feminist therapy (Chapter 11; see also multicultural counseling and therapy in Chapter 12, and developmental counseling and therapy in Chapter 13. These theoretical orientations recognize that part of the empowerment process is helping each client find a balance of self, other, and environmental awareness (D'Andrea & Daniels, 2005).

Different Skill Patterns for Different Theories

By mastering the foregoing skills, you can "mix and match" foundational patterns and apply alternative helping theories in your professional practice. Table 4.4 summarizes four of the major theoretical forces in terms of their differential usage of the microskills that are described in this chapter. In this table, it can be seen that existential/humanistic theory primarily uses attending skills and very few questions. Psychodynamic theory makes extensive use of interpretation. Both approaches tend to focus on individual issues. By way of contrast, multicultural-feminist-social justice counseling focuses on self-in-context and takes a more action-oriented approach to helping.

Each therapeutic system is based on varying conceptual frameworks and skill patterns that must be mastered if you are to work effectively and ethically within that orientation. However, all systems use basic listening skills to some extent, and once you have mastered these fundamental skills, it is easier to move across theoretical orientations into new ways of functioning in the helping process. You will become better able to intentionally employ different skill patterns as you learn more about the various theoretical orientations that are presented in this book and by completing the competency-building activities included in each chapter.

The Five-Stage Interview: A Viable Model for All Theories

Each interview has a beginning and an end. In between, clients need to share their problems and personal stories, with the practitioner helping clients define goals for the session and working with clients to find new solutions to old issues. The five-stage

Table 4.5

The Five-Stage Structure of the Interview

Definition of Stage	Function and Purpose	Cultural and Individual Issues
1. Establishing rapport and structure "Hello. This is what we'll be doing today."	To build a working alliance with the client and to enable the client to feel comfortable with the interviewer. Structuring may be needed to explain the purpose of the interview. Structuring functions to help keep the session on task and to inform the client what the counselor can and cannot do.	With some clients and some cultural groups, rapport development may take a long time so that trust can grow. Methods of rapport development and decision making will vary with individuals and cultures.
2. Gathering data and identifying assets "Tell me your story." "What's your concern?" "What are your strengths?"	To find out why the client has come to the interview and how he or she views the concern. Skillful problem definition will help avoid aimless topic jumping and give the interview purpose and direction. Also to identify clearly positive strengths of the client.	Not all clients appreciate the careful delineation of issues typical of middle-class helping. Solution-oriented approaches minimize this stage.
3. Determining outcomes and goal setting "What do you want to have happen?"	To find out the ideal world of the client. How would the client like to be? How would things be if the "problem" were solved? This stage is important in that it enables the interviewer to know what the client	If work is clear and concrete here, specific resolutions may be immediately apparent. Many cultural groups and individuals prefer to start here. If we know goals, the concern may be clear and we can move to stage 4. This

continued on next page

interview model (Ivey & Ivey 2007; Ivey & Matthews, 1984) provides a practical framework for organizing the interview into distinct and overlapping phases, regardless of the theoretical orientation you may use. While therapist behaviors in each stage of the interview will vary, there is a common coherent framework in most effective sessions.

If you develop expertise in the basic listening and influencing skills and work toward infusing these skills into the five-stage model, you will move to acquiring a foundation for a mastery of the theories presented in this book. The competency-building exercises are based on the five-stage framework of interviewing and will help you grasp the full range of skills necessary to engage in a complete interview

---

Table 4.5, continued

The Five-Stage Structure of the Interview

Definition of Stage	Function and Purpose	Cultural and Individual Issues
	wants. The desired direction of the client and counselor should be reasonably harmonious. With some clients, skip stage 2 and define goals first.	is also characteristic of solution-oriented therapy.
4. Generating alternative solutions "What are we going to do to generate new ideas?" "How could we look at the story differently?"	To work toward resolution of the client's issue. This may involve the creative problem-solving model of generating alternatives (to remove stuck-ness) and deciding among those alternatives. It also may involve lengthy exploration of personal dynamics. This phase of the interview may be the longest.	It is critical that individual and cultural differences in decisional style be acknowledged. What is the "correct" decision from your point of view may be highly inappropriate to another. With some groups, a highly directive style on the counselor's part may be appropriate. In general, listen and let the client decide.
5. Generalizing and transferring learning "Will you do it?"	To enable changes in thoughts, feelings, and behaviors in the client's daily life. Can the new story be generalized to the real world?	The degree of generalization will also relate highly to how effectively you took cultural and individual differences into account in the early stages of the session(s).

using the basics of each theory. With the foundation provided by the five-stage interview theory and your own personal experience, you will have an excellent base to develop your own future integrated practice of helping, and with competence in multiple modes of counseling and therapy, regardless of your primary orientation. Table 4.5 presents the five-stage interview model in brief form, identifying key counselor "leads" (lead-in comments) for each stage.

As presented, the five-stage framework appears to be linear and moves step by step. But, once you are acquainted with the basic steps of this foundational framework, you may find yourself changing the order as appropriate to whatever individual client you may be working with. For example, some clients may be anxious to talk and will start immediately with stage 2, bypassing the traditional rapport and structuring in stage 1. In brief therapy, you may choose to bring goal setting into the counseling and therapy process very early, sometimes even before the problem has been discussed in detail. You will also find yourself recycling between and among the five stages in this model. In the middle of longer-term therapy, you may want to address new rapport-building issues and return to the structuring dimension of therapy to establish an even more solid base of trust.

Stage 1. Establishing Rapport and Structure

The specific microskills that are particularly important to implement at this stage of counseling and therapy include (1) the implementation of culturally and individually appropriate attending behavior, (2) the ability to accurately observe and make meaning of client reactions to the counseling process as it unfolds, and (3) the ability to change the structure and pace of the interview to meet individual and cultural needs of your clients. Your ability to establish rapport both early in the session and later in the helping process will be important in building an empathic bond between the client and yourself.

When working with delinquent acting-out youngsters, Stage 1 may take a number of counseling sessions, perhaps even weeks of work on your part, before a sufficient level of trust is developed in the client to move forward with the helping process. In Aboriginal Australia, social workers often spend more than half of the interview focusing on family and social interconnections before even asking about the issue or problem to be discussed. With many middle-class people in North America, this stage can almost be omitted, as clients often start talking about their problems quickly. Nonetheless, the continual development of rapport and trust throughout the session is vital.

Stage 2. Gathering Data and Identifying Assets

The microskills most associated with this phase of the interview are those of the basic listening sequence. Counselors and therapists use these listening skills to draw out clients' narratives or stories and also to identify clients' strengths. Your ability to summarize clients' stories or issues in their own words is an important part of empathic understanding. Brief counseling and therapy (Chapter 3) gives prime attention to clients' strengths, with secondary emphasis directed to their perceived "problems." This is done in the belief that people are able to resolve their issues by becoming more aware of and willing to use their personal assets and resources in dealing with their life challenges, and not by simply dwelling on their problems or weaknesses.

Social constructivism and focus analysis remind us that defining the problem is not as easy as it seems (Sexton & Griffin, 1997). The way we define and tell stories about a problem often decides how the issue will be resolved. Is the problem "in the client" and thus an issue of internal attribution and locus of control, or is it "in the environment" and concerned with external attribution and contextual issues?

Feminist theory (Chapter 11) points out that environmental contingencies of sexism are vital issues in any work with women. Traditionally trained rational-emotive behavioral (REBT) theorists, on the other hand, make the point that "it is not things, but how we think about things" that underlies our sense of mental health and personal well-being. REBT therapists have historically insisted that the problem to be solved is in the individual and is to be resolved by thinking and behaving differently. The multicultural-feminist-social justice approach to counseling seeks to balance individual and environmental issues by acknowledging internal and external attributions in the helping process.

Different approaches to problem definition result in different ways of constructing meaning of a particular client "problem." The existential-humanistic approach seeks to locate problematic concerns within the client's personal meaning-making system and then strives to help the person self-actualize by learning to think, feel, and act in new ways. The psychodynamic therapist seeks to find connections of past and present behavior.

Some point out that the very use of the word *problem* starts counseling off on the wrong foot. Brief counseling theorists argue strongly that counseling and therapy are too much about "problems" and suggest that mental health practitioners would do well to change their vernacular by using the terms *issues, challenges,* or *concerns* in the helping process. Many African-Americans object to the concept of "problem" and respond more readily to the use of the latter terms (Lanier, cited in Ivey & Ivey, 2007). Experience with other racial and ethnic groups reveals that many clients prefer the more open and positive language suggested by Lanier.

Regardless of your theory, we recommend identifying positive client strengths in each session. These strengths may include positive childhood experiences, accomplishments in sports or the arts, something the individual is proud of doing, images of supportive relatives, times things were "going right" in the person's life, or the ability to survive a trauma. Positive stories and images about gender, sexual orientation, and ethnicity/race help center clients and give them strength to delve more deeply into the difficult areas of their lives.

Stage 3. Determining Outcomes and Goal Setting

The basic listening sequence and balancing internal and external attribution of problems are central tools at this stage. However, at this point the listening sequence focuses on helping the client find positive, clear, and reachable goals. Concreteness and specific reachable goals are essential to promoting successful counseling outcomes that are of personal relevance to our clients. Too often, counselors fail in this area, as clients are often willing to talk endlessly about their issues but reluctant to talk about what they specifically want to have happen in their lives.

Many clients can benefit from an immediate focus on goals. Brief counseling and solution-oriented therapy (Sklare, 2004) gives minimal attention to stages 1 and 2, choosing instead to find out what the client wants to have happen. This approach makes the excellent point that if clients can achieve what they want, there is no need to bother with long stories and definitions of problems and personal concerns or frustrations in counseling and therapy.

Moving directly to goal setting and establishing mutual outcomes within the context of counseling and psychotherapy may help you work more effectively with clients who are culturally different than yourself. Clients often find it difficult to tell a counselor their stories of life issues and problems if there is a lack of trust due to a history of racism, sexism, heterosexism, or spiritual oppression between themselves and people with whom the counselor might be identified.

Finally, the goals of counseling are sometimes established by theorists before the client walks in the door. There are some practitioners who believe that every client needs to understand their unconscious, become self-actualized, or "really look at themselves" in a racially or gender-fair society. Although all of these goals may be laudable, the field increasingly is moving away from this "top-down" approach and is involving clients in establishing their own goals.

Stage 4. Generating Alternative Solutions

Influencing skills become more important at this stage of counseling and therapy. Any of a variety of skills or theoretical alternatives may be employed to help clients create new ways of thinking about their stories. Clear discussion of clients' stories and strengths, followed by precise goal setting, is often enough to help many clients brainstorm their own solutions.

Implied in this phase of the change process is the basic confrontational statement, "On the one hand, your issue/problem/concern is . . . and on the other hand, your goal is . . ." Images and stories of strengths may be brought in to help clients act on their personal challenges as they are encouraged to reframe their thinking about solution-based approaches to whatever issue they bring to counseling.

A better sense of self and life's meaning is often a goal for existential-humanistic helping, and thus influencing skills, such as interpretation and directives, will be seldom used. The cognitive-behavioral tradition, however, may be very active, with directives, instructions, and use strategies oriented to help clients understand their cognitions and behaviors in new ways. Psychodynamic strategies tend to focus on free association, with extensive interpretation of past events, in an effort to help clients generate alternative solutions to current life challenges.

Stage 5. Generalizing and Transferring Learning

Influencing skills are particularly important at this stage, because you as the counselor want to ensure that the client actually does something as a result of the session. Special attention to **relapse prevention** (Marlatt & Gordon, 1985; Marlatt, & Donovan, 2005) is given in Chapter 8 in the discussion on cognitive-behavioral methods.

Unless you plan for the transfer of decisions and actions discussed in therapy sessions to real-life situations, much of your work will be for naught. Not all theories give this important area sufficient attention. After a demanding interview, it is all too easy for the therapist to skip this stage of the helping process.

Some of the questions you can ask clients to bring therapy sessions to an effective close include: "What stands out for you today from our session?" "What one thing

Professional Development Extension

Using the Five-Stage Counseling Model and the Microskills Framework in Career Counseling

Young practitioners can derive a great deal of pragmatic benefit from keeping the microskills framework in mind when providing counseling and therapy services to their clients. The following case example is of Maureen, a 32-year-old counselor who recently graduated with a master's degree in community counseling, specializing in career counseling. Although she was excited about receiving her degree, Maureen was nervous about her ability to provide the kind of high-quality services she expected of herself when working with clients. Maureen chose to use the five-step model and microskills framework to help her "stay on track" when working with her first client, a 28-year old male.

After greeting Mr. Garcia and exchanging brief pleasantries, I found myself becoming so nervous about wanting to do a good job with him that I began to draw a blank as to what I should say next. When this happened I shifted my thinking to the five-stage counseling model and the microskills framework that I had learned in graduate school.

As I did this I remembered the importance of using various attending skills to communicate a genuine sense of empathy and positive regard when trying to build rapport with my client (stage 1).

After Mr. Garcia made positive reference to his Latino ancestry on a couple of occasions early in our session, I thought of the notion of multicultural intentionality. This led me to intentionally take time to enable Mr. Garcia to get to know me as I learned about him. As I did this, I sensed we were developing what many Latinos and Latinas commonly refer to as *personalismo* early in the counseling process.

Feeling that we had begun to develop a positive relationship, I thought it might be a good time to intentionally shift to the second stage of the five-stage model by asking Mr. Garcia what

brought him to counseling today. As he began talking about career concerns, I was reminded of the importance of using another important microskill — the positive asset search.

Like many clients, Mr. Garcia began talking about many of his limitations that prevented him from securing the career he was interested in. By identifying some of his personal assets, I was able to help Mr. Garcia gain a more balanced view of his own career capabilities.

Shortly thereafter, I used summarization to make sure I had heard everything Mr. Garcia said. After he acknowledged that I did understand him, I asked him to state what his goal for counseling was (stage 3).

The ensuing conversation made it clear that Mr. Garcia wanted to learn about local resources he could access to become a chef. By identifying this counseling goal, I was able to provide specific information that increased Mr. Garcia's knowledge of the chef training programs available in the area as well as the requirements and costs of these programs.

As we continued this discussion, Mr. Garcia talked about some of the problems he thought he was likely to encounter in being accepted to a chef training program. I could feel us moving into stage 4 of the process. We discussed some of the steps he could take in becoming a chef and what some of the consequences might be. In doing so, I was able to assist Mr. Garcia in generating new ideas about the things he could do to overcome the barriers he perceived in becoming a chef.

Before scheduling our next meeting, I was mindful to encourage Mr. Garcia to transfer what he had learned in our first session by taking some action that would help him realize some aspect of his career development (stage 5). He responded by stating that he would contact two of the chef training schools we talked about to get more specific information about their requirements so he could better ascertain his suitability to enroll in either of them.

After Mr. Garcia left our meeting, I reflected on how helpful it was to refer to the microskills framework when working with him. Not only was I able to overcome the nervousness that caused me to blank out on what I should be doing with him, but it enabled me to implement many of the

continued on next page

specific microskills (e.g., communicating a sense of warmth, genuineness, authenticity, and respect; using the basic listening sequence; paraphrasing; being concrete in my suggestions; using open-ended statements as well as reflection of feeling and thinking questions) to help my client. Although I know I will be able to feel more relaxed and confident in my counseling skills as time goes on, the microskills model provides the sort of guidelines I need to help my clients at different points during the helping process.

might you remember from today?" These open-ended questions often have surprising results. What we thought was our brilliant intervention in counseling may not have even been noticed by the client. Data obtained from these questions often tell us what to do next to ensure that the client returns and/or takes action on the decisions reached.

Limitations and Practical Implications of the Microskills Framework

The microskills approach is noted for its precision and clear description of interview behavior. Although early presentations of the model did not take cultural issues into account, the evolution and precision of the microskills approach have led to its current, more culturally sensitive presentation. It is now an axiom of the microskills approach that all interviews must take into account both individual and multicultural differences.

Allen Ivey has worked with Matthew Rigney, a highly skilled Aboriginal social worker in Australia, in jointly examining the multicultural implications of using one of the most important parts of the microskills model—attending skills. Matthew was videotaped interviewing a client in the "Aboriginal way," which involves the therapist demonstrating limited eye contact, offering more self-disclosing comments in the session, and generally promoting a more participative interviewing style. On reviewing the tape, Allen and Matthew noted various strengths in how the therapist modified his attending skills to match the cultural expectations and interpersonal style of his client. In responding to the role-play and the discussion that ensued from it, Matthew stated, "You mean it's OK to do counseling in our people's way?"

Matthew had been taught that he should do counseling in the Western style, and his own cultural background had been denied. Despite his obvious skill as an Aboriginal therapist, Matthew had come to believe that the European-American style of listening was a more appropriate way of conducting counseling and therapy than the listening behaviors that characterize his own cultural group. He was encouraged to maintain and sharpen his traditional ways of listening as a result of the new insight he gained into the cultural relevance of counseling approaches. Matthew Rigney is very much alive in the ideas presented in this chapter, and we are grateful for the ways he has helped to expand our own thinking and sensitivity about cultural issues in the helping process.

At the present time, many people in Australia, Canada, and the United States continue to teach and practice microskills in a culturally insensitive manner. Some books still discuss attending without attention to cultural differences. This gap between theory and culturally respectful counseling practices is not solely associated with the microskills approach. Individualistic psychodynamic and client-centered theories are also transported to relational cultures and presented as "the way to conduct interviewing and therapy." Powerful and intrusive Gestalt techniques may be effective in North America, but they can be inappropriate in other settings. Cognitive-behavioral techniques are often useful in culturally diverse settings but require serious modification to ensure that they are appropriate and respectful of persons with differing cultures and experiences.

The Professional Development Extension further explores some of the ways that the microskills model and the five-stage interview framework might be used in other aspects of your professional practice beyond individual counseling and psychotherapeutic settings. The microskills and five-stage interview model can be easily transferred to a broad range of professional and personal interactions and can promote a greater sense of professional and personal empowerment for your clients.

Summary

This chapter provides you with an overview of the foundational skills you will need to effectively conduct counseling and therapy sessions in the future. By describing the various microskills presented in the above sections and discussing the five-stage framework for conducting counseling and therapy interviews, it is hoped that you have a greater level of confidence in understanding how the helping process may unfold in your professional practice in the future.

You should view the presentation of the microskills and the five-stage interview model as guidelines and not hard and fast ways of doing counseling and therapy. Certain microskills are readily used when counselors and therapists implement some of the theoretical orientations discussed in the preceding chapters while other skills are more frequently utilized by mental health practitioners who adopt different helping approaches. By presenting the broad range of microskills early in this book, you will have the opportunity to more easily exercise these skills as you learn more about the various counseling and therapy theories that are described in greater detail in the ensuing chapters.

The microskills presented in this chapter, however, have much applicability in whatever theoretical approach you may be attracted to as you work through this textbook. Regardless of whatever theories you eventually use in your work, you will be ethically challenged to thoughtfully reflect on how the helping strategies and microskills you intentionally use in counseling and therapy complement your clients' cultural identity, worldview, and constructions of what constitutes appropriate helping strategies.

Multimedia Resources for This Chapter

The following online resources offer video and other resources of particular relevance to this chapter of your text.

Companion Website

Go to **www.ablongman.com/Ivey6e** to view the following video clips:

- Video clip 4.1 serves as an example of how a White male therapist addresses a number of issues related to sexism and racism early in the session with an African-American female client. How does the therapist's use of microskills positively affect his work with the client?
- Video clip 4.2 demonstrates how a therapist can develop a positive and trusting relationship with the client while also working toward gaining a mutually agreeable format for structuring the counseling process. Many of the microskills used by the therapist in this role-play can be used to implement multicultural intentionality in your own counseling style.

As you review these video clips, consider the following questions:

- What microskills is the therapist using in the session?
- Which microskills seemed to work best with this client?
- Which microskills did not seem to work well with this client?
- What would you have done differently in implementing the various microskills discussed in this chapter?

MyHelpingLab

If a MyHelpingLab passcode was included with your textbook and you have activated your passcode:

- go to **www.ablongman.com/myhelpinglab**
- enter the "Counseling" area of the site by clicking on that tab
- select "Video Lab" from the toolbar to the left of the page
- select "MyHelpingLab Videos by Theoretical Approach"
- select any of the following modules—"Existential Humanistic," "Family Systems," "Narrative"—to view various video clips of a therapist using various microskills with clients

part two

The First, Second, and Third Forces in Counseling and Psychotherapy

Although more than 250 theories for counseling and therapy exist, psychodynamic, cognitive-behavioral, and existential-humanistic theories continue to play a significant role in the work of mental health professionals. The impact of these historical forces is reflected in the manner in which they shape counselors' and therapists' thinking about the roles and approaches they use to promote their clients' mental health and sense of well-being in their professional practices.

Chapters 5 and 6 explore the first force, psychodynamic theory, and the works of early theorists in the area—Sigmund Freud, Alfred Adler, and Carl Jung—as well the more recent works of John Bowlby and Mary Ainsworth, whose theory of attachment offers many practical considerations for practitioners. You will see how theorists who followed Freud addressed important questions and criticisms that multicultural and feminist adovcates have long raised about Freud's traditional psychoanalytic approach to therapy.

Chapters 7 and 8 then examine the second major theoretical force, which is tied to the emergence of behavioral theory and its more recent derivative cognitive-behavioral therapy (CBT). The genesis of the second force has long been associated with the work of B. F. Skinner, despite Skinner's belief that the mind and cognitions were relatively unimportant constructs in people's behavior. Researchers such as Donald Meichenbaum and Aaron Beck extended Skinner's foundational work by describing why and how mental health practitioners need to address the complex interplay of people's thinking (mind) and their behaviors in counseling and psychotherapeutic practice. Albert Ellis's rational-emotive-behavioral-contextual therapy and William Glasser's reality therapy represent further extensions of the second force.

Finally, Chapters 9 and 10 explore the third force in counseling and psychotherapy, existential-humanistic theory, which originated in European philosophy but achieved its maximum influence in counseling and therapy through the work of Carl Rogers. In addition, many of the practical implications of Viktor Frankl's logotherapy and Frederick (Fritz) Perls's Gestalt therapy are highlighted. Particular attention is directed to the ways in which multicultural and feminist constructs can be incorporated into these important theoretical helping approaches.

chapter 5

The Psychodynamic Tradition: Theoretical Constructions and Practical Applications

chapter goals

This chapter is designed to:

1. Summarize the psychodynamic frame of reference and illustrate that it is far from a single orthodox helping framework.

2. Describe the central constructs of psychodynamic theory.

3. Expand your understanding of the psychodynamic frame of reference by presenting an overview of attachment theory, giving special attention to the contributions of John Bowlby and Mary Ainsworth in this area.

4. Outline specific applications of psychodynamic theory for professional practice, including the use of free association, interpretation, dream analysis, analysis of resistance, and issues related to transference and countertransference.

5. Give special attention to multicultural-feminist-social justice counseling issues as they relate to psychodynamic theories.

6. Explore the limitations of psychodynamic approaches to counseling and therapy.

7. Extend your thinking about some of the ways that psychodynamic theories and practices can be used in other areas of your work.

Introduction

The psychodynamic frame of reference represents the first major theoretical force that helped shape the fields of counseling and psychology. The genisis of the psychodynamic perspective can be traced to the pioneering work of Sigmund Freud, who developed his theory of psychoanalysis in the early 1900s. While Freud's psychoanalytic theory has had a profound effect in shaping the work of many counselors and therapists, it is often viewed as an antiquated and irrelevant perspective by many persons in the mental health professions today. This is unfortunate, because many aspects of this rich theoretical framework can be very useful when effectively and respectfully implemented with persons from diverse groups and backgrounds.

Later in the chapter, you will see modifications to Freud's psychoanalytic theory, particularly those by John Bowlby, Mary Ainsworth, and Bruce Taub-Bynum, that have particular relevance to current life and multicultural thought. Bowlby's (1969) attachment theory is one of the most researched psychodynamic systems in the world today. Bowlby and Ainsworth's concepts demonstrate how many of Freud's ideas apply to the development of both children and adults.

Taub-Bynum (1992, 1999) introduced the concept of the African unconscious. This concept extends some of the unique dimensions of unconsciousness that Freud failed to address. Taub-Bynum's description of the African unconscious also expands the understanding of the comprehensive nature of psychological attachment to our families and cultural groups. His description of these issues provides new insights into the psychodynamic perspective that complements and adds to the earlier work of Freud, Bowlby, and Ainsworth. Nonetheless, any discussion about psychodynamic theory must begin with Sigmund Freud.

Sigmund Freud and Psychoanalytic Counseling and Therapy: An Overview

Sigmund Freud was born in Moravia on May 6, 1856. His father was 40 years old and a widower when he married his second wife, who was only 19 years old at the time. While Freud's father had two sons from his first marriage, his second wife gave birth to seven additional children. Freud was the oldest of these seven children and reportedly his mother's favorite.

Freud's mother was a warm and nurturing woman who had an important impact on his life. His father was a successful merchant and had a demanding but gentle disposition. Freud greatly admired and respected his father's commitment to his family and the value he placed on hard work and personal responsibility (Freud, 1925/1964).

Seligman (2001) discusses two family events that had a lasting impact on Freud's life. The first involved the death of his eight-month-old brother Julius when Freud was 19 months old. Commenting on this significant event in early childhood, Seligman notes that "Freud recalled feeling jealous and resentful of his younger brother and later reproached himself when his brother died. Early memories such as these are very likely to have contributed to Freud's later emphasis on the formative power of early childhood experiences" (p. 51).

The second aspect of Freud's family life that had a lasting effect on his development relates to his Jewish identity and background. Commenting on this influence, Seligman (2001) points out:

> His Jewish heritage, with its emphasis on learning and family, contributed to Freud's appreciation for study, history, and in-depth analysis. It also influenced his place of residence and his career choice, probably colored the reception his work received, and eventually meant that he had to flee from Austria when Hitler came into power (p. 51).

These familial/cultural/religious influences led Freud to develop as a serious student and to eventually choose medicine as a career. He worked hard as a medical student from 1873 to 1881 at the University of Vienna, where he earned a degree in neurology. During medical school, he met Martha Bernays, whom he married in 1886. The couple had six children in the first 10 years of their marriage.

Seligman (2001) summarizes the value that Freud placed on his career and family:

> Freud's work and his family were the most important parts of his life. Jones (1955) speaks of the "unshakable devotion and a perfect harmony of understanding" between Freud and his wife and of Freud's efforts to raise his children in an atmosphere that would keep anxiety low, minimize limitations and criticism, and allow personalities to develop freely. (p. 52)

It is not possible to adequately chronicle Freud's career here, but it is important to point out that the mentoring he received from two neurologists, Jean-Martin Charcot and Josef Breuer, helped set the foundation for his psychological perspective on the condition of hysteria.

As Freud began to work with persons suffering from hysteria, his interests shifted from primarily theoretical endeavors related to neurology to a greater interest and involvement with patients themselves. These clinical experiences ultimately led him to develop what he referred to as the **psychoanalytic theory** of personality development.

Out of this clinical work came Freud's belief that a person's behavior is determined by both interpersonal and intrapsychic forces. He referred to this aspect of his psychoanalytic theory as **psychic determinism.** Accordingly, "human beings, in Freud's view, are not masters of their own destinies; rather, their behaviors are driven by the need to gratify basic biological needs and instincts. Behavior is not random but determined by past experiences. In this context, behavior is lawful and connected" (Hansen, Rossberg, & Cramer, 1994, pp. 21–22).

It could be argued that Freud brought order out of the chaos of ideas about psychological development. Until his brilliant and insightful work was publicized in the early part of the 20th century, mental operations and behavior seemed unknowable and almost mystical. His place in history ranks with the major influences of Darwin, Einstein, and Marx. Although discussions about Freud's legacy sometimes elicit more heat than light, there can be no disputing his importance in the development of Western psychological thought.

What relevance do Freudian concepts have for the work of today's counselors and therapists? First, his extensive writings help us to be more cognizant of the ways in which unconscious thoughts and emotions underlie many of the seemingly irrational behaviors some clients manifest in their lives.

Second, his many disciples have provided a constant impetus for change in psychotherapy by adding to and modifying a number of Freud's original concepts. Those who started from a Freudian orientation include close followers like Ernest Jones and other neo-Freudians such as Alfred Adler, Carl Jung, Eric Erikson, Karen Horney, Melanie Klein, and Harry Stack Sullivan. When names such as Fritz Perls (Gestalt therapy), Alexander Lowen (bioenergetics), and Eric Berne (transactional analysis) are added, it is easy to see the profound influence Freud has had and continues to have on the mental health profession.

Freud's Psychoanalytic Worldview

The Unconscious and a Person's Developmental History

Of all of Freud's theoretical contributions, one of the most important is the emphasis he placed on the **unconscious** and its connection to human development and psychological problems. The word *unconscious* means lack of awareness of one's own mental functioning. More broadly, it refers to all of the thoughts, feelings, and memorable experiences—both biological and psychological—we are not aware of at a given moment. From Freud's psychoanalytic worldview, it is believed that individuals are routinely unaware (unconscious) of what is impelling and motivating them toward action. The following discussion describes some of the other central components of Freud's psychoanalytic worldview and their implications for psychodynamic counseling and therapy.

1. *Client developmental history is important and needs to be considered for full client understanding.* Freud is often considered to be the first developmental psychologist. He was among the first to explain how experiences that occurred at an earlier state in one's development continue to impact an individual's current psychological functioning. Basic to his orientation and the psychodynamic frame of reference is the importance of childhood experiences in determining how we act and behave in the present.

2. *Important in our developmental history are the key people we have experienced in our lives.* In psychodynamic language, **object relations** is the term given to the relationships we have developed with important people and the continuing impact these relational experiences have on our lives. More specifically, it is noted that we all develop in relationship to other people—our family, friends, and peers. From a psychodynamic perspective it is important to help clients become more fully conscious of their historical connections with others and how these connections directly impact their present way of being.

3. *We are unaware (unconscious) of the impact of biological needs, of past developmental attachments, and of cultural determinants on our present behavior.* One of the most important aspects of psychodynamic theory involves the refinement of our thinking about the unconscious dimension of human development. From a Freudian perspective, the unconscious is viewed as the reservoir of our memories and biological drives, most of which we are generally unaware.

4. *We constantly act out our developmental history and our unconscious biological drives.* Freud's worldview embraces the notion that we are all heavily ruled, sometimes even completely determined, by forces outside our awareness. Although some psychodynamic theorists claim that biology is central in a person's unconscious development, others focus more on people's life-span developmental issues, including the impact of a person's experiences with one's parents in childhood. Increasingly, the influence of multicultural factors in unconscious development is being recognized by many persons who embrace psychodynamic approaches to counseling and therapy.

5. *The task of counseling and therapy is to help clients become more conscious of the ways in which past influences impact their present thinking, feeling, and behaving.* Although this is a common consideration in psychodynamic counseling and therapy, the designation of which part of the past we need to pay attention to varies. Orthodox psychoanalysis gives special attention to past experiences related to people's sexual development, particularly during the Oedipal period (ages 5 through 7). Attachment theory, on the other hand, focuses on the long-term impact of infancy and early childhood experiences on later human development.

Feminist theory (see Chapter 11) concentrates on how cultural gender roles influence our present way of being, whereas Jungians (see Chapter 6) search for cultural archetypes that influence how we live our lives today. Practitioners who are oriented toward family therapy (see Chapter 14) typically direct their attention to how intergenerational family issues affect their clients' development and their current ways of thinking, feeling, and behaving. The sort of attention that family therapists commonly give to intergenerational issues is also reflected in many recovery movements such as Adult Children of Alcoholics.

Whereas feminist, Jungian, and family-oriented counselors focus on different aspects of their clients' lives, psychodynamic therapists typically direct attention to the roots of their clients' behaviors, emotions, and present thinking patterns. They do so by encouraging clients to talk about various unresolved (and often unconscious) conflicts that are linked to their childhood and adolescent experiences.

As clients talk about their earlier life experiences, psychodynamically oriented counselors and therapists proceed to make interpretations about the possible ways in which unresolved conflicts and anxieties from the formative years may continue to affect clients' present functioning. These interpretations are, in large part, based on the psychodynamically oriented counselor's understanding of the various tasks and challenges individuals undergo at different stages of childhood and adolescence. Thus, to understand the developmental roots of clients' behaviors, emotions, and thought patterns from a psychodynamic frame of reference, it is important to be knowledgeable of the life developmental stages that Freud postulated.

Freud's Stages of Development: The Roots of Behavior, Emotion, and Thought

One of the reasons Freud is considered the first developmental psychologist is because he viewed childhood and adolescence as critical developmental stages in a person's life. He pointed out that the distinct patterns, challenges, and problems commonly manifested at these developmental stages have a lasting, although generally unconscious, impact throughout the rest of life.

Among the central tenets included in Freud's perspective is the idea that each developmental stage requires individuals to face key tasks as part of their development. As you read about each stage, notice the multicultural-feminist considerations included in the brief desciptions. These additional considerations are drawn from the work of Bruce Taub-Bynum, John Bowlby, Mary Ainsworth, and other feminist theorists who have helped to greatly expand the thinking about psychodynamic theories of counseling and therapy.

The Oral Stage and the Issue of Trust. The child in the oral stage (roughly birth through 2 years) must learn how to be dependent, trust others, and relate with the primary caregiver, usually the mother. If the child does not accomplish these age-related developmental tasks adequately, interpersonal relationships will likely be disturbed and then reappear as adult problems later in life.

Freud viewed infants and young children as being dominated by internally driven biological factors that provide them with an id-oriented frame of reference. (The three major components of personality development associated with psychodynamic theories—namely, the id, ego, and superego—are discussed in greater detail later in this chapter.) While the importance of the id-oriented framework in young children's psychological development is generally accepted by most psychodynamically oriented practitioners, multicultural and feminist theorists have extended thinking in this area by pointing to other factors that also affect children's development.

Drawing on an African-centered view of psychological development, Taub-Bynum (1984, 1999) emphasizes that a person's family of origin (and superego processes initially fostered within one's familial context) has an equal if not a greater role in influencing a person's psychological development. His discussion of the ways in which an individual's family of origin has a lasting impact on the child and adolescent's long-term psychological development is consistent with feminist theorists, who emphasize that what occurs in the familial/societal context heavily impacts an individual's development from childhood through adulthood (Brown, 1994).

The Anal Stage and the Issue of Control. According to Freud's developmental view, one of the central tasks of the anal stage (2 through 4 years) involves the acquisition of a greater level of self-control. At this stage, individuals must learn how to move beyond total dependence on the primary caregiver, take control over their own lives, and become separate and eventually individuated persons. The "terrible two's," with characteristic strife and temper tantrums, are illustrative of the child's struggle to become her or his "own person" during this developmental period.

Freud (1925/1964) pointed out that the individual is often constituted in negativity or opposition at this stage. He also asserted that while children may have the capacity to develop positive relationships in the oral period, the individual may remain overly fused and dependent on or generally distant from others as an adult unless successful psychological separation from the primary caregiver occurs at the anal stage.

In addition to psychologically separating from one's primary caregiver, the task of toilet training is another important characteristic of the anal stage. It would be a vast oversimplification to talk about the control of feces as the major issue of this period, however. This type of conceptualization is naive and makes it easy for many to reject the Freudian framework as being overly simplistic.

It is more meaningful to view the central task of this period as that of gaining control over one's life. Gaining such control leads individuals to learn about their unique individuality by becoming separate and autonomous human beings. According to Freud's psychoanalytic perspective, the development of a greater sense of independence and psychological separateness is significantly influenced by earlier attachments youngsters make with key persons during the preceding (oral) stage.

It is important to keep in mind that Freudian theory, like any counseling and therapy theory, is embedded in a host of cultural values and biases that are tied to the theorist's own cultural/historical context and socialization. Consequently, while the cultural values and biases embedded in Freud's worldview may make sense to individuals who share similar cultural perspectives, these views are likely to conflict with the perspective that people from different cultural/racial/ethnic backgrounds hold about human development and mental health.

Such differences are clearly noted in the emphasis that Freudian theory places on the importance of gaining control over one's environment and developing oneself as a separate human being during the anal period. Whereas the theoretical values and biases that Freudian theory places on control, separateness, and autonomy complement Western constructions of the world, these values and biases conflict with multicultural-feminist theories, which emphasize the interdependence and interconnectedness of all persons and things (Duran & Duran, 1995; Parham, 2002; Parham, White, & Ajamu, 1999).

The Phallic Stage and Sex Role Development. The phallic stage (4 through 7 years) is a time when children learn to understand the sex roles they are to undertake in life. As can be seen in the oral and anal periods, children have already received considerable training in sex roles through their holding environment and the manner in which the control issues of the anal period have been handled in their cultural context. What is distinctive about the phallic period is that the child develops an awareness of the meaning and importance of sex roles in a way that brings together all previous learnings about these socially constructed role definitions.

The interpretation of the phallic period has given rise to much controversy. Feminist theorists have been particularly critical of the gender biases inherent in some of the descriptions of this developmental stage (Brown & Ballou, 1992; Enns, 1993). Other psychological theorists, who focus on a lesbian frame of reference, present similar criticisms of traditional psychoanalytic theory in this area (Greene, 1997).

The Latency Stage and Shifting Interests. According to Freud, the increased sexual energy manifested during the phallic stage is subdued during the latency stage. Freud noted that between the ages of 5 and 11, youngsters exhibit an enhanced sense of social curiosity as their sexual energy is quieted. As the sexual drive becomes less dominant, children increasingly exhibit outward interests as they strive to form new relationships with others. The drive to form new relationships during the latency stage is complemented by children's progression through elementary school and their growing interest in exploring new hobbies and activities.

Freud pointed out further that children's emotional development is greatly affected by the successes youngsters experience when they attempt to achieve new goals during this developmental stage. Thus, "children who successfully negotiate this stage typically develop feelings of empowerment and exercise initiative, while those who cannot deal with the demands of this developmental stage may develop feelings of low self-esteem" (Seligman, 2001).

The Genital Stage and Dealing with Ongoing Challenges. Freud referred to the final stage in his theoretical model as the genital stage, which begins around 11 years of age and continues throughout the life span. During this ongoing stage, adolescents and adults are challenged to address several important developmental issues. These include solidifying their personal identities, developing caring and altruistic feelings toward others, establishing positive and loving sexual relationships, and progressing in successful careers (Seligman, 2001).

Freud acknowledged that each stage is built on and integrates the learning that individuals experience from previous life experiences. He acknowledged that this learning resulted in a limited conscious awareness of who one is and why one does what she or he does in life. However, Freud also stressed that people's understanding of themselves and their behavior is greatly limited by an overarching unconscious psychic component. Thus, the essential goal of Freud's helping theory is to assist clients in becoming more aware of the unconscious aspects of their personality. This aspect of Freud's theory and other related concepts are discussed in more detail below.

Feminist, lesbian, and multicultural theorists have the important notion that traditional Freudian interpretations of these developmental stages need to be adjusted to address variations in gender, sexual orientation, and other cultural influences. Much more attention is directed to these variations later in the book in Chapter 12, where you will be introduced to Tamase's (1991) culturally relevant developmental framework. By exploring this culturally relevant framework, you will gain a greater understanding of the ways in which persons in different cultures have differing needs at differing times in the developmental process. You also will better understand how the psychodynamic views presented in this chapter can be modified to more effectively fit the cultural variations that are manifested in your clients' lives.

Other Key Freudian/Psychoanalytic Concepts

Psychodynamic helping methods in general and Freud's theoretical model in particular can be thought of as "uncovering therapies." This is because the focus is on assisting clients discover how the past affects their present ways of thinking, feeling, and behaving.

The earlier discussion of postmodernism (Chapter 1) reminds us that the emphasis that psychodynamic therapists place on the connection between past and present behaviors is not a universally accepted premise for all counselors and therapists. For instance, rational-emotive-behavioral-contextual therapy (REBCT) holds that it is an irrational idea to think that "the past has a lot to do with determining the present" (Davis, Eshelman, & McKay, 1995, p. 143). Thus, what seems to be an accepted truth in one theoretical orientation is not considered so in another.

Despite the different views many practitioners may have about the impact of clients' past history on present psychological functioning, it is apparent that this fundamental psychodynamic belief has gained much acceptance in the general public as well as in the fields of counseling and psychology.

Psychodynamically oriented practitioners who embrace this fundamental Freudian concept use different therapeutic strategies to help clients become more fully conscious of the ways in which childhood experiences may unconsciously impact current ways of thinking, feeling, and behaving. Once these unconscious processes are revealed, it is believed that clients will be better able to reconstruct their personalities in ways that foster an increased sense of health, well-being, and personal satisfaction. Working to reconstruct an individual's personality in ways that enhance these positive psychological outcomes requires the therapist and client to explore how the various components of a client's personality continue to be unconsciously affected by previous experiences.

In the past, psychodynamic practitioners were trained to help clients explore unconscious issues on an individual level of analysis. Multicultural theorists have "pushed the envelope" in this area by encouraging counselors to help their clients explore how their family and cultural unconscious affect their overall development as well.

The Individual, Family, and Collective Cultural Unconscious

Multicultural theorists identify three interrelated levels of unconscious functioning: the individual (Nobles, 1998), the family (Nobles, 1997; Taub-Bynum, 1984), and the collective cultural unconscious (Akbar, 1994; Parham et al., 1999). From a multicultural perspective, the individual level of unconscious and the defense mechanisms that are rooted in this aspect of people's psyche are substantially influenced by the values, traditions, and myths that distinguish one's cultural group from others. The individual level of unconsciousness is also impacted by the level of personal attachment and identification that individuals develop toward their cultural group in general and the worldview espoused by their group in particular.

The family is the fundamental culture-bearing unit in every society. As such, it is the primary system where we first learn about the beliefs, values, and worldview of whatever culture we are a part. Beyond the fundamental knowledge we acquire about the world in this system, our family experiences lead us to develop an unconscious storehouse in which we acquire a broad range of thoughts and feelings about ourselves and the world in which we live.

It is further acknowledged that we are not aware of many of the thoughts and feelings generated from our familial experiences because they are often embedded in strong emotional reactions that are linked to past interactions we encountered with important persons in our family system. Taub-Bynum (1984) succinctly summarizes this point, noting that "the family unconscious is composed of extremely powerful affective (emotional) energies from the earliest life of the individual" (p. 11).

Taub-Bynum's view of the family unconscious complements the fundmental premises of feminist counseling theories, which direct particular attention to the ways in which family experiences unconsciously impact our constructions of the world in general and our views about sex roles in particular. Consequently, from both a multicultural (Taub-Bynum, 1984) and a feminist (Hill & Ballou, 2005) theoretical perspective, a person's family experiences are unconsciously transmitted to the child and become very much a part of her or his family unconscious.

Several experts in Black psychology have extended our thinking about the individual and family unconscious even further, emphasizing that these aspects of a person's psyche are subsumed within a broader level of unconsciousness referred to as the collective cultural unconscious (Nobles, 1997, 1998; Parham et al., 1999; Taub-Bynum, 1984). Similar to Carl Jung's (1960) notion of the collective unconscious (Chapter 6), the **collective cultural unconscious** develops from the cumulative experiences individuals encounter in the overarching cultural context within which they and their families are situated. This expansive view of people's unconscious is leading psychodynamically oriented practitioners to consider the importance of acknowledging all three unconscious levels (e.g., the individual, family, and collective cultural unconscious) when working with culturally diverse clients.

To deal with these different levels of the unconscious effectively and respectfully, mental health practitioners need to communicate the kind of cultural empathy that is described in Chapter 4. Culturally competent practitioners are not only aware of the importance of developing cultural empathy, but they also can effectively implement this important therapeutic skill when using Freudian concepts in multicultural counseling and therapy settings.

From a multicultural perspective, it is not really possible to separate the impact that individual, family, and cultural factors have on a person's overall psychological development, because the interplay of these factors is so powerful and persistent. You will be able to better understand how these factors affect human development by learning about different cultural traditions and practices, especially as they relate to child-rearing practices.

For example, within a traditional Japanese cultural context, an infant is immediately placed on the mother's body at birth, and the two mold—or bond—together as one. In European cultures, the newborn traditionally is taken from the mother and held separately. Emotional body attachments and relational thinking are thereby reinforced in Japanese child-rearing practices, whereas the focus in European societies is on separation and autonomy. These small examples illustrate how individual constructions of self (or self-in-relation) are subtly and unconsciously shaped by family and cultural conditions very early in life.

Additional similarities between psychodynamic and multicultural theories are reflected in the term *soul wound*. This term is used to describe the unconscious psychic conflicts and pain many Native Americans continue to experience as a result of having their cultural way of life destroyed by White European settlers (Duran, 2006; Duran & Duran, 1995). According to Duran (2006), the horrific treatment imposed on the indigenous people of this nation has resulted in a deep-seated, intergenerational, collective cultural trauma that continues to unconsciously and adversely impact the psychological health and spiritual well-being of many Native Americans today. In discussing the relevance of this concept for psychological practice, Duran and Duran (1995) explain:

> If one accepts the terms *soul, psyche, myth, dream,* and *culture* as part of the same continuum that makes people's experience of being in the world their particular reality, then one can begin to understand the soul wound. The notion of soul wound is one which is at the core of much of the suffering that indigenous peoples have undergone for several centuries. This notion needs to be understood in a historical context to be useful to the modern therapist who provides therapeutic and consultation services to the Native American community. (p. 24)

The Id, Ego, and Superego

What all of the theoretical tenets described above have in common is the belief that a person's psychological development is impacted by conscious and unconscious dynamics that continually affect the way people think, feel, and behave. This basic Freudian concept is more fully understood when one learns about the three major psychic components Freud believed influence everyone's psychological functioning—the id, ego, and superego. Imperative for uncovering unconscious functioning from a traditional psychodynamic perspective is an understanding of how the id, ego, and superego operate.

The Id. The id is characterized by basic drives and needs. In discussing the concept of the id, Nugent (2000) observes that it involves "unconscious instinctual processes that are potentially destructive unless controlled and channeled" (p. 105). Although Nugent points to the destructive potential of the id, this aspect of a person's psychological development can also be manifested in playful and creative ways. Biological drive theory is important for those who focus on the id.

The Superego. By way of contrast, the superego develops as the child matures in the family and society. Freud believed that one's conscience, ideals, and values all comprise the realm of the superego. Whereas the id is marked by uncontrolled impulses, the superego seeks to control one's primordial energy.

The superego is largely comprised of the internalized rules and expectations generated by one's family and cultural history. The superego represents the warehouse in which constructions of appropriate gender roles, acceptable social behaviors, attitudes toward one's affectional orientation, and preferences about cultural values are generated and stored.

Psychodynamic counselors and therapists often consider such experiences as the posttraumatic stress reactions many war veterans manifest, the psychological problems of homeless persons, or the fears some gay and lesbian persons exhibit about "coming out of the closet" to be connected to unconscious superego conflicts. From a psychodynamic perspective, such unconscious conflicts may arise due to the incorporation of society's discriminatory attitudes during childhood and adolescence. According to a psychoanalytic perspective, these unconscious attitudes often lead many traumatized war veterans, homeless persons, or gay and lesbian individuals to blame themselves for their present problems.

The Ego. The ego serves as a mediator between the superego (as manifested in the unconscious incorporation of the ideals, rules, and expectations put forth by society in general and one's family in particular) and the id (as expressed in an unconscious rebellion against such ideals, rules, or expectations). In traditional Freudian theory, the ego is sometimes seen as being at the mercy of these two competing forces. More contemporary psychodynamic theorists, such as Erik Erikson, present an alternative view that describes how healthy ego functioning can be enhanced in counseling and therapy in ways that give clients more conscious control and power over their own lives.

Ego strength may be increased by assisting clients to understand the interplay of the ego with the id and the superego. The ego operates at the conscious, preconscious, and unconscious levels of experience. However, it is primarily manifested at the conscious level in counseling and psychotherapy.

If you decide to work from a psychodynamic perspective, you will have to take a position on the respective roles and importance of how the id, ego, and superego function in your clients' lives. If you place the id as central in importance, you will find orthodox, traditional psychoanalytic theory most helpful in uncovering the roots of anxiety. If you take this id, or drive-oriented, position, you may be more interested in and supportive of medication as a supplement to your therapeutic practice. If you place the ego as central to your therapeutic theory, you may find that the theories of Erikson (1963) and Loevinger (1986) are helpful in your work.

It is important to note that Freud is often credited for "discovering" the notion of the ego. However, from a multicultural perspective, it should also be pointed out that the concept of the ego has recurred in diverse cultural groups across the course of human history.

For example, the ancient Chinese philosophy of Taoism places emphasis on the importance of developing a healthy and enlightened mind by becoming a more fully conscious being. According to Taoist principles, this is achieved by intentionally striving (usually through meditation) to increase one's conscious understanding of the ways in which instinctual-biological drives and the pressure to conform to societal ideals and values impact a person's psychological and spiritual development (Simpkins & Simpkins, 1999).

Anxiety and Ego Defense Mechanisms

From a Freudian perspective, the psychic tensions that continually exist between id urges, superego mandates, and ego drives underlie much of the anxiety people experience in their lives. According to Freud's frame of reference, anxiety is a universal human characteristic that is routinely experienced by everyone, regardless of the individual's cultural background or group identification. Many people can and do consciously identify some of the sources of their anxiety. However, psychodynamic theory asserts that we all experience a great deal of "free-floating" anxiety that is not accurately or consciously understood in our personal psyches.

When people experience this free-floating anxiety and are not able to give a rational explanation for its source, they may experience uncomfortable and threatening thoughts and feelings. To deal with these uncomfortable and threatening inner experiences, Freud asserted that individuals commonly use various ego defense mechanisms. Some of the more commonly known defense mechanisms include repression, denial, projection, displacement, and sublimation. Table 5.1 provides a more detailed description of these and other defense mechanisms.

Attachment Theory

Other psychodynamic theorists, particularly John Bowlby and Mary Ainsworth, have extended Freudian thinking about these psychological mechanisms. In their work on attachment theory, these two theorists describe additional defense mechanisms that are relevant for the work mental health practitioners do with children as well as adults.

Attachment theory emphasizes a couple of important points that are embedded in Freud's psychoanalytic frame of reference. First, this theoretical framework describes the ways that individuals unconsciously develop personal attachments to key individuals, objects, and ideas in early childhood. Second, it explains how early attachments unconsciously impact people's thinking, feeling, and behaviors later in their development (Peluso, Peluso, White, & Kern, 2004).

Like most psychodynamically oriented theorists, attachment theorists such as Ainsworth (1985) and Bowlby (1988) acknowledge the important role that biological and unconscious factors play in personality development. The work of these theorists greatly extends Freud's traditional psychoanalytic frame of reference by describing the ways that ecological/environmental variables also influence human development.

As the creator of attachment theory, John Bowlby directed particular attention to these issues in his early writings. For this reason, Bowlby is considered to be one of the earliest developmental ecologists in psychology. The ecological nature of his work is reflected in the way he clearly articulates how each individual is impacted by the unique psychological attachments developed in childhood. These attachments result in a conscious and unconscious identification with various persons, objects, and ideas encountered in the formative years.

Table 5.1

Examples of Defense Mechanisms

Defense Mechanism	Description
Repression and continuation	A generic concept of all defense mechanisms is that some of our behavior, thoughts, and actions are repressed developmental continuations from the past. Winnicott (1988) maintains that all defense mechanisms are methods the child (and adult) uses to repress pain. These mechanisms stem either from denial of internal drives (id wishes) or hurts from external reality (superego pressures).
	In a broad sense, defense mechanisms are all repressed continuations of past biological and environmental issues and stressors. Many, perhaps even most, of your clients will be continuing old behavior, thoughts, and emotions in some form from their developmental past.
	The remainder of the defense mechanisms discussed in this table are elaborations of this basic point. Your task as a therapist is to find the underlying structure of the anxiety and the purpose of particular defense mechanisms used by your clients.
Denial	This is the most difficult and troublesome defense mechanism to deal with in counseling and psychotherapy. Many of your clients will refuse to recognize their traumatic and troublesome past. Veterans from the Vietnam and Iraq wars will often be observed to psychologically split off and deny the origins of their distress in combat; antisocial clients will deny their needs for dependency and attachment; and survivors of abuse or rape may unconsciously forget (deny) that they were abused earlier in their lives.
	Denial, at the same time, can be healthy. If we allow ourselves to be in touch with our past and present pain all the time, we can become easily and routinely depressed. From this frame of reference, then, depression is at least a partial failure of the positive aspects of the defense mechanism of denial.
Projection	When clients refuse to recognize behaviors or thoughts in themselves and see or project these behaviors and thoughts onto someone else, the defense mechanism of projection is likely to be in operation. We are most often troubled by behavior in others that is similar to our own behavior.
	At an extreme level, you will find projection in the paranoid client. Individuals with a paranoid style often have a history of real persecution in the family of origin or developmental past. They have learned to project onto others anticipated persecution. As it happens, anticipating persecution often results in a self-fulfilling prophecy. However, there can be positives to paranoia. For example, when buying a used car, it might help to be a bit paranoid.
	Similarly, one of the most important helping skills may be related to projection. In empathy, we try to see the world as others see it and project ourselves into the client's worldview. Some of us become so empathic and entwined with others that we literally project ourselves into the problems

Table 5.1 continued

Examples of Defense Mechanisms

Defense Mechanism	Description
	our clients may be experiencing and fail to accurately identify their strengths and personal assets (Ivey & Ivey, 2007).
Displacement	This defense mechanism involves transference in the sense that the client's feelings or thoughts are transferred or directed toward a person other than the originating source. The worker who has a bad day on the job and then treats her or his spouse badly is an example of displacement. If antisocial clients act out against you for no apparent reason, they are likely to be displacing anger and aggression around past maltreatment onto you.
	You may notice that each of the defense mechanisms relates to others. In a sense, displacement is behavior *repressed and continued* from the past. Displacement *denies* what is really happening and often *projects* onto others the events of the day or the past. The displacement may enact itself in an opposite form of the conscious intent—that is, *reaction-formation.*
	It is important to note that these defense mechanisms are not clearly distinct entities. Rather, defense mechanisms are simply alternative constructions of the same continued event from the past. Consequently, you may find that clients use one defense mechanism in certain situations and implement another (that is at first seemingly a totally different defense mechanism) in other situations.
Sublimation	A more positive defense mechanism, sublimation takes repressed instinctual energy and unconscious continuations from the past and channels them to constructive work such as artistic, physical, or intellectual endeavor. A person who is frustrated sexually or a survivor of abuse may turn to movie making, athletics, or creative writing and be rewarded well by society for these efforts.
	Many survivors of child abuse sublimate past hurt and become counselors and therapists themselves. The danger here is that wounded helpers who have denied or sublimated their own history of abuse may unconsciously prevent clients who have been abused from looking at their own past history.
Other mechanisms	
• Fixation	Being immobilized at an earlier developmental stage
• Rationalization	Making up rational reasons for irrational or inconsistent behavior
• Regression	Returning to earlier childhood behavior when faced with a life event that somehow resembles an old traumatic injury
• Conversion	Translating unconscious mental functioning into physical symptoms such as headaches
• Identification	Acting and behaving like someone else
• Reaction-formation	Doing the opposite of unconscious wishes
• Provocative behavior	Acting in a way such that others are provoked to do to one what one is unable to do to oneself, such as showing anger or love

Early Research

Bowlby's (1969) original formulation of attachment theory emphasized the impact that the mother-child relationship has on psychological development. His early work in this area involved research with young children who were separated from their parents in England during World War II. As a result of being subjected to constant bombing by the Germans, many parents living in London moved their children to rural parts of England, where their youngsters might be safe.

Bowlby used psychodynamic principles to describe his observations of the positive and negative ways that the youngsters in his study reacted to their mothers when they were separated and then reunited during periodic visitations. These observations led Bowlby to theorize that the different reactions these children had to being temporarily reconnected with their mothers were largely based on the quality of the psychological attachments the youngsters had developed with their mothers in early childhood.

Bowlby (1940, 1951, 1969, 1973) theorized that the primary task in the mother-child relationship in early childhood is for youngsters to become securely attached to their primary caregiver. According to Bowlby, children respond in positive and satisfying ways to their parents and other persons in their environment when they develop what Bowlby (1988) refers to as "secure attachments" with their mothers. Such psychological attachments commonly occur when young children are nurtured in an environment that is characterized by consistently positive and caring mother-child interactions.

Bowlby further emphasized that the development of secure attachments in early childhood helps youngsters acquire a lasting sense of self-esteem and confidence. He further noted that these psychological traits not only enable youngsters to interact with others in positive and cooperative ways in early childhood, but also contribute to many positive and lasting psychological outcomes that are manifested later in life.

Bowlby's protégé, Mary Ainsworth (1967, 1977, 1985), later conducted numerous studies of children in other settings. Her research findings confirmed Bowlby's earlier research conclusions regarding the positive developmental outcomes that ensue when youngsters develop secure attachments with their mothers in early childhood.

Several other researchers have further validated Bowlby's and Ainsworth's findings, offering additional support regarding the positive and lasting effects of such attachments. Some of these findings include the following:

1. The pattern of attachment identified at 12 months was still present at 6 years of age (Goldberg, Muir, & Kerr, 1995).

2. Young children identified as securely attached to their mothers were described as being cheerful, cooperative, and popular three and a half years later in nursery school, whereas children shown to develop anxious avoidant and anxious resistant patterns of attachment were emotionally insulated, hostile, and antisocial in later childhood (Bowlby, 1988; Gunner & Sroufe, 1991).

3. Children who were securely attached in early life were later found to respond to failure with increased effort, whereas less securely attached youngsters were observed to do the opposite (Parkes, Stevenson-Hinde, & Morris, 1991).

Bowlby's and Ainsworth's psychodynamic theory and research findings also suggest that the positive developmental outcomes manifested when youngsters developed secure psychological attachments in early childhood significantly changed when youngsters experienced major disruptions in their attachments to key persons in their lives. Research into the psychological effects that these disruptions had on youngsters' psychological development led Bowlby and Ainsworth to note that children commonly use unique defense mechanisms to deal with the anxiety generated from such disruptions.

New Defense Mechanisms Associated with Attachment Theory

In constructing his own theory about the nature and function of defense mechanisms, Bowlby observed that the young children in his studies became depressed and morose when they were separated from their parents. In spite of their depressed reactions, many of these youngsters gradually learned to cope in unique ways with their personal loss and began to behave more "normally" with the passage of time. Bowlby also found it interesting that most of these youngsters did not greet their parents enthusiastically when they periodically visited their children during the war. While many of the youngsters remained generally cautious in drawing close to their parents during their visitations, others displayed anger and some even tried to hurt their parents when they approached them during their visitations.

These observations led Bowlby to conclude that the children in his studies used two unique defense mechanisms to cope with the anxiety they experienced as a result of being separated from their parents. Bowlby refers to these defense mechanisms as **acting-out behavior** and **avoidant behavior.** Bowlby suggested that it was functional for children to use these defense mechanisms to defend themselves against further anxiety and the threat of experiencing repeated personal losses.

Acting-Out Behavior. This aspect of attachment theory complements the more contemporary notion of self-in-relation highlighted in most feminist theories of human development (Hill & Ballou, 2005). Like Bowlby, many feminist theorists describe the various ways that a person's environmental experiences influence one's construction of the world and the psychological and interpersonal attachments that unconsciously drive a person's meaning-making system (Comstock, 2005). From a feminist perspective, these psychological attachments not only influence the way people make meaning of themselves and the world at large, but also underlie much of the free-floating anxiety that is linked to a disruption of personal attachments in a person's life. Much like the children in Bowlby's studies, adolescents and adults commonly use acting-out and avoidant defense mechanisms to unconsciously cope with anxiety associated with disrupted personal attachments (Worell & Remer, 2003).

Bowlby found that acting-out behaviors were typically linked to what he referred to as **anxious resistant attachment reactions.** These reactions were frequently manifested by children whose maternal relationships were alternatively marked by acceptance and rejection. According to Bowlby and Ainsworth, the contradictory messages that youngsters get from such maternal responses create ambivalent feelings when they are separated from their mothers. These ambivalent feelings result in the development of anxious resistant attachment reactions.

It was Freud (1982) who actually coined the term *ambivalence*. He used this term to refer to the simultaneous existence of two conflicting and unconscious feelings, such as love and hate. Building on Freud's definition of ambivalence, Bowlby and Ainsworth indicated that children's acting-out behaviors could be traced to unconscious ambivalent feelings when their need for positive and secure attachment with their mothers was disrupted (Ainsworth, 1985; Bowlby, 1969).

Avoidant Behavior. The second defense mechanism that Bowlby and Ainsworth discuss in their writings relates to avoidant behaviors the children in their studies often exhibited when they were reunited with their mothers after a period of separation. These behaviors were associated with what Bowlby originally referred to as **anxious avoidant attachment reactions.**

Attachment theory suggests that children commonly exhibit anxious avoidant attachment reactions when they are consistently rejected by their mothers or subjected to general environmental impoverishment in early childhood (Ainsworth, 1985; Ainsworth & Bowlby, 1991). When using this defense mechanism, children withdraw from anxiety-provoking situations and become generally apathetic in their reactions to the world. Ainsworth (1985) suggested that such unconscious reactions in early childhood can and often do lead to more lasting and generalized forms of withdrawal and apathy when individuals are confronted with other anxiety-provoking situations in adolescence and adulthood.

The attachment reactions that Bowlby and Ainsworth discuss in their work represent new ways of thinking about the unconscious psychological defenses youngsters commonly use to deal with anxiety-provoking experiences. These concepts expand our view of Freud's original list of defense mechanisms (see Table 5.1). They also increase our thinking about the unique ways that children may cope with free-floating and situation-specific stressors that threaten their sense of personal safety and psychological well-being.

Adult Resistant and Avoidance Defense Mechanisms

Although attachment theory has historically focused on the unique defense mechanisms children develop in response to various environmental stressors, recent efforts have been aimed at using these concepts to explain the types of acting-out and avoidant defense mechanisms that adults commonly use in their own lives (D'Andrea, 2006a; Peluso, Peluso, White, & Kern, 2004). Attachment theory can help in understanding the defense mechanisms adults use when experiencing anxieties tied to situations in which their constructions of the world are challenged by people who hold different perspectives about reality.

Like children and adolescents, adults construct certain ways of viewing themselves and the world. Developmental researchers point out that adults not only develop such constructions but become psychologically and emotionally attached to them, as they provide a sense of meaning and purpose in life (Daniels & D'Andrea, 1996). As a result, most adults experience a heightened sense of anxiety and frustration when these psychological attachments are threatened by other people who confront them with alternative values, beliefs, and constructions of the world. Adults often respond in predictable ways, including expressing frustration and anger at having their beliefs and values challenged (D'Andrea, 2006a).

Another response of adults is feeling "alienated" or "put off" by encounters that contradict their construction of themselves and their world. These reactions typically lead many adults to avoid people or situations that represent potential threats to their beliefs, values, and constructions of the world, to which they have become psychologically and emotionally attached.

Applying attachment theory, it can be theorized that adults use defense mechanisms similar to the anxious resistant attachment reactions and the anxious avoidant attachment reactions that Bowlby and Ainsworth describe in their work with young children. This is especially the case in situations where adults feel that their beliefs and values are being threatened by alternative constructions of the world that conflict with their own meaning-making systems.

Researchers have noted that many adults normally react to such threats by projecting blame on other people (avoidant resistant attachment reactions) or actively avoiding individuals (anxious avoidant attachment reactions) who may potentially threaten their psychological attachments and constructions of the world (Cassidy & Shaver, 1999; D'Andrea, 2006a). Competency-Building Activity 5.1 is designed to further your thinking about the ways in which you and other adults you know may use these defense mechanisms. By becoming more aware of some of the unconscious defense mechanisms you may use in your own life, you will be able to realize the "psychological liberation" (Ivey & Ivey, 2001, p. 220) that represents more advanced levels of human development. Such development is useful in becoming an effective mental health professional (Montgomery & Kottler, 2005).

Psychodynamic Counseling and Therapy Strategies: Applications for Practice

Psychodynamically oriented counselors and therapists draw from a broad range of therapeutic techniques that are intentionally aimed at addressing various defense mechanisms clients may use in their lives. Some of these psychodynamic techniques include the use of free association, interpretation, dream analysis, regression techniques to reexperience past trauma, analysis of resistance, analysis of transference and countertransference, and projective identifcation. The primary goals of these therapeutic

Competency-Building Activity 5.1

Extending Bowlby and Ainsworth's Concepts about Attachment Theory to Adult Development

Instructions: To begin this activity, find a quiet place where you can spend about 20 minutes to complete this exercise without being disturbed.

Step 1. *Think about a situation in which you felt alienated or frustrated by something that someone recently said to you.* If you are in a professional training program, it would be particularly helpful to think of a situation in which your instructor or another student in your class stated something that made you feel uncomfortable, frustrated, or even angry.

Step 2. *Take a couple of minutes to write down why you think you felt alienated or frustrated by the things the other person had to say.* In doing so, address the following questions:

- What cultural beliefs and values do you think were being expressed by the other person in this situation?

- How did these beliefs and values conflict with your own beliefs and values about the topic being discussed?

- How do you think your own psychological attachment to the beliefs and values that you have developed may have contributed to your reactions to this situation?

Based on your understanding of attachment theory, did your response include reactions similar to the acting-out (anxious resistant attachment) or the avoidance (anxious avoidant attachment) reactions that Bowlby and Ainsworth describe in their work?

Write down any new insights you may have gained about yourself in using attachment theory to assess how you may have used these defense mechanisms to unconsciously deal with the situation.

Finally, write down any ways that you think this activity might help clients become more conscious of the personal attachments they have developed that contribute to their own acting-out or avoidant behaviors with other people. Be sure to include all of these written reactions in your personal/professional development portfolio.

techniques are to help clients become more aware of the unconscious aspects of their personality and to address the various defense mechanisms clients commonly use to protect themselves against free-floating and situation-specific anxieties.

Free Association

Free association is a basic psychodynamic technique designed to tap into the client's unconscious. In using this therapeutic technique, counselors encourage clients to express their thoughts, regardless of content, in response to a specific cue such as a word, number, dream image, or any other idea that may enter clients' thinking in the context of psychotherapy.

Freud developed free association in his early work on hysteria as a way to encourage his patients to search for underlying unconscious factors. He refined this technique in his own self-analysis, particularly of his dreams. Through using dream analysis in this way, Freud discovered the "royal road to the unconscious." He found that allowing oneself to say anything that came to mind (no matter how seemingly irrelevant)

Competency-Building Activity 5.2

Focused Free Association

Instructions: Complete this exercise yourself by following the instructions provided below. You can use the same instructions when working with clients you think may benefit from this therapeutic technique.

Step 1. *Focus now on a current concern or issue.* Take time and consider it fully. It sometimes helps to visualize an image of the problem or issue that has come to mind. It can help to ask: "What are you seeing, hearing, and, especially, feeling as you think about the issue?" Make this exercise as "here and now" as you can.

Step 2. *What emotions do you have around this issue?* Focus now on your feelings. Locate these feelings physically in your body and really focus on them.

Step 3. *Allow your mind to drift to an earlier time in your life (the earlier the better) that is associated with these feelings.* What comes to your mind? You may experience visual images or fragments of feelings or remember a specific situation. Allow yourself to experience these old thoughts and feelings once again. When using this technique in therapy with a client, be careful not to suggest specific possibilities. These should be the client's associations, not yours.

Step 4. *Give some thought to these questions:* "How do you connect your present concern with the past?" "How are the past and present similar?" "Does the association between past and present give you some new thoughts about the meaning of the present concern?"

Step 5. *Think about your gender, family of origin, and your cultural/ethnic identity.* How do these factors relate to your experience? (Free association too often focuses just on the individual. If you ask your client to freely associate to gender, family, or cultural issues, you have moved a long way to adapting psychodynamic theory to multicultural, feminist, and perhaps even social justice issues.)

Take a few minutes now to write down your reactions to this activity and include them in your personal/professional development portfolio.

would often reveal a pattern that helped explain the meaning of a behavior, dream, or a seemingly random thought.

Competency-Building Activity 5.2 introduces you to the technique of focused free association. This simple, but often very powerful, exercise encapsulates both the theory and practice of the psychodynamic approach to counseling and therapy. The exercise is based on the idea that whatever comes to mind from the past is important and somehow connected to current life issues.

Free association can be made more powerful and understandable if sensorimotor elements involving images and bodily sensations are added, as is done in the competency-building activity. This exercise asks you to concretely describe your present issues and relate them to past events—that is, to make connections or patterns. Making connections is a formal operational process that is basic to the psychodynamic approach. Such formal operational thought requires verbal ability and depends on a relationship of trust between therapist and client. Completing the exercise will make many of the concepts presented in this chapter more useful and understandable. This exercise can be used with your clients, not only in psychodynamic practice, but also in conjunction with other helping theories.

Therapists and counselors often ask questions in their interviews that relate to free association. For example, when you ask a client such questions as "What comes to your mind?" "What do you think of next?" or even "What is the *last* thing that comes to mind?" you are inviting the client to freely associate to an idea. Free association is an invaluable technique, regardless of one's theoretical orientation to counseling and therapy, because it focuses on clients' constructions of various issues. It also provides you, the therapist, with access to clients' inner dialogues, thoughts, and feelings that you might miss when using other techniques. Free association gives you and your clients access to often surprising and valuable information, such as indicators of otherwise unsuspected abusive history.

Although having much therapeutic utility, it is important to point out that the use of psychodynamic techniques (such as free association) among persons from diverse cultural/ethnic/racial backgrounds has been criticized for failing to focus on social injustices that undermine the mental health of many people from devalued groups in our society (D'Andrea, 2005a). These techniques have also been criticized as being "alien" to culturally different individuals who may not wish to disclose personal thoughts and feelings to a relative stranger early in counseling and psychotherapy (Ponterotto & Casas, 1991).

Nonetheless, it is quite possible to blend multicultural, feminist, and social justice counseling issues with psychodynamic techniques such as free association in many diverse helping situations. To increase your understanding of ways in which counselors and therapists can use free association techniques in culturally competent ways, complete Competency-Building Activity 5.3, an exercise in free association and imagery that uses gender-related, spiritual, and cultural symbols. This activity, if presented well and timed carefully, can be helpful in bringing to the fore important images from the past that can help clients think about issues from new perspectives.

Other basic psychodynamic counseling techniques are described in the following sections of this chapter. However, one central fact stands out: Free association is the basis for all the techniques discussed. This is because free association is considered to be the most direct route to reach unconscious experiences. The following counseling techniques—interpretation, dream analysis, regression, analysis of resistance, and analysis of transference and countertransference—all rely on free association in some way.

Interpretation

Psychodynamic counseling approaches are interpretive. Interpretation is a sophisticated and complex skill in which intellectual knowledge of psychodynamic theory is integrated with clinical data generated from the client. The microskill of interpretation can be defined as the renaming of client experience from an alternative frame of reference or worldview. Applied specifically to dynamic approaches, the skill of interpretation comes from the worldview of psychoanalysis and seeks to identify and give meaning to wishes, needs, and patterns from the client's unconscious world.

There are some specific guidelines therapists and counselors are encouraged to follow when making interpretations. First, the counselor must use attending skills carefully so the data point clearly to the interpretation.

Competency-Building Activity 5.3

Focused Free Association and Guided Imagery with Gender, Spiritual, and Cultural Symbols

Instructions: The following exercise is designed to help clients recognize and use strengths based on their gender, religion, and/or cultural backgrounds.

Step 1. *Inform your client about the process and intent of this activity.* Rather than surprise the client, tell him or her what is about to happen and why it may be potentially helpful. For instance, you can say that we all carry images around with us that can be personally helpful and supportive when we recall them in stressful situations. That is what we will be trying to do in this exercise.

Step 2. *Generate an image.* Ask your client to relax and then to generate a positive image that can be used as a personal resource in the future. Suggest that the image be related to his or her gender, religion, or cultural background. It is possible that a single image may encompass all three dimensions. A Franco-American woman, for example, might focus on Joan of Arc. Alternatively, a Jewish-Canadian might focus on the Star of David; a Navajo, on a mountain or religious symbol; a Mexican-American, on the Christian cross or the pyramids near Mexico City.

Step 3. *Focus on the image.* Ask your client to see the image in the mind's eye. What is seen,

heard, felt? Locate the positive feelings in the body. Identify the image and bodily feeling as a positive resource always available to the client. (Body anchoring of resources will make them more readily available when needed in counseling and therapy.)

Step 4. *Take the image to the problem.* Using relaxation and free association techniques, ask the client to keep the positive image in mind and encourage her or him to think of some personal challenge or problem that is currently occurring in her or his life. Suggest that the client use the positive image to help work with the personal challenge or problem that has come to mind. It is important to stress to the client that although the image can be a resource, it may or may not resolve the concern. If the challenge or problem the client is experiencing seems too large, the positive image that was generated at the beginning of this activity can be used to work on a smaller part of the problem rather than attempting to find a complete solution.

Step 5. *Process this experience with the person you are working with.* Take a few minutes to see what reactions your client had to using the positive image to deal with whatever personal challenge or problem she or he may be experiencing.

Take a moment to write your own reactions to facilitating this activity with another person and include your written reactions in your personal/professional development portfolio.

Next, the interpretation should be stated and the client given time to react. The helper may "check out" the interpretation with the client by asking such questions as "How do you react to that?" "Does that ring a bell?" or "Does that interpretation make sense to you?" Such questions encourage clients to think through and assimilate or reject the interpretation that is presented in counseling and therapy.

One of the goals of intentional psychodynamic therapy is to encourage clients to make their own interpretations of their life experiences. When clients are encouraged to do so, they often gain insight or the ability to look at old information from new perspectives.

Insight is directly related to intentionality and creative responding to life's challenges. Clients who are able to interpret life experiences by gaining new insights into their lives are better positioned to generate new ways of describing and responding to the world. It is important to point out that these new descriptions are almost invariably verbal. It is also helpful to note that the insights gained from these new descriptions are most useful if clients are able to take the new information out of the session and use it in daily life.

Multicultural counseling advocates raise an important criticism about the use of various psychodynamic techniques that are primarily aimed at helping clients gain new insights about past experiences while they continue to have difficulty coping with present-day living situations. Commenting on the multicultural implications of using psychodynamic techniques such as free association and interpretations to promote clients' insight, Sue and Sue (2003) state:

> We need to realize that insight is not highly valued by many culturally different clients. There are also major class differences as well. People from lower socioeconomic classes frequently do not perceive insight as appropriate to their life situations and circumstances. . . . After all, insight assumes that one has time to sit back, to reflect and contemplate about motivation and behavior. For the individual who is concerned with making it through each day, this orientation proves counterproductive.
>
> Likewise, many cultural groups do not value insight. In traditional Chinese society, psychology has little relevance. It is interesting to note that many Asian elders believe that thinking too much about something can cause problems to worsen. . . . "Think about the family and not about yourself" is advice given to many Asians as a way of dealing with negative affective elements. *This is totally contradictory to Western notions of mental health— that it is best to get things out in the open in order to deal with them.* (pp. 109–110) (emphasis added)

Interpretation in the psychodynamic model has traditionally been made from an individualistic, ego psychology frame of reference that locates the problem and decision making in the individual. There is an increased awareness of how the psychodynamic model can be extended by including interpretations made from a family or multicultural frame of reference as well. The following example illustrates multicultural interpretation with a client suffering from depression:

Client: I'm really depressed. It's taken a long time for me to understand myself. I can only be happy if I do something for others, but they always seem to want more. I feel I'm never liked for myself.

Counselor (individualistic interpretation): Your pattern seems to be that you try to do things for others while directing little attention to yourself. That would seem to go back to the way you solved problems as a child. You didn't feel adequate, so you tried to please others. Here again we see you continuing the behavior now.

Counselor (family interpretation): Your role in your family was the placater. Everyone else was arguing, and you took it on yourself to take this role. Then they kept you in it and still do even today. You're very good at keeping your new family flowing smoothly.

Counselor (gender-oriented multicultural interpretation): Women in North American culture are expected to take the caring role. We've learned to define ourselves through relationships with others. It's natural, but the question is what do you want?

Counselor (ethnic/racially oriented multicultural interpretation): Puerto Rican women are expected to put the family interests ahead of their own; it's in our tradition of *Marianismo*. How can we respect that tradition and find a place in U.S. society?

Each of these interpretations might be helpful when used with the same client at various points in therapy. The danger of taking a strictly individualistic psychodynamic approach and ignoring family, gender, and multicultural issues is that it places the primary burden for change on the individual and ignores self-in-relation.

Dream Analysis and Current Real Issues

Dream analysis is another important psychodynamic technique that can be useful in counseling and therapy. An effective approach to dream analysis is to use the five-stage interview structure that was described in Chapter 4 and emphasize focused free association on any important client topic that may emerge in the process. Although dreams may be, as Freud suggested, "the royal road to the unconscious," free association is too useful a technique to be reserved only for dreams.

Competency-Building Activity 5.4 illustrates how you can conduct a psychodynamic interview to analyze a dream or other issues of relevance to your clients. The purpose of this exercise is to illustrate how to conduct a basic interview from a psychodynamic perspective. Analysis of a dream or a client's reaction to an authority figure works well in the following framework. Alternatively, you may identify a repeating life pattern in which the client tends to have a certain style of response, thought, feeling, or behavior in several situations.

Keep in mind that dreams have different values in different cultures. For instance, Australian Aboriginals consider "dreamtime" more real than daily "reality." In other cultures, dreams are thought to be an important and useful avenue to spiritual issues. Many dreams and life experiences can be interpreted from a spiritual or cultural perspective. Roman Catholic, Baptist, Muslim, or Buddhist clients will tend to have dreams that relate to their particular spiritual tradition. Thus, from a multicultural perspective we do not just incorporate individual interpretations of the world; we also make family, spiritual, and cultural experiences part of our being.

Analysis of Resistance

Another important theoretical and methodological issue in psychodynamic counseling and therapy is **analysis of resistance.** Resistance includes everything in the words and

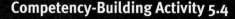

Competency-Building Activity 5.4

An Exercise in Psychodynamic Interviewing

Instructions: Before conducting this interview with someone else, first go through the following stages by yourself, thinking about one of your own dreams, your reactions to authority, or your own repeating patterns in your own life.

Stage 1. Establishing Rapport and Structure

Develop rapport with the client in your own natural way. Inform the client that you will work through some basic psychodynamic understanding about a dream, a relationship with authority, or a life pattern. Mutually decide the issue to be worked on before proceeding.

Stage 2. Gathering Data and Identifying Assets

Use the basic listening sequence (BLS) of questioning, encouraging, paraphrasing, and reflection of feeling to bring out the issue in greater detail. If you are working with a dream, be sure that you bring out the facts, feelings, and organization of the dream. If you are working with an authority issue, draw out a concrete situation and obtain the facts, feelings, and organization of the issue. In the case of repeating patterns, draw out several concrete examples of the pattern. Once you have heard the issue presented thoroughly, summarize it using the client's main words and check it out to ensure that you have understood the client correctly.

At this point, it is often wise to stop for a moment to use the positive asset search technique described in Chapter 4. In doing so be sure to use the BLS to draw out the facts, feelings, and organization of something positive in the client's life. This may or may not be related to the dream or authority figure. Clients tend to move and talk more freely from a base of security and awareness of their personal strengths.

Stage 3. Determining Outcomes and Goal Setting

Setting up a specific goal of understanding may be useful at this point in the activity. A general goal here may be to find earlier life experiences that relate to the dream, authority issue, or repeating life pattern. Use the BLS to specify what the client would like to gain from this interview.

Stage 4. Generating Alternative Solutions

Depending on your purpose and your relationship with your client, there are three major alternatives for analyzing the problem that may be helpful to consider using at this stage in the exercise.

Alternative 1. Summarize the dream, authority issue, or pattern and the desired outcome of the session. Ask your client, "What comes to mind as a possible explanation of this dream or issue?" If you have communicated the fact that you have been listening, you will often find that clients will generate new ideas and interpretations on their own. The structure provided by the interview and by effectively listening is often sufficient to help clients analyze and understand their own problems.

Alternative 2. Summarize the issue and then reflect on the central emotion you may have noted expressed in the client's description of her or his problem or ask the client what one single emotion stands out from the first part

continued on next page

behaviors of the client that prevents access to unconscious material. The temptation in many helping approaches is to avoid areas of resistance and find other routes toward client verbalization.

The effective psychodynamic counselor or therapist, by contrast, often pays prime attention to areas of resistance. In the process of counseling, clients often fail to hear important statements from the counselor. The client may say "What?" and of the interview. Ask the client to focus on that emotion and to stay with that feeling.

Through the use of the focused free association exercise, encourage the client to concentrate on that emotion and then to free associate back to an earlier life experience in which this emotion was also elicited—the earlier the better. (Free associations are more valuable if made from an emotional state rather than from a state of clear cognitive awareness.) Many clients' first associations are linked to some experience they encountered in their teenage years, whereas others may be associated with a more recent event. In either case, draw out the association using the basic listening sequence.

You now should have the facts, feelings, and organization of the dream, reaction to authority, or other life pattern as well as the facts, feelings, and organization of the first free association. Based on a clear summary of these issues, you and the client should be able to find some consistent pattern of meaning. The discovery and notation of these patterns are examples of a basic psychodynamic interpretation.

Key words will often be repeated in both the free association and the discussion of the original dream or problem. Deeper understandings may come from continuing the exercise as outlined below.

Alternative 3. Continue alternative 2, but ask your client to free associate to an even earlier life experience. Again, use the focused free association technique. Draw

out these earlier free associations with the BLS. Over time, you may assemble a group of recollections. In doing so you are likely to find several patterns in the associations that repeat themselves in the client's daily life at the present time.

At this point, the client may make interpretations of meaning or you may add your own interpretations. Generally speaking, interpretations generated by the client are longer lasting.

Stage 5. Generalizing and Transferring Learning

Psychodynamic therapy is not typically oriented to transferring the insights and learnings gained from the interview to daily life. However, it may be helpful to ask the client to summarize the interview. What did the client summarize as the main facts, feelings, and organization of the interview? As appropriate, you may want to add to the client's perspective and work toward some future action plan.

Comment

The five-stage structure of the interview plus the microskills discussed earlier are basic to a successful psychodynamically oriented interview. Cultural and individual empathy, client observation skills (both of verbal and nonverbal behavior, incongruities, pacing, and leading), and the positive asset search are all critical dimensions of a successful session. What psychodynamic theory adds to the process is a content, a specific direction, and a purpose to use these skills in uncovering life patterns and relating them back to earlier life experiences, with specific interpretations.

look puzzled. Alternatively, the client may hear the therapist but forget what was said within a minute or two or between interviews. Such behavior may indicate an area of resistance. Other indicators of resistance can be when the client blocks while trying to say something, leaves out a key part of a dream, comes late to an interview, or refuses to free associate. Resistance shows up in many ways, as the client unconsciously tries to sabotage the treatment process.

The "Freudian slip," in which the client accidentally substitutes one word for another or mixes two words together, often provides a clue as to underlying issues and resistance. For example, a client reported that he had recently visited his mother-in-law, with the goal of tape-recording her comments on family history, and had told her "I want to record you for mortality." The implications of such slips go beyond being amusing and can offer useful access to unconscious functioning.

Analysis of Transference and Countertransference

Transference refers to feelings and thoughts clients have toward the counselor. Clients do not have a clear picture of the nature of the helper in psychodynamically oriented counseling and therapy situations. This is, in large part, due to the manner in which psychodynamically oriented counselors and therapists strive to operate from a neutral and objective position in the helping process. Given this aspect of psychodynamic counseling and therapy, clients will sometimes project an imagined image on the therapist, literally transferring the feelings and thoughts they have toward other people onto the counselor. The transference of such thoughts and feelings in the counseling setting provides the therapist with here-and-now information on the life experience of clients. For example, a client may relate to the therapist as a parental figure, revealing that the client is struggling with family-of-origin issues.

The techniques for coping with a transference situation are similar to those for dealing with resistance. The transference is identified and labeled, and free association techniques are used to clarify meaning. Premature and too-direct examination of transference feelings can confuse and trouble the client. Consequently, analysis of transference is usually done in the middle or later stages of therapy.

Virtually all counselors and therapists, regardless of their theoretical orientation, will observe some form of transference in their clients' comments. However, differing theories vary widely in their use of analysis of transference, and some ignore this area completely.

A nontraditional, but perhaps more multiculturally relevant, approach is to consider transference through family-of-origin work. Many of the examples in this chapter focus on how clients transfer learnings from their families to their daily lives through personality style and/or defense mechanisms. Clients often feel more comfortable talking about how they experienced life and learned modes of behavior in their families. Thus, analysis of transference often works more smoothly if discussed from a family frame of reference (Taub-Bynum, 1999).

Countertransference, defined broadly, consists of feelings and thoughts the therapist has toward the client. Countertransference often results in counselor "blind spots" and can be destructive and disruptive to the interview process. Feelings the counselor has toward the client must be isolated, identified, and worked through. A major portion of training in psychoanalytic work is devoted to a form of counselor therapy, in which the counselor shares feelings, attitudes, and fantasies held toward the client with a psychodynamically trained supervisor. The supervisor also analyzes countertransference feelings through use of free association and other concepts and methods of psychodynamic counseling.

Supervision for the psychodynamic therapist is very much like that of the counselor-client interview. From the perspective of professional ethics, strong countertransference feelings and feelings of resistance toward the client may preclude counselors from working with some clients until personal counseling or therapy is undertaken. Awareness of feelings toward the client and the ability to cope with these feelings are essential theoretical elements that psychodynamic counselors and therapists are encouraged to be mindful of when working with their clients. Supervision when dealing with complex issues of transference and countertransference is particularly important for any professional, beginning or advanced.

Practical Implications and Limitations of Psychodynamic Methods

Psychodynamic approaches require extensive study, reading, and supervised practice by carefully trained individuals who have completed years of study themselves. Full-blown psychodynamic practice is not for the beginner in that training in this theoretical perspective requires the most rigorous intellectual discipline of all Western therapeutic methods.

Nonetheless, the psychodynamic theoretical perspective may be helpful to counselors and therapists in that it can create an awareness that the presentation of a surface problem, concern, or behavior may not be the essential issue that the client is actually grappling with. Underlying the description of a problem may be a vast array of unconscious or unknown forces, ideas, and thoughts. As Freud, Bowlby, Ainsworth, and Taub-Bynum all remind us, the force of unconscious experience is extremely powerful and should not be overlooked.

Psychodynamic approaches have been criticized as being antithetical to and irrelevant for anyone other than highly verbal middle-class clients. Furthermore, there are many practicing psychodynamic therapists who have yet to come to terms with the multicultural-feminist-social justice challenges described in Chapters 1 and 2. Focusing solely on the individual, they may miss other environmental/contextual issues that are critical for client change and growth.

Lastly, as has been pointed out earlier, it is vital to be aware of your own cultural and personal issues and biases when implementing psychodynamic theory in counseling and therapy. Taub-Bynum warns that cultural and family considerations must be a central part of our interventions when using psychodynamic approaches with persons from diverse client populations or you may unintentionally transmit various forms of psychological oppression in the counseling process.

Critics of the psychoanalytic framework also often find the approach to be too closely associated with different forms of patriarchy and male domination. Sayers (1995) argues that, given the pervasive ways in which patriarchy and male domination continue to exist in society, these forms of cultural oppression impact the collective unconsciousness of everyone, including mental health professionals.

Professional Development Extension

Using Freudian Concepts in a School Setting

The psychodynamic frame of reference continues to have a tremendous impact on the thinking of many people in the general public. Some psychodynamic principles that have been inculcated into the public consciousness include unconscious conflicts between past experiences and present-day thinking, feeling, and acting; the use of defense mechanisms when confronted with anxiety and stress; and the impact of early childhood experiences on later psychological development. Counselors and therapists frequently refer to these concepts in their work, including when working with children. Consider the case of Bruce, a 13-year-old client referred to therapy for problems he was experiencing at school.

Bruce was frequently referred to the principal's office for bullying other students as well as acting aggressively toward his teachers and school counselor. His aggressive behavior was unpredictable. Some days he functioned as well as or better than other students in his class. On other days, Bruce would exhibit heightened anger with the smallest provocation.

Having tried many interventions without much success, Bruce's teachers and the school counselor were at a loss. They encouraged Bruce's mother to schedule an appointment to have Bruce seen by one of the therapists at a local mental health center who was known for effectively using psychodynamic principles and techniques with young adolescents.

During her first meeting with Bruce's mother, Jean (the therapist) learned that Bruce had a strong connection with both parents but "took after his dad in many ways." She also learned that Bruce's parents were separated and going through a contentious divorce. The mother further stated that Bruce's dad was physically violent with her in the past and often used spankings to discipline Bruce.

Bruce appeared very frustrated during his first therapy session and stated that "there is nothing wrong with me." When asked how things were going at school, Bruce angrily said, "I can't stand the kids in my class. They are always bothering me, and the teachers always stand up for them. So I have to take care of myself."

Bruce then directed his anger toward Jean and made numerous disparaging comments, in particular, "You're just like my mom. You should leave me alone. I can't stand it when people try to change me."

Jean hypothesized that much of Bruce's aggression was tied to his unresolved anger about his parents' divorce, his identification with his father, his disconnection with his mother, and his unconscious use of various defense mechanisms (e.g., repression, denial, projection), which he utilized to cope with the anxieties that were linked to these issues. Jean proceeded by using a number of Freudian principles with this young client.

Jean Baker Miller's (1986) classic work, entitled *Toward a New Psychology of Women,* is particularly influential in advancing a critical understanding of the sexist underpinnings of many traditional approaches to psychodynamic counseling and therapy. Miller asserts that one of the central issues that is missing from the traditional psychodynamic frame of reference is an awareness that women's sense of self is typically generated within a family and cultural context.

This feminist view of human development is in sharp contrast to the approaches that many traditionally trained psychodynamic therapists use in practice. According to Miller (1991), most traditionally trained psychodynamic therapists overemphasize individualistic and autonomous psychological considerations in counseling

In her second session with Bruce, Jean invited him to play a game in which he would agree to say the first thing that came to his mind when presented with a series of cards that had different words written on them. When Bruce agreed to play this "silly game," it became apparent that his thoughts and feelings were dominated by a general sense of anger and frustration as he participated in this free association. Although Jean believed that Bruce was not fully conscious of the amount of anger he harbored toward his mother and father, she was able to help Bruce acknowledge that he was very frustrated about many things in his life, including his parents' upcoming divorce. Bruce's anxiety increased as he talked about these issues, and he would make hostile comments to Jean. Rather than responding negatively to his comments, Jean patiently tried to find ways to help Bruce think about why he was feeling angry with her.

Jean worked to help Bruce become more conscious of the ways in which his parents' divorce was affecting him in general. She also helped him recognize how his love for and identification with his father often led him to act like his father when he became frustrated with other students and teachers at school. When implementing these strategies, Jean frequently had to address various forms of negative transference that Bruce directed at her as she tried to help him make new interpretations of his thoughts, feelings, and behaviors.

By directing particular attention to the impact of the family unconscious, Bruce was able gain a new understanding of some of his thoughts, feelings, and actions. Over the course of several therapy sessions, this new understanding contributed to changes in Bruce's behavior. Although his aggressive and hostile behavior did not completely disappear, Bruce demonstrated improved control over his anger at school. He continued his work with Jean for a total of 15 therapy sessions over four and a half months.

During his last session with Jean, Bruce stated, "I may come back to see you if I need to, but I feel that I know a lot more about why I used to act so mean before." While it is important to note that the time Bruce spent working with Jean did not result in the complete elimination of all of his aggressive behavior, his improvement was significant enough to enable him to return to school, where he advanced to the next grade and exhibited more positive social interactions with the other students and teachers.

Counselors often encourage teachers to consider the possibility that the hostile and aggressive behaviors some students manifest in their classes may be a reflection of unresolved conflicts in their home and family situations. These conflicts often are unconsciously displaced at school. Recognition of this encourages teachers to think in new and more empathic ways about the troublesome behaviors some students exhibit in their classes. Parents can also benefit from understanding how important early childhood experiences are for the long-term psychological development of their children.

and therapy without directing equal time to the ways in which relational and contextual issues unconsciously underlie the anxiety many female clients experience in their lives. Miller and other feminist theorists (Brown, 1994; Brown & Ballou, 1992; Hill & Ballou, 2005) argue that by continuing to overemphasize individualistic and autonomous considerations in psychodynamic therapeutic situations, practitioners unintentionally help to perpetuate various forms of patriarchy and male domination that are antithetical to women's mental health and spiritual well-being.

To complicate matters, the cultural conditioning of women in society leads many females to consciously and unconsciously adapt roles that restrict their ability to recognize the various forms of sexism, patriarchy, and male domination that continue to exist in our contemporary society. This cultural society undermines many women's ability to effectively deal with conflicts that are tied to these forms of cultural oppression. In terms of therapeutic work with women, Miller (1991) points out that psychodynamic techniques are dangerous unless issues of gender, patriarchy, and male domination are made central in the helping process.

Being aware of the negative and pervasive impact that various forms of cultural oppression such as patriarchy and male domination have on the collective unconscious, multicultural and feminist theorists hold that a critical issue in modern psychodynamic therapy is helping women and persons from other devalued groups learn how their present concerns are related to past histories of domination. From this frame of reference, insight becomes a valuable tool with the potential to lead clients to new and more liberatory ways of thinking and acting in the future (Ivey & Ivey, 2001).

Despite the numerous limitations of this theoretical perspective, Freudian concepts have proven to be useful in fostering many clients' mental health and sense of personal well-being. The Professional Development Extension demonstrates the process and some of the positive outcomes that can result.

Summary

This chapter provides foundational information about the first theoretical force that emerged in the fields of counseling and psychology—the psychodynamic frame of reference. This chapter starts with the theories of Freud and then moves to the more multiculturally relevant attachment theory of John Bowlby, which is supported by the research of Mary Ainsworth. The innovative work of Bruce Taub-Bynum is also presented, showing how family and cultural influences can be made more explicit in the psychodynamic model. Particular emphasis is placed on the importance of considering the cultural limitations of this theoretical perspective when working with women and persons from diverse cultural groups and backgrounds.

Despite the numerous limitations of this theoretical perspective, psychodynamic principles in general and Freudian concepts in particular are useful in much of the work done in and outside of individual counseling and psychotherapeutic settings. Your understanding of the complexity and utility of this important theoretical force will be further stimulated in Chapter 6, where you will learn about two other leaders in psychodynamic counseling and therapy—Alfred Adler and Carl Jung.

Multimedia Resources for This Chapter

The following online resource offers video resources of particular relevance to this chapter of your text.

Companion Website

Go to **www.ablongman.com/Ivey6e** to view the following video clips:

- Video clip 5.1 demonstrates how sublimation can be used to achieve positive outcomes. You will see how the therapist uses a psychodynamic approach with the client. You will also hear how this client describes her efforts to sublimate her anger and frustration by engaging in more productive and satisfying endeavors. Although the use of sublimation in this situation may temporary serve to alleviate the client's sense of frustration and anxiety, the continued use of this defense mechanism may fail in the long term, as repressed anger and hurt will well up in unexpected ways unless they are more effectively addressed in the helping process.

- Video clip 5.2 provides a glimpse of some of the ways that a White male counselor addresses these issues early in the therapeutic encounter with a woman of African descent.

chapter 6

Adlerian and Jungian Counseling and Therapy

Introduction

As noted in Chapter 5, Freud's theory of therapy provides the basis of psychoanalytic thought, and as such, he should be credited with the birth of all intrapsychic and psychodynamic theories. However, it is equally important to acknowledge the ways in which Freud's traditional views have been modified and extended by other psychoanalytic proponents. This chapter focuses on the important contributions two of Freud's closest protégés have made in expanding our thinking about the psychoanalytic view of counseling and therapy.

Alfred Adler and Carl Jung have had a profound impact on psychodynamic thinking in the mental health professions. Both also had close relationships with Freud, although each ended in bitter disagreement over issues related to Freud's psychoanalytic theory. Nonetheless, many positive outcomes ensued from the disagreement and personal estrangement with Freud. Among them is that the psychoanalytic perspective was greatly expanded as a result of the different theoretical contributions of Adler and Jung. The new concepts of Adler and Jung that contributed to their break with Freud are more consistent with multicultural counseling theories than are the views Freud espoused.

This chapter is designed to increase your understanding of the lives and work of Adler and Jung and to provide an overview of their theories of counseling and therapy. In addition, you will learn about some of the basic competencies needed when using Adlerian and Jungian helping approaches in your professional practice.

Alfred Adler and Adlerian Counseling

Alfred Adler was born on February 7, 1870, in Vienna, Austria. He lived with both of his parents and was the third child in the Jewish family. His father worked as a grain merchant, providing a middle-class lifestyle for his family.

Adler's childhood was marked by a series of illnesses that greatly limited his ability to play outdoors. According to one of his biographers, "Alfred developed rickets, which kept him from walking until he was four years old. At five, he nearly died of pneumonia. It was at this age that he decided to be a physician" (Boeree, 2004, p. 2).

Despite his chronic childhood physical problems, Adler demonstrated a determination, outgoingness, and zest for life that carried over to his adolescent and adult years. His strong determination helped him achieve his goal of becoming a physician, and he acquired his medical degree from the University of Vienna in 1895.

During his college and medical school years, Adler became attached to a group of socialist students. Among them was his wife-to-be, Raisa Epstein. She was an intellectual and social activist in her own right who had come from Russia to study in Vienna. Alfred Adler and Raisa married in 1897 and eventually had four children, two of whom became psychiatrists themselves.

His encounters with socialist philosophy significantly impacted Adler's thinking about the need for psychiatry and psychology to address the concerns of all the people, not just those affluent enough to afford the services of mental health professionals. Unlike Freud, who served persons of the upper middle class, Adler worked early in his medical career as a general practitioner in a lower-class part of Vienna (Boeree, 2004). These early professional experiences impacted his later thinking about the way people experience difficulties in their lives and develop psychological strengths.

Adler turned to psychiatry in the early 1900s and was invited to join Freud's inner circle in 1907. His close association with Freud led Adler to thoughtfully reflect on Freud's psychoanalytic perspective. This reflection resulted in the development of an alternative perspective on the Freudian view of psychological growth and development.

Overview of Adler's Theory of Individual Psychology

Adler's alternative theory, referred to as **individual psychology,** included numerous criticisms of Freud's fundamental psychoanalytic propositions. The theoretical differences between these two important figures ultimately resulted in a formal split in 1911. Shortly thereafter, Adler's psychological theory became institutionalized into The Society for Free Psychological Thought, which was organized in Vienna in 1912. This society began publishing the *Journal for Individual Psychology* shortly thereafter (Gilliland & James, 1998).

Another factor that contributed to the development of Adler's psychological theory involved his participation in World War I. During this military conflict, Adler served as a physician in the Austrian army, first on the Russian front and later in a children's hospital. As a result of this experience, Adler "saw first hand the damage that war does, and his thought turned increasingly to the concept of social interest. He felt that if humanity was to survive, it had to change its ways" (Boeree, 2004, p. 3).

These life experiences led Adler to become what Corey (1995) describes as a "politically and socially oriented psychiatrist who showed great concern for the common person; part of his mission was to bring psychotherapy to the working class and to translate psychological concepts into practical methods for helping a varied population meet the challenges of life" (p. 186).

Although Adler's unique psychoanalytic views on "bringing psychology to the people" gained acceptance by mental health professionals in Europe during the early 1900s, they were much slower in coming to the attention of psychological practitioners in the United States. In fact, it was not until the mid 1900s that Adlerian theory was introduced to American psychology by Rudolf Dreikurs. Commenting on Dreikurs's contributions in introducing Adlerian theory to the field of psychology in the United States, Gilliland and James (1998) point out:

> If not for Rudolf Dreikurs, the fledging Adlerian movement might have ceased to exist. Dreikurs pushed hard for the adoption of child guidance centers in American that were based on Adlerian principles. His prolific writings about Adlerian psychology and his own innovations, such as the use of group therapy, the modeling of real-life counseling sessions before audiences (Dreikurs, 1959), multiple therapist procedures, and a comprehensive counseling approach to children did much to bring Adlerian psychology to the attention of the general public. (pp. 42–43)

While the work of Dreikurs was instrumental in bringing Adlerian theory to the awareness of many counselors and psychologists in the United States in the mid 1900s, it was Don Dinkmeyer and his son, Don Dinkmeyer, Jr., who promoted the widespread use of Adlerian concepts in the United States through their commercial enterprises. These enterprises include two psychoeducational resources— *Developing Understanding of Self and Others* (DUSO) (Dinkmeyer & Dinkmeyer, 1982) and *Systematic Training for Effective Parenting* (STEP) (Dinkmeyer, McKay, & Dinkmeyer, 1998)—that many counselors have found useful in promoting the healthy psychological development and effectiveness of children and parents.

As Adler's theoretical perspective became better known in the mental health professions, it notably impacted many of the other major theories of counseling and psychotherapy that were being used in the United States. Commenting on this point, Gilliland and James (1998, p. 43) note:

> A number of Adlerian concepts such as the idea of inferiority and superiority complexes, goal orientation, lifestyle, the will to power, dependency, and over protection have become so widespread that few realize they were originated by Adler. The logotherapy of Frankl (1970), the humanism of Maslow (1970), the existentialism of May (1970), and the rational-emotive approach

of Ellis (1971) all owe much to Adler. A number of other approaches, such as Glasser's reality therapy, Satir's family therapy, Berne's transactional analysis, and Perls's gestalt therapy, have also borrowed from Adlerian techniques. (Mosak, 1989; Sweeney, 1989)

The Adlerian Worldview

Alder's theoretical perspective of human development catalyzed a major shift in thinking from Freud's psychoanalytic theory. As noted in his theory of individual psychology, Adler's worldview is distinguished from a Freudian perspective in several fundamental ways. First, while Freud emphasized the important role that the unconscious plays in a person's psychological functioning, Adler placed a greater value on people's consciousness in their development. Thus, from an Adlerian perspective, "consciousness rather than unconsciousness is the primary source of one's ideas, values, and sense of psychological health" (Gilliland & James, 1998, p. 44).

Adler agreed with Freud's assessment of the important impact that biological factors and early childhood experiences have on one's personality development. He did not, however, share the same convictions as Freud about the ways in which these factors were thought to determine an individual's personality development. While Adler agreed that biological, sexual, and aggressive drives as well as one's childhood experiences increase the probability that an individual will develop in certain ways, he placed a much greater emphasis on people's creative ability to realize their personal goals and live purposeful lives (Adler, 1963).

The Teleological Nature of Humankind. The notion that human development is largely impacted by goal-directed drives and purposeful actions is referred to as the **teleological nature of humankind.** Writing about these key Adlerian concepts, Seligman (2001) notes:

> For Adler, those characteristics of human development that were determined by heredity and early upbringing were less important than what the person made of them. He believed that all behavior was purposeful and goal directed, and that we can channel our behavior in ways that promote growth. For Adler, what matters to people is finding success, fulfillment, and meaning in life. Their actions reflect their efforts to achieve those goals, and the goals they value and how they seek to reach them are major factors in their development. (p. 78)

Another factor that distinguishes an Adlerian worldview from Freud's psychoanalytic perspective involves the notion that the goals people strive to achieve in life are grounded in social considerations. Adler theorized that everyone is innately driven to explore new and untapped dimensions of their being by a uniquely human characteristic he termed *social interest.*

Social Interest, Personal Competence and Superiority, and Belongingness. Social interest is a central construct in Adler's theory of individual psychology. According to Adler, this innate drive is grounded in a universal urge to satisfy three fundamental human needs:

- the innate drive to realize a state of perfectibility
- the need to achieve a sense of personal competence (or what Adler refers to as superiority)
- the desire to experience a increased belongingness with other persons

There is a close fit between these three aspects of Adler's worldview and similar concepts reflective of the multicultural-feminist-social justice movement. The notion that humans are driven by nature to realize a state of perfectibility is consistent with the Black psychology model known as **Maat** (Obasi, 2002, p. 71). In explaining this construct, Black psychology theorists point out that the drive to realize a state of perfectibility is one of the seven character principles that comprise Maat. This innate drive is manifested in a person's social interactions with others and is a key indicator of an individual's mental health (e.g., the degree to which an individual consciously strives to realize her or his perfectibility within the context of the broader community of which one is a part) (Parham, 2002). Like Adler, multicultural theorists emphasize that the drive for perfectibility begins in early childhood as youngsters move beyond a state of dependence and toward a state of greater competence (or feeling of superiority, as Adler refers to it).

The emphasis that Adler placed on people's innate drive to move beyond a pervasive sense of inferiority that marks early childhood is balanced by his belief that everyone can realize new and untapped dimensions of their humanity when afforded the opportunities to do so. Adler (1959, 1963) insisted that individuals move from feelings of inferiority to a greater sense of superiority and confidence when they have the opportunities to develop new knowledge and skills and are encouraged to do so.

Early Supporter of Women's Rights. As an early proponent of women's rights, Adler repeatedly argued that women should be provided the same opportunities as men if they were to move beyond their own innate sense of inferiority to feelings of competence and personal superiority. While this dimension of Adler's worldview distinguished him from most of his colleagues, it is consistent with the call for equal treatment in the psychological development of females that is asserted by many feminist writers (Worrell & Remer, 2003). The emphasis that Adler placed on creating social conditions that more effectively enable individuals to move from the feelings of inferiority that characterize early childhood to a greater sense of personal competence and superiority later in life is consistent with the views of other multicultural-social justice counseling advocates (Ponterotto, Casas, Suzuki, & Alexander, 2001).

Consistency with Multicultural-Social Justice Theories. Martin Luther King, Jr. (1986), referenced Adler's work in one of his best-known speeches, "The Drum Major Instinct." In doing so, Dr. King gave credit for the way this noted psychoanalyst explains the process that enables people to successfully move beyond a pervasive sense of inferiority and dependence to an increased and healthy sense of personal distinction and self-worth when opportunities are available for them to do so. King (1986) went on to point out that the healthiest manifestation of the drive for distinction (or competence and superiority, as Adler refers to it) occurs when individuals express their love for others by working to create a greater level of social justice in the world.

Adler's notions about people's feelings of inferiority and superiority are also consistent with the writings of other multicultural theorists, who use similar considerations in describing the psychology of White racism and White superiority. One example of this is found in Welsing's (1991) psychological analysis of these complex problems as they continue to manifest in our contemporary society. In presenting her assessment of these problems, Welsing suggests that many White persons intentionally or unintentionally perpetuate various forms of White racism and White superiority by using a host of defense mechanisms to compensate for feelings of inferiority and fear. According to Welsing, these feelings of fear and inferiority are linked to many White people's perceived threats to their historical position as the dominant cultural/racial group in our society.

D'Andrea (2004b) builds on Welsing's work by describing the different defense mechanisms that many White people use to deal with this anxiety. Among these are the use of denial, which helps to disengage individuals from the awareness of the complex ways in which White racism and White superiority continue to exist in our nation (D'Andrea, 2001). Also included is the use of projection, which is frequently exhibited when individuals blame other persons for bringing up issues related to White racism and White superiority for discussion and analysis. Welsing (1991) and D'Andrea (2006b) insist that many White persons unconsciously employ these and other defense mechanisms to reduce their feelings of fear and inferiority and to reinstate their feelings of superiority.

Other multicultural-social justice counseling advocates note that the striving for this kind of superiority results in a widespread state of psychological disorder among many in the United States (Myers, 1992). The disordered state of being rooted in this unhealthy striving for superiority contributes to the creation and maintenance of unjust social, economic, educational, and political conditions (Myers, 1992).

Other theorists point out that the racialized psychological and societal arrangements that characterize our contemporary society effectively maintain White people's feelings of superiority by bestowing many unearned cultural privileges on them and reducing the opportunities that persons of color might otherwise have to realize their own competencies and to achieve a heightened sense of belongingness in our contemporary society (McIntosh, 1989; Scheurich, 1993; Scheurich & Young, 1997).

Life Tasks. According to Adler (1963), the urge to experience a heightened sense of belongingness with others is a universal drive. The drive for belongingness motivates individuals to become engaged in a host of **life tasks** that are of vital importance in a person's psychological development and mental health (Adler, 1959). The three original life tasks that Adler discussed in his theory of individual psychology include:

- the need to develop friendships with others
- the urge to realize a loving relationship with another person
- the drive to be involved in a satisfying and productive occupation

From an Adlerian perspective, a person's mental health is significantly impacted by the ability to establish friendships and maintain meaningful relationships with others. People who have difficulty establishing and maintaining meaningful friendships commonly experience varying degrees of depression, frustration, anger, and social alienation. Adler believed these negative psychosocial experiences lead many people to seek help in counseling and therapy.

Adler also described the vital role that more intimate and loving relationships play in fostering healthy personality development. His views on these issues represent additional ways in which he disagreed with Freud. Adler rejected Freud's view that the urge to develop loving and intimate ties with others is primarily rooted in biologically based libidinal drives. Instead, Adler suggested that the universal need to give and receive love represents a vital dimension of every person's social interest. From an Adlerian point of view, this dimension of social interest enables individuals to develop their capacity to experience and communicate a deep and genuine sense of empathy, compassion, and respect for others. Realizing these aspects of their humanity, people normally experience a heightened sense of psychological well-being and mental health (Adler, 1959).

Adler's theoretical perspective of what constitutes a loving relationship and its relevance for a person's mental health is consistent with many feminist counseling theorists, who emphasize the centrality of self-in-relation (Comstock, 2005). These considerations have relevance not only for female development, but also for the psychological health of men. Consequently, from an Adlerian and feminist point of view, healthy male development is reflected in those men who are able to experience loving, intimate, and respectful connections with women as well as other males. This requires men to transcend stereotypic and antagonistic views about gender differences and embrace the notion that women and men are equal partners in life and love (Adler, 1959; Taylor, 2002).

Spirituality. The evolution of Adlerian theory has resulted in the identification of another important life task. This task involves the need to develop a relationship to the spiritual (Mosak, 1989; Mosak & Goldman, 1995). In describing this component of the Adlerian worldview, Gilliland and James (1998) point out that "people do not live by bread alone and must define a spiritual self in relation to the cosmos, God, and universal values and how to relate to these concepts to obtain a spiritual centeredness such that the other life tasks all take on meaning" (p. 45).

Directing attention to spiritual issues reflects another way that Adlerian theory differs from traditional psychoanalytic theory. Freudian psychoanalytic theory does not place much credibility on spirituality as a major factor in healthy human development. By including spiritual factors as important considerations in the tasks that people face in their lives, Adlerian theorists further expand the traditional parameters of psychoanalytic thinking. It is also useful to point out that the task of developing a relationship with the spiritual is consistent with the emphasis that many multicultural counseling theorists place on the special role that spirituality plays in the healthy psychological functioning of persons from diverse groups and backgrounds (Fukuyama & Sevig, 1999).

A Prevention Focus. A final point to be made about Adler's worldview relates to the ways in which he used many of his theoretical premises to promote preventive counseling strategies in his professional practice. Adler implemented prevention counseling interventions in his work throughout much of his career by providing outreach services to persons in the greater community where he lived (Dreikurs, 1981; James & Gilliland, 2003).

Among the preventive outreach intervention strategies Adler implemented were setting up a number of child guidance centers in the Vienna public schools. The child guidance centers Adler established were intentionally designed to foster youngsters' healthy psychosocial development through the use of teaching and learning approaches based on his principles of individual psychology.

Adler's pioneering work in prevention intervention distinguished him from other theorists and practitioners of his time. Speaking from a more contemporary perspective, his pioneering efforts in this area are consistent with calls by multicultural-social justice counseling advocates for the development and implementation of more prevention interventions aimed at fostering the psychological health and collective empowerment of persons in diverse groups (Lewis & Bradley, 2002; McWhirter, 1994; Ponterotto et al., 2001). Competency-Building Activity 6.1 is designed to help you develop some of the basic skills necessary when using Adlerian principles in preventive counseling settings.

Other Key Adlerian Concepts

Fictional Goals. Competency-Building Activity 6.1 highlights the importance of acknowledging the goal-directed drives and purposeful actions that emerge from the teleological nature of our clients' and our own development. Elaborating on these positive and growth-oriented aspects of human development, Adler suggests further that people develop **fictional goals.** Adler believed that these fictional goals develop during a person's childhood and remain largely at the unconscious level of awareness throughout one's life. Although the genesis of a person's fictional goals can be traced

Competency-Building Activity 6.1

Implementing Preventive Counseling Strategies from an Adlerian Perspective

Instructions: To complete this competency-building activity, you will need the assistance of someone who is willing to participate in an interview that will last about 30 minutes. After you have found someone to participate in this activity, explain to her or him that you hope to achieve three goals in conducting this interview. First, explain that you want to provide an opportunity for her or him to learn about some life tasks from Alfred Adler's theory of individual psychology.

Second, say that you would like the interviewee to identify those life tasks that he or she has had the greatest success in achieving up to this point in time.

Finally, let the interviewee know that you will ask her or him to talk about how to experience a more satisfying and productive life by consciously working on one or two aspects of a life task that would be helpful in this regard.

Once you have explained what you will be doing in this exercise, ask the interviewee if he or she has any questions or comments.

After you have answered any questions, describe the following life tasks discussed in Adler's theory.

- Life task 1 relates to people's need to develop friendships with others.
- Life task 2 relates to the drive that all people have to realize a more intimate and loving relationship with another person.
- Life task 3 relates to the drive to be involved in a satisfying and productive occupation or career.
- Life task 4 relates to the need and satisfaction one derives from developing a spiritual perspective in life.

Step 1. *Take a few minutes to explain any aspects of these life tasks that the interviewee may have questions about.*

Step 2. *Ask the interviewee to identify the life task(s) that he or she is doing well with and derives a great deal of satisfaction from.* Be sure to use the microskills described in Chapter 4 to help the interviewee discuss thoughts and feelings about this issue(s) in as much detail as possible.

Step 3. *Focus attention on the life task or tasks that may represent more of a challenge at this time.* Let the interviewee know that researchers in the fields of counseling and psychology have noted that people can prevent problems from occurring in the future and experience a greater level of personal satisfaction and productivity in their lives when they take time to reflect on personal strengths developed as a result of successful accomplishment of various tasks. Ask the interviewee to identify specific areas he or she is committed to improving.

Step 4. *Talk with the interviewee about the specific life task(s) he or she would like to more effectively address in the future.* Then explore what action she or he would be willing to take to address this life task(s) in the next 30 days. Be sure to assist the interviewee in (1) identifying practical strategies to implement in the near future, (2) discussing how such action strategies will lead to a greater sense of personal satisfaction and productivity, and (3) making a commitment to take such action in the next 30 days.

Mental health professionals can be helpful in assisting clients to develop the knowledge and skills that are useful in leading more satisfying and productive lives. They can do so by using some of the ideas that are reflected in an Adlerian worldview of counseling and therapy. This competency-building activity is designed to assist you in

continued on next page

Competency-Building Activity 6.1, continued

developing some of the competencies necessary to effectively implement preventive counseling interventions by supporting clients' sense of personal empowerment as they address the various life tasks described in Adler's theory of individual psychology.

When you have completed this competency-building activity, take a few minutes to write down your reactions to this exercise. We encourage you to then add your written reactions to your personal/professional development portfolio. This will enable you to keep a record of the different ways that you are affected by the exercises presented in this book.

to her or his childhood and family experiences, these unconscious and personalized goals strongly influence the way people think, feel, and act throughout their lives.

It is important to understand that fictional goals essentially develop in conjunction with people's subjective interpretation of their life experiences and personal understanding of their place in the world. This is a key concept that Adler referred to as the **phenomenological nature of human development.**

Private Logic. From an Adlerian point of view, people's phenomenological nature leads them to construct unique meaning of the experiences they have in life. These unique personal constructions and interpretations of the world lead people to unconsciously develop their own **private logic.** Though typically situated at the unconscious level of a person's awareness, this private logic significantly affects the way individuals think and feel about their purpose in life and the manner in which they strive to achieve their fictional goals (Adler, 1959).

Dreikurs (1981) expanded Adler's original description of the phenomenological nature of human development and the private logic people use to realize their fictional life goals. He maintained that these Adlerian concepts include unconscious beliefs about who one is, convictions about who one should be, thoughts about what the rest of the world should be like, and notions about what is ethically right or wrong.

Within the context of an Adlerian perspective, healthy human development occurs when individuals become more conscious of the unique ways in which they have unconsciously constructed meaning of the world. This consciousness-raising process is central to Adlerian counseling and therapy and represents what is called a **phenomenological approach to helping** (Adler, 1959).

Family Factors. Adlerian counseling strategies are based on the belief that clients' mental health and sense of well-being are enhanced when practitioners use a phenomenological approach to assist clients in becoming more fully conscious of their fictional goals and the private logic that underlies their striving to achieve these goals. Adler believed that practitioners need to help clients explore how their family history and experiences impact their development. In doing so, he directed particular time in discussing how one's **family constellation** contributes to the formation of an individual's fictional goals and private logic (Adler, 1963; Sweeney, 1989).

The term *family constellation* refers to the composition of an individual's family and one's position within that primary social system. Gilliland and James (1998) point out that "the family constellation mediates the genetic and constitutional factors the child brings into it and the cultural factors the child learns from it. The personality characteristics of each family member, the sex of the siblings, family size, and the birth order of the children all influence how the individual finds their niche in life" (p. 49).

Adler directed particular attention to the ways in which a person's family experiences and birth order affects her or his **style of life.** This multifaceted concept holds a central position in Adlerian theory. Lundin (1989) outlines several factors that comprise this important aspect human development. These include an individual's

- problem-solving style and skills
- unique expression of her or his creativity
- attitudes toward life
- opinions about oneself
- ways in which an individual strives to fulfill her or his social interest and drive for competence/superiority
- expressions of one's entire personality

Adler (1963) discussed at length how a person's style of life is significantly affected by her or his **birth order** within the individual's family constellation. He described how four different birth order positions commonly impact an individual's personality development. These birth order positions are described as follows:

1. *The firstborn.* The first child occupies a unique position in the family constellation. She or he starts out as the only child, who is commonly showered with a great deal of love and attention by her or his parents. The firstborn child is put in a position as being a pioneer—the first to travel the birth canal, the first to challenge adults' parenting abilities, the first to lead the way for younger siblings.

   Although the first child is often given much attention and love, he or she is dethroned from this position when a second child enters the family constellation. Unless parents are careful to prepare the first child for this dethroning event by continuing to direct much attention and love to the first child, problems are likely to occur.

   Adler believed that the firstborn is more likely to become a leader, since younger siblings manifest a greater level of inferiority and dependence in the family constellation than the oldest child, who has had more time and opportunity to develop various competencies.

2. *The second born, or middle child.* Second-born, or middle, children are cast into a situation that fosters a heightened sense of competition. Their lives are a continuous race to catch up with the firstborn. The competitive attitude stimulated in some middle children may be so strong that they become revolutionaries or fearless and outspoken leaders in their careers.

However, Adler noted that the competitive attitude second-born youngsters acquire because of their position in their family constellation usually operates within reason. As such, the second child is thought to be less vulnerable to psychological problems later in life that either the first- or the last-born child.

3. *The last born.* The youngest child is the most likely to be the pampered one in a family constellation, as many parents realize that this will be their last child. The pampering treatment many last-born youngsters receive during childhood influences their development in many ways.

On the positive side, Adler cited numerous cases where the last born strives to excel in whatever she or he endeavors during adulthood. He also noted how this positive potential is reflected in many fairy tales, where the youngest child in a family is portrayed as a hero, heroine, or winner.

On the other hand, last-born children may experience a heightened sense of egocentricity as a result of the special treatment they receive from their parents early in their lives. This may result in difficulties later in life, especially in interpersonal situations that demand a heightened level of mutuality and reciprocity to function effectively with others.

4. *The only child.* Like the youngest child, the only child is likely to be pampered. Given the unique position of the only child in the family constellation, Adler suggested that he or she is not likely to develop a competitive lifestyle.

Because only children are often the center of attention in the family constellation, they may develop exaggerated opinions of their own importance. Adler suggested that the only child may also develop a lifestyle that is marked by timidity and overdependence on others.

Adler's birth order hypothesis has become popular in the media, but research data have not really substantiated these ideas. Nonetheless, with so many people aware of birth order, it is very likely that the Adlerian story has entered the cultural consciousness. Because people expect birth order to make a difference, it is very likely that it sometimes does. As such, used carefully, birth order can be a useful counseling construct.

As is the case with all of the counseling and psychotherapy theories presented in this textbook, Adler's theory of individual psychology has its strengths and weakness. It is our hope that you will refrain from overgeneralizing any aspects of Adlerian theory in your work with clients. We believe that, like the pieces of a complex puzzle, each theory presented in this textbook will provide useful concepts that can be pieced together to foster the psychological development and well-being of clients who experience different challenges in their lives. We do not believe that any one single theory is the best or should be used universally among all the clients we serve.

Some of the strengths and shortcomings of Adler's theory of individual psychology are discussed later in this chapter. That discussion is aimed at helping you think about the types of clients that are likely to benefit from the concepts included in Adler's theory. Before embarking on that discussion, your attention is now directed to the application of Adlerian counseling and therapy in professional practice.

Adlerian Counseling and Therapy Strategies: Applications for Practice

Most clients come to counseling and therapy in the hope that they will find new ways to deal with different problems and challenges they are experiencing in their lives. Adlerian counselors and therapists operate in a certain way to achieve specific outcomes that are consistent with the theoretical worldview and concepts described above. These outcomes include assisting clients to realize a greater level of social interest and gain a better understanding of the beliefs, motives, and feelings that underlie their lifestyles. In addition, these practitioners help clients develop new insights into mistaken goals and self-defeating behaviors as well as explore alternative ways of thinking, feeling, and acting in the world (Carlson & Sperry, 2001).

As they attempt to achieve these outcomes in counseling and therapy, Adlerian counselors strive to help people acquire new insights, knowledge, and abilities that are necessary to develop a lifestyle that is more personally satisfying and productive than their current lifestyle. This is often accomplished when counselors and therapists facilitate clients' movement through four stages of the Adlerian counseling process, as presented in the following subsections.

Stage 1. Building a Trusting Relationship

Adler (1959) emphasizes the importance of taking time to develop a respectful, mutual, and empathic relationship with clients in the first stage of the helping process. One of his reasons for doing so relates to the tendency of clients to engage in what is referred to **safeguarding.** Safeguarding is an unconscious defense mechanism many clients use to defend themselves against examining and altering the fictional goals they acquired earlier in their lives, regardless of how unsatisfying, unrealistic, and self-defeating these goals may be.

Another reason Adler gives for establishing a positive and trusting relationship at the initial stage of counseling and psychotherapy relates to the fears and dangers clients commonly experience when entering the therapeutic situation (James & Gilliland, 2003). These include the fear of

- becoming overly defensive in counseling
- being exposed for who one truly is
- being disapproved of by the counselor
- being ridiculed

- being taken advantage of
- getting the help clients want in counseling
- having to accept personal responsibility for one's difficulties
- experiencing unpleasant consequences as a result of participating in counseling and therapy (Shulman, 1973, pp. 106–107)

Intentionally communicating a genuine sense of respect, warmth, acceptance, and empathic understanding (as discussed earlier in this textbook; see the section on microskills in Chapter 4) is important in effectively addressing the challenges associated with the first stage of Adlerian counseling and therapy. The first stage of the five-stage interview described in Chapter 4 is very close to Adler's first stage.

Stage 2. The Assessment Stage

In addition to building a trusting relationship, helping clients to assess various dimensions of their lifestyle is also critical in this counseling framework. In conducting this lifestyle assessment, counselors take time to assist clients in talking about their beliefs and feelings as well as their motives and fictional goals (Carlson & Sperry, 2001).

Such assessment includes encouraging clients to talk about their early recollections and memories of their family atmosphere and constellation, to consider the impact of their birth order on their development, and to explore their dreams. Using these approaches in the assessment stage of Adlerian counseling enables clients to explore aspects of themselves they rarely take time to consider in the context of the busy and rapidly changing world in which we live and work. This stage is different from the second stage of the five-stage interview (Chapter 4), which focuses on defining problems, concerns, issues and finding positive strengths of the client.

Stage 3. Promoting Insight

At this stage of the helping process, Adlerian counselors assist clients in developing new insights regarding unsatisfying aspects of their fictional goals and self-defeating behaviors. To assist their clients in becoming more conscious of these unconscious aspects of their psychological development, Adlerian counselors frequently make use of the kinds of the interpretation and confrontation skills that are described in Chapter 4. This portion of the session closely approximates the fourth stage of the microskills framework.

It is important to emphasize that Adlerian counselors are interested not only in promoting intellectual insights into their clients' lifestyle and fictional goals, but also in stimulating changes in the way clients act so that they can develop new and more satisfying lifestyles grounded in the personal insights gained in therapy. Commenting on the importance of using the above-mentioned skills to foster the development of such insights, James and Gilliland (2003) explain that "the client gains insights through the counselor's interpretation of his or her ordinary communications, dreams, fantasies, behavior, transactions with the counselor, and other interpersonal interactions. The purpose in interpretation is on purpose rather than cause, on movement rather than description, on use rather than possession" (pp. 113–114).

Stage 4. Reorientation

The challenge of helping clients move from developing new insights to more effective and satisfying actions is the focus of the final stage of Adlerian counseling and therapy. To facilitate these important changes, Adlerian counselors begin by gently offering alternative ideas for the client's consideration (Dinkmeyer, Dinkmeyer, & Sperry, 1987). As a result of building an increasing sense of trust and mutual respect with the client, Adlerian counselors move to using a more confrontational approach to intentionally assist clients in committing themselves to trying out new and more effective ways of responding to the challenges and problems in their lives. This includes getting clients to express a personal commitment to implement new ways of acting in their daily lives during this fourth stage of counseling and therapy. This stage is virtually identical with the fifth stage of the microskills interview.

Practical Implications and Limitations of Adler's Theory

Adler's individual psychology theory is unique in its emphasis on human perfectibility and innate propensity to engage in positive social interests. The teleological or goal-directed nature of humankind that represents the core of Adler's theory sharply contrasts with the deterministic view of humanity put forth by Freud.

These positive aspects of Adler's theory resulted in his strong advocacy for the use of encouragement in counseling and psychotherapy. By serving as a source of encouragement, counselors and therapists implicitly provide clients' with a sense of personal affirmation and hopefulness that is often missing in other traditional psychoanalytic helping approaches (Lewis et al., 2003).

Of all the psychodynamic theories, Adler's has had the most pervasive impact in that it has been extended to other aspects of counseling beyond individual therapeutic interventions and to other professional fields as well. The effects of many of Adler's theoretical concepts are reflected in various forms of group counseling, parent education interventions, and family system counseling strategies.

Adler's writings complement many of the current contributions offered by various multicultural-feminist-social justice counseling advocates in the field today. The positive attention Adler directed toward the psychological needs and social interests of women distinguishes him from most other psychodynamic theorists of his time. In many ways, Adler's theoretical concepts in these areas were precursors of some of the central psychological issues presented by contemporary feminist counseling and psychotherapy theorists. As alluded to earlier, contemporary concepts related to the self-in-relation or the relational self that represent a cornerstone of most feminist counseling theories reflect the importance Adler placed on the connections people make with others.

Adler's social interest concept and his emphasis on the innate human drive to realize an increased sense of one's perfectibility complement the worldviews of persons in other diverse cultural/racial groups. These Adlerian constructs fit well into an African-centered cosmology, as reflected in the Black psychology model referred to as Maat (Obasi, 2002).

While it is important to acknowledge the different ways that Adler's contributions complement the writings of many contemporary feminist and cultural theorists and researchers, it would not be accurate to portray Adler as a vociferous multicultural-feminist-social justice advocate during his time. However, he might well have been at the forefront of the present paradigm shift that is emerging in the fields of counseling and psychology, given the ways in which his writings match the views expressed by many multicultural-feminist-social justice advocates in the field today.

One of the notable limitations of Adler's theory of individual psychology relates to the emphasis he placed on the need to explore the impact of the family constellation and birth order in the helping process. While it is reasonable to assume that it is important to promote a clearer understanding of the ways in which a client's family experiences and birth order unconsciously contribute to the challenges and problems faced in life, an overemphasis of these considerations may lead to an underexamination of other aspects of a client's unconscious. As you will find later in the description of Carl Jung's theory, other aspects of a client's unconscious (such as the personal and collective unconscious) are thought to be equally important when using a psychodynamic approach in counseling and therapy.

Another limitation of Adler's theoretical framework relates to the question of the empirical validation of the central concepts associated with individual psychology. Although researchers have validated Adler's ideas about the impact of birth order on psychological development (Lombardi, 1996), empirical support for other Adlerian concepts and counseling approaches is generally wanting (Seligman, 2001).

While it is important to be cognizant of the weaknesses associated with individual psychology, the tremendous benefits that can be derived from implementing many of Adler's concepts about human development into counseling, psychological, and educational practices outweigh the limitations.

Carl Jung and Jungian Therapy

Carl Gustav Jung was born in Kesswil, Switzerland, on July 26, 1887, to Emile Freiswerk Jung and her evangelical minister husband. Jung had two siblings. His older brother died in his infancy, and his younger sister was born nine years after himself. From his own reports, Jung was a lonely and introverted child who experienced terrifying dreams that helped shaped his later thinking about the role that these psychic phenomena play in psychological development (Jung, 1960, 1964).

Jung's parents had a significant impact on both his personal and professional development. Although a well-respected Christian minister, Jung's father often expressed doubt about his own religious faith. While Jung experienced disappointment in his father's inability to fully accept the religious faith that he ministered, much of the emphasis Jung placed on spirituality as a critical factor in human development can be traced to his father's influence (Schwartz, 1999).

Jung's mother also had an important impact on his later thinking about human development. Seligman (2001) describes this impact in the following way:

> Just as his father seemed to reflect polarization (the minister who was a disbeliever), so did his mother, a woman who followed socially accepted and often repressive standards in her own outward behavior but seemed to have a different almost clairvoyant inner self. The divergent personalities of his parents offered yet another polarity. The concepts of polarities and the persona (the parts of ourselves we show to the world) in Jung's theory very likely originated in his family environment. (p. 101)

As an adolescent, Jung was an avid reader with interest in a broad range of fields. This broad interest led him to study philosophy, anthropology, the occult, and parapsychology on his own. In his early adulthood he attended medical school in Switzerland and initially directed his attention to internal medicine. He subsequently shifted his attention to psychiatry. Upon graduating from medical school as a psychiatrist, he was employed at a psychiatric hospital in Zurich. During this time, he gained experience working with individuals diagnosed as experiencing schizophrenia under the tutelage of Eugene Bleuler, a well-respected pioneer in the area at that time. Shortly thereafter, Jung married Emma Rauschenback, who was the daughter of a wealthy industrialist. The couple had five children—four daughters and a son.

A major turning point in Jung's career occurred in 1907, when Freud invited him to help build the psychoanalytic movement. This invitation was largely due to Jung's defense of Freudian theory in an attack by a professor at the University of Heidelberg (Kelly, 1990). While Freud welcomed Jung into his inner circle as a disciple and eventual successor, these two psychodynamic giants experienced a serious parting of the ways due to a number of major theoretical disagreements (Seligman, 2001). In an effort to distinguish his theoretical approach to counseling and therapy from Freud's psychoanalytic framework, Jung referred to his conceptual framework as **analytic psychology.**

The Jungian Worldview

Carl Jung's analytic psychology differs from Freud's and Adler's theories in a number of ways. First, unlike Freud's emphasis on the negative instinctual nature of human development (which is highlighted in Freud's description of innate sexual and aggressive energies), Jung wrote about people's positive developmental potentials. This aspect of Jung's worldview is grounded in the belief that people realize their human potential by finding ways to have a unique and positive impact in the world (Jung, 1954).

As discussed in Chapter 5, Freud maintained a staunch belief in the overarching impact that libidinal (e.g., sexual and aggressive) energy has on psychological development. This perspective underlies the belief in the biologically determined nature of human development that is reflected throughout much of Freud's psychoanalytic work. Jung, on the other hand, stressed positive, cultural, and strength-based factors in a person's development, maintaining that these factors have an equal if not a more substantial effect on healthy psychological growth.

Another aspect of Jung's work that distinguishes it from both Freud's and Adler's theories relates to the way each of them described the process of psychological development. Freud and Adler argued that an individual's personality development undergoes predictable changes across the life span. For Freud, these changes are manifested in the way individuals deal with the different tasks that are outlined in his psychoanalytic stages (see Chapter 5). Adler, on the other hand, promoted the notion that a person's development can be largely traced to the manner in which one deals with a fixed set of life tasks (as described earlier in this chapter).

The Jungian perspective, in contrast, presents a more flexible and dynamic description of human development. This perspective highlights the notion that people are constantly undergoing various physical, cognitive, emotional, psychological, and spiritual changes throughout their lives. Jung's fluid and dynamic view of human development is consistent with long-standing Buddhist beliefs about the constant changeability of all people (including people's thoughts, feelings, and behaviors) as well as more contemporary insights from quantum physics about the fluidity all animate and inanimate entities in the world as described by quantum physics (Chopra & Simon, 2001; Levine, 2000).

One of the important dynamic factors that Jung directed particular attention to is the powerful and complex interaction of the individual's ego (e.g., one's conscious understanding of the world), personal unconscious, and collective unconscious. Jung's description of the collective unconscious has been the focus of much attention among many psychodynamically oriented counselors and therapists (Jung, 1960).

Another important factor that Jung addressed in his work is the transcendental nature of human development (Jung, 1971). While this aspect of Jung's theoretical framework has been viewed with skepticism by some traditionally trained psychodynamic professionals, it represents a central consideration of multicultural counseling theorists (Fukuyama & Sevig, 1999; Parham, 2002).

Like Freud and Adler, Jung believed that counseling and psychotherapy provide a useful means for people to transcend the unconscious parameters of their personalities and realize untapped dimensions of their potential for psychological development. These three theorists all agreed that it is important to help clients become more conscious of their personal unconscious and the ways in which it impacts their thoughts, feelings, and behavior. Jung greatly expanded the notion of the personal unconscious by postulating a deeper, more universal and collective unconscious that also affects everyone's psychological development.

The Personal Unconscious. Like Freud, Jung believed that each individual possesses a unique **personal unconscious** that develops over one's lifetime. According to Jung (1971), the personal unconscious includes memories of thoughts, feelings, and experiences that have been forgotten or repressed; that have lost their intensity and importance over time; or that have never had enough psychic energy to enter one's consciousness.

Jung agreed with Freud that the personal unconscious exerts much influence over our current thoughts, emotions, and behaviors. He also emphasized that helping individuals become more conscious of the unconscious aspects of their psychic lives is a central dimension of counseling and psychotherapy. However, unlike Freud, Jung had a more positive view of the personal unconscious. While Jung agreed with Freud in acknowledging that the personal unconscious was a holding place for negative and unacceptable psychological images, Jung also believed that this level of the unconscious provides people with a source of creativity and guidance (Seligman, 2001).

Jungian counselors strive to help clients access the creative and guiding potential of their personal unconscious by fostering a greater awareness of the **psychological complexes** that influence their lives.

Psychological complexes represent different types of psychic processes that, although usually unconscious, affect a person's way of thinking, feeling, and being in the world. These complexes have a broad impact on a person's psychological functioning, ranging from minimal disruption to more serious consequences on an individual's personality (Schwartz, 1999).

Commenting further on the meaning and purpose of addressing psychological complexes in counseling, Schwartz (1999) states:

> Jungian counseling aims to separate psychological complexes from the unconscious into conscious awareness. Jung says we all have complexes and the real issue is whether or not they are controlling us. Complexes either repress or promote consciousness, inhibit or inspire, hinder development or provide the seeds for new life. Complexes are like magnets, drawing psychological and archetypal experience into a person's life. They occur where energy is repressed or blocked, point to unresolved problems and weaknesses, and develop from emotional wounds. When a complex is touched, it is accompanied by exaggerated emotional reactions and may also be experienced physically.
>
> A complex does not completely disappear, but the arrangement of energy changes with awareness. The psychic energy caught in the complex is accessed for personality development. No complex should entirely control the personality, but the ego complex dominates during waking life. The particular makeup of a complex is apparent through images pertaining to the unconscious psychological situation occurring in dreams and the synchronous events of waking life. One's destiny can be adversely affected by a complex and psychological issues can remain unresolved for generations. For

example, a woman with a negative father complex may transfer a limited purview into everything male and operate from negatively biased perceptions that are rooted in her personal unconscious (pp. 98–99).

Although the personal unconscious is an important domain to address in counseling and therapy, Jung also believed that the collective unconscious plays an equal and perhaps an even more powerful role in a client's mental health.

The Collective Unconscious. Not only did Jung use his description of psychological complexes to extend Freud's view of psychic functioning, but he also introduced a new and controversial concept into the psychodynamic perspective, which he referred to as the collective unconscious. Jung's description of the **collective unconscious** represents one of the most intriguing aspects of his theoretical worldview (Gilliland & James, 1998). In discussing this dimension of an individual's personality, Jung asserted that it is comprised of a complex, universal, and primordial set of psychic images that are common to all of humanity (Jung, 1960). He referred to these universal psychic images as **archetypes.** In explaining the "collective" nature of the collective unconscious, Jung pointed out that archetypes are transmitted biologically across generations and cultures in the form of memory traces that are located in the cortex of an individual's brain (Jung, 1960).

Adding to this point, Seligman (2001) explains that the collective unconscious is the "storehouse of latent memory traces inherited from the past that predispose people to react to the world in certain ways. The collective unconscious transcends individual experience and the personal unconscious and includes primordial motives or images passed on from our ancestors" (p. 104). The work of Bruce Taub-Bynum (1984, 1999) on the family unconscious (discussed in Chapter 5) closely relates to these ideas.

The Shadow Within. One aspect of the primordial motives associated with our ancestral archetypes that Jung wrote extensively about involves what he referred to as the **shadow.** The shadow represents the dark side of an individual's personality. It includes those motives, images, thoughts, and feelings that we do not wish to acknowledge but that are a part of our psychological constitution. The shadow exists in both the personal and collective unconscious, where we attempt to psychologically hide it from ourselves and others (Jung, 1960, 1971).

Seligman (2001) describes this component of Jung's theoretical worldview:

> The shadow includes morally objectionable traits and instincts and has the potential to create thoughts, feelings, and actions that are socially unacceptable, shameful, and evil. At the same time, the shadow's unrestrained and primitive nature is a wellspring of energy, creativity, and vitality. The shadow is, in a sense, the opposite of the persona. The persona seeks social acceptance and approval, while the shadow embraces the socially reprehensible. (pp. 105–106)

The Family Unconscious: Expanding Jungian Concepts through Multicultural Psychodynamic Theory

Multicultural psychodynamic counseling theorists identify three interrelated levels of unconscious functioning: the individual (Nobles, 1998), the family (Nobles, 1997; Taub-Bynum, 1984), and the collective cultural unconscious (Akbar, 1994; Parham et al., 1999). The **individual unconscious** that is described by multicultural psychodynamic theorists is similar to Jung's personal unconscious. However, from a multicultural perspective, the individual unconscious and the defense mechanisms that are rooted within this level of the psyche are substantially influenced by the values, traditions, and myths that distinguish one's cultural group from others, as well as by the level of personal attachment (e.g., personal identification) that individuals develop toward their cultural group.

Family and Culture. The family is where we first experience and learn our culture. The family unit is the culture bearer, and the nature of the family and its functions varies widely among cultures. Taub-Bynum (1984) speaks of the "powerful affective energies" we experience in the family. The interplay between individual and family affective experience is the formative dialectic of culture. It is not really possible to separate individuals, families, and culture, for their interplay is so powerful and persistent.

The interaction of family and culture is reflected in the psychodynamic life of the individual. When the individual is considered within the expanded context of the **family unconscious,** we readily see how each person's psychodynamic functioning is implicated in the functioning of significant others who share the same field of consciousness, energy, and experience. This interrelationship can be seen in the choice of symptoms and behavior, both somatic and psychological, that are presented in counseling and psychotherapy.

A hologram provides a useful analogy. In a hologram, each image and area in the overall field reflects and dynamically enfolds each other area but from a slightly different angle. That different angle significantly can be seen as the perception and experience of "individuality" in the interdependent family system. Each family member contains the experience of the family and the culture, but each member has varying perceptions and experiences.

The Family and the Collective Cultural Unconscious. According to Taub-Bynum (1984), "the family unconscious is composed of extremely powerful affective (emotional) energies from the earliest life of the individual" (p. 11). This statement is in accord with the description of Jung's personal and collective unconscious but extends these concepts by specifically directing attention to the unconscious domain that develops from our familial experiences. Essentially, our life experience in our family of origin enters our being in both positive and negative ways. Experience in the family (as contrasted with experience solely with a single caregiver) is transmitted to the child and becomes very much a part of the child's being (and later, of course, the adolescent and adult being). Thus, the construction, development, and recognition of the family of origin become of key importance in understanding the individual's development.

There is a marked relationship between these formulations and those of K. Tamase, another multicultural psychodynamic theorist (Tamase, 1998; Tamase & Inui, 2000). Both Taub-Bynum and Tamase maintain that many of the social and environmental constructions of reality the individual absorbs come from the family, which itself is located in a cultural context.

Like Freud and Adler, these multicultural theorists acknowledge the power of the individual unconscious in shaping people's psychological development. Like Jung, they also underscore the power of what they refer to as the **collective cultural unconscious.** Additionally, they emphasize that the family unconscious is yet another vital domain to consider in counseling and therapy situations.

In discussing the notion of the collective cultural unconscious, multicultural theorists (Nobles, 1997, 1998; Parham et al., 1999; Taub-Bynum, 1984) use concepts similar to those presented by Jung (1935). As noted above, Jung describes the collective unconscious as drawing on all the thought and behavior patterns that characterize various cultural groups over time. According to Jung (1935), Nobles (1997), and Taub-Bynum (1984), much of the collective unconscious is the repository of clients' experiences in their families. Consequently, when you work with an individual, his or her family and culture are also present (Nobles, 1997; Parham et al., 1999). From this multicultural psychodynamic frame of reference, the construct of the collective cultural unconscious becomes closely allied with issues of multicultural empathy and understanding (see Chapter 4).

Therapeutic Implications. You as counselor or therapist can assume that the client is in some way acting out his or her family and cultural unconscious. In some cases, the client will present a unique personal construction of the problem, but in other cases, family or cultural influences are more powerful and important than are individual forces.

The microskill of focus is a simple way to approach these complex issues. If a client presents an issue and you focus on that issue by emphasizing personal pronouns ("*You* seem to feel") and "I" statements, the client will talk about the problem on an individual basis. If you focus on the family in connection with the individual, the process of therapy changes ("How did *you* learn that in your *family?*" "How does that experience relate to *your family of origin?*"), and the client will talk about issues from a family orientation.

At the cultural level, the focus changes to the impact of context and culture on the client's development and present worldview ("How does the *Irish* experience of Yankee oppression in Boston relate to how *your* family generated its ideas in the world, and how does that play itself out in *you?*" "What does being *African-American* [or other minority group] have to do with your *family* experience and *your* own view of *yourself?*"). These example questions are designed to illustrate the interrelationship of the individual, the family, and the cultural context; specific questions and clarifications should be appropriate to the context of the interview.

Cheatham (1990) challenges the above constructions by suggesting that counselors not only need to understand what is happening in the client's family and multicultural context, but also need to take action. More specifically, this multicultural theorist asserts that counselors and therapists need to (1) help families deal with the cultural setting which they are a part and (2) work to change a culture that often is more responsible for problems and pathology than are individuals or families.

At a more complex level, Taub-Bynum talks about the intergenerational transmission of symptoms in a family. If you construct a family history/genogram of an alcoholic client, you often find several alcoholics in the family over the generations. Family counseling theory (see Chapter 14) gives central attention to this dynamic.

The story of Kunta Kinte in Alex Haley's popular book *Roots* (1977) illustrates the above point. Kunta Kinte, taken into slavery from Africa, provided his family with an image that played itself out over generations, right to the time when Haley wrote his book. Family members acted out this story over the generations in differing ways, but much of their thinking and behavior could be traced to this ancestor. For example, an upstanding member of the family might be acting out the positive intergenerational family script, whereas another family member might be in trouble with the law and acting out the negative family script. Each of these family members could be said to be engaging in a set of defense mechanisms that could be explained by tracing individual, family, and cultural history.

From both a Jungian and multicultural psychodynamic perspective, these defense mechanisms are used to ward off anxieties that are generated from psychological memories and images anchored within an individual's personal, family, and/or cultural collective unconscious (Taub-Bynum, 1999). Counselors who use Jungian and multicultural psychodynamic helping strategies in their work intentionally strive to assist individuals in developing a new level of self-knowledge that enables clients to transcend the limits of being psychologically encumbered by their personal, family, and/or cultural unconscious (Parham et al., 1999).

The Transcendental Function and Individuation

There is a set of psychological and behavioral goals that is common to most mental health practitioners who use individual counseling and therapy services in their work. These goals typically include assisting clients to experience healthy catharsis of pent-up emotions, gain new insights into their lives, and learn new and more effective ways of addressing their life challenges and problems. Although Jung agreed that these are important aspects of counseling and therapy, he also introduced another important function that counseling and therapy can potentially serve. He referred to this as the **transcendental function** of counseling and therapy.

One of the central purposes of the transcendental function is to assist individuals in becoming more conscious of the psychic tensions that are embedded in what Jung called **psychological opposites.** Jung (1971) indicated that "psychological oppo[site]s are the ineradicable and indispensable preconditions for all psychic life" (p. 169[). He] pointed to the conscious and unconscious aspects as general psychological opposites that need to be reconciled to attain a healthy state of self-realization. He also speci-fied other archetypal opposites common to persons in all cultural groups, which he believed need to be reconciled and integrated to into clients' consciousness if they are to achieve the highest level of psychological health and development. One of the main opposites Jung discussed in this regard relates to the need for individuals to integrate the masculine (**animus**) and feminine (**anima**) archetypal dimensions of their personality (Douglas, 2005).

As a scholar who spent much of his career studying the psychology of people in a broad range of cultures and religions, Jung noted that cultural and religious/spiri-tual beliefs, practices, and **symbols** serve important roles in helping individuals rec-oncile conflicting psychological attitudes and emotions that emerge from **archetypal opposites.** This, in part, occurs in cultural, religious, and spiritual practices that acknowledge the existence of opposing and unseen forces that transcend concrete and commonsense interpretations of life.

The process of reconciling and integrating the psychological and archetypal opposites that Jung wrote about involves the process of **individuation.** From a Jungian worldview, individuation is "an instinctual force that continuously pushes us toward wholeness and realization of our particular meaning in life" (Kaufmann, 1989, p. 120). The growing sense of self-realization that emerges from the indi-viduation and transcendental processes is a hallmark of psychological health and development that guide the work Jungian counselors and therapists do with their clients.

Other Key Jungian Concepts

Like Adler's theory of counseling and therapy, Jung's view of helping is grounded in the belief that people are **teleologically oriented.** As such, Jung believed that people are goal directed. More specifically stated, Jung's theory asserts that people are driven by an innate propensity to realize an integrated sense of who they are as they move from childhood to adolescence to adulthood.

From a Jungian perspective, the process of becoming a psychologically healthy and mature individual fundamentally involves becoming aware of and integrating contrasting dimensions of one's psychic life. Jung referred to these psychic dimen-sions as **psychological types** (Jung, 1971). The psychological types that Jung wrote about represent different ways that people consciously perceive and construct mean-ing of themselves and the world.

Jung used the terms **introvert** and **extrovert** to describe two general psychologi-cal types that are manifested in different "attitudes for perceiving the world and one's relationship to it" (Schwartz, 1999, p. 97). An extrovert is an individual whose inter-est centers on surrounding people and things rather than on her or his inner thoughts and feelings. An introvert focuses on her or his inner thoughts and feelings before responding to the external world. Schwartz points out that "the extrovert is influenced by collective norms, the introvert by subjective factors. Jungian analysts are predominately introverts, as are often those who come for this kind of counseling or psychotherapeutic treatment" (p. 97).

In addition to these two general psychological types, Jung described four psychological functions that determine that way individuals process internal and external stimuli. These four functions help clarify the different psychological types:

1. *Thinking.* People whose thinking function is dominant react cognitively and intellectually, seeking to interpret and understand their interpersonal interactions, cultural experiences, and other life events that affect their psychological development.

2. *Feeling.* The feeling function is the opposite of the thinking function. People whose feeling function is primary react emotionally, focusing on pleasure, dislike, anger, and other feelings stimulated by their life experiences.

3. *Sensation.* Sensation involves receiving and identifying physical stimuli through the senses and relaying them to perceptual consciousness. People who have sensation as their dominant function look at the facts and the substance of their experiences in life, seeking concrete evidence of its meaning and value.

4. *Intuition.* Intuition is the opposite of sensation. People whose intuition is their dominant function rely on hunches about where a stimulus has come from, where it is going, and what its possibilities are to determine their reactions and decisions related to the stimulus.

The Myers-Briggs Type Indicator (MBTI) is a popular psychometric test that provides a measure of the four bipolar psychological functions that are described in Jung's theory: introversion-extroversion, sensing-intuition, thinking-feeling, and judging-perceiving. With appropriate training, counselors and therapists can use the MBTI to guide the approaches they intentionally decide to take in helping clients' transcend their current psychological state as they move to a greater level of self-understanding and individuation.

Jungian Counseling and Therapy Strategies: Applications for Practice

Jungian counselors and therapists keep several fundamental goals in mind when using this theoretical model in practice. These goals include facilitating clients' personality transcendence, transformation, and integration in such a manner as to stimulate a greater conscious understanding of their true selves (Jung, 1960, 1971). To realize their potential for psychological transcendence, transformation, and integration, clients are encouraged to explore and make new sense of material that is anchored in their personal, family, and collective (cultural) unconscious. By becoming more conscious of these unconscious dynamics, clients are able to learn about the ways in which their persona (the socially acceptable side of one's personality), shadow (the socially unacceptable side of one's personality), and psychological opposites impact their personality development and daily functioning. From a Jungian perspective, the new insights and learning gained from these areas in counseling and psychotherapy increase the possibility that clients will be able to experience a greater understanding of their true selves as they realize transcendental, transformative, and integrative individuation.

To achieve these fundamental goals, Jungian counselors and therapists normally assist clients in moving through four stages in the helping process.

Stage 1. Catharsis and Emotional Cleansing

One of the main objectives of the initial stage of Jungian counseling is to develop a positive and trusting relationship with the client that allows her or him to feel safe in expressing feelings about various situations of concern. As the therapeutic alliance strengthens between the client and the counselor, clients are able to establish contact with the feeling tone of their unconscious complexes through the emotional cleansing process, which accompanies the effective catharsis that occurs in this stage of Jungian counseling and therapy.

Rychlak (1973) points out that the catharsis and emotional cleansing that occurs in the first stage of Jungian counseling is similar to the release of feelings about one's problems that often occurs in the confessional rite of Christian religions. Jung (1971) explained that the catharsis and emotional cleansing that occurs in the initial stage of analytic counseling and therapy as well as in the Christian confessional rite are also manifested in the ceremonies, initiatory practices, and rites of passage of many diverse cultural groups.

The catharsis and emotional cleansing that are common to all of these human activities help foster the unfolding of the individuation process. As people are able to move beyond the limits of their persona by openly expressing emotions related to different experiences and problems within a supportive and affirming context, they are able to experience new dimensions of their humanity. The expression of these emotions enables clients in Jungian counseling, just as with those engaging in psychologically cathartic and emotional cleansing rituals in their cultural and religious contexts, to gain a deeper understanding and appreciation of the different psychological forces that impact their lives. They also experience a greater sense of psychological wholeness and realization of their meaning in life (Kaufmann, 1989).

Stage 2. Elucidation

Recognizing that catharsis and emotional cleansing are necessary but insufficient components of successful counseling and therapy, Jung stressed the importance of dealing with other therapeutic challenges in the second stage of the helping process. In the elucidation stage, Jungian counselors help clients construct new meaning of their life situation and problems. This involves offering new interpretations about their clients' physical and psychological symptoms by clarifying how their clients' anima, animus, and shadow as well as their personal, family, and collective cultural unconscious impact their psychological functioning.

Issues related to transference and countertransference are keystones of this stage of Jungian counseling and therapy. The process of assisting clients to become more conscious of the unconscious factors that affect their psychological perspectives often involves the projecting of unconscious thoughts, feelings, and past experiences onto the therapist, as clients bring these psychic memories to the forefront of their consciousness. As transference emerges in Jungian counseling and therapy, counselors are also susceptible to experiencing countertransference, as their own unconscious dormant thoughts, feelings, and psychic memories are stimulated and projected onto clients.

Jung believed it is vital that counselors effectively handle the different types of transference and countertransference that are manifested at this stage in the helping process. It is important to do so, because clients' individuation (e.g., the innate teleological propensity that drives people toward realizing a greater sense of personal wholeness and meaning in life; see Kaufman, 1989) is greatly enhanced when transference and countertransference issues are effectively dealt with at stage 2. To underscore the importance of this point, Jung insisted that counselors and therapists need to participate in analytic therapy themselves when working with their clients. He believed that, in doing so, counselors and therapists are better able to acquire new insights that will enable them to effectively address transference and countertransference issues as they emerge in Jungian counseling and therapy.

Stage 3. Education

The individuation process that was stimulated at stage 2 becomes extended and concretized in new ways of acting that clients are encouraged to manifest in their daily lives. Jung talks about the psychological risks clients experience as they strive to move beyond the familiarity and security of less conscious ways of being. In doing so, they have to break away from habitualized behavioral and thought patterns that provide a sense of personal predictability and control. As clients become more conscious of the many ways they project unconscious thoughts, feelings, and psychic memories onto other persons and situations in stage 2 of Jungian counseling and therapy, they are better positioned to exercise new behaviors that reflect a heightened consciousness and self-understanding.

Jungian counselors and therapists play an important role in the third stage of this helping process by being "supportive and encouraging, helping people to take risks to improve their lives" (Seligman, 2001, p. 109). Unlike other counseling and psychotherapy theorists presented in this book, Jung notes that it is not possible to describe specific counseling techniques that are likely to be effective in helping all clients move through the third stage of his helping framework. Commenting on this issue further, Rychlak (1973) asserts that at this stage "the therapist must now help clients to educate themselves in all aspects of life that have been found lacking. Jung proposes no particular way of doing this, except to say that whatever needs doing will be made plain by this stage of therapy, and the therapist will need to act as a friend, by lending moral support and encouragement to the client's efforts" (pp. 177–178).

Other Jungian experts point out that the first three stages are enough for many clients and therapy will be ended at the third stage. This occurs when clients feel their lives have been sufficiently enriched as a result of acquiring new knowledge and insights that enable them to realize a greater semblance of psychological balance (Gilliland & James, 1998). Jung (1954) forthrightly responds to this issue by stating that for some clients, "to educate them to normality would be their worst nightmare because their deepest need is to march to the tune of a different drummer" (p. 70). Understanding the true uniqueness that underlies the "abnormal" lives of these clients challenges therapists to encourage them to plunge into the fourth and most complex stage of Jungian counseling and therapy (Gilliland & James, 1998).

Stage 4. Transformation

Gilliland and James (1998) assert that the final stage of Jungian counseling is "unlike any other in psychotherapy" (p. 86). At this stage, clients work toward developing a new level of self-realization by increasing their capacity for personal transformation. The increased individuation and transformative processes that occur in stage 4 of Jungian counseling and therapy unfold as the client struggles to learn more about the shadow side of her or his personality.

Learning about the shadow side of one's personality necessitates a dialogue with the ego (the conscious domain of one's personality) and the self (the personal, familial, and collective cultural unconscious domains of one's personality). Jungian therapists can facilitate this dialogue by helping clients become increasing aware of the role their persona (the socially acceptable side of one's personality) plays in defending against becoming more aware of the shadow side of their personality.

This is a very challenging and difficult therapeutic task that requires a great deal of time and concentrated effort from both the client and the therapist. In successfully achieving this task, clients are able to experience a greater level of psychological individuation and realize new aspects of their human potential through the transformative process that characterizes the fourth stage in Jungian counseling and therapy.

Throughout the process of Jungian counseling and especially in the fourth stage, counselors and therapists work to assist clients to reduce the threshold of their current state of consciousness so that unconscious memories and images can emerge and ultimately become integrated into their consciousness. Jungian counselors and therapists use a broad range of intervention strategies to facilitate this consciousness-raising experience in the helping process. This includes identifying various images and symbols that emerge in clients' consciousness as they proceed through the four

sional Development Extension

Adlerian and Jungian Theories in eling Practice

Counselors and therapists often use a combination of approaches when working with clients. The following case demonstrates how a university counselor utilized both Adlerian and Jungian concepts with one client. Both approaches incorporate techniques aimed at helping clients develop greater understanding of themselves so they can make decisions that have a positive effect on their lives.

Habib, a 21-year-old Arab-American college student, went to the university student counseling center seeking help with a general sense of depression that he started experiencing shortly after leaving home to attend school. During his first session, Habib discussed his apprehension in getting counseling, saying that he feared other people would think he was either crazy or weak because he could not deal with his depression on his own. He stated further that he was a happy and highly motivated person before coming to college but that now he found himself becoming depressed, withdrawn from others, and less interested in studying or even attending classes.

Habib's counselor was trained in both Adlerian and Jungian theories and decided to use Adler's teleological principle to first address Habib's apprehension about counseling. The counselor did so by explaining that another way to think about people who seek counseling is that their taking this action was purposeful and goal directed. Habib said that he thought that was an interesting idea and wanted to hear more about it.

As Habib demonstrated more comfort and interest in the discussion, the counselor described Adler's concepts of social interest and belongingness. Both ideas resonated with Habib, and he said he experienced much more interest in and belongingness with other people before coming to college. As he spoke, Habib noted that

his social interest and sense of belongingness was directly tied to the Muslim community where he resided.

Recognizing the important role this community played in his life, the counselor informed Habib about two mosques located fairly close to the university. The counselor then asked Habib if he would be willing to visit either of the mosques and then talk about his experiences as part of his "homework" for the next counseling session.

After Habib agreed to do this "homework," the counselor and Habib brainstormed other practical things he could do to regain his motivation and involvement with others. This resulted in Habib agreeing to attend 90 percent of his scheduled classes and doing at least three things with his roommates during the upcoming week.

At the next counseling session, Habib reported feeling less depressed. He attributed some of this progress to the fact that he had attended all of his classes and had done a "couple of things" with his roommates during the week. He also indicated that much of the change was tied to the fact that he had attended two religious activities at one of the mosques and had met several people his age who shared similar religious beliefs and values. Habib went on to say, "It sure helped to attend the services at the mosque and meet people my age there. I felt a lot like I do when I am at home."

In an effort to build on the positive outcomes, the counselor talked about Jung's concept of the collective unconscious. As the counselor began to explain the deep unconscious psychological connections that constitute Jung's collective unconscious, Habib's face lit up. "I know what you are talking about. I have met Muslims to whom I feel very connected, although I have only met them for a short period of time."

During the next two counseling sessions, the counselor helped Habib learn about other Adlerian and Jungian concepts. This included exploring Adler's private logic (e.g., the way individuals think and feel about their purpose in life) and exploring some of Jung's archetypes.

Together they explored the degree to which Habib thought these concepts might have personal relevance for his own life and the challenges he currently faced.

The client ended his final session by voicing appreciation for the counselor's assistance in helping him overcome his depressed feelings and in assisting him to learn about Adlerian and Jungian principles, which he said "made a lot of sense to him."

By exploring Jungian and Adlerian concepts, Habib learned about the importance of extending his social interests beyond college. He came to understand what gave him satisfaction and fulfillment and became more motivated to identify specific strategies to keep such connections in his life.

stages. It also involves exploring the symbolic meaning of clients' fantasies and making interpretations about dreams clients may recall in counseling sessions.

Dream interpretation is a particularly important intervention that Jungian counselors use to assist clients in becoming more conscious of their personal, family, and collective cultural unconscious. Although you may not seek intensive training in dream analysis in your professional career, it is useful to develop some facility in helping clients explore and make sense of their dreams if you decide to use this aspect of Jungian counseling in your work. Counselors and therapists can develop basic dream analysis skills by taking time to analyze their own dreams from time to time. Competency-Building Activity 6.2 on page 176 is provided to assist you in exercising your dream analysis skills and interpretative abilities. This activity is designed to help you in thinking about the meaning of your own dreams. By completing this activity, you may feel more comfortable helping some of your clients to talk about the meaning of their dreams, when appropriate. In doing so, you may assist them in becoming more conscious of unconscious aspects of their psychic lives. From an ethical perspective it is important to emphasize that this competency-building activity is **not** designed to make you a dream analysis expert.

Practical Implications and Limitations of Jung's Theory

Jung's interest in Eastern philosophy, mystical religions, and cultural mythology is reflected in many aspects of his theory of analytical psychology. These interests have much relevance for people from diverse groups and backgrounds, whose cultural worldviews and religious/spiritual beliefs do not resonate with many concepts embedded in much of Western psychology. Thus, from a multicultural perspective, Jung's helping theory provides more affirmation for the legitimacy of many indigenous healing practices that have heretofore been viewed with much skepticism by traditionally trained counselors and psychologists (Moodley & West, 2005).

As noted earlier in this chapter, Jung's theory of counseling and therapy may be particularly useful to implement with clients who reflect the sort of psychological maturity and intellectual capabilities that are necessary to comprehend such complex concepts as one's persona, shadow, psychological complexes, and personal, family, and collective unconscious. However, it should also be noted that much of Jung's

Competency-Building Activity 6.2

Analyzing Your Dreams

Step 1. *Commit yourself to analyzing your dreams over a five-day period.* To do so you will need to keep a notebook close to your bed and write each dream you recall having over five consecutive days in your notebook as soon as you awake. Do not become frustrated if you cannot recall your dream on any of the five days you have set aside to do this exercise. What is important is to write down as much of the dream as you can recall immediately on awakening and to do so for five consecutive days.

Step 2. *Set aside 30 minutes when you can review the content of the dreams that you wrote down in your notebook.* Make sure the 30 minutes you set aside will be a time when you will not be interrupted and can fully attend to the dream images you recorded in your notebook.

Step 3. *Ask yourself the following questions and record your answers in your notebook:*

- What general thoughts and feelings are generated from reviewing your dream images?

- Are there any specific images, themes, and/or symbols that you can identify that seem to repeat themselves in your dreams? If so, what meaning can you give to these repeated images, themes, and/or symbols?

- What, if anything, do your dreams say to you about your personal unconscious?

- Given your understanding of Jung's theory, can you identify any symbols, themes, or images that were manifested in your dreams that might reflect a part of your collective unconscious?

In responding to the last question, it is useful to think about some of the archetypal images that are commonly revealed in people's dreams. This includes, but is not limited to, dreams about persons who represent the archetypes of the mother (e.g., nurturing and caring persons in one's dreams), warrior (authoritarian, intimidating dream images), magician (magical, integrating, and healing dream images), and teacher (dreams that include images of persons or animals who are instructive, information giving, and/or directive).

Personal insecurities are commonly manifested by dreams in which one sees oneself falling or appearing naked in public settings. The shadow is frequently revealed in images that reflect socially inappropriate behaviors or other symbolic dream images.

Step 4. *Reflect on any new insights you may have gained from completing the first three steps.* It may also be helpful to consider how you might use any new insights you gained from completing these steps in changing the way you act in your life. The behavioral changes you decide to try to make will reinforce your learning from this activity and may help you increase the individuation process that Jung describes in his theory of analytic psychology.

When you have completed this competency-building activity, take a few minutes to write down your reactions to this exercise; then add your written reactions to your personal/professional development portfolio. This will enable you to keep an ongoing record of your professional development.

thinking about the importance of helping clients learn about the symbolic meaning of their behaviors has been incorporated into various forms of play therapy and sand therapy with children.

Another important implication of Jung's theory involves his positive and growth-oriented view of human development. Unlike many of his contemporaries, who used pathological terms to describe clients' problems, Jung used nonpathological constructs to define the challenges his clients faced in life. In doing so, he viewed clients' depressed, angry, and confused experiences as unconscious messages that provide individuals a means to greater health and personal individuation rather than as indicators of mental illness. This aspect of Jung's theory influenced the thinking of many other existential, humanistic, and Gestalt counseling theorists who followed him.

Despite these positive aspects of Jung's work, his theory of counseling and therapy is not without notable limitations. One of the apparent limitations relates to his dense and challenging writing style, which is complicated by specialized terminology (Seligman, 2001).

Jung does not provide clearly spelled-out helping tools, counseling techniques, or psychotherapeutic techniques that are easily accessible to practitioners. Also, mastery of this theoretical approach requires extensive training and supervision. All of these factors contribute to the fact that Jungian counseling and therapy has not been as extensively researched as many of the other theories described in this book.

From a multicultural-feminist-social justice counseling perspective, Jung's theory reflects a major weakness that is similar to the other traditional frameworks that have dominated the mental health professions. This weakness relates to the fact that while Jungian counseling and therapy directs much attention to clients' inner psychic lives, little effort is aimed at addressing the various environmental conditions, injustices, and forms of cultural oppression that are known to adversely affect human development and healthy psychological functioning.

Despite the limitations noted in Jung's analytical psychology, his theoretical contributions have had a significant impact on the work of many counselors and psychologists. The Professional Development Extension on page 174 discusses one of the most well-known offshoots of Jungian theory.

Summary

Thinking back to the beginning of this chapter, you may recall that we outlined several goals that guided the knowledge and skill-building exercises presented in above sections. These chapter goals included

- fostering an increased understanding of the Adlerian and Jungian theories of counseling and psychotherapy

- assisting you in exercising some of the skills associated with Alfred Adler's and Carl Jung's helping theories

- deepening your thinking on the strengths and limitations of Adlerian and Jungian counseling from a multicultural-feminist-social justice perspective.

- expanding your understanding of some of the ways that Adlerian and Jungian concepts can be used in other aspects of your work

We hope you feel that you have achieved the above-listed goals as a result of completing this chapter. In doing so, you are likely to now possess (1) a greater understanding of the ways in which Adler's and Jung's work has contributed to the ongoing evaluation of the first force (*psychodynamic counseling and therapy*) in the mental health professions; (2) a deeper appreciation of the relevance of Adlerian and Jungian theories from a multicultural-feminist perspective; and (3) an increased sense of confidence in using some of the helping strategies, skills, and techniques associated with these two psychodynamic theoretical frameworks in counseling and therapy settings as well as in other professional situations in which you are involved.

Multimedia Resources for This Chapter

The following online resource offers video and other resources of particular relevance to this chapter of your text.

MyHelpingLab

If a MyHelpingLab passcode was included with your textbook and you have activated your passcode:

- go to **www.ablongman.com/myhelpinglab**
- enter the "Counseling" area of the site by clicking on that tab
- select "Video Lab" from the toolbar to the left of the page
- select "MyHelpingLab Videos by Theoretical Approach"
- select "Adlerian" and "Adlerian Play" modules to view various video clips of a therapist using these approaches with clients

Cognitive-Behavioral Counseling and Therapy

This chapter is designed to:

1. Foster a greater understanding of the development of cognitive-behavior therapy (CBT) as an important force in the mental health professions.

2. Stimulate new knowledge of the evolving worldview of CBT, which has moved from an emphasis on observable behavior and action to include the inner world of cognitions.

3. Point out the multicultural implications of CBT theory and its practice.

4. Present central constructs of CBT that are basic to both behavioral and cognitive interventions.

5. Enable you, through practice exercises, to become familiar with practical strategies and skills in CBT.

Introduction

Currently the most frequently used counseling and therapy orientation in practice, cognitive-behavioral therapy (CBT) has had considerable research and clinical experience that attest to its effectiveness and ability to produce significant change among clients. One of the reasons for this is that CBT is an action theory that is closely tied to direct interviewing practice. Thus, this chapter is unique in that the space given to theory is less than that given to the many specific and highly practical strategies that CBT has developed over the years. Whether or not you make CBT your central helping approach, you are likely to find yourself using many of the techniques and strategies presented in this chapter in your own practice.

Cognitive-behavioral therapy (CBT) constitutes the second major force in the fields of counseling and psychology. The force is grounded in a theoretical worldview that is significantly different from the psychodynamic force described in Chapters 5 and 6. Among the key theoretical assumptions that distinguish CBT from the psychodynamic and existential-humanistic (Chapters 9 and 10) perspectives is the belief that

- the proper concern of counseling and therapy should primarily focus on clients' observable behavior and their responses to life, not on a person's unresolved unconscious issues (which CBT counselors believe cannot be meaningfully defined)

- people are born as "blank slates" and that whatever people learn to do (meaning all behavior) depends on their interactions and experiences with the environment
- changes in behavior (i.e., learning) follow the Law of Effect. Thorndike (1905) defined this law by stating that "behavior that is followed by satisfying consequences will be more likely to be repeated and behavior that is followed by unsatisfying consequences will be less likely to be repeated" (p. 74)
- changes in behavior or learning can occur automatically as people discover contingency in relationships between sequences of events and behaviors, which is also called associative learning (Wolpe, 1990)

A more recent development has been the acknowledgment that even some behaviors that are not directly observable can be addressed using cognitive behavioral practices. For example, **self-talk** refers to words and ideas that occur in the client's head that are only available by what the client verbalizes. Research and clinical practice has shown that many behavioral strategies can change the way individuals think. And when they think differently, they may act differently.

Cognitive-Behavioral Therapy: An Overview of Behaviorism

To understand the emergence of the second force in counseling and psychology, you need to understand the four stages that mark the development of this major theoretical force. This understanding begins with the first three stages, which represent the behavioral aspects of CBT: classical conditioning theory, operant conditioning theory, and social learning theory.

Classical Conditioning Theory: Pavlov and Watson

The first stage in the evolution of CBT can be traced to the work of the early learning theorists. Some of the most notable learning theorists who had a significant impact in the development of behavior psychology include Ivan Pavlov (1927), John B. Watson (1925), and Joseph Wolpe (1982, 1990).

His research with dogs led Pavlov (1927) to be among the first theorists to write about a specific type of learning that became known as **classical conditioning.** According to this Russian physiologist, classical conditioning takes part in three phases. First, an unconditioned stimuli (US) (e.g., a piece of meat) was presented to hungry dogs. This resulted in an unconditioned response (UR) (e.g., a salivation response by the dogs).

Second, Pavlov regularly introduced a neutral stimulus (e.g., the ringing of a bell) with the US (e.g., the piece of meat), which resulted in the UR (a salivation response).

Third, over a period of time in which the neutral stimulus (the ringing bell) was matched with the US (the piece of meat), Pavlov found that the dogs became conditioned to salivate to the ringing of the bell alone (even when the piece of meat was not presented). (See Figure 7.1.)

Figure 7.1 The Three Phases of Classical Conditioning

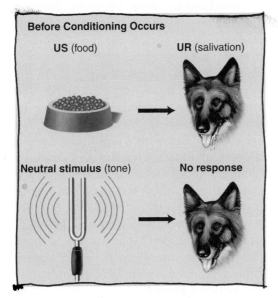

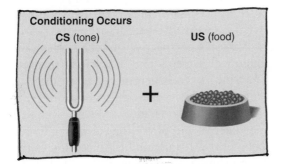

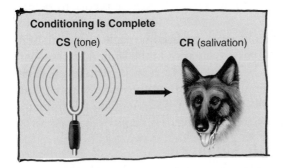

Before conditioning occurs, the CS does not lead to a conditioned response, but the US does.

Then the CS is paired with the US—here, the tone is sounded and then the food is presented.

Classical coditioning is complete when the CS elicits the conditioned response—here, the dog salivates after hearing the tone.

Source: S. M. Kosslyn & R. S. Rosenberg, *Psychology in Context* (3rd ed., 2006). Needham Heights, MA: Allyn and Bacon. Reprinted by permission.

When this occurred, Pavlov asserted that a new kind of learning had taken place. This new learning (or classical conditioning) occurred when the dogs manifested what Pavlov referred to as a conditioned response (CR) (e.g., the automatic salivation of the hungry dogs) to what now was a conditioned stimulus (CS) (e.g., the ringing of a bell without the presentation of a piece of meat).

John Watson (1925) expanded Pavlov's learning theory by applying the principles of classical conditioning to humans, most famously to a young boy named Albert. In his experiments with Albert, Watson first introduced an unconditioned stimulus (e.g., a loud noise), which resulted in an unconditioned response (e.g., an automatic startle response).

When the loud noise was routinely matched with a conditioned stimulus (the introduction of a white rat), Albert eventually learned to respond to the presentation of the white rat with a startled response without the accompaniment of a loud bell. Watson also pointed out that the new learning (which was manifested by the conditioned response) not only occurred when a white rat was presented, but this CR also became generalized to the presentation of other similar objects like white cotton. While this research provides important information that helps explain human learning, it also can help you to understand why the early stages of the behavioral approach brought about considerable resistance among many people. Needless to say, this type of research would be considered unethical today.

Watson's research findings led him to be recognized as the originator of the major theory of psychology known as **behaviorism.** This theoretical perspective attempts to trace all behavior to physiological responses to various types of stimuli. Watson's research findings and theoretical writings were also precursors to the newly emerging field of neuropsychology. Like Watson's perspective of behaviorism, neuropsychology describes humans as mechanical systems that essentially respond to the world according to the biological "wiring" of their nervous systems. Fundamentally speaking, both behaviorism and neuropsycholgy suggest that we become who we are through our physiological responses to the environment.

Despite using his mechanistic perspective and physiological wiring hypothesis to explain human development and behavior, Watson paid little attention to the impact of heredity and instead focused on environmental influences. As a result of embracing this mechanistic view of human development, Watson considered alternative psychological theories and particularly Freud's psychoanalytic theory to be unscientific and even mystical.

Watson eventually left academic work to become vice president of J. Walter Thompson, one of the largest advertising agencies in the United States. Many advertising principles that continue to be in use today rest on Watsonian behaviorism. However, it is also apparent that Freud's views about the unconscious are also incorporated in the strategies many advertising companies employ to stimulate interest among potential consumers who view their advertisements in the media.

Operant Conditioning Theory: B. F. Skinner

The second stage in the evolution of the CBT was largely propelled by the work of B. F. Skinner, who built on Watson's legacy. Skinner's (1953, 1969) theoretical worldview suggests that humans can have the closest approximation to "freedom" through recognizing that they can control and shape behavior in their culture and families if they choose. This perspective is referred to as **operant conditioning** and is grounded in the belief that we can choose what behavior to reinforce in our own lives. According to Skinner's behavior theory, four types of operant conditioning exist: **positive reinforcement, negative reinforcement, punishment,** and **extinction.**

Positive Reinforcement. In positive reinforcement, a particular behavior is strengthened by experiencing a positive condition. As Skinner noted in his research, a hungry rat presses a bar in its cage and receives food. The food is a positive condition for the hungry rat. The rat presses the bar again, and again receives food. The rat's behavior of pressing the bar is thus strengthened by the consequence of receiving food. From operant conditioning theory, it is believed that that a rat learns to control or direct its behavior to ensure that positive conditions or outcomes will continue to ensue from such actions. (See Figure 7.2.)

Negative Reinforcement. Negative reinforcement, on the other hand, results when a particular behavior is strengthened by the consequence of stopping or avoiding a negative condition. Skinner described how this form of learning occurs by reporting on the reaction of a rat that was given a mild electrical shock on its feet when it was placed in a cage. The shock is a negative condition for the rat. However, the rat is able to press a bar in the cage that stops the electrical shock. Shortly thereafter, the rat receives another shock and, on pressing the bar again, stops the shock from occurring once again. Skinner concluded that the rat learned to associate the pressing of the bar in the cage with the alleviation of a negative condition. This principle resulted in his definition of negative reinforcement in his theory of operant conditioning.

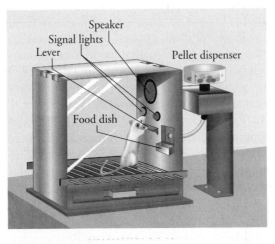

Figure 7.2 Skinner Box
Source: S. M. Kosslyn & R. S. Rosenberg, *Psychology in Context* (3rd ed., 2006). Needham Heights, MA: Allyn and Bacon. Reprinted by permission.

Punishment. Skinner also noted that punishment often contributes to learning. From the perspective of operant conditioning theory, the term *punishment* describes those behaviors that are weakened as a result of experiencing negative conditions in the environment. For example, a rat presses a bar in its cage and immediately receives a mild electrical shock. The electrical shock is a negative condition for the rat. The rat presses the bar again and again experiences the negative condition by receiving another shock. On further observation, Skinner noted that the rat's continued behavior of pressing the bar was weakened by the consequence of receiving a shock each time that action was initiated by the rat.

Extinction. Skinner also introduced the concept of extinction to behavioral psychology. This concept describes behavior that is weakened or ceases to be elicited as a result of not experiencing a positive or a negative condition in the environment. Skinner's experiments demonstrated how extinction occurred when a rat presses a bar in a cage and nothing happened. That is, neither a positive nor a negative condition resulted when the rat initiated this behavior. Skinner observed that the pressing of the bar in the cage was greatly weakened and in many instances completely extinguished when the rats experienced neither a positive nor a negative outcome from this initiating behavior.

Although Skinner's experiments were primarily done with animals in highly controlled experimental settings, his operant conditioning theory gained much popularity and was applied in many human settings during the 1950s and 1960s. This included the incorporation of many of his behavior psychology concepts in education settings, psychiatric hospitals, prisons, and workplaces.

Although there is a tendency today to downplay the importance of Skinner's influence and methods, his contributions have had a lasting impact on the work counselors and psychologists do at the present time. Skinner's emphasis on observable behavior remains foundational to behavioral therapy and to much of cognitive-behavioral therapy at the present time. In addition, applied behavioral analysis, a specific analysis of behavioral sequences used by many mental health practitioners in the field today (discussed in greater detail later), is based on Skinner's work. Finally, the microskills approach of noting specific behaviors engaged in by therapists was lauded by Skinner as making a mystical activity clear and observable (Skinner, 1969; personal communication to Allen Ivey). The clarity in describing effective and ineffective counseling skills and therapeutic strategies—the cornerstone of the microskills model—fits well into Skinner's views about the importance of identifying the specific behaviors that have a positive impact on the way clients respond in counseling and therapy.

Despite the practical utility of behavioral psychology, critics point to a particular limitation of this psychological perspective. This criticism centers around the fact that Skinner directed little attention to internal mental processes and cognitions and focused instead on direct, observable behavior. Recognizing that human development, learning, and behavior is too complex to be fully explained by the stimulus-response contingencies Skinner outlined in his theory, other learning theorists sought to provide a more comprehensive explanation of the way people learn and behave. This resulted in the third stage of the evolution of the CBT—the emergence of social learning theory.

Social Learning Theory: Albert Bandura

Although Albert Bandura was significantly influenced by the theoretical perspectives of all of the above-mentioned behaviorists, he recognized that people commonly exhibit behaviors that are rooted in factors that go beyond an interest in simply earning a reward or avoiding a negative environmental condition. Seeking a more comprehensive explanation of the way people behave, Bandura began a series of field studies at Stanford University in 1953. These studies led to the formation of his theory of social learning and aggression.

Working with Richard Walters, his first doctoral student at Stanford, Bandura directed his attention to researching antisocial aggression in boys who came from intact homes in advantaged residential areas. These researchers intentionally selected youngsters from intact families and economically advantaged backgrounds to demonstrate that factors other than adverse familial and socioeconomic conditions helped to spawn behavior problems in these youngsters. This research, which underscored the paramount role of modeling in human behavior, led to a series of additional studies into the determinants and mechanisms of what Bandura called **observational learning.**

Modeling. Bandura and Walters found that hyperaggressive adolescents often had parents who modeled hostile attitudes. Although the parents would not tolerate aggression in the home, they demanded that their sons be tough and settle disputes with peers physically if necessary. When this resulted in their sons getting into trouble at school, the parents sided with their sons against the school staff. These parents not only displayed aggression toward the school system but also toward the other youngsters, whom they believed were giving their sons a difficult time (Bandura, 1976).

From this research, Bandura concluded that the aggressive behavior of these youngsters was better explained by the modeling of their parents' hostile attitudes and aggressive actions rather than by the tenets of classical or operant conditioning theories. Bandura further explained that, for these aggressive adolescents, the vicarious influence of seeing a model meting out punishment outweighed the suppressive effect of receiving punishment when behaving in aggressive ways themselves.

These findings contradicted the Freudian assumption that direct parental punishment would internally inhibit children's expression of aggressive drives (Freud, 1982). Bandura's research findings also conflicted with Skinner's views of negative reinforcement and punishment. His research in this area resulted in the formation of **social learning theory,** which is outlined in his first three books: *Adolescent Aggression* (Bandura, 1959), *Social Learning and Imitation* (Bandura, 1962), and *Social Learning and Personality Development* (Bandura, 1975).

Bandura continued to extend previous thinking about behaviorism by conducting additional studies that tested his social learning theory in other situations. As was the case with his research on aggressive adolescents, other studies focused on ways people learn by observation and modeling. His research endeavors in these areas included studies that Bandura did with Dorrie and Sheila Ross on social modeling among children, which involved the now-famous inflated plastic Bobo doll.

The children who participated in the Bobo doll studies were exposed to social models that demonstrated either violent or nonviolent behaviors toward the rebounding Bobo dolls. Children who viewed violent models in these studies subsequently displayed novel forms of aggression toward the Bobo dolls. In contrast, children who observed models who exhibited nonviolent behaviors to the Bobo dolls rarely exhibited violent behaviors themselves when left on their own. (See Figure 7.3.)

The results of these studies helped to validate his concept of observational learning. This concept was used to explain the different behaviors that the children in the Bobo doll studies manifested in the absence of direct reinforcements. In this way, Bandura and his colleagues demonstrated that children could learn new patterns of behavior vicariously, without actually performing the observed behaviors or receiving rewards from others for manifesting specific behaviors.

Bandura's work created much controversy both in and outside of the field of psychology. For example, his findings have been consistently attacked by television executives. It is likely that he would be attacked today by the supporters of video games, especially violent video games, in light of the implications of his concept of observational learning on people's behavior.

The work Bandura did in this area has since resulted in the generation of an amazingly extensive body of additional research that validates that what people see, they often do. It is clear that violence in the media and in the video game world are highly influential in the psychosocial and behavioral development of children and adolescents today. Despite the findings by Bandura and other behavior scientists who demonstrate that there is a linkage between observational learning and the manifestation of violent behaviors, there exists consistent denial of this fact from corporate

Figure 7.3 Bandura's Bobo Doll
Source: S. M. Kosslyn & R. S. Rosenberg, *Psychology in Context* (3rd ed., 2006). Needham Heights, MA: Allyn and Bacon. Reprinted by permission.

executives and other media professionals. This denial is partially fueled by the large profits generated from the marketing of violent media products, in spite of the evidence that Bandura's observational learning concept helps account for the increasing level of violence that is manifested among many children and adolescents in our contemporary society.

Bandura's research findings in this area led him to conclude that modeling was indeed a powerful and pervasive process that accounted for much learning that people experience. This theory was particularly discordant with the behaviorist views in vogue at the time, which asserted that learning is a consequence of positive reinforcement, negative reinforcement, or different forms of punishment, as defined by Skinner and other operant conditioning advocates. Until that time, behaviorally oriented psychologists focused almost exclusively on learning through the consequences of one's actions.

However, Bandura now showed that the tedious and hazardous process of trial-and-error learning could be shortcut through social modeling. The expanded views Bandura gained as a result of conducting ongoing research in social learning also led him to distinguish between the cognitive effects of modeling on **behavioral acquisition** and the motivational effects of rewards on **imitative performance.**

Self-Regulation. Later in his career, Bandura launched a research program that focused on children's self-regulatory capabilities. This line of research led to the formation of his concept of **human agency,** in which people are viewed as self-initiating, self-regulatory, and self-reflective organisms, not just entities reactive to environmental influences.

Bandura worked with another one of his doctoral students, Carol Kupers, in studying various dimensions of human agency. These efforts resulted in an increased understanding of the ways in which individualized performance standards and self-rewarding processes stimulated human agency. Their research in these areas included using a bowling game where children were able to reward themselves with candy for whatever performance level they felt merited a self-reward.

The children in these studies watched other adults or peer models bowl and reward themselves according to either a high- or a low-performance standard that they established for themselves. When it was time for the young research participants to bowl, Bandura and Kupers noted that those children who witnessed a model that set a high standard for a self-reward adopted a more stringent performance criterion for their own self-reward.

In comparison, those children who watched a model that set lower-performance standards set similarly low-performance standards in order to gain their own self-rewards. Bandura also noted that children who established high-performance standards for themselves generally achieved more when they received self-rewards in comparison to other children who were provided with external rewards when striving to attain similar performance standards (Bandura, 1982).

These studies led Bandura and his colleagues to build on initial thinking about human agency by including a new concept referred to as **self-efficacy** (Bandura,

1997). Bandura's ongoing research on human agency and self-efficacy led him to discover that people's thinking about their ability to control what they perceive as threats to themselves is accompanied by specific physiological changes.

The physiological changes that Bandura noted to ensue from a heightened sense of self-efficacy included the release of increased levels of neurotransmitters and stress-related hormones into the bloodstream. Bandura also found that people can regulate the level of neurotransmitters and stress-related hormones released into the bloodstream by altering their thinking about their own self-efficacy in different environmental situations.

Bandura's research and theoretical contributions in all of these areas represent important contributions in the evolution of the CBT force in counseling and psychology. His many discoveries of the role that cognitions play in learning and behavior has been extended further by other CBT theorists as well. These theorists built on Bandura's work by outlining additional ways that people's thinking (cognitions) could be effectively addressed in counseling and psychotherapy situations to promote new and more satisfying ways of acting.

Behavioral Counseling and Therapy Strategies: Applications for Practice

Before exploring the cognitive side of CBT further, it is important to understand the various ways traditional behavioral concepts can be used in a variety of counseling, psychotherapeutic, and other helping situations.

Applied Behavioral Analysis

One of the basic competencies counselors and psychologists need to acquire to conduct behavioral counseling and therapy effectively involves their ability to complete an **applied behavioral analysis.** Briefly defined, applied behavioral analysis is a systematic method of collaboratively examining the client and the client's environment in which client and mental health practitioner jointly develop specific interventions that are aimed at altering the client's life conditions. Successful applied behavioral analysis rests on four foundations: the relationship between the counselor and the client, the definition of the problem through operationalization of specific client behaviors, the understanding of the full context of the problem through functional analysis, and the establishment of socially important goals for the client.

The Client-Counselor Relationship. It was once thought that those who engaged in behavioral approaches were cold, distant, and mechanical. A classic research study in 1975 by Sloane and others forever changed this view, however. This research examined expert therapists from a variety of theoretical orientations and found that behavioral therapists exhibited higher levels of empathy, self-congruence, and interpersonal contact than other therapists and that levels of warmth and regard were approximately the same for practitioners from different theoretical orientations. Behavioral therapists may be expected to be as interested in rapport and human growth as those working from any other orientation.

Behavioral therapists have very specific methodologies and goals. In addition to working toward building positive rapport with their clients, behavioral therapists engage in careful structuring of the interview. They are willing and eager to share their plans collaboratively with the client in the expectation that the client will fully share with them in the therapy process.

Relationship variables have differing meanings, according to clients' individual and cultural backgrounds. With this in mind, it is important that eye contact, body language, vocal tone, and verbal following be culturally appropriate. Too many reflective listening skills can result in mistrust unless culturally appropriate sharing is included. A relationship can develop slowly or quickly, depending on the client's cultural background and the counselor's approach to helping.

For instance, working with urban Aboriginals in Australia or with the Inuit or Dene in the Arctic, the professional helper may take half an interview or more simply to become acquainted, learn the family system, share personal anecdotes, and so on before trying to find out what the client wants to talk about. At the other extreme, a relationship between therapist and client can develop quickly with many urban White professionals, who can be fully intimate and open with a therapist immediately on entering the room.

Operationalization of Behavior. Clients often bring to the therapist clouded, confused, and abstract descriptions of their issues. You can help clients become much clearer if you focus on the concreteness and specifics of their behaviors. The temptation for many counselors is to think and talk abstractly. **Operationalization of behavior** will help you and the client "get down to specific cases" and discover what is really happening in the client's life. Consider, for example, that you have a client who is depressed and talks about feeling sad. In psychodynamic therapy, you might seek to discover the roots of the sadness, whereas in cognitive or humanistic therapies, you might want to help the client alter the way he or she thinks about the world. However, in behavioral therapy, particularly with applied behavioral analysis, the task is to determine what the client does specifically and concretely when he or she feels depressed, as the following dialogue illustrates:

Counselor: You say you feel depressed. Could you tell me some of the specific things you do when you are depressed?

Client: Well, I cry a lot. Some days I can't get out of bed. I feel sad most of the time.

Counselor: When you say, "I feel sad most of the time," how does your body feel?

Contrary to some stereotypes, behaviorally oriented therapists are very attuned to their clients' emotions and stress the importance of emotional issues in the helping process. Many therapists would settle for the client's description of "sad," but here special effort is taken to make the emotion more based in actual sensorimotor experience.

Client: It feels tense and drawn all over, almost like little hammers are beating me from inside. It gets so bad sometimes that I can't sleep.

The counselor's two questions have made the behaviors related to the general construct of depression far more obvious. Crying, failure to get out of bed, feelings of bodily tension, and inability to go to sleep are operational behaviors that can be seen, measured, and even counted. The feelings of sadness, however, are still somewhat vague, and further operationalization of the sentence "I feel sad most of the time" might result in the following, more specific, description of behaviors:

Counselor: A short time ago you said you feel sad much of the time. Could you elaborate a little more on that?

Client: Well, I cry a lot and I can hardly get moving. My wife says all I do is whine and complain.

Counselor: So sadness means crying and difficulty in getting moving and you complain a lot. You also said you felt tense and drawn inside like hammers were hitting inside yourself I think you said.

Here the counselor ties in the vague feelings of sadness with the more concrete operational behaviors mentioned by the client and locates them more specifically in the sensorimotor space of the client's body.

The objective of operationalization of behavior, then, is the concretizing of vague words into objective, observable actions. Virtually all behavioral counselors and therapists will seek this specificity at some point in the helping interview, believing it is more possible to work with objective behavior than with vague nonspecific concepts such as depression and sadness.

A simple but basic question to ask yourself when engaging in the operationalization of behavior is "Can I see, feel, hear, or touch the words the client is using?" The client may speak of a desire for a "better relationship" with a partner. Since the behavioral therapist cannot see, feel, hear, or touch a "better relationship," the therapist would seek to have this concept operationalized in terms of touching, vocal tone, or certain verbal statements (e.g., "I wish my partner would touch me more and say more good things about me").

Again, making vague terms as specific as possible can be useful in other theoretical orientations. The clarity that comes with a careful applied behavioral analysis often provides a basic understanding for truly appreciating the client's worldview and environmental situation.

Functional Analysis: The A-B-Cs of Behavior. An individual's behavior is directly related to events and stimuli in the environment. Consequently, another task of the behavioral therapist is to discover how client behaviors occur in the "natural environment." To accomplish this task, behavioral counselors and therapists talk about the "A-B-Cs" of functional analysis—that is, the study of antecedent events, the resultant behavior, and the consequence(s) of that behavior. The behavioral counselor is interested in knowing what happened just prior to a specific behavior, what the specific behavior or event was, and what the result or consequence of that behavior was on the client and the environment. Chapter 8, which describes Albert Ellis's cognitive-behavioral counseling theory, explores parallel "A-B-Cs" for inner thoughts and feelings.

In the following examination of functional cause-and-effect relationships, the counselor comes to understand the sequence of events underlying the overt behavior of a client. Out of such functional patterns, it is possible to design behavioral programs to change the pattern of events reported by the client.

Counselor: So far, I've heard that you are generally depressed, that you get these feelings of tiredness and tension. Now could you give me a specific example of a situation when you felt this way? I want to know what happened just before the depression came on you, what happened as you got those feelings and thoughts, and what resulted afterward. First, tell me about the last time you had these feelings.

Client: Well, it happened yesterday. (Sigh.) I came home from work and was feeling pretty good. But when I came in the house, Bonnie wasn't there, so I sat down and started to read.

Counselor: (interrupting) What was your reaction when your wife wasn't home?

Client: I was a little disappointed, but not much, I just sat down.

Counselor: Go ahead.

Client: After about half an hour, she came in and just walked by me. I said hello, but she was angry at me still from last night when we had that argument. Funny, I always feel relieved and free after we have an argument almost like I get it out of my system.

Counselor: Then what happened?

Client: Well, I tried to get her to talk, but she ignored me. After about ten minutes, I got really sad and depressed. I went to my room and laid down until supper. But just before supper, she came in and said she was sorry, but I just felt more depressed.

Counselor: Let's see if I can put that sequence of events together. You were feeling pretty good, but your wife wasn't home and then she didn't respond to you when she did get home because she was angry. You tried to get her to respond and she wouldn't. [antecedents] Then you got depressed and felt bad and went to your room and lay down. [resultant behavior] She ignored you for a while, but finally came to you and you ignored her. [consequences] This pattern seems to be similar to what you've told me before. That is, how you try something; she doesn't respond; you get discouraged, depressed feelings and tensions—sometimes even crying; and she comes back to you and apologizes, but you reject her.

From a cognitive-developmental frame of reference, the counselor summarized the concrete cause-and-effect sequence through the A-B-C analysis. This awareness of sequence is characteristic of persons who operate from a late concrete operational stage of thinking. Then, the counselor used the word *pattern,* thereby helping the client see that this one concrete example is representative of repeating behavior. If the client is not cognitively able to think in patterns (formal operations), it is preferable to stay with a single example and work on that specific situation in counseling and psychotherapeutic situations like this.

Important in performing functional analysis is being aware of how behavior develops and maintains itself through a system of rewards or reinforcers and punishments. At the simplest level, whatever follows a particular piece of behavior will influence the probability of that behavior happening again.

In the above case, the husband gained no attention from his wife until he became depressed. At this point, and at this point only, she came to him. Therefore, the wife's behavior heavily influences the probability of his becoming depressed again. On this subject, Skinner (1953) notes:

> Several important generalized reinforcers arise when behavior is reinforced by other people. A simple case is attention. The child who misbehaves "just to get attention" is familiar. The attention of people is reinforcing because it is a necessary condition for other reinforcements from them. In general, only people who are attending to us reinforce our behavior. (p. 78)

Patterns of attention are particularly important in understanding human relationships. In the above case, the husband gets attention only when he becomes depressed, and his wife's attention at that time only reinforces further feelings of depression and hopelessness. If she were to attend to him when he initiated behavior, it is possible—even likely—that certain portions of his pattern of depression would be alleviated. However, neither does the husband attend to (reinforce) his wife's coming to him in the bedroom. He ignores her and thereby continues the pattern of mutual lack of reinforcement. Either individual could break this self-defeating pattern of antecedents, behavior, and consequences.

Any meaningful functional analysis must examine the reinforcement patterns maintaining the system of an individual or couple. As mentioned above, examining patterns in life requires individuals to develop formal operational thinking ability. Since many clients have not developed this cognitive ability and operate instead from concrete operational thinking, it will be necessary to work only with one single situation at a time and examine in detail the concrete A-B-C sequence for each situation that is causing them distress. Once several single situations have been mastered by the client, it may then be possible to examine formal patterns of behavior later in counseling and psychotherapy.

The social reinforcers of attention and approval are particularly potent and vital in human relationships. However, other reinforcers (money, grades, or other tangibles, as well as social rewards such as smiles, affection, and recognition) must be considered in any functional analysis. In many cases, negative attention (punishment) is often preferred to being ignored. Ignoring a human being can be a very painful punishment (Eisenberger, Lieberman, & Williams, 2003).

Establishing Behavior Change Goals. If a counselor is to help clients, the intended behavior change must be relevant to clients' psychological concerns and their specific environmental challenges. Behavioral counseling and therapy is designed to assist clients in making specific behavior changes that enhance their personal development and foster a greater sense of psychological well-being. When using these therapeutic interventions, counselors and psychologists should clearly communicate how they can help clients learn new ways of acting that can lead to more effective functioning.

It is important for mental health practitioners to take time to explain how striving to achieve specific behavioral goals in therapy will not interfere with the client's or their community's short- and long-term goals. It is equally important to acknowledge that in using behavioral counseling and therapy approaches with their clients, counselors and psychologists will not serve the interests of other individuals or institutions/agencies whose goals may be detrimental to their clients or to their cultural groups.

During the goal-setting phase of the interview, the counselor will work with the client to identify highly specific and relevant goals (Nugent, 2000). Rather than setting a generalized goal such as "My goal is not to be depressed anymore," the behavioral counselor will work toward detailing much more specific goals. One early goal might be as basic as going to a movie or learning to dance. Later goals might be to join a community club, start jogging, or find a job.

Applied behavioral analysis breaks the abstract idea of depression down into manageable behavioral units and teaches clients how to live their lives more happily and effectively. One can do something about specifics, and as concrete goals are achieved, there is a greater probability that a client's depression may lift.

Throughout applied behavioral analysis, there is an emphasis on concrete doing and action. The individual must do something that can be seen, heard, and felt. Thoughts are less important, but these become central in cognitive psychology, behavioral psychology's offshoot. Interestingly, behavioral psychotherapy often tends to be especially effective with depressed clients, as its emphasis on doing and acting rather than on self-reflection gets many clients moving. Applied behavioral analysis will have a more lasting meaning for you if you actually practice it. Competency-Building Activity 7.1 provides you an opportunity to do so.

Other Behavioral Strategies

Competency-Building Activity 7.1 offers you the opportunity to experience the rudiments of an applied behavioral analysis. The following sections offer a more expansive understanding of other practical techniques in behavioral counseling and therapy based on the findings of behavioral analysis.

Pinpointing Behavior. Assume that you are working with a hyperactive child. A teacher or parent may complain about the child's overactivity and tell you that the child is "difficult to control." These are not directly observable behaviors. Your task is to pinpoint very precise behaviors, such as the number of times the child interrupts a classmate or teacher, the number of times the child leaves his or her seat during a specified time period, or the child's "time on task" (percentage of time the child is actually working on schoolwork).

Your skill in applied behavioral analysis is basic to pinpointing specific behavioral targets for change or reinforcement. Your challenge here is to operationalize behavior concepts to pinpoint very specific behaviors associated with depression, arguments, or sexual harassment (see Competency-Building Activity 7.1).

Competency-Building Activity 7.1

Applied Behavioral Analysis

Instructions: Interview a friend or colleague using the exercises below as examples for implementing successful behavioral counseling and therapy.

Operationalization of Behavior

The following are vague statements a client might present in the interview:

"I'm depressed."

"I'm no good as a parent."

"He argues all the time."

"I'm unhappy."

"She doesn't love me anymore."

"The boss doesn't like me."

"The boss harassed me."

When clients give you vague statements such as the above, your task is to help them become more concrete and specific. For example, if the client said, "The boss harassed me," your task would be to obtain the concrete specifics of "harassment." You can obtain these concrete specifics by asking:

"Could you give me a specific example of what the boss did?"

"What do you mean, all the time?"

"What happened specifically?"

"What words does he use?"

"How loudly does he talk?"

"Where did he touch you?"

"Who holds the power?"

"What's the boss's behavior toward other men/women/minorities?"

When you hear a vague statement such as those described above, ask open questions, using the above guidelines, until you get the concrete specifics of the behavior.

At times, you will want to concretize a sequence. In the example below, the focus is on making an argument specific. You can do this simply by asking:

"What happened in the argument?"

"What did she or he say?"

"What did you say?"

"What happened before?" (to obtain antecedents)

"What happened afterward?" (to obtain consequences)

To ensure that you have heard the person you are interviewing correctly, use the microskill of summarization to lay out the sequence of events you heard the person describe to you during this meeting. Also be aware of the social context of your analysis. Your efforts will often be most effective if conducted with contextual awareness and action in mind. Again, using these ideas with your friend or colleague, draw out the sequence of events in your interview. You may simply begin the interview by asking the individual you are working with to talk about a situation that occurred recently that she or he found frustrating or anxiety producing.

Functional Analysis

The questioning techniques outlined above are basic to a functional analysis. In conducting a functional analysis, think about the A-B-Cs of behavior. In the following examples, note the importance of the word *doing,* which focuses on action.

A—Antecedent Events

Examine preceding behavioral facts as well as feelings and emotions when conducting your interview. Ask such questions as:

"What happened just before the argument?"

"What were you doing?"

"What were they doing?"

"Could you just step back and describe the event step by step—give me lots of details?"

continued on next page

"What did you feel beforehand?"

"How did the other person seem to feel?"

It may also be useful to explore the environment, using such questions as:

"Where did this occur?"

"What else was going on?"

"Who else was there?"

You may think of the guidelines newspaper reporters follow in reporting a story and asking questions that begin with the words "who, what, when, where, why, and how" to enrich background information related to the interviewee's issues.

A critical question that should be asked at each segment of any careful functional analysis is "Have we missed anything important?" Summarize the antecedents to ensure that you have heard them correctly.

B—Behavior That Occurred (Resultant Behavior)

Here you focus on the sequence of events or interactions that occurred during the critical period in which your friend or colleague experienced the situation he or she describes in this exercise. Use variations of the same questions suggested above and pay special attention to feelings and emotions that accompanied the behavior. Again, summarize the behavior and check to see if you missed something important.

C—Consequences

Most essential here is what specifically happened as a result of A (the antecedent events) and B (the behavior that occurred). Some helpful questions include:

"What was the end result of the whole event?"

"Could you explore what happened for you as a result of this situation and what happened for the other person?"

"How did you feel when it was over?"

"Are there situational, environmental checks on you or others that may have power and influence over the total situation?"

Again, summarize the behavior and check to see if you missed something important. This completes the A-B-C analysis of behavior. In completing this analysis in counseling and therapy, you will gain a clearer understanding of what is occurring for clients who are experiencing problem situations in their lives.

Establishing Behavior Change Goals

Having completed an A-B-C functional analysis, the next task in behavioral counseling is to identify, with the client's participation, specific goals for behavioral change.

Many clients can participate very effectively in analyzing behavioral sequences, but when you ask them "What is your goal for change?" they often will return to vague, nonspecific concepts. Your task as a therapist once again is to help them become more specific about their goals for change. Some useful questions that can assist you in helping clients get more specific are:

"Given that we have discussed your parental argument (your depression, the issue of harassment) and conflict in detail, what specifically would you like to change?"

"We could work on how you behave before the argument occurs, how you talk and behave when one does occur, or what you do after an inevitable argument happens. Which one would you like to work on first?"

The information that is gained from the client's responses to these questions often suggests that change can be sought in the areas of the antecedents, the behavior itself, the consequences, or some combination of these three. If these questions are too complex for clients, the following concrete questions may be more useful.

"Ideally, what one single thing would you most like to change?"

continued on next page

Competency-Building Activity 7.1, continued

"Let's explore that in more detail. What would you have to do differently to make that situation better?"

It is also helpful to use a fantasy directive at this point in behavioral counseling and therapy. An example of such a directive might be stated as follows:

"Fantasize an ideal solution as if everything were exactly like you'd wish it to be."

A situational question such as "What can we do to help change the system in which this happened?" will help add a multicultural-feminist-social justice focus.

Again, take a friend or colleague through the specifics of operationalizing behavior, defining the A-B-C sequence, and establish clear, measurable goals for behavioral change. After you have completed your interview, take time to write down your reactions to exercising these behavior counseling and therapy skills in this competency-building activity. Be sure to file your written reactions in your personal/professional portfolio.

Positive and Intermittent Reinforcement. Perhaps the most direct behavioral technique is the provision of rewards for desired outcomes. The systematic application of positive reinforcement to human beings began with an important experiment by Greenspoon (1955), who demonstrated that it was possible to condition people to "emit" more plural nouns whenever the "counselor" smiled or nodded his head. In the context of what appeared to be a normal counseling session, Greenspoon conducted a typical interview, with the exception that whenever the client uttered a plural noun, the interviewer smiled and nodded. Very soon the client was providing him with many plural nouns.

Smiles, nods, and the attention of others are particularly reinforcing events. Reinforcement and rewards appeal to everyone, and those who provide the rewards tend to be looked on favorably. Those who do not tend to be ignored or avoided. Money can be another powerful positive reinforcer. In any fully effective applied behavioral analysis, the counselor will be able to note the positive reinforcers and rewards that maintain the client's behavior. The search for the A-B-Cs of behavioral sequences will often unravel seemingly complex and mystical behaviors.

Intermittent reinforcement represents a random dispersal of reinforcement, whether negative or positive. This type of reinforcement can be very helpful in understanding client behavior. For example, a woman may suffer from spousal abuse but refuse to leave the home, even if in danger of her life. From a behavioral frame of reference, this behavior could be explained as follows: (1) the woman has a strong history of positive reinforcement from the male in some form; (2) many abusive men apologize and provide immediate promise of positive reinforcement, even after dangerous physical incidents; (3) the woman has no place else to go for positive reinforcement if she leaves the male; and (4) behavioral research indicates that a random mixture of negative and positive events at different times can be even more powerful in maintaining behavior than unmixed positive reinforcement. Thus, the intermittent reinforcement pattern in abusive relationships is one of the hardest to break, whether one works from a psychodynamic, behavioral, humanistic, multicultural-feminist, or other frame of reference.

When learning theory concepts, such as extinction, shaping, and intermittent reinforcement, are joined together, extremely powerful and effective programs of human change can be developed. At the most sophisticated level, elaborate economies have been developed in prisons, psychiatric hospitals, schools, and other settings in which tangible reinforcers in the form of tokens are given for desired acts immediately after they have been performed. At a later point, the tokens may be exchanged for candy, cigarettes, or privileges. Important to the success of positive reinforcement and token economies is the clear identification, by the client, of the desired behavior with the reward. Too long a delay in reinforcement dulls its effectiveness in changing behavior.

Charting. One route toward identifying whether or not progress is being made with a behavioral change program is charting the changes manifested by a client. Charting is the recording of the number of specific occurrences of important behaviors before, during, and after treatment. For example, a teacher may be concerned with "out-of-seat behavior" of a hyperactive child. The goal of the behavioral program is to reduce this behavior using a modified token economy in which the child is rewarded for staying at her or his desk.

Figure 7.4 illustrates the daily frequencies for out-of-seat behavior before the intervention was instituted, during the treatment, and after treatment was terminated.

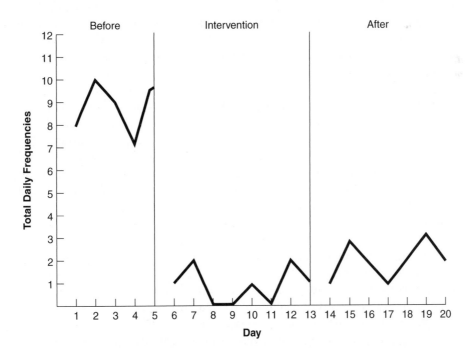

Figure 7.4 Charting Out-of-Seat Behavior

It is important to record behavior before the program is instituted so the effectiveness of the behavioral program can be examined. Charting after program completion is important because, when the intervention is removed, the behavior sometimes returns to the previous level. This is an indication that the behavioral program was unsuccessful in maintaining desired outcomes. When charts indicate failure, another type of behavioral program (or even another type of counseling intervention, such as a psychodynamic or an existential-humanistic intervention) may need to be instituted. In such cases relapse prevention programs can be particularly useful.

Charting is often used in weight control programs, family communication skill training, aiding a child in keeping a room clean, smoking cessation programs, and a wide variety of interpersonal or classroom situations. The very act of self-recording (charting) sometimes helps an individual modify her or his behavior without further instruction or counseling.

Many therapists, particularly those who work with children and adolescents, find that pinpointing behavior and conducting a thorough A-B-C analysis are vital if change is to occur. Once a change plan has been collaboratively agreed on with the client (and parents, if you are working with a child), charting is helpful for studying whether or not your intervention is effective and whether or not change is maintained after the intervention ceases.

Relaxation Training. Physical body tension is characteristic of many clients who enter counseling and therapy. This tension may show itself in a variety of ways, including statements of fear or tension in social situations; direct complaints of sore, constantly tense muscles; impotence and frigidity; difficulties with sleep; and high blood pressure. There is clinical evidence that borderline clients reduce the number of suicidal gestures and "cutting" (slashing themselves) if they are supported with a relaxation training program. Many seriously depressed clients can benefit from relaxation training as part of their treatment regimen as well.

Surprisingly, simply teaching people the mechanics of systematic relaxation techniques has been sufficient to alleviate many seemingly complex problems. Rather than search for the reasons that a client is unable to sleep, for example, behavioral counselors have found it more effective in many cases to teach the client relaxation techniques. The simple procedure of training clients in relaxation can be an important way to bring totally new views of the world to them. Through finding that they can control their bodies, clients can move on to solve many complex personal difficulties later in counseling and therapy.

For this reason, virtually all counselors and therapists today are becoming skilled at training clients in relaxation techniques similar to the exercises presented in Competency-Building Activity 7.2. A client may learn the rudiments of relaxation training in a fifteen-minute session, but careful planning and training are needed if relaxation techniques are to become part of a client's life.

A variety of systematic relaxation tapes is now available commercially, making it possible for the busy behavioral counselor to delegate this training to such resources and to spend more time training the client how to use relaxation in specific situations.

Competency-Building Activity 7.2

Two Relaxation Exercises

Instructions: To use the following exercises most effectively, have a friend or family member read them to you slowly while you go through the procedures yourself. Then change roles and help the other person enter the same relaxed state you have just enjoyed. As a final step, adapt the material below into your own relaxation program and place it on audiotape for your own and others' use.

Tension-Relaxation Contrast

Many people exist at such a high level of tension that they find it difficult to start relaxing. Tension-relaxation contrast shows the beginner in relaxation exercises what tension is and how it may be controlled systematically. The person who is to go through relaxation training should be seated comfortably in a chair or lying on the floor. An easy, casual manner and good rapport are essential for the counselor. The following steps provide specific guidelines that will enable you to try one type of relaxation training that you may use with individuals you work with in the future.

Step 1. *Suggest that the client close her or his eyes and take a few deep breaths, exhaling slowly each time.*

Step 2. *Tell the client, "We are going to engage in a systematic relaxation program."* Go on to say, "You'll find it's something you'll enjoy, but we must go at your pace. If you find I'm moving too fast or too slowly, let me know. In general, I'll know how you are doing as I can watch your response and will time what I'm doing to where you are. First, I'd like you to tighten your right hand—that's right—hold it tight for about five seconds—one, two, three, four, five. Now let it go, and notice the difference between the relaxation and tension in your hand. Notice the feeling of ease as you let your hand go. What we'll do is go through your body in much the same fashion, alternately tightening

and letting go of each muscle group. Let's begin . . ."

Step 3. *Continue by having the client tighten and loosen the right hand once again.* Remember to have the client notice the difference between relaxed and tense body states. Awareness of muscle tension is one key goal of relaxation training. After you have done the right hand for a second time, continue through the rest of the body in the order suggested below. Each time, have the client (1) tighten the muscle group, (2) hold the tension approximately five seconds, (3) let the tension go, and (4) notice the difference between tension and relaxation. A suggested order for muscle groups follows:

right hand

right arm

left hand

left arm

neck and shoulders together

neck alone

face and scalp

neck and shoulders again

chest, lungs, back

abdomen-stomach

entire upper body—chest, back, lungs, abdomen, face, neck, both arms, followed by a deep breath held and then exhaled slowly and gently

abdomen-stomach again

buttocks

thighs

feet

entire body

As the training progresses, it is not necessary to comment on awareness at each muscle group, but mention awareness of the contrasting feelings

continued on next page

Competency-Building Activity 7.2, continued

from time to time. Occasionally, it is helpful to suggest taking a deep breath, holding it, and then exhaling while noting the contrast between tension and relaxation.

Step 4. *Suggest that the client continue to sit or lie still, enjoying the feelings of relaxation and ease.* When he or she wishes, suggest opening her or his eyes and returning to the world.

Direct Relaxation

Many people prefer this form of relaxation if they find the alternate tensing and loosening tiring and/or uninteresting. However, it has been found that the tension-relaxation contrast procedure is often a good place to start with as a beginner to relaxation training. Eventually, many people will want to shift to some form of direct relaxation.

One form of direct relaxation is to use the above order of muscle groups and go through them one at a time. However, no tension is used, and the client simply lets each muscle group relax, one at a time. With practice and experience, the relaxation can be as complete without the practiced tension.

A second form of direct relaxation involves visualization and imagery. The following is one brief example of this approach to relaxation training. As in the tension-relaxation exercise described above, the client is encouraged to sit or lie down. In direct relaxation training, the relationship between the counselor and client is even more important.

Step 1. *Suggest that the client close her or his eyes and notice the feelings inside the body.* Take some time to encourage the client to notice the breath going in and out of her or his lungs, the feeling of the chair or floor on the buttocks and back, the feeling of the temperature in the room. All this should be done slowly, easily, and comfortably. The effort focuses on bringing the client to a here-and-now awareness of body experience.

Step 2. *Suggest that the client freely think about a scene in the past where he or she felt at ease and comfortable and happy.* Suggest that the client go to the scene and enjoy the feelings and thoughts that go with that happy time, noticing as many details and facts as possible. The client may wish to notice the feelings in the room and her or his body at that time. This may include becoming more aware of the movement of the air, temperature, and body sensations at the immediate moment. Let the client continue with the visualization as long as desired and then become silent, letting him or her determine when to come back.

Step 3. *Tell the client to take some time to enjoy the scene and experience, but that she or he will come back in a while.*

Step 4. *After about 5 minutes, gently say, "It is time to return to this room."* Suggest that the eyes remain closed and that he or she note once again the feelings in the body connected with this room, as in the first part of the exercise. Suggest that the eyes may open when the client wishes.

After you have completed your interview with a friend or colleague, take time to write down your reactions to exercising these behavior counseling and therapy skills in this competency-building activity. Be sure to file your written reactions in your personal/professional portfolio.

Relaxation may, for example, be an important part of assertiveness training. If a client describes physical tension in the stomach when talking with members of the family or the boss, it is possible to teach the client to deliberately relax the stomach muscles and remain calm as part of a larger program of assertiveness training. Most relaxation training programs are based on a tension-relaxation or direct relaxation procedure. These two approaches to relaxational training are discussed in Competency-Building Activity 7.2.

Biofeedback and Self-Regulation. It is now possible to use biofeedback instrumentation to monitor tension in muscles, heartbeat, and blood flow as part of a treatment plan to help clients alleviate tension. Biofeedback combines many of the relaxation procedures of behavioral psychology for analysis and treatment of a variety of client tension patterns.

Biofeedback has become an increasingly popular treatment technique for tension headaches and general stress reactions (Schwartz & Andrasik, 1998). It has been used to support behavioral treatment of patients on insulin (Bailey, Good, & McGrady, 1990) and in many cases of pain control (Schwartz & Andrasik, 1998). Biofeedback may have an even more important future in medicine and stress control. When faced with stress, blood vessels constrict. Relaxation training, biofeedback, and stress management all can help people relax and ease blood flow.

There are some important multicultural issues that need careful consideration concerning environmental and life stressors and the ability to manage these stresses. Clark and his colleagues (1999) present one of the most comprehensive reviews of the literature related to the impact of racism on the physiological functioning of African-Americans. These researchers point out the numerous ways that stressors associated with various forms of perceived racism adversely impact African-Americans' immune and cardiovascular system functioning as well as neuroendocrine responses (Clark, Anderson, Clark, & Williams, 1999). An ongoing stressor for African-Americans (and most likely for other minorities as well) is a general environment that is nonsupportive and, in many instances, hostile to their cultural/racial differences.

Given the data reported by Clark and his colleagues (1999), it follows that biofeedback, relaxation, and stress management may be important programs to facilitate not only the mental health, but also the physical health of many persons subjected to various forms of oppression and social injustice. Cheek (1976) might add that such behavioral strategies could be accompanied by cognitive counseling strategies that are aimed at stimulating one's consciousness about issues of powerlessness and how clients in marginalized and devalued groups can work to effectively promote positive and empowering environmental changes. Several other multicultural-social justice counseling advocates emphasize that direct action by the therapist or counselor in the community that produced the stress is what is also needed (Lewis et al., 2003; Parham et al., 1999).

Reciprocal Inhibition and Systematic Desensitization. Joseph Wolpe (1982) introduced the concepts of reciprocal inhibition and systematic desensitization into behavioral therapy theory. Reciprocal inhibition is a form of behavior therapy that is based on the inhibition of one response by the occurrence of another response that is incompatible with it. Relaxation training utilizes this aspect of behavioral therapy theory when clients are assisted in learning to implement deep breathing and muscle relaxing techniques in response to situations that normally elicit heightened stress and anxiety.

Behavior therapists also use the principle of reciprocal inhibition when implementing systematic desensitization strategies in counseling and therapeutic settings.

This powerful therapeutic tool matches relaxation techniques with controlled exposure to a feared stimulus such as the fear of heights or the fear of frightening animals. Systematic desensitization conditioning techniques continue to be widely used when behaviorally oriented counselors work with clients who experience various phobias such as irrational fear of heights, objects, or animals. It is also used with clients who manifest heightened anxiety and stress in social situations.

The assessment portion of systematic desensitization is useful in helping you understand the specific nature of a wide variety of client difficulties. The collaborative generation of an anxiety hierarchy will help identify the client's issues in a very concrete way. This information can be combined with typical behavioral change methods or with psychodynamic therapy, brief counseling, and other treatment alternatives.

Systematic desensitization consists of three primary steps: (1) training in systematic deep muscle relaxation, (2) construction of anxiety hierarchies, and (3) matching specific objects of anxiety from the hierarchies with relaxation training. It is impossible to be simultaneously relaxed and anxious; thus, the purpose of systematic desensitization is to train an automatic relaxation response in conjunction with a previously feared object. Systematic desensitization has proven effective with anxieties or phobias such as those about snakes, heights, death, sexual difficulties, and examinations.

Examination anxiety is an area that is particularly appropriate for desensitization. As such, the use of systematic desensitization procedures have proven to be very useful with students in many academic institutions. The first steps in using systematic desensitization with students involve training in relaxation and applied behavioral analysis of the antecedents, resultant behavior, and consequences relating to the student's examination problems. To assist individuals experiencing anxiety, it often is useful to help them construct an **anxiety hierarchy**.

An anxiety hierarchy is a scale of the client's various fears. Wolpe and Lazarus (1966) offer the following suggestions in developing an anxiety scale in clinical practice: "Think of the worst anxiety you have ever experienced or can imagine experiencing, and assign to this the number 100. Now think of the state of being absolutely calm, and call this 0. Now you have a scale. On this scale how do you rate yourself at this moment?" (p. 73).

This type of scale allows the counselor and the client to develop a common understanding of how anxious the client was or is at any time in the past or present. It clearly identifies the beginning and end points of the anxiety hierarchy. Through questioning and further applied behavioral analysis, it is possible to fill in and rate stress-producing experiences. An example anxiety hierarchy for a student suffering from examination anxiety is presented in Figure 7.5.

The importance and value of this type of individualized, collaborative behavioral assessment cannot be overstressed. Such a hierarchy provides a greater awareness of how anxiety plays itself out in the interview and in the daily lives of clients. Competency-Building Activity 7.3 helps you practice constructing an anxiety hierarchy as well as become familiar with desensitization techniques.

Figure 7.5 Anxiety Hierarchy

___	0	School is over and I have no more exams for another year.
___	10	On the first day of class, the professor tells us the course plan and mentions examination plans.
___	30	About a week before the examination, I realize it is coming.
___	50	Two days before the examination, I get particularly nervous and begin to find it hard to concentrate.
___	70	The day before the examination, I get sweaty palms and feel I am forgetting things that are important.
___	85	The night before the exam, I can't sleep and wake up in the middle of the night.
___	90	As I walk to the exam, I find myself shaking and feeling almost ill.
___	95	As I enter the room, my hands sweat; I fear I am forgetting everything; I want to leave.
___	99	When the tests are passed out, I feel totally tense, almost unable to move.
___	100	As I look at the examination I see a question or two that I really don't know, and I absolutely panic. I leave the room.

Modeling and Social Skills Training. Seeing is believing, it is said, and behavioral psychologists have found that watching films or videotapes of people engaging in successful behavior is sufficient for clients to learn new ways of coping with difficulties. Bandura (1976) found that live modeling of snake handling was even more effective than systematic desensitization in teaching snake phobics to cope with their anxieties.

> After observing the therapist interacting closely with the snake, clients were aided through other induction procedures to perform progressively more frightening responses themselves. At each step the therapist performed the activities fearlessly and gradually led the clients to touch, stroke, and hold the midsection of the snake's body with gloved and then bare hands for increasing periods of time. As clients became more courageous, the therapist gradually reduced the level of participation and control over the snake until eventually clients were able to tolerate the squirming snake in their laps without assistance, to let the snake loose in the room and retrieve it, and to let it crawl freely over their bodies. (p. 256)

In a sense, modeling is one of the most simple and obvious ways to teach clients new behaviors. Seeing and hearing directly, either live or via film or tape, brings home a message much more clearly than direct advice and description. Modeling can be combined with relaxation and assertiveness training as well as with other behavioral techniques in developing uniquely individualized programs for clients. Modeling is a key ingredient in social skills training.

The three stages of behavioral psychology described earlier in this chapter and the behavioral counseling strategies discussed above represent important aspects of the development of the second theoretical force in counseling and psychology. The continuing evolution of this force has moved from an emphasis on observable behavior and action to the fourth stage in CBT, which includes the inner world of cognitions.

Competency-Building Activity 7.3

Constructing an Anxiety Hierarchy and Systematic Desensitization

Instructions: You can practice constructing an anxiety hierarchy or scale using the following approach.

Step 1. *Develop rapport with a volunteer or real client.* Again, work mutually and tell the client what to expect. Ask the client to tell you about something that is anxiety producing. Good topics include examinations, specific fears (heights, animals, public speaking), and even the degree of physical tension and anxiety felt in the "here and now" of the therapeutic interview.

Step 2. *Coconstruct with the client an anxiety scale numbered from 1 to 10.* The lowest point should represent a feeling of calmness; the highest, a feeling of maximum anxiety or tension. Define specific situations and behaviors for points 1 and 10. You may find doing an applied behavioral analysis helpful in this process. Then, identify specific behaviors, situations, and feelings for the remainder of the scale.

Step 3. *Develop a second anxiety scale that directs attention to the level of anxiety and tension the client experiences in the counseling session.* You and your client can do so by modifying the above scale so you are able to communicate about the level of tension in your interview. For

example, it is often helpful to ask clients how physically tense and anxious they are as you move from topic to topic. An occasional question about where the tension is located in the body will help you understand the client's emotional state more clearly.

Desensitization can be done most effectively by either teaching brief relaxation methods or by asking the client to develop a positive image along with focusing on positive body sensations, as follows:

1.　Ask the client to relax and/or visualize a positive image while simultaneously viewing the absence of the problem at the 0 point on the anxiety scale. Check to make sure that the client feels calm before moving on.

2.　Work through the anxiety hierarchy in a similar fashion, making sure that the positive visualization and relaxed body sensations are paired with the negative experience the client encounters in his or her life. Gradually, the client will be able to monitor and control anxiety levels throughout the hierarchy. Some people can construct and work through a full anxiety hierarchy and desensitization in one session. More likely, several sessions may be needed.

3.　In actual therapy, you may want to add live experiences in the client's environment with the use of imagery

continued on next page

This has resulted in the development of a broad range of cognitive-behavioral therapies (CBT) that are widely used by many mental health practitioners today.

The Cognitive Revolution

Albert Bandura's work led the way to the realization that change in thought patterns could change the way we behave, just as behaving in new ways can change the way we think. Albert Ellis's rational-emotive behavior therapy and William Glasser's reality

---

Competency-Building Activity 7.3, continued

and relaxation. For example, if the client is fearful of crowds, you may jointly plan homework exercises in which the client gradually moves into larger groups of people. In some cases, you may want to go with the client to the place in which anxiety is the greatest and practice the new behavior in the "real world."

Using the Hierarchy for Treatment

Following completion of the anxiety hierarchy, the client is asked to sit with eyes closed and visualize a variety of scenes close to the o point of anxiety. These scenes may be of school being over or an enjoyable activity, such as a picnic or walking in the woods. The therapist asks the student to note the easy feelings of relaxation and then moves gradually up the hierarchy, having the client visualize each scene in the hierarchy. If tension is felt, the client may indicate this by a raised finger. Thus, if tension was experienced as the client visualized the situation two days before an examination, the therapist and client would work to note the tense muscles and relax them while still thinking of the usually tension-producing scene.

Gradually, the client learns to visualize all the scenes in the anxiety hierarchy while relaxed. This type of training may take several interviews, but it has been demonstrated to be quite effective. When students find themselves in similar tension-producing situations, they are then able to generate relaxation behaviors to counteract the feelings of tension, anxiety, and panic (Stuart, Treat, & Wade, 2000).

Similar work with anxiety hierarchies has proven equally effective in many anxiety and phobic situations. Some of the most dramatic demonstrations of desensitization procedures have been with snake phobics who, as a final test, allowed a snake to crawl over them (Wolfe & Maser, 1994).

Frigidity and impotency also have been successfully treated with this therapeutic method. In these cases, couples construct anxiety hierarchies related to sexual experimentation and the sex act. Generally, it is found that the sex act is the most tension-producing experience of all. Assuming there is no biological component, couples are instructed in systematic relaxation and go through the anxiety hierarchy visualization, much as did the student with examination anxiety. When transferring the newly learned behavior to the bedroom, the couple is often instructed to stop further sexual experimentation until full relaxation is regained.

After you have tried out these new skills and interventions with the person who volunteered to take part in these activities, take a few minutes to write down your reactions to using this theoretical approach. File these written reactions in your personal/professional development portfolio when you are finished.

---

therapy, which will be discussed in Chapter 8, were prominent in expanding the cognitive portion of the cognitive-behavioral movement. Their emphasis was much more on thinking, with behavior expected to change as a result of developing new cognitions.

Donald Meichenbaum, however, is often seen as the integrative force that brought cognitive psychology and behavioral psychology together. His basic tenets of CBT, along with those of Aaron Beck, offer important insights into the field.

Meichenbaum's Theory of Cognitive-Behavioral Therapy

Donald Meichenbaum (1991, 1994, 2003) has been one of the primary forces in moving behavioral therapy to its present cognitive-behavioral orientation. In

Meichenbaum's view, CBT is concerned with helping clients define problems cognitively as well as behaviorally and with promoting cognitive, emotional, and behavioral change and preventing relapse in the process.

Meichenbaum (1991) outlined 10 central tenets of CBT. As you read them, note how the fundamental CBT constructs expand your overall thinking of the helping process.

1. *Behavior is reciprocally determined by the "client's thoughts, feelings, physiological processes, and resultant consequences"* (p. 5). No one of these elements is necessarily most important. Thus, the therapist can intervene in the interacting system by focusing on thoughts or feelings, using medication, or changing consequences. Meichenbaum points out that with clients suffering from depression, the amount of criticism coming from the spouse (resultant consequences in the environment) is the most important predictor of relapse.

2. *Cognitions do not cause emotional difficulties; rather, they are part of a complex interactive process.* A particularly important part of the cognitive process is "metacognitions" in which clients learn to comment internally on their own thinking patterns and thereby act as their own mentor or therapist. "Moreover, CB therapists insure that clients take credit for behavioral changes they implement" (p. 6).

   The cognitive structures we use to organize the experiences we have in life are our **personal schemas.** We develop these personal schemas from past experience. From a CBT worldview, changing ineffective schemas is an important part of therapy. For instance, clients who are diagnosed with anxiety disorders have particular concerns about issues of loss of personal control and physical well-being. Depressed individuals are prone to be concerned about issues of loss, rejection, and abandonment. Individuals who are particularly concerned about issues of equity, fairness, and justice commonly have problems with anger.

3. *"A central task for the CB therapist is to help clients come to understand how they construct and construe reality"* (p. 7). In this statement, Kelly's (1955) early personal construct theory has been joined with the behavioral tradition. Meichenbaum stresses that clients and counselors can work collaboratively to explore cognitions, personal constructs of the world, and desired behavioral changes.

   According to Meichenbaum (1991), *"CBT does not hold that there is 'one reality'"* (p. 4). He also emphasizes that it not the task for the therapist to educate or correct clients' misperceptions (e.g., errors in thinking, irrational thoughts). Rather, CBT holds that there are "multiple realities." Consequently, from Meichenbaum's worldview, the collaborative task for clients and CB therapists is to help clients appreciate how they create such realities.

4. *"CBT takes issue with those psychotherapeutic approaches that adopt a rationalist or objectivist position"* (p. 8). This is an important and radical position that challenges Albert Ellis's theoretical model (Chapter 8). Meichenbaum's

approach is more existential-humanistic in nature and directed toward understanding how clients subjectively experience the world. He stresses the importance of reflecting key words and phrases used by clients and of mirroring their feelings back to them "in an inquiring tone" (the microskills of encouraging and reflection of feeling are particularly useful in addressing these aspects of Meichenbaum's CBT theory). By mirroring clients in these ways, Meichenbaum seeks to help clients understand how they have constructed meaning of themselves and the world.

5. *"A critical feature of CBT is the emphasis on collaboration and on the discovery processes"* (p. 8). Meichenbaum talks about the importance of having clients make their own discoveries. He recommends using a variety of behavioral techniques, such as those presented in this chapter, to facilitate the discovery process.

6. *"CBT holds that the relationship that develops between the client and the therapist is critical to the change process"* (p. 10). Empathy and listening skills are critical as well as the important relationship dimensions stressed by Rogers (Chapter 9).

7. *"Emotions play a critical role in CBT"* (p. 11). Much like psychodynamic theory, Meichenbaum's view of CBT suggests that clients bring into the therapy session the emotional experiences they have had with others. Past life experiences are seen as affecting how clients react with you in the session, and emotions are the route toward understanding the nature of the relationship.

8. *"CBT therapists are now recognizing the benefits of conducting CBT with couples and families"* (p. 12). In this sense, CBT is moving toward the network treatment constructions that are advocated by multicultural counseling theorists such as Attneave (see Chapter 12).

9. *"Relapse prevention is a central dimension of CBT"* (p. 17). Unless we specifically help clients generalize their learning from counseling and therapy to the larger world of which they are a part, the positive effects of the helping process will soon wear away (Marlatt & Donovan, 2005; Stevens-Smith, 1998). Stevens-Smith's (1998) relapse prevention framework has much applicability for many different approaches to counseling and psychotherapy including CBT.

10. *"CBT can be extended beyond the clinic setting for both prevention and treatment"* (p. 18). Meichenbaum points out that CBT techniques have been used in probation offices, schools, hospitals, the military, and infant home visitations. It is becoming clearer that many CBT concepts can also be effectively incorporated into psychoeducational interventions that are used to prevent drug and alcohol abuse as well.

Aaron Beck, Cognitive Therapy, and Automatic Thoughts

Aaron Beck first became known for his success in treating depression. The personal strength and warmth of Beck are perhaps best illustrated by a case from his well-known book *Cognitive Therapy and the Emotional Disorders* (1976) in which he describes a depressed patient who had failed to leave his bed for a considerable period of time. Beck asked him if he could walk to the door of his room. The man said he would collapse. Beck said, "I'll catch you." Through successive steps and longer walks, the man was shortly able to walk all over the hospital and in one month was discharged.

The example illustrates how Beck focuses on cognitive change to produce behavioral change. Key to the client walking was belief that he could do it. Beliefs about self and others are central to cognitive therapy. Note also in the case above that the client had faith in his relationship with Beck. The power of your relationship and rapport with your client is basic to effective cognitive-behavioral therapy of all types.

Relationship as Central to Change in CBT. How are such "miracles" accomplished? First, Beck is a powerful and caring individual who himself believes that change is possible. He is willing to provide himself as a support agent and has specific goals and behaviors in mind for the client. In the case described above, he sought to change the way the depressed person thought about himself. Through slow, successive approximations, from shorter to longer walks with Beck's help, the client was able to change his behavior.

This case illustrates the importance of building a positive relationship as one directs attention to behavioral as well as cognitive change. It also points out that you may at times need to move out of the office and work in the community. In Beck's framework, this basic cognitive change would be a move from "I can't" to "I can."

Basic to much of behavioral work is to take small steps toward success. Somewhere along the continuum of change, clients will likely realize that they can do something to help themselves. It is this attitude of "I can" that is basic to generalizing learned behavior and ways of thinking from the therapy hour to real life.

Beck has outlined important principles for working with many types of patients. Since his early work with depression, he has demonstrated that his concepts are equally effective with personality disorders (Beck & Zebb, 1994), anxiety disorders (Beck, 1996), and many other issues.

Beck gives central attention to the cognitive process. He points out that there is a constant stream of thoughts going through our minds, not all of which we listen to. These thoughts move so rapidly that Beck calls them **automatic thoughts** and points out that it is difficult to stop them. In counseling and therapy, Beck is concerned with helping clients learn how to stop negative and harmful automatic thoughts. His theory of cognitive therapy suggests that this can be done by assisting clients in examining their mode of thinking and eventually developing new forms of cognition during the counseling and psychotherapeutic process.

Changing Faulty Thought Patterns. In Beck's theoretical model, the therapist seeks to change clients' thinking patterns and way of constructing their worldviews. This requires the following steps:

1. *Recognize maladaptive thinking and ideation.*

2. *Note repeating patterns of ideation that tend to be ineffective.* Beck terms such repeating patterns *automatic thoughts.* The therapeutic task here focuses on helping clients break down their illogical thinking patterns by assisting them to realize the distinctions between more logical and less logical ways of thinking about problems and life situations.

3. *Distance and decenter.* These counseling strategies involve helping clients remove themselves from the immediate fear, thought, or problem. Clients are encouraged to think about whatever issue they are dealing with from a "distance." Distancing strategies have been found to be very effective in fostering a "decentering" of clients' constant preoccupation with nonproductive ways of thinking.

4. *Change the rules.* This strategy is important in working with faulty thinking and negative automatic thoughts and involves talking. The therapist talks with the client about the logic of the situation. For example, a client may be encouraged to rethink her dog phobia through realizing that the chances of being bitten by a dog are at best one in a thousand.

As noted earlier, Beck's system has proven to be particularly effective with depressed clients, whose worldview is full of pessimistic automatic thoughts that forcefully affect their behavior. Beck and Beck (1995) provide a list of "faulty reasonings" that are commonly manifested by depressed persons. This list is, in many ways, similar to Ellis's conceptualizations of irrational ideas (Chapter 8). Beck's and Ellis's lists include such concepts as dichotomous reasoning (assuming things are either all good or all bad—"I'm either perfect or I'm no good"), overgeneralization ("If my husband leaves me, I'm totally alone"), magnification (Ellis terms this catastrophizing), and flaws in inference or logic. Clients will commonly manifest a multitude of variations on perfectionism.

These automatic thoughts and irrational ideas tend to be obsessive in nature, as they are repeated over and over again. However, what makes ideas particularly irrational is their unattainability, overgeneralization (one must reach 100 percent of everything), or significant distortion of occurrences.

Beck's cognitive therapy assumes that clients can examine themselves in more thoughtful ways. Many people, particularly depressed persons, are embedded in their own negative constructions of the world. Beck recognizes that clients' particular worldviews may indeed be accurate, but if one thinks about alternatives in counseling and psychotherapy, these alternative constructions may be even more useful and certainly more growth producing.

Beck's theory has important parallels to Kelly's (1955) personal construct theory in that depressed individuals commonly believe that they have to adhere to a particular set of personal constructs. According to both Beck and Kelly, these personal constructs reflect ineffective hypotheses about the depressed client's world. Thus, the task of the therapist is to change the client's constructs with the expectation that if the way one views the world is changed, the way one acts in the world will also change.

Table 7.1

An Obsessive-Compulsive Personality's Daily Record of Automatic Thoughts

Date	Situation (describe briefly)	Emotions	Automatic Thoughts	Rational Response	Outcome
5/12	Office	Anxiety, fear	If I don't do the report perfectly, I'll get fired.	Do the best you can. Nobody's perfect.	Felt better. Boss liked report.
	Dinner	Anger	Why doesn't my wife have things ready on time?	I'm lucky she cooks at all. I need to help her more.	I helped with meal.
	Movie	Tears, sadness	Why am I doing this? It always happens in sad places.	Just enjoy the movie. It's OK to cry.	More tears? Why?

The Daily Record of Automatic Thoughts. Another counseling technique Beck recommends is the use of the daily record of automatic thoughts. Table 7.1 depicts a portion of the record of the automatic thoughts of a male who was diagnosed as having an obsessive-compulsive personality disorder. Using the daily record method can help the client learn how to identify thinking patterns using one or more of the four steps on page 209.

Experience has shown that automatic thoughts often reappear unless closely monitored for a period of time outside of the interview. The client is instructed to mark on the daily record each time an automatic thought intrudes and the client feels uncomfortable. Just the act of recording such automatic thoughts in itself reinforces and promotes change.

It is crucial that the therapist monitor this daily record form and encourage clients to continue using the form for a sufficient time period to ensure that automatic thoughts do not relapse. If the daily record is discontinued too soon, the client will likely relapse into old patterns of automatic thoughts.

Table 7.1 reveals that the obsessive-compulsive client was able to monitor emotions and thoughts in two situations and change the outcome to a more positive one. His record notes he was in tears at the movie. Many obsessive-compulsive types, contrary to popular stereotype, cry easily yet feel uncomfortable about it. The data gained from the daily record provide the counselor with new information for further cognitive-behavioral treatment. At this point, the cognitive-behavioral therapist can focus on a variety of techniques to understand the meaning of the tears, such as the use of images at the sensorimotor level.

Adding Family/Multicultural Dimensions. The recording of automatic thoughts tends to put the responsibility for most change within the client. As such, multicultural theory would point out that this method fails to consider contextual issues. Gender and multicultural dimensions can be added to the automatic thoughts chart by including a column that specifically focuses on context.

In the above example, the obsessive-compulsive male could review the entire record as an example of sex-role stereotyping learned in the family of origin. In this case, cognitive consciousness raising about the oppressiveness of male roles may be a new and beneficial addition to Beck's orginal theoretical model.

For many individuals, reviewing automatic thought patterns from a gender, family, or multicultural perspective can be very helpful. Women and minorities, for example, may sometimes blame themselves for lack of job advancement. If the record of automatic thoughts is reviewed for examples of sexism or racism, this may change the meaning and the cognitions of the client. At the same time, it is important to balance internal and external responsibility for change.

Multicultural Approaches to CBT

Traditional psychodynamic, humanistic-existential, and cognitive-behavioral theories can be used effectively to foster the mental health of many clients who come from culturally diverse populations. However, to do so, counselors and therapists must acquire knowledge about the values, beliefs, and worldviews of persons who come from different cultural backgrounds to work ethically, effectively, and respectfully with them. Paniagua (2005) stresses the importance of implementing concrete cognitive-behavioral techniques and strategies, as contrasted with humanistic or psychoanalytic approaches in multicultural counseling settings.

Donald Cheek (1976), a pioneer in multiculturally sensitive assertiveness training, demonstrates the validity of traditional behavioral counseling concepts with African-American clients. He was also an early proponent of cognitive methods being used concurrently with assertiveness training, calling this approach "didactic assertiveness training." An example of how Cheek's didactic assertiveness training method is used to address the complex issue of male-female African-American relations in the counseling setting follows:

Therapist: I understand you have trouble rapping with sisters [Black women].

Patient (African-American male): Yeah, that's right. I can seem to talk with White women, but I can't seem to get across to sisters. Like at the last social we had—there was this fine number I wanted to rap with—you know—just get to know her—but I didn't know how to go about it.

Therapist: What if the woman was White?

Patient: Well, I would put on my gentleman act and break it on down.

Therapist: And with a sister?

Patient: Well, I'd either just go along with the program or cuss her out.

Therapist: OK, then maybe you're satisfied with that approach.

Patient: No—that's not the way it should be. I've got feelings and ideas that I really would like to get across—but I don't want her laughing at me or thinking I'm square—you dig?

Cheek interprets this behavior as representative of an underlying anxiety and the need for assertiveness. Cheek (1976) starts the session at the point where the client is most uncomfortable in order to get therapy moving, as "Blacks have little time (or money) to fool around" (p. 67). In this example, some standard techniques of cognitive-behavioral approaches are used, but gender and cultural issues are addressed directly as well. The cognitive work in this dialogue provides a base for the assertiveness training to follow.

Cheek's (1976) pioneering work demonstrates how a CBT approach to counseling and psychotherapy can be effectively used with African-American clients when modified to meet the client's unique linguistic style and life experiences. While Cheek shows how this approach can be used with persons of African descent, he cautions practitioners against simply thinking that modifying traditional forms of counseling and psychotherapy is all that is needed to work ethically and effectively with persons from diverse client populations. In an imaginary dialogue, Cheek speaks directly to this point by noting some of the problems underlying assertive behavior with African-Americans:

Me [Cheek]: A Black person has got to know when to be assertive and when to kiss ass. [*Knowing is a cognitive act. Cheek focuses not just on assertive behavior, but also on the thinking, cognition, and emotion that guide that behavior.* Cheek's 1976 book can now be read as one of the earliest presentations of cognitive-behavioral counseling from a multicultural perspective.]

You: But so does everybody.

Me: I mean it in terms of survival, baby—survival—I mean whether or not the man even lets you live. Ain't that many Whites who got to worry about being killed because they want to be assertive enough to vote. You see the authors on assertiveness have not sufficiently considered the social conditions in which Blacks live—and have lived. That blind spot in many ways alters or changes the manner that assertiveness is applied. Current assertive authors have a great approach—it's an approach which can really aid Black folks, in fact they need it—but at the same time these authors are unable to translate assertiveness training into the examples, language, and caution that fit the realities of a Black lifestyle. (pp. 10–11)

Cheek points out that assertive behavior varies between African-American and White cultures and that both groups need to understand the frame of reference of the other. He also points out that the passive nonviolent stance of the Black freedom movement represented a particularly powerful type of Black assertiveness.

Assertiveness is not aggression; rather, it is culturally relevant behavior and thinking in which people or groups stand up for their rights. In short, Cheek stresses that, when using assertiveness training or other CBT techniques, it is important to be sensitive and respectfully acknowledge how contextual factors impact clients' lives.

Hill and Ballou (2005) welcome the shift of behavioral and cognitive-behavioral theories from a strict individual orientation to a growing awareness of how the social context affects people's development. For example, if a woman has a behavioral difficulty, no longer can we find "fault" with her and her alone. CBT therapists are increasingly encouraged to more accurately see how environmental conditions (such as the pervasive problem of sexism and various forms of patriarchy in our contemporary society) affect their clients' behavior and internal thoughts.

Kantrowitz and Ballou (1992) earlier pointed out that "individuals are still expected to improve their adaptive capacities to meet the environmental conditions, which serve to reinforce the dominant (male) social standards" (p. 79). With this in mind, these feminist theorists argue that assertiveness training is in itself an insufficient form of helping for a woman suffering harassment in the workplace. Kantrowitz and Ballou explain further that action in the community and challenging standard social norms must be considered part of the therapeutic process.

CBT uses the word *cognitive* and as such gives primacy to thinking over feeling. How a person develops in the culture, particularly around issues of gender, is given relatively little attention in most traditional CBT theories. Despite its many positive qualities, feminist authors maintain that CBT needs to be used with caution and sensitivity. Cheek's (1976) early work, discussed above, and Meichenbaum's later constructions of CBT are important in addressing some of the important concerns raised by multicultural and feminist critics of CBT.

The origins of behavioral psychology obviously lie in concrete behavior, with minimal attention given to philosophic constructs. As a result, behavioral counseling and therapy has presented somewhat of a puzzle to those committed to a multicultural-feminist-social justice approach to helping. Behavioral techniques tend to be successful in producing change and, owing to their clarity of direction and purpose, are often understandable and acceptable to minority populations.

At the same time, the behavioral approach can run into problems in multicultural situations over the issue of control. Early ventures in behavioral psychology often gave the therapist, counselor, or teacher almost complete power, and decisions sometimes focused on controlling clients rather than helping them control themselves. Behavioral psychology has been forced to overcome some of these early problems and the resultant fears among minority clients and their advocates (McMullin, 2000).

Meichenbaum has increasingly come to recognize the importance of understanding how cultural and gender differences influence clients' cognitions and behaviors when using CBT, in general, and assertiveness training, in particular. In speaking specifically to multicultural issues, Meichenbaum (1985) notes:

Given the marked variability of reactions to stressful events, stress training programs should take into consideration cultural differences in determining adaptive coping mechanisms. Attempting to train clients to cope in ways that may violate cultural norms could actually aggravate stress-related problems. In some cultures, people tend to cope with stressors passively, by trying to endure them rather than viewing them as challenges and problems to be solved. Stress management training must reflect these cultural preferences. (p. 17)

CBT Strategies: Applications for Practice

The following discussion builds on your present understanding of CBT theory by describing useful ways this theoretical framework can be implemented into your professional practices in the future.

Stress Management

Stress management training programs involve three distinct phases: (1) helping clients develop a cognitive understanding of the role stress plays in their lives, (2) teaching specific coping skills so they can deal with stress more effectively, and (3) working with clients' thoughts and feelings about stressful situations so they will be motivated to do something about stress outside of the counseling and therapy setting. Meichenbaum (1993) makes the important point that cognitive awareness of stress is not enough to produce change, nor are learning new coping skills. One must actually decide to do something. Ultimately, a change in behavior as well as in a client's thoughts and feelings must occur.

As an example, consider a professional couple who may be faced with difficulties in their lives and may frequently argue with each other. Their problem could be defined as "marital difficulty," or it could be defined as a problem in coping with stress. The couple may work full time, be responsiible for two children, and be active in the community. There simply is not time to "do it all" effectively, and this becomes a major stressor in itself.

The first task in stress management counseling is to help the couple define the problem as one of stress. This itself can be useful, as they no longer have to "blame" each other for their difficulties and now can see the impact of environment stressors on their marriage.

Second, this couple may benefit further from learning stress reduction procedures (such as relaxation training), applying new decision-making strategies and social skills (often via a form of assertiveness training), and developing a better understanding of alternative activities they can become engaged in to reenergize themselves from the demands of their careers. These behavioral skills can lead to important life changes and involve the use of a variety of CBT techniques, including, but not limited to, modeling, role-playing, and direct instruction.

Finally, knowing that one has a problem with stress and having some skills to cope with the stressors of life are often not enough to enable clients to lead healthy, satisfying, and productive lives. Will the couple decide for action? At the point of generalization, will the couple's emotional and cognitive world again become stress engendering and result in the reemergence of maladaptive thinking (and the accompanying dysfunctional emotions) that will prevent them from taking effective action in the future?

The various forms of racism that continue to exist in our contemporary society can be particularly damaging for many persons of color (Parham & Parham, 2002). McNeilly (1996) found that racist comments from Whites "triggered significant rises in blood pressure and heart rate in 30 Black women. Racism can act as a potent stressor that may contribute to hypertension and heart disease" (p. A7).

Similarly, a woman who encounters sexual harassment, a gay or lesbian who is attacked for sexual preference, and people in other oppressed groups that experience either short-term or systematic discrimination also suffer physically from stress. When implemented by culturally competent mental health practitioners, stress management training can be an important strategy to use when working with persons from diverse client populations (Lewis et al., 2003).

Stress Management Training. Most therapists and counselors today find themselves required to do some sort of stress inoculation or stress management training as part of individual therapy. Moreover, as a therapist you might well be called on to conduct a group training program in stress management.

Stress management programs combine many of the behavioral techniques described in this chapter plus important cognitive techniques discussed in Chapter 8, as well as the microskills of listening (Chapter 4). You may use any of a large number of strategies in individual counseling and therapy for helping clients deal with stress. For example, you might teach a lonely or shy person the microskills of listening and then use assertiveness training to help this individual become more socially effective. You can teach relaxation training or desensitization to phobic clients to help reduce their stress level. Most cognitive-behavioral techniques can be used for individual or group stress management programs. Competency-Building Activity 7.4 asks you to generate your own stress management program for use with clients in small groups.

Stress Management Training and Trauma. The concepts of stress management and stress inoculation have been expanded to include specific suggestions on how to work with survivors of trauma (rape, abuse, terrorist attacks). Stress management is increasingly vital as a treatment framework in its own right. Meichenbaum (2003) elaborates his innovative ideas about CBT and includes suggested clinical interventions for working with posttraumatic stress clients. Stress management training will not "cure" extremely severe stress issues, but it can be an important part of the therapeutic approach.

One example of an effective stress management training group for traumatized persons is a nine-session stress inoculation counseling program that was used with rape survivors by Foa and others (1991). This innovative intervention was found to be more effective than traditional counseling in that long-term follow-up revealed significant improvement in posttraumatic stress disorder was manifested by the

Competency-Building Activity 7.4

Developing Your Own Stress Management Program

Instructions: To experience the powerfulness of stress management training, get together a small group of three or more individuals with similar issues and spend at least an hour teaching them some of the basic principles of stress management. A model group stress management program includes, but need not be restricted to, the following:

1. *Establishing rapport and relating program goals to your group's special needs.* Usually, there is a special topic or need that the group shares. For instance, your group might be comprised of teenagers, adult children of alcoholics, women dealing with job stress, or an inpatient group diagnosed as borderline. Spend time with your group so they feel part of the process.

   Your task at this stage of this intervention is to share the program goals and learn about the individual needs of your members. Modify your program to meet their wishes and needs.

2. *Providing cognitive instruction that focuses on the origins of stress and what it does to people.* Following the collaborative model, draw out from your group the nature of stressors in their lives. Storytelling and personal sharing will draw your group together and help define a common purpose.

You can share a brief lecture on the nature of stress and what it does to our bodies and to our minds. An analysis of the antecedents, behaviors, and consequences of stress can be especially helpful. In addition, you may want to brainstorm the many stressful events we all face in our daily lives. This list may include various common stressors such as commuting, conflict with supervisors, family arguments, loss of a job, medical issues, or the neighbor's dog barking.

3. *Stress management training.* Select your own favorite stress management techniques for this first session. Review your own special skills and experience and make your first try at stress management training from what you know best. Usually, stress programs include some form of relaxation training, meditation or yoga, personal sharing of coping mechanisms, listening skills training, and assertiveness training. Do not overplan and be sure your program itself is not rushed and stressful.

4. *Homework.* Relapse prevention techniques are an important part of stress management training programs. Unless your trainees are encouraged to "take home" what they have learned, their experience with you is likely to be forgotten. Follow up with your workshop participants a week later to see how effective your program was.

Be sure to take a few minutes to record your reactions to completing this competency-building activity and file these written reactions in your personal/professional portfolio.

---

participants in the stress inoculation intervention in comparison to the clients receiving traditional counseling services. The overall content of the sessions was similar to the general concepts presented in this chapter, with particular emphasis also given to cognitive variables that are similar to those described in Chapter 8.

Foa, Hearst-Ikeda, and Perry (1995) also examined the effectiveness of brief cognitive-behavioral therapy with recent assault survivors and found that a combination of education about common reactions to assault plus CBT resulted in significantly fewer symptoms of posttraumatic stress disorder five and a half months after the assault.

Working with clients who have experienced trauma requires special training beyond the scope of this book. Further directions for working with these clients can be found in Donald Meichenbaum's *A Clinical Handbook/Practical Therapist Manual for Assessing and Treating Adults with Post-Traumatic Stress Disorder (PTSD)* (Meichenbaum, 1994).

Social Skills Training

An important part of the cognitive-behavioral method is life skills training—teaching clients and others specific modes of responding effectively to various life challenges. Social skills training is a popular dimension of life skills training (Dowd & Tierney, 2005; Ivey, Pedersen, & Ivey, 2001). A variety of systematic formulations are used for teaching communication skills, life skills for difficult/delinquent adolescents, marital skills, and skills for psychiatric patients, among others. Life skills training interventions represent theories of counseling and change in their own right. Most often, social skills training involves the following cognitive-behavioral components:

1. *Rapport-building/structuring.* Clients/trainees are prepared cognitively and emotionally for the social skills instruction.

2. *Cognitive presentation and cuing.* Usually, some form of explanation and rationale for the importance of social skills training as a means to realizing a more satisfying and productive life is presented.

3. *Modeling.* Role-plays, videotapes, audiotapes, and demonstrations are commonly used in social skills training interventions so trainees can see and hear effective social skills in action.

4. *Practice.* One does not always learn a skill by cognitive understanding and watching various forms of modeling alone. Most social skills trainers require their clients/trainees to engage in role-played practices that can be supplemented by videotape and audiotape feedback.

5. *Generalization.* All social skills training interventions emphasize the need to take the learning outside and beyond the immediate training setting.

One cognitive-behavioral skills training program that has been found to be effective with persons in different populations and settings involves the use of the microskills framework (see Chapter 4). This framework involves teaching counseling and communication skills to trainees. Researchers have found that teaching these microskills is useful not only for training students in professional counseling and psychology training programs, but also for persons in a wide variety of client groups (Ivey, 1971b, 1991a).

The early research that was done in this area included a series of studies in which Allen Ivey videotaped depressed psychiatric patients talking about their issues with a therapist. The patients viewed the videotape and observed and counted behaviors they themselves identified as being poor social skills (for example, poor eye contact, slumped body posture). The patients were then provided social skills training using the microskills framework and encouraged to practice these skills in role-plays with their therapist (Ivey, 1971b).

On reviewing videotapes of these role-plays, the psychiatric patients counted and charted changes to pinpointed behaviors. This "media therapy" project proved effective in helping patients who had been in the hospital for up to four years to move out of the hospital within from one to two months (Ivey, 1971b).

In addition to psychiatric patients, many other people have benefited from this form of training, including management interns, medical personnel, and hospice workers. Social skills training is a major theoretical and practical form of treatment itself. It is also closely related to assertiveness training strategies.

Assertiveness Training

Some individuals passively accept whatever fate hands them. You may know someone who acts as a "doormat" and allows friends and family to dominate her or him. This person may allow others to make decisions, let strangers cut in front while standing in line, or accept being ignored by a waiter for an hour. Individuals who may be overly passive in their behavior can benefit from assertiveness training and learn to stand up for their rights.

You may also know someone who is overly aggressive and dominating, who tells others what to do and what to think. This person may interrupt conversations rudely, cut in front of others in line, and yell at waiters. This aggressive individual can also benefit from assertiveness training.

Assertiveness training involves learning to stand up for your rights, while simultaneously considering the thoughts and feelings of others. While emphasizing overt behavior, assertiveness training also focuses on client cognitions.

The specifics of assertiveness training are outlined in Competency-Building Activity 7.5. If you can conduct a basic applied behavioral analysis and pinpoint behavior with some precision, you should be able to conduct assertiveness training with sensitivity and skill. As you will see, Competency-Building Activity 7.5 emphasizes a behavioral approach to assertiveness training, with minimal attention directed to internal cognitive states.

This approach is likely to be useful with many persons who are interested in receiving assertiveness training to more effectively deal with the challenges of their lives. However, it is important to note that, if your depressed, agoraphobic, or normal clients do not have some attention paid to their internal states of thinking and feeling, change is much less likely to occur and be maintained. The cognitive dimensions of CBT stressed in Chapter 8 are critical for producing enduring change with these and other clients who participate in assertiveness training interventions.

Multicultural Considerations in Assertiveness Training. Imagine you are working with a woman or an individual from a marginalized group who is dealing with discrimination and other associated stressors. In doing so, it is useful to keep in mind that one important dimension of being able to engage in assertiveness training is

Competency-Building Activity 7.5

An Exercise in Applied Behavioral Analysis and Assertiveness Training

Instructions: The purpose of this exercise is to integrate many of the concepts presented in this chapter in a practical format that you can use to implement assertiveness training in your own counseling practice. With a role-played client who is willing to discuss a specific situation in which he or she may have been too passive or too aggressive, work carefully through the following interview:

Step 1. *Building rapport and structuring.* Remember that data indicate that behaviorally oriented counselors and therapists offer as much or more warmth than counselors who embrace other helping orientations. Recognizing the importance of this point, it is imperative that you establish a positive rapport with your client in your own unique way. You can use attending behavior to "tune in" to the client and client observation skills to note when you have established positive rapport with the individual you are working with.

Give special attention to structuring the interview and telling your client ahead of time what he or she can expect to happen in your meeting. In doing so, you will demonstrate your awareness that behavioral counseling operates in mutuality between counselor and client.

Step 2. *Gathering data.* Your goal here is to get a clear, behavioral definition of the problem your client is experiencing. The basic listening sequence (BLS) (see Chapter 4) will help you draw out the specific behaviors that are associated with the client's difficulty.

Identify a clear, specific instance in which the individual was not sufficiently assertive. Asking for concrete examples will facilitate operationalizing the overly passive or overly aggressive behavior.

Use applied behavioral analysis to find out the antecedents of the behavior. What was the context, and what happened before the behavior occurred? Define the problem behavior even more precisely. Finally, find out what the consequences were after the behavior occurred? In each case, use questioning skills to help the client describe the behavior.

A role-play is a particularly useful way to obtain further behavioral specifics. Once you have a clear picture of the antecedents-behaviors-consequences, have your client role-play the situation, with you acting as the other person(s). Make the role-play as real and accurate as you can.

Finally, draw out positive assets of the client and situation. What strengths does the client have that will be useful in later problem solution? You may find it necessary to provide your client with positive feedback, as nonassertive clients often have trouble identifying any positives in themselves or the situation.

Step 3. *Determining outcomes.* Develop clear, specific behavioral goals with your client. You will want to use listening skills and operationalization of behavior methods. Is the goal established by your client clear, specific, and attainable? Will it lead to change?

Step 4. *Generating alternative solutions.* At this point in the activity you should have identified the client's goal(s) and contrasted his or her goal(s) with the presenting problem. In addition, you should have also identified some of the client's positive assets and strengths.

Now, with your client, review her or his goal(s) and practice in a role-play the new behaviors your client wants to develop to achieve his or her stated goal(s). Continue practicing with your client until she or he demonstrates the ability to engage effectively in the desired behavior.

You may find relaxation training, charting, modeling, and other CBT techniques useful to supplement and enrich your behavioral program.

Step 5. *Generalizing.* It is easy for the successful therapist to stop at the fourth stage. However,

continued on next page

Competency-Building Activity 7.5, continued

it is critical that specific behavioral plans be made with your client for generalization of the behavior beyond the counseling session. Use the relapse prevention workshop (presented later in this chapter) with your client. Be clear and specific with your behavioral goals and anticipate the likely relapse potential. Behavior that is not reinforced immediately after training is likely to be lost two weeks later.

Step 6. *Following up.* One week after the interview, follow up with your client and determine if behavior actually did change. Later follow-ups can be useful to both you and the client. As necessary, use the relapse prevention worksheet to analyze any difficulty with behavioral generalization.

Be sure to take a few minutes to record your reactions to completing this competency-building activity and file these written reactions in your personal/professional portfolio.

feeling good about oneself. Sometimes people who experience discrimination believe that the problems they suffer are "their fault" and that "if only" they behaved more effectively, their problems would be resolved.

In addressing these attitudes, cognitive instruction, as discussed in Chapter 8, can be a vital part of assertiveness training. Furthermore, the ideas of feminist counseling and therapy (FCT) and multicultural counseling and therapy (MCT) (Chapters 11 and 12) clearly show that the focus of your intervention must often be directed to changing the environment, not just the individual. In assertiveness training language, there is a need to help individuals change cognitions about themselves and their environments so they can be more effective and assertive in their lives.

Cheek (1976), for example, talks of the importance of "a foundation for the Black perspective" when providing assertiveness training and other types of psychological services among persons of African descent. When mental health practitioners operate from this perspective, they do not seek to have African-Americans behave or think like European-Americans or to have women think like men. Rather, assertiveness training services that are provided by culturally competent practitioners are presented in ways that reflect a heightened recognition and respect for the perspective and worldview of persons from different multicultural and gender groups. Parham and his colleagues (1999) note that the African-American cognitive perspective includes:

- familiarity and experience in both the African-American and European-American perspectives

- a frequent distrust of European-Americans, with accompanying emotions such as anger and rage

- an emphasis on race and its importance for daily living

Professional Development Extension

Using the CBT Frame of Reference in a School Setting

It could be argued that more aspects of the CBT frame of reference are used in nontherapeutic settings (e.g., educational, business, life skills training settings, etc.) than all the other theoretical approaches discussed in this book. An example of the ways CBT concepts are used in an elementary school setting is presented here.

School counselors developed and implemented a Peace Project among children in a combined kindergarten–first-grade class. This peace education intervention was designed to stimulate a greater understanding of the meaning of peace and its application in daily living and to foster the acquisition of new skills that children can use to realize a greater level of peace at school and in their lives.

The counselors used a broad range of CBT concepts to achieve these goals, including the use of social skills, assertiveness, and relaxation training. To assist the children in acquiring new social skills that could be used to resolve inter-personal differences in respectful and nonviolent ways, such CBT techniques as role-playing and modeling were frequently used in this classroom-based psychological intervention.

Another important component of the Peace Project involved teaching the children meditation techniques to complement the relaxation training they received in this intervention. This part of the project was aimed at using CBT techniques to assist the youngsters in acquiring new self-regulation skills that would be helpful when dealing with the various stressors they encountered in their lives.

To accomplish this objective, the counselors read the youngsters a book entitled *Peaceful Piggy Meditation* (MacLean, 2004) as they sat in a circle on the floor. This easy-to-read, beautifully illustrated book provides clear instructions about simple meditation activities that can help in developing the basic behavioral skills children need to develop to realize a greater level of self-regulation.

After reading the book, the counselors asked the youngsters a number of questions to see if they understood the concepts covered in the story. The counselors then told the children that they could meditate like the Piggy in the story by getting quiet, placing their hand over their hearts, and quietly feeling their heartbeats. As the children got quieter, the counselors asked them to think about their breathing and asked them to think about the air coming in and going out of their bodies as they continued to breathe slowly and deeply.

After the children continued to use these deep breathing and meditation techniques for about three minutes, the counselors asked them to stop and talk about how they felt. Several children said they felt "good," "quiet," and "relaxed." The counselors followed this format two more times by asking the children to continue to relax, breathe deeply, keep their hands on their hearts, and feel their heartbeats. They then asked for the children's reactions to this meditation exercise. After this, the counselors talked about the ways that people can use deep breathing and meditation to stay calm in busy or frustrating times of the day. The counselors provided the chil-dren with paper and crayons and asked them to draw a picture of themselves meditating and getting calm and peaceful. The counselors ended the session by saying they would have the children practice these new skills at different times throughout the rest of the school year, especially whenever the youngsters appeared to be more agitated or distracted than usual.

The students' teachers and parents commented that they were impressed with how well these young children learned these skills and how effective they were in calming students at different times of the day. The teachers indicated that the children participating in the Peace Project demonstrated increased self-regulatory behaviors during the school year and manifested more effective and peaceful interpersonal problem-solving skills while they were at school. Many parents even reported that they had begun incorporating some of the CBT techniques used in the Peace Project at home.

- internal conflict as to whether to talk in White or Black language; African-Americans are often bidialectical in this regard
- an ability to "fake it" with European-Americans

Similar issues of the meaning of assertiveness training with other cultural/racial groups can be raised. For example, assertiveness training for Latinas needs to be conducted with unique gender and cultural sensitivity, for women from a Spanish-speaking tradition face different problems when they adapt assertive behaviors that are reflective of a European-American assertive perspective. This point might be summed up by pointing out that what is considered to be assertive behavior in European-American cultures may be viewed as being intrusive and aggressive by persons in other cultural groups (hooks, 2000).

European-American women usually find assertiveness training helpful, but it is most helpful if combined with a discussion of related issues about being a woman in a sexist society. Ballou and West (2000) give special attention to these issues by pointing out that assertiveness training should not be used to teach women a man's style of being but rather be based on models of liberation psychology that are grounded in feminist principles of mental health (Hill & Ballou, 2005).

Most counselors and psychologists are likely to agree that it is important to be culturally respectful and responsive when using CBT interventions among persons from diverse client populations. A second point of agreement is likely to be found in the expressed need to develop and implement relapse prevention strategies among all clients we serve.

Relapse Prevention

In counseling sessions and CBT-based training interventions (e.g., stress management, social skills, assertiveness training interventions), you are likely to see some positive changes in clients' attitudes and behaviors. Helping clients maintain these changes becomes challenging when they return to their home or work environment and encounter the same problems that led them to seek professional help in the first place. For instance, an alcohol abuser or a teenager suffering from bulimia must live with the same family and/or job circumstances that are likely to have played a role in generating their original difficulties.

Clients will often lose the insights and new skills gained in counseling and therapy if the counselor does not assist clients in developing plans to maintain these gains. For this reason, relapse prevention (RP) is an important consideration when providing counseling, psychotherapeutic, and other training services.

Research on relapse has shown that the initial lapse in treatment is predictive of future and continued lapses (Stevens-Smith, 1998). For example, in weight control therapy, the way the overeater handles the first failure to stay on the diet is highly predictive of what will happen in the future. Because skills developed in counseling and therapy have not yet been tested in real-life situations, we can expect relapse in nearly 100 percent of our clients in some form.

Your task as a mental health practitioner is to help your clients construct individualized relapse prevention programs to ensure that newly learned behaviors and insights are not lost shortly after the interview. Research on RP clearly indicates that a systematic program can help clients learn more from their participation in counseling and therapy and help maintain their behavioral change for a longer time (Marlatt & Donovan, 2005).

Helping Clients Cope with the Environment. Environmental realities (family, job, the availability of cigarettes, drugs, and so on) often conspire to make long-term behavioral maintenance almost impossible. To combat the difficulties of the environment, Stevens-Smith (1998) outlines four points that are helpful in assisting clients to become more prepared to manage the postcounseling environment.

1. *Anticipate difficult situations.* Clients can often predict the circumstances likely to be threatening to their resolve to maintain their behavioral change program. Clients, with the counselor's assistance, can identify high-risk situations that might sabotage new learning and serve as early warning signs so that they will be on guard against relapse.

2. *Regulate thoughts and feelings.* Emotions can sometimes get out of control and make us feel incompetent, upset, or temporarily irrational. This is when clients experience some sort of relapse. However, relapses are less likely to occur if clients can anticipate these temporary responses and then return to a rational approach and learn from their mistakes.

3. *Diagnose necessary support skills.* Although we may help clients change behavior, their old patterns may reemerge when they are in a hurry or when faced with other stressors. Techniques such as assertiveness training, time management, or key cognitive skills may be useful in helping clients avoid eventual relapse.

4. *Regulate consequences.* A key behavioral concern is to provide appropriate consequences for behavior. When a client maintains a new behavior, there will be no thunderous applause. That support must come from the client, who must learn how to create meaningful rewards for good actions and behavioral maintenance.

Making Relapse Prevention Work for You. Competency-Building Activity 7.6 summarizes a RP program that you are encouraged to use with a real or role-played client. Note that RP is skill specific. For example, a client may want to stop overeating. The task of the therapist is to help the client understand several strategies that are available for controlling overeating. Once clients have learned the behavioral techniques to slow down the rate of eating (that is, eat only in specified places and times, monitor calories, understand how emotions affect eating, and eliminate discretionary eating), they are ready to begin preparing for the hurdles in the environment once counseling is over and they must manage on their own.

Competency-Building Activity 7.6

Relapse Prevention Worksheet

Instructions: Go through the worksheet below by yourself, perhaps using a behavior you have difficulty maintaining. Alternatively, use the form to go through the danger of relapse with a real or role-played client.

I. Choose an appropriate behavior to retain

Describe in detail the behavior you intend to retain.
How often will you use it?
How will you know when a slip occurs?

II. Use relapse prevention strategies

1. Strategies to help you anticipate and monitor potential difficulties (regulating stimuli)

   - Do you understand the relapse process? What is it?
   - What are the differences between learning the behavioral skill or thought and using it in a difficult situation?
   - What is your support network? Who can help you maintain the skill?
   - What are high-risk situations? What kind of people, places, or situations will make retention especially difficult?

2. Strategies to increase rational thinking (regulating thoughts and feelings)

- What might be an unreasonable emotional response to a temporary slip or relapse?
- What can you do to think more effectively in tempting situations or after a relapse?

3. Strategies to diagnose and practice related support skills (regulating behaviors)

   - What additional support skills do you need to retain the skill? Assertiveness? Relaxation? Microskills?

4. Strategies to provide appropriate outcomes for behavior (regulating consequences)

   - Can you identify some likely outcomes of your succeeding with your new behavior?
   - How can you reward yourself for a job well done? Generate specific rewards and satisfactions.

III. Predict the circumstance of the first lapse

Describe the details of how the first lapse might occur, including people, places, times, emotional states.

After you have completed this competency-building activity, take a few minutes to write down your reactions to this exercise and file it in your personal/professional development portfolio.

Source: Adapted from R. Marx, *Self-management strategies for skill retention*, University of Massachusetts. Used by permission.

Practical Implications and Limitations of CBT

Ineffective and careless counseling can endanger clients. No matter how good the theory or the potential power of a counseling or therapeutic intervention is, the counselor has the professional and ethical responsibility to be aware of manifestations of false practice. The term *manipulative cognitive-behavioral counseling* can be used to describe the misuse of the techniques presented in this chapter.

Manipulative cognitive-behavioral counseling occurs when the counselor makes a decision for the client without client awareness or when the counselor has so much power in the client's life that the client has no choice but to go along with the CBT program whether or not he or she agrees with it. For example, a focus of behavioral counselors has been to increase "time on task" (amount of time spent working at one's desk) in elementary classrooms. This can be a desirable educational goal, but sometimes these behavioral interventions have been implemented without child or parent awareness that anything was being changed.

Cognitive-behavioral techniques are often readily accepted by many clients in diverse cultural/racial groups due to their clarity and effectiveness. At the same time, effectiveness does not equate with cultural appropriateness. As Cheek reminds us, cognitive-behavioral techniques need to be applied with the gender and culture of the client in mind.

The several competency-building exercises included in this chapter provide a solid beginning in CBT. Relapse prevention is an especially useful set of techniques to add to the final stages of the interview, regardless of which therapeutic technique or theory you are using. The fifth stage of the interview (generalization), follow-up with clients after the interview, and relapse prevention are critical elements for therapy.

Behavioral techniques "work," and clients often benefit from and enjoy the specificity of these techniques. At the same time, some clients will change their behavior but still feel that "something is missing." These clients may benefit from the addition of more cognitive methods (see Chapter 8) to your treatment plan, or some may want to examine the reasons their behavior developed as it did. In short, you may find that behavioral counseling benefits from association with other helping theories. The Professional Development Extension on page 221 presents how a multifaceted CBT approach was used in an elementary school setting.

Summary

Now that you have completed this chapter, you should have a greater understanding of many of the factors that have contributed to the development of the cognitive-behavioral therapy (CBT) perspective as an important second force in the mental health professions. More specifically, we hope the information presented in this chapter has increased your knowledge of the evolving worldview of CBT, which has moved from an emphasis on observable behavior and action to include the inner world of cognitions.

It is also hoped that you have found the competency-building activities included in this chapter helpful in developing some of the fundamental skills that are employed by cognitive-behavioral counselors and therapists. These competency-building activities are intentionally designed to increase your ability to implement a broad range of behavioral counseling and therapy strategies into your professional practices. This includes activities to help you develop some of the basic skills necessary to implement applied behavioral analysis, relaxation training, systematic desensitization, social skills and assertiveness training, and relapse prevention strategies in your work.

Throughout this chapter you have been encouraged to keep in mind the importance of working in a culturally respectful and sensitive manner when using cognitive-behavioral strategies with persons from diverse groups and backgrounds. This important point is reexamined in Chapter 8, where you will be introduced to the important contributions Albert Ellis and William Glasser have made in fostering the ongoing evolution of the second theoretical force (cognitive-behavioral counseling and therapy) in the mental health professions.

Multimedia Resources for This Chapter

The following online resources offer video and other resources of particular relevance to this chapter of your text.

Companion Website

Go to **www.ablongman.com/Ivey6e** to view the following video clips:

- Video clip 7.1 demonstrates one approach to establishing yourself as a helper in multicultural settings. You will see that some of the basic requirements include skills in observation and listening, some beginning knowledge of multicultural differences in style, and a willingness to share part of yourself.

- Video clip 7.2 provides an opportunity to see and hear some of the ways that a counselor can use CBT approaches in an interview with a Black female client.

MyHelpingLab

If a MyHelpingLab passcode was included with your textbook and you have activated your passcode:

- go to **www.ablongman.com/myhelpinglab**
- enter the "Counseling" area of the site by clicking on that tab
- select "Video Lab" from the toolbar to the left of the page
- select "MyHelpingLab Videos by Theoretical Approach"
- select any of the following theory modules—"Behavioral," "Cognitive," and "Cognitive-Behavioral"—to view various video clips of therapists using these approaches with clients

chapter 8

Rational-Emotive Behavioral Therapy and Reality Therapy

This chapter is designed to:

1. Present the worldview provided by the more cognitive portion of the cognitive-behavior therapy (CBT) tradition.

2. Illustrate the work of two important cognitive-behavioral theorists—Albert Ellis and William Glasser.

3. Enable you to gain an understanding of the skills required for rational-emotive behavioral analysis of cognitions and reality therapy.

4. Relate the cognitive orientation to multicultural counseling and therapy.

5. Expand your thinking about the many ways that rational-emotive-behavior-contextual therapy (REBCT) and reality therapy concepts can be used in a broad range of helping settings.

Introduction

Chapter 7 described the evolution of behavioral psychology from its beginnings in scientific psychology to a more cognitive orientation as exemplified by Aaron Beck. Commenting on Beck's contributions in fostering the evolution of the cognitive-behavioral force, Gladding (2000) states that Beck "developed a cognitive approach to mental disorders at about the same time that Albert Ellis was developing his ideas about rational-emotive behavioral therapy in the late 1950s and early 1960s. In doing so, Beck emphasized the importance of cognitive thinking in his theory, especially *dysfunctional thoughts,* thoughts that are nonproductive and unrealistic" (p. 235).

As discussed in Chapter 7, Beck's work, along with the theoretical contributions of Donald Meichenbaum, greatly extended the thinking of earlier behavioral theorists such as Pavlov, Watson, and Skinner. As a result, Beck and Meichenbaum are thought to be major contributors to the current cognitive-behavioral perspective that has gained tremendous popularity in the mental health professions. By reading this chapter, your knowledge of the cognitive-behavioral theoretical force will be further expanded by learning about the work of two additional theorists—Albert Ellis and William Glasser.

In different ways, Ellis and Glasser have played significant roles in extending the purview of CBT. Both of these leaders underscore the importance of two goals in counseling and therapy: (1) examining how clients think about themselves and their world and, if necessary, helping them change these cognitions, and (2) ensuring that clients act on those changed cognitions by exhibiting new behaviors in their daily lives—thus the term *cognitive-behavioral*.

Cognition and the Cognitive-Behavioral Force: A Worldview

Most reviewers of the cognitive frame of reference trace the history of the movement to the stoic philosopher Epictetus, who noted that people "are disturbed not by events, but by the views they take of them." Changing how one thinks about the world, then, becomes a major goal of the cognitive-behavioral point of view. A worldview in which thinking and ideas about the world are central can also be traced beyond stoicism to Plato and to the philosophies of idealism.

The philosophies of idealism emphasize that the idea one has about the world is more important than what is "real." In fact, the concept of "reality" may be dismissed by the idealists as mere "ideas about things." More recent adaptations of the idealistic philosophic tradition are manifested in the work of Kant and Hegel.

The work of Freud fits the philosophic tradition of stoicism. As a stoic, Freud felt that little could be done about the human condition except to know it and understand it. Behavioral change may be helpful in the psychodynamic frame of reference but is still viewed as relatively limited in scope from this theoretical perspective.

Few persons in counseling and psychology would disagree with the important role that cognitions play in fostering self-understanding and healthy psychological functioning. However, many individuals in these fields also ask, "But what about 'reality' and people's reactions to the stressful situations they routinely face in their daily lives?"

The British and American logical positivists and pragmatists (Bentham, Mill, James, and Russell) have questioned that cognition and good thinking are meaningful or sufficient for living in the real world in and of themselves. Out of their philosophic work has arisen the optimistic scientific tradition of hypothesis testing and direct action on the world. Behavioral psychology, as represented by Skinner and the cognitive-behavioral work of Meichenbaum and Beck, is an obvious extension of this scientific, realistic orientation.

Existentialist philosophers such as Kierkegaard, Tillich, and Sartre question both idealistic and realistic philosophers by emphasizing the act of individual choice and the process of intentionally choosing and deciding in life. Rogers and Perls clearly represent this philosophic helping orientation in their existential-humanistic theories as well (Chapters 9 and 10).

The cognitive-behavioral worldview may be described as a beginning attempt to integrate the three major philosophic traditions of idealism, realism, and existentialism. There is no better place to find these three philosophic traditions integrated in counseling and psychology than in Albert Ellis's rational-emotive behavioral therapy (REBT), which has recently been expanded to rational-emotive-behavioral-contextual therapy (REBCT).

Albert Ellis, considered a pioneer of cognitive-behavioral theory, first maintained a psychodynamic practice. He then started to work on his theory of rational-emotive therapy, which was classified in the existential-humanistic tradition for many years. Throughout his career, Ellis has consistently stressed the importance of action in his theoretical writings and clinical practice.

Ellis also helped to integrate the three philosophical traditions mentioned above by emphasizing three fundamental points in his theoretical framework. In doing so, Ellis pointed out that we live in a kind of world that we may not always wish it would be (existentialism). Despite the limitations that mark the situations faced in life, Ellis asserted that people can strive for a more ideal way of thinking and acting in their world (idealism).

Ellis stressed that, in striving to think and act in new and more rational ways, people would be able to realize a greater level of personal satisfaction as a result of learning to more effectively deal with the day-to-day challenges they face in their lives (realism).

William Glasser's reality therapy theory represents another important integrative force in the evolution of the CBT movement. Simply stated, Glasser's theory acknowledges that some of the environmental conditions encountered in life are not susceptible to being significantly altered, at least in the foreseeable future (existentialism). Nevertheless, Glasser insists that people can all realize a more ideal state of being in the world by making a commitment to control those aspects of their lives that are indeed controllable—namely, thoughts and actions (realism). Glasser acknowledges that in doing so, people must constantly assess the degree to which the implementation of new ways of thinking and acting actually lead to a greater level of satisfaction and productivity in the real world we face every day (realism).

Ellis and Glasser both have used their techniques successfully with culturally different clients. As these two theorists have demonstrated, part of what is involved in surmounting discrimination, prejudice, and unfairness is generating a new cognitive view of self and the ability to change environmental situations. These points are reflected in the work of some contemporary reality therapy practitioners. However, they are even more apparent in Ellis's early work as an advocate for the rights of women and gay persons as well as in his recent acknowledgment of the importance of incorporating contextual considerations into his REBT framework (Rigazio-DiGilio, Ellis, D'Andrea, Ivey, & Gutterman, 1999).

The worldview of the cognitive-behavioral therapy movement reflects an evolving synthesis of the three major philosophic traditions of the Western world. Therefore, the cognitive-behavioral counselor or therapist is interested in knowing how individuals develop ideas or cognitions about reality, choose to implement some of these ideas from the many possibilities, and act and behave in relationship to reality.

The growing popularity of CBT has resulted in the proliferation of many theoretical models in this area over the past 40 years. The theories of Ellis and Glasser, however, lead the way because of the significant impact they have had in the ongoing evolution of the second major theoretical force in counseling and psychology to the present time.

Albert Ellis and Rational-Emotive Behavior Therapy

Born into a Jewish family in Pittsburgh, Pennsylvania, on September 17, 1913, Albert Ellis was the eldest of three children. Ellis's father had limited success in a series of business ventures and did little better in expressing affection to his children.

Ellis described his mother as a self-absorbed woman with a bipolar affect: "a bustling chatterbox who never listened" (Ellis, Abrams, & Abrams, 2005, p. 1). As emotionally unavailable as his father, Ellis's mother was often still asleep when he left for school and frequently was not at home when he returned. Additional insights into Ellis's childhood experiences follow:

> Instead of feeling bitter [about his parents' lack of emotional responsiveness], Ellis took on the responsibility of caring for his siblings. He purchased an alarm clock with his own money and woke and dressed his younger brother and sister. Despite the emotional paucity, his family had very little privation until the Depression. That historic event necessitated Albert and his brother and sister to seek work to assist the family.
>
> Young Albert was a frail young man who suffered numerous health problems throughout his youth. At the age of five, he was hospitalized with a kidney ailment. He was also hospitalized with tonsillitis shortly thereafter, which led to a severe infection requiring emergency surgery. He reported that he had eight hospitalizations between the ages of five and seven. One of these hospitalizations lasted nearly a year. His parents provided little or no emotional support for him during these years, rarely visiting or consoling him. Ellis stated that he learned to confront his adversities as he had "developed a growing indifference to that dereliction" (Ellis, Abrams, & Abrams, 2005, p. 3).

Ellis's Early Training

Ellis attended City University of New York in the mid 1920s, majoring in business. On graduating from this institution, he briefly tried to secure a business career only to find that this was not his life's calling. During these early adult years, Ellis explored his literary capabilities by writing fiction. Although he discovered that he was not an effective fictional writer, he did learn that he had a talent for nonfiction.

Much of his early nonfiction writing focused on a broad range of issues related to human sexuality. Since there were virtually no experts in human sexuality at the time, Ellis soon developed a respected reputation for his expertise in this area. Consequently, he was increasingly called on to counsel individuals who were experiencing various sexually related problems and concerns.

Partly due to the success in providing these lay counseling services, Ellis decided to enroll in the clinical psychology doctoral program at Columbia University in 1942, where he received training in the psychoanalytic tradition. After acquiring his doctoral degree in 1947, Ellis began working full time in private practice. While working as a clinical psychologist, Ellis continued to receive psychoanalytic training and supervision from Robert Hulbeck, a leading training analyst at the Karen Horney Institute. Horney, a psychoanalytic leader in her own right, was a very influential force in Ellis's professional development. It was Horney who introduced Ellis to a number of other psychoanalytic leaders, including Alfred Adler, Erich Fromm, and Harry Stack Sullivan, to name a few, who influenced his early thinking about counseling and psychotherapy.

While Ellis's extensive training and personal involvement in psychoanalysis led him to develop a sound understanding of the psychoanalytic worldview, it also resulted in him becoming disgruntled with various aspects of this helping perspective. His increasing disagreement with many of the central tenets of the psychoanalytic perspective resulted in the formation of his own theory of counseling and psychotherapy.

Ellis's New Approach

Ellis formulated what he originally referred to as rational-emotive therapy (RET) in the mid 1950s as he became increasingly aware of the ineffectiveness of psychoanalysis to produce lasting change in his patients. Although he had an extremely successful private psychoanalytic practice, he was dissatisfied with the results he was obtaining. Gradually, Ellis found himself taking a more active role in therapy, attacking his clients' logic, and even prescribing behavioral activities for patients to follow after they left therapy (Ellis, 1983).

As his own thinking about counseling and psychotherapy evolved, Ellis increasingly found it useful to link clients' irrational thoughts with their ineffective behaviors. As a result, Ellis can be credited with pioneering a method of cognitive therapy connected to classic behavioral theory and method.

In a revision of his classic *Reason and Emotion in Psychotherapy* (1995), Ellis changed the name of his 40-year-old therapeutic method from rational-emotive therapy (RET) to rational-emotive behavior therapy (REBT). He provides a detailed explanation for this name change in the following illustrative summary:

> RET is a misleading name because it omits the highly behavioral aspect that rational-emotive therapy has favored right from the start. RET has always been one of the most behaviorally oriented of the cognitive-behavior therapies. In addition to employing systematic desensitization and showing clients how to use imaginal methods of exposing themselves to phobias and anxiety-provoking situations (Wolpe, 1982), it favors in vivo desensitization or exposure. [It is] more behavioral than the procedures of other leading cognitive-behavioral therapies. RET has really always been rational-emotive behavior therapy (REBT). (pp. 86–89)

Central Theoretical Constructs and Techniques of REBT

Ellis and the REBT approach focus more on dysfunctional thoughts than do other therapies, although the importance of emotional reactions is also stressed (Ellis, 1999). The REBT view is that people often make themselves emotional victims by their own distorted, unrealistic, and irrational thought patterns.

Ellis takes an essentially optimistic view of people, but criticizes some humanistic approaches as being too soft at times and failing to address the fact that people can virtually "self-destruct" through irrational and muddled thinking. Consequently, the task of the REBT therapist is to correct clients' thought patterns by minimizing irrational ideas while simultaneously helping them to change their dysfunctional feelings and behaviors.

Emotion and REBT

Emotion is central in REBT theory (Ellis, 2000). Unless the "E" in REBT is present, change is unlikely to occur. Ellis, himself, is often seen personally as a highly rational and logical person. Yet awareness of others' emotions and constructions of reality is central to his approach. Weinrach (1990) provides the following personal anecdote in which he describes his observations of Ellis in action as he supervises a beginning helper:

> One of the students played a tape which reflected virtually no mastery of the RET concepts or techniques which had been exhaustively taught and demonstrated over the previous three days. As the tape played, other group members and I expected Al to show some understandable frustration or exasperation. To the contrary, Al proved to be the ever-patient, tender, and gentle master teacher. He started at the very beginning and taught this student the basics of RET, step-by-step. That experience forced me to reconcile the discrepancy between Al's public and private personae. (p. 108)

Ellis unconditionally accepts all manner of clients, just as does Rogers (Chapter 9). And, like Perls (Chapter 10), Ellis is searching for authenticity. Ellis encourages clients to think rationally and be in touch with their emotions. In doing so, he may use bibliotherapy and ask clients to write journals to increase their self-understanding. He may use humor or sarcasm, as appropriate, with other clients. He constantly stresses "homework" as important to the change process, seeking to have clients generalize ideas from the interview to their daily lives.

Examining Philosophy and Belief Systems

Ellis distinguishes REBT from other cognitive-behavioral theories, putting an emphasis on philosophy (Ellis, 1994).

> CBT of course emphasizes cognitive processes, but it does not have a specific philosophic emphasis, as REBT does. Donald Meichenbaum, a leading proponent of CBT, covers many techniques, but often significantly omits any stress

on a distinctly philosophic outlook. REBT, on the other hand, emphasizes that humans are born (as well as reared) as philosophers and that they are natural scientists, creators of meaning, and users of rational means to predict the future. One of its main goals, therefore, is to help clients make *profound philosophic changes* that will affect their future as well as their present emotions and behaviors. (pp. 241–242)

One of the central constructs of REBT relates to clients' **belief systems**. Belief systems are organized ways of thinking about reality and one's personal experience. Belief systems are the concrete operations of abstract formal philosophy. The language clients use constantly tells us about their personal philosophy and belief systems. For example, as a gay male talked about his concerns in psychotherapy, Ellis carefully followed this client's language to ascertain the degree to which the client had adopted oppressive ideas from society. The clients' belief system resulted in a negative self-view that reflected the client's own internalized oppression.

It is important in a cognitive approach to have the client examine this negative belief system and strive to find positive ways of thinking about him- or herself. This is an important step in realizing what social justice counseling advocates refer to as a **psychology for liberation** (Martin-Baro, 1994). As one goes further into this helping process, it is possible to examine the client's overarching belief systems and personal philosophy of life in greater depth, which can lead to more sophisticated forms of a liberated psychology (Ivey & Ivey, 2001).

Ellis (1994) believes in free will, pointing out that clients "*create* their own emotional disturbances by strongly believing in absolutistic, irrational beliefs" (p. 248). Clients can actively choose their belief systems and philosophies, but all too often they choose a language and philosophy that are irrational and cause them cognitive and behavioral difficulties. REBT is an attempt to bring these irrational views to consciousness and effect change.

If clients are to change, Ellis (2000) suggests that it is important for counselors and therapists to help them (1) examine the ways in which they construct meaning in their lives, (2) understand the irrational beliefs that underlie many of their mental constructions, (3) reconstruct more rational cognitions, and (4) use their free will to commit themselves to make behavior changes that are based on new and more rational constructions of themselves and the world in which they operate.

Thus, as the counselor or therapist helps clients identify and work with irrational thoughts, it becomes possible to organize these ideas into larger and more rational philosophic patterns. Effective REBT can help clients solve specific, concrete problems and then examine their philosophy of life. For the gay client referred to earlier, we might expect that attacking specific irrational ideas would eventually lead to a new philosophy of being gay in a homophobic society and, hopefully, the motivation to act in new, more satisfying, and psychologically liberated ways.

There are many steps one must take in becoming an effective REBT practitioner. One of the first steps an individual needs to take in becoming proficient in this helping framework involves learning to identify irrationality in the language of the client.

Identifying Irrational Statements

In counseling and psychotherapy, clients will frequently use such irrational statements as "If I don't pass this course, it is the end of the world," "Because my parents have been cruel to me as a child, there is nothing I can do now to help myself," "Since the economy is lacking jobs, I can't have a good life," "If I can't get that scholarship, all is ended," and "The reason I have nothing is that the rich have taken it all." All of these statements at one level are true, but all of them represent "helpless" thinking, a common end result of irrational thought.

People learn to incorporate many irrational or dysfunctional ideas into their belief systems during the course of their lives. Ellis and Dryden (1997) note the following irrational and dysfunctional ideas that many persons commonly use. As you review these statements, you will find that there is an underlying demand for perfection accompanied by a denial of the impossibility of such perfection. As you read these examples, think about those that might apply to yourself.

1. It is a *necessity* to be loved and approved of by *all* important people around us.
   "If he (or she) doesn't love me, it is awful."

2. It is *required* that one be *thoroughly* competent, adequate, and achieving if a person is to be worthwhile.
   "If I don't make the goal, it's all my fault."

3. Some people are bad and *should* be punished for it.
   "He (or she) did that to me and I'm going to get even."

4. It is better to *avoid* difficulties and responsibilities.
   "It won't make any difference if I don't do that. People won't care."

5. It is *awful* or *catastrophic* if things are not the way they are supposed to be.
   "Isn't it terrible that the house isn't picked up?"

Assess these statements for "all-or-none" thinking—irrational thinking that helps the client avoid the complexity of life. This list can be amplified, but more at issue is your ability to recognize irrational thinking in the forms it takes. Listen carefully to those around you, and you'll discover that the world is full of irrational ideas and thoughts. As you listen to others talking around you, keep in mind that the words *should, ought, never,* and *must* are useful indicators of irrational thinking (Ellis, 1999).

The basic therapeutic strategy in REBT is always to be on the alert for irrational thinking and, when it is observed, to confront it directly, concretely, and immediately. REBT counselors vary in their use of microskills, but Ellis uses a large number of open and closed questions, directives, interpretations, and advice giving in his approach. The listening skills of paraphrasing and reflection of feeling play a less prominent role in his theory. Confrontation of cognitive discrepancies is central.

Integration of Theory and Action

By his own account, Ellis may or may not spend time developing rapport with clients. His unique personal style is known for starting the interview in a direct, rather confrontive manner. Despite this unique approach to helping, Ellis demonstrates a nonjudgmental attitude about lifestyle issues. This nonjudgmental approach includes insisting that clients need to make more rational decisions that are based on a growing awareness of their own personal preferences rather than "absolute musts" they have somehow acquired in their thinking. Then they need to learn to live comfortably with the implementation of these rational decisions in their daily lives.

The following transcript illustrates how Ellis (1971) rapidly moves into direct action with one of his clients. The primary goal of this intervention is to help the client decide how he wants to live with being gay. Ellis's work with this client reflects much of his thinking about his cognitive-behavioral helping theory. If the same client were treated today, some attention might also be paid to other contextual aspects of a gay person's life, such as the issue of discrimination against gay men and lesbians in contemporary society.

1. *Therapist:* What's the main thing that's bothering you? [*Open question*]

2. *Client:* I have a fear of that I'm gay—a *real* fear of it!

3. *Therapist:* A fear of *becoming* gay? [*Encourager*]

4. *Client:* Yeah.

5. *Therapist:* Because "*if* I were gay—," what? [*Open question, oriented to helping the client think in terms of logical consequences, a skill basic to RET work. Note that Ellis here focuses on thoughts or cognitions about being gay rather than on behavior. "It is not things, but how we view things" that is most important.*]

6. *Client:* I don't know. It really gets me down. It gets me to a point where I'm doubting every day. I do doubt everything, anyway.

7. *Therapist:* Yes. But let's get back to—answer the question: "If I were gay, what would that make me?" [*Directive, open question*]

8. *Client:* (pause) I don't know.

9. *Therapist:* Yes, you do! Now, I can give *you* the answer to the question. But let's see if you can get it. [*Opinion, directive*]

10. *Client:* (pause) Less than a person?

11. *Therapist:* Yes. Quite obviously, you're saying: "I'm *bad* enough. But if I were gay, that would make me a *total* shit!" [*Interpretation, logical consequences. Ellis often uses language to shock, and in this process, the client realizes that even if the "worst" is said, the client still survives and is respected by Ellis. Underneath the "tough" demanding exterior, Ellis demonstrates immense positive regard for the strengths within each individual. This particular interpretation also focused on the logical consequences of the client's thinking. Note that A = the possible facts, B = the beliefs about the facts at A, and C = the emotional consequence. Ellis is particularly skilled at drawing out the cognitive thought patterns or sequences in client thinking and emotion.*]

12. *Client:* That's right.

13. *Therapist:* Now, why did you just say you don't know? [*Open question*]

14. *Client:* Just taking a guess at it, that's all. It's—it's just that the fear really gets me down! I don't know why.

15. *Therapist:* (laughing) Well, you just gave the reason why! Suppose you were saying the same thing about—we'll just say—stealing. You hadn't stolen anything, but you thought of stealing something. And you said, "If I stole, I would be a thorough shit!" Just suppose that. Then, how much would you then start thinking about stealing? [*Expression of content—sharing information/instruction, closed question*]

16. *Client:* (silence)

17. *Therapist:* If you believed that "If I stole it, I would be a thorough shit!"—would you think of it often? Occasionally? [*Closed question*]

18. *Client:* I'd think of it often.

19. *Therapist:* That's right! As soon as you say, "If so-and-so happens, I would be a thorough shit!" you'll get obsessed with so-and-so. And the reason you're getting obsessed with being gay is this nutty belief, "If I were gay, I would be a total shit!" Now, look at that belief for a moment. And let's admit that if you were gay, it would have real disadvantages. Let's assume that. But why would you be a thorough shit if you were gay? Let's suppose you gave up girls completely, and you just screwed guys. Now, why would you be a thorough shit? [*Encourager, interpretation, directive, open question. Here we see the more inclusive microskill of logical consequences as discussed in Chapter 4, used in its fullest sense.*]

20. *Client:* (mumbles incoherently; is obviously having trouble finding an answer)

21. *Therapist:* Think about it for a moment. [*Directive*] (pp. 102–103)

In later stages of the interview, Ellis seeks to have the client decide what he wants to do for logical reasons that are satisfactory emotionally—thus the terms *rational* and *emotive*. The individual must think and feel a decision is correct.

This interviewing style may be most appropriate for Ellis, as it is congruent with his personality. You may not choose to be as forceful and direct if this style is not personally authentic for you. However, it is possible to use the theory of rational-emotive behavior therapy in a fashion that is authentic to you.

The goal of the client and therapist in this session was to change cognitions about the idea of being gay (cognitive), to make decisions about how one wants to live (cognitive-existential), and to then act according to those decisions (behavioral). This reflects the integration of the three basic philosophic traditions of idealism, existentialism, and realism discussed earlier.

When encouraging clients to act on their cognitions, Ellis is likely to use role-plays similar to those of social learning theory (modeling) or Kelly's (1955) fixed-role therapy. He almost certainly would recommend "homework" in the final stages of the interview to ensure that the client does something different as a result of the session. In the follow-up interview, Ellis would likely check carefully on whether or not the client had done anything differently in the time between sessions. Current therapeutic work with clients debating sexual orientation would possibly include homework assignments to help build awareness of the gay pride movement and examine the role of the media in stereotyping as well as creative uses of bibliotherapy.

Ellis has a long history of tolerance for human diversity. Ellis was one of the first to recognize the importance of viewing gay and lesbian persons as individuals who are exercising an alternative lifestyle and should not be considered as being "pathological" or a "clinical problem" because of their sexual orientation (Ellis, 1958). Consequently, he would support a gay male or lesbian client in activities oriented toward helping the community become more aware of the group's special needs. While working with a client, Ellis would continue to challenge the basic assumptions and logical structure of the client's thinking, never hesitating to challenge any client whose thought and emotional patterns were self- or socially defeating.

An abbreviated REBT self-help form is presented in Competency-Building Activity 8.1. This form may be useful in aiding you to identify your own and your clients' faulty thought patterns. In addition, this exhibit summarizes the A-B-C/D-E-F patterns discussed in the subsection that follows.

The A-B-Cs of Cognition

Perhaps Ellis's most important concrete methodological contribution is his A-B-C theory of personality, which can be summarized as follows:

A—the "objective" facts, events, behaviors that an individual encounters
B—the person's beliefs about A
C—the emotional consequences, or how a person feels and acts about A

People tend to consider that A causes C, or that facts cause consequences. Ellis challenges this equation as naive, pointing out that it is what people think about an event that determines how they feel. Applying the A-B-C framework to the preceding interview with the gay client, we see that

A—The "objective fact" is the possibility of being gay.
B—The client believes being gay is bad and self-denigrating.
C—Therefore, as an emotional consequence, the client experiences guilt, fear, and negative self-thoughts.

In this case the client has short-circuited B, concluding that "if I am a gay, I am bad." Ellis's goal is to attack this belief system. What the client thinks about being gay causes his anxiety and difficulties, not the objective facts of the situation. There are obviously numerous gay, lesbian, and heterosexual people who believe that alternative lifestyles are valid and who do not come to the same conclusion (C) that this client did.

Ellis's approach in this case was to challenge the client's logic: "If I were gay, I would be a total shit." He points out the A-causes-C conclusion and challenges the irrationality of this "logic." Again, it can be seen that it is not the specific beliefs that are challenged, but rather the unfoundedness of those beliefs that leads to illogical conclusions.

Competency-Building Activity 8.1

Rational-Emotive Behavior Therapy Self-Help Form

Instructions: This form can be used for examining yourself. It also can be used with equal effectiveness in the interview with your clients and/or as a homework assignment for them.

1. *Identify objective facts, events, or behaviors.* List and describe the activating events, thoughts, or feelings that happened just before you felt emotionally upset by some situation or acted in some self-defeating way.

2. *Identify irrational beliefs.* Look at your description of events, thoughts, or feelings and then examine them for irrational thinking. Circle all those that apply or add other irrational beliefs you may be operating from. Examples:

   I *must* do well or very well.

   I am a *bad* or *worthless person* when I act weakly or stupidly.

   I *must* be approved or accepted by people whom I find important.

   I *need* immediate gratification for my needs.

   Other people *must* live up to my expectations or it is *terrible*.

   It's *awful* or *horrible* when major things don't go my way.

   I *can't stand it* when life is really unfair.

   Additional irrational beliefs.

3. *Identify emotional consequences.* How did you feel after the fact, event, or behavior? What did you do to produce it?

4. *Identify disputes.* Look at the irrational belief and then challenge it. Examples: "Why *must* I do so very well?" "Where is it written that I am a *bad person*?" "Where is the evidence that I *must* be approved or accepted?"

5. *Develop rational beliefs.* These can replace irrational beliefs. Examples: "I would prefer to do well, but I don't *have to be* that perfect." "I am a person who acted badly, but I am not a *bad person.*" "There is no evidence that I *have to be* approved, although I would like to be."

6. *Commit to more positive and rational feelings and behaviors.* Finally, list the feelings, behaviors, and thoughts you are experiencing after challenging and working on your irrational beliefs. Can you make the following commitment? "I will work hard to repeat my effective rational beliefs forcefully to myself on many occasions so I can make myself less disturbed now and act less self-defeatingly in the future."

Be sure to take time to write down your reactions to this activity when you have completed this exercise and file your reactions in your personal/professional portfolio.

Source: Adapted from J. Sichel and A. Ellis (1984), copyrighted by and available from the Institute for Rational-Emotive Therapy, 45 East 65th Street, New York, N. Y. 10021. It is used here by their permission.

Ellis does not challenge the client's goals and values (that he doesn't *want* to be gay) but instead attacks his *absolute demands* about achieving these values (that under *no* conditions *must* he be gay; that he would be a worthless "shit" if he were gay). The emphasis of the therapy is on changing the way the client thinks about the behavior, rather than on changing the behavior itself. Recall Epictetus: It is not events but our view of events that is critical.

The A-B-C framework is really the golden nugget of Ellis's theory. It is not the event that really troubles us, but instead the way we think about the event. Ellis's theory is closely akin to humanistic therapies that focus on meaning and the importance of how a person interprets the world. Frankl (Chapter 10), for example, survived the horrors of a Nazi concentration camp. He comments on how his survival depended on his ability to believe certain things about the events around him and to find something positive on which to depend. Beliefs were more important to survival than objective facts. Although the A-B-C framework is a key part of Ellis's theory, it is only half of his helping formula.

The D-E-Fs of Promoting and Maintaining Change

"D" stands for disputing irrational beliefs and thinking. It is at this point that Ellis's work first became controversial. When the logic of the client's A-B-C thought patterns is noted to be ineffective, Ellis becomes directly challenging and confrontative: "But why would you be a thorough shit if you were a gay? Let's suppose you gave up girls completely, and you just screwed guys. Now, why would you be a thorough shit?"

This language and style offended many people in the 1950s and 1960s, a time when Rogerian listening and respect were at their greatest influence. Furthermore, Ellis's tolerance and openness to cultural difference were well ahead of his time.

It is now widely recognized that disputing and challenging clients' logical systems is an effective mode of intervention and that rational disputation is an important therapeutic strategy. In the later sections of this chapter, you will see that William Glasser uses disputation, but in a more gentle manner than Ellis.

"E" is the effect that disputation (or other interventions) has on the client. At this point, the client generates a more effective belief system or philosophy about the situation. In the above example, the fact of being gay has not been changed, but the client generates a new way of thinking about himself: "It's OK to come out of the closet and be a gay man—if I wish to take that direction."

"F" stands for new feelings and behaviors. The client has new emotions associated with the situation. "I'm gay and I'm proud and I feel good about myself." REBT emphasizes emotional change as foundational. Although much REBT work focuses on logical thinking, unless logic is ultimately integrated with emotion, change is unlikely to last. Emotional change is basic if we are to prevent relapse into old ways of thinking and feeling. Behavior change follows from new feelings about the self.

REBT and Multicultural Factors

Despite the advanced thinking and tolerance Ellis demonstrated in the 1950s and 1960s about issues related to individuals' sex roles and identity, his REBT approach to counseling and psychotherapy has been sharply criticized in recent years by multicultural counseling advocates. These criticisms have specifically focused on Ellis's failure to address contextual-situational factors that adversely impact clients' lives (Rigazio-DiGilio, Ivey, & Locke, 1997) and an ethnocentric approach to mental health care that is inherent in a traditional REBT approach to helping (D'Andrea, 2000).

Chen (1995) provides an important critique and supplement to Ellis's system. In doing so, this multicultural advocate points out that Chinese philosophy values rationality and stresses the importance of perception over real events, as does Ellis. Given this cultural perspective, Chen points out that REBT may have value for many traditional Chinese clients. However, he also adds that the confrontational style of some REBT practitioners may be personally and culturally offensive to Chinese persons as well. Chen suggests an emphasis on relationship and a soft, yet strong, approach to challenging a Chinese client's rationality is important when working with persons from this cultural group. Building trust is foundational in this approach.

By way of contrast, Scorzelli and Reineke-Scorzelli (1994) studied cognitive therapy in India and found that this helping approach conflicted with many clients' religious/spiritual beliefs and their connections with family and culture. In fact, religious/spiritual beliefs were a particularly important factor in those cases in which REBT was found to be less effective.

The comments of these researchers suggest that REBT does have multicultural relevance but that major changes in how this form of counseling and psychotherapy is conducted may be required. Moreover, clients' strong cultural or religious/spiritual orientations may necessitate changes in the way REBT is presented to persons from diverse backgrounds. Later in this chapter, Glasser's reality therapy is explored as a way to work through some of these issues from a cognitive perspective.

Moving from REBT to REBCT: A Significant Advancement

One criticism of REBT is that Ellis consistently failed to address the different ways that irrational beliefs are manifested by persons who come from diverse cultural groups and backgrounds. He also failed to stress the importance of having practitioners acquire a broad range of multicultural counseling competencies, as outlined by the American Counseling Association, before using this theory with clients from diverse populations (D'Andrea, 2000).

Debate over these concerns has grown and was evident in an exchange on this topic held at a 1999 national convention for professional counselors. The primary focus of the debate was on the ways in which counselors and psychologists can make CBT and REBT more relevant to the various contextual-situational challenges and cultural worldviews that characterize clients from diverse populations (D'Andrea, 2000; Ellis, 1996, 1997, 2000; Guterman, 1994, 1996, 1997; Guterman, Ellis, Rigazio-DiGilio, & D'Andrea, 1999; Ivey, Locke, & Rigazio-DiGilio, 1996; Rigazio-DiGilio, Ivey, & Locke, 1997).

Clearly, more discussion about these issues needs to occur if mental health practitioners are to learn how they can work more effectively and ethically in a culturally diverse, postmodern, 21st-century society. Rigazio-DiGilio and her colleagues (1997) have written specifically about the cultural and contextual relevance of Ellis's theory, suggesting that, like other forms of cognitive-behavioral therapy, REBT would have a greater impact if practitioners were to direct their attention to doing more than helping clients learn to change their inner thoughts. An expansion in REBT's cultural-contextual purview needs to include intentional efforts to help clients learn "new behaviors that have an ameliorating effect within their own personal sphere while also interrupting constraining interactions that may exist in the wider sociocultural and social political context" (Rigazio-DiGilio et al., 1997, p. 236).

Ellis himself actively participates in the discussion about the need for counseling and psychology to become more sensitive and responsive to situational and cultural factors influencing clients' lives. In this way, Ellis models the type of professional leadership that is needed to foster changes in our thinking about CBT and REBT—changes that will increase the cultural and contextual relevance of these powerful theoretical helping frameworks. As Ellis states, "Personally, I favor counselors taking this kind of sociocultural and sociopolitical stand" (2000, p. 100).

Ellis expressed an even clearer commitment to having his REBT theory become more culturally and contextually relevant during a public debate about these issues at the 1999 American Counseling Association's annual convention in San Diego, California. Ellis agreed to include the "C" (contextual/cultural) factor in REBT. By moving his cognitive-behavior theory from REBT to REBCT (rational-emotive-behavior-contextual therapy), Ellis demonstrated a growing understanding of the need to incorporate contextual considerations into traditional theoretical models of counseling and psychotherapy. Acknowledgment from a leading theorist such as Ellis is particularly important as the mental health professions seek more effective and respectful ways of working with diverse clients in a country undergoing unprecedented changes in its cultural/racial makeup.

Failure to promote such change in traditional counseling and psychotherapy will jeopardize the relevance and viability of the mental health professions in the coming decades (D'Andrea & Daniels, 2005). With this in mind, Ellis's public statement of support to move his REBT theory to a new REBCT model represents "a giant step" in promoting cultural-contextual considerations into the CBT movement.

Ellis's "giant step" in this area is welcomed by multicultural counseling advocates. However, other CBT theorists and researchers will need to follow Ellis's example by further extending their understanding of the additional changes that need to occur in the CBT movement if this vital theoretical force is to remain relevant and viable within the context of a culturally diverse 21st-century society (Rigazio-DiGilio, Ellis, D'Andrea, Ivey, & Gutterman, 1999).

Working with Clients

REBCT practitioners need to work with their clients to assist them in developing new behaviors that have an ameliorating effect within their own personal sphere while also interrupting constraining interactions that may exist in the wider sociocultural and social political context. An important first step in doing so involves helping clients from diverse cultural groups avoid operating from irrational thoughts that seemingly occur automatically. Competency-Building Activity 8.2 encourages you to exercise some of the skills that are useful in helping individuals avoid such automatic irrational thoughts as they strive to develop more rational thinking abilities in counseling and psychotherapy.

Competency-Building Activity 8.2

Automatic Thoughts within Gender and Multicultural Contexts

Instructions: With yourself or a real or role-played client, work through this automatic thoughts exercise by focusing on an issue of concern. To make the task clear at the beginning, use only one specific situation that concerns you or the person you are working with. Later, identify more situations so that you can search for patterns. Note that the search for one situation is an example of concrete thought processes. When we combine several situations, we develop formal operational thought patterns.

For this practice exercise, ask yourself or your client to develop a sensorimotor image of the situation. You can do this by asking yourself (or your client) to describe the bodily feeling that comes with thinking about the situation. Imaging in this way will help concretize the situation and make the emotional reactions you or your client have to this issue more accessible. The addition of gender and multicultural contexts enables a dialectic/systemic view of the situation you (or your client) are thinking about. The following steps are provided to give you a clearer idea as to how you can present this exercise.

Step 1. *Situation.* Ask the client to tell you a brief story or narrative of the situation. Then, ask her or him to identify the emotions associated with the narrative.

Step 2. *Emotions.* If appropriate, seek an image of the situation by asking the client to select one key scene and keep it in mind. Through the use of images, the past situation can be brought into the here and now. Again, ask the client to identify the emotions associated with the image. Usually, this will be a more powerful experience than that in step 1; as such, special care should be taken. Do not lead the client, but simply ask for whatever image comes to mind.

Step 3. *Automatic thoughts.* Ask the client, "What occurs in your mind during the situation?" or "What thoughts go through your head when you experience that image?" Discovering automatic thoughts requires questioning skills.

Clients who have been used to external control will require considerable help in looking inside themselves. Automatic thought analysis forces overexternalized clients to look inward.

Step 4. *Rational response.* Think of a logical response as you or the client reflect on the situation, the resulting emotions, and the automatic thoughts. This process will involve some coconstruction with the client. Whereas REBCT tends to dispute client cognitions, cognitive therapy is more likely to work with the client in generating a rational approach to reality. This rational response provides the foundation for a new stylistic approach to life.

When working with a daily record of automatic thoughts, you have the opportunity to generate patterns of thought and action and to then examine broader lifestyle issues and move to more comprehensive changes.

Step 5. *Gender and multicultural issues.* There is a pronounced tendency in cognitive-behavioral psychology to ignore gender and multicultural matters. However, multicultural theorists often stress that external reality must be dealt with if clients are to achieve mature cognitions and emotions (Parham, 2002).

Ask yourself or your client, "Reflect back on your system of emotions and automatic thoughts. How do your gender and cultural, religious, and other frameworks speak to these issues?" Through adaptations of this core question, your clients will be able to see their situations in a broader context. In this way, external reality can be brought into the cognitive paradigm. This may be helpful in answering the following critical question: "Is the client or the external situation irrational?"

Step 6. *Outcome.* Ask clients what occurs for them if they change their responses to the situation. Also, you may wish to encourage them to think about whether or not gender and multicultural issues are related to the entire process. At issue in this approach to automatic thoughts is balancing internal and external reality.

Be sure to take time to write down your reactions to this activity when you have completed this exercise and file your reactions in your personal/professional portfolio.

Limitations and Practical Implications of Ellis's Theory

Ellis's personal style is considered by some to be abrasive, which has led some persons in the field to discount his important and seminal work. However, it would be a mistake to confuse personal style with theoretical merit. As with any therapy, it is important that you find your own way of integrating Ellis's work into your array of skills and theories.

The constructs of REBCT have been vastly influential. Ellis's three major tenets are critical additions to the skills and understandings of any professional helper, regardless of theoretical orientation. These major tenets include the following:

- REBCT points out that it is possible to change the way we think about things and that cognitive change is often sufficient for significant improvement.

- The A-B-C and D-E-F frameworks for analyzing irrational client cognitions have become a standard in the field.

- Ellis has provided significant leadership in generating a more culturally equitable approach to CBT helping.

Albert Ellis's REBCT could be summarized by the following statement: "Be rational and think about things logically." This therapeutic mantra underscores the need for clients to accept their own responsibility in creating both the psychological distress that is rooted in the maintenance of irrational thinking as well as an increasing sense of psychological liberation and well-being that accompanies more rational thinking.

William Glasser and Reality Therapy

The importance of accepting one's own responsibility for creating psychological health and personal satisfaction or fostering psychological distress and dissatisfaction with one's life is the centerpiece of William Glasser's reality therapy. Glasser's theory could be summarized by saying, "Take responsibility and control of your own life and face the consequences of your actions." Glasser's theory complements Ellis's REBCT model in many ways. It also represents an important theoretical aspect that contributes to the ongoing evolution of the CBT force in counseling and psychology.

William Glasser was born in Cleveland, Ohio, in 1925. He was educated at Case Western Reserve University (Cleveland, Ohio) where he received a B.S in 1945 and an M.A. in clinical psychology in 1948. He received his M.D. in 1953 and completed a psychiatric residency between 1954 and 1957 at UCLA and at the Veterans Administration Hospital of Los Angeles.

During his early years as a psychiatrist at the Veterans Administration Hospital in Los Angeles, Glasser became disgruntled with the practice of traditional psychiatry. His dissatisfaction with this form of mental health care was based in a few key points.

First, he was frustrated with the overuse of many traditional psychoanalytic principles, especially those that focus on the unconscious and unresolved conflicts individuals are believed to develop from their childhoods.

Second, Glasser was not pleased with the goal of primarily promoting clients' insight into their problems without placing equal value on the need to foster new behaviors that enable clients to become more satisfied and productive in their lives.

Third, Glasser thought that the extensive investment of time and money individuals had to pay for receiving services from psychiatrists was not necessary. These concerns led him to develop a new mode of helping that (1) focused on clients' present challenges and problems rather that past events, (2) stressed the importance of stimulating behavioral as well as cognitive changes, and (3) outlined a more efficacious manner for psychological helping that sharply contrasts with the time-consuming process used by traditionally trained psychiatrists.

Glasser developed his original theory of reality therapy in 1965. Since then, he has been continually updating and expanding this approach to counseling and psychotherapy. In the 1970s, Glasser began referring to his body of work as control theory. Currently, his counseling and therapeutic approaches are based on what he now calls **choice theory,** which he explains in detail in his 1998 book of the same title. His theory of reality therapy has been recently upgraded in a new book entitled *Counseling with Choice Theory: The New Reality Therapy* (Glasser, 2001). All in all, Glasser has written 21 books, including his best-selling *Reality Therapy* (1965), *Schools without Failure* (1969), *Positive Addiction* (1976), and *The Quality School* (1990).

Central Theoretical Constructs of Reality Therapy

In describing the basic tenets of reality therapy, Glasser (1998) states that clients are generally responsible for being unsuccessful in meeting their needs. Their lack of success in doing so is often due to the ways in which they select ineffective behaviors that virtually ensure their failure. Like Ellis's theoretical framework, Glasser's theory stresses the importance of helping clients learn to think in new ways about the responsibility and control they have in authoring their lives. Glasser further emphasizes that assisting clients to construct new cognitions about their lives represents the foundation on which positive behavioral and affective changes can be fostered.

The following three tenets represent additional principles of reality therapy that distinguish Glasser's approach from other forms of counseling and psychotherapy. (These points are taken from Glasser's [1998] updated ideas on reality therapy, which are published in one of his more recent books on the topic entitled *Choice Theory: A New Psychology of Personal Freedom*.)

1. There is no need to probe at length about a client's problem in counseling and psychotherapy. Usually, a person's problem is obvious even if many clients deny that it is the case. If counselors and psychologists accept their client's denial, they are likely to spend much time probing for something or someone in the client's

past that is thought to be responsible for their current problems. Thus, one of the main tasks early in counseling is to help clients get beyond their use of denial to obstruct new and more responsible ways of thinking and acting in the present.

2. Since clients' problems are always in the present, there is no need to make a long intensive investigation into their past. A long examination of the past may inadvertently lead clients to believe that so much has happened there that they will never be able to live effective lives in the present or future. It is much more important for counselors and therapists to simply tell clients the truth: The past is over; clients cannot change what they or anyone else did in the past. All clients can do now is work to build a more effective present.

3. In traditional counseling, a lot of time is spent both inquiring into and listening to clients complain about their symptoms, the actions of other people, the world they live in, and on and on—the list is endless. Reality therapy emphasizes what clients can do to help themselves and to improve the current situation in which they have negative feelings. Doing so not only saves a lot of time but focuses the counseling and makes it more effective. (pp. 116–117)

Reality therapy can best be described as a common-sense approach to counseling. What Glasser advocates is (1) finding out what people want and need, (2) examining their failures and their present assets, and (3) considering factors in the environment that must be met if their needs are to be satisfied.

According to Glasser, a person cannot meet one's needs except in the real world. Consequently, people must face a world that is imperfect and not built to their specifications. With this realistic understanding of the world in mind, people are then encouraged to act positively, given the situation at hand.

The worldview of reality therapy is essentially based on the premise that people can do something about their fate if they will consider themselves and their environmental/contextual conditions realistically and accurately. In this sense, reality therapy has much in common with brief counseling (Chapter 3). Variations of brief reality counseling meetings are often used in correctional facilities, schools and universities, and employee assistance programs at the workplace.

The Importance of Responsibility

As might be anticipated, reality therapy focuses on conscious, planned behavior and gives relatively little attention to underlying dimensions of transference, unconscious thought processes, and the like. The essential goal of reality therapy is to assist clients in understanding the past as being past and done with; the present and the future are what are important at this point in their lives.

Yet reality therapy does not emphasize applied behavioral analysis or the detailed plans of assertiveness training or systematic desensitization. Rather, almost like REBCT, reality therapy focuses on responsibility and choice. What is central is that clients examine their lives to see how specific behaviors undermine their psychological well-being in general and what they want to get out of life in particular. The more important step, however, is to encourage clients to take responsibility for their lives, which Glasser (1965) defined early as "the ability to fulfill one's needs and to do so in a way that does not deprive others of the ability to fulfill their needs" (p. 13).

Learning responsibility is a lifelong process. Given the population that reality therapy often serves (clients of street clinics, prison inmates, schoolchildren, and others in institutional settings), it is clear that establishing a positive and trusting relationship is very important. However, it is also clear that the institutions of which many of these clients are a part do not engender the trust that characterizes traditional client-therapist relationships. With this in mind, the personhood of the reality therapist becomes especially important in the helping process. The qualities of warmth, respect and caring for others, positive regard, and interpersonal openness are particularly crucial in fostering positive outcomes by using this therapeutic modality.

Reality therapy is much more likely to be practiced in settings other than the counseling office, although this method is also used in standard clinical settings. The individual practicing reality therapy may be out on the playground or in a delinquent detention center or may be a classroom teacher or a prison guard. The possible multiplicity of relationships requires a special type of person to maintain consistency. This challenge provides an opportunity for the reality therapist to serve as a continuing model of personal responsibility to the client outside the counseling environment (Glasser, 1999).

Cognitive Trends in Reality Therapy

A critical part of reality therapy is client awareness of the consequences of her or his actions: "If you do X, then what is the consequence?" Reality therapy, in a highly nonjudgmental fashion, attempts to help individuals learn what they can expect when they act in certain ways.

In this sense, you may again note a similarity and a difference from Ellis's cognitive helping theory. In REBCT, the consequences are those inside the person (feeling depressed and so forth), whereas in reality therapy, the consequences may indeed be inside, but the emphasis is on what happens in the outside world when the client fails to face reality and be responsible.

Glasser has continually expanded his thinking but has remained true to the basic constructs of the method and theory described above. In his 1998 book, *Choice Theory: A New Psychology of Personal Freedom*, he builds on his earlier writings about the differences that characterize the "external world" and the "internal world of the mind" (p. 16). Glasser repeatedly emphasizes that because individuals have much less control over the "external world" than they do over their "internal world," it is important for clients to learn new ways to control their thinking in order that they might experience more positive and empowering psychological and behavioral outcomes.

This important theoretical tenet underscores the emphasis Glasser places on helping clients understand the significant personal power they have in (1) controlling the types of thoughts they have about themselves and the world in which they live and (2) exerting intentional control over the direction of their lives and making intentional choices about how they want to act and feel in different situations.

In reality therapy, clients are encouraged to recognize that some of the reasons they may choose misery as a way of life is because it can provide an excuse from trying harder or may win help or pity from others. Psychosomatic illness is considered a specific type of internal control that helps individuals avoid reality. For example, "headaching" individuals may benefit from having headaches because it gives them a reason to lie down and rest. Drugs and alcohol are still other ways people exert control to avoid facing reality.

Careful analysis of Glasser's recent work suggests that he is moving closer to Ellis's position in that he gives increased attention to the way people think about things. However, Glasser still uses the basic structure of reality therapy to produce behavior change. His control theory provides an important additional tool for therapists working with individual clients. The therapist insists that the client "own" her or his thoughts, behavior, and feelings and be responsible for them. The logic underlying this perspective is that if one can exert control over seemingly unsatisfactory ends, such as drugs, headaches, stealing, and interpersonal conflict, then one can reframe control more positively (Glasser, 1998).

Glasser talks about "positive addictions," which range from spending time with friends to jogging to movies to meditation—anything from which an individual can obtain a "high" in a more satisfactory and healthy way. The world offers us many opportunities to replace negative additions with positive addictions. Glasser argues that we all choose our addictions and our fate. Consequently, we can choose headaches or we can choose joy. The choice is ours. We are in control.

Theory in Action

Glasser's reality therapy can be considered a cognitive-behavioral therapy, but one that focuses very much on realism and how to treat difficult clients. Although research on reality therapy is limited, it is a frequent treatment of choice in working with resistant clients, particularly acting-out or delinquent youth or adults. In reality therapy, there is more focus on external reality than in Ellis's helping theory.

Counseling sessions within reality therapy can range from a regularly scheduled 50-minute hour to brief personal encounters in the dining room, classroom, or other environmental settings. Many clients do not want to come to the office for the highly verbal and sophisticated treatments that we as counselors and therapists might prefer to offer. Reality therapy offers a viable alternative that you can use as a basis for working with difficult clients; later, other forms of helping can be incorporated.

Especially in the early stages of therapy, some younger clients, particularly those who are acting out or delinquent, will not "stand still" for Ellis's REBCT approach. However, after you establish a working alliance with such clients, perhaps through reality therapy, you can return successfully to other cognitive-behavioral techniques later in the helping process. The following case study of reality therapy with an acting-out younger client provides a general sense of how Glasser's cognitive-behavioral theory can work in practice.

The client is an 18-year-old man on probation for repeated offenses of a minor nature, including selling alcohol to minors, assault, and petty theft. The counselor in this case is a county probation officer. The meeting occurs in a community halfway house. They are just finishing a game of ping-pong (Glasser, 1998).

1. *Counselor:* Got ya! 21 to 18. Took me three games, but I finally got one.

2. *Client:* Yeah, you pulled it off finally. Man, I'm pooped. (They sit down and have a cup of coffee.)

3. *Counselor:* So, how have things been going? [*Open question*]

4. *Client:* Well, I looked for jobs hard last week. But nothing looked any good. The bastards seem to know I'm coming and pull the help wanted sign down just as I come walking in.

5. *Counselor:* So, you've been looking hard. How many places did you visit? [*Paraphrase, closed question; search for concrete behavior*]

6. *Client:* Oh lots. Nobody will give me a chance.

7. *Counselor:* Maybe I can help. Tell me some of the places you've been. [*Directive, with continued emphasis on concreteness. Where Ellis often moves clients to formal operational thought, the Glasser approach focuses on specifics—one of its values for the many concrete operational clients.*]

8. *Client:* I tried the gas station down the street. They gave me a bad time. Nobody wants me. It's really tough.

9. *Counselor:* Where else did you go? [*Closed question*]

10. *Client:* I tried a couple other stations too. Nobody wants to look at me. They don't pay too good anyway. Nuts to them!

11. *Counselor:* So you haven't really done too much looking. Sounds like you want it served on a silver plate, Joe. Do you think looking at a couple of gas stations is really going to get you a job? [*Paraphrase, interpretation, logical consequences. Here is a lead, particularly typical of reality therapy, that places considerable emphasis on the consequences of actions. The point is similar to applied behavioral analysis, but the way of reaching consequences is different.*]

12. *Client:* I suppose not. Nobody wants to hire me anyway.

13. *Counselor:* Let's take another look at that. The economy is pretty rocky right now. Everyone is having trouble getting work. You seem to think "they" are after you. Yet I've got a friend about your age who had to go to 35 places before he got a job. How does that square with you looking at three places and then giving up? Who's responsible—you, the service station owners, or the economy? [*Directive, information giving, open question; note confrontation and emphasis on the word* responsible. *Responsible action is the formal operational concept toward which most of reality therapy aspires.*]

14. *Client:* Yeah, but, there's not much I can do about it. I tried . . .

15. *Counselor:* Yeah, at three places. Who's responsible for you not getting a job when you only go to three places? At a time like this you've really got to scramble. Come on, Joe! [*Interpretation plus logical consequences*] (p. 171)

The interview continues to explore Joe's lack of action, with an emphasis on responsibility. At points where a Rogerian counselor (see Chapter 9) might paraphrase or reflect feelings and attitudes (such as in numbers 4, 8, and 10), the reality therapist opts for more behavioral specifics through questions and interpretation. The process of examining Joe's behavior is closely akin to that of the behavioral counselor using applied behavioral analysis. However, the use of the behavioral data is quite different in reality therapy. Instead of seeking to change behavior, the reality therapist works on changing awareness of responsibility. Once the focus of responsibility has been acknowledged and owned by the client, it is possible to start planning a more effective job search. Later in the interview, the process of planning evolves.

51. *Counselor:* So, Joe, sounds like you feel you made a decision this past week not to really look for a job . . . almost as if you took responsibility for not getting work. [*Reflection of meaning, interpretation. Note that placing the locus of decision in the client can be a helpful strategy in any approach to helping. It is here that reality therapy truly becomes cognitive-behavioral. At the same time, this is a clear example of moving away from a societal, contextual focus.*]

52. *Client:* Yeah, I don't like to look at it that way, but I guess I did decide not to do too much.

53. *Counselor:* And what about next week?

54. *Client:* I suppose I ought to look again, but I really don't like it. (p. 172)

The reality therapist at this point moved to a realistic analysis of what the client might expect during the coming week on the job market, constantly emphasizing the importance of the client, Joe, taking action and responsibility for his life. A practice role-played job interview was held, and several alternatives for generating a more effective job search were considered. Joe tried to escape responsibility at several points ("I couldn't do that"), but the counselor confronted him and allowed no excuses or ambivalence.

A reality therapist will use the skills and ideas of other theoretical orientations when they serve the purpose of assisting the client to confront reality more effectively. More likely, the reality therapist will be her or his natural self and use humor, sarcasm, and confrontation in very personal ways to assist the client in understanding behavioral patterns and developing new action strategies. Role-playing, systematic planning, and instruction in intentional living are important tools in reality therapy as well.

Although many who practice reality therapy may be in power situations (guards, principals, rehabilitation counselors), they still tend to be themselves and use reality therapy as an extension of themselves. This adds a tone of genuineness and authenticity to the process at a more significant level than would be possible with other therapeutic approaches. For example, a prison guard trained in reality therapy can simply state his position realistically as one of power and control. Then, with the role relationships clearly established, the process of involvement, teaching of responsibility, and relearning can occur.

Reality Therapy and Multicultural Counseling and Therapy

Multicultural experts have questioned the effectiveness of reality therapy when used among persons from diverse cultural/ethnic/racial groups and backgrounds. Recently, however, Wubbolding and his colleagues (2004) reviewed research projects that assessed the effectiveness of reality therapy among persons from a broad range of culturally diverse groups. This review resulted in several important findings that are briefly summarized below.

One study reviewed by Wubbolding and his colleagues involved research conducted by Okonji (1995), who studied the level of satisfaction of African-American clients after participating in counseling and psychotherapy. One group of research participants received reality therapy and the other group received Rogerian counseling. Okonji found more statistically significant satisfaction reported among those African-American clients who participated in reality therapy groups in comparison to those receiving person-centered counseling services.

Another study included in their review involved research completed in Korea to test the efficacy of using reality therapy among delinquent adolescents in that Asian country. The researchers who were responsible for overseeing this two-year study reported a significant increase in the levels of self-esteem, planning ability, and sense of internal control among the adolescents receiving reality therapy (Kim & Hwang, 2001).

A third study testing the use of reality theory included in Wubbolding et al.'s (2004) review "involved former residents of a correctional institution in Visnja Gora, the former Yugoslavia" (p. 227). The areas of improvement reported in this study included positive gains in participants' employment stability and the quality of their family lives. At the same time, significant reductions were reported in the research participants' stealing behaviors, the expressed need for psychiatric help, and lower contacts with police due to legal violations on being released from prison (Lojk, 1986).

The last study included in the review of reality therapy's cross-cultural utility was done among another group of delinquent teenagers but this time in Hong Kong. In this research project, Chung (1994) found significant improvements among the teenagers who received Glasser's approach to CBT in the areas of punctuality, problem solving, and communication skills.

Beyond the positive findings reported in the above-mentioned studies, there are other reasons to suggest that reality therapy has much to offer multicultural counseling and therapy. One factor in particular relates to the emphasis Glasser's theory places on having clients recognize, accept, and act on their responsibility to themselves, others, and society at large. This value is in accord with Native American Indian and Asian-American value systems that stress the need to accept responsibility for one's own life and actions in ways that keep the dignity of others in mind. Competency-Building Activity 8.3 illustrates concretely how reality therapy can be tied to multicultural counseling and therapy in other ways.

Competency-Building Activity 8.3

Facing Reality: Adding Context to Cognitive Therapies

Instructions: Most work in cognitive therapies focuses on the client's internal thoughts and feelings. Reality therapy adds an important dimension to this theoretical tradition as it balances considerations of the person-environment interactions. Not only is the client looking at her- or himself, but the client is also challenged to see her- or himself-in-context. In this sense, reality therapy offers some useful ideas for a multiculturally sensitive approach to helping. The following exercise provides practical guidelines that help illustrate this point:

Step 1. *Find a volunteer client.* Ask a friend or classmate to volunteer as a client. Show your volunteer this exercise in advance so that you can work mutually in a coconstructive relationship. A suggested topic for this exercise is examining an interpersonal conflict.

Step 2. *Use the basic listening sequence to draw out the client's story.* Be sure to obtain the central facts and emotions and clearly summarize what you have heard. You may also wish to use the concepts of applied behavioral analysis so that the story is really clear.

Step 3. *Review the story from three perspectives—client, other person, and context.* First, point out that the client has told the story from a personal perspective. Ask the client to describe how the other person would tell the same story. Give special attention to what the client and other person need to have happen to make the situation better. Finally, consider with the client how multicultural or other contextual issues, such as gender, socioeconomic status, sexual preference, religion, race/ethnicity, workplace, and physical space, might affect the conflict. Specifically, if a person from one or more of these backgrounds described the story, which elements might be the same and which might change?

Step 4. *Introduce the issues of responsibility and what is realistic in this situation.* Reality therapy stresses that we must look beyond clients' internal needs and also examine the facts of external reality. Traditional cognitive therapy does not deal with external facts as directly. In this practice exercise, explore with your client issues of personal responsibility and how best to face the realities of this context. Encourage the client to seek fulfillment for self, others, and the broader context.

Step 5. *Review possible consequences of cognitive and behavioral change.* You may wish to brainstorm the future results of varying actions on the part of the responsible client. Encourage your client to take specific behavioral action on the conflict. Or you may even encourage your client to take action on the context affecting the problem. Here you may wish to utilize some of the behavioral techniques described in Chapter 7 or consider using some of the concepts underlying the community action programs of multicultural counseling and therapy presented in Chapter 12.

Be sure to take time to write down your reactions to this activity when you have completed this exercise and file your reactions in your personal/professional portfolio.

Limitations and Practical Implications of Glasser's Theory

Glasser's increasing emphasis on the control and choices clients have in their lives suggests that he is moving toward a more immediate, confrontational, and cognitive point of view. From his perspective, many clients need and benefit from direct and forceful confrontations of existing thought patterns, active teaching of alternative perceptions of reality, and an emphasis that focuses more on internal states and thoughts. Needless to say, the client must be ready for these new psychological and cognitive challenges.

The "how" of Glasser's control theory has not really been addressed, except by implication. At the moment, traditional reality therapy and the new dimensions of control and choice theory seem somewhat at odds. We may anticipate for the future, however, a more complete integration of Glasser's thinking with illustrations of how a new theory of reality therapy may be used in more practical ways. In the past, Glasser seemed to stress the importance of the client adapting to the world as it is. He now appears to be adding a more sophisticated dimension of internal cognitive states that directs greater attention to contextual/environmental factors to his original theoretical perspective (Glasser, 1998, 2001).

For some, categorizing Glasser's reality therapy as a cognitive-behavioral helping approach may seem unusual, as Glasser tends to work outside the therapeutic mainstream of the second theoretical force. With its clear emphasis on logical consequences of personal actions and the importance of personal control and choice, Glasser's reality therapy will remain appropriate when working with difficult clients in institutional settings where regular psychotherapeutic sessions and time-intensive treatment plans are not always feasible.

The theories of Ellis and Glasser both tend to put the problem "in the client." This, of course, is true for most individualistically oriented helping theories. Reality therapy, for example, stresses the need for the client to adapt to necessary environmental contingencies. Sometimes clients come from oppressive families, neighborhoods, and cultural histories. Although it is important that the client adapt to reality, such adaptation can result in clients returning to oppressive systems with the idea that the "fault" is in them rather than in the environment. Ellis's REBCT approach also can fall prey to what some call "blaming the victim" by overemphasizing the need to cure the "ills" of the client, when family and society are also responsible for fostering the client's thoughts, feelings, and actions.

Cognitive-behavioral methods and strategies often make quick and decisive change possible and are especially practical in this era of managed care and its increasing emphasis on promoting positive psychological and behavioral changes in a limited time. For this reason, many mental health professionals find it important to be conversant with and competent in this helping framework. The Professional Development Extension provides an example of cognitive-behavioral methods is professional practice.

Professional Development Extension

Using REBCT and Reality Therapy Principles in Practice

Cognitive-behavioral therapies, in general, and the theories of Ellis and Glasser, in particular, embrace the ancient wisdom in the ancient Greek philosopher Epictetus's statement that people "are disturbed not by events, but by the views they take of them." At a fundamental level, the approaches of Ellis and Glasser encourage clients to develop a new mind-set by disregarding ideas that are not only ineffective in helping them get what they want in life, but are also psychologically and physically destructive to their well-being.

Ellis encourages clients to become aware of the automatic thinking that underlies many of the irrational thoughts that contribute to their psychological distress, depression, and personal dissatisfaction with life. He invites them to consider the positive psychological benefits that inevitably ensue from stopping this sort of automatic thinking and by becoming more mindful of their thought processes. Glasser stresses the importance of individuals accepting the responsibility of making positive choices that affect their lives, minds, and bodies. Both stress the importance of moving from thinking to implementation of new cognitions in the practice of daily living. This can be seen in the following case of Angela, a 55-year-old woman who entered therapy because of the stress she was experiencing in her marriage.

According to Angela, she had become increasingly unhappy with the lack of love and respect her husband of 30 years demonstrated to her. Angela stated, "While he has never been physically abusive to me, he acts like he isn't interested in me and doesn't love me." She stated that she had felt like this for several years and had tried to talk to her husband about her feelings, but he was unwilling to discuss these concerns.

In her first therapy session, Angela said she thought the difficulties she was experiencing could relate to things she unconsciously learned from her mother and father's relationship. The therapist (Marrietta) pointed out that while analyzing one's past history can be beneficial for some people, she believed it might be more useful to explore how Angela's present thoughts about her relationship with her husband were affecting her feelings.

After Angela agreed that this might be a useful perspective to explore in their meetings, Marrieta asked Angela what she wanted in her life. Angela paused for a moment and then said she wanted to "be happier and feel more respected." Angela continued by saying that she wished she could get a greater sense of happiness and respect from her husband.

Marrietta then asked Angela to identify a recent time she felt unhappy and not respected by her husband. After Angela talked about an incident that happened the preceding evening, Marrietta helped her analyze this situation by using Ellis's A-B-C model. In doing so, the therapist and client talked about "A"—the antecedent events—as Angela recalled the facts of interaction that occurred between her and her husband. Then the counselor focused on "B"—Angela's beliefs about her husband's behavior—then moving on to "C"—emotional consequences that ensued from Angela's beliefs about her interaction with her husband. Angela responded to this discussion by saying that she found this method of analyzing her thoughts and feelings interesting.

Marrietta continued on, using the D-E-F components of Ellis's theory. The therapist confronted Angela with "D"—disputing the ineffectiveness of her A-B-C thought patterns. Marrietta saw that this disputation had a positive "E"—effect on Angela—as Angela expressed interest in knowing what she could do about her A-B-C thought patterns. The therapist continued the therapy session by helping Angela begin to develop a more effective belief system about her relationship with her husband.

The therapist and client then explored several things Angela could do to think and act in new

continued on next page

ways that would enhance her feelings of happiness and respect without totally relying on her husband's reactions to her. Angela stated that she was beginning to feel better as they brainstormed these ideas and talked about "F"—the new feelings she might experience as a result of implementing new ways of behaving in her life.

Marrietta ended this session by referring to two fundamental reality therapy principles. She did this by emphasizing that Angela's future success would largely depend on her willingness to accept her responsibility to make new choices that would increase her sense of happiness and respect, regardless of her husband's willingness to listen to or act on her concerns.

Angela participated in six additional therapy sessions. During this time she was able to more clearly identify the irrational underpinnings of some of her thinking about her relationship with her husband. She also expressed pride in the way she demonstrated greater responsibility for the new choices she was making, which contributed to her growing sense of happiness and self-respect.

Summary

The changes that have and continue to occur in the CBT movement represent important and complementary views that foster the ongoing evolution and integration of this important theoretical force in counseling and psychology. This is clearly reflected in Donald Meichenbaum's original work (Chapter 7) on the behavioral side of the cognitive-behavioral continuum, but more recently with a newly developed cognitive orientation that is in many ways as strong as that of Albert Ellis.

Ellis's approach to therapy provides yet another perspective to consider as you think about the actions you will implement in your own professional practices. The theoretical principles of Ellis's rational-emotive behavior contextual/cultural therapy are summarized here to highlight their practical utility in counseling and psychotherapy:

1. Expect your clients (and yourself, your family, and your friends) frequently to make impossible, perfectionistic statements about themselves and others.

2. The basic treatment rule is to dispute the rationality of perfectionistic cognitions and to teach clients how to do their own realistic, open-minded disputation.

3. In therapy, it may be useful to work through several irrational statements in a step-by-step A-B-C process and search for repeating patterns of thought and emotion.

4. Agreed-on homework can help your clients take their new knowledge into the real world.

5. Do not hesitate to add other techniques to the REBCT structure if you feel it helps you and your client reach your joint goals.

William Glasser added another perspective to the cognitive end of the CBT continuum with his reality therapy, which focuses on the importance of personal responsibility. Some key aspects of reality therapy include:

1. Reality therapy considers the behavior and cognitions of other people and not just the client's. For this reason, it is important to assess the facts of cognitive and behavioral consequences in person-environment interactions. This dimension moves reality therapy closer to the precepts of multicultural counseling and therapy.

2. The typical office setting of most counseling and therapy may not reflect the reality of life. If counselors and therapists move out into the real world, they will quickly find that even the best theory must change in practice.

3. Responsibility for clients' actions is central. Adding dimensions of personal ethics, responsibility, and analysis of consequences for clients' behavior are particular strengths of reality therapy.

At this point, your expanded knowledge of the CBT theories should help you understand the profound impact this second theoretical force continues to have in the mental health professions. Adding this new knowledge to your understanding of the first force (psychodynamic counseling and therapy) should offer clarity regarding many of the key theories that have impacted and continue to impact the fields of counseling and psychology. At issue for you is how you will decide to integrate the powerful methodology that has evolved from the CBT movement over the past several decades in ways that lead to your own effectiveness as a mental health professional.

Multimedia Resources for This Chapter

The following online resource offers video and other resources of particular relevance to this chapter of your text.

MyHelpingLab

If a MyHelpingLab passcode was included with your textbook and you have activated your passcode:

- go to **www.ablongman.com/myhelpinglab**
- enter the "Counseling" area of the site by clicking on that tab
- select "Video Lab" from the toolbar to the left of the page
- select "MyHelpingLab Videos by Theoretical Approach"
- select the "Cognitive-Behavioral" or "Reality" modules to view various video clips of therapists using this approach with clients

chapter 9

The Existential-Humanistic Tradition

This chapter is designed to:

1. Describe the general worldview of existential-humanistic theory, an orientation that greatly influences the practice of most counseling and therapy.

2. Examine person-centered theory and its possible relevance for work with multicultural populations.

3. Present central theoretical and practical constructs from the work of Carl Rogers.

4. Present the work of Clemmont Vontress, which integrates existential, Rogerian, and multicultural thought.

5. Introduce through practice exercises the skills necessary to use a "nondirective" approach to helping and integrate existential-humanistic and multicultural issues.

Introduction

The existential-humanistic tradition has impacted counseling and psychotherapy in two important ways. First, it added several major helping theories—existential, person-centered, logotherapy, and Gestalt theories—that have greatly expanded practitioners' approaches to promoting their clients' mental health.

Second, this third force in counseling and psychology represents an attitude toward the human condition and the interview that now permeates virtually all practice, regardless of theoretical persuasion. The foundational concept of empathy is derived from Carl Rogers's person-centered theory, and the listening microskills (Chapter 4) are closely allied with his early work in nondirective counseling. Cognitive-behavioral, psychodynamic, and multicultural approaches often draw from existential-humanistic theory and practice when they address the importance of the client's relationships. More than any other group of theories, the existential-humanistic tradition focuses on the nature and meaning of the client and counselor relationship.

Although the roots of the existential-humanistic tradition lie in philosophy, Rogers and his person-centered approach to counseling have been most influential in popularizing the existential-humanistic point of view and making it accessible and relevant to clinical practice. Rogers's techniques are designed to help you enter the worldviews of your clients and then to assist them in finding their own new directions and frames of thinking.

Also discussed in this chapter is the work of Clemmont Vontress, whose ideas on relationships differ from those of Rogers and add a new dimension to the constructs of existential humanism. Vontress (1995) speaks of the therapeutic relationship as being central in existential-humanistic counseling and therapy:

> The existential-humanistic counseling relationship is best described as an interaction in which two co-equal humans benefit from the encounter. The focus is, however, primarily directed to one of the interactants only because that one declares him- or herself to be in need of help from the other. Undergirding the relationship is existential ideas such as death, sympathy, psychotherapeutic eros, and an I-Thou personal relationship. (p. 1)

The Rogerian and existential-humanistic perspectives delve into the rich, complex, and, at times, disturbing elements of human experience. The existential-humanistic tradition does not have all the answers for helping victims and survivors, but its deep tradition of caring and the promotion of individual free choice are important parts of any treatment you may engage in. The philosophic aspects of this theoretical tradition are well received in virtually all cultures, and its major theorists have had wide impact and acceptance throughout the world.

The Existential-Humanistic Worldview

The existential-humanistic worldview focuses on men and women as people who are empowered to act on the world and determine their own destiny. The locus of control and decision to lead a more satisfying and productive life lies within the individual, rather than in his or her past history or in environmental determinants. At the same time, the humanistic aspect of this tradition focuses on people in relationship one to another. It is this combination of individual respect and the importance of clients' relationships with others that gives this framework its long-lasting strength.

Existentialism's roots may be traced to the Danish philosopher Kierkegaard, but the movement came into full bloom following World War II with the writings of Sartre (1946, 1956) and Camus (1942, 1958). Heidegger (1962), Laing (1967), Husserl (1931), and Tillich (1961) loom large among the many existential philosophers, psychologists, and theologians that influenced this approach. Rollo May (1958, 1961, 1969) played a key role in bringing existential thought to the awareness of counselors and psychologists in the United States. Binswanger (1958, 1963) and Boss (1958, 1963) also have been instrumental in pulling together the many threads of existentialism into the practice of counseling and therapy.

Being-in-the-World

Being-in-the-world is regarded as the most fundamental concept of existentialism. From this viewpoint, it is believed that we act on the world while it simultaneously acts on us. Any attempt to separate ourselves from the world alienates us and establishes a false and arbitrary distinction.

According to existential theorists and philosophers, human alienation results either from separateness from others and the world or from one's inability to choose and act in relationship with the world. The central task of therapy and counseling, then, is to enable alienated clients to see themselves in relationship to the world and to choose and act in accordance with their own self-evaluated standards and beliefs.

The existential-humanistic worldview also acknowledges that racism, sexism, heterosexism, and the failure to understand and respect human differences lead to major forms of alienation that are pervasive in our contemporary society. These forms of human alienation share a common characteristic in that they all produce a heightened sense of separation from others. They are also viewed as being a main cause of anxiety and aloneness from an existential-humanistic perspective.

To facilitate an effective analysis of a person's psychological development, existentialists often think of the individual in terms of the **eigenwelt** (the person and the body), the **mitwelt** (other people in the world), and the **umwelt** (the biological and physical world). The **überwelt** (spiritual dimension) is added to this framework by Vontress (1995), who states that assessing the client's relationship to larger issues is a vital part of counseling and therapy. Spirituality and religion connect the individual to the past and to spiritual images and traditions. These issues provide a gateway for counselors and psychologists to address some of the larger existential issues clients face, including the various forms of personal alienation that many clients commonly experience in their lives.

Alienation can be experienced in one or more areas: the person may be alienated from self and her or his own body, from other people, or from the world at large. A general process of existential analysis requires individuals to explore and reflect on these aspects of life (the *eigenwelt, mitwelt, umwelt,* and *überwelt*). As a result of successfully examining the meaning of these personal, interpersonal, world, and spiritual dimensions, it is believed that individuals will learn to become freer to act, rather than only to be acted on.

As stated earlier, the existential-humanistic worldview includes a unique analysis of the ways in which a person's action or lack of action in the world results in a heightened sense of mental health and personal satisfaction or personal alienation and existential anxiety. Although most existential theorists are likely to agree that existential anxiety may result from alienation, many would also readily acknowledge that such anxiety may also result from failure to make decisions and to act in the world.

Existential-humanistic theorists recognize that choices and decisions are often difficult to make. This is so, in part, because people realize that any time they make a decision to act in a certain way in the world, they must accept the fact that they deny other alternatives and possibilities in their lives. Consequently, although choice may be painful, it is likely to be less so than the anxiety that may be created by not choosing to act.

Existential Commitment, Intentionality, and the I-Thou Relationship

Existential commitment is manifested when a person makes a decision to consciously and intentionally act in the world. Such action is expected to alleviate the generalized anxiety that is a part of the human condition. Being-in-the-world means a person must constantly make choices, which inevitably reactivates other anxieties related to the changing situations faced in life. This circle of choice and anxiety causes some existentialists (such as Sartre and Kierkegaard) to be pessimistic and dubious. Others (such as Buber and Tillich) regard the issue of choice as an opportunity to intentionally exercise one's personal freedom rather than being a problematic aspect of the human condition.

Intentionality, a key existential construct, holds that people can be forward moving by consciously acting on their world. Existential philosophers, however, encourage people to temper their understanding of the importance of acting with intentionality in the world by remaining cognizant that the world constantly acts on themselves as well. The existential notion of intentionality provides a bridge to humanism that is in full bloom in the theoretical writings of Carl Rogers and Martin Buber.

Both of these theorists have done much to link existential-humanistic concepts to counseling and psychotherapy, with a heightened recognition of the value and dignity of all persons. In doing so, they have contributed greatly to an existential-humanistic tradition that recognizes the tremendous opportunities for personal growth and increased self-understanding that may be realized from the variety of life experiences that people may encounter. Basic to this philosophy is assuming responsibility for the many choices one can make in life and then consciously deciding to act in positive ways in the world.

In adopting this existential-humanistic position in life, individuals make an intentional commitment to move toward what is positive and possible in human relations. In discussing this construct in greater detail, Buber (1970) talks of the importance of "I-Thou" relations between people—that is, a relationship in which others are seen as people rather than as objects. The intentional individual seeks I-Thou relationships as opposed to I-it relationships. Buber's concept of I-Thou relationships speaks directly to multicultural concerns. Thus, from an existential-humanistic perspective, the central challenge we all face in living in the context of an increasingly diverse society may be summed up in the following question: "How can we learn to develop positive, respectful, and caring relationships with people who are different from ourselves?"

The Rogerian Revolution: Carl Rogers's Theoretical Worldview

The word *self-actualization* is now a basic part of North American culture. This term can be traced to Rogers's influence, as can be seen in the following comments of Rogers and Wallen (1946):

> Counseling [is] a way of helping the individual help him- or herself. The function of the counselor is to make it possible for the client to gain emotional release in relation to problems and, as a consequence, to think more clearly and more deeply about oneself and one's situation in life. It is the counselor's function to provide an atmosphere in which the client, through exploration of the situation, comes to see one's self and his [or her] reactions more clearly and to accept (personal) attitudes more fully. On the basis of this insight [the client] is able to meet life's problems more adequately, more independently, and more responsibly than before. (pp. 5–6)

This aspect of Rogers's worldview, now commonplace in counseling and therapy and in Western society as a whole, represented a radical departure from the psychodynamic and behavioral traditions following World War II. Whereas psychodynamic and behavioral theories viewed humankind as the often unknowing pawn of unconscious forces and environmental contingencies, existential-humanistic psychology (particularly as interpreted by Rogers) stressed that the individual could "take charge" of life, make decisions, and act positively on the world.

At the heart of Rogers's worldview is a faith that people are positive, forward moving, basically good, and ultimately self-actualizing. Self-actualization may ultimately be defined as experiencing one's fullest humanity. Self-actualizing people enjoy life thoroughly in all its aspects, not only in occasional moments of triumph. From Rogers's perspective, the fundamental task of the counselor is to assist clients in attaining the intentionality and the health that are natural components of self-actualization and one's inner authentic self. When a person becomes truly in touch with the inner self, that individual will move to positive action and personal fulfillment (Bozarth, 1999; Lago & MacMillan, 1999).

Adding Multicultural Dimensions to Self-Actualization Theory

Lerner (1992) notes that the positive view of human nature and the desire for an egalitarian approach to living make existential-humanistic theory and counseling appealing to women and other multicultural groups. However, she criticizes the view of Rogers as particularly limited in terms of placing responsibility for development, growth, and change almost totally within the individual. According to Lerner (1992), Rogers "pays almost no attention to the so-called 'real world' or 'reality'" (p. 11). For women and other groups, Lerner maintains that Rogers's and other humanistic practices are potentially harmful because "no person constructs their own reality without external influences. These theories do not take into account exactly how influential external forces really are" (p. 13).

Some might propose that Rogers would agree with Jean Baker Miller's (1986, 1991) concepts of self-in-relation, as described in this feminist counseling theorist's writings. Rogers, after all, was a relationship therapist himself. At the same time, the very term *self-actualization* could be read as self-centered and self-focused, even though this was not Rogers's meaning or desire. With all of this in mind, it is safe to say that Rogers's work has meaning as well as limitations when applied to multicultural and feminist counseling and therapy (Hwang, 2000).

Different cultures and social classes place different emphasis on *eigenwelt* (the person and the body), *mitwelt* (other people in the world), *umwelt* (the biological and physical world), and *überwelt* (spirituality). Some upper- and middle-class clients have learned to believe that the *eigenwelt* (the person and the body) is perhaps the only desirable mode of being. This focus has led to some alienation of women and others from self-actualization counseling and therapy (Hwang, 2000; Vontress, Johnson, & Epp, 1999).

The microskill of focus can be a simple, but effective, way to balance *eigenwelt*, *mitwelt*, and *umwelt* considerations in counseling and psychotherapy. For example, assume the following lesbian client is oriented to her relationship with another person as well as being motivated to realize a greater level of self-actualization. Note the variation in responses as the therapist focuses on different dimensions of the client's psychological constructions of herself and others in her world.

Client: The professor just doesn't understand. He keeps talking about self-actualization and finding one's own way. I can't find my own way. My lover, Jenny, and I are very close. I don't want to be separate from her—we are as one. Right now she's sick and how can I find my own way if she's not OK? I don't even feel able to go out and work right now.

Therapist: (focusing on *eigenwelt*) *You're* feeling overwhelmed, and *you* don't quite know what to do. What can *you* do to work through *your* present difficulties? [*The italics highlight "you," "you're," and "your" as representative of possible* eigenwelt *responses that may lead the client to self-actualization.*]

Therapist: (focusing on *eigenwelt* and *umwelt*) Jenny's terribly important to *you*. The *relationship* sounds like the most important thing in *your* life right now. The question is how *the two of you* can survive this difficult time. *You're both* worried and upset and feel lost.

Therapist: (focusing on *umwelt*) The possibility of losing your *job* sounds very worrisome. You are wondering if issues of discrimination aren't part of the picture as well. Tell me some more about what's going on *at work*.

Therapist: (focusing on *überwelt*) I've heard your pain and sense your confusion. Tell me about your *spiritual history*. Where do you find strength and power *outside and beyond yourself*? What values or concepts are most meaningful to you?

The first three therapist responses can be useful in a Rogerian existential approach. Rogers constantly sought to help people work together. In some ways, the very terms *person-centered* and *client-centered*, attractive though they may be, can obscure the theoretical and practical value of Rogerian theory for non-middle-class and non-European-North American clients.

The fourth response addresses the *überwelt* (spiritual dimension) of Vontress's theoretical perspective as a way of enriching and expanding the therapy and counseling process with this client. Vontress suggests that truly existential-humanistic helping approaches, including Rogerian counseling and therapy, must consider *überwelt* issues if they are to be relevant from a multicultural point of view (Vontress, Johnson, & Epp, 1999).

Fusion and Boundaries in Relationships

The foregoing example focuses on an issue in relationship—namely, **fusion**—that has controversial interpretations in the field. Fusion is an important concept in counseling and therapy with lesbian clients (Mencher, 1990) as well as heterosexual couples. Fusion represents deep closeness between individuals so that at times the two individuals feel as one.

Fusion in this sense is seen by Mencher as a strength of lesbian relationships. The interpersonal closeness that characterizes such fusion is very reassuring, giving each individual a sense of secure being-in-relationship. However, many traditional Western counseling and psychotherapy theories hold that this sort of fusion is pathological and something to be avoided. These theories further assert that what is important is maintaining firm interpersonal boundaries in one's relationships with others.

Fusion operates in many, perhaps most, heterosexual relationships as well. The best human relationships include some dimension of fusion. However, just as with all dimensions of human experience, one can experience "overfusion" and lose a sense of self. What is desirable is a balance. Moreover, what in some cultures is considered fusion may be normal closeness of relationship in another. The well-defined relationship boundaries of a New England Yankee or a German-American, for instance, may be seen as being "overly distancing" from another cultural standpoint.

If, as a therapist, you focus totally on the North American male values of individuation, self-actualization, and autonomy, you will view things in terms of boundary and distancing issues and may miss important relational issues of interpersonal closeness (Comstock, 2005). Because Rogers was always open to expanding his helping theory, he would likely now argue that a balance of self-actualization (*eigenwelt*) and relationship (*mitwelt*) is most desirable (Mearns & Thorne, 1999).

Rogerian therapy is a highly verbal approach and may require complex cognitive skills on the part of the client (Bozarth, 1999). As such, the theory tends to be less effective in actual practice with children, adolescents, and less verbal clients. The economically disadvantaged often find most immediate benefit from a direct action approach rather than a self-reflective one. Behavioral, family systems, consciousness-raising, community organization, and developmental counseling methods and techniques therefore are often the treatment of choice for these groups.

The Influence of Rogers

Despite the above-mentioned difficulties of using a Rogerian approach to counseling and therapy with persons in the above-mentioned groups, his humanistic philosophy remains important in all counseling and therapy and has been supported by much research over the years (see Research Exhibit 9.1). Most practitioners who have adopted other theories or taken an eclectic or metatheoretical approach to

Research Exhibit 9.1

Research on Person-Centered Theory: Significant Findings

Rogers's methods have had an immense influence on the entire helping field. Even if one does not accept his theory as sufficient, most counselors and therapists find themselves constantly falling back on many of his theoretical concepts. The following discussion presents some research highlights on person-centered theory dating back to the 1950s.

Landmark Research

A landmark series of studies by Fiedler (1950a, 1950b, 1951) sought to define the ideal therapeutic relationship. In attempting to achieve this research goal, Fiedler studied therapists of psychoanalytic, Adlerian, and Rogerian persuasion. Fiedler found that expert therapists of these various persuasions appeared more similar to each other than they did to inexperienced therapists within the same theoretical orientation. An equally important study was conducted by Barrett-Lennard (1962), who found higher levels of facilitative conditions among experienced therapists.

Relationship as Central in Many Theories

The above-mentioned research findings prompted an avalanche of studies of the Rogerian qualitative dimensions during the ensuing years. Useful reviews of this body of research may be found in Anthony and Carkhuff (1977), Auerbach and Johnson (1977), and Garfield and Bergin (1986).

The influential study by Sloane and others (1975) found that behavioral therapists exhibited higher levels of empathy, self-congruence, and interpersonal contact than did psychotherapists using a psychodynmaic approach, whereas levels of warmth and regard were approximately the same. There was no relationship, however, between these measures and eventual effectiveness of the therapy.

Therapist Warmth

It is interesting to note that behavioral therapists, often thought of as cold and distant, proved warmer than did psychodynamic therapists in studies conducted by Sloane and his colleagues (1975, 1984). In summarizing their findings about therapist warmth, as reported by clients who worked with behavioral and psychodynamic therapists, Sloane and Staples (1984) pointed out that "successful patients in both therapies rated their personal interaction with the therapist as the single most important part of treatment" (p. 225). It is difficult to deny or disregard such a powerful statement by clients.

Research Findings

In a comprehensive review of psychotherapy research, Strupp (1989) comments: "The first and foremost task for the therapist is to create an accepting and empathic context" (p. 718). The Psychotherapy Research Project of the Menninger Foundation, which compared different types of therapy, found that "supportive mechanisms infiltrated all therapies, psychoanalysis included, and accounted for more of the achieved outcomes (including structural changes) than anticipated" (Wallerstein, 1989, p. 195). Coming nearly 40 years after the Fiedler studies, the consistency of research on the Rogerian model is notable.

A Different View

However, Mitchell, Bozarth, and Krauft (1977) read the literature on Rogerian theory quite differently. These researchers concluded that "the recent evidence, although equivocal, does seem to suggest that empathy, warmth, and genuineness are related in some way to client change, but that their potency and generalizability are not as great as was once thought" (p. 483). Work by Lambert, DeJulio, and Stein (1978) severely criticizes empathy research, suggesting that research methods

continued

Research Exhibit 9.1

have not always been adequate in studying these aspects of counseling and psychotherapy. A major study using person-centered methods with schizophrenics (Rogers et al., 1967) was also noted not to be truly effective in this regard.

Matching Therapeutic Style to Client Needs

Rogers pointed out that many therapists fall short of offering empathic conditions and that as a result, therapy and counseling can be "for better or worse." Strupp and Hadley (1976) and Strupp (1989) have illustrated this point further. In doing so, they reviewed a large number of studies indicating possible deterioration as an effect of the psychotherapeutic process. Their results point to the importance of a solid relationship appropriate to the need level of the client.

Strupp (1977) catches the essence of this argument, saying that "the art of psychotherapy may largely consist of judicious and sensitive applications of a given technique, delicate decisions of when to press a point or when to be patient, when to be warm and understanding, and when to be remote" (p. 11). Strupp suggests that simple application of a few empathic qualities is not enough. These qualities also must be in synchrony with the client at the moment in the interviewing process (see especially Strupp, 1989).

Lambert and Bergin (1994) conducted a careful review of process and outcome variables in counseling and therapy and found, once again, that the Rogerian conditions of relationship are vital to the interview.

counseling and psychotherapy still employ Rogers's interviewing skills and humanistic attitudes.

Rogers was never content with the status quo. His life was a personal demonstration of intentionality and self-actualization, as he constantly changed, shaped, and adapted his ideas over the years, increasingly emphasizing in his later years the importance of awareness and action on social issues (Rogers, 1995). His work could be broken down into three main stages of the development of his existential-humanistic theory of counseling and therapy. Although his methods changed at each stage of his development, his underlying faith in humanity and the individual-in-relationship remained constant. Segments of his interviews with different clients at each period are included to help you better understand the ways in which Rogers's approach to counseling and therapy changed over time.

Stage 1. The Nondirective Period (1940 to 1950). The nondirective stage emphasizes the acceptance of the client, the establishment of a positive nonjudgmental climate, trust in the client's wisdom, and permissiveness in the counseling and psychotherapeutic encounter. It uses clarification of the client's world as the main helping technique. Rogers's writings give a central emphasis to these skills and conditions in the counseling process.

Rogers brought a new openness to the interview process during this stage in the development of his existential-humanistic helping theory. Through detailed notes and the then-new medium of audio recording, Rogers shared in great detail what he did in the counseling interview. Up to that time, the training of counselors and therapists had taken place in formal classrooms and through lectures and discussions of what a therapist remembered from an interview.

A classic research study by Blocksma and Porter (1947) revealed that what therapists say they do in an interview and what they actually do are two different things. Rogers's ability to share what he was doing, coupled with the work of Blocksma and Porter, has forever changed the nature of counseling and psychotherapy training. There remains, however, strong resistance to this openness, particularly among some psychoanalytic therapists, who often prefer more abstract discussions of underlying unconscious conflicts to what actually happens in helping sessions.

Gendlin (1970) summarizes in a few brief words the change process of nondirective therapy:

> By saying what the client said, something new will occur, the client will soon say something new, and then we can respond to that. By featuring responsivity at every small, specific momentary step, the therapist carries forward not only what the client verbally stated, but also the client's experiential process. This responsivity to specific felt meaning at each step engenders, carries forward, and changes the individual's ongoing experiential process. This is the underlying principle that is implicit in nondirective therapy and its early quaint rules for therapist responding. (pp. 32–33)

In effect, Gendlin suggests that when clients share their experiences with the counselor and the counselor responds with accurate listening, clients move forward by the interaction. Even if the counselor just directly repeats what clients say, clients' worlds will be changed by the very act of being heard. Being heard by another person can thus be considered an action on the world.

Many, perhaps most, clients do not feel they have power and influence on others or their surroundings. By giving of themselves to their clients through empathic attending skills, counselors empower their clients. Clients speak; therapists listen carefully and attempt to understand clients' perceptions of the world. Having been heard and understood, clients can then move forward.

Figure 9.1 provides a typescript taken from Rogers's nondirective phase. Note how he explicitly tries to draw out the client and impose as little of his orientation as possible (Rogers & Wallen, 1946). His belief was that interference from the counselor would only slow natural client growth. The microskills used in this interview are all attending skills. As a useful competency-building exercise, fill in the blank space to the left of the counselor response with both the focus and the microskill(s) being used. (A listing of the microskills used in each counselor response can be found at the end of the exercise.)

The exchange in Figure 9.1 was really the summary of a longer session. However, in the interactions presented in this transcription of the counseling process with this

Figure 9.1 Sample Transcript from Rogers's Nondirective Period
Focus/Microskill

1. *Client:* I wish I knew how to pray.

_____ _____ 2. *Counselor:* Do you want to tell me some more about that?

3. *Client:* I'm all in a mess. I can't sleep. Last night I walked the streets most of the night in a pouring rain. I haven't been able to sleep all the time I've been on leave. I was home for a while, and I couldn't even talk to my folks there. You see, my buddy was killed, and I just can't get over it.

_____ _____ 4. *Counselor:* That's been a pretty upsetting blow to you.

5. *Client:* Well it is. You see, my buddy was my only real friend—I don't make friends easily, never have had very many—and he and I always stuck together. [Tells how they met and some of the things they had been through.] We worked on the same gun crew, and we knew each other so well we never had to tell each other what to do. We could just signal by the way we looked. In this particular scrap the enemy planes were coming over plenty. It was pretty hot. The ammunition box was getting empty, and I just glanced at my buddy. He knew what I meant, and he went to get another box. While he was doing that a shell exploded right near him and killed him. (pause) I just can't get over it. I feel—I feel as though I caused his death.

_____ _____ 6. *Counselor:* You feel that somehow you are to blame for the fact that he was killed.

7. *Client:* Yes I do. I don't see why. Well, there's one thing I haven't mentioned. Maybe that has something to do with it. My buddy and I, we got along swell. We hardly ever quarreled, but just the day before this all happened we had quite an argument. [He relates the details of the argument.] We really got sore at each other. I wouldn't even speak to him for several hours afterwards. You know, I think that does have something to do with it. I guess that quarrel makes me feel that I am to blame for what happened.

_____ _____ 8. *Counselor:* You feel that your being angry at him in some way was responsible for killing him.

9. *Client:* You know, I think that's it. I haven't thought that through before. Maybe I was scared to think it through. Somehow it helps to talk about things like this. You see, I didn't usually quarrel with my buddy, and I guess it hit me hard to think that we had an argument just the day before he was killed. It doesn't seem so bad when you talk about it. He was really a great guy. [He goes on to tell at some length about his buddy and his buddy's accomplishments and the good relationship they had together. The conversation then turns into other channels, and he talks about his own family and again mentions the fact that he had been very upset while

continued

home on leave.] I don't know what you've done, sir, but this has sure helped me a lot. I don't see why I felt so much to blame as I did.

_____   _____   10. *Counselor:* It seems to have helped to get it off your chest. Is that it?

11. *Client:* It sure has. I wonder, sir, if it would be too much if I could write to you if I ever feel this way again. I'm probably shipping out pretty quick so I don't think I'll have a chance to see you again, but maybe I could write you a letter.

_____   _____   12. *Counselor:* I'd be delighted to get a letter from you even if you're not feeling upset. I hope you will write to me.

13. *Client:* Well, thanks a lot for talking with me. I've got to go now but you may be hearing from me. (pp. 120–121)

(Answers: 2. Client, topic (focus)/closed question (microskill); 4. Client/reflection of feeling; 6. Client/paraphrase; 8. Client, other/paraphrase; 10. Client/reflection of feeling/paraphrase—note checkout, "Is that it?"; 12. Mutual/expression of content and feeling—self-disclosure.)

Source: C. Rogers and J. Wallen, *Counseling with returned servicemen.* Copyright 1946 from McGraw-Hill, Inc. Used by permission.

client it is important to note that every one of Rogers's leads was a listening skill much like the basic listening sequence discussed in Chapter 4. The example also illustrates issues of focusing on the *eigenwelt* and *umwelt*. Rogers's leads at numbers 2, 4, and 10 focus solely on the client (*eigenwelt*). Critical leads at numbers 6 and 8 focus on the client-in-relation to his buddy. Rogers's last statement (number 12) brings the counselor directly into the relationship.

Rogers provides an interesting personal analysis of this interview and points out that the counselor does not direct the depth of the interview but rather attempts to establish conditions so that the client can determine how far or deep to go (Bozarth, 1999). Whereas many CBT-oriented counselors might have wanted more concreteness and specifics about the situation, the counselor in this case accepts the client's definition of what has happened.

Another view of this same interview is that Rogers is more directive than he thinks. By focusing on the individual and selecting certain key words (e.g., *blame* and *anger*), Rogers actually does shape the interview. If the interviewer had been an antiwar activist and had focused on the *umwelt* (environmental, contextual, and multicultural issues) and the horrors of war, the interview likely would have been very different.

Reinforcement theorists suggest that even in the nondirective and listening approaches, counselors and therapists unconsciously encourage clients to talk about their issues in certain ways. Competency-Building Activity 9.1 can help you become aware of your listening style and how it might shape the interview.

Rogers tended to reply in a particularly disarming fashion to those who criticized his work. He suggested that therapists find their own ways of being authentic with others and that those whose views differed from his would select counseling theories

Competency-Building Activity 9.1

An Exercise in Nondirective Counseling

Instructions: The following practice exercise is designed to help you become aware of your own listening style and how it may influence the manner in which your clients tell their stories to you. The exercise will work most effectively if you audio record the three brief storytelling sessions and listen to them together with the client. Keep your use of the skill of questioning to a minimum.

Step 1. *Ask a client or a volunteer if she or he would be willing to have you tape-record an interview in which he or she talks about an issue of concern to her- or himself.* Use the basic listening sequence (BLS) to draw out the issue related to the volunteer client's story. Summarize the story at the end, feeding back to the client as accurately as you can the main facts and behaviors, thoughts, and feelings related to the story.

Step 2. *Use the BLS to draw out the same story once again.* This time attempt to focus solely on the *eigenwelt*—the client before you. Summarize as before, but make sure this time that your summary focuses almost totally on the individual. What are the client's behaviors, thoughts, and feelings? How does the client "live with" the story?

Step 3. *For a third time, use the BLS.* This time focus solely on the *mitwelt* (other people, family) and the *umwelt* (environmental, contextual, and multicultural issues). Again, summarize the client's story from these frames of reference.

Step 4. *Discuss this experience with your volunteer client.* Consider how these issues of "nondirective" counseling relate to you and your work. Then consider the following question as it relates to using a Rogerian approach in counseling and therapy: "Can we ever be truly nondirective as we listen to and work with clients?"

Be sure to take time to write down your reactions to this activity when you have completed this exercise and file your reactions in your personal/professional portfolio.

---

that worked best for them. As a result, Rogers exhibited unusual congruence within himself. Not only did he emphasize and respect clients' rights to determine what was appropriate for them, but he also respected his critics' ability to determine what was right for themselves as well.

The importance of listening is illustrated dramatically in studies by Inbar and others (1989) of soldiers who experience combat stress. These researchers found that combat-stressed soldiers benefited from talking about their difficulties with supportive staff personnel. Because combat stress was treated as a normal response to an abnormal situation, these soldiers were able to return to their posts with minimum long-term effects. If combat difficulties are ignored, as they were in the Vietnam War, there is evidence that stresses will reappear later as posttraumatic stress disorder.

Rogers's nondirective style has continuing relevance in many other areas of counseling and psychology as well as those noted above. One particular issue that Rogers repeatedly emphasized in the early formation of his nondirective theory relates to the way mental health practitioners can effectively and respectfully respond to their clients in counseling and psychotherapy.

Commenting on this critical issue, Rogers pointed out that when clients are involved in talking about their own experiences, it is important to focus totally on them. Clients need to be heard, and we as counselors and therapists need to learn about their constructions of the world. Through empathy and by using listening skills, we provide clients with a chance to learn what they themselves think.

However, a pure listening approach, as represented in the foregoing transcript, is not always appropriate. At times, the nondirective style can bring about difficulties in multicultural counseling. For example, African-American clients working with a European-American therapist might sometimes mistrust the Rogerian mirroring response. They might want to know who you are as a person and reject a helping approach that is solely focused on mirroring back what is said. Sue and Sue (2003) found that some traditional Asian-American clients often prefer a more directive approach and do not respect a counselor who cannot and will not give advice and direction.

Thus, although listening is considered a central skill in counseling and therapy, it is one of many techniques that form the total strategy of professional helping. During the client-centered period, Rogers was increasingly willing to interpret and influence clients.

Stage 2. The Client-Centered Period (1950 to 1961). The client-centered period centers on reflecting the feelings of the client, helping the individual to resolve incongruities between the ideal self and real self, avoiding personally threatening situations for the client, and using reflection as the main technique in counseling and therapy. Other skills and techniques are not emphasized at this stage in Rogers's theoretical development. Rather, the major emphasis is placed on the counselor as an accepting and authentic person in Rogers's helping model.

Most excerpts from this period of Rogers's work are highly verbal and relevant to clients who are deeply interested in introspection. Consequently, there may be less value in this period for multicultural counseling than in his other two periods. The client-centered style of helping is currently used relatively infrequently and thus is of limited historical interest.

The following interview segment illustrates the work of the second period of Rogers's (1961) theoretical development. The client, Mrs. Oak, talks about how hard it is for her to accept any help or positive reactions from others. The complexity of the counselor's sentences has greatly increased compared with those in the nondirective period interview. Although the emphasis is still very much on the client and the client's perceptions, there is also an interpretive dimension in that the counselor seems to lead the client at times.

Client: I have a feeling that you have to do it pretty much yourself, but that somehow you ought to be able to do that with other people. [She mentions that there have been "countless" times when she might have accepted personal warmth and kindliness from others.] I get the feeling that I just was afraid I would be devastated. [She returns to talking about the counseling itself and her feeling toward it.] I mean there's been this tearing through the thing myself. Almost to—I mean, I felt it—I mean I tried to verbalize it on occasion—a kind of—at times almost not wanting you to restate, not wanting you to reflect, the thing is mine. Of course, I can say it's resistance. But that doesn't mean a damn thing to me now. The thing is—I think in—in relationship to this particular thing, I mean, the—probably at times, the strongest feeling was, it's mine, it's mine. I've got to cut it down myself. See?

Counselor: It's an experience that's awfully hard to put down accurately into words, and yet I get a sense of difference here in this relationship, that from the feeling that "this is mine," "I've got to do it," "I am doing it," and so on, to a somewhat different feeling that "I could let you in."

[*The counselor's reflection of meaning catches the main points of Mrs. Oak's statement in brief form, feeding back to her what her inner world is truly like. In addition, the basic incongruity between her real and ideal self is reflected back to the client. Mrs. Oak's statement has a vagueness that would prompt many other counselors to search for more concreteness and to ask for specifics. A psychodynamic therapist might observe the sexual symbolism in the words "I've got to cut it down myself" and the therapist's response "I could let you in."*]

Client: Yeah. Now I mean, that's—that it's—well, it's sort of, shall we say, volume two. It's—it's a—well, sort of, well, I'm still in the thing alone, but I'm not—see—I'm—

Counselor: M-hm. Yes, that paradox sort of sums it up, doesn't it.

Client: Yeah.

Counselor: In all of this, there is a feeling, it's still—every aspect of my experience is mine and that's kind of inevitable and necessary and so on. And yet that isn't the whole picture either. Somehow it can be shared or another's interest can come in and in some ways it is new.

[*There is an interpretive flavor to the last two therapist statements as new meanings are put on old experience. Yet as they very much come from the client's worldview, these leads are a reflection of meaning but close to a paraphrase. The increased involvement of the therapist since Rogers's first period is apparent. Note also that the therapist goes so far as to use "I" when talking about the client rather than "you"; this could be considered a sign of strong empathy in that the counselor can see the world through the client's eyes.*]

Client: Yeah. And it's—it's as though, that's how it should be. I mean, that's how it—has to be. There's a—there's a feeling, "and this is good." I mean, it expresses, it clarifies it for me. There's a feeling—in this caring, as though—you were sort of standing back—standing off, and if I want to sort of cut through to the thing, it's a—a slashing of—oh, tall weeds, that I can do it, and you can—I mean you're not going to be disturbed by having to walk through it, too. I don't know. And it doesn't make sense. I mean—

Counselor: Except there's a very real sense of rightness about this feeling that you have, hm?

Client: M-hm. (pp. 84–85)

[*It is particularly important to note the emphasis in the paraphrase. The therapist has selectively attended to the positive aspects of the client's message ("this is good") and simultaneously ignored the negative aspects ("it doesn't make sense"). Behavioral counselors have often pointed out that Rogerian counseling involves selective attention and that as complete a verbal "shaping" process occurs in this mode of counseling as in more systematic behavioral approaches. Regardless of whether this view is accepted or not, the selective attention to positive, forward-moving aspects of the client is an example of the positive emphasis of this theory.*]
[*Rogers goes on to comment that this was a turning point for Mrs. Oak, who learned that it was all right to accept others and to discover positive things in herself. This acceptance is, of course, crucial in the development of a positive self-actualizing personality.*]

The focus in the foregoing interview is still very much on the individual (*eigenwelt*) and her construction of events. Very little attention is paid to how others might view the same events. The goal of the interchange seems to focus on Mrs. Oak finding her own "space." Rogerian theory holds that after Mrs. Oak has found herself, she will be better able to relate with others. A feminist or multicultural critique might be that Mrs. Oak could find herself even more rapidly given a more immediate focus on relationships and the role of women in society, with a secondary focus on her own self-perceptions.

A critical issue in Rogerian counseling is the discrepancy that often occurs between the real self and the ideal self. Individuals need to see themselves as worthy of personal affirmation and dignity. Often individuals lose sight of what they really are in an effort to attain an idealized image (Lago & MacMillan, 1999). This discrepancy between thought and reality, between self-perception and others' perceptions, or between self and experience leads to incongruities. These incongruities in turn result in areas in which individuals are not truly themselves. The father who strikes the child lacks congruence. The objective of therapy with this client is to resolve the discrepancies between ideal and real self, thus eliminating the tension and substituting forward-moving self-actualization.

From a multicultural frame of reference, the emphasis in Rogerian theory on the client's ideal self and real self tends to obscure relational and broader environmental issues. As such, it may be helpful to add a broader focus when working with many clients from diverse cultural backgrounds. For example, it would be within the Rogerian tradition to help clients focus on real relationships and ideal relationships. Such a focus would help individuals think of themselves as persons-in-relation to significant others. This focus would entail a change in the style of counseling and therapy usually associated with Rogers. But considering Rogers's life development, these concepts likely would fit with the direction he was heading at the end of his life. Clearly, Rogers was focusing on a more ideal world as contrasted with the real world (*umwelt*).

Furthermore, theorists of a more psychodynamic orientation have suggested that Rogers's emphasis on the self as a central construct goes back to his own roots in a strict German family. From this frame of reference, his self-referenced counseling approach represents an unconscious rebellion against and an attempt to cope with family and cultural controls.

Rogers, who once studied for the ministry, constantly stressed the importance of a natural relationship among human beings. He rejected the concepts of psychoanalytic transference and countertransference as being unnecessary in the helping process. Research Exhibit 9.2, however, presents data supporting the idea that Rogers was not as free from his own past developmental history as he stated in his writings.

The emphasis in the first two periods of Rogers's work was on individual counseling and therapy. LaFromboise and Low (1989) comment that a broader approach than just individual problem solving may be necessary with Native Americans:

> Traditionally, Indian people live in relational networks that serve to support and nurture strong bonds of mutual assistance and affection. Many tribes still engage in a traditional system of collective interdependence, with family members responsible not only to one another but also the clan and tribe to which they belong. The Lakota Sioux use the term *tiospaye* to describe a traditional community way of life in which an individual's well-being remains the responsibility of the extended family. When problems arise among Indian youth, they become problems of the community as well. The family, kin, and friends join together to observe the youth's behavior, draw the youth out of isolation, and integrate that person back into the activities of the group. (p. 121)

If Mrs. Oak were a Lakota Sioux, the individual-focused approach of the interview likely would be inappropriate. Although it would be important to listen to her individual constructions (as in the nondirective period), the focus of counseling interventions would probably emphasize the *mitwelt*, the family, extended family, and community. For a Lakota Sioux, an individual issue remains unsolved until it is considered in the broader network of relationships.

In addition, it would be important for you as therapist to present yourself in the interview as a real person with real thoughts and feelings. In multicultural settings, the boundaries between therapist and client change, which presents a challenge to the practice of traditional counseling and therapy. Rogers was moving toward a multicultural emphasis and understanding in his final, person-centered period.

Stage 3. The Person-Centered Period (1961 to 1987). The person-centered stage is characterized by increased personal involvement, with more stress on relational issues in counseling and therapy. While maintaining consistency with all of his past work, Rogers increasingly emphasized present-tense experience, a more active and self-disclosing role for the counselor, the use of group as well as individual counseling, and increased consideration of broader issues in society, such as cultural differences and the use of power. The focus on skills and techniques remains minimal at this

Research Exhibit 9.2

A Controversy in the Field: Does Transference Exist in Rogerian Therapy?

In a famous film entitled *Three Approaches to Psychotherapy* (Shostrum, 1965), a client named Gloria is interviewed by Carl Rogers, Fritz Perls, and Albert Ellis. The film had an immense influence on the acceptance of Rogers's work at the time. In the film, he appears warm and accepting toward Gloria, who indicates that she enjoys his work with her above the others.

In the second period of the formation of his helping theory, Rogers emphasized the importance of here-and-now interactions between client and counselor and felt that transferential concepts and discussion of the past were not useful dimensions of the counseling process. Rogers commented in some detail that the film is evidence that transferential concepts are not needed and used the film to stress the importance of focusing on the person. This film and Rogers's negation of transference have influenced many counseling and therapy training programs, which prefer to ignore psychodynamic concepts.

Weinrach (1990) discovered that a final extra 249 words were deleted from this famous film. Just prior to the deleted words, Gloria comments, "Gee, how nice I can talk to you and I want you to approve of me and I respect you, but I miss that my father couldn't talk to me like that. I mean I'd like to say, 'Gee, I'd like you for my father.'" Rogers comments that Gloria would make a "pretty nice daughter." The film concludes as they discuss Gloria's father's inability to accept her as she is. At this point, Rogers makes a point against a transferential interpretation.

Weinrach presents the full text that continues the father-daughter issue. The following interpretation missing from the published film is an example of a psychodynamically oriented statement that one would not expect of Rogers: "*Rogers:* The phrase that comes to my mind—I don't know if it is appropriate or not—you're slapping your father in the face, aren't you?"

[*Interpretation: the focus is on Gloria transferring unconscious feelings toward her father to her present behavior.*]

Weinrach points out that transferential relationships can complicate our interventions unless we are aware of them and their implications. He also points out that Rogers himself may be seen as involved in a complex countertransferential relationship with Gloria. Weinrach comments that if the full film had been shown, Rogers might have been seen less as a role model and more as a "mortal therapist who missed or unintentionally ignored an important clinical issue."

Bohart (1991) takes issue with Weinrach, commenting that transferential concepts are highly intellectualized and miss the essence of the Rogerian relational approach. He describes the above missing segment of the interview as more evidence of Rogers's caring and empathy.

Beaver (1991) adds additional comments on the failure of Rogers to consider Gloria as a woman in a society dominated by men. Rogers's focus was on a single person in front of him, and he did not consider any contextual issues except as Gloria constructed them. Clearly, Gloria faced many multicultural issues in terms of male-female relationships, societal expectations, and her father-daughter relationship. From a multicultural-feminist-social justice counseling perspective, these matters must be considered in understanding how a woman's self-in-relation is established.

This is the type of controversy you as a therapist or counselor will encounter again and again. Given the discussion in this chapter, do you endorse Weinrach's, Beaver's, or Bohart's interpretation of the data? Recall that more than one perspective may be "correct" and that the meaning of "correctness" depends on the constructed worldview of the observer. On this last point, we might expect Rogers to concur.

stage. Instead, the counselor's attitude toward the client is stressed. Coupled with this is an emphasis on experiencing oneself as a person-in-relation to others. A review of Rogers's transcripts reveals an interpretative helping style emerging at this phase of his professional development that often focuses on the above issues.

This final phase of Rogers's career brought forth a flowering of new ideas and continuous additions to his framework. He became interested in encounter groups and was deeply affected by his learnings in group work at this phase of his professional development. During this period, he also developed an interest in couples counseling (1972), personal power (1977), the learning process (1969), and world peace (Gendlin, 1988). Despite these diverse interests, which continued to grow and expand until his death at the age of 85 in 1987, Rogers maintained his consistent respect for the individual, stressed the importance of research, and constantly emphasized the ability of individuals to find their own direction, but always in relationship to other human beings.

To the traditional skills of paraphrasing, reflection of feeling, and summarizing, he added new skills of self-disclosure, feedback, and questioning. In this period, he also seemed to be less interpretive than he was in the client-centered period. In the following interview, Rogers (1970) acts as facilitator for an encounter group:

Art: When the shell's on it's, uh . . .

Lois: It's on now?

Art: Yeah, it's on tight.

Susan: Are you always so closed in when you're in your shell?

Art: No, I'm so darn used to living with the shell, it doesn't even bother me. I don't even know the real me. I think I've, well, I've pushed the shell away more here. When I'm out of my shell—only twice—once just a few minutes ago—I'm really me, I guess. But then I just sort of pull in a cord after me when I'm in my shell, and that's almost all the time. And I leave the front standing outside when I'm back in the shell.

Facilitator: And nobody's back in there with you?
  [*Art is the focus of group interaction at the moment. He describes his feelings of being shut off from people in a vivid metaphor of life in a shell. As a group member Art is using effective self-disclosure skills. Lois and Susan, through completion of Art's sentence and the focused closed questions, show that more people than group leaders and counselors can be helpful in this therapeutic modality. The facilitator's interpretation is critical because it brings past and present experience together in one existential moment. Art is experiencing being alone in the shell at this moment as he has in the past in other situations. Yet, paradoxically, he is alone with a supportive facilitator and group. This integration of past and present experiences in "moments of truth" appears in most theories of helping and is particularly important in person-centered counseling and therapy.*]

Art: (crying) Nobody else is in there with me. I just pull everything into the shell and roll the shell up and shove it in my pocket. I take the shell, and the real me, and put it in my pocket where it's safe. I guess that's really the way I do it—I go into my shell and turn off the real world. And here—that's what I want to do here in this group, y'know—come out of my shell and actually throw it away.

Lois: You're making progress already. At least you can talk about it.

Facilitator: Yeah. The thing that's going to be hardest is to stay out of the shell.

Art: (still crying) Well, yeah, if I can keep talking about it I can come out and stay out, but I'm going to have to, y'know, protect me. It hurts. It's actually hurting to talk about it. (p. 26)

[*Lois provides a good example of a feedback statement, and the facilitator expresses his opinion and reaction. Together, the two support Art in the immediate moment and help him clarify his own experience.*]

The title of Rogers's best-known book, *On Becoming a Person* (1961, 1995), is a reflection of the man and his theory. In the Rogerian view, there seems to be no definable end to counseling work. The emphasis on process toward possible futures is particularly illustrative of the existential-humanistic orientation, which stresses individual choice.

At the same time, there is a potential problem in the term *person-centered* in that counselors and therapists have sometimes limited the scope of what Rogers meant by relating to others and to the world. Although Rogers did not use the language of German existentialism, he was very concerned that persons extend their view beyond themselves to others and to the world at large. As his later writings reveal, Rogers worked toward expanding his and others' humanistic concepts to issues that extend beyond the individual.

In expanding our view beyond the self, one of the most powerful things we can do in groups and in other human settings that involve complex negotiations is to hear how others construct meaning of the world. An interview conducted with an 82-year-old Rogers (*APA Monitor*, 1984) highlighted this point:

His work over one weekend with Irish Protestants and Catholics joined by a representative of the British government achieved what he called "surprising results" and led to a film that the participants hoped to take to schools, churches, and similar neutral settings. The proof of its success, he added, came when paramilitary groups on both sides, who were opposed to his attempt to overcome centuries of hostility, destroyed four copies of the film before it could be shown.

This summer he attended a conference in Hungary in which 300 persons from 27 countries—Western democracies as well as Eastern-bloc communist countries—grappled with issues that divided their nations. Although participants were often more revealing in private conversations than in public sessions, Rogers said the conference was extremely successful in teaching individuals to listen to the views of others. (p. 15)

In these workshops, Rogers encouraged the participants to explore their hostile attitudes and feelings, thus helping remove irrational aspects of their thinking. He also focused on persons and attitudes, thereby forging an important beginning once the underlying rage was accepted and understood. He fostered "direct confrontation of opponents in a confined area." Rogers found that in a group environment where members listened and sought to understand one another, group members who were previously combatants could learn to accept one another and work toward mutual goals together.

The theoretical movement of Rogers seems to begin and end with careful listening. Rogers fostered a greater awareness that listening could serve as a foundation for challenging feedback, interpretations, and even direct confrontations. The first step toward mutual understanding is listening and learning how others construe events (Patterson, 1999; Rogers, 1995).

Spirituality, Multiculturalism, and Existential-Humanistic Counseling

Clemmont Vontress has long been a proponent of multicultural counseling and therapy (Vontress, 1979, 1986). His more recent writings direct attention to the ways in which the existential-humanistic perspective complements the multicultural worldview (Vontress, 1995a, 1995b).

Vontress has been particularly drawn to Rogers's concepts of empathy and positive regard. He has also helped to expand Rogers's theoretical perspective in these areas by describing, in more depth, how the therapeutic relationship can serve as a truly healing experience when the client-therapist relationship is characterized by expressions of intimacy, openness, and real human exchange.

Vontress's concern is that the therapist's reliance on techniques may obscure the possibility of building an intimate, open, and real relationship with the client. Only in a situation of genuine caring and authenticity, Vontress and his colleagues believe, can true healing and growth occur (Vontress, Johnson, & Epp, 1999). The following interview of Vontress indicates why he reconsidered the Rogerian approach.

Lee: What was your theoretical position, and how would you describe your ideas on multicultural counseling in the early years of your degree?

Vontress: Well, when I left Indiana University with a Ph.D. degree in 1965, the professors and students were excited about the Rogerian approach to counseling. I remember Dr. Rogers came to Indiana University to make a presentation, and I occupied the stage with him to ask questions; that was a big honor. So, when I left graduate school I was, I thought, a Rogerian. But, during my years at Crispus Attucks High School as director of counseling, I learned from counseling the students that that approach wouldn't work with them. I remember once I was asking a Black student, "How do you feel about this and that?" The student finally exploded with great frustration and said, "What is all this 'how do you feel' stuff? I feel like you feel when something like that happens to you." (Lee, 1994, p. 68)

Although Rogerian philosophy is a useful and popular approach, the skills and strategies for implementing this philosophy should change with the individual and cultural background (Chung & Bemak, 2002). Vontress did not abandon the Rogerian position but rather integrated it with an important new understanding of existentialism. Whereas multicultural counseling and therapy tend to focus on differences, Vontress emphasizes commonalties among people.

One of the most vital commonalties emphasized by Vontress is being together with another person in relationship (*mitwelt*). Vontress (1995) illustrates the importance of "being with" another person in ways that respect cultural uniqueness (*umwelt*). Counseling and therapy are usually thought of as highly verbal occupations, but Vontress notes that many Appalachian Whites and Native American Indians spend considerable time together without saying a word. Consequently, silence can be a way of respecting the individual (*eigenwelt*), developing a trusting relationship (*mitwelt*), and working within the client's culture (*umwelt*). As an existential therapist, Vontress would remind us that all three dimensions of existentialism must exist as a whole for counseling and therapy to be effective.

This point is echoed by work in Japan, where Rogers's approach was originally accepted with great enthusiasm but later fell into some disrepute. Hayashi and others (1992) state that originally Rogers's work was accepted uncritically in Japan, resulting in a dogmatic approach that at times was highly inappropriate for the cultural setting. Although Rogerian and existential philosophies remain important in Japan, newer approaches add a focus on culture and *umwelt* that has been vital in the ongoing evolution of the existential-humanistic worldview in general and Rogerian counseling in particular.

Vontress believes that spirituality is a vital part of any truly multicultural encounter. He is one of the few theorists to state unequivocally that the spiritual/religious *überwelt* is critical to understanding not only the person but also the client's culture. Japanese culture is heavily based in Buddhist and Shinto spiritual dimensions. Buddhist holistic concepts and Shinto veneration of human-nature connections are key aspects of the very being of many Japanese people. Any revision of the Rogerian approach in a Japanese context would benefit by considering these particular religious/spiritual influences (D'Andrea, 2004c).

The Japanese example illustrates how important it is to include the spiritual dimension for a more complete understanding of the individual and cultural dimensions of human experience. The individual lives in relationship to a cultural and spiritual frame of reference. According to Vontress (1995):

> Human beings need the respect, devotion, love, and affection of parents, elders, departed ones, and spiritual figures. In Africa, the spirit world connects the living with people who have been here before and who therefore still reside in the living via genetics, culture, and the collective unconscious. Ancestors are invisible neighbors of the living. Their love sustains them and often directs their lives. (p. 2)

From the perspective of traditional Western counseling and therapy, this statement may seem radical and controversial. Spirituality and the connection with the distant past are seldom associated with here-and-now action-oriented counseling and

Competency-Building Activity 9.2

Reviewing the Meaning of One's Being-in-the-World

Instructions: This exercise will take a half hour or more and requires a volunteer or real client who is willing to explore the meaning of a significant stressful experience. The five-stage interview format described in Chapter 4 is used to provide a structure for the suggested activities of this session.

Stage 1. Establishing Rapport and Structuring

As you start, outline with your client the purpose and general structure of this session. Talk with the client in appropriate language about the idea of making meaning of old situations in new ways through the multiple lenses of *eigenwelt, mitwelt, umwelt,* and *überwelt.* The goal is to review a stressful incident from the distant or recent past and to see what sense can be made of it. Before you start, spend some time examining the degree of rapport and trust between you and the person you are working with.

You can do this by using words or through nonverbal awareness. Your own and the client's comfort are vital. Vontress often speaks of the importance of finding commonalties between people. What are your commonalties with this client? Are you coequal with your client, or have you established a therapist-client hierarchy? Is your relationship real and authentic?

Stage 2. Gathering Data

Ask your client to tell you about her or his concern or issue. Use the basic listening sequence to draw out the facts, feelings, and thoughts associated with the client's story as it unfolds. On listening to the client's narrative, note how much of the expressed concern is directed to the individual, others, and/or the environment/context in which the concern/issue occurred. Listen for underlying spiritual dimensions.

As you listen to the story, pay special attention to the client's positive assets as well as the strengths in his or her relationships with other people and the cultural/environmental context of which she or he is a part. These positive resources in the *eigenwelt, mitwelt, umwelt,* and *überwelt* can lead to positive reframing and new meanings for future action. You may wish to directly ask where the client stands on each of these dimensions. As in the approaches of Vontress, feminist therapy, and multicultural counseling and therapy, you may wish to share some of your own beliefs briefly and concisely, making sure not to take the lead away from the client.

Stage 3. Determining Outcomes

Your client has very likely indicated or implied a desire for how things should be ideally. The clarification of the "real world," as compared to the "ideal world," is an important part of Rogerian theory. Clarification of the discrepancy between the real and the ideal often impels clients to more serious thought, feeling, and action.

Once there is a clear understanding of the present and possible future, summarize the interview to this point, including the original story, and contrast this summary with the ideal narrative. Of course, a complete resolution may not be possible in one session. Thus, you may want to ask your client which part of the discrepancy should be considered at this time.

Stage 4. Generating Alternative Solutions and Meaning

The word *solutions* may not always be appropriate in a therapeutic setting. Instead, the goal might be rephrased as finding new meanings in old situations and narratives. There are a variety of ways to explore new meanings, including drawing on other theories (cognitive-behavioral, multicultural, etc.) at appropriate points in the helping process. However, within the existential-humanistic tradition, the focus is on finding positive new meanings. Two concrete intervention styles that may be useful in helping clients generate positive alternative solutions and new meaning to their concerns are multiple storytelling and developing a shared or coconstructed narrative.

continued on next page

Competency-Building Activity 9.2, continued

Multiple Storytelling. Most likely the client has focused the narrative on a personal frame of reference. Ask the client to tell the story from the frame of reference of significant others—How would other people tell the same story? Then, ask the client to tell the story from a gender, ethnic/racial, spiritual, or other multicultural perspective. If the client told the story from an external perspective (significant other [*mitwelt*] or cultural [*umwelt*]), it might be necessary to ask the client to tell you a story focusing on "I" statements in which the *eigenwelt* becomes the focus.

Vontress notes that the body stores these stories and that one's narrative can even affect immune system functioning. You may wish to make bodily experience part of this discussion (see Chapter 13 for a review of skills in this area).

At another level, consider retelling the story from the spiritual (*überwelt*) perspective. For many of us, this will be uncomfortable. However, this is a time to test and experience new dimensions of meaning making in a coequal relationship with your client.

Then review the multiple stories and ask the client what meanings were found. Useful questions here may include:"What sense do you make of the different stories?" "What one idea stands out for you?" "We've looked at your situation from several perspectives now—how would you integrate them into a new story?"

Developing a Shared or Coconstructed Narrative. This is a more difficult task, as it requires you to share your own struggles with meaning with the client. The focus is on commonalties and differences between you and the client, which emphasizes the relationship (*mitwelt*) between the two of you. This approach also requires a judicious use of self-disclosure and an effort not to force your meaning on the client.

Buber might consider this a focus on the I-Thou relationship of the counselor and the client. This intervention can be supplemented by focusing on cultural, environmental, and contextual issues (*umwelt*) you and the client encounter.

Stage 5. Generalizing Learning

Existential-humanistic philosophy often views therapy as a process of personal exploration and discovery. This perspective embraces the essence of existential thinking, which fosters a search for new meaning as an end in itself in counseling and psychotherapy.

However, it is also clear that thinking in new ways about old stories can change bodily functioning and may lead automatically to new actions. With this in mind, you and the person you are working with may choose to end this activity by doing more than developing new meaning about the client's concern. More specifically, the person you are working with may agree to generalize the new meaning gained in this exercise in other situations outside of the helping process. If this is the case, it will useful to spend a few more minutes exploring with your client the answer to the following question: "How can I use the new meaning I acquired about this concern in the world of which I am a part?"

After exploring some of the possible things she or he can do to use the new meaning generated in this exercise in her or his life, set a time to follow up with this individual in the coming week to check on success in this area. In doing so, you will be exercising a level of ethical responsibility that is important to demonstrate in your future professional practices.

An alternative to using the generalizing technique described above is to ask if the client would like to select one specific task for "homework." If so, the task may be behavioral and based on the cognitive-behavioral paradigm. Or the client may set a goal of thinking in new ways about old situations. You may wish to have the homework focus on Ellis's rational-emotive behavior-contextual therapeutic system or Glasser's more externally focused reality therapy.

Be sure to take time to write down your reactions to this activity when you have completed this exercise and file your reactions in your personal/professional portfolio.

therapy (Duran & Duran, 1995; Moodley & West, 2005; Parham, White, & Ajamu, 1999). Nonetheless, there is a precedent for Vontress's views in the work of Carl Jung (1958). Jung constantly stressed the importance of spirituality, and his idea of the collective unconscious represents a foundation for much of what is considered spiritual.

Whether you find Vontress's views of spirituality compatible with your own worldview or not, it is nonetheless true that many cultures in different ways subscribe to the spiritual foundations he suggests. Many Africans and African-Americans, Chinese, Japanese, Jews, Mormons, Native American Indians, Hindus, Roman Catholics, Muslims, and others would find counseling and therapy incomplete without the inclusion of spiritual and religious concepts and traditions infused into the helping process (Fukuyama & Sevig, 1999).

As an example of the importance of including the spiritual dimension in counseling, consider the anger many African-Americans feel as they experience various forms of racism in our contemporary society. This anger can become internalized, affecting the mind, body, and spirit. Vontress (quoted in Lee, 1994) makes a connection between spiritual and bodily disease in speaking of middle-class African-American men:

> It's terribly fascinating to try to understand why these Black men die in their sleep more than any other men. I maintain it's because they are working in the mainstream culture around White people and have to suppress their hostility during the day. It's only when they're sleeping at night that their system allows that hostility to express itself, and it expresses itself very often in sleep. This helps to explain why there's such an inordinate number of Black middle-class men who die in their sleep at night. (p. 71)

In working with clients suffering emotional distress, existential-humanistic understanding and spiritual connection can elevate not only clients' thinking but also their bodily functioning (Chissell, 2000; Chopra & Simon, 2001; Moodley & West, 2005). Applying these ideas in counseling practice requires you as therapist or counselor to seek a full Rogerian relationship, but with a balanced focus on *eigenwelt*, *mitwelt*, *umwelt*, and *überwelt*. Competency-Building Activity 9.2 is designed to integrate ideas of Carl Rogers with those of existentialism, particularly as suggested by Clemmont Vontress. Vontress emphasizes the importance of the meaning one makes of one's life and the situations one encounters. Through meaning making, we can redefine our world and develop more effective means of making sense of who we are, our relationships with others, and our being-in-the-world.

Limitations and Practical Implications of the Existential-Humanistic Tradition

The beauty and strength of the existential-humanistic tradition lie in its strong faith in humankind, the unlimited opportunity for personal growth, and the infinite possibility of experience. However, some naive therapists and counselors have taken only the concept of "infinite possibility" and have led clients into destructive, closed circles of existence.

As with psychodynamic theory, the existential-humanistic approach tends to be highly verbal. Concerned with the meaning of life and individual satisfaction, the therapy can be a way to avoid reality and the need for taking action in one's life. This latter aspect of existential-humanistic counseling and psychotherapy is antithetical to those multicultural-feminist-social justice counseling advocates who stress the need for mental health practitioners to help clients effectively combat those environmental-contextual conditions that negatively impact the physical and psychological health of millions of people in our society (NIMC, 2000).

The positive philosophy of Carl Rogers is applauded by some multicultural advocates as a much needed alternative to the negative views presented by the traditional psychoanalytic worldview and the deterministic perspective reflected in behavioral theories (Vontress, 1995). But the nature of Rogerian methods—slow reflection and a lack of action and immediate problem solving—seems inappropriate for many clients in marginalized groups, who are routinely subjected to various forms of social injustices that adversely affect their mental health and psychological well-being (Sue & Sue, 2003).

The tendency for existential-humanistic counseling to ignore person-environment transactions can be a major limitation of this theoretical force. The intense preoccupation with the individual and free choice is at times incompatible with more environmentally oriented and contextually aware helping approaches.

However, the existential-humanistic philosophic tradition does speak to multicultural concerns in that, perhaps more than any other set of theories, it focuses on human relationship. We can supplement the basic ideas of Rogers with a more focused emphasis on the *mitwelt* and *umwelt*.

Vontress adds a challenging dimension to existential-humanistic thought, in general, and Rogerian counseling, in particular, by suggesting an increased emphasis on the cultural/environmental context (*umwelt*) and a focus on the holistic and spiritual dimensions of counseling (*überwelt*). As noted in Chapter 1, mainstream counseling and therapy theories have tended to ignore spirituality. For this reason, Vontress's ideas, although controversial for some, add an important dimension to the existential-humanistic worldview.

What does the existential-humanistic movement offer the beginning counselor or therapist that is immediately useful? Perhaps the major contribution of Rogers has been his emphasis on empathic and accurate listening (Chung & Bemak, 2002) and his willingness to open the interview to inspection and research through audiotape and film (Cornelius-White, 2002).

Attending skills are basic to Rogers's classifications and discussion in his early work. The qualitative conditions of warmth, respect, and concreteness (Chapter 4) are derived from his seminal thinking. Rogers's methodological message is that we as counselors and therapists must listen to the client and open the interview and ourselves to scrutiny. Only in this way can we grow and learn about our own possibilities to enrich the lives of others. The Professional Development Extension provides an example of existential-humanistic principles in professional practice.

Professional Development Extension

Using Existential Principles in Practice

One of the most important principles of existential-humanistic approaches to counseling and therapy centers around the concept that people are empowered to act on the world and determine their own destiny. Events in a client's life can foster alienation, which commonly results in negative psychological outcomes (e.g., an increased sense of hopelessness, depression, frustration, and anger). This in turn can lead to an increased sense of separateness from others and the world. The existential therapist strives to reshape this line of thinking. Consider the case of Thomas.

Thomas is a 68-year-old retired teacher who came to counseling after the unexpected death of his wife. He was reportedly depressed about her death and complained of feeling too anxious to do anything except "mope around the house all day." Even though he knew that he would continue to grieve the loss of his wife "probably for the rest of my life," Thomas wanted to know what he could do to move beyond the increasing depression and anxiety he was experiencing.

The therapist (Dorothy) followed Carl Rogers's suggestions about building a positive relationship with the client by communicating a genuine sense of warmth, positive regard, and empathy for the client as she carefully and respectfully listened to Thomas's stated concerns during their first therapy session. During their second session, Dorothy continued to build on her relationship with Thomas in this way but also talked to him about the importance of making an existential commitment while facing his present challenges. Dorothy further explained that people demonstrate this commitment when they intentionally move forward by consciously acting on their world.

Although Thomas found this to be an interesting concept, he said that he was not sure where or how he could begin to make this commitment. Dorothy responded by saying that they could take time to explore the degree to which the depression and loss Thomas experienced resulted in a generalized anxiety that caused him to become alienated from himself and his body (his eigenwelt), other people (his mitwelt), the world at large (umwelt), and his sense of spiritual connection in the world (his überwelt).

By taking time to explore all four of these areas with Thomas during their second and third therapy sessions, the therapist could see that the anxiety and depression Thomas was experiencing over the loss of his wife was adversely impacting each of these areas. A summary of their discussions about these areas indicated that he had essentially stopped taking his regular walks and was not eating as regularly or as healthily (eigenwelt) as he had in the past. He had stopped participating in various informal social events (like playing cards and going food shopping) with some of his friends (mitwelt). He also no longer watched the news or participated in the community group at his church (umwelt). Also he had grown cynical about why God would have let his wife (who was several years younger than Thomas) die before himself (überwelt).

The therapist helped Thomas discuss the ways in which he had disengaged or grown cynical in these areas. Dorothy then asked Thomas what changes he would be willing to make to move beyond his disengagement and cynicism. Over the next 12 sessions, Thomas began to make small steps in implementing changes in all four of these areas. Three months later, he stated that he had gained much from working on these areas and felt less depressed and anxious about life. He also said that by improving his diet and exercise as well as his involvement with his friends and reestablishing his relationship with God, he was feeling more like "my old self, even though I continue to miss my wife greatly."

The case of Thomas demonstrates some of the positive psychological outcomes that can ensue when practitioners use an existential-humanistic approach to helping. Although Thomas's genuine grieving for the loss of his wife did not totally dissipate, he was able to move forward. By introducing Thomas to the concepts of existential commitment and intentionality and helping him assess the degree to which his eigenwelt, mitwelt, umwelt, and überwelt were disrupted by his personal loss, he was able to think about the specific actions he was willing and able to take to move forward.

Summary

The existential-humanistic point of view is an attitude toward the counseling interview and the meaning of life that contains many assumptions and concepts. The key assumptions and concepts of the existential-humanistic perspective clearly distinguish it from the psychodynamic and cognitive-behavioral forces discussed in the preceding chapters.

The most significant theorist who is responsible for propelling this theoretical worldview into the fields of counseling, education, and psychology is Carl Rogers. The following points summarize the key considerations that characterize the existential-humanistic force, as they are all included in one way or another in Rogers's theory of counseling and therapy.

1. We are all in the world. Our task is to understand what this means. It is clear that the meanings we generate about ourselves and the world vary from culture to culture.

2. We essentially come to know ourselves through our relationships with the world and, in particular, through our relationships with other people.

3. Anxiety can result from a lack of relationship (with ourselves, with others, or with the world at large) or from a failure to act and choose in our lives.

4. We are responsible for our own constructions of the world. Even though we know the world only as it acts on us, it is we who decide what the world means and who must provide organization for that world.

5. The task of the existential-humanistic therapist or counselor is to understand clients' worlds as fully as possible and ultimately to encourage them to be responsible for making more conscious and intentional decisions in their lives. However, existential-humanistic counselors and therapists will also share themselves and their worldviews with clients as appropriate.

6. A special problem in living involves the notion (as asserted by some existential philosophers) that the world is not necessarily meaningful. In this regard, existentialists such as Sartre and Kierkegaard often develop a negative and hopeless view of what they observe to be the absurdity and cruelty of life. However, humanistic existentialists such as Buber and May suggest that the very confusion and disorder in the world represent wonderful opportunities for growth and beauty.

7. The distinction between existential and existential-humanistic positions can be defined as one of philosophy or faith. If individuals see the many possibilities in the world as a problem, they will predictably experience problems in their lives. On the other hand, if individuals see the array of possibilities in the world as infinite opportunities, they are likely to act in ways that increase the probability of realizing their potential for self-actualization.

8. The spiritual dimension (*überwelt*) of life is given credence by the work of Clem-mont Vontress. Vontress suggests that a truly holistic experience must include something beyond the individual (*eigenwelt*), our relationships with other people (*mitwelt*), and our connectedness with the cultural/environmental context (*umwelt*) in which we are situated.

Multimedia Resources for This Chapter

The following online resources offer video and other resources of particular relevance to this chapter of your text.

Companion Website

Go to **www.ablongman.com/Ivey6e** to view the following video clips:

• Video clip 9.1 offers an example of how one therapist connects with his client by presenting himself as a real person. The therapist discloses his own thoughts and feelings on various racial and gender issues early in the therapeutic session. Contrary to traditional counseling and psychotherapy theories, which strongly encourage maintaining strict boundaries in the counselor-client relationship, the therapist also asks the client what she would like to know about him before proceeding with the helping process.

In doing so, the therapist exhibits *client-centered* counseling, which is intentionally aimed at building a greater level of trust and authenticity in the client-therapist relationship. This kind of counseling is based on a recognition of (1) the importance of dealing with the suspicions that many persons of color and women bring to counseling sessions that include a White male therapist, and (2) the need to let clients from different gender and cultural/ethnic/racial backgrounds know who the therapist is as a person. Although the client-centered counseling approach is different than traditional counseling theories discussed in this book and contrasts with Rogers's approach to helping, it is consistent with many of the recommendations made by multicultural-feminist-social justice counseling theorists (Ponterotto, Casas, Suzuki, & Alexander, 2001; Sue & Sue, 2003).

• Video clip 9.2 serves as a demonstration of Buber's (1970) I-Thou concept. In his interview with the client, the therapist demonstrates one way to develop a shared narrative with his African-American female client. Compare this demonstration of existential-humanistic counseling and therapy with the way you think you might develop in the future a coconstructed narrative with culturally and racially different clients.

MyHelpingLab

If a MyHelpingLab passcode was included with your textbook and you have activated your passcode:

- go to **www.ablongman.com/myhelpinglab**
- enter the "Counseling" area of the site by clicking on that tab
- select "Video Lab" from the toolbar to the left of the page
- select "MyHelpingLab Videos by Theoretical Approach"
- select the "Existential-Humanistic" module to view various video clips of a therapist using this approach with a client

chapter 10

Logotherapy and Gestalt Counseling

This chapter is designed to:

1. Extend your understanding of the evolution of the third force in the fields of counseling and psychology.

2. Present Frankl's logotherapy—its central constructs, example techniques, and a multicultural examination of this approach to helping.

3. Describe Perls's Gestalt therapy theory—its central constructs, example techniques, and a multicultural examination of this theoretical approach to helping.

4. Enable you, through practice exercises, to gain an understanding of the skills required in a helping interview using logotherapy or Gestalt therapy approaches.

Introduction

The existential-humanistic tradition has many variations, but its core focuses on clients' lived experiences and their interpretations of life events. In the existential-humanistic helping approach, understanding the client's story is central in the counseling and therapy process.

As a counselor or therapist, you will likely work with individuals who have suffered severe life difficulties and trauma; physical, sexual, and emotional child abuse; rape; or extreme racism and discrimination. You may work with individuals who find that they carry the HIV virus, actually have AIDS, or have some form of cancer that is undermining their physical health and sense of psychological well-being. Each of these clients has suffered major personal assaults. How can you help them make any sense of what has happened?

Two theories that have greatly contributed to the evolution of the third force in counseling and psychology may be helpful in answering this question. These include the reflective, meaning-oriented logotherapy of Viktor Frankl and the experiential Gestalt therapy of Fritz Perls.

Fritz Perls takes a separate direction from Rogers, Vontress, and Frankl by offering a different existential-humanistic view of the individual. In sharp contrast to Rogers, Perls's techniques are extremely directive. Whereas Rogers would listen, Perls would be much more active in directing the change process.

Viktor Frankl, on the other hand, provides a balancing force between Rogers and Perls. While Rogers might be described as an attending or listening therapist and Perls as an influencing therapist, Frankl appears to use both attending and listening skills according to the varied needs of the client. All three individuals offer much that is of practical value to the practice of existential-humanistic counseling and therapy.

Viktor Frankl and Logotherapy: An Overview

Logotherapy holds that the critical issue for humankind is not what happens to a person but, rather, how one views or thinks about what happens in one's life. Similar to the cognitive-behavioral perspective discussed in Chapters 7 and 8, logotherapy is concerned with action and changing behavior in the real world. The originator of logotherapy is Viktor Frankl, who was born in Vienna in 1905 and died there in 1997. While some identify Frankl as a forerunner to the cognitive-behavioral movement (Frankl, 1985a; Mahoney & Freeman, 1985), it is more accurate to view his theoretical position as providing an important bridge between existential-humanistic and cognitive-behavioral theories.

Frankl's Early Years

Frankl grew up in the early 1900s in Vienna, Austria, with a very disciplined father and a tenderhearted and pious mother (Boeree, 2004). He is described as being a very precocious child who at the age of 4 announced to his family that he knew he wanted to be a physician.

Frankl's interest in psychosocial-political issues began to be manifested during adolescence, when in high school he became actively involved in a local Young Socialist Workers organization. Although having a keen interest in local, national, and world politics in his youth, Frankl was increasingly attracted to the study of philosophy and psychology. On finishing his high school studies, he had an article published in the *International Journal of Psychoanalysis,* which, in turn, led to the beginning of regular correspondence with Sigmund Freud.

Frankl attended medical school in Vienna in the early 1920s. It was here that he had the opportunity to first meet Freud. On studying psychoanalytic theory, Frankl accepted Freud's concept of the unconscious. However, Frankl also asserted that the will to create meaning in one's life is stronger and more fundamental than the unconscious pleasure drive that Freud espoused.

Despite his interest in Freud's work, Frankl became more attracted to Alfred Adler's theory of individual psychology and published an article in Adler's *International Journal of Individual Psychology* in 1925. It was around this time that Frankl received training in individual psychology directly from Adler.

As his interest in the psychoanalytic tradition and Adler's theory increased, so too did his efforts in developing his own psychotherapeutic theoretical framework—a theory he would first call **logotherapy** in a public lecture in 1926 (Boeree, 2004). Some of the basic concepts of logotherapy—such as the drive to construct meaning in life, personal freedom, and responsibility—bear the imprint of Adler's influence on Frankl's thinking (Wong & Fry, 1998).

Following Adler's example of providing psychological services in the greater community where he lived, from 1928 through 1930 Frankl established several counseling centers in six different cities in Austria. These centers provided free counseling services to teenagers in their local communities.

He completed his doctorate in medicine in 1930 and worked at the Psychiatric University Clinic from 1930 through 1933. Frankl became the director of a ward for suicidal women at the clinic in 1933. One year later, Hitler's army invaded Austria and occupied Vienna.

Personal Tragedy

During the Nazi occupation of Austria, Frankl was made head of the neurological department of Rothschild Hospital. This was the only hospital for Jews in Vienna at the time. Boeree (2004) reports that Frankl "made many false diagnoses of his patients in order to circumvent the new Nazi policies requiring euthanasia of the mentally ill. It was during this period that he began his manuscript, *Arztliche Seelsorge*—in English, *The Doctor and the Soul*" (p. 2).

Frankl married in 1942, but in September of that year, he, his wife, his father, mother, and brother were all arrested and brought to the concentration camp at Theresienstadt in Bohemia. His father died there of starvation; his mother and brother were killed in Auschwitz in 1944; his wife died at Bergen-Belsen in 1945. Of his immediate family, only Frankl's sister would survive as a result of immigrating to Australia a short time earlier.

He continued to develop his theory of logotherapy while imprisoned in Nazi concentration camps from 1942 through 1945 (Wong & Fry, 1998). Unlike Freud and Adler, who both focused on the impact of past events on a person's development, "logotherapy focuses rather on the future, that is to say, on the meanings to be fulfilled in one's future" (Frankl, 1984, p. 12). This fundamental theoretical premise was severely tested in Frankl's personal triumph over the unimaginable trauma he experienced in the Nazi concentration camps. When he was moved to Auschwitz, his manuscript of *The Doctor and the Soul* was lost in a "disinfection chamber" (Frankl, 1946/1959, p. 49). His strong desire to complete this manuscript and his hope to some day be reunited with his wife and family kept Frankl from losing all hope in what seemed like a hopeless situation (Boeree, 2004). Although suffering from typhoid fever while imprisoned, Frankl kept himself awake and psychologically resilient by reconstructing on stolen pieces of paper the manuscript that was destroyed.

Frankl's Search for Meaning

After his liberation from the concentration camps in April 1945, Frankl completed his book *The Doctor and the Soul*. Shortly thereafter, he dictated his most famous work, which was completed in only nine days, entitled *Man's Search for Meaning*, which details the development and central concepts of his theory of logotherapy.

Frankl continued an illustrious career that included being promoted to full professor in psychiatry at the University of Vienna, becoming the first president of the Austrian Medical Society for Psychotherapy in 1950, being nominated for the Nobel Peace Prize, and authoring 32 books that have been translated into 27 languages. Although Viktor Frankl died on September 2, 1997, of heart failure in Austria, his impact on the evolution of the existential-humanistic force in counseling and psychology continues. Considering the traumatic circumstances under which his theoretical model was born, his life and work are inseparable.

Frankl is a cognitive theorist with an existential-humanistic message of faith and hope. His logotherapy is concerned with the search for meaning in life. Frankl was able to reframe his life situation while in a Nazi concentration camp and find positive reasons for living in the midst of negatives. He faced the existential dilemma of the meaning of life under the most extreme conditions.

By finding positive meaning in extreme suffering, Frankl offers new hope. His psychological theory has profound implications for multicultural counseling and therapy and especially for clients who have suffered from various forms of trauma as a result of being oppressed, marginalized, and discriminated against because of their cultural identity and background.

Frankl's view of the human condition reflects a lifetime of struggle to find the positives in humankind. In his highly affecting book *Man's Search for Meaning* (1946/1959), Frankl relates his experiences in German concentration camps during World War II. Although Frankl describes the horrors of the concentration camp in great detail, the book is more a testimony to the power of the human spirit and its capability of survival under the most inhumane conditions.

Following are some passages from Frankl's book that will help to illuminate your understanding of Frankl's important existential-humanistic approach. Despite the dehumanizing environment, Frankl finds something meaningful that enables him and others to survive. In the following passages, the positives in a very negative situation have been highlighted with italics.

We stumbled on in the darkness, over big stones and through large puddles, along the one road leading from the camp. The accompanying guards kept shouting at us and driving us with the butts of their rifles. Anyone with very sore feet supported himself on his neighbor's arm. Hardly a word was spoken; the icy wind did not encourage talk. Hiding his mouth behind his upturned collar, the man marching next to me whispered suddenly: "If our wives could see us now! I do hope they are better off in their camps and don't know what is happening to us."

That brought thoughts of my own wife to mind. And as we stumbled on for miles, slipping on icy spots, supporting each other time and again, dragging one another up and onward, nothing was said, but we both knew: *each of us was thinking of his wife.* Occasionally I looked at the sky, where the stars were fading and the pink light of the morning was beginning to spread behind a dark bank of clouds. *But my mind clung to my wife's image, imagining it with an uncanny acuteness. I heard her answering me, saw her smile, her frank and encouraging look. Real or not, her look was then more luminous than the sun which was beginning to rise.*

A thought transfixed me: for the first time in my life I saw the truth as it is set into song by so many poets, proclaimed as the final wisdom by so many thinkers. The truth—that love is the ultimate and the highest goal to which man can aspire. Then I grasped the meaning of the greatest secret that human poetry and human thought and belief have to impart: The salvation of man is through love and in love. I understood how a man who has nothing left in this world still may know bliss, be it only for a brief moment, in the contemplation of his beloved. In a position of utter desolation, when man cannot express himself in positive action, when his only achievement may consist in enduring his sufferings in the right way—an honorable way—in such a position man can, through loving contemplation of the image he carries of his beloved, achieve fulfillment. For the first time in my life I was able to understand the meaning of the words, "The angels are lost in perpetual contemplation of an infinite glory."

In front of me a man stumbled and those following him fell on top of him. The guard rushed over and used his whip on them all. Thus my thoughts were interrupted for a few minutes. *But soon my soul found its way back from the prisoner's existence to another world, and I resumed talk with my loved one: I asked her questions and she answered; she questioned me in return, and I answered.* (pp. 48–49)

In the winter and spring of 1945 there was an outbreak of typhus which infected nearly all the prisoners. The mortality was great among the weak, who had to keep on with their hard work as long as they possibly could. The quarters for the sick were most inadequate, there were practically no medicines or attendants. Some of the symptoms of the disease were extremely disagreeable: an irrepressible aversion to even a scrap of food (which was an additional danger to life) and terrible attacks of delirium. The worst case of delirium was suffered by a friend of mine who thought that he was dying and wanted to pray. In his delirium he could not find the words to do so. *To avoid these attacks of delirium, I tried, as did many of the others, to keep awake for most of the night. For hours I composed speeches in my mind. Eventually I began to reconstruct the manuscript which I had lost in the disinfection chamber of Auschwitz, and scribbled the key words in shorthand on tiny scraps of paper.* (p. 46)

These passages show how Frankl shifted attention from the immediate horror of the here and now to other issues. Particularly, he thought of his wife and his relationship with her. His was a sane response in an insane situation. At a more basic level, Frankl found meaning outside the horror of the immediate situation, which gave him strength to cope with life's difficult reality.

When problems cannot be solved, how one thinks about what has happened and the meaning of life—cognitions—are as important as or more important than any concrete behavioral change the person can make.

Central Theoretical Constructs of Logotherapy

In coining his theory of logotherapy, Frankl used the Greek word *logos,* which can mean study, spirit, God, or meaning. It is this last definitional concept that Frankl focused on, although the other meanings are never far off in his writings. Comparing himself with Freud and Adler, he suggested that Freud essentially postulated a will to pleasure as the root of all human motivations; and Adler, a will to power. **Logotherapy,** in contrast, postulates a will to meaning (Boeree, 2004). Consequently, the task for the logotherapist is to help the client find meaning and purpose in life—and then to support her or him to act on those personal meanings. Logotherapy could be described as a therapy balanced between the listening skills of Rogers and the influencing skills of Perls, with a greater stress on the importance of generalizing change to the real world.

Logotherapists are interested in carefully learning how the client constructs meaning of the world. Once they have this understanding, they move actively to promote client change. Logotherapy, like much of the cognitive-behavioral tradition, is also a metatheoretical orientation in that its practitioners will not hesitate to use techniques from other orientations to help clients find new meaning, establish new real-life goals, and implement new personal strategies to achieve those goals.

Cognitive Change and Finding Positive Meanings

Many war veterans will raise issues of the meaning of life in therapy. So will a minority youth who feels hopeless because of frequent discrimination, as well as the young, poor mother who is routinely subjected to domestic violence. Almost all clients of any cultural background will bring problems relating to meaning to counseling and therapy. Since the definition of *meaning* sometimes depends on the religious, ethnic, and cultural background of your client, you need to be prepared to deal with a variety of meaning and belief systems ranging from Christian and Jewish to Buddhist and Islamic. Being a woman, a gay male or lesbian, or a person who is physically challenged, economically disadvantaged, or from a particular ethnic/racial group will also change the structure of the client's meaning system.

The route to working with intentionality to gain a clear understanding of a client's meaning-making system is to carefully listen to the client's construction of the world. Then, if necessary, the logotherapist will intervene directly and actively to facilitate change in the client's meaning-making system, but always in accord with the cultural tradition of the client. Frankl is keenly aware that meaning is constructed not only in the individual, but also from the cultural tradition of the client.

Understanding different cultural and family traditions is key in facilitating meaningful change in clients from diverse groups and backgrounds. This change in meaning may be represented in new thoughts or played out in direct actions in one's environment. It is important that you be aware of the differing types of meaning-making systems manifested among individuals from varying cultural backgrounds. Again, the most important skill counselors and therapists can use to accurately understand the meaning clients give to their lives in logotherapy is the skill of listening.

The listening aspect of Frankl's logotherapy seems close to that of Rogers, and the influencing aspect is almost as powerful and direct as that of Perls. Yet logotherapy extends existential-humanistic thinking and practice in its awareness of cultural traditions as an essential part of clients' meaning making.

To help clients find personal meaning and make more sense of their lives, Frankl offers a positive philosophy, as exemplified by his life and influential writings. Talking with or listening to Frankl personally is an exercise in life itself—a sermon in motion—and in this sense, Frankl is very similar to Rogers. This is a reminder that the person you are in the interview with is as important as or more important than your therapeutic skills. In addition, you must find the person in your client and what is meaningful to that child, adolescent, man, or woman before you.

Many clients suffer from day-to-day problems that, from Frankl's (1985a) perspective, are fundamentally linked to their inability to find positive meaning in their lives. How does one make sense of a meaningless job, learn to cope with a less-than-satisfactory personal relationship, or relate to difficult parents or in-laws? Helping clients find positive meanings obviously is not a technical helping skill. There is no formula that can be easily applied to any one client or group of clients who are in need of finding more positive meaning in life. Adapting Frankl's basic philosophy in your own personal and professional life may enable you to more effectively search with your clients as they find their unique meanings—perhaps differently constructed meanings than yours, but nonetheless positive and workable for them.

Logotherapy Strategies: Applications for Practice

Frankl (1946/1959, 1969) framed a theory and a method of helping that has gained prominence in the fields of counseling, psychology, and psychiatry (see Mahoney & Freeman, 1985). The techniques he developed—dereflection, paradoxical intention, and change of attitude strategies—are important methodological and research areas (Fabry, 1984; Frankl, 1985b; Lukas, 1984). Frankl's change of attitude strategies and the dereflection technique may be found in varying forms in cognitive-behavioral modification, rational-emotive therapy, and structural/systemic family counseling and therapy theories. Paradoxical intention is considered one of the relatively "new" therapeutic methods that is used to produce rapid change in cognitive-behavioral therapy, yet it was implemented by Frankl as early as 1929.

Lukas (1984), a major logotherapy theorist and practitioner, describes the three main logotherapy techniques listed above and adds a fourth helping strategy, the appealing technique.

Modification of Attitudes. Clients can hold negative attitudes toward themselves despite overtly positive life situations. For example, many attractive and personable clients may see themselves quite negatively. Other clients may have serious problems and be unable to do anything about them. In each case, the logotherapeutic task is to help the client change the way one thinks about her or his situation—a goal similar to that of the cognitive approach to helping.

Modification of attitudes is most often conducted directly through sharing opinions, arguing (as in Ellis's REBCT theory), or offering positive suggestions for the client. The essential challenge in all of this is to assist the client to take a new view of her or his life situation.

Reframing attitudes. The positive asset search (Chapter 4), or what proponents of Frankl's theory would call **positive reframing,** is one technique used in logotherapy to help clients modify their attitudes about themselves and other aspects of their lives. When using this technique, it is of crucial importance to first listen carefully to clients' negative meanings and constructions of their life situations in the early phase of counseling and therapy. Clients need to tell their stories fully and completely and to feel heard. If you use the techniques of positive reframing or the positive asset search too early in the helping process, the client may likely be put off. An important guideline is: Do not try to modify attitudes or cognitions until the client feels thoroughly and respectfully heard. The following brief example from a videotaped interview by Ivey (1984) illustrates the specifics of finding positive meanings in negative situations:

Counselor: (after listening to the client's deepest fears and hearing how he thought himself close to death in quicksand—the client had talked about feelings of guilt about survival—"Why me?") Is there anything positive? I mean I know it sounds like a totally negative experience. But was there anything you could see that was positive about what happened? [*This short counselor comment catches the essence of the search for positive meanings. It is a simple point, so direct that its importance is sometimes lost in professional jargon and theorizing.*]

Client: Well, it sure felt good when they saved me. I was scared, I felt guilty, but at least they came and got me.

Counselor: So you felt that help was there even though you were afraid.

Client: And you know what, one of the guys who helped me get out I thought didn't like me before. But he asked me to work for him the following week. I never thought of that before.

This example illustrates the central dimensions of cognitive reframing. The client's story about his near-death experience was listened to carefully and respectfully. The cognitions associated with the experience in the original narrative were all negative, being associated with guilt and shame. Many clients who share stories of trauma focus on the negative. Frankl would call this negative focus **hyperreflection,** in that the individual only reflects on one aspect of the experience.

The simple question "But was there anything you could see that was positive about what happened?" opens the way for positive reframing of attitudes around a basically negative experience. There is sometimes a tendency for counselors and therapists to focus solely on the negative. The search for positives in even the most difficult of situations is basic to Frankl's logotherapy and to cognitive reframing.

Obviously, finding positive reframes will not be as easy with many clients as it was in this brief example. Nonetheless, the reshaping of negative events through positive reframing is a basic dimension of all counseling and psychotherapy and particularly in logotherapy. It may be helpful to review the video vignette included on the Companion Website that accompanies this book and try to identify the time when the therapist uses positive reframes with the African-American female client he works with. You might be interested in seeing how this client responds in both positive and negative ways to this therapist's efforts to interject positive reframes into the counseling session. In doing so, you may want to ask yourself how you might respond similarly or differently in addressing the client's expressed concerns about the problem she brings to the counseling session.

Changing the client's meaning-making system in a more positive direction has been a major theme in this book. The positive asset search (Chapter 4) and the positive reframing discussed here stress that clients can best effect such change by acknowledging and using positive resources available to them. These ideas have been influenced by Frankl's theoretical perspective, which emphasizes the importance of helping clients develop new meaning in their lives by finding positives in the midst of stressful problems and challenging situations.

Deciding for the future. Although what is past is indeed past, one can modify and change the way one thinks about past experiences. Thinking of the past negatively is making a negative "decision for the past." By questioning the client's past interpretations, the therapist can help her or him make a positive "decision for the future." Those who suffer trauma often make negative decisions about the past, since it is difficult not to focus on the negatives of trauma. The modification of attitudes, as demonstrated in the foregoing interview, undergirds complex survivor issues. Combining an understanding of the specific needs of trauma survivors with the basic approaches of Frankl's logotherapy will give you a good foundation for helping your clients live and cope with the effects of trauma.

Frankl (1985b) reminds us that some people must live with impossible situations and disturbing memories:

> This was the lesson I had to learn in three years spent in Auschwitz and Dachau: those most apt to survive the camps were those oriented toward the future, toward a meaning to be fulfilled by them in the future. But meaning and purpose were only a necessary condition of survival, not a sufficient condition. Millions had to die in spite of their vision of meaning and purpose. Their belief could not save their lives, but it did enable them to meet death with heads held high. (p. 37)

The ultimate existential issue is survival and finding something positive in the simple act of being-in-the-world. Those who have experienced war, child abuse, rape, domestic violence, serious illness, or other trauma have all survived. Mere survival for some will be sufficient to satisfy existential needs, but the issue will be more complex for others.

Modification of attitudes cannot change the past, but it can help people more intentionally live with the past in the present. The point is to find something positive, something to live for beyond the trauma experience. As a therapist or counselor, you will need a good deal of patience, strength, belief, knowledge, and power to help your clients modify their attitudes toward these seemingly impossible traumatic situations.

Paradoxical Intention. Frankl was the first therapist to use the concept of paradox in individual counseling and psychotherapy. In 1929, Frankl had a phobic client who was suffering from severe agoraphobia. Analysis and other methods were not working. Improvising, Frankl suggested that instead of being afraid of fainting on the street, the patient should deliberately try to collapse. Frankl (1985a) unequivocally defines his paradoxical intention technique as "encouraging the patient to do, or wish to happen, the very things [she or] he fears—albeit with tongue in cheek." The next week the client was cured. Frankl did not recall what he had advised, so the patient told him, "I just followed your advice, Doctor. I tried hard to faint but the more I tried, the less I could, and consequently—the fear of fainting disappeared!" Thus the technique of **paradoxial intention** was born.

Paradoxical intention has become an important therapeutic skill in other theoretical modalities as well. Ascher and Turner (1979) were the first to experimentally validate the clinical effectiveness of paradoxical intention in comparison with other behavioral strategies. Prior to this work, Solyom and others (1972) proved experimentally that paradoxical intention was useful in therapeutic settings.

However, Frankl (2000) warns about the tendency of confusing paradoxical intention with so-called symptom prescription. In symptom prescription, clients are told to exaggerate their symptoms—for instance, the manifestation of a fear of a particular animal or object. In paradoxical intention, however, patients are encouraged to wish to happen what they fear will happen. In other words, the fear itself is not dealt with but rather the object of fear.

In the hospital where Frankl worked, there was a patient suffering from a severe washing compulsion. This client would wash her hands several hundred times a day. One of the doctors suggested that instead of being afraid of bacteria, the patient should instead desire to contract an infection. She was advised to tell herself: "I can't get enough bacteria. I want to become as dirty as possible. There is nothing nicer than bacteria." The patient diligently followed this advice. She asked other patients to let her borrow from them as many bacteria as possible and came up with the resolution no longer to wash "the poor creatures" away but instead to keep them alive. This approach of paradoxical intention worked well with this patient. In this case, it would have been less effective to use symptom prescription (to exaggerate symptoms), since the patient already was manifesting excessive symptoms.

As one can see from this case example, "an integral element in paradoxical intention is the deliberate evocation of humor" (Lazarus, 1971). A sense of humor is an aspect of the helping process that logotherapy regards as a specifically human capacity, namely, to be self-distancing.

Some authorities (Bandler & Grinder, 1982; Lankton, 1980) argue that the client should not know that a paradoxical intervention is being used. However, research data suggest that clients can profit from knowing that a paradoxical technique is being used. It may even be helpful to explain to the client your theory as to why the technique works (Wong & Fry, 1998).

Dereflection. Dereflection, according to Lukas (1984), uses our ability to "forget ourselves" and brings about a therapeutic reordering of attention—turning our attention away from the problem toward other, more positive content of our thinking. Many of us "hyperreflect" on our problems and our negative feelings and experiences. The objective of dereflection is systematically to change the focus of our attention. Put in its most simple and direct terms, the task of the therapist is to encourage the client to think about something else other than the problem.

Techniques of dereflection may be as simple as encouraging a person who has lost a limb to start thinking about a new career, helping a cancer patient focus on helping others rather than on her- or himself, or encouraging a retired person to find an interesting hobby. It is true that the facts of the situation cannot be changed and that it is difficult to reframe problems of illness, age, and loneliness as having positive components. However, it is possible to find something else on which to focus one's attention.

Instead of being depressed about the loss of a limb, the disabled person, through refocusing of attention, can work toward a new goal, the cancer patient can think about others, and the aging individual may make new friends in the process of enjoying a new hobby. The concept of refocusing has many important variations that are clearly described by Frankl (2000) in a chapter on dereflection, in which he also devotes special attention to issues of sexual functioning. Lukas (1984) is another useful source for ideas about this concept.

Dereflection may be especially useful in therapy that involves persons experiencing sexual dysfunction. For example, impotence can be caused when a man directs excessive attention on whether or not he will have an erection. In doing so he is hyperreflecting on himself and his fear, which in turn causes more impotence. The logotherapist would help this client dereflect and possibly focus attention on his wife and particularly on some sexual stimuli that is particularly relevant and meaningful to her. When one focuses attention on another, it is difficult to think about oneself; at such a time, natural autonomic functions start working more effectively.

A similar approach may be used with a person suffering from insomnia. Instead of trying to fall asleep, the individual may decide to use this time to study or for an enjoyable activity. After a relatively short period of time, many clients will naturally get tired and fall asleep.

This simple technique is partly born of logic and common sense. However, it takes considerable creativity and expertise to find out what negative situation or experience each individual client needs to avoid hyperreflecting on. Furthermore, changing patterns of attention may require you to use different attitude modification techniques (such as the positive asset search) as well as some form of paradoxical intention.

The Appealing Technique. Lukas (1989) suggests that using the **appealing technique** may be particularly effective for clients experiencing drug/alcohol detoxification or for individuals you cannot reach via other therapeutic methods. The appealing technique is reminiscent of the concepts used by Alcoholics Anonymous (AA) and other drug therapy groups.

In this approach, one simply appeals to the client to do better and to change. The counselor takes the position that the client's situation is not hopeless and directly attempts to bring the client to a similar awareness. For example, the drug-abusing client may be asked to state out loud, "I am not helpless. I can control and direct my fate."

In some situations, with an understanding and supportive counselor/therapist, the appealing technique can work. However, it is clearly different than the "sophisticated" techniques of psychoanalysis or cognitive-behavioral therapy discussed in earlier chapters.

Some counselors choose not to implement this logotherapy technique in their work because of its simplicity. Others feel it does not have sufficient theoretical implications to be useful in clinical practice. However, if you believe in what you say, some clients will respond to your exhortative approach, which appeals to the human spirit. Witness the effectiveness of AA and other drug treatment programs that use techniques similar to the appealing process.

By applying the above-mentioned techniques in the helping process, counselors and therapists demonstrate an intentional approach to change. There are theoretical and practical reasons for trying to help clients change in a certain direction, but if the first technique does not work, logotherapy does not hesitate to "mix and match" and change the approach to meet the unique human needs of the client. Competency-Building Activity 10.1 offers an opportunity to exercise some dimensions of logotherapy that you may find beneficial in your own work in counseling and psychotherapy in the future.

Logotherapy, Spirituality, and Medicine

In exploring the border between medicine and logotherapy, Van Pelt (1993, 2000) asserts that the healthy human spirit is important to a person's psychological and physiological well-being. Moreover, she points out that if broad human issues are considered from the philosophic framework of logotherapy, new dimensions for mental and physical health, and even world peace, can be the result.

Although the issue of spirituality was previously discussed in Chapters 1 and 9, the discussion is enlarged here because of the important role spirituality plays in logotherapy. Van Pelt (1993) points out:

> Many therapists tend to avoid getting involved with religious thoughts or struggles. They feel ill equipped or see it as inappropriate to deal with religious quests or meaning issues; it does not fit into the traditional therapeutic model.

Competency-Building Activity 10.1

An Exercise in Logotherapy

Instructions: Viktor Frankl and his colleague Elisabeth Lukas give almost as much attention to listening and understanding the worldview of the client as does Carl Rogers in his person-centered therapy. Thus, you can easily adapt Competency-Building Activity 9.2 (see Chapter 9) to this logotherapy exercise.

Step 1. *Establishing rapport.* As you use the same structure of the interview as you did in Competency-Building Activity 9.2, take time to first indicate to your real or role-played client that you are going to be talking about a particular problem she or he is currently experiencing in her or his life. Explain that you would like to find out what the problem means and that the actual solving of the problem will be a secondary consideration in this activity. Particularly good topics for this exercise include procrastination, a difficulty with a colleague or housemate, boredom, or concern over illness or the loss of someone important.

Steps 2 and 3. *Gathering data and determining outcomes.* Use your listening skills and the basic listening sequence to draw out the problem in the second stage of this process. However, be sure to add one central dimension by asking your client, "What does this problem mean to you?" "What does this say about your deeper values?" "Why is this important?" Ask these meaning-oriented questions after you have heard the problem defined clearly by the person you are working with.

As you reach the third stage of the interview and the goal is established, ask what the desired outcome means to the client and why the client values that goal. In the process of asking questions about the meaning of the problem as well as the goal, you will find that a new depth is added to the interview and that clients frequently start talking about their lives when before they were primarily focused on their problems.

In this process you will want to add the skill of reflection of meaning. Reflection of meaning is similar to the paraphrase but focuses more on deeper issues underlying the surface structure sentence.

Step 4. *Generating alternative solutions and meaning.* Once having heard the client and the client's meaning, you have two main alternatives:

continued on next page

The logotherapist addresses primarily the client's healthy human spirit. By awakening this human spirit, one opens up the road toward meaning and fulfillment in life. For the logotherapist, it will be irrelevant whether the client's search for meaning will lead to the discovery or rediscovery of religious faith—the emphasis is on meaningful living from moment to moment. Meaning, and certainly higher meaning, however, contains a "faith factor."

Logotherapy bridges the gap between psychology and religion. Outreach to others, transcendence, is known as loving your neighbor. Higher meaning is known as God's Will, a Higher Power. Logotherapy even acknowledges the redeeming factor of forgiveness. (pp. 106–107)

Van Pelt (1994) provides an example in the form of treatment for chronic headaches and conflict resolution. She presents several case histories in which issues of meaning appear to be central to the documented physiological condition. For example, a 58-year-old Greek woman at a headache clinic was able to reduce aspirin use from three hundred tablets a month to five. The treatment focused on the client's loneliness and homesickness and the refocusing of internal conflicts over

> **Competency-Building Activity 10.1, continued**
>
> 1. You may summarize the problem and its meaning to the client and contrast it with a summary of the ideal goal and its meaning. Throughout the summary, you will point out possible discrepancies and mixed messages in the client's meaning-making system. Then, through listening skills and reflection of meaning, you can encourage further self-exploration. The goal here is to discover the underlying, more deeply felt meanings guiding the client's action.
>
> 2. If the client wishes to act on the new meaning that has been constructed in this activity, select one of the four major techniques of logotherapy (modification of attitudes, paradoxical intention, dereflection, or the appealing technique). If one technique does not work, try another. Logotherapy does not hesitate to try several approaches in an attempt to meet your clients' unique needs.
>
> The goals of this portion of your interview are to (1) further assist the client in examining the new meaning she or he has developed about her or his problem and (2) through the influencing approach described above, help your client change and act on the new meaning making that has ensued from this helping approach.
>
> **Step 5.** *Generalizing learning.* As with other existential-humanistic orientations, logotherapy does not give extensive attention to the generalization and maintenance of behavioral change. It is suggested that you may ask your client to "think about" the interview over the next few days and talk with you personally or by phone. If it seems relevant, ask your client to try one thing differently during the time period before you have a follow-up talk.
>
> When you have completed this competency-building activity, take a few minutes to write down your reactions to this exercise. Then add your written reactions to your personal/professional development portfolio. This will enable you to continue to keep a record of the different ways that you are being affected by the various exercises that are presented in this book.

personal loss to a positive approach to the meaning of life and an awareness of new possibilities.

Critical in this client's case was an emphasis that the logotherapist directed to the power of the human spirit and the ability of this client to transcend present-day experience. Van Pelt notes that conflicts between personal values *(eigenwelt)* and societal expectations *(umwelt)* are critical issues in logotherapy in general and in this client's case in particular. In addition to exploring these values and expectations, the *überwelt,* or spiritual connection (as described by Vontress in Chapter 9), was a vital aspect of the helping process that contributed to the positive outcomes this Greek woman experienced as a result of participating in logotherapy (Van Pelt, 1994).

Spirituality and Psychotherapy as Reconciliation

In a paper entitled "From Self-Actualization to Global Responsibility," Lukas (1989) talks about "education toward responsibility" and maintains that individual self-examination is a most limited way to view therapy and counseling:

> We must be concerned about a *future worthy of human beings.* This concern deserves the trouble to look up from our navels and focus our feelings on

something beyond our Ego—feelings which in turn could release energies for the spiritual renaissance of our generation. (p. 5)

Lukas argues for three sensitivities: the feeling for the sacred, the feeling for the necessary, and the feeling for Otherliness. The sacred is spiritual being—our relationship with transcendence and nature. The necessary represents our ability to deal with challenging situations—for example, trauma, oppressive situations, physical disfigurement. Life, as Frankl discovered in the Nazi concentration camp, is not all positive; one must, however, do everything to cope with the impossible.

The feeling for Otherliness speaks of relations with friends, family, and strangers. "The Otherliness of the other person is not something just to be tolerated; it is, instead, something to behold, something that in fact enriches the beholder" (p. 15). Lukas stresses that we must learn to accept and appreciate the Other—"The I and the very different You can be integrated in a common We."

Embracing this perspective enables us to reconcile all differences we may have with others in ways that foster human dignity and development through our diversity. Lukas asserts that logotherapy is a useful way for us to become "agents of reconciliation." This is possible because logotherapy seeks to reconcile us to God and nature, to the most difficult challenges we face in our lives, and to each other.

Multicultural Implications of Logotherapy

Logotherapy grew out of cultural oppression—the German treatment of Jews during the Holocaust. Frankl's (2000) powerful existential-humanistic approach appeals to the human spirit and is, thus, particularly adaptable to multicultural counseling and therapy. Many culturally diverse groups may find Frankl's philosophy and specific methods particularly applicable because they represent a response to personal and cultural oppression.

Frankl's theory provides a useful means of fostering the sort of psychological liberation that many multicultural-feminist-social justice counseling advocates indicate is essential in moving women and persons in other devalued groups to healthier states of psychological and spiritual functioning (hooks, 2000; Ivey, 1995b; LaFromboise, & Jackson, 1996). One of the essential aspects of a psychology for liberation involves facilitating a greater understanding of the ways in which historical forms of oppression and injustice adversely impact the way people view themselves, their constructions of the world, and their thoughts about their ability to effect positive changes in that world.

Another aspect of a psychology for liberation relates to the need to assist women and people in other marginalized cultural/racial groups to learn about the interconnections that exist between their own feelings of depression, hopelessness, and cynicism and those contextual-environmental arrangements that perpetuate various forms of injustice, oppression, and privilege in our contemporary society. Martin-Baro (1994) has written extensively about both the theoretical and pragmatic strategies counselors and psychologists can use to foster a psychology of liberation. In doing so, he details the challenges that multicultural-feminist-social justice counselors face in moving their clients beyond a state of hopelessness, cynicism, despair, and self-devaluation to more a more hopeful, empowered, healthier, and liberated psychological disposition.

The three logotherapy techniques described above may be particularly helpful in fostering a psychology of liberation among culturally diverse clients whose mental health is negatively affected by the various forms of injustice and oppression they commonly encounter in their lives. The first, dereflection, is aimed at bringing about a therapeutic reordering of attention by turning clients' focus from the negative impact of their problems toward more positive and less self-depreciating thinking.

Many clients who are victimized by various forms of injustice, discrimination, and oppression internalize these problems. In doing so they often view themselves as being totally responsible for the negative consequences they are experiencing. This kind of hyperreflective thinking inevitably leads to increased feelings of self-depreciation and hopelessness and fosters a general sense of cynicism about making positive changes in life. As Frankl notes in his writings, this "hyperreflective" cognitive process invariably promotes negative psychological outcomes and robs people of alternative ways of thinking that would otherwise lead to more positive and satisfying actions.

By using the dereflection technique in counseling and therapy, mental health practitioners can assist culturally different clients to change the focus of their attention. They can do so by encouraging clients to exercise more hopeful and empowering thought processes. To accomplish this, counselors and therapists challenge their clients in a supportive manner to shift their attention from the negative attitudes they have developed about themselves and the challenges they face in life to more positive and hopeful ways of thinking about the meaning of their lives.

The second logotherapy technique that is useful in fostering a more liberated psychological disposition involves the appealing technique. As described earlier, the appealing technique simply involves appealing to the client to do better and to change. When implementing this therapeutic technique, the counselor or therapist takes the position that the client's situation is not hopeless and directly attempts to bring the client to a similar awareness. This helping strategy can complement the practitioner's use of dereflection and lead the helping process toward a more action-oriented direction—a direction that is necessary in stimulating a psychology of liberation among clients who suffer from various forms of cultural oppression and social injustices.

The third logotherapy technique that facilitates the process of psychological liberation in multicultural settings involves the use of Frankl's strategy of deciding for the future. The aim of this counseling strategy is to assist clients to increase their understanding that while they cannot change past events, they can make decisions about the future that are based on the lessons they learned from the past.

Frankl recognized that people who suffer from injustices and trauma often find it difficult not to focus on the negatives of unjust and traumatic events. However, it is also understood that a preoccupation with the negative, unfair, and traumatic situations that occurred in the past produces a form of mental incarceration that impedes a person from thinking and acting in positive and constructive ways in the future (Parham, 2002).

Thus, after listening carefully to the client's thinking about her or his situation and possibly employing a combination of the deflection strategy (to stimulate alternative ways of thinking) and the appealing technique (to reinforce the notion that the client's situation is not hopeless), counselors and therapists would do well to implement the technique of deciding for the future. This can be done to help clients not only take the new meaning they developed about their lives into concrete action but also assist them in realizing new dimensions of their own psychological liberation.

Logotherapy leaves you considerable room to generate your own culturally relevant integration of theory and practice. Frankl would endorse drawing from indigenous helping traditions and practices from the client's particular culture. Perhaps more than any other single theory of helping, logotherapy is supported throughout the world with commitment and passion from its adherents.

To underscore one of the practical implications of using Frankl's theoretical constructs outside of individual counseling and psychotherapy, the Professional Development Extension feature on page 313 discusses some of the ways that Frankl's constructs can be useful in maintaining your own positive psychological perspective. After all, much of the healing power of counseling and therapy is dependent on the sense of optimism and hopefulness you are able to genuinely communicate to your clients and maintain in your personal life.

As you continue with this chapter, you will learn about the development of Gestalt therapy as described by Fritz Perls. The discussion of Perls's theory will add further to your knowledge about another theoretical model that has contributed to the evolution of the existential-humanistic force in the mental health professions.

Fritz Perls and Gestalt Therapy: An Overview

Frederick "Fritz" Perls was born in 1893 in Berlin, Germany, the middle child and only son of middle-class parents. Although he reportedly had a fairly happy early childhood, Perls described significant tensions in his parents' relationship.

During his adolescence, Perls began to experience a strong dislike for school as well as a psychiatrist he was referred to for assistance. He also expressed a preoccupation with sexual matters during this stage in his development. In his own unique writing style, Perls (2005) describes these issues in his diary:

> 1910—Gymnasium unloving, cruel teachers. Brightness lost, hate school. Masturbation conflicts; can't conquer forbidden sex. Psychiatrist prescribes bromides and exercise. Don't believe him. Helper is no help. Confusing. (p. 1)

Perls earned his medical degree in 1926 and proceeded to work at the Institute for Brain Damaged Soldiers in Frankfurt. While working at this institute, Perls invested much time and energy studying existential philosophy and Gestalt psychology. It was at this point in his career that he was also introduced to Karen Horney. Horney was influential in getting Perls interested in psychoanalysis, an interest that ultimately resulted in him training to become a psychoanalyst himself (Maples & Sieber, 1999).

The early 1930s were marked by two important happenings in Perls's life. This includes his marriage to his wife, Laura, and his escape from Hitler's rule to South Africa, where he increasingly became disenchanted with Freudian psychoanalysis. Again, taking from his own writings in *A Life Chronology of Frederick Perls,* which was recently published on the Gestalt Therapy website, Perls (2005) describes these events and related outcomes in the following manner:

> 1930—Marriage. Later two children, four grandchildren. Sideline. No square husband. Wife Laura involved in expressive movement—Gindler. No integration yet of soma and psyche. Mind-body relationship still confusing.

> 1934—An early refugee from the Hitler regime. Still deeply involved in orthodox analysis, I go to teach Freud's gospel in South Africa. Still confused. (p. 2)

While living in South Africa, their growing dissatisfaction with psychoanalysis led Perls and his wife to develop what they referred to as **Gestalt therapy.** Gestalt psychology, with its emphasis on the whole person, was a useful principle in the development of this new therapeutic framework. Perls's theoretical worldview as it relates to Gestalt therapy was initially published in 1946 in a book entitled *Ego, Hunger, and Aggression: A Revision of Freud's Theory and Method,* which he wrote while living in South Africa.

In the early 1950s, Perls and his family moved to New York City, where he wrote *The Beginning of Gestalt Therapy* (with Ralph Hefferline and Paul Goodman) in 1951. Perls and his wife also organized the New York Institute of Gestalt Therapy during this time. Among Perls's other important publications were his 1969 autobiography, *In and Out of the Garbage Pail* (1992), and *Gestalt Therapy Verbatim* (1969a), a description of his therapy.

Perls moved to California in 1960, where as a result of striving to fill what he believed were serious gaps in classic psychoanalysis by developing his own theoretical approach to counseling and psychotherapy, he came to be regarded as a "guru" of existentialism (Gaines, 2000). So popular was Perls that his "Gestalt Prayer" was widely available in poster form:

> You do your thing, and
> I'll do my thing, and
> If by chance we meet, it's beautiful.

Perls continued to live in California where he offered Gestalt therapy workshops until his death in Indianapolis in 1970. A relatively large group of admirers waited outside the hospital as he passed away. This symbolically marked the end of an important era in the evolution of this particular school of thought in the existential-humanistic movement.

Central Theoretical Constructs and Techniques

The statement "Do your own thing" in many ways captures the essence of Perls and his approach to therapy. It also describes the relationship of his theoretical model to the existential-humanistic force. Perls deeply believed that individuals who become aware of themselves and their experience in the immediacy of the here and now can become more authentic and purposeful human beings. Consequently, many of his techniques are directed to helping individual clients and groups become more fully conscious of who they are and what they really want in their lives (Perls, 1992a).

The Gestalt Worldview

Perls saw human nature as holistic, consisting of many varied parts that make a unique individual. According to Perls (1969a), everyone starts life more or less "together," but as they grow and develop, they encounter experiences, feelings, and fears in life that cause them to lose parts of themselves. These "splits" from the whole, or the gestalt, must be reintegrated if they are to live intentional, authentic, and self-actualized lives. Thus, Gestalt therapy is centrally concerned with integrating or reintegrating our split-off parts into a whole person (Perls, 1992a).

The Gestalt worldview also includes the notions that people can be responsible for their actions in the world and, further, that the world is so complex that very little can be understood at any given moment. Consequently, Gestalt therapy tends to focus extensively on the present-tense, immediate, here-and-now experience of the client (Perls 1992b). These two key constructs are indicative of the basic existential premises underlying Perls's approach to Gestalt therapy.

The following excerpt is typical of Perls's approach to Gestalt therapy (1969a). In this case, he was working with a client's dream. In Gestalt dreamwork, each part of the dream is believed to represent a part of the dreamer. The task of the Gestalt therapist is to find how the parts relate together as a unity. Note particularly the consistent present-tense immediacy in the session and the willingness to direct client action.

1. *Meg:* In my dream, I'm sitting on a platform, and there's somebody else with me, a man, and maybe another person, and—ah—a couple of rattlesnakes. And one's up on the platform, now, all coiled up, and I'm frightened. And his head's up, but he doesn't seem like he's gonna strike me. He's just sitting there and I'm frightened, and this other person says to me—uh—just, just don't disturb the snake and he won't bother you. And the other snake, the other snake's down below, and there's a dog down there.

2. *Fritz:* What is there? [*Open question*]

3. *Meg:* A dog, and the other snake.

4. *Fritz:* So, up here is one rattlesnake and down below is another rattlesnake and the dog. [*Paraphrase; note how Perls works in the present tense. The emphasis*

is on immediate sensorimotor and concrete experience rather than formal operational analysis.]

5. *Meg:* And the dog is sort of sniffing at the rattlesnake. He's—ah—getting very close to the rattlesnake, sort of playing with it, and I wanna stop—stop him from doing that.

6. *Fritz:* Tell him. [*Directive*]

7. *Meg:* Dog, stop! /*Fritz:* Louder. /*Meg:* Stop! /*Fritz:* Louder. /*Meg:* (shouts) STOP! /*Fritz:* Louder. /*Meg:* (screams) STOP! [*This example is particularly representative of Gestalt repetition exercises. Repeating words again and again often leads to deeper, more emotional experience.*]

8. *Fritz:* Does the dog stop? [*Closed question*]

9. *Meg:* He's looking at me. Now he's gone back to the snake. Now—now, the snake's sort of coiling up around the dog, and the dog's lying down, and—and the snake's coiling around the dog, and the dog looks very happy.

10. *Fritz:* Ah! Now have an encounter between the dog and the rattlesnake. [*Directive*]

11. *Meg:* You want me to play with them?

12. *Fritz:* Both. Sure. This is your dream. Every part is a part of yourself. [*Directive, interpretation*]

13. *Meg:* I'm the dog. (hesitantly) Huh. Hello, rattlesnake. It sort of feels good with you wrapped around me.

14. *Fritz:* Look at the audience. Say this to somebody in the audience. [*Directive*]

15. *Meg:* (laughs gently) Hello, snake. It feels good to have you wrapped around me.

16. *Fritz:* Close your eyes. Enter your body. What do you experience physically? [*Directing. This type of sensorimotor body technique is particularly emblematic of Perls and Gestalt therapy. Emotions are to be experienced immediately rather than reflected on abstractly. As such, Gestalt exercises should be used with care with children and many less-verbal clients.*]

17. *Meg:* I'm trembling. Tensing.

18. *Fritz:* Let this develop. Allow yourself to tremble and get your feelings. (Her whole body begins to move a little.) Yah. Let it happen. Can you dance it? Get up and dance it. Let your eyes open, just so that you stay in touch with your body, with what you want to express physically. Yah. (She walks, trembling and jerkily, almost staggering.) Now dance rattlesnake. (She moves slowly and sinuously graceful.) How does it feel to be a rattlesnake now? [*Directive, open question. The building and magnification of sensorimotor experience are considered basic to Gestalt work.*]

19. *Meg:* It's—sort of—slowly—quite—quite aware, of anything getting too close.

20. *Fritz:* Hm? [*Encourager*]

21. *Meg:* Quite aware of not letting anything get too close, ready to strike.

22. *Fritz:* Say this to us. "If you come too close, I—" [*Directive*]

23. *Meg:* If you come too close, I'll strike back!

24. *Fritz:* I don't hear you. I don't believe you, yet. [*Feedback*]

25. *Meg:* If you come too close, I will strike back!

26. *Fritz:* Say this to each one, here. [*Directive*]

27. *Meg:* If you come too close, I will strike back!

28. *Fritz:* Say this with your whole body. [*Directive*]

29. *Meg:* If you come too close, I will strike back!

30. *Fritz:* How are your legs? I experience you as being somewhat wobbly. [*Open question, feedback. Perls was often concerned about clients' bodies being physically grounded on the earth.*]

31. *Meg:* Yeah.

32. *Fritz:* That you don't really take a stand. [*Interpretation*]

33. *Meg:* Yes, I feel I'm kind of, in between being very strong and—if I let go, they're going to turn to rubber.

34. *Fritz:* Ok, eh, let them turn to rubber. (Her knees bend and wobble.) Again. Now try out how strong they are. Try out—hit the floor. Do anything. (She stamps several times with one foot.) Yah, now the other. (Stamps other foot.) Now let them turn to rubber again. (She lets her knees bend again.) More difficult now, isn't it? [*Directive, closed question*]

35. *Meg:* Yeah.

36. *Fritz:* Now say again the sentence, "If you come too close—"(She makes an effort.) (laughter) [*Directive*]

37. *Meg:* If—if you

38. *Fritz:* Ok, eh, change. Say "Come close." (laughter) [*Directive*]

39. *Meg:* Come close.

40. *Fritz:* How do you feel now? [*Open question*]

41. *Meg:* Warm.

42. *Fritz:* You feel somewhat more real? [*Interpretation*]

43. *Meg:* Yeah.

44. *Fritz:* Ok, eh. So what we did is we took away some of the fear of being in touch. So, from now on, she'll be a bit more in touch. [*Interpretation and the beginning of formal reflection on the experience*] (pp. 162–164)

It is useful to compare Perls and Rogers on their use of microskills. In Rogerian counseling, attending and listening skills are primary, whereas Perls predominantly used the influencing skills of directives, feedback, and interpretation. Whereas Rogers emphasized empathy, warmth, and positive regard, Perls was somewhat personally distant and remote during the session. His respect for others showed only when they became truly themselves. Although both Rogers and Perls sought genuine encounters with others, Rogers tended to wait patiently for them, whereas Perls demanded that authentic relationships develop quickly and strongly.

Gestalt therapy is fundamentally concerned with the totality of the individual's being-in-the-world. The complexity and possibility of the world can be dealt with, according to existential thought, in a wide variety of ways. Perls chose to emphasize here-and-now present-tense experiencing as a way to integrate people in relation to themselves, others, and the world. There is thus a corresponding decrease in emphasis on past or future.

In explaining this central theoretical construct, Perls (1969a) writes: "Whenever you leave the sure basis of the now and become preoccupied with the future, you experience anxiety" (p. 30). Perls suggested that the mode of being-in-the-world is to center on oneself and get in touch with one's own existential experience; this makes for a very "I-centered" individualistic view of therapy.

Gestalt Techniques

Perls was a charismatic, dynamic therapist who was trained in classical psychoanalysis but profoundly aware of its limitations. He brought his formal knowledge and a formidable clinical talent to the counseling interview. He and his coworkers have been able to document both Gestalt therapy theory and technique in a rather complete form (Fagan & Shepherd, 1970; Perls, 1992a, b; Perls, Hefferline, & Goodman, 1951). However, the most effective way to understand Gestalt therapy is to experience it.

It can be argued that Perls's major contribution is methodological rather than theoretical. Over the years, he developed a wide range of techniques that vitalize existential experiencing. The following techniques should always be used in a working relationship and with a full sense of ethics. Reading about them will be of no value unless you practice them experientially. These methods are easily integrated into interviews, regardless of theoretical orientation.

Here-and-Now Experiencing. Most techniques of Gestalt therapy are centered on helping the client experience the world now rather than in the past or future. What is done is done, and what will be will be. Although past experiences, dreams, or future thoughts may be discussed, the constant emphasis is on relating them to immediate present-tense experience. In the transcript, Perls again and again directs the client to awareness of the here and now.

Directives. Gestalt therapists constantly tell their clients what to do in the interview, although decisions for their own later actions are clients' own. For example, Meg (number 5) talks in a nondirect way about the dog in her dream. Perls, through the simple directive "Tell him," brings her to an active, present role in the dream. Throughout this session, Perls constantly directs the movement of the client. Feedback (number 24), questions related to physical feelings (number 30), and interpretations (number 32) give additional strength to the directives.

Language Changes. Gestalt clients are encouraged to change questions to statements in the belief that most questions are simply hidden statements about oneself. For example, "Do you like me?" may actually be the statement "I am not sure that you like me." The therapist suggests that the client change questions to "I" statements. Clients are also often asked or told to change vague statements about some subject to "I" statements, thus increasing the personal identification and concreteness in the interview.

The client is frequently directed to talk in the present tense ("Be in the here and now"), as this also adds power and focus to the problem. Gestalt therapists point out that the counselor can see and understand only what is before him or her. Talking about problems is considered less effective than experiencing them directly. Although questions are generally discouraged, "how" and "what" questions are considered more acceptable than "why" questions, which often lead to intellectualization.

The Empty Chair Technique. Perhaps the best-known and most powerful of the many Gestalt techniques, the empty chair technique, is also one of the easiest to use in counseling practice. When a client expresses a conflict with another person, she or he is directed to imagine that the other person is sitting in an empty chair and then to talk to that person. After the client has said a few words, the counselor directs the client to change chairs and answer as the other person might. The counselor directs a dialogue between the client and the imaginary other person by constantly suggesting chair changes at critical points. Through this exercise, clients learn to experience and understand feelings more fully. Clients also often learn that they were projecting many thoughts onto the other person. Research on the empty chair technique is provided in Research Exhibit 10.1. After reviewing the research findings related to this Gestalt therapy technique, you can exercise some of the skills that are necessary to effectively use the empty chair technique in your own professional practice by completing Competency-Building Activity 10.2.

Talking to Parts of Oneself. A variation of the empty chair technique is to point out client splits, immobility, or impasses to the client. The two sides of an issue, or conflicting parts within the person, are drawn out. Sometimes the therapist seeks details for clarity; at other times, the counselor moves immediately to the exercise. The two sides of the person then engage in a dialogue, using the empty chair technique. By discussing the conflicted issues reflected by the split, the person often spontaneously generates a new solution or answer to her or his problem or concern.

A variation on the foregoing often occurs when the counselor notes incongruities or mixed messages in client body language or between client body language and her or his stated words. For example, in some cases a Gestalt therapist may have the client's tense right hand talk to the loose left hand or the client's jiggling right leg talk to his or her upset stomach. Through such imaginative games of body dialogue, quick and important breakthroughs in understanding often occur.

Top Dog and Underdog. Gestalt therapists constantly search for the authoritarian and demanding "top dog" of the personality, which is full of "shoulds" and "oughts."

Research Exhibit 10.1

Studies on the Empty Chair Technique

Research demonstrating the effectiveness of Gestalt techniques is finally beginning to bear some positive fruit. Paivio and Greenberg (1995) examined the empty chair technique as a method to help clients work through "unfinished business." Unfinished business can include the failure to resolve emotional issues around divorce, difficulties with parents, or other interpersonal conflicts.

The authors note that clients with unfinished business tend to have unresolved anger and sadness, which in turn result in anxiety, depression, and other clinical symptoms. When clients talk about their issues using the empty chair technique, they can release their emotions. Greenberg and Saffran (1987) and Foerster (1990) note that resolution often occurs and clients tend to see themselves as less weak and more empowered after using this technique.

Paivio and Greenberg (1995) provided empty chair therapy for twelve weeks of treatment. In the sessions, the therapists guided clients to express their unresolved feelings to an imaginary person. A comparison group of clients engaged in a lecture and discussion around issues of unresolved business for the same period of time. The empty chair technique was found to be more effective in producing clinically meaningful changes with a large effect size. Some of the changes that ensued from using this therapeutic intervention were less hostility, more self-acceptance, and more understanding of the other person's point of view.

Clients who profited most from this experience were those "able to experience anxiety . . . [and allow] accessing of the emotional memory" (Paivio & Greenberg, 1995, p. 424). In effect, those able to handle stress most effectively were those who gained most from the twelve-week experience. This finding is typical of psychotherapy and counseling research in general, which often reveals that those who are "most well" benefit the most from professional helping.

Despite some methodological difficulties, this study is important, as it demonstrates that areas previously thought to be inaccessible to research are indeed measurable. Clinicians intuitively have known for years that strong emotional discharge often leads to improvement. The type of study done by Paivio and Greenberg needs replication and extension. One possibility would be to include Gestalt empty chair work in the lecture and discussion group sessions. This, of course, is classic Gestalt group work, and it is possible that the effectiveness of the empty chair technique could be demonstrated in other than one-on-one counseling and psychotherapeutic interviews.

In contrast, the "underdog" is more passive, apologetic, and guilt ridden. When these two personality dimensions are observed, the empty chair technique or a dialogue often helps the client to understand and experience them more fully.

Staying with One's Feelings. When a key emotion is noted in the interview, particularly through a nonverbal movement, the Gestalt therapist will often immediately give attention to the feeling and its meaning. Perls's suggestion to Meg to let her trembling develop (number 18) exemplifies the use of this technique. This is a simple technique, but it can be an invaluable one, whether you are a Rogerian, a psychodynamic helper, or a feminist therapist.

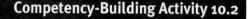

Competency-Building Activity 10.2

Using the Empty Chair Technique to Resolve Unfinished Business

Gestalt techniques often focus on the here and now. How can one talk about past issues in the present? The empty chair technique is particularly suited to this purpose, as it provides you and the client with a way to bring the past into the present and to work toward a new, more positive future. The techniques and strategies of the empty chair are powerful and should be used with care and a full sense of ethical responsibility.

In this activity the four techniques of Gestalt therapy are used: here-and-now experiencing, therapist directives, language changes, and the empty chair technique.

Instructions:

Step 1. *Fully inform the client (real or role-played) about what to expect.* Mention that the client can stop at any point.

Step 2. *Use the basic listening sequence to draw out a story of the unfinished personal business from the client.* As always, listen carefully and be sure to summarize the story's major facts and feelings to the client's satisfaction.

Step 3. *Inform the client about the nature of the exercise.* For example, you might state something like the following:

"You seem to have unfinished business with your uncle. We have found that if you imagine that he is sitting in that empty chair over there it may be helpful in resolving and understanding some of your issues. I'd like you to talk directly to your uncle as if he were there right now."

Step 4. *Use prompts.* Appropriately used, these directives may be helpful in bringing the conversation more into the here and now:

"Look at your uncle sitting in that chair, not at me."

"Don't say 'I would say X to him.' Rather, use his name and talk as if he were there right now."

"Use here-and-now language, not there-and-then language."

To make the situation more powerful, ask the client to tell the other person the same thing again (and again) with increasing feeling. The Gestalt technique of repetition often builds emotion quickly, so work with the client rather than on the client.

Step 5. *Ask the client to move to the chair and take the role of the other person.* The client is encouraged to physically move to the empty chair, become the uncle, and answer the now-imaginary self in the empty chair. Many Gestalt therapists will continue this back-and-forth exchange until a resolution to the problem seems to have been reached.

Step 6. *Spend sufficient time "talking down" your client.* The emotional release that often occurs during this exercise is powerful. Encourage deep breathing in the here and now to help the client readjust to present reality and leave the recently completed work in the there and then.

When you have completed this competency-building activity, take a few minutes to write down your reactions to this exercise. Add your written reactions to your personal/professional development portfolio. This will enable you to continue to keep a record of the different ways that you are being affected by the various exercises presented in this book.

Dreamwork. In dreamwork, the Gestalt approach most closely resembles its psychoanalytic foundation. Yet, unlike psychoanalysis, Gestalt does not use dreams to understand past conflicts but rather as metaphors to understand present-day, here-and-now living. The parts of a dream are considered as aspects of the client. Any piece (person, object, scene, or thing) of a dream is a projection of the client's experiential work. Through acting out the dream, the client can integrate the split pieces of her or his personality into a whole person.

Each of these techniques can be used in multicultural settings, providing there is a base of sufficient understanding and trust between client and therapist. For example, Gestalt dreamwork can be expanded to include the multicultural dream concepts mentioned in Chapter 5. When combined with other Gestalt interventions, dreamwork can be very powerful and emotional. The empty chair technique can be used to increase women's or gay males' understanding of how others may have mistreated them. The top dog/underdog technique also is made to order for discussion of oppression in multicultural Gestalt counseling and therapy sessions.

Through the development of these and other powerful Gestalt techniques, Perls made an impressive impact on the practice of counseling and psychotherapy. More than any other therapist, he has been able to show that clients can rapidly be moved to deep understanding of themselves and their environmental-contextual conditions. Although his theoretical foundations have been criticized and there is little empirical evidence validating the effectiveness of his therapeutic approaches, there is no question that his work and life are important expressions of the existential-humanistic tradition.

Individualism and Other Cultural/Contextual Considerations

Perls's focus on individuals making decisions alone—"doing their own thing"—is similar to the emphasis Rogers placed on self-actualization, but Perls carries the idea considerably further. In terms of actual practice, Perls did not give much attention to the individual-in-relationship. Yet when his clients truly were able to find themselves, to identify themselves as authentically in real relationship to others, Perls would often embrace them with joy.

Thus, although Perls's system does not focus on relationships, it should be stressed that real and authentic relationships were important to him. In the final stages of his life, he established a Gestalt community on Vancouver Island, British Columbia. The idea of developing this community was to extend Gestalt ideas of the "whole" to group and community interactions. Unfortunately, Perls died before his ideas could be tested. Clearly, in his last works he was moving toward linking his views of Gestalt therapy to broader interpersonal interactions to foster positive environmental, contextual, and social changes.

To make Gestalt therapy more culturally relevant, it is important that practitioners extend the work that Perls (1992a, b) was involved in at the end of his career.

This includes directing greater attention to the impact environmental/contextual factors have on clients' development. Such attention is especially important, given the rapid cultural/racial transformation of the United States and, in the past, the general failure of Gestalt theorists and practitioners to address cultural/contextual issues.

To become more culturally relevant and respectful when using Gestalt counseling theories in practice, therapists will need to move beyond the individualistic biases that are embedded in Perls's helping approach. The "Gestalt Prayer" presented earlier provides one example of the many ways in which traditional Gestalt therapy is rooted in highly individualistic constructions of mental health and personal well-being.

While such individualistic constructions and biases about psychological health are appropriate for many persons in the dominant cultural group in the United States, this slant sharply contrasts with the values, traditions, and worldviews of clients from other cultural/racial backgrounds. In light of the unprecedented demographic changes occurring in the United States (D'Andrea & Daniels, 2005), the failure to expand the cultural/contextual relevance of Gestalt therapy will predictably undermine the potential usefulness of this important counseling and psychotherapeutic approach in the coming decades.

Some of the specific things counselors and psychologists can do to make Gestalt therapy more relevant and helpful for culturally different clients include:

1. directing greater attention to the importance of human interconnectedness (as Perls increasingly emphasized toward the end of his life)

2. demonstrating a heightened sensitivity to the various ways that persons from diverse client populations experience different forms of oppression (i.e., sexism, racism, classism, etc.)

3. communicating a genuine sense of empathic understanding as to how these environmental conditions negatively affect clients' sense of personal well-being

4. implementing new Gestalt approaches that effectively help clients deal in positive ways with the negative impact of oppressive contextual stressors

5. considering how the three major domains of the multicultural counseling competencies discussed in Chapter 2 (e.g., the multicultural awareness, knowledge, and skills domains) can impact the implementation of Gestalt therapy with persons from diverse client populations

As stated in Chapters 1 and 2, counselors and psychologists will be increasingly challenged to extend their thinking about what constitutes mental health and therapeutic help within the context of a multicultural society. This will necessitate critically examining and reformulating some of Perls's foundational theoretical concepts, such as the importance of "doing your own thing" (Perls, 1992a, b).

Counselors and therapists who use Perls's helping framework with persons from diverse groups and backgrounds are encouraged to reassess individualistic notions of mental health and psychological well-being within the context of multicultural postmodern society. They also need to consider the benefits that can be derived from

Professional Development Extension

Applying Gestalt Principles of Emphasizing the "Here and Now" in Wellness Counseling

Fritz Perls's approach to Gestalt therapy emphasizes clients' ability to release themselves from thinking about past events and future possibilities to more fully experience the "here and now" of their lives. In doing so, Perls instructed his clients to focus on their present bodily reactions to become more fully self-aware and personally integrated. The case of Dominque demonstrates how this aspect of Perls's theory was used by the therapist.

Dominque is a 26-year-old community counseling student who is majoring in psychology. She came to the counseling center because of what she referred to as "generalized nervousness that gets in the way of my studies and social life." The counselor (David) probed this issue further and found that Dominque had become more and more nervous since she was a teenager. She stated that she believed she is too concerned about what other people will think about her grades and how she looks and acts. "I just don't know what I can do to get rid of this constant feeling of nervousness. It is driving me crazy."

As Dominque talked more, the counselor noted that Dominque was preoccupied with past reactions people had had to her and with anxiety about future events that might occur in school or in her social life. What became increasingly clear in their first session was that Dominque had difficulty simply talking about or being calm in the present moment.

When David pointed this out to her, Dominque started to cry and said, "You're right. My mind is always going a million miles a second with thoughts about what happened in the past or concerns I have about what is going to happen in the future. I just don't know how to stop it."

The counselor responded by using one of one of Perls's favorite Gestalt counseling strategies. First, David explained the positive effects individuals commonly experience when they shift their attention from thinking about past events or future expectations to becoming more fully conscious of the "here and now." He said this could be done by directing attention to one's present bodily reactions. He then asked Dominque to focus on how her body was feeling and what this told her about her present state of being.

Initially, Dominque had difficulty talking about her bodily feelings. But after a couple of minutes she said, "I feel very tight around my neck and my chest. I am surprised at how fast my breathing is. I never really noticed that."

Recognizing that the latter statement was a subtle reference to her past, David immediately asked to continue by asking her how the rest of her body was feeling "right now." Dominque noted, "My foot is tapping kind of fast, like it is releasing nervous energy. Now it is kind of slowing down as I become more aware of it."

The counselor responded by saying that her foot was slowing down in part because Dominque had moved her thinking from past worries and future concerns to being in the "here and now" by focusing on her present bodily reactions. Dominque stated that she found this simple technique to be interesting and helpful, as "I really did slow down the busy chattering going on in my head, where I am constantly thinking about the things I should have done in the past or what I ought to do in the future."

Dominque participated in four additional sessions in which David combined several other Gestalt techniques with a number of wellness counseling strategies. This was done to assist Dominque in developing both a greater awareness of her present state of being and an increased sense of responsibility for nurturing a healthy and calmer lifestyle.

promoting new Gestalt approaches that stimulate a greater sense of collective responsibility and care. Such notions are implicitly reflected in a different version of the Gestalt Prayer, which is called the "Getsmart Prayer":

> You are you, and I am I,
> And if by chance we find
> Our brothers and sisters enslaved
> And the world under fascist rule
> Because we're doing our thing—
> It can't be helped. (Author unknown, *Rough Times,* 1972, p. 7)

Although the Getsmart Prayer was published by an unknown author in the journal *Rough Times* in 1972, it is particularly relevant for the present discussion as it underscores the need to remember that we as individuals are interconnected and that "doing our own thing" has consequences for those around us. As counselors and therapists, the social commentary in the Getsmart Prayer serves as a reminder of the importance of keeping collectivistic, cultural, and contextual considerations in mind when using Gestalt therapy approaches in the helping process.

Counselors and psychologists who are interested in learning more about the practical ways in which they can use Gestalt techniques in a culturally respectful way are encouraged to review Ivey's (1995b) "psychotherapy as liberation model" (p. 53). This model outlines numerous suggestions for helping clients explore their feelings about oppressive environmental conditions from a sensorimotor perspective (see Chapter 13). Ivey's strategies for helping clients experience their problems from this perspective complement several Gestalt therapy techniques, including talking to parts of oneself and staying with one's feelings.

Critiquing Perls's Work from a Multicultural-Feminist-Social Justice Perspective

Lerner's (1992) critique of Perls is more gentle than her commentary on Rogers (Chapter 9), as she recognizes that Gestalt therapy is more concerned with environmental realities than is person-centered theory. However, she feels that Perls gave insufficient attention to the role of trauma in therapy in that he uncritically accepted Maslow's (1971) hierarchy of needs in explaining the ways that counselors can deal with traumatized clients in therapy. In her view, the emphasis on helping traumatized clients to strive to realize self-actualization misses the importance of self-in-relation (see Chaper 11 for clarification of the meaning of this term).

Enns (1987) gives special attention to Gestalt therapy's implications for women by suggesting that Gestalt exercises can be helpful for female clients in three ways:

1. helping women become aware of themselves as distinct individuals having their own power (particularly as "I" statements are used in the helping process)

2. facilitating the expression of anger through a variety of Gestalt exercises

3. enabling women to become more aware of their life choices as they move beyond the splits in their personality and become more integrated and authentic persons

Gestalt therapy is highly concerned that individuals make their own choices and, as such, can be very helpful to women who have been culturally discouraged from doing so in life. Of course, these three advantages may be less applicable with individuals in other marginalized cultural groups.

Also, Gestalt therapy contains a strong confrontational element and quickly moves clients to direct emotional expression. The emotional expressiveness required in Gestalt therapy may be seen as immature in some ethnic communities, and the confrontational nature of this therapeutic approach may not be welcomed by many persons in these cultural groups.

Building trust between the client and the therapist is needed before people from various backgrounds would be willing to reveal themselves fully, as is strongly encouraged in Gestalt therapy. Rigney (1981) speaks to the condition of the Australian Aboriginal, making specific comments on how unsuitable much of traditional counseling and therapy is for many cultural groups, particularly the Aboriginal, even when trust building has occurred between the Aboriginal client and non-Aboriginal therapist.

However, the word *gestalt* itself implies that the individual is a whole in a context of family and community. Consequently, clients from many cultural backgrounds might respond positively to Gestalt interventions that emphasize the interdependent, holistic, contextual nature of human development, especially if such an approach is used by culturally competent mental health practitioners. Underlying your work as a culturally competent practitioner is the respectful manner in which you check to make sure that your client is ready and cognizant as to why you are using these particular interventions.

Limitations and Practical Implications of the Existential-Humanistic Tradition

The basic tenets of the three major existential-humanistic theorists complement each other quite well. For example, it is easy to integrate the views of humankind put forth by Rogers and Frankl; from a technical perspective, the listening style of Rogers is particularly compatible with Frankl's theoretical approach to logotherapy. Each was an admirer of the other's work.

Unfortunately, research studies comparing Rogerian, logotherapy, and Gestalt methods are virtually nonexistent. In fact, there is very little research on Gestalt therapy itself. However, opinion is that Gestalt therapy facilitates change faster than Rogerian methods but that it also has the potential for more destructive impact on the client if the therapist moves too fast. The Gestalt therapist has often been viewed by the client as a kind of "guru," which means that the therapist has even more power in the helping process. Strupp and Hadley (1976) have documented thoroughly the dangers of the charismatic therapist for fragile clients.

Like many other orientations to helping, the evolution of Gestalt therapy has been influenced by the Rogerian tradition. This is reflected in Yontef and Simkin's

(1989) commentary on Gestalt therapy, which places a greater emphasis on the client-therapist relationship. These authors argue for more softness rather than the "hard-ball" approach of Perls.

It seems wise, particularly for beginning counselors and therapists, to use the powerful techniques of Gestalt therapy with a real sensitivity to the worldview and experience of the client. Be advised to seek specific training and supervision before implementing these techniques, especially at the early stage of your professional practice. The Professional Development Extension provides an example of how Gestalt practices were used to emphasize the here and now with a client.

Of all the existential-humanistic approaches, Frankl's logotherapy sometimes can be overly verbal, reflective, and formal operational in nature, whereas Perls's direct sensorimotor approach may be inappropriate for clients who are uncomfortable with the emotional realm. Also, if Gestalt exercises are used too soon, they may be personally and culturally offensive to some clients.

Current theory and practice suggest that Frankl's balanced listening and influencing approach may become the most prominent existential-humanistic theory. This approach deals openly and honestly with issues of pain and how to surmount these difficulties through personal action, with the support of the therapist or counselor. However, manipulative and insensitive therapists are the greatest danger in the field. Theories may not always be personally and culturally sensitive, but if you are aware and growing, you almost always can adapt theory to meet the needs of the client you are working with.

Summary

This chapter marks the end of Part Two of this textbook. Hopefully, the combination of information presented about Rogers's person-centered framework (Chapter 9) as well as Frankl's theory of logotherapy and Perls's Gestalt therapy (as presented in this chapter) has expanded your understanding of the evolution of the existential-humanistic force in the fields of counseling and psychology.

Clearly, these three giants (Rogers, Frankl, and Perls) have played significant roles in the development of this third theoretical force in the mental health professions. Their individual and collective impact is most readily acknowledged in the benefits that clients derive from their theoretical constructs, as applied in counseling and psychotherapy.

Multimedia Resources for This Chapter

The following online resource offers video and other resources of particular relevance to this chapter of your text.

Companion Website

Go to **www.ablongman.com/Ivey6e** to view the following video clips:

- Video clip 10.1 demonstrates how a therapist uses techniques of logotherapy in a counseling session. Review this video clip to see how this therapist uses positive reframing with a client.

MyHelpingLab

If a MyHelpingLab passcode was included with your textbook and you have activated your passcode:

- go to **www.ablongman.com/myhelpinglab**
- enter the "Counseling" area of the site by clicking on that tab
- select "Video Lab" from the toolbar to the left of the page
- select "MyHelpingLab Videos by Theoretical Approach"
- select the "Gestalt" module to view various video clips of a therapist using this approach with a client

The Fourth Force in Counseling and Therapy: Multicultural and Feminist Perspectives

Historically, we talk of first-force psychodynamic, second-force cognitive-behavioral, and third-force existential-humanistic counseling and therapy theories. Counseling and psychotherapy really began with Freud and psychoanalysis. James Watson and, later, B. F. Skinner challenged Freud's emphasis on the unconscious and focused on observable behavior. Carl Rogers, with his person-centered counseling, revolutionized the helping professions by focusing on the importance of nurturing a caring therapist-client relationship in the helping process. All three approaches are still alive and well in the fields of counseling and psychology, as discussed in Chapters 5 through 10. As you reflect on the new knowledge and skills you exercised by reading the preceding chapters and completing the competency-building activities in those chapters, hopefully you will see that you have gained a more sophisticated foundational understanding of the three traditional theoretical forces that have shaped the fields of counseling and therapy over the past one hundred years.

Efforts in this book have been intended to bring your attention to both the strengths and limitations of psychodynamic, cognitive-behavioral, and existential-humanistic perspectives. With these perspectives in mind, the following chapters examine the fourth major theoretical force that has emerged in the mental health professions over the past 40 years: the multicultural-feminist-social justice counseling worldview. The perspectives of the fourth force challenge you to learn new competencies you will need to acquire to work effectively, respectfully, and ethically in a culturally diverse 21st-century society.

Part Three begins by discussing the rise of the feminist counseling and therapy perspective (Chapter 11) and multicultural counseling and therapy (MCT) theories (Chapter 12). To assist you in synthesizing much of the information contained in all of the preceding chapters, Chapter 13 presents a comprehensive and integrative helping theory referred to as developmental counseling and therapy (DCT). Chapter 14 offers a comprehensive examination of family counseling and therapy theories to further extend your knowledge of ways that mental health practitioners can assist entire families in realizing new and untapped dimensions of their collective well-being. Finally Chapter 15 provides guidelines to help you develop your own approach to counseling and therapy that complements a growing awareness of your own values, biases, preferences, and relational competencies as a mental health professional. Throughout, competency-building activities offer you opportunities to continue to exercise new skills associated with the different theories discussed in Part Three.

chapter 11

Feminist Counseling and Therapy

Judy Daniels
University of Hawai'i, Manoa

Introduction

There are a number of important commonalities that characterize the three major theoretical forces that continue to have a significant impact on the work counselors and therapists do.

1. The fact that the majority of persons who developed the psychodynamic, cognitive-behavioral, and existential-humanistic theories discussed in Part Two of this book are men.

2. These men also worked from a middle- and upper-middle-class socioeconomic position.

3. The vast majority of them come from White European-American backgrounds.

All of these factors (a person's gender, socioeconomic background, and cultural/racial group affiliation) are known to significantly affect one's psychological development and relational empowerment. In addition, feminist theorists and researchers point to the impact of a person's gender in shaping one's psychological perspective and meaning of the world. Feminist theorists and researchers direct particular attention to the negative economic, social, psychological, and spiritual consequences that commonly ensue from being socialized within a societal context that perpetuates various forms of institutionalized sexism and patriarchy.

These forms of institutionalized sexism and patriarchy are manifested and maintained in hierarchical power arrangements in which men are consistently placed at higher, more privileged positions in our society. Specific manifestations of these hierarchical power arrangements include, for example, the fact that men typically have higher-paying career positions and the continuing disparity in pay women with the same qualifications receive for doing the same work as men (Evans, Kinade, Marbley, & Seem, 2005).

An example of how patriarchy is manifested in counseling and therapy is when practitioners are viewed (and commonly view themselves) as experts who have the right and responsibility to impose specific helping theories and perspectives of mental health on persons experiencing psychological distress, regardless of the fact that cultural, racial, or gendered biases are reflected in these theoretical viewpoints (Cartwright, D'Andrea, & Daniels, 2003). The perpetuation of these complex forms of social injustice not only result in the privileging of men by continuing the oppression of women but also adversely affect the mental health and psychological well-being of millions of women and men through creating other forms of cultural stratification and oppression (hooks, 2000).

Feminist counseling and therapy (FCT) advocates have long noted that the imposition of gender-biased helping strategies that are embedded in the three major theoretical forces discussed earlier constitute unique forms of social injustice that continue to be perpetuated in the fields of counseling and psychology (Brown & Root, 1990). The imposition of gender-biased theories by persons in positions of power (e.g., by counselors and therapists) on those with less power (e.g., female clients seeking help during times of personal vulnerability) is one way in which social injustice is played out in many traditional counseling and therapy settings.

The continued emphasis by traditional helping theories on having clients reenter the environmental settings that contributed to their psychological distress also characterizes the inherent social injustice of traditional counseling and psychotherapy (Comstock, 2005; Ridley, 2005). Feminist and multicultural counseling theorists consistently question the ethics of such practice (hooks, 2000; Parham, 2002).

This chapter aims to increase your understanding of the ways in which FCT advocates have worked to overcome these forms of sexism and patriarchy in the helping professions. It is also designed to assist you in developing some of the skills necessary to implement feminist counseling and therapy strategies in your future professional practices.

The Feminist Counseling and Therapy Movement: An Overview

While the feminist counseling and therapy (FCT) movement emerged during the cultural revolution that took place in the United States in the 1960s and 1970s, much earlier in our nation's history many women set the tone for the spirit and principles that underlie this movement. The calls for freedom and social justice by many contemporary feminist counseling and therapy theorists are in accord with efforts of Harriet Tubman, who assisted hundreds of Black slaves to freedom through the Underground Railroad during the early and mid 1880s. Many other female abolition and women's suffrage advocates, such as Elizabeth Stanton, Sojourner Truth, and Susan B. Anthony, played pivotal roles in fostering an expanded consciousness related to the rights to life, liberty, and the pursuit of happiness as they applied to all people, including women, duing the mid 1800s and early 1900s.

Although the social justice principles and spirit that underlie the FCT movement have roots in a long history of the struggle for women's personal and political empowerment, mental health, and collective well-being, the genesis of this movement can be found in the publications of feminist counseling theorists of the 1960s and 1970s. At that time, increasing numbers of women actively took a stand against the various ways in which institutionalized forms of sexism and patriarchy undermined women's human dignity, mental health, and full citizenship rights. The early pioneers in the FCT movement directed much attention to three areas of relevance:

- uncovering the ways in which the gender biases that are embedded in the three traditional theoretical forces are routinely played out in the work of mental health practitioners
- describing how the use of gender-biased counseling and therapy theories and practices are harmful to women (and men)
- developing an alternative helping paradigm that is better suited for women's health, development, empowerment, and psychological liberation

Space limitations restrict a detailed description of the numerous pioneers who created the FCT paradigm that continues to significantly shape the way many mental health professionals operate in the field today. What follows is a brief description of some of the key persons and the contributions they made in building the FCT force in the United States, a force that has helped formulate a new psychology of women.

Developing a New Psychology of Women

As noted earlier, the traditional counseling and therapy theories that have been implemented in the field over the past one hundred years reflect the gender, economic class, and cultural values, preferences, and biases of the men who developed them. FCT pioneers focused on these values, preferences, and biases as they sought to build new helping frameworks that reflected greater respect for and understanding of the unique psychological development of women.

Jean Baker Miller

The efforts of the early FCT pioneers took place during the fervor of the 1960s and 1970s, when the United States was in the midst of major social, political, and cultural change. The opening sentence in Jean Baker Miller's (1986) book entitled *Toward a New Psychology of Women* captures the zeitgist of that time. In her opening sentence, Miller notes that "there is a new spirit abroad among women today, a new kind of collective and cooperative devotion to each other and to the search for the knowledge about important matters" (p. ix).

As one of the early pioneers in the feminist counseling and therapy movement, Miller recognized that this "new spirit" held the potential to create a new helping paradigm in the fields of counseling and psychology by bringing a more expansive understanding of human development into view. The new and more expansive view of human development that Miller helped to unveil relates to the distinctly different psychological strengths and challenges that women typically face as they navigate their lives within the context of a sexist and patriarchical society.

Among the important contributions Miller made in this area was her description of the central role relationships play in women's development, the psychological challenges women face in dealing with conflict in their lives, and the tendency for women to unconsciously adopt a negative perspective of womanhood.

Miller makes the point that several premises common to most traditional counseling and therapy theorists conflict with women's psychological needs and development. One of the central premises of traditional counseling theory that Miller and other FCT pioneers challenged at the time (Chodorow, 1978; Rawlings & Carter, 1977) included the high value placed on the individual's capacity to develop a sense of autonomy and independence.

The concepts of autonomy, individuality, separateness, and independence that have been associated with healthy human development reflect the Western, male perspective that underlies the three major theoretical forces that have dominated the fields of counseling and psychology for the past one hundred years. Miller and other FCT advocates provided empirically based evidence that verifies the ways in which women's healthy development is fueled by their sense of connection and interdependence with other people. The important roles that these factors play in women's development has been further substantiated by the work of more contemporary FCT advocates, including Carol Gilligan (1982) and Dana Comstock (2005).

The second major contribution Miller made to the fields of counseling and psychology concerns the unique challenges women face when they experience interpersonal conflicts in their lives. In discussing these challenges, Miller (1986) points out that women are socialized to suppress feelings of anger and frustration that are often natural outcomes of interpersonal conflicts. She explains that this socialization process leads many women to experience negative psychological and physical outcomes because they are fearful of expressing their thoughts and feelings about conflicts they are having with people, especially interpersonal conflicts that occur among individuals women are emotionally close to (e.g., boyfriends, husbands, family members, etc.). Comstock (personal communication, April, 18, 2006) refers to these dynamics as "prohibitions against women's anger."

The third point Miller focused on in formulating her theory of a new psychology of women relates to the tendency for women to unconsciously adopt a negative perspective of womanhood. Although the devaluation of a woman's own gender group is not a psychologically healthy perspective, it is understandable, given the developmental barriers that commonly emerge from living within a social context that

- maintains gender power imbalances that perpetuate various forms of sexism and patriarchy
- affirms male psychological characterisitics of autonomy, independence, and separateness as indicators of a more mature and well-developed person
- works to silence the legitimate frustration and anger many women experience
- devalues women's strengths as the keepers of connection, the paradox being that this role is essential to human survival (D. L. Comstock, personal communication, April, 18, 2006)
- continues to inaccurately describe the feminist perspective in oppositional terms in which feminist advocates are projected as being in opposition to men

Miriam Greenspan

Other early and contemporary FCT theorists supported Miller's claims about these issues and discussed the ways in which many counselors and therapists contribute to these problems (Contratto & Rossier, 2005; Greenspan, 1983; Rawlings & Carter, 1977). One of the early feminist theorists to support Miller's thinking in these areas was Miriam Greenspan. In her 1983 book entitled *A New Approach to Women and Therapy*, Greenspan extended many of Miller's theoretical concepts. In doing so, she helped shape the early stage of the FCT movement by asserting that many counselors and therapists operate from three general myths. Greenspan further argued that, in operating from these myths, mental health practitioners fail to address the social/contextual factors and injustices that underlie women's oppression and ensuing psychological difficulties. They also underestimate the frustration and anger that many woman experience as a result of being routinely subjected to these environmental conditions.

Myth 1. It's All in Your Head. According to Greenspan, this myth is commonly manifested when counselors and psychologists focus on unconscious and unresolved conflicts thought to be the cause of many female clients' feelings of frustration, anger, or depression. In perpetuating this myth, counselors and psychologists conveniently avoid directing attention to the oppressive and unjust stressors that occur in women's workplaces or within their families and their other relationships and instead primarily direct time and energy to "fixing" the female clients who seek their help. This results in an overemphasis on the intrapsychic issues female clients experience and a neglect of the environmental/contextual factors that undermine women's mental health, psychological liberation, relational competence, and collective empowerment.

Myth 2. The Medical Model of Psychopathology. This myth suggests that all emotional pain can be treated the same way that one would treat medical problems, by prescription (Contratto & Rossier, 2005). Similar to the first myth, the underlying assumption of this second myth is that the problem lies within the client. Consequently, corrective actions are aimed at changing those aspects of the individual that are causing psychological distress. Culturally and gender-biased diagnostic and assessment tools that are contextually insensitive are used to further legitimize the use of an intrapsychic approach, which is aimed at addressing the individual's perceived deficits and psychopathology.

In viewing their problems in the terms set forth by myths 1 and 2, female clients (and many male clients as well) fail to consider the important personal strengths they bring to the helping situation. This may often result in a disempowering process that is antithetical to the strength-based approaches to counseling and therapy so central to the microskills approach to helping (Chapter 4), the positive psychology paradigm (Chapter 5), and the multicultural counseling and therapy framework (MCT) (Chapter 12).

Myth 3. The Doctor as "The Expert." This myth helps perpetuate the power imbalance that is noted to exist between the doctor, therapist, and/or counselor and the female clients who seek assistance with their medical, psychological, or emotional difficulties. Contratto and Rossier (2005) point out that this myth not only increases the disempowering process noted above but also leads clients to adopt a sense of powerlessness, which can carry over to other social relationships outside counseling and psychotherapy.

The FCT movement has directed much time and energy to debunking these myths. It has done so by helping women and other persons recognize that their problems are often rooted in their environmental contexts. In addition to assisting clients to realize this fundamental aspect of their own psychological liberation (and not merely accept the myth that their problems are "in their head" or a reflection of their personal deficits), FCT-oriented practitioners provide opportunities for clients to exercise new and untapped empowerment capabilities. Thus, from a FCT theoretical perspective, it is not enough that mental health practitioners help clients feel better about themselves in counseling and therapy. They must also

- continually strive to become aware of the ways in which their social/professional context and conditioning impact their own psychological development, in general, and their biased views about helping, in particular
- understand how clients' social/cultural/environmental contexts affect their development, mental health, and sense of individual and collective well-being

- implement counseling and therapy strategies that stimulate a greater sense of personal and collective empowerment and psychological liberation in the counseling and psychotherapy setting

- work intentionally to stimulate clients' relational capacities/competencies

- exercise advocacy services that are aimed at promoting positive environmental changes that help to sustain and amplify the above-mentioned counseling and psychotherapeutic outcomes

The latter point is the focus of increasing attention in the mental health profession, as the practitioner's role as client advocate is being more fully and explicitly encouraged and defined by various professional groups and organizations. For more information on this emerging issue, review the advocacy competencies that have been developed and formally endorsed by the American Counseling Association (ACA) in 2003 (**www.counseling.org**).

These and many other changes occurring in the fields of counseling and psychology are fueled by new ideas put forth by supporters of the FCT theoretical movement. Although these new ideas contribute to the ongoing evolution and transformation of the mental health professions, there continues to be a great deal of resistance to implementing an FCT approach in counseling and therapy settings. Competency-Building Activity 11.1 aims to help you assess your own resistance or proclivity to use some of the FCT concepts in this chapter in your professional practice.

The FCT Worldview

Three concepts are of particular importance to the FCT worldview: the notion of power and its many manifestations in our contemporary society; the adverse impact that sexism has on women and men's psychological development; and the important place that the self-in-relation (or person-in-relation) concept holds in this theoretical worldview. Traditional theories of counseling and therapy direct little attention to the ways in which the appropriation of societal power affects people's mental health and psychological well-being. In contrast, FCT theorists acknowledge that societal power, or the lack thereof, plays a major role in the way people, in general, and women, in particular, develop psychologically, how they come to view themselves and their place in the world, their sense of human agency, their connections with others, and their constructions of fairness and justice (Gilligan, 1982; Hill & Ballou, 2005).

FCT theorists direct specific attention to the ways that the various forms of social-political-economic power that are disproportionately appropriated to men in our society help maintain complex forms of individual, institutional, and cultural sexism. From this worldview, sexism is viewed both as a pervasive form of injustice that not only undermines women's social, political, and economic standing in society, but also fosters a disordered psychological state that adversely impacts millions of people's (e.g., both women and men's) development and mental health (hooks, 2000).

Competency-Building Activity 11.1

Where Do You Stand on the Three Myths?

Instructions: It is useful to complete this competency-building activity with a small group of colleagues or students in your professional training program who are familiar with some of the foundational concepts put forth by FCT theorists. To begin this activity, provide the other members of the group with a copy of the three myths described above.

Make this a semistructured group conversation in which you encourage an open discussion of these myths as they relate to each person's thinking about his or her own philosophy of counseling and therapy. In addition to hearing everyone's own thinking about these myths, ask each person to comment on the following questions:

1. How does your own philosophy of counseling and psychotherapy complement or conflict with the three myths that Greenspan and other FCT theorists have written about?

2. If your philosophy of counseling and psychotherapy complements the ideas presented in the description of the three myths presented above, briefly explain why you think these concepts are helpful in assisting female and/or male clients effectively address their personal concerns and problems.

3. If your philosophy of counseling and psychotherapy conflicts with the ideas presented in the description of the three myths presented above, briefly explain why you think your own theory of helping is more useful in assisting female and/or male clients to effectively address their personal concerns and problems.

4. Can you think of any additional "myths" that could be asserted about either the traditional approaches to counseling and therapy (e.g., the psychodynamic, cognitive-behavioral, existential-humanistic theories) or about FCT as you understand it at the current time?

Although you may serve as the facilitator of this group activity, be sure to participate in an open and honest manner by expressing your own views in addressing the questions listed above. After you have completed this competency-building activity, take a few minutes to write down your reactions to this exercise and file them in your personal/professional development portfolio.

Although the early FCT theorists primarily focused on the adverse psychological effects that sexism has on women, attention has increasingly been directed toward recognizing the negative psychological outcomes that men commonly experience as a result of being raised within a sexist environmental/societal context. It is helpful to use concepts that are associated with the three traditional theoretical forces discussed in Part Two to understand some of the ways in which men are negatively affected by the perpetuation of sexism in our society, in general, and address the stereotypic feminine and masculine social expectations that guide how we relate to each other, in particular.

From a psychodynamic perspective, many men employ defense mechanisms regarding the unfair treatment and inferior power status of women in our contemporary society. One defense mechanism is denial, which allows men to psychologically divorce themselves from consideration of the existence of sexism as well as other social injustices in our society (e.g., racism, ableism, heterosexism, classism) and the tremendous psychological, social, and economic difficulties and injustices they place on many women and men subjected to these cultural oppressions.

Repression is another defense mechanism that helps protect men from feelings of guilt and anger about the unfair and destructive ways in which sexism undermines women's rights and their psychological and spiritual well-being. These and other defense mechanisms adversely impact men's psychological development because they lead to serious distortions of the sociopolitical realities that continue to adversely impact many women's lives in the United States (hooks, 2004). If people value their connections with others, as encouraged in the feminist perspective, they will more likely begin talking about these problems as "mutual concerns" that are not exclusive to women or persons in other devalued groups.

From a cognitive-behavioral perspective, the perpetuation of sexism in society often results in the development of a number of irrational beliefs about women. These often include, but are not limited to, the belief that women are innately inferior to men in many ways, are often to blame when they are sexually assaulted (e.g., because of the provocative way they dress or act), and are destined to play particular social roles, as prescribed by certain religious and political doctrines.

Although many mental health professionals would likely agree that these statements represent inaccurate stereotypes of women, there is a danger in identifying these ideas as being "irrational" without also commenting on the social/contextual forces that tend to "normalize" them. Comstock (personal communication, April 20, 2006) points out that "these ideas are actually taught to (and violently instilled in) us from our socialization and through the media and in advertising. Recognizing the systemic underpinnings from which these ideas are produced, it might be dangerous to say they are irrational, since some counselors and therapists might simply conclude, 'It's not rational; it really is in these women's heads. So we need to help them change the way they think.'"

While psychodynamic, cognitive-behavioral, and existential-humanistic counseling and psychotherapy theories have many strengths, they are not always helpful in enabling men to become aware of their own unconscious sexist ideologies or to be cognizant of their irrational beliefs about women's lives and development. The emphasis on intrapsychic issues and the individual's meaning-making system directs men's attention away from the ways in which their own unearned gendered power and privileges contribute to the complex problem of sexism and adversely affect women's psychological health and sense of empowerment.

Self-in-Relation: The Importance of Relational Considerations

Another important factor that characterizes the FCT worldview involves the notion of **self-in-relation.** Unlike traditional theories of counseling and psychotherapy, which place a high value on clients' autonomy, separateness, and unique individuality, FCT theorists assert that women's psychological health is anchored in their relational connections with others. The term *self-in-relation* refers to the important part that interdependent and mutually respectful relationships play in women's mental health and collective well-being (Gilligan, 1982).

In short, the concept of self-in-relation acknowledges the intimate linkages that exist between people and their environment. It affirms that human development, psychological health, and spiritual well-being are all significantly affected by one's cultural/contextual history and relational experiences with the world and with other people.

From a multicultural perspective, this aspect of the FCT theoretical worldview is consistent with Buddhist principles of the interdependence of all animate and inanimate elements in the world (Levine, 2000). It also complements many Native American Indian (Smith, 2005) and African-centered (Graham, 2005) constructs about the manner in which contextual factors and a relational consciousness impact a person's sense of personal wellness.

Factors That Disrupt Relational Connections and Undermine Psychological Health

As noted earlier, FCT theorists point out that the fields of counseling and psychology are situated within a broader social-political context that perpetuates various forms of social injustice and cultural oppression, including overt and covert manifestations of sexism (Robb, 2006). It is within this broader social-political context that theorists from each of the three traditional theoretical forces (psychodynamic, cognitive-behavioral, existential-humanistic) developed gender-biased views of helping, human development, and mental health. These gender-biased approaches continue to be implemented by many practitioners in the field today.

FCT researchers provide clear evidence that substantiates the ways in which cultural and gender-biased values related to autonomy, separateness, and independence undermine women's psychological health (Hill & Ballou, 2005). These and other feminist researchers have directed particular attention to the ways in which these values commonly come into play in counseling and psychotherapy and lead to ineffective and harmful outcomes for many female clients (Worrell & Remer, 2003).

Other FCT theorists and researchers point out that while these biases contribute to disconnection between therapist and client, this situation is not limited to counseling and therapy settings. Such unhealthy disconnections also ensue from the perpetuation of the cultural and gender-biased values embedded in broader societal hierarchical power arrangements that privilege those in certain cultural and gender groups at the expense of people in less privileged positions in our society (Comstock, 2005).

The hierarchy of societal power arrangements in the United States results in people being effectively relegated to particular social positions in life (Scheurich, 1993). This social positionality not only impacts our psychological development and orientation to life but also contributes to various forms of human disconnection that diminish our ability to relate in mutually empathic and respectful ways to one another (hooks, 2000; West, 1999). Scheurich (1993) describes this phenomenon:

> Each of us is socially positioned or located by major sociological categories, such as race, class, and gender. Those in different positional intersections, like lower-class females or Asian middle-class males, are socialized in different ways.

These positional intersections, however, are not equal in our society. There is a hierarchy of positions, with upper-class White males at the top and lower-class males and females of color at the bottom. Resources and power—economic, intellectual, and emotional—are largely distributed according to this hierarchy. Whites as a group get more resources and power than people of color. The upper class as a group gets more resources and power than the middle class as a group, which gets more resources and power than the lower class. Men as a group get more resources and power than women.

This inequitable distribution of resources and power by social group is concealed by middle- and upper-income White people's and men's investment in the idea of individualism. Despite the grouping effect of racism and sexism in our society, many people of color and women are not seduced by the idea of individualism and the myth of meritocracy. People of color and women, through their socially positioned experiences, know that they are a part of racialized and gendered groups rather than separate individuals.

Although we live in a culture that distributes its resources most disproportionately to middle- and upper-class White males, this does not mean that there are not exceptions to this arrangement or that groups do not persistently resist the inequitable distribution of power and privilege in our society. Middle- and upper-class White males, nonetheless, consistently reap the most benefits and have done so for a very long time within Western culture. The result of this historical dominance is that the styles of thinking, acting, speaking, and behaving of the dominant group have become the socially correct or privileged ways of thinking, acting, speaking, and behaving. (p. 7)

The social positionality, power arrangements, and cultural privileges described above are maintained and reinforced in the social-economic-educational-political institutions that mental health practitioners and their clients are a part of. They are largely sustained by organizational policies and practices, educational curricula, and mental health care practices that promote social conformity and control over the way individuals think, talk, feel, and behave (Daniels et al., 2002; Martin-Baro, 1997).

The focus of traditional counseling and therapy theories is on the individual rather than on the client's environmental context and the impact that this context has on mental health. Ignoring clients' environmental context and the impact of their social positionality is considered by feminist therapists to be a major shortcoming of traditional helping theories.

Self-Reflection by Counselors and Therapists

Unlike traditional theoretical approaches to counseling and therapy, the FCT worldview (like the multicultural counseling worldview) is more expansive, in that it directs much attention to contextual issues, power dynamics, and the psychological impact of social positionality and how these factors affect the client. Adapting this expansive and contextualized worldview leads FCT-oriented therapists to place much emphasis on understanding how the hierarchy of societal power and the social positionality that ensues from it affect their clients' development as well as their own personal and professional development. As a result, feminist counselors and therapists routinely reflect on the ways that various environmental/contextual factors in their own lives and their professional training influence

- their thinking about the process and goals of counseling and therapy

- their ability to effectively connect in mutual and empathic ways in gender-similar and gender-different helping relationships

- their interest in their clients' and their own psychological liberation and empowerment

- how these factors might facilitate or block mutuality in the therapeutic relationship

Such self-reflection and self-assessment are essential in implementing FCT. By regularly engaging in this process, counselors and psychologists can become more mindful of the relative strengths and limitations of all helping theories and more cognizant of the ways in which counseling and therapy can either contribute to the maintenance of the status quo or can serve as a liberating force (Prillitensky, 1997).

The self-reflective therapist will also be better able to avoid becoming intellectually limited in the use of a single theoretical helping perspective for various persons from diverse groups and backgrounds. The self-reflection processes not only enhances counselors' and therapist's understanding of the many ways their context and experiences affect their clients' development and worldview (as well as their own) but also facilitate the kind of psychological liberation that is a cornerstone of the FCT and MCT theories.

The commitment that FCT-oriented practitioners make to understanding the impact of contextual factors on their own development is manifested in their work with clients in counseling and psychotherapy. This commitment results in a helping approach that is intentionally designed to facilitate a greater understanding of the ways in which clients' relationship with their social/environmental contexts (e.g., clients' self-in-relation) affects their mental health and sense of psychological well-being. This approach helps FCT practitioners avoid the first myth Greenspan (1983) discussed—"It's all in your head."

Avoiding "Victimology"

By taking a self-in-relation approach to helping, FCT counselors and therapists intentionally avoid fostering a sense of **victimology** among the clients they serve. The term *victimology* refers to the belief that a person is the helpless victim of one's environmental/contextual circumstances. FCT-oriented practitioners work toward increasing women's (and men's) understanding of the responsibility to learn new ways to more effectively address unique stressors, injustices, and oppressive treatment within different environmental contexts.

To avoid promoting a sense of victimology in counseling and therapy, FCT-oriented practitioners utilize many helping strategies associated with the three major theoretical forces (e.g., psychodynamic, cognitive-behavioral, and existential-humanistic) to stimulate clients' psychological liberation as well as their individual and collective empowerment. These include, but are not limited to, the following:

- psychodynamic strategies aimed at increasing clients' understanding of contextual factors and experiences that contribute to repressed frustration and anger (Miller, 1986)

- cognitive-behavioral approaches that foster more effective and assertive communication skills, self-management abilities (e.g., through stress management and meditation training), and the eradication of irrational beliefs resulting from various forms of internalized oppression (Hill & Ballou, 2005)

- existential-humanistic helping skills that stimulate a greater acceptance for responsibility in making choices to realize new and healthy connections with others (Comstock, 2005)

These strategies incorporate some of the constructs associated with the three major theoretical forces of counseling and psychology into an FCT approach to helping. By including concepts of social positionality, hierarchies of power, and self-in-relation in the work of psychodynamic, cognitive-behavioral, and existential-humanistic oriented counselors, these traditional theoretical frameworks can become more respectful of client differences and needs. This is true for female clients as well as males, who are also adversely impacted by the various forms of sexism, patriarchy, and "gender straitjacketing" that continue to be perpetuated in our contemporary society.

Dealing with Sexism in Counseling and Therapy

Gender issues and sexism are, of course, central to feminist therapy. In their critique of the mental health professions, Hill and Ballou (2005) explain the numerous ways that gender issues and sexism are embedded in the fields of counseling and therapy. They point out that traditional systems of counseling and psychotherapy make a serious error by operating from sexist assumptions about mental health and human development. Consequently, traditional counseling and psychology research paradigms, personality theories, clinical practices are all suspect, from a feminist helping perspective.

Besides becoming knowledgeable of the various ways that gender issues and sexism impact the mental health professions, counselors and psychologists have an ethical responsibility to take into account the interface between gender and other characteristics of diversity. For example, Islamic women will have different issues than those of Jewish or Christian women; African-American men will have differing ideas on the pace of therapy than will Native American Indian or Irish-American men. Those with physical issues, gay or lesbian identity issues, spiritual issues, or other issues also will have unique perspectives. With this in mind, FCT practitioners realize that they must not assume a common context for all client concerns and issues.

A particular value conflict within feminist theory focuses on the issue of when and how female clients should be encouraged to explore issues of sexism and their impact on clients' psychological well-being and perspective on womanhood. Clearly, a fragile individual could be overwhelmed and disturbed if suddenly confronted with the social facts of her life. Marriages can be broken by the anger that often comes as a client moves from lower to higher levels of feminist consciousness. Some practitioners believe that traditional therapy is more appropriate for the "traditional woman" and that feminist therapy can be used later, when the individual has achieved a greater level of social insight. Alternatively, some see difficulty and personal pain as a necessary part of the route toward a larger, evolving feminist consciousness, psychological liberation, and collective empowerment.

It is clearly risky to promote a feminist consciousness by challenging gender roles in many women's lives. The literature on domestic violence demonstrates that raising one's voice in protest about these issues can lead to increased assaults within some male-female relationships. In some cultures, standing up for one's rights as a woman is sometimes treated as a crime. For example, under the rule of the Taliban in Afghanistan, women's "allies" were often criminalized as well, including men who fought against sexism and related issues, which was perceived as taking power away from the dominant male group.

The following transcript illustrates some of the issues and therapeutic approaches one might take into consideration when dealing with the problem of sexism from a FCT perspective. The method presented in the following transcript is different than other theories of helping, particularly in the mutual exploration by both therapist and client and the manner in which socioeconomic factors undergirding the interview are included.

Client: Yes it is, but what should I do?

Counselor: Let's see if we can explore this a bit more. For example, imagine what would happen if Joe was an apartment-mate, not a boyfriend/partner?

Client: His demands for so much attention and sex would go away, and the help with the money and the baby would still be there. My family and church would approve. But I would be lonely, and you are supposed to love and give sex to your boyfriend.

Counselor: Let's look at the hidden views under your ideas. One is that your family and the church can and should define your choices. Another is that male-female relationships are a bargain—money and childcare for attention and sex—and OK if you love him. A third is that you cannot make new choices about how to meet your own needs. The final one is that there are realities outside of our control, for example, money needed for food, rent, medical care. These factors affect us deeply but are outside of our control. Do I understand correctly?

Client: I think so but I never thought of it that way.

Counselor: In fact many social and economic arrangements often benefit one party over the other. Many people just follow the rules, assuming it's the way it is. Often the reasons behind the rules and just who benefits are not very clear. Options are not talked about. I think the key is to see all the reality and make our own choices. How does this strike you?

Client: It means I have to think about everything and then decide. That's scary and hard.

Counselor: Making decisions about what to value and how to live instead of following preset answers and patterns is difficult, and yet it can be exciting. There are conditions that are givens, like responsible childcare and needing money, about which there is little real choice. But there are also some options to sort through and choices to be made. The decisions are yours to make, and although it is hard, whatever you decide is not cast in stone. Decisions can be looked at and remade. I think the keys are to claim the power to make decisions and to make them carefully and with the complicated pieces in mind. Now, these are my ideas and I have been talking a lot. I want to listen to your ideas.

Client: I'd like to talk about deciding about Joe, especially the apartment-mate idea and relationships being mutual rather than bargains. Both are very different from the way I've thought about things.

Counselor: Maria, last week we talked about your relationship with Joe, the baby's father. You said he is living with you and the baby again. We identified the positives as meeting your family's wishes, more money to pay the bills, help with childcare and transportation, and your sense of rightness as defined by the church rules and your community's standards. We also identified the negatives as more yelling at home, which is disliked by you and upsetting for your daughter; more physical and emotional caretaking responsibilities for you; conflict about sexual demands and other relationships; a recent episode of his hitting you; and your sense of Joe's immaturity and dependence rather than experiencing him as a partner. Is this how you remember our session, and is there more to add from your thinking this week?

Client: That covers last week pretty well. This week I've been thinking that I do not love him but I need him and think he should be here. I just don't know what to do.

Counselor: What is the need to do something?

Client: I must love him and make him be a partner or have him leave and raise my baby alone.

Counselor: Are those the only options?

Client: What do you mean? I don't love him so he should go, but we need him to make it as far as money, babysitting, and transportation.

Counselor: What I mean is, you are thinking of the situation as either/or. Maybe there are some other ways to think about it. It seems instead of mutuality your relationship is a bargain, with lots of tension and conflict.

Several aspects of this interview illuminate key concepts associated with FCT. Among these are the egalitarian nature of the counselor-client relationship. The egalitarian nature of this interaction was enhanced by the active participatory manner in which both the counselor and client explored the various challenges and problems the female client brought to this helping session.

Obviously, this client was in a good place, cognitively and emotionally, to engage in the sort of counseling process that involves an in-depth exploration of the various forms of sexism that are adversely impacting her life, sense of well-being, and the level of growth that fosters mutuality in her current relationship. As a result of realizing she possesses these qualities, the client is able to actualize a new relational awareness through working with the counselor in this session.

Not all clients come to counseling and psychotherapy with this psychological disposition. What can counselors and therapists do to better understand female clients' readiness for such an approach to helping or to recognize the need to implement other intervention strategies? Feminist identity development theory can be a particularly useful resource in answering this question.

Feminist Identity Development Theory

Feminist identity theory was developed by Downing and Roush (1985) and is based on the theoretical constructs of William Cross's (1971) model of Black identity development. This theory consists of five developmental stages that describe how women construct meaning of themselves, others, and the world as a result of being subjected to various forms of sexism in society.

Stages of Feminist Identity Development Theory

According to the feminist development framework, women typically manifest qualitatively different ways of thinking about themselves, others, their social context, and the hierarchies of power in which they are situated when they enter counseling and therapy. Movement through these stages involves a shift from a general lack of awareness of the ways in which various forms of sexism affect women's mental health to an increasing understanding of these issues and a growing commitment to actively address different forms of oppression and injustice in their lives. What follows is a description of some of the indicators of a raised feminist consciousness.

Passive Acceptance. The first stage of feminist identity development is called **passive acceptance.** In this stage, women embrace traditional gender roles and see these roles as advantageous to their lives. Women either deny or are unaware of issues related to oppression, prejudice, and discrimination that occur as a result of sexism in society and in their own lives. These women are typically situated in a social context that supports traditional sex roles and is structured to maintain a hierarchy of power and privilege for a male worldview over a feminist perspective.

Operating within this gender hierarchy of power and privilege, many women exhibit an automatic acceptance of traditional female sex roles and commonly acknowledge that men are indeed superior to women in many ways. As a result, men and their roles and contributions are valued more than those of women.

Revelation. When a woman experiences a crisis or series of events that are so powerful that they call into question traditional sex role assumptions, she may move into the stage of revelation. In this stage, sexism is no longer denied, and feelings surface that cannot be ignored. Women often experience anger and guilt regarding their previous lack of awareness and general acceptance of sexism. Persons operating from this developmental stage commonly manifest dualistic thinking, where men are devalued and viewed as being oppressive while women are held in high esteem.

Embeddedness-Emanation. As women nurture closer bonds and relationships with other females who embrace a feminist consciousness, they often begin to realize new ways of thinking and acting, described as the **embeddedness-emanation** stage. In this third stage of feminist identity development, women explore and solidify new ways of thinking and feeling about womanhood and the importance of confronting the various forms of sexism that continue to exist in our contemporary society. These new ways of thinking and feeling are nurtured and supported through the connections that women have with other individuals who embrace a feminist worldview. The dualistic ways of thinking and behaving that are manifested at the second stage (the stage of revelation) begin to be replaced by more relativistic ways of conceptualizing life experiences, particularly as they relate to women's experiences with men.

Synthesis. At the fourth stage, called the **synthesis** stage, a more positive and consolidated personal identity emerges. The psychological disposition associated with the synthesis stage is marked by a more complex understanding of the important linkages that exist between the hierarchy of power arrangements that continues to disempower women, the unjust social positionality in which women are situated, and the personal problems that individual women experience in their daily lives.

The developmental advancements that occur at the synthesis stage enable women to more clearly see multiple sources of oppression that occur at different levels of their ecological context and that affect their and other women's lives. Woman operating from this stage typically value the support of other woman but increasingly voice independent views about a broad range of issues related to women's and men's lives and development.

Active Commitment. The fifth stage is called **active commitment.** While women continue to exhibit a complex understanding of the impact of sexism and become more knowledgeable of the ways in which hierarchical power arrangements negatively affect women's and men's development, those at this stage also demonstrate an active commitment to promote social justice, especially as it relates to women's rights.

Women in the active commitment stage set personal priorities based on their unique talents for effecting societal change. It is recommended that counselors and psychologists implement helping strategies that are different from those used with clients operating at the other four stages.

How can counselors/therapists intentionally work toward addressing the unique psychological perspectives manifested by female clients operating from different stages of feminist identity development? Before we address this important question, complete Competency-Building Activity 11.2. This exercise will help you think about how you would presently work with female clients who are operating from different stages in this model.

Working Intentionally with Women

It is hoped that your increased understanding of feminist identity development theory will extend your thinking about the different ways female clients may construct meaning of themselves and the challenges they experience in their lives. Competency-Building Activity 11.2 is provided to help personalize the new knowledge you may have gained by reading about Downing and Roush's theoretical framework. By considering the types of women you prefer to work with and believe you are prepared to effectively serve, you will be better positioned to reflect on the types of approaches you might intentionally use to foster the psychological health, liberation, and empowerment of all the female clients you are called on to serve in the future. **Intentionality** in counseling and therapy, highlighted in Chapter 4, is described as follows:

> Intentionality is a goal of effective counseling and therapy. This goal has two dimensions. First, from the practitioner's perspective, intentional counseling involves selecting a theoretical approach and using various skills in a deliberate and purposeful manner. The deliberate and purposeful manner in which one selects a given theoretical approach and various counseling skills depends upon a host of cultural and gender factors.
>
> Second, rather than trying to find a single correct response to clients' issues, intentional counseling is aimed at assisting individuals to look at their life situations in a new light with an increased sense of hopefulness and direction.

The feminist identity development model represents one resource that counselors and therapists can use to guide their work with women and enhance their intentionality in the process. To work effectively and intentionally with female clients, mental health practitioners need to accurately assess their clients' and their own level of feminist identity development. They also need to use therapeutic strategies and counseling skills that complement and extend clients' current constructions of themselves, the world in which they are situated, and the challenges and problems they are experiencing.

One of the strategies many feminist counselors and therapists use early in the helping process involves the implementation of a developmental-ecological assessment to

Competency-Building Activity 11.2

Becoming Aware of Your Own Approach to FCT

FCT theory suggests that counselors/therapists need to provide effective services among women who are operating at different stages of feminist identity development. Given their own personal biases and professional preparation, counselors/therapists are likely to prefer and to be better prepared to work with female clients operating from some of the stages of Downing and Roush's feminist identity development model than from other stages.

This activity is designed to serve multiple purposes. First, it is aimed at helping you gain a better understanding of the feminist identity development theory from a personal perspective. Second, it encourages you to reflect on the types of female clients you would presently prefer to work with as well as those that you have less personal interest in working with. Third, it provides an opportunity to have you reflect on the types of female clients you believe you are best prepared to work with at the present time as well as those female clients that you are not as prepared to work with professionally, given their unique feminist identity. Finally, this activity will encourage you to consider what you can do in the future to become better prepared to work with female clients.

Instructions:

Step 1. *Review the description of the five stages of Downing and Rouch's feminist identity development model.* The stages are (1) passive acceptance, (2) revelation, (3) embeddedness-emanation, (4) synthesis, and (5) active commitment.

Step 2. *Think about those you know personally or professionally who may embody some or all of the characteristics associated with each stage.*

Step 3. *Think about the types of female clients you would most prefer and be best prepared to work with at the present time.* Use the feminist identity development model as a guide. List the stage or stages that these women are likely to be operating from on a blank piece of paper.

Step 4. *List general goals you think might be appropriate to work toward with these female clients.* Then, briefly describe the counseling and psychotherapeutic approaches (e.g., psychodynamic, cognitive-behavioral, existential-humanistic, multicultural, feminist counseling) you might use to achieve the goals you listed. Try to be as specific as you can when listing the approaches and skills.

Step 5. *Think about the types of female clients you would least prefer and think you are least prepared to work with at the present time.* Use the feminist identity development model as a guide. List the stage or stages that these women are likely to be operating from on a blank piece of paper.

Step 6. *Describe general goals you think might be appropriate to work toward with these female clients, even though they are not who you would prefer to work with.* Then, briefly describe the counseling and psychotherapeutic approaches (e.g., psychodynamic, cognitive-behavioral, existential-humanistic, multicultural, feminist counseling) you might use to achieve the goals you listed for these female clients. Try to be as specific as you can when listing these approaches and skills.

Step 7. *Think about what you could do to better prepare yourself personally and professionally to work with those female clients you may not prefer to serve or believe you are not prepared to work with professionally at this time.* It is likely that you may be called on to work with female clients who manifest some or all of the characteristics associated with each stage of the feminist identity development model. It is your ethical responsibility to provide effective counseling and therapeutic services to all the clients you work with.

Step 8. *List at least two things you will commit yourself to doing in the next 30 days to increase your personal readiness and/or professional effectiveness when working with*

continued on next page

Competency-Building Activity 11.2, continued

those female clients you least prefer to work with and/or believe you are not professionally prepared to serve at the present time.

As you read further in this chapter, you may have additional ideas that will help you address the personal and professional areas

for improvement you have identified in this competency-building activity. Add any additional ideas you may come up with to the list of things you can do in step 8.

After you have completed this exercise, take time to write down some of your reactions to completing this activity and file it in your personal/professional development portfolio.

determine the client's strengths and needs. This includes thoroughly analyzing with the client how social, political, and cultural contexts impact her or his psychological development and current functioning. In doing so, counselors/therapists carefully consider the ways in which a female or a male client's ecological contexts (1) contribute to the strengths clients have developed, (2) underlie the challenges and problems they are encountering, and (3) create a certain way of viewing the world at large and oneself as a woman or a man.

It is important to point out that in directing attention to clients' personal assets, resources, and strengths as well as the specific challenges and problems that bring them to counseling and therapy, the FCT approach is similar to other helping theories discussed in this book. This includes the positive psychology/wellness counseling paradigm (Chapter 3), the microskills counseling model (Chapter 4), and the multicultural counseling and therapy metatheory (Chapter 12).

By working in an egalitarian and collaborative manner with female (and male) clients and using feminist identity development theory as a guide, practitioners can effectively learn about their clients' strengths, resources, needs, challenges, and problems from their clients' perspective. Because feminist identity theory is grounded in developmental-ecological considerations of clients' psychological processes, it leads practitioners to direct attention to the impact of multiple contexts on clients' mental health and sense of individual and collective well-being.

Focusing Intentionally on Women's Strengths

FCT theorists emphasize the importance of intentionally using a strength-based helping approach with women (and men). They do so because they are cognizant of the many ways that female clients have been (and in many instances continue to be) pathologized by traditionally trained counselors and therapists.

Brown (2000) discusses the importance of not assessing women from a pathological orientation but rather in terms of how their life experiences and coping strategies are related to the various forms of sexist oppression women encounter in life. The tendency to pathologize women's expressed concerns and problems represents one of the common ways that sexism continues to be manifested in the fields of counseling and psychology at the present time.

Feminist identity development theory provides mental health professionals with a practical framework for assessing female clients in a nonpathological manner. It also provides guidelines for working intentionally from a strength-based perspective to stimulate women's mental health, psychological liberation, and personal/collective empowerment. To assist you in thinking of some of the ways that you can work more intentionally to foster these counseling and therapy outcomes, we present the following discussion, which focuses on the different helping strategies counselors/therapists can use with women who are operating at different stages of Downing and Roush's feminist identity development model.

Working with Persons at Stage 1: Passive Acceptance. Clients operating from the passive acceptance stage may be the most difficult to help develop a more complex feminist identity. This is because they are embedded in a sexist orientation to life and willingly accept traditional sex roles. As such, female clients operating from this stage may prefer a male therapist, since males are often viewed as being generally superior to and more competent than female counselors.

Women at this stage may have difficulty accepting many of the major tenets of feminist therapy. This may include having difficulty with the egalitarian relationship that FCT counselors work to establish with their clients. Consequently, it may be useful to operate in a direct manner and assert the role as "expert" to build a trusting relationship with passive acceptance stage clients early in the helping process. This is useful to do before trying to create a more egalitarian helping approach with women who exhibit characteristics of the passive acceptance stage.

Because passive acceptance stage persons are usually not interested in exploring women's issues and the impact of sexism on their own and other women's mental health, it is important that counselors and therapists affirm the dignity of these clients as it is manifested in their current stage of feminist identity development. This can be done by addressing the expressed needs and concerns of clients in this stage and not examining feminist considerations until a more trusting therapeutic relationship has been developed.

Once a positive therapeutic relationship has been established with these clients, it may be appropriate for the counselor or therapist to introduce gender-related issues into the helping process. Clients who continue to resist exploring these issues will signal the counselor that they are not ready or interested in probing these issues further. When this occurs, the counselor should respectfully refrain from pursuing these issues.

However, if the client signals a readiness to begin to explore these issues, the counselor should proceed slowly and cautiously, so as not to outpace the client beyond her state of readiness. After exploring how gender issues may relate to the client's current challenges, the practitioner may want to help the client examine some of the ways she might benefit from the current arrangements of power in her relationships. This discussion may eventually include an examination of the ways in which the client plays a subservient role to maintain these benefits.

If the client continues to exhibit an interest in probing the meaning of gender issues for her life as well as the lives of other women, the counselor or therapist may consider the appropriateness of exploring other important factors related to FCT. This may include, but is not limited to, exploring how issues related to dependence, passivity, patriarchy, and gender socialization affect women's and men's psychological development.

As the client demonstrates a greater level of trust and openness in counseling and therapy, FCT-oriented counselors can make an intentional effort to build a more egalitarian relationship with passive acceptance individuals. The counselor can begin this process by intentionally asking the client if they can work together to assess the progress the client believes she has made up to that point in time in counseling. They then can talk in a mutual manner about benefits the client may derive from modifying previous goals or establishing new goals.

By intentionally striving to build an egalitarian relation in this way, the counselor can help foster a new sense of empowerment among female clients who have grown accustomed to operating in a generally subservient manner in the stage of passive acceptance. This strategy can be further nurtured by introducing these clients to bibliotherapy and cinematherapy—that is, recommending that as a part of their therapeutic "homework" they read books and view videos that depict other women who are grappling with gender-related issues. This exposure can help stimulate new ways of thinking about the traditional roles women are expected to play versus newer roles of psychological liberation and empowerment. In this way, counselors and therapists may help stimulate a shift in the these clients' way of thinking toward the next stage of feminist identity development.

Working with Persons at Stage 2: Revelation. When a woman experiences a crisis or series of powerful events that confront her previously unquestioned traditional sex role assumptions, she is often catapulted into the second stage of feminist identity, called the revelation stage. As a result, the problem of sexism can no longer be denied. The increasing awareness and acknowledgment of this complex problem and the adverse impact it has on women typically results in heightened feelings of anger and guilt.

This level of feminist consciousness is often an entry point into therapy, as many women experience a growing need to deal with their heightened feelings of anger and guilt. Since men are often viewed as oppressors at this stage, these clients likely will gravitate to female therapists.

At this stage, clients are more receptive to examining how external conditions and gender socialization have impacted and continue to impact their mental health and sense of empowerment. Counselors and therapists can play an important role in helping clients in this stage uncover how their socialization and stereotypic views of the roles and functions of men and women have contributed to their own psychological incarceration and disempowerment. Working with these issues in counseling and therapy includes an intentional and in-depth analysis of the costs and benefits of maintaining a traditional sex role orientation in life.

While it is vital to communicate a genuine sense of empathy in affirming the client's anger and guilt at this stage, it is equally important to assist these clients in exploring how they think these feelings can be used as a catalyst for positive change rather than an excuse for personal immobilization and nonaction. By affirming these clients' feelings and helping them extend their thinking about the ways in which their feelings are connected to external sources of sexism and injustice, counselors and therapists will be better able to assist these women in shifting from a reactive mode characterized by anger and guilt to a more proactive cognitive-behavioral approach to their life situation.

FCT-minded counselors and therapists are likely to more readily offer advice and use appropriate self-disclosure when working with revelation stage female clients than traditionally trained practitioners. There are several reasons for intentionally using these strategies when working with these clients. First, offering advice can facilitate new ways of thinking among many clients at the revelation stage. The new insights female clients can gain from this advice may help balance the heightened and disruptive emotions they are experiencing as a result of their awareness of the impact that sexism has on their lives and the lives of other women in society.

Second, although most traditional helping theories discourage giving advice in individual counseling and psychotherapy situations, this counseling strategy can help these clients think about what they can do to more effectively deal with their feelings of anger and guilt. It should be emphasized that the advice giving should not be done in an authoritarian manner, but, rather, it should be presented as suggestions for the client to consider and respond to within an egalitarian relationship. In this sort of relationship, clients are given the space to agree or disagree with the advice offered by the counselor or therapist.

Third, FCT-oriented counselors and therapists who also intentionally use appropriate levels of self-disclosure can serve as a model for the client needing to find new ways to more effectively channel her feelings of anger and guilt, which, unless addressed, could lead to increased feelings of hopelessness and cynicism. Similar to the advice-giving strategy, the intentional utilization of appropriate self-disclosure should be done in the context of an egalitarian relationship. Counselors can encourage individuals to apply whatever insights they may gain from the therapist's modeling to their own unique life situations if they think this will be useful.

By maintaining an egalitarian relationship, which most revelation stage clients prefer, practitioners can serve as a positive model to the client and avoid the inappropriate imposition of power dynamics that imply that the client should do what the therapist would do. When used appropriately, self-disclosure can foster clients' empowerment and psychological liberation. This occurs when individuals genuinely feel free to use all, some, or none of the information they receive from the counselor's self-disclosure.

Many cognitive-behavioral approaches discussed in Chapter 7 are also helpful to implement with revelation stage clients. This includes the use of meditation and relaxation training as well as assertiveness training. While meditation and relaxation training can be useful in helping clients at this stage more effectively mange their heightened feelings of anger and guilt, assertiveness training can increase the skills they will need to actively and effectively deal with future sexist situations. All three of these cognitive-behavioral approaches (meditation, relaxation training, and assertiveness training) can help promote the development of a greater sense of empowerment and psychological liberation, which are foundational in FCT.

Working with Persons at Stage 3: Embeddedness-Emanation. Persons functioning at the embeddedness-emanation stage are distinguished from individuals operating at the two preceding stages by their increased motivation to explore and solidify new ways of thinking and feeling about womanhood and the need to confront various forms of sexism and other social injustices. These new ways of thinking and feeling are nurtured and supported through the connections women at the embeddedness-emanation stage have with other individuals, particularly those who embrace a similar feminist worldview and experience similar struggles in realizing a greater level of psychological liberation and collective empowerment.

As a greater collective consciousness emerges at this stage, the therapy of choice for these women is group counseling. Counselors/therapists who work with female clients at the embedded-emanation stage are well positioned to help these clients understand the benefits of moving into a group counseling situation.

Group counseling modalities that are intentionally aimed at helping female clients consolidate a more expansive feminist identity can be quite effective with persons at the embeddedness-emanation stage. To facilitate this outcome, counselors/therapists need to refer these clients to a group that provides a safe place to nurture their growing feminist values.

Among the tasks that are helpful to address in stimulating the psychological development of women who exhibit characteristics associated with the embeddedness-emanation stage include

- consciousness raising

- naming issues related to sexism, gender oppression, and social injustice

- discussing power issues, especially as they relate to the gender/cultural/racial hierarchies of power in society

- exploring clients' thoughts and feelings about these issues in greater depth

- providing opportunities for female clients operating at the embeddedness-emanation stage to bond with other women experiencing similar challenges

Practitioners can use Fritz Perls's empty chair technique (Chapter 10) to assist female clients at the embeddedness-emanation stage come to a deeper understanding of the impact that others' mistreatment has had on them. Perls's top dog/underdog technique (Chapter 10) may be another useful helping strategy.

Group counseling and therapy provide an opportunity for women to explore these issues and discuss other developmental tasks in a safe, respectful, challenging, and empowering environment. In addition to these interventions, there are a number of other "therapeutic" activities designed to further promote the psychological liberation and empowerment of women at the embeddedness-emanation stage, including (1) linking female clients to community events that honor and showcase women, (2) encouraging women to see movies and plays that deal with feminist issues, and (3) introducing them to other female role models through the use of bibliotherapy. If the therapist's level of feminist identity is beyond that of the clients, real-life examples from the therapist's own struggles for liberation and empowerment may provide powerful models for development and transformation. In providing these examples, the therapist is able to model the relational competencies that clients at this stage can aim to attain and realize.

FCT counselors and therapists also intentionally utilize helping strategies aimed at assisting these clients to view men in a different light. Whether it is done within the context of individual or group counseling and therapy or in follow-up conversations, practitioners can encourage discussions that assist women to view men less as a stereotypic collective group and more as individuals. By intentionally facilitating these discussions with clients operating at this stage, counselors/therapists can assist female clients to move beyond dualistic thinking about men and women (e.g., men are oppressive and women are empowering) that characterizes persons at the earlier stages of feminist identity development.

Working with Persons at Stage 4: Synthesis. At this stage, the central task for counselors and therapists is to facilitate a more differentiated understanding and affirmation of their female clients' identity. This process includes assisting women to develop a more complex understanding of their similarities and differences with other women as well as of the impact that different environmental contexts they are a part of have on their lives. By working to extend women's understanding of these issues, FCT practitioners intentionally assist synthesis stage clients in exploring new and uncharted dimensions of their own personal identity as it relates to and extends beyond their identification with their gender group.

Individual counseling and therapy may be a particularly appropriate helping modality to use in addressing these issues. Within individual counseling and therapy settings, synthesis stage women have the opportunity to more freely examine the costs and benefits of engaging in the sort of "group think" that women at the revelation and embedded-emanation stages commonly exhibit.

Self-reflection is a key psychological process in acquiring a more differentiated sense of psychological liberation and empowerment at the synthesis stage. Recognizing this, counselors and therapists can intentionally employ helping strategies that encourage clients at this stage to (1) reflect on their past histories and present life situations from a contextual-ecological perspective, (2) more fully analyze from a feminist perspective how they have come to be the person they are, and (3) explore the choices they can make in the future to realize new and untapped dimensions of their humanity.

Some of the traditional counseling and therapy theories discussed in this book are helpful in assisting female clients at the synthesis stage to achieve these objectives. The nondirective helping approach developed by Carl Rogers (Chapter 9) is helpful in assisting women to reflect on their past histories and present life situation in a nonjudgmental and affirming manner. Rogers's insistence on exhibiting genuine empathy in counseling and therapy is another important consideration when working with women at the synthesis stage.

Communicating a nonjudgmental and empathic attitude is vital when working with all women, regardless of their stage of feminist identity development. However, the Rogerian approach is particularly helpful in enabling individuals at the synthesis stage to develop a more differentiated and integrated sense of who they are as individuals and as a part of a gender group that continues to be oppressed and unfairly treated in our society.

Viktor Frankl's logotherapy theory (Chapter 10) is another traditional therapeutic approach that has relevance for work with synthesis stage clients. Practitioners may find Frankl's dereflection technique to be particularly helpful when working with clients who have reached an impasse from fixating on negative aspects of their past experiences as females.

The dereflection technique may also be useful when these clients exhibit a growing sense of cynicism and hopelessness over the harmful impact of sexism and other social injustices. FCT counselors/therapists can implement this helping strategy by encouraging their female clients to not lose sight of the positive potentiality that can be attained by engaging in the difficult and ongoing struggle to realize untapped aspects of women's psychological liberation and collective empowerment.

Working with Persons at Stage 5: Active Commitment. Women operating at the active commitment stage pose unique challenges for mental health practitioners. First, women at the active commitment stage possess an understanding of the adverse impact that sexism and other forms of cultural oppression (e.g., racism, heterosexism, ageism) have on women's and men's development. This awareness extends beyond the knowledge and sensitivity many other people have about these issues, including many counselors/therapists.

These women are also very cognizant of the hierarchical power arrangements that underlie such social injustices and know how such arrangements effectively disempower women and negatively affect men. Their understanding of these societal dynamics is further enhanced by a clear understanding of the many ways in which sexism and other social injustices are deeply ingrained in the organizational and institutional structures that make up our society. This includes being knowledgeable of the many ways that sexism and gender biases continue to be concretely manifested in our nation's religious, economic, educational, health care, media, political institutions, organizations, and communities.

In addition to possessing a complex understanding of the world from a feminist perspective, women at this stage are also highly motivated to actively participate in endeavors designed to promote organizational, institutional, community, and societal changes that are congruent with their social justice principles. The breadth and scope of their understanding of these issues and their commitment for action represent unique strengths that clearly distinguish individuals operating from this fifth stage of feminist identity development from women at other stages of this theoretical framework.

Paradoxically, these strengths also represent major sources of stress, which can negatively affect the psychological health and well-being of women at this stage. Having this expanded psychological perspective is not common, and thus operating at this stage can be a lonely endeavor that may result in a heightened sense of stress and disconnection from others.

Another major source of stress for women at the active commitment stage involves the various ways in which their understanding of sexism and other forms of cultural oppression are dismissed and marginalized in society. Women at the active commitment stage commonly experience feelings of marginalization in different ways. One the one hand, the sophisticated knowledge these women have about how sexism and other forms of social injustice get concretely played out on a daily basis in our society is easily dismissed by many men, whose motivation in doing so is grounded in an interest in maintaining the status quo and their privileged position in it.

On the other hand, many persons at this stage can be marginalized by other women who are not operating from the same perspective of psychological liberation and empowerment. This marginalization frequently results in individuals at this stage being viewed with suspicion, distrust, and trepidation by women at the first stages. This sort of marginalization is communicated in different ways by women who are comfortable with the status quo (passive acceptance), preoccupied with heightened anger and guilt over their experience with sexism (revelation), in need of exploring and solidifying new ways of thinking and feeling about their womanhood (embeddedness-emanation), or simply are less committed to feminist and social justice activism (synthesis). These forms of marginalization can lead to an increased sense of disconnection that can contribute to the unhealthy stressors many active commitment stage women encounter in their lives.

Numerous feminist theorists have discussed the negative outcomes that many women (and men) experience when they are psychologically disconnected from other people, especially from individuals with whom they would like to have a more authentic and mutually respectful relationship (Hill & Ballou, 2005; Jordan, 2001). In focusing on these issues, feminist theorists have extended the FCT paradigm by developing what is referred to as relational-cultural theory (RCT). This theoretical model directs attention to the ongoing challenges women (and men) face in negotiating the connections and disconnections that represent a normal part of life and people's interactions with others (Comstock, 2005).

Although discussed in greater detail later in this chapter, it is suggested that RCT approaches to counseling and therapy can be an effective way to assist women at the fifth stage of feminist identity development in dealing with the unique stressors they commonly encounter in their lives. RCT directs particular attention to the ways in which clients' connections and disconnections with others contribute to their feelings of stress, frustration, and shame.

Comstock (2005) explains this further by noting that "basic to RCT is the process of moving through connections, disconnections, and back into new, transformative, and enhanced connections with others" (Comstock & Qin, 2005, p. 32).

Thus, this helping theory suggests that, while a sense of disconnection with others is a normal and inherent part of life and human development, all individuals have a fundamental yearning for connection. Consequently, one of the central challenges that underlie human development is to have women (and men) learn how to effectively negotiate disconnections that predictably occur during one's life in ways that lead to increased mutual empathy, understanding, respect, and authenticity with others. This may be especially helpful when women at the active commitment stage express concern about their sense of marginalization by and disconnection with others.

By communicating mutual empathy in counseling and therapeutic sessions with active commitment stage women, mental health practitioners can help build a unique collaborative alliance that enables these female clients to explore new dimensions of their potential connections with others as well as analyze some of the underlying factors that contribute to their sense of disconnection and marginalization. This therapeutic exploration and analysis is aimed at intentionally stimulating an increased level of differentiation in clients' self-understanding and assisting clients to develop new images of their present and future relationships with others (Miller & Stiver, 1995). These new relational images can help illuminate how clients can more effectively

- accept themselves and others for who they are

- use this increased awareness and acceptance to enact new interpersonal interactions that stimulate a greater sense of mutual respect and authenticity with others

- determine when it is important to disconnect from interpersonal relationships that result in an undermining of mutual respect and authenticity

- reflect on how and if they can or should move beyond their sense of disconnection with specific persons

- make an effort to reconnect (if they determine that this is the course of action to take) in ways that are intended to foster transformative relational changes with others

RCT theorists' claims about the positive psychological benefits that ensue from intentionally promoting mutual empathy, increased differentiation, and new relational images in counseling and therapy are supported by a growing body of research in this area (Comstock, 2005; Jordan, 2001; Miller & Stiver, 1997). In addition to these therapeutic approaches, it is important to reflect on the qualities that counselors and therapists themselves need to bring to the helping encounter to work effectively with these clients.

It is also important for FCT practitioners to possess some of the same psychological characteristics as their active commitment stage clients. This includes (1) understanding the adverse impact that sexism and other forms of cultural oppression (e.g., racism, heterosexism, and ageism) have on women's and men's development, (2) being cognizant of the hierarchical power arrangements that underlie these social injustices,

Competency-Building Activity 11.3

Expanding Your Thinking about Using FCT Strategies

Instructions: Take a few minutes to read over the personal/professional development entry you wrote after you completed Competency-Building Activity 11.2. Now that you have read about the different helping strategies counselors and therapists might intentionally implement when working with clients operating at different feminist identity development stages, write down any new thoughts you may now have about this issue. Be sure to file your reactions to this exercise in your personal/professional development portfolio when you have finished.

---

(3) being knowledgeable as to how such power arrangements effectively disempower women and negatively affect men, (4) cultivating an awareness of the many ways that sexism and other social injustices are deeply ingrained in organizational and institutional structures, and (5) possessing a personal understanding of what it means to be marginalized for one's beliefs and actions.

In Competency-Building Activity 11.2, you were encouraged to reflect on some of the counseling and therapy strategies you thought you might employ when working with female clients. By completing Competency-Building Activity 11.3, you can assess how your thinking about counseling women may have been affected by reading the counseling and therapy approaches described above.

FCT and Multicultural Counseling and Therapy

There are many aspects of FCT that can be applied to the practice of multicultural counseling and therapy (MCT) (Chapters 2 and 12). For example, the emphasis that FCT-oriented counselors/therapists place on external reality and its impact on their clients is central to MCT theory. Although the concept of power is often missing in psychodynamic, cognitive-behavioral, existential-humanistic, and other psychotherapeutic theories, it is an essential concept in both FCT and MCT theories. The idea that working in a community context can be more important than one-on-one counseling is challenging to the psychotherapy and counseling establishment but central to feminist and multicultural practitioners.

Despite the ways that FCT complements MCT, feminist counseling theorists have received sharp criticsm in the past from multicultural advocates (Barret, 2005, hooks, 2000). These criticisms largely focus on the cultural and racial biases and insensitivies that many FCT theorists and researchers reflect in their earlier writings.

Over the past several years, many FCT theorists, researchers, and practioners have worked to address these criticisms. As a result, FCT theorists and researchers have directed increasing attention to the linkages that exist between clients' gender and their cultural/ethnic/racial background and group identity. Competency-Building Activity 11.4 is designed to help you adapt some of the ideas of feminist and MCT theory in an interview setting.

Competency-Building Activity 11.4

Applying Feminist Theory in Practice

Instructions: The following exercise can be useful in learning how to adapt the ideas of feminist with multicultural counseling theory when conducting an interview that focuses on issues of reality and possible oppression. You will need the assistance of a client or a volunteer to complete this exercise by following the five steps presented below.

Step 1. *Storytelling.* Ask the person you are working with to recall an incident in which she or he felt vaguely uncomfortable. For example, you may encourage the volunteer to think of an incident of feeling embarrassed about her or his appearance, awkward behavior, or somewhat inferior to others. One specific example might be a situation in which the individual encountered people of a different social class or cultural background.

Step 2. *Identifying themes.* Draw out the story of the uncomfortable or embarrassing incident using the basic listening sequence described in Chapter 4. Be sure to summarize key facts, feelings, and thoughts as your volunteer expresses them.

Step 3. *Gender analysis.* Proceed by conducting a feminist or gender analysis of the story. You can do this by asking, "How does being a man or a woman affect this story?" Often people tend to first look internally and "blame" themselves for what happened. The general purpose of reviewing the narrative from a gender perspective is to consider how these issues might change the way we look at reality.

Step 4. *Oppression/harassment analysis.* It is particularly important to look for real issues of oppression or harassment that may occur in the story. Oppression may come from others to the client or can originate unconsciously as self-oppression (e.g., internalized oppression). It also can be helpful to review the same story from an ethnic/racial perspective. Religious or spiritual dimensions may provide still other views of the same story.

Step 5. *Informing the client/volunteer about oppression or other contextual issues.* One of the major tenets of feminist and MCT theories is the emphasis these theoretical models place on explaining clients' development and behaviors from an environmental/contextual perspective. Many times clients will continue to blame themselves when it is obvious that responsibility for the events lies outside the person. Counselors and therapists can carefully assist clients to construct alternative views about their contextual reality by using FCT and MCT helping approaches in their clinical practices.

You can try to do this at this point in the interview by spending a few minutes brainstorming alternative ways of analyzing the client's story. Then discuss with your client or volunteer other reactions to the situation now that she or he has looked at it from a different perspective.

Be sure to end this activity by asking your volunteer what she or he thought of this exercise. Also, take time to write down your own reactions to this competency-building activity and file it in your personal/professional development portfolio.

Relational-Cultural Theory

As briefly stated earlier, the ongoing evolution of feminist counseling and therapy movement has led to the creation of another new theoretical framework called **relational-cultural theory** or **RCT.** Comstock and her colleagues (2002) describe RCT as follows:

The relational-cultural model was conceived after the publication of *Toward a New Psychology of Women* (Miller, 1976). . . . What followed was the unfolding of what is sometimes referred to as "self-in-relation" theory or the "relational-cultural model" of counseling and therapy.

The relational-cultural model looks at all interpersonal dynamics through a relational lens. Miller and Stiver (1997) suggested that although individuals yearn for connection with others, they develop a repertoire of strategies that keep them out of connection. Such strategies, for example, include withholding love and affection, withdrawing from others, criticizing loved ones, and hiding authentic feelings (Hartling, Rosen, Walker, & Jordan, 2000). At worst, these strategies are destructive and could involve addictions, compulsions, abrasive behaviors, eating disorders, and workaholism. Each of these strategies has the potential to keep individuals out of relationships and subsequently to evoke a deep sense of shame (Hartling et al., 2000; Jordan & Dooley, 2000).

The relational model provides an alternative perspective to traditional ways of viewing both internal processes and relational dynamics in counseling and therapy. For example, traditional therapies value the identities of individuation, separation, and autonomy and generally honor the concept of the "self" (Fedele, 1994). In contrast, this model espouses that we become increasingly relationally complex rather than more individuated and autonomous over the life span. The uniqueness of relational therapy is its focus on achieving growth by enhancing each individual's capacity to create, build, sustain, and deepen connection as a life-long goal. (pp. 254–256)

As with multicultural counseling theories, the creators of RCT realize that many clients blame themselves for problems that are linked directly to the sociocultural contexts of which they are a part. Consequently, much attention is placed on clients' environmental contexts to understand their problems and challenges as well as to identify their sources of personal and collective strength and support.

RCT differs from multicultural counseling and therapy theories by the emphasis it places on the relational connections and disconnections people experience in their lives. RCT theorists readily acknowledge that people normally encounter various relational connections and disconnections throughout their lives. However, they also assert that the way people navigate through these relational changes significantly affects their mental health, psychological development, and sense of empowerment across the life span. Comstock et al. (2002) explain these points further:

According to this model, understanding one's relational capacities in a sociocultural context allows one to move out of a place of shame and frustration and into the possibility for more mutually empathic and authentic connections (Hartling et al., 2000; Walker, 2001). As such, the relational model can be used with both women and men from diverse backgrounds and in counseling settings that address a multitude of issues (Jordan & Dooley, 2000). (p. 256)

Key Concepts Associated with RCT

Mutual empathy, connections and disconnections, the central relational paradox, and relational images are key concepts associated with RCT. As stated earlier, **mutual empathy** extends our thinking about the more common expression of "one-way" empathy, which was popularized in Rogers's counseling theory (Chapter 9).

Rogers emphasizes the importance of communicating a genuine sense of empathy to enable clients to experience greater personal acceptance, validation, and psychological well-being. Mutual empathy, on the other hand, refers to more empowering and psychologically liberating human experiences that go beyond Rogers's theoretical views. According to RCT theorists, these experiences occur when the listener (e.g., the therapist) shows that she or he has been affected by the experiences of the other (e.g., the client). The client not only experiences acceptance and affirmation by the therapist but also recognizes that she or he has impacted and changed the counselor in this way (Comstock, Duffey, & St. George, 2002).

The increasing personal power people experience in mutual connection with others stimulates a greater level of psychological liberation. This occurs as individuals move from feelings of self-doubt, shame, and frustration to a clearer understanding of how they can affect others who engage in mutually empathic, respectful, and authentic relations. Thus, mutual empathy results in more empowering and liberating relational development as a result of (1) the heightened authenticity and mutuality that is manifested in such connections and (2) a more differentiated understanding of the connections and disconnections we have with people in our lives.

Commenting on empathy as discussed by the ideas of Rogers and RCT on mutual empathy, Comstock (2006, personal communication) pointed out that "Rogers never much addressed how he handled or named the 'disconnections' or 'empathic failures' that happen all the time. It is important to understand that our empathic capacities grow in relationship like everything else and expand/transform when we name our disconnections, not by pretending we don't have them."

Also, one of Rogers's goals for his clients was helping them become more aware of themselves as unique individuals. In contrast, RCT involves developing increased relational competencies and an increased capacity for authentic relating and resistance to the forces of disconnection, both interpersonally and sociopolitically, as these are often one and the same. Rather than asserting that individuating is key in one's development (as the three traditional theoretical forces in counseling and therapy agree), RCT maintains that the acquisition of new and more differentiated relational competencies and mutual empathy are vital for healthy human development across the life span.

In essence, mutual empathy broadens and deepens both the counselor's and the client's experience and perspective. Miller and Stiver (1997) point out that this results in people becoming more "empathically attuned, emotionally responsive, authentically present, and open to change" (p. 11).

Building mutual empathic bridges in counseling and therapy provides a means for clients to explore the various ways in which their **connections** and **disconnections** with others affect their development. Miller (1986) explains that when authentic and mutually empathic connections occur:

> Each person feels a greater sense of "zest" (vitality, energy); each person feels more able to act and does; each person has a more accurate picture of her/himself and of the other person(s); each person feels more connected to the other person(s) and feels a greater motivation for connections with other people beyond those in specific relationships (p. 3).

The opposite characteristics are manifested when people experience unhealthy disconnections with others, including "decreased energy; an inability to act; a lack of clarity or confusion regarding self and other; decreased self-worth; and the turning away from relationship with others" (Jordan & Dooley, 2000, p. 13).

It is important to reiterate that the process of experiencing connections and disconnections with others is a natural and reoccurring part of life. From an RCT perspective, it is equally important to understand the transformative, empowering, and liberating potential that is inherent in moving through our connections and disconnections and then reconnecting with others. Jordan (1992) addressed this potentiality by stating:

> In cases of disconnection, transformation involves awareness of the forces creating the disconnection, discovery of a means for reconnecting, and building a more differentiated and solid connection. The movement into and out of connection becomes a journey of discovery about self, other, and relationship—about "being in relation." (p. 8)

RCT practitioners realize that, while everyone yearns for connection, we all employ strategies that result in various kinds of disconnection from others, from the world at large, and from ourselves. This common human phenomenon is referred to as the **central relational paradox** (Miller & Stiver, 1997).

While it is agreed that disconnections are an inherent part of life, RCT counselors and therapists take time to explore the reasons why clients implement strategies for disconnection in their lives. They also work with clients to examine the creative and empowering potential that is linked to enlarging mutual empathy in their connections with others. According to RCT theorists, this empowerment stimulates a growing sense of relational resilience and competence, both of which are critical aspects of mental health and psychological well-being from this theoretical perspective (Comstock et al., 2002). Thus, some of the central roles RCT practitioners play in counseling and therapy include helping clients to

- recognize where mutual agreement and empathy are possible in relationships that are becoming disconnected
- understand how such agreement and empathy can strengthen their relational competencies and resilience
- determine when, how, and why they may need to employ strategies for disconnection with certain persons who are clearly having a toxic impact on their lives

The process of collaborating with clients about these issues leads to the development of new, more empowering, and liberating **relational images.** It is important to assist clients in developing these kinds of new relational images, because many people go through life engaging in relationships in which they are denied empathic possibilities. When this occurs, people learn to adapt to relational images that are devoid of meaningful connection, mutual empathy, and authenticity. Such images "are frustrating and binding because they negate the possibility for new relational possibilities. In reality, individuals may have more relational possibilities than they are able to construe. In RCT counseling and therapy situations, clients create the possibilities of the here and now as they struggle with the disappointments, abuses, and violations of the past" (Comstock et al., 2002, p. 261).

Implementing RCT in Practice

Jordan (1992) describes four stages of RCT, which include movement from (1) supported vulnerability to (2) flexibility, (3) empowerment and conflict, and (4) relational confidence and awareness. At the beginning stage of RCT, the challenge is to create a space of safety in which clients are willing to make themselves vulnerable to discussing and working through disconnections in their lives. RCT counselors and therapists intentionally assist clients in becoming more conscious of the possible patterns that underlie their clients' disconnections and openly explore what prevents them from seeking support and connection from their disconnected relational experiences. This is a creative and difficult phase in RCT, given the **vulnerability** that clients experience when they explore these relational issues.

As clients develop trust in the RCT therapist and further explore the meaning of their relational connections and disconnections, they are ready to move to the second stage of RCT. This involves developing new and more differentiated ways of thinking about how they can relate to themselves, other people, and the world in which they are situated. In doing so, clients develop greater **relational flexibility** as a result of making finer distinctions between disconnected relationships that may be potentially growth fostering and in need of reengagement from those disconnections that act as protection from nonmutual and toxic relationships.

At the third stage of RCT, counselors and therapists and clients work together to explore the interconnections that exist between clients' newly emerging sense of **empowerment** and **conflicts** they experience with others. Clients become more empowered as a result of learning to more effectively manage the predictable relational changes they encounter throughout their lives. The sense of empowerment that clients experience as a result of learning how to better manage these relational changes leads to a sense of **relational confidence** and **resilience.**

During the final stage of RCT, clients and counselors work together to discover how issues related to vulnerability, flexibility, empowerment, and conflict facilitate the realization of a greater sense of relational confidence and resilience. As clients acquire new insights and develop new abilities that enable them to rework their disconnections and empathic failures, they are better able to handle other relational challenges that occur. These developmental advancements constitute the essence of a person's relational confidence and resilience, characteristics that are viewed from an RCT perspective as the cornerstones of psychological health and well-being.

Clearly, not all clients are suitable for RCT. Counselors and therapists need to consider a host of factors regarding a person's readiness to engage in RCT. This includes assessing clients' level of self-awareness, their willingness to be influenced by others, and their cognitive and communication capacities related to these skills (Comstock et al., 2002). As noted previously, however, RCT may be particularly helpful to implement when working with women who are operating in the fifth stage (active commitment) of Downing and Roush's (1985) feminist identity development theory.

The Professional Development Extension summarizes the impact of the feminist perspective on contemporary society. It also briefly describes some of the contributions that counselors and therapists can make to advance this perspective in their work as mental health professionals.

Summary

Many of the constructs and theories discussed in this book are open to feminist critique. This is done to illuminate the ways in which traditional helping theories complement and conflict with the psychological strengths, needs, challenges, and problems female clients bring to counseling and therapy.

This chapter provides information that is aimed at increasing your understanding of the development of the feminist counseling movement in the United States. Key characteristics of FCT include:

1. *Building an egalitarian relationship.* Feminist therapists consider themselves partners with their clients and value women and their need for mutual support and exploration. Self-disclosure of one's own personal experiences as a therapist is a particularly important part of the therapeutic process. Important here is the concept of power. Feminist therapy emphasizes sharing power and working against domination by any group.

2. *Valuing pluralism.* Feminist theory values difference. Although focused on women, the feminist approach also recognizes the many dimensions of the RESPECTFUL counseling framework (D'Andrea & Daniels, 2001b). Again, the issue of power is critical. One cannot be free if others are restricted. A basic tenet of feminist counseling and therapy is the awareness of the need to respect the multidimensionality of other persons.

3. *External emphasis.* Whereas much of cognitive-behavioral theory focuses on internal thoughts, feminist theory stresses that oppressive aspects of reality (such

Professional Development Extension

How the Feminist Perspective Has Revolutionized Thinking about Human Development

The emergence of the feminist perspective in the latter half of the 20th century has had a revolutionary impact on how people think not only about the way that women need to be treated in our society but also about the role that mental health professionals can play in promoting human development. While much more work needs to be done in addressing the various forms of sexism and the hierarchies of power that sustain sexist thinking and behavior in our nation, the progress that has been made in promoting women's dignity and development over the past 40 years is indisputable.

Much of this progress can directly be attributed to many of the principles that are embedded in a feminist worldview in general and reflected in FCT practices in particular. For instance, the emphasis that feminist advocates place on building egalitarian relationships between men and women (a concept that is also key in FCT) has led to the empowerment and psychological liberation of countless numbers of women in various settings over the past several decades. Not only has this resulted in the realization of a higher level of justice in our society, but it has also contributed to an enhanced sense of psychological well-being among many women as individuals and the growth of an empowered group identity.

This collective empowerment is further enhanced by a growing understanding and respect for the different perspectives, strengths, and needs of women from diverse cultural/ethnic/racial groups. The increased recognition and acceptance of these differences has led to greater solidarity among women from diverse backgrounds who are committed to ameliorating the unique forms of sexism that are tied to other social injustices, such as racism, heterosexism, ableism, and classism, to name a few.

Counselors and psychologists can make important contributions to further advance the feminist perspective by advocating for a continued and increased guarantee of equal rights for all women. They can do this in the work they do as organizational development consultants in schools, businesses, government agencies, and communities. They can also do this when consulting with individual

as sexism and heterosexism) may need to be addressed directly—"It is not what we think of things, but rather what is which must be addressed" (M. Ivey, 1994).

4. *Using community resources.* Feminist counseling and therapy does not end with the completion of the psychotherapeutic interview. Many clients are referred to women's support groups, community action work, legal aid, and other relevant community services.

5. *Implementing an active, participatory counseling style.* Feelings are considered important, but confrontation of discrepancies in the client and between the client and society are also viewed as being important in the helping process. For example, the therapist might work with a client who is full of conflict to understand the emotional aspect of one's problems but also confront the client with the need for growth and resolution. Although the therapist may be warm and supportive, a gradual move toward more differentiated thinking on the client's part is emphasized. The therapist is likely to use most of the techniques discussed in this book (such as assertiveness training, Frankl's dereflection, dream

parents and teachers about the growth and development of girls and boys in our public schools and community agencies.

A number of issues covered in this chapter represent important considerations that counselors and psychologists might keep in mind when implementing these consultation services in the field. In addition to emphasizing the psychological benefits associated with building egalitarian relationships among people from diverse gendered groups and cultural/racial backgrounds in school, business, and community settings, mental health professionals can provide additional information that focuses on other key concepts related to the FCT worldview. This includes:

1. providing information about those community resources that may be helpful in addressing the needs of schools, businesses, organizations, and communities interested in promoting the mental health and well-being of all of its constituents from a feminist perspective

2. encouraging the use of active and participatory approaches to decision making that include all the members of the school, business, organization, and/or community where one works

3. noting the empowering potential that commonly is realized when individuals have the opportunity to become more fully engaged in community service projects that are intentionally aimed at promoting social justice and eradicating various forms of cultural oppression that continue to exist in our society

4. emphasizing the positive psychological benefits that predictably ensue when leaders in these environmental settings routinely provide personal validation for the work that the persons do who make up the schools, businesses, and communities

These are some of the practical suggestions that highlight how the feminist perspective can complement and extend the work mental health professionals do in a variety of settings. You can probably think of other ways you might implement the ideas presented in this chapter to have a more positive and lasting psychological impact on larger numbers of persons from diverse groups and backgrounds.

analysis, and so forth) but will do so with an awareness of the feminist context of the helping process.

6. *Information giving.* A strong educational component exists in feminist counseling. The client may be instructed in social/historical facts concerning sexism and the impact of cultural conditioning. Sex-role analysis may be used so that women can understand how they have become culturally conditioned to respond in certain ways (Robinson & Howard-Hamilton, 2000).

7. *Personal validation.* Many women come from oppressed situations in which they have little or no awareness of their own inherent personal worth. Feminist therapy seeks to validate the individual and her cultural heritage as unique and valuable.

Multimedia Resources for This Chapter

The following online resource offers video and other resources of particular relevance to this chapter of your text.

MyHelpingLab

myhelpinglab   If a MyHelpingLab passcode was included with your textbook and you
have activated your passcode:

- go to **www.ablongman.com/myhelpinglab**
- enter the "Counseling" area of the site by clicking on that tab
- select "Video Lab" from the toolbar to the left of the page
- select "MyHelpingLab Videos by Theoretical Approach"
- select the "Feminist" module to view various video clips of a therapist using this approach with a client

chapter 12

Multicultural Counseling and Therapy

chapter goals

This chapter is designed to:

1. Create understanding of the multicultural worldview from a universal and culture-specific perspective.

2. Identify and discuss six central theoretical propositions of multicultural counseling and therapy (MCT).

3. Help you examine your own level of cultural identity development and awareness of cultural issues in the helping process.

4. Explore how strategies and techniques of various theories may be adapted to multicultural counseling and therapy practice.

5. Identify key MCT techniques and strategies that you can integrate into your daily clinical practice.

6. Foster your personal and professional development as a culturally competent mental health practitioner by helping you develop such skills as

   • working with individuals who are culturally different from yourself

   • examining family rules and roles

   • implementing a structured approach to psychological liberation

   • generating your own counseling and therapy theory for a multicultural group

   • implementing basic consciousness-raising strategies

   • learning your personal place in cultural identity theory

Introduction

Multicultural counseling and therapy (MCT) may best be described as a metatheoretical approach to helping that recognizes that all helping methods ultimately exist within a cultural context. This integrative helping approach is comprised of an array of therapeutic strategies and techniques that assist counselors and psychologists to work more effectively, respectfully, and ethically with persons from diverse groups and backgrounds.

MCT starts with awareness of the psychological differences that are commonly manifested among persons in different cultural/ethnic/racial groups (between-group differences) and within the same group (within-group differences). In this way, MCT can be viewed as a highly person-centered approach to helping. However, MCT also stresses the importance of acknowledging how family and cultural factors affect the way clients view the world and the types of problems and challenges individuals in different groups experience in their lives. In this way, MCT is also culture centered (Ivey, Pederson, & Ivey, 2001; Pedersen & Carey, 2003).

MCT challenges practitioners, theoreticians, and researchers to rethink the meaning of helping and to give attention to unique individuals and their family and cultural contexts. Making these factors central in the helping process leads counselors and therapists to implement differential treatment strategies when working with persons from diverse cultural, ethnic, and racial groups. This point was explicitly addressed by Cheek (1976) more than a quarter of a century ago in his discussion about the need to implement differential helping strategies when working with African-American clients. In that discussion, Cheek (1976) emphatically stated: "I am advocating treating one segment of our population quite differently from another. This is implicit in my statement that Blacks do not benefit from many therapeutic approaches to which Whites respond. And I have referred to some of these approaches of counselors and therapists as 'White techniques'" (p. 23).

In the years following Cheek's comments, increasing attention was directed to generating culturally appropriate theoretical frameworks and helping strategies (Baruth & Manning, 2003; Pedersen, Dragons, Lonner, & Trimble, 1981; Sue & Zane, 1987). These new theoretical frameworks and helping strategies were intentionally aimed at moving the fields of counseling and psychology to a greater level of cultural sensitivity and understanding to lessen the dangers of imposing culturally biased helping strategies on clients from diverse groups and backgrounds.

Cheatham (1990) expands on these important points, noting that counselors and psychologists violate the integrity of African-American clients if they insist on using culturally biased helping approaches. Commenting on this point, Cheatham (1990) argues:

> The helping professional doubtless will violate the Black client's sense of integrity or "world view." Blacks are products of their distinct sociocultural and sociohistorical experience. Counseling and therapy are specific, contractual events and thus may proceed more effectively on the basis of understanding of the client's cultural context. (pp. 380–381)

Cheatham argues further that the role of the therapist is not just to work with an individual, but also to work with the family and with the extended networks that may be important to clients in culturally diverse groups. He also urges counselors and therapists to address specific contextual factors that are known to undermine the psychological health and spiritual well-being of culturally diverse clients.

Cheatham suggests that an African-American client who suffers from depression should be treated both as an individual and as an individual within a cultural context. The existence of racism can often contribute to depression among many African-Americans. According to Cheatham (1990), Cheek (1976), Parham (2002), and others (Ponterotto, Casas, Suzuki, & Alexander, 2001), multicultural counseling and therapy will not be effective unless counselors and therapists focus on and effectively intervene in issues of racism, sexism, and other forms of cultural oppression.

Numerous MCT researchers and theorists (D'Andrea et al., 2001; Helms & Cook, 1999; Parham, 2002) have documented the various ways in which the fields of counseling and psychology operate as "instruments of oppression" (Sue & Sue, 2003, p. 32). One way this is manifested is through the individualistic cultural values that are embedded in counseling and psychology training programs and reflected in many traditional intervention approaches. These individualistic values are potentially harmful because they are clearly antithetical to the worldviews and values of many persons in diverse client populations.

Feminist theorists provide additional support for these claims, pointing out that individualistic cultural biases are harmful when used with many women, especially with those who experience mental health problems directly linked to the impact of sexism and patriarchy (Hill & Ballou, 2005) (see Chapter 11).

Multicultural counseling theorists describe how traditional approaches to counseling and psychotherapy perpetuate the status quo rather than fostering the psychological liberation and well-being of many persons from culturally and racially different groups in our society. Sue and Sue (2003) note that traditional therapists are frequently guilty of serving as "handmaidens of the status quo" (p. 32).

Freire (1972) uses the term *conscientizacào* to describe his view of the essential goal of education and, by extension, of multicultural counseling and therapy. *Conscientizacào* focuses on the liberation of individuals from the various forms of internalized oppression that are commonly tied to different personal, social, and economic injustices. Many women and persons from other culturally diverse groups come to therapy blaming themselves for their life conditions (Liu, 2001). The culturally competent counselor's task is to help liberate these clients from self-blame, encourage them to see their issues in a social context, and facilitate personal action.

In an effort to formulate a new multicultural perspective that will move beyond ethnocentric theories and practices, Sue and his colleagues (1996) generated a set of principles that represent the cornerstones of MCT theory. These principles form the basis of much of the information presented in the rest of this chapter.

Multicultural Counseling and Therapy as Metatheory

MCT is a complex metatheory concerned with counseling and psychotherapy as liberation—the view of the self in relation to others and to social and cultural contexts. Interdependence is basic to the philosophy and actions of this metatheory. Although MCT can be described in many ways, Sue et al.'s (1996) presentation of six propositions succinctly describes this metatheory. These propositions are presented throughout this chapter to help you enhance your effectiveness as a culturally competent mental health practitioner.

Proposition I. *MCT is a metatheory of counseling and psychotherapy. It is a theory about theories and offers an organizational framework for understanding the numerous helping approaches humankind has developed to promote people's psychological health and personal well-being. It recognizes that theories of counseling and psychotherapy developed in the Western world and those indigenous helping models intrinsic to other non-Western cultures are neither inherently "right" or "wrong" nor "good" or "bad." Rather, MCT holds that each helping theory represents a different worldview and holds the potential to foster psychological health in different ways.*

Each theory of counseling and psychotherapy was developed in a particular cultural context and, to some extent, will likely be biased toward that cultural context. Different theoretical worldviews lead to different constructions of client concerns. As noted earlier, psychodynamic approaches may view client issues as originating in unconscious developmental history, whereas cognitive-behavioral approaches may see the same issues as a result of social learning. These differing theoretical worldviews result in different modes of conceptualizing and working with clients.

The worldviews, values, and assumptions reflected in all of the helping theories explored in this book are likely to differ from the constructions of psychological health care that people in diverse cultural groups bring to counseling and psychotherapy. For this reason, MCT emphasizes the importance of making these values, assumptions, and philosophical tenets clear early in the helping process.

MCT recognizes the utility of Western counseling and psychotherapy theories and practices. MCT does not present itself, as some counselors and therapists may think, in opposition to psychodynamic, cognitive-behavioral, or existential-humanistic counseling and psychotherapeutic approaches. Rather, MCT strives to complement and extend many of the ideas that comprise these three traditional theoretical forces by putting cultural considerations at the center of these conceptual frameworks (Pedersen & Carey, 2003).

In addition, MCT points to the importance of seeing the individual-in-context by emphasizing the need to consider the cultural background of the client, acknowledge each client's multidimensionality, and find culturally appropriate solutions to the individual's problems and concerns. This helping approach necessitates changes in the way counseling and psychotherapy has historically been conducted.

These changes include helping clients to view their problems in context, drawing group or family members into the treatment process, and using non-Western therapeutic approaches as appropriate. This sharply contrasts with many traditional Western approaches to counseling, therapy, and diagnostic procedures (such as those outlined in the DSM-IV), which locate the client's "problem" within the individual who seeks professional assistance.

Although the MCT perspective is fueled by an increasing recognition of the pivotal role cultural factors play in the helping process, it is anchored in the following important point: *Counseling and psychotherapy are likely to result in ineffective and even harmful outcomes if practitioners overemphasize either cultural differences or similarities in helping situations.*

This key point reflects the culturally competent counselor's understanding that an overemphasis on cultural differences in counseling and therapy can easily lead to stereotypic, exclusionary, politicized, and antagonistic helping services. On the other hand, culturally competent practitioners are equally cognizant that an overemphasis of cultural similarities in counseling and psychotherapy can lead to adverse outcomes as well. The latter point is fueled by the recognition of the many ways that individuals in more powerful groups can use cultural similarities as a pretense to promote a "melting pot" environment that disregards essential features of cultural identity (Parham, 2002).

As an additive force in the mental health professions, MCT encourages counselors and psychologists to modify traditional helping strategies as they strive to communicate respect for human diversity and foster positive outcomes among persons from different groups and backgrounds. To work ethically and effectively with persons from diverse cultural/racial/ethnic populations, culturally competent counselors and psychologists are comfortable consulting with and obtaining assistance from the indigenous healers in their clients' host communities (Lee & Armstrong, 1995; Moodley & West, 2005). In doing so, these counselors and psychologists encourage their clients to utilize many different resources and services that have been used to foster the physical health and psychological well-being of many persons in diverse groups (Lewis et al., 2003). These include, but are not limited to, the use of acupuncture, herbal therapies, the I Ching, and therapeutic massage as well as concepts drawn from an Afrocentric approach to mental health and Japanese Naikan therapy to name a few (Moodley & West, 2005).

Generating New Theory from an MCT Perspective

Efforts to build a more expansive metatheory that integrates many Western theoretical perspectives and indigenous helping traditions is one of the central challenges multicultural counseling advocates presently face. The following section directs your attention to this important challenge by discussing an Afrocentric worldview of mental health and explaining how this perspective ties into the ongoing evolution of the MCT metatheory. Although this perspective is derived from an Afrocentric theoretical worldview, it is possible to adapt this perspective to other cultural helping frameworks (Parham, Daniels, & D'Andrea, 2006).

The Afrocentric Worldview. The Afrocentric worldview proposes that the African-American experience in the United States represents a continuation of African history and culture. Years of slavery and racism have not dimmed the African intergenerational legacy of family relationships, interdependence, and group solidarity. Molefi Kete Asante's (1987) controversial and influential book *The Afrocentric Idea* has brought these concepts to national prominence. However, many other authors have also described these ideas in great detail as well (Blassingame, 1972; Gutman, 1976; Myers, 1988; Taub-Bynum, 1999).

Cheatham (1990) elaborates on the Afrocentric idea, noting:

> Unlike the Western philosophic system, the African tradition has no heavy emphasis on the individual; the individual's being is authenticated only in terms of others. Nobles writes that there is a sense of corporate responsibility and collective destiny as epitomized in the traditional African self-concept: "I am because we are; and because we are, therefore I am." (p. 375)

Black theorists further assert that psychological linkages with Africa have been retained even with the forced transplantation of millions of African persons and the continuing press by the dominant cultural group to have African-Americans forget the past and divorce themselves from their cultural roots (West, 1999). This was made possible, in part, because of the rigidly enforced isolation of Blacks through formal and informal forms of segregation that continue to be manifested in many parts of our contemporary society (Jones, 1997; Ridley, 2005). The various forms of segregation and isolation that mark this nation's treatment of people of African descent allowed (and perhaps even required) retention of a deep psychic orientation toward self-in-connection.

The Afrocentric or African worldview is holistic, emotionally vital, interdependent, and oriented toward collective survival. Additionally, the Afrocentric perspective emphasizes an oral tradition, uses a "being"-in-time orientation, focuses on harmonious blending and cooperation, and is highly respectful of the role of elderly persons in their cultural community (Parham, 2002). In doing therapy with persons of African descent, the therapist or counselor should consider this multidimensional perspective and be aware that each individual client will be affected by this worldview differently.

In contrast, the North American–Eurocentric worldview tends to divide the world into discrete, "knowable" parts; handles emotion somewhat carefully, even to the point of emotional repression; focuses on self-actualization and independence as a goal of life; emphasizes the clarity and precision of the written word; is oriented toward a linear "doing" view of time; stresses individuation and difference rather than collaboration and interconnectedness; and is more oriented toward youth than the elderly. Traditional counseling theories tend to support this cultural worldview (Ponterotto et al., 2001).

MCT metatheory emphasizes that neither the Afrocentric or North American–Eurocentric or any other cultural frame of reference or worldview is "right" or "wrong" per se. Rather, each is thought to provide a different way of constructing meaning of the world. What can be harmful in counseling and psychotherapy, however, is to impose any particular theoretical frame of reference or worldview on clients whose cultural perspective, values, and assumptions about mental health and mental health care are in conflict with those implemented by practitioners in clinical settings.

It should also be added that MCT operates from the belief that clients will at times benefit from exposure to a culturally different helping frame of reference. Thus, sharing new helping perspectives and narratives from other cultures might be beneficial to some clients in some counseling and therapy situations. However, the consistent imposition of a foreign worldview is to be avoided in all multicultural counseling and therapy situations.

Moreover, each individual you work with is likely to operate from some mixture of different cultural frames of reference. An African-American or Japanese-American client, for example, is likely to have been influenced by North American culture and may have incorporated many values of the Eurocentric frame into her or his own personal psychology. The MCT metatheory also asserts that many women who adopt a feminist orientation to life consciously or unconsciously manifest many Afrocentric psychological ways of being and meaning making (Barrett et al., 2005).

The Afrocentric Worldview Related to Other Cultures. Many of the sons and daughters of southern Italian, Chinese or Japanese, or Puerto Rican and Mexican families have a life orientation that is closer to the Afrocentric worldview than the North American–European worldview. Sue and Sue (2003) provide an important summary of key issues in multicultural counseling and development. In doing so, they point out that constructions of the world are very different among Asian, African-American, European-American, Latina/o, and Native American populations, but that issues of relationship are more highly valued in non-Eurocentric cultures.

We should also recall that each individual is unique and special. There are some African-American clients whose worldview is more similar to midwestern culture than to that of their ethnically related brothers and sisters. Similarly, there are some religious cultures that are dominated by persons from White Western European backgrounds that adopt a more relational and family-centered orientation than do some African-Americans.

As always, it is important to never stereotype your clients. From a practical point of view this suggests that if you do not begin your interview by learning from the client, your assumption that you are being a "culturally aware" helping practitioner may result in more oppressive therapeutic interventions than if you knew nothing about cultural differences at all.

It is important to adopt a RESPECTFUL approach to counseling and psychotherapy, as described in Chapter 2. Many of your clients will identify with more than one cultural or ethnic tradition. These multiple cultural identities can be a major strength. However, due to conflicting cultural expectations, racism, and/or social status differences, multicultural experiences may often need to be the focus of counseling and psychotherapy when working with persons who have been negatively impacted by various forms of oppression in their lives.

The microskills approach (Chapter 4) offers some direction in generating more culturally relevant theory and practice. One route toward this objective is to examine a specific African culture and then see how the findings may relate to African-Americans, European-Americans, and persons from other cultural groups identified in the RESPECTFUL counseling framework (Chapter 2).

Using Nwachuku's Helping Theory from an MCT Perspective

Uchenna Nwachuku, a Nigerian Igbo, provides relevant guidelines for counseling and therapy in multicultural helping situations. His writings provide the concrete beginnings of a specifically Afrocentric theory and method of helping. Of particular importance is that he provides a basis for developing new theoretical strategies for counseling persons from a broad range of cultural groups and backgrounds that are consistent with the principles of MCT metatheory (Nwachuku, 1989, 1990; Nwachuku & Ivey, 1991) and of numerous feminist counseling theorists (Evans et al., 2005).

Drawing on his personal experience and knowledge of Western helping methods, Nwachuku developed several steps in generating a new counseling theory that he used with his native Igbo people in Nigeria. These steps are described below, as they may be useful when you work with persons from diverse cultural groups and backgrounds in the future.

Step 1. *Examine the culture of your clients and identify some of the important personal and interpersonal characteristics manifested in their cultural group.*

This step entails doing field research by interviewing persons who come from your client's cultural group and reading about this group from a psychological and anthropological frame of reference. In doing field research, Nwachuku examined five key characteristics of the Igbo culture: group orientation, decisional style, developmental progressions, attitude toward change, and language. Although these key characteristics may be of greater or lesser importance in varying cultures, they nevertheless form the foundation of Nwachuku's Afrocentric theory, as reflected in the psychological development of the Igbo.

Reflecting on the orientation to life of the Igbo, Nwachuku talks about going for walks with his mother as a child. Rather than running ahead or holding his mother's hand as a Western child might, Nwachuku recalls his mother holding him and placing his hand under her armpit so he could feel the beat of her heart.

He comments that the beat is still with him and provides him with an important and continuing sense of interconnectedness with the world that he draws from when he encounters challenging and stressful events in his life. This aspect of Nwachuku's personal history provides an interesting example of how the relational orientation of his cultural group is reflected in his group's child-rearing practices.

In the Igbo culture, the focus is on the child in relation to the community and the mother. The Western child may experience a different sort of socialization, one more oriented to individualism, by being encouraged to move ahead separately when taking a walk with one's mother or father. In one society, children are kept closer to the mother; in another, children are encouraged to go out on their own.

The Igbo have much in common with other African cultures, but there is much that is distinctive about their own group as well. Thus, it would be best to not overgeneralize lessons learned from the Igbo to the Nigerian Yoruba or other African groups. African cultures differ, just as do French and German, or Haitian and Cuban cultures.

As you work with different groups, you may want to add additional dimensions related to a particular group's special interests. For instance, in developing a theory for gay and lesbian persons, you would want to direct particular attention to the process of "coming out" and its personal and interpersonal ramifications. In developing a theory for clients from differing backgrounds, it is important to learn about the developmental history and the personal and interpersonal strengths that characterize the mental health and psychological liberation of persons in each group.

Several multicultural theorists encourage mental health practitioners to develop new competencies that will enable them to more effectively address the complex problems of racism, sexism, heterosexism, anti-Semitism, anti-Muslim sentiments, ageism, and classism as they are presently manifested in our contemporary society (Arredondo & D'Andrea, 1999; Jones, 1997; Ponterotto, Utsey, & Pedersen, 2006; Ridley, 2005). Failure to effectively deal with these and other forms of oppression and power imbalances in our contemporary society will undermine the viability and relevance of the mental health professions in a culturally diverse 21st-century society (Lewis et al., 2003).

Step 2. *Identify concrete skills and strategies to be used in multicultural helping relationships.*

Drawing out the client's story using empathic listening skills is a central part of both MCT and Nwachuku's helping model. As Nwachuku notes, traditional Igbo culture assists individuals in solving their problems by having them tell their life stories and use these stories to help clarify the challenges and problems they are presently encountering in their lives. As the helping encounter proceeds, the task of the Igbo helper is to use specific strategies that assist these individuals to develop new ways of thinking, feeling, and acting. The Igbo helper listens empathically to their stories and then commonly uses an authoritarian and directive helping approach once the client's issues are understood.

Nwachuku also encourages the use of the microskill of focusing to promote clients' psychological development. Most Western counseling and therapy theories use focusing skills to help clients direct attention to their individual needs and problems. In contrast, Nwachuku's Afrocentric theory serves a broader purpose of encouraging clients to focus primarily on the ways in which their personal challenges are directly linked to their extended family and their community. A secondary focus is on the individual and the nuclear family, if appropriate.

Another similarity between Nwachuku's helping model and MCT metatheory is that both emphasize the need to help clients direct attention to the internal and external factors contributing to psychological health and personal distress. Balancing attention to internal/intrapsychic and external/environmental factors and their impact on clients' lives distinguishes Nwachuku's model and MCT metatheory from other theoretical approaches to counseling and therapy.

This perspective represents a particular challenge to cognitive-behavioral helping theories (Chapters 7 and 8), because these theories emphasize that it is what one thinks, more than the external factors, that determines one's mental health. In contrast, counselors and therapists who adopt an MCT perspective recognize that external reality at times may be far more important than clients' internal cognitive structures, unconscious processes, or even empathic conditions. This metatheoretical perspective illuminates the point that racism, sexism, discrimination, and other forms of cultural oppression impact people's sense of psychological well-being and cannot be dealt with solely by helping clients to make internal cognitive changes.

Step 3. *Test the new helping theory and its skills in action.*

Nwachuku videotaped two different counseling sessions: one implemented a traditional Western approach to helping; the second session was approached from Nwachuku's Afrocentric theoretical perspective. Both sessions focused on the same question: Should an African student return home from graduate school in the United States and meet family responsibilities in his African homeland? In the traditional Western counseling session, the helper focused immediately on the problem, used an "I" focus, and encouraged the client to make an independent autonomous decision regarding his problem. The helper demonstrated excellent listening skills throughout the session. Throughout this process, the client was consistently supported to find his own independent decision in his situation.

The session employing the Afrocentric Igbo model of helping was quite different. The helper spent more time building rapport at the beginning of the session, to help the client feel comfortable. Although a "we" focus was used early in the session, it became clear that the Igbo helper was establishing himself as an authority who expected to take charge of the session.

The Igbo helper used effective questioning skills as he encouraged the client to tell his story. After briefly probing the client's thoughts about the issue, the interviewer then focused on the client's extended family. In doing so, it became apparent that a broader network of decision makers was involved in addressing this client's dilemma.

As the counseling sessions continued, it was obvious that the African Igbo client had been influenced by North American individualism as a result of living in the United States. It was also evident, however, that he needed help from the counselor in dealing with the clash in cultural beliefs and values that were related to the decision he faced. As the counselor continued working with this person, he reminded the client that more people than just himself would be affected by this important life decision.

The counselor then told the client a traditional Igbo story about family values and looked at the client. The client understood the meaning of the story and acknowledged that he had lost some of his traditional values as a result of accommodating the more individualistic values associated with the culture of the United States.

The counselor proceeded with this session by helping the client explore specific ways that the client could balance the strengths of an individualistic culture with the positive dimensions of a relational culture. Being able to see both cultural perspectives helped clarify the consequences of the decision he would have to make.

Implications of Nwachuku's Model for the MCT Metatheory

Beginning or experienced professionals in counseling and psychotherapy may not be comfortable with Nwachuku's helping model. The idea that the family and the counselor lead the client in making decisions may seem antagonistic to the traditional goals of counseling and therapy, which focus on individual outcomes. However,

Nwachuku's framework can help increase counselors' understanding of the different worldviews clients bring to counseling and therapy; as such it can be applied to a variety of cultural contexts. Understanding multiple worldviews from Afrocentric, European-American, Native American, Asian-American, Latino/Latina, and other cultural perspectives will lead to new insights that can greatly impact your own approach to counseling and therapy.

It should also be noted that many clients from different cultures may find strengths in the European–North American cultural worldview, just as European-Americans may be motivated to adapt Afrocentric or other cultural values as they learn about the diverse traditions of people in various groups. Helping clients sort out these issues is an important part of many MCT counseling sessions.

Being Mindful of Multiple Identities, Contexts, and Experiences

> **Proposition II.** *Counselor and client identities are formed and embedded in multiple levels of experiences (individual, group, and universal experiences) and contexts (individual, family, and cultural). The totality and interrelationship of these experiences and contexts need to be considered in any treatment plan.*

MCT therapists acknowledge that everyone possesses an individual, group, and universal identity. Even though we are unique individuals, we share commonalties with our multicultural reference groups (cultural, racial/ethnic, gender, spiritual/religious, sexual orientation, socioeconomic class, etc.) as well as the universal identity that we are all human beings. These levels of identity are fluid and ever changing, and the salience of one over the other is also changing. Consequently, a client may at one moment focus on individual needs, at another moment on an issue related to multicultural reference group identity, and at still another time on universal human experience.

The effective culturally competent helping professional validates all levels and strives to relate to that which is most salient and important to the person at the time of contact. Unfortunately, traditional counseling and psychotherapy have tended to relate primarily to the individual or universal levels of human development, thereby negating or minimizing multicultural reference group identities as important considerations in the helping process.

In contrast, MCT metatheory stresses the importance of understanding how people develop multiple identities as a result of the person-environment interaction. Thus, working effectively with clients requires an understanding of how the individual is embedded in the family, which in turn requires an understanding of how the family is affected by a culturally diverse society. Increasing one's understanding of the interfacing impact of familial/cultural/societal influences on clients' psychological development can be attained by using community and family genograms in counseling and therapy (see Chapters 1 and 14).

MCT therapists presume that the salient feature of a client's personal identity (e.g., individual, multicultural group, or universal identity) will change during the process of counseling and psychotherapy. Furthermore, these therapists are able to accurately track the change from one cultural referent group to another in the helping process.

As noted before, culturally competent practitioners are ever mindful that they bring their own families, communities, and cultural backgrounds, values, and biases into their helping sessions. This self-understanding is extended by the culturally competent practitioner's awareness of the ways in which the salience of various components of her or his own multiple identities changes during multicultural counseling and therapy encounters.

For instance, while counselors and therapists may begin the helping interview with their professional identity being most salient at the beginning of counseling and therapy, the client may say or do something that consciously or unconsciously stimulates some aspects of the practitioner's sexual, socioeconomic class, or spiritual/religious identity. MCT counselors and therapists are aware of the changing salience of different components of their clients' and their own identities during the helping process and are sensitive to the ways in which these changes might affect the process and outcome of counseling and therapy.

Culturally competent mental health practitioners are able to assist clients in gaining a better understanding of the ways in which their personal identity has changed over the course of their lifetime as well as in the helping setting. These practitioners are also sensitive to the ways in which their own identities have shifted over time and within the context of multicultural counseling and therapy endeavors. Tamase's (1991) introspective developmental counseling (IDC) model provides a useful framework to assist clients and practitioners develop new insights about these and other personal changes that occur during the lifespan.

Life-Span Review: Introspective Developmental Counseling

Introspective developmental counseling (IDC) seeks to help clients learn how their life histories affect their present experiences. This theory was generated from a multicultural framework in Japan by Tamase (1991). IDC draws on past and present strengths in working on and resolving problematic life issues. In developing his IDC theory, Tamase integrates many Eastern and Western psychological theoretical concepts. This includes concepts that are drawn from Eric Erikson's life-span theory (1950/1963), developmental counseling and therapy theory (Ivey, Ivey, Myers, & Sweeney, 2005) (Chapter 13), and a Japanese helping model referred to as Naikan therapy (Krech, 2002; Reynolds, 1990).

Erikson's life-span theory (summarized in Table 12.1) has been severely criticized on the grounds that it is based on a Northern-European White male model of human development (Gilligan, 1982; Robb, 2006). Nonetheless, it remains a popular developmental model for many counselors and therapists, one that can be made even more useful from a multicultural perspective when modified by Tamase's IDC theory.

Table 12.1

Erikson's Developmental Stages throughout the Life Span as Modified by Multicultural Counseling and Therapy

Life Stage (approximate age and major developmental crises derived from Eurocentric norms)	Key Environmental Systems (will vary with the cultural experience of the individual)	Developmental Tasks (will vary with family, community, and culture)	Example of How Life Stages Differ among Multicultural Groups
Infancy (birth–1) Balancing trust in others vs. mistrust	Caregiver and family. Families may be traditional, single-parent, blended, grandparent, adoptive, gay or lesbian, rich or poor. Seek out the nature of the early attachment experiences and how they may be unique to the person, family, and culture.	Attachment to caregiver, individual, or network. Sensorimotor intelligence. Basic motor coordination.	Caregiver and nuclear family are the focus in European-American situations, but extended family may be central in many groups. The "holding environment" of Japan may produce closer attachments than in Eurocentric cultures.
Early childhood (2–4) Autonomy vs. shame and doubt (learning one's responsibility to others)	Family, extended family, preschool play group	Need to determine how much emphasis is to be placed on individual need vs. the group. Self-control. Language learning. Attachment to family is basis for developing a beginning sense of self and others. Walking and play activities are central.	Autonomy is a Eurocentric construct. In Japan, for example, the child is often encouraged to develop a sense of closeness and dependence on others. Too much autonomy is viewed as selfishness in some cultures.
Middle childhood (5–7) Initiative vs. guilt (responsibly representing one's family and culture—initiative exists within a context)	Family, neighborhood, school	Gender identity. First stages of moral development. Concrete mental operations.	Boys and girls have been taught since infancy to behave differently and dress differently and are rewarded for different types of behaviors in virtually all cultures. Initiative may be defined as aggressiveness in some groups.

Table 12.1, continued

Life Stage (approximate age and major developmental crises derived from Eurocentric norms)	Key Environmental Systems (will vary with the cultural experience of the individual)	Developmental Tasks (will vary with family, community, and culture)	Example of How Life Stages Differ among Multicultural Groups
Late childhood (8–12) Industry vs. inferiority. Most cultures expect some form of productivity from the child at this stage, yet the focus is on doing. Some cultures would emphasize the importance of "being vs. doing."	Family, neighborhood, school, and peer group	Basic time of learning social relationships through work and play. Team membership may be as important as building self-esteem and feelings of competence. Egocentric learning. Learning of many basic life skills in the culture. Late concrete mental operations. "If . . . then" reasoning. Moral development in terms of right vs. wrong.	Children of poverty may not be surrounded by a stimulating material environment and may have less chance to learn self-esteem and basic skills, which are considered natural to children of a more economically advantaged background. The word *industry* is related to a "doing orientation" of Eurocentric culture. as contrasted with Afrocentric and Arabic ideas of "being."
Puberty and adolescence (13–19) Identity vs. role confusion. Role confusion might be translated by feminist theory as a time of developing multiple roles and recognizing that identity can be defined only in relationship to others.	Peer group, school, family, neighborhood, work setting	Sexual maturation. Formal operational thought. Generation of self-concept and awareness of personal identity in Eurocentric culture as a move toward independent living. In traditional Latina/o experience, the movement may be toward taking one's place in organized society and recognizing relational responsibilities.	Piagetian theorists estimate that between 25 and 40 percent of the population never reaches full formal operations. Gay or lesbian adolescents may have a particularly difficult time at this stage due to cultural expectations.

Table 12.1, continued

Life Stage (approximate age and major developmental crises derived from Eurocentric norms)	Key Environmental Systems (will vary with the cultural experience of the individual)	Developmental Tasks (will vary with family, community, and culture)	Example of How Life Stages Differ among Multicultural Groups
Young adulthood (20–30) Intimacy vs. isolation. Intimacy may be defined in Chinese culture as being part of a larger extended family. Most cultures focus on issues of connection, but in varying ways.	In Eurocentric culture, new family and living mate(s) may become central. Friendship network may move away from family of origin. Work setting becomes more important.	Finding one's own sense of self in a family relationship of love and commitment. Initial parenting. A new relationship with parents and extended family. Major career decisions and financial decisions.	Adolescent women in U.S. culture work on issues of intimacy during adolescence, perhaps even more so than identity. In some African and Italian cultures, the extended family remains especially important in living and decision-making arrangements.
Adulthood (31–64) Generativity vs. stagnation. The definition of generativity in one culture may focus on work, whereas in another it may be on family. Stagnation may be interpreted by some as a contemplative state of being.	Family and children, friendship network, work setting, community	Reworking of all the issues above from a new perspective of maturity. Special emphasis on career and family changes. Particularly important are the physical, cognitive, and emotional changes that come with each new decade.	Women's career and life patterns do not easily fit into Erikson's framework. Rather than move systematically through the stages one by one, as suggested by Erikson, some women work on many at once. Maturity may be flexibility in the use of all stages. Each culture will define maturity differently. The thirty years of adulthood are more complex than allowed for in the Erikson time frame.
Old age (65–death) Ego integrity vs. despair. The concept of ego again	Family, friendship network, community, caring and health	Reworking all previous developmental crises	Experts now concede that many are still in middle age at 70. A

Table 12.1, continued

Life Stage (approximate age and major developmental crises derived from Eurocentric norms)	Key Environmental Systems (will vary with the cultural experience of the individual)	Developmental Tasks (will vary with family, community, and culture)	Example of How Life Stages Differ among Multicultural Groups
focuses on the individualistic aspects of Erikson's framework. Is integrity to be defined by an individual or a self-in-relation?	agencies (as one faces illness and nears death)	once again. Life review and finding meaning in what one has done. Coping with physical changes and illness. Dealing with the death of family and friends. Financial/living concerns and decisions.	new and rapidly increasing category is the "old old" who are 85 and over, many of whom still have good health and enjoy full lives, contrary to cultural stereotypes. Age is valued far more in Native American Indian culture.

Erikson defines the task of early childhood (ages 2 through 4) as developing a sense of autonomy. Elsewhere, however, such as in Africa, Japan, or South America, the goal of this developmental period is not autonomy but rather a sense of connectedness to the caregiver. In fact, an overemphasis on autonomy and separation is considered pathological in many cultures.

Tamase avoids labeling any developmental period as being focused on a particular task. He maintains, instead, that different cultures will focus on different issues at different stages than those proposed by Erikson. Tamase also points out that a person's psychological development is shaped with the network of relationships of which one is a part. His IDC theory further acknowledges that the Western concepts of cognitive accommodation and assimilation (Ivey et al., 2005; Piaget, 1985) are very useful in understanding the psychological changes individuals experience as they proceed through several basic life stages or phases within their own relational networks.

Tamase's Basic Life Stages. Tamase identifies four age-related developmental phases in his IDC theory: birth through preschool, elementary school, adolescence, and present-day life. Early research and clinical practice using Tamase's theoretical model suggest that the use of structured questions that focus on the four phases of his framework can provide a substantial base of information that has much relevance for multicultural counseling and therapy endeavors (Tamase, 1991; Tamase & Rigazio-DiGilio,

1997). Examples of the types of structured questions that practitioners can use to garner such information in counseling and therapy are presented in Competency-Building Activity 12. 1.

It is important to point out that while Western developmental theories such as Erikson's psychosocial development theory traditionally focus on the individual, IDC operates from a self-in-relation perspective. Consequently, much attention is directed to how a client's past relational experiences contribute to her or his identity development. In this way, IDC complements many of the central tenets associated with feminist counseling (Chapter 11) and MCT metatheory.

Making Meaning from the Past: An Essential Component of IDC. The goals of IDC are in some ways similar to psychodynamic therapy theories in that the client's past history is believed to significantly affect her or his present state of being. However, Tamase avoids giving theoretical interpretations in counseling and therapy. Rather, the IDC interviewer simply listens and helps the client review her or his past. Often, if the counselor listens to past events carefully, clients begin to discover repeating patterns, make their own interpretations of their life history, and identify the impact of their past experiences on their identity development.

Ivey et al. (2005) suggest that when you review clients' early school-age experiences, they are likely to provide concrete descriptors of specific situations and events that occurred at that point in their developmental history. In contrast, clients often demonstrate more reflective and formal operational thinking when describing experiences and events that occurred during their adolescence. The dialectic/systemic perspective that is described in Ivey et al.'s developmental counseling and therapy model (Chapter 13) challenges you and the client to reflect on life and its multiple systems from an even more complex, multidimensional, and contextual perspective when using Tamase's theory in counseling and therapy.

By using some of the specific questions that Ivey et al. (2005) present in their DCT approach (Chapter 13), you can bring out sensorimotor, concrete, formal/reflective, and dialectic/systemic thinking as your client reviews each stage of Tamase's theoretical model. This can greatly help foster clients' psychological liberation and well-being by stimulating new insights about their past life experiences and their present psychological disposition.

Completing Competency-Building Activity 12.1 will help make Tamase's adaptation of life-span theory more meaningful to you by extending your own thinking about the practical ways IDC can be used in multicultural counseling and therapy situations.

Essentially, Tamase's IDC theory is designed to raise clients' consciousness about the ways in which various contextual/relational factors impact personal identity development and current way of being. MCT counselors and therapists may complement this helping strategy by encouraging clients to participate in consciousness-raising groups, which can help clients discover new and untapped dimensions of their psychological development and liberation.

Competency-Building Activity 12.1

Using Tamase's IDC Framework in Practice

This exercise will help you understand how you or your client have generated key construct systems and beliefs about the world that impact your client's and your own identity development. The exercise can be quite lengthy, as it is designed to assist you and your clients to do an introspective review of the four stages in Tamase's IDC theory (birth through preschool, elementary school, adolescence, and present-day life).

A review of each life stage can take an hour or more. Alternatively, you can relate a brief story from each stage to help you understand how some life patterns have developed at the different developmental stages included in Tamase's IDC theory.

Instructions: You can use the following format to review each life stage. After presenting a brief description of the key areas to focus on when reviewing each stage of the IDC model, a set of structured questions are provided to guide your review of these stages.

1. *Key environmental systems.* The focus here is on the individual and key environmental support systems.

   - What was the family situation during this life stage (birth through preschool, elementary school, adolescence, and present-day life)?
   - What important life events or stressors affected your family or caregivers during this period?
   - What is the nature of your family or extended family at this stage in your personal history?
   - Where did you obtain support during this life stage?

2. *Life stage developmental story.* The focus here is on the individual recollections, although the recollections are usually in a context.

   - Tell a story about or describe a significant event that stands out for you from this life stage. (Examples might be a birth story, a fragment of a childhood memory, a repeatedly told family story.)
   - What are additional stories from this life stage (birth through preschool, elementary school, adolescence, and present-day life)?

3. *Multicultural issues.* The focus here is on the individual and how he or she relates to the community and the multicultural environment.

   - How did gender, religion, ethnic/racial status, or other multicultural issues affect your development during this period (birth through preschool, elementary school, adolescence, and present-day life)?
   - Tell me a story you recall about the role of men or women, a religious figure, or ethnic/racial figure from that time period in your personal history.
   - Who were your heroes during that stage?
   - Whom did you look up to and respect at that point in your life?

4. *Relating the past to the present.* The focus here is on balancing the individual with family and multicultural issues.

   - Given the data you've discussed during this time period (birth through preschool, elementary school, adolescence), how does this relate to your present life experience?
   - Do you see any patterns that relate to how you are now and/or how you relate to others?
   - What do you see as the influence of family and culture on where you are now?

If you wish to work through the framework at a deeper level, return to this activity after reading Chapter 13 and add the four-level questioning framework of DCT to your interview. This involves exploring recollections and reactions to Tamase's four life stages from the sensorimotor, concrete,

continued on next page

Competency-Building Activity 12.1, continued

formal operations, and the systemic/dialectic perspective. For example, in discussing the family situation in the first question, you might ask for an image and what is seen, heard, and felt; then ask for a concrete situation; then you could ask yourself or your client what patterns stand out in your

or your client's family history. You could end the interview with a systemic multicultural examination of the family system.

Be sure to take time to write your reactions to completing this competency-building activity, whether it involved working with yourself or with another person, and file your written reactions in your personal/professional development portfolio.

Focus and Consciousness-Raising Groups

The essence of consciousness raising is group discussions that can help individuals to better understand how past events have impacted their present level of development and then to plan for future action. An example can be found in the project initiated by the Aboriginal Educational Foundation to help native people discuss their issues, strengths, and desires for the future with the goal of empowering families and groups.

The Aboriginal project brought families and groups together to tell their stories in an intensive two-hour helping session. The objective was to draw out their daily life struggles as they related to schooling or study and employment. The task of the group leaders was simply to listen and learn from the discussion among the group members. There was an emphasis on group sharing of experiences in a safe atmosphere. As the participants discussed their concrete issues, they soon discovered many commonalities and patterns. This was described in greater detail in the report of the Aboriginal Educational Foundation (1992):

> Most group members have strong criticisms of their schooling. All are very critical of the employment choices open to them. Few reported satisfaction with their current employment and training situation. Many hoped that their children and grandchildren could be spared similar experiences. (p. 1)

These comments might be similar to those of many nonmajority people throughout the world. Irish migrant workers in Britain, Ukrainian farmers in Canada, and African-Americans in the United States might have similar concerns.

Group consciousness raising can also be the foundation for further theory development. For example, as noted in Chapter 11, feminist theory and practice evolved out of women's consciousness-raising groups and their concrete naming of common experiences of oppression and injustice. Consciousness-raising groups can also be an effective complement to individual approaches to MCT. Competency-Building Activity 12.2 provides a specific set of consciousness-raising strategies that can be employed with either individuals or groups.

Consciousness-raising groups provide a means for individuals to learn about the common experiences and reactions they have with other people who encounter

Competency-Building Activity 12.2

Basic Consciousness Raising

Instructions:

1. Establish a group of at least three participants. The topic for your session can be as broad as what it means to be male or female; gay, lesbian, bisexual, or heterosexual; or a member of some other racial/ethnic or multicultural group. Being a White Canadian or White U.S. citizen also represents a multicultural group. You might have group members share an experience they have had with oppression as a result of being of member of such groups.

2. Discuss the general issue(s) raised by the persons participating in this competency-building activity. Begin by asking each person to tell a story that represents what membership in their particular group means to them. Allow time for sharing after each story. The persons participating in this activity are likely to find common patterns as they continue to discuss their individual experiences.

3. Divide the time by focusing on three dimensions. In a consciousness-raising session, one-third of the time may be profitably spent focusing on personal stories and narratives of oppression or group identity; one-third, on group process and participants' reactions to one another's stories; and one-third, on the cultural/environmental contexts surrounding the issues discussed. The microskill of focus is particularly helpful to use in this activity. Time may be structured formally along these three dimensions, or you may wish to simply balance discussion along the three above-mentioned dimensions from time to time.

4. Establish an action commitment. Ask the participants for one thing they might do differently as a result of this interaction. Examples could be a new behavior or a new way of thinking about various issues discussed in this group activity.

Be sure to take time to briefly write your own reactions to facilitating this small-group discussion and include your reactions in your personal/professional development portfolio.

---

similar life situations. It also helps foster a more positive identification with a cultural/racial group that people may not have experienced previously.

The following section of this chapter directs your attention to the important role cultural/racial identity plays in people's lives and the pivotal position cultural/racial identity development theory holds in the MCT metatheory. This topic is central to the third major proposition underlying the MCT metatheory.

Cultural/Racial Identity Development Theory

Cultural/racial identity development represents a cognitive, emotional, and behavioral progression through identifiable and measurable levels or stages of consciousness. Theorists vary in their description of the specific characteristics that are associated with the different cultural/racial identity development theories that have emerged in the professional literature over the past 35 years. However, all of these theorists agree to several common issues that are associated with a person's cultural/racial identity development. These common issues include:

- a naive awareness of oneself as a cultural being

- an encounter with the reality of cultural/racial issues that disrupts the naiveté of the previous stage

- the naming of these cultural/racial issues (which fosters an increase in cultural/racial pride and identification)

- a reflection on the meaning of self as a cultural/racial being that fosters heightened personal introspection

- the internalization of a more differentiated and integrated cultural/racial identity that is grounded in multiperspective thought about self-in-system

Each stage of cultural/racial identity development involves the manifestation of different attitudes toward oneself (self-identity) and others (group identity and/or recognition of group differences). This brief description of cultural/racial identity development leads to the third proposition underlying the MCT metatheory.

> **Proposition III.** *Cultural/racial identity development is a major determinant of both the counselor's and client's beliefs and attitudes toward oneself, other persons in the same group, and other persons in different cultural/racial groups. These beliefs and attitudes, which may be exhibited in affective and behavioral dimensions, are strongly influenced by cultural/racial variables and the dynamics of dominant-subordinate relationships that exist between and among persons in diverse cultural and racial groups in our contemporary society. The level or stage of a client's cultural/racial identity development influences how the client and counselor define the problem presented in therapy and dictates what they believe to be appropriate goals in counseling.*

The essential idea of cultural/racial identity theory is that individuals have varying levels of awareness about the multidimensional nature of their development. As counselors and therapists, we must be able to recognize our own and the client's level of cultural/racial identity development in the helping encounter. Recognition of these factors enables practitioners to be better positioned to intentionally match their interviewing style and helping strategies to their clients' cultural/racial consciousness.

The most highly developed models of cultural/racial identity have been generated by African-American (Cross, 1971, 1991, 1995; Helms, 1990, 1995; Jackson, 1975, 1990) and Asian-American theorists (Sue & Sue, 1999, 2003). Cultural/racial identity theories have been developed for many other multicultural groups as well, including Latinas/os (Casas & Pytluk, 1995), biracial/multiracial groups (Kerwin & Ponterotto, 1995; Wehrly, Kenney, & Kenney, 1999), and White persons (Helms, 1995; Ponterotto, Utsey, & Pedersen, 2006).

Although Thomas (1971) and Cross (1971, 1995) are generally regarded as the originators of cultural/racial identity development theory, the foundational concepts associated with this theoretical perspective have come from a multitude of persons in

Table 12.2

Cultural/Racial Identity Development Theory

Stage 1. *Naiveté.* The individual has little focused awareness of self as a cultural/racial being. This is most clearly represented by children who do not distinguish skin color as an important feature. Helms (1995) points out that many White individuals lack awareness of the meaning that "Whiteness" has in our society. Naive understanding can also be manifested by successful and educated professionals who fully or partially deny that they have been oppressed and discriminated against.

Stage 2. *Encounter.* Despite lack of contact or efforts to shield oneself from racism, sexism, or other discrimination, the individual encounters experiences in the environment that clearly demonstrate that the earlier naive view was inadequate. For example, the African-American goes through a critical transformation and recognizes that discrimination is real and that being African-American is different than being White or Asian.

Stage 3. *Naming.* The act of naming is transformative. When Betty Freidan (1963) named the "problem that has no name" as sexism, she forever changed the way women viewed themselves and their issues. The gay liberation movement named itself gay, and thus took on what was previously a negative slur as its own positive identity. At this stage, the individual may feel much anger and may actively or passively refuse to work with those considered oppressors—most often European White males. For White and majority people seeking to support liberation of consciousness, the naming phase represents a real challenge, as it often leaves the White person without any sense of a positive identity.

Stage 4. *Reflection on self as a cultural being.* The development of a keener awareness of being Asian-American, bisexual, or culturally deaf continues. However, at stage 3, the Black individual may turn away from White culture and become totally immersed in reflecting on African-American history and the Black community. The lesbian may move away from confronting men and focus within her own community. At this point, the majority society is less relevant. The developmental task is the establishment of a definite cultural consciousness.

Stage 5. *Multiperspective internalization.* The individual develops pride in self and awareness of others. This individual makes use of the important dimensions of all stages of development and thus recognizes and accepts the worthwhile dimensions of predominant culture; fights those aspects that represent racism, sexism, homophobia, and oppression; and integrates all the stages in a transcendent consciousness. The individual is able to view the world through multiple frames of reference.

various disciplines. Table 12.2 provides a synthesis and summary of the five stages of cultural/racial identity development theory.

As you review the five-stages presented in Table 12.2, you will become more knowledgeable of the key psychological characteristics that mark people's changing consciousness about their own cultural/racial identity development from a naive lack of awareness to a highly sophisticated and action-oriented awareness of self-in-relation to society.

Jackson and Hardiman's (1983) Black identity development theory emphasizes the evolution of consciousness—the growing awareness of oneself in relationship to others and society. Cross (1995, 2001) points out that each developmental stage has a special value in the culturally and racially different person's life.

In reply, Jackson (1975) argues that all but the first and second stages of Black identity development are of particular value for African-Americans. It could be argued, however, that the denial characteristic of those in stage 1 (naiveté) might be necessary to maintain survival and sanity, especially if such persons are constantly subjected to various forms of racism and cultural oppression.

The counterpoint to the advantages in the fifth level of consciousness in the cultural/racial identity development model described in Table 12.2 is that it involves the use of a multiperspective consciousness that sometimes makes action in a racist society difficult. This level of critical consciousness can also be emotionally and cognitively exhausting. Parham and others (Parham et al., 1999; Parham, 2002) further point out that many persons constantly cycle through the five levels again and again as new issues are discovered and new cultural/racial experiences are encountered. It is clear that the development of consciousness as a cultural/racial being is always evolving.

Table 12.3 presents the cultural/racial identity development model and two related frameworks. The first theoretical framework includes a description of the stages in women's identity development. This model describes how both European-American and minority women develop consciousness of womanhood over time.

The second theoretical framework explores how cultural/racial identity constructs can be related to war veterans who are experiencing posttraumatic stress. Trauma survivors are themselves a special cultural group and need highly sensitive treatment designed for their levels of awareness.

Any individual may have more than one set of multicultural issues. For example, let's say you are called on to work with an African-American or Chinese-American nurse who suffers from posttraumatic stress as a result of working with injured members of the armed forces during the war in Iraq. It is possible that this client may not only exhibit thoughts, feelings, and behaviors commonly associated with posttraumatic stress, but she may also be adversely affected by being treated differently by the bureaucracy, colleagues, and others because she is a woman and a minority person. It is also possible that her level of consciousness may be high in terms of her African-American or Asian-American identity, but she may be at different levels on awareness of women's issues and the meaning of being a war veteran. All of these factors need to be taken into consideration when implementing MCT with this individual.

Culturally competent practitioners are also highly aware that each client has multiple cultural identities that do not typically progress or expand at the same rate. Different clients experience various challenges related to their personal/cultural/racial identities, which can have varying degrees of psychological salience. For example, a client's identity as a Navajo may be quite high, whereas her awareness of herself as a heterosexual or war veteran may be less developed. Some African-American college students may focus on issues related to their racial identity, whereas other dimensions of their cultural identity may be less central (see the discussion of other dimensions of multidimensionality as described in the RESPECTFUL counseling framework presented in Chapter 2).

Table 12.3

Cultural/Racial Identity Developmental Theory as Related to Women and War Veterans

Cultural/Racial Identity Development Theory	Women's Developmental Identity Theory	War Veterans' Developmental Identity Theory
Naiveté	Lacks awareness of system; "buys into the status quo."	Feels guilty and at fault for participation in war; frequent physical/emotional concerns.
Encounter	Becomes aware of women's oppression through contact with multiple issues that illustrate the failure of naiveté.	Becomes aware that he or she is not "at fault." Begins to see a new and broader picture of the war.
Naming	Identifies issue as sexism; angry with men and takes action to produce change.	May become angry at being a tool for the system. Becomes angry with governmental lack of support and sensitivity.
Reflection on self as cultural being	Pride in being a woman. Often separates from men to find self in relation to other women.	Generates increased pride for role in defending country. Often with the help of other veterans, develops an understanding of self in relation to others and the war.
Multiperspective internalization	Views male-female relationships in cultural/historical perspective. Values aspects of maleness, sees men selectively, is able to take parts of women's identity theory interchangeably and accept, act, and reflect, as the situation warrants.	Multiperspective—sees war and participation in war as both individual and social phenomena. Able to accept the status quo at times, able to become angry and use action when appropriate, and can reflect on both self and situation from multiple perspectives.

Identity Development Theory for European–North American Counselors and Therapists

Ponterotto and his colleagues (1993, 2006) developed a cultural/racial identity development theory for White counselor trainees. Their four-stage model is similar to those described above. According to Ponterotto et al. (1993, 2006), European–North American White counselor trainees often work through the following stages when confronted with cultural/racial issues in counseling and therapy.

Stage 1. Preexposure. White counselor trainees operating from this developmental stage typically have not thought about counseling and therapy as a multicultural phenomenon. The trainee may say that "people are just people" and in counseling practice may engage in unconsciously and unintentionally perpetuating various forms of institutional racism, sexism, or other forms of cultural oppression as they strive to treat all clients the same.

Stage 2. Exposure. When multicultural issues are introduced in counseling and psychotherapy, White therapist trainees (or experienced professionals) are given the opportunity to learn about cultural differences and matters of discrimination and oppression. This often leads to the realization that previous professional training experiences may have been incomplete in effectively addressing these factors as they relate to the work mental health practitioners do in multicultural situations. Trainees operating from this stage may become perturbed and confused by the many incongruities that exist in their professional training experiences and the issues presented by culturally and racially different clients in counseling and therapy.

Stage 3. Zealotry or Defensiveness. Faced with the challenge of multicultural issues, students and professionals at this stage may respond in different ways to cultural/racial concerns manifested in counseling and therapy. Some become angry and active proponents of multiculturalism, even to the point of offending their colleagues when discussing issues related to this topic with others.

Another common response to the incongruities experienced in Stage 2 is to retreat into quiet defensiveness. Criticisms of European-American White culture, "the system," and culturally biased aspects of therapeutic theory are taken personally. These students become passive recipients of information and "retreat back into the predictability of the White culture" (Helms, 1985, p. 156).

Stage 4. Integration. At this stage, White trainees and practitioners acquire a greater awareness of and respect for cultural/racial differences. They also (1) become more knowledgeable of their clients' and their own personal family and cultural history and (2) better understand how these factors might affect the way they develop a treatment plan and provide counseling and psychotherapeutic services. There is also an acceptance that one cannot know all dimensions of multicultural counseling and therapy at once. With this understanding in mind, White counselors, therapists, and trainees operating from this developmental stage make plans for a lifetime of learning in this area.

Although the above model was generated for White European-Americans, it has implications for counselor and therapy trainees from other cultural backgrounds as well. Competency-Building Activity 12.3 outlines a way to further stimulate your own personal awareness of multicultural issues as a counselor and therapist.

Competency-Building Activity 12.3

Your Personal Journey as a Professional Helper from a Cultural/Racial Identity Development Perspective

Instructions: Take time to think about the following questions as they relate to your own personal and professional development.

Ethnic/Racial Identity

1. Given your understanding of the five stages of the cultural/racial identity development model or the four stages of Ponterotto et al.'s model described above, what stage do you see yourself operating from most often?

2. Think back to earlier stages of your life when your identity as an ethnic/racial human being might have been different than what it is now. How did you think and feel then? What led you to change?

Counselor/Therapist Identity and Multiculturalism

Take time to describe how your cultural/racial identity development has been impacted by your counseling and therapy training program.

Take a few minutes to write down your reactions to these questions and include them in your personal/professional development portfolio.

Coconstructing Culturally Appropriate Techniques and Strategies in MCT

> **Proposition IV.** *Counseling and therapy's effectiveness is enhanced when the counselor uses techniques, strategies, and goals that are consistent with the client's cultural/racial identity, life experiences, and values. No single helping approach or intervention strategy is equally effective across all populations and client situations. Consequently, the ultimate goal of multicultural counselor and therapist training is to expand the repertoire of helping responses available to the professional, regardless of the theoretical orientation one finally embraces for her or his professional practice.*

One way to effectively ensure that your counseling approaches, strategies, and goals are consistent with the needs and preferences of culturally diverse clients is to openly discuss these issues early in the helping session. This leads to a coconstruction of the preferred process, content, and outcomes of counseling and therapy with both of the persons involved in the helping endeavor—the client and the counselor.

Coconstruction of the goals and strategies of therapy implies a nonhierarchical relationship with the client. The search for an egalitarian client-counselor relationship must be modified when working with individuals from traditional cultures in which the counselor or therapist is expected to take the expert or leader role. This issue is explored in greater depth later in this section.

MCT metatheory emphasizes that interventions that are appropriate for one client in one cultural context may be inappropriate for another client in another cultural context. For this reason, it is important to increase your repertoire of helping strategies and skills so that you will be better positioned to match an appropriate strategy and skill with the right client at the right time during the helping process. Feminist therapy offers perhaps the most complete framework for considering how to mutually coconstruct a working alliance with the client. This issue is demonstrated in the video clips which are included on the Companion Website that accompanies this textbook.

Applying Multicultural Counseling and Therapy with Culturally Different Clients

The counseling process can be more complex when there are ethnographic, demographic, status, or affiliation differences. When the counselor and client are similar along these factors, the counseling process can be more easily facilitated. However, too much similarity can lead to blind spots for counselor and client in the psychotherapeutic process.

Finding the appropriate blend of similarity and difference is the goal. In matching and blending client and counselor styles, considerations of cultural similarity must be secondary to client preferences. For example, some clients may prefer a counselor who is culturally or racially different from themselves. Automatically assuming that clients will prefer culturally similar counselors is itself an example of stereotyping and should be avoided.

Counselors/therapists who are culturally different from their clients can acquire multicultural competencies that will increase their probability of working respectfully and effectively with diverse clients. Under some conditions, cultural differences may actually enhance the counseling relationship, providing that the counselor has developed the various multicultural counseling competencies outlined in Chapter 2.

Researchers have noted that many clients who are culturally and/or racially different from the counselor may not return for a second interview (Sue & Sue, 2003). Reasons for this vary with the cultural group; some contributing factors include the formality of counseling, counselor-client hierarchy, and, particularly, the lack of sensitivity to varying cultural norms on the part of the helper (Pope-Davis, Coleman, Liu, & Toporek, 2003).

Paniagua (1994, 2001) provides some general guidelines for preventing attrition and establishing appropriate relationships with African-American, Hispanic, Asian-American, and Native American Indian clients. Although these guidelines are not all-inclusive, they clearly point to the need to modify the helping approach to address multicultural dimensions in counseling and therapy.

General Guidelines for Working with Persons in Specific Groups

In working with African-American clients, Paniagua recommends that counselors discuss racial differences early in multicultural counseling/therapy settings. It is also important to focus the culturally and racially different clients' expression of environmental and contextual factors, as these may affect the problems these clients are experiencing.

Paniagua (2001) suggests that it is useful to explore religious and spiritual issues with clients of African descent early in the counseling and therapy process in order to assess the salience of these issues on the client's cultural/racial identity development.

Paniagua further states that many African-American clients may view medication as an impersonal and inappropriate helping strategy. He points out that repeated suggestions by the therapist that an African-American client consider the use of medication may be viewed as the therapist's avoidance of the environmental/contextual factors that contribute to the client's problems.

Latino/Latina clients often feel more comfortable with a formal approach (*formalismo*) at the beginning of counseling and therapy. Paniagua (1994) suggests that using a more formal approach during the early stage of the helping process can be followed by a gradual introduction of a more personal helping style (*personalismo*). Again, religious/spiritual considerations may be important to include in the assessment and treatment of persons in this cultural group.

Also, given his status in the family, the Latino father will often need to be given special regard in counseling and therapy. In doing so practitioners communicate sensitivity for the cultural values of respect (*respecto*) and manhood (*machismo*) that are commonly shared by many Latino/Latina clients.

Paniagua suggests that, with Latino/Latina clients, specific recommendations be made for taking action on the presenting problem, even in the first counseling and psychotherapy session. He notes that these clients may expect suggestions about the use of medication, and therefore, the counselor should be prepared to discuss medication early in treatment. The counselor is encouraged not to make an issue of a Latino/Latina client's being late for a session, should this occur, as many Latino/Latina persons do not view time as specifically as individuals in the dominant cultural/racial group in the United States.

Paniagua encourages the use of a more formal counseling/therapeutic approach with Asian-American clients throughout the helping process. He also indicates that it may be useful for you as the counselor to discuss your educational background and other professional credentials when working with persons in this cultural/racial group. Paniagua particularly stresses the importance of waiting for the clients in this cultural group to initiate discussions about their problems, as many experience a sense of shame for having problems and needing to see a professional.

Many Asian-American clients are likely to have positive dependent relationships with their parents. Paniagua suggests that these relationships should be supported rather than viewed as pathological or an impediment to independent and autonomous development.

It may be important to refer Southeast Asian immigrant clients to social service agencies for housing or school-related issues, as these immediate needs may, from the client's perspective, be a priority over psychological concerns. Also, clients from Cambodia, Laos, or Vietnam may have a history of trauma from war or other immigrant-related experiences. These issues need to be addressed carefully, sensitively, and respectfully in the counseling and psychotherapeutic process.

Native American Indian clients, according to Paniagua, tend to prefer a listening rather than a talkative counselor. Time is viewed very differently by many persons of Native American descent than it is by those within a Eurocentric context. This Native American cultural perspective may often be manifested with a focus on being-in-time rather than the linear, Western being "on time" frame of reference.

Coconstructing counseling/therapy plans and actions is important when working with Native American Indian clients, as is your participation in the broader Native American community. Paniagua points out that medication may be viewed with suspicion by many Native American Indian clients, and the overuse of authority in counseling and therapy needs to be avoided. While Paniagua asserts that it is important to be respectful when working with Native American Indian clients, he also emphasizes the importance of not trying to become overly personal with these clients. All of Paniagua's recommendations reflect an emphasis on respect for humankind and a clear indication that Eurocentric norms of behavior and action must constantly be modified when working with culturally and racially diverse persons.

MCT Practice and Multiple Helping Roles

As you think about the different helping strategies that you can use to foster the mental health and psychological well-being of clients from culturally and racially diverse groups, you might consider how you would include the use of community resources to further complement traditional Western helping approaches to counseling/psychotherapy. In doing so, you can take advantage of the natural helping networks of which your clients are a part.

A natural helping network that can support individual counseling or family therapy may include extended family members, people in the neighborhood, spiritual advisers, government officials, coaches working with youths, and many other people who impact your clients' overall health and sense of well-being. The idea of expanding your impact by using multiple helping strategies and roles that include collaborating with persons in your clients' natural helping networks is the basis of the fifth proposition of the MCT metatheory.

> **Proposition V.** *MCT stresses the importance of multiple helping roles and strategies that are employed by many culturally different individuals, groups, and societies. These multiple helping roles and strategies emerge from culturally diverse family and community networks that have helped sustain and strengthen persons in different cultural/racial groups long before counselors and psychotherapists came on the scene. The MCT metatheory recognizes that conventional Western counseling and psychotherapy represent only one of many theoretical techniques and strategies available to helping professionals. These additional helping approaches extend beyond one-on-one*

therapy and include traditional healing practices, outreach strategies, systems interventions, and prevention interventions involving persons in the client's family, cultural community, and larger social units in which she or he is situated.

MCT metatheory distinguishes itself from traditional counseling and therapy theories in many ways. One of the key distinctions lies in the importance MCT counselors and therapists give to the idea that clients are first and foremost individuals-in-context. The individual-in-context perpective results in the provision of a broad range of mental health care services that include the whole system of individuals, families, groups, and communities of which the client is a part.

Network Therapy

From a multicultural therapeutic orientation, there is something paradoxical about working with the individual alone when that person comes from a relational culture. With this point in mind, Carolyn Attneave developed a new helping approach that integrates Native American concepts of relationship and community with family therapy (Attneave, 1969, 1974, 1982; Speck & Attneave, 1973). She refers to this new helping model as **network therapy** (1969, 1982).

Attneave was not satisfied to limit her mental health interventions to the individual. For example, if the presenting problem was alcoholism, Attneave brought the individual together with the family and community network, which included the nuclear family, the extended family, important neighbors, and key figures from the community such as the priest, teacher, police officer, and perhaps even the local bartender.

These group meetings generated a network of helpers who were aware of the individual alcoholic's problem. Alcoholism is often a hidden behavior, and family and community members often remain silent, even if they suspect the problem. Attneave's network approach brings group awareness and help for the individual's issues.

Attneave's network interventions inevitably changed the way those in the community thought about themselves and their relationships with one another. For example, the bar owner could not sell drinks to the alcoholic without being aware that the priest or a neighbor might observe this and inquire why he was doing something that would negatively affect the client and his family. The teacher, now aware of the family difficulty, could not simply dismiss the acting-out child. The police would be more aware of their responsibility as network support agents and might be motivated to work more closely with the community to address this client's issues.

Attneave's original work has since been updated and used by other Native American advocates (LaFromboise & Jackson, 1996) and community counselors (Lewis et al., 2003). D'Andrea and Daniels (2005) have recently extended many of the ideas presented in Attneave's network therapy model in discussing the importance of building "beloved communities" as a way to promote the mental health and personal well-being of those from diverse cultural/ethnic/racial groups in the United States.

Recognizing the psychological benefits that can be derived from fostering positive and supportive interpersonal interactions, these theorists discuss numerous helping strategies that are effective in building respectful, caring, and supportive interpersonal connections among persons from diverse groups and backgrounds.

Network therapy addresses the individual and the family, but it also relates to the broader community of which our clients are a part. Underlying the network approach are Native American conceptions of interdependence, which form the basis of this type of therapy, as contrasted with the independent orientation that characterizes traditional Western counseling theories. LaFromboise and Low (1989) explain the Native American traditions underlying network therapy in the following manner:

> Traditionally, Indian people live in relational networks that serve to support and nurture strong bonds of mutual assistance and affection. Many tribes still engage in a traditional system of collective interdependence, with family members responsible not only to one another but also to the clan and tribe to which they belong. The Lakota Sioux use the term *tiospaye* to describe a traditional, community way of life in which an individual's well-being remains the responsibility of the extended family. When problems arise among Indian youth, they become problems of the community as well. The family, kin, and friends join together to observe the youth's behavior, draw the youth out of isolation, and integrate that person back into the activities of the group. (p. 121)

Where to Start with Network Therapy. When you work with a European-American child, you can begin to implement network therapy by working with the individual and her or his family, later expanding to larger networks. However, if you are working with a Laotian or Cambodian child, you may want to start by going into the community and learning about the customs of the group. In doing so, you may find that developing a relationship with a respected Buddhist monk in the child's community may be more important in the overall helping context than beginning by using play therapy to assist the youngster in problem solving.

When working with African-American clients, there will likely be some measure of distrust if you are of a different cultural group (Helms & Cook, 1999; Parham, 2002). Working in the community to combat racism may be a step you can take that will aid you in developing a meaningful counseling relationship with children or adolescents who live in that community. Cooperation is often best developed by framing your intervention in terms of an egalitarian relationship with the African-American client or family.

You can follow these guidelines when using the network approach in your own professional practice:

1. *Don't expect to do it all by yourself.* As a counselor or therapist, you cannot do all that is involved in the network approach on your own. Network therapy

relies on a treatment team working together. Case management skills and the ability to work with organizations can be as important as your individual helping skills.

2. *Use multiple theoretical approaches.* Also implied in the network approach is that different theories may be useful with different clients at different points in the helping process. At one time a child may need art therapy to work out certain issues, play therapy at another, and traditional talk therapy at still another. Surprisingly, most adult therapy techniques work well with children if you use appropriate language.

3. *Consider the value of network treatment for all clients.* If you work with a traumatized individual, you can expect that the family is also traumatized in some way. In addition, anticipate that the extended family as well as the neighborhood and community are influenced as well by your client. Network therapy has value for adult European-American clients just as it does for Native American and other groups.

Traditional Healing

Working with clients' familial and community networks enables counselors and therapists to learn about the alternative helping and healing traditions that many culturally and racially diverse people use to realize enhanced health and well-being. MCT counselors and therapists are not only respectful and knowledgeable of many of the traditional healing practices that people in diverse cultural networks use, but they also facilitate the use of these important cultural and community resources and traditions.

Although counseling and psychotherapy developed within a European-American academic setting during the 20th century, other helping strategies have been used throughout history and across cultures when individuals need assistance with emotional and personal problems. Formal methods in formal settings and informal methods in informal settings have been used, as required by those experiencing psychological distress, depending on the cultural setting.

Traditional healing is a form of helping and health promotion employed by people in diverse cultural/racial groups, networks, and communities. It is therefore important that the multicultural therapist develop an understanding of indigenous helping and traditional healing approaches. Traditional healing practices may provide a more viable and effective way of promoting the physical, psychological, and spiritual health and well-being with culturally different clients who are less receptive to Western counseling and psychotherapy theories and interventions (Moodley & West, 2004).

Traditional healing paradigms as well as those of European–North American culture have similar structures. Both are based on the epistemology and belief systems that represent the cultural context. Achebe's (1986, 1995) description of traditional healing in other cultures describes divination processes that focus on the spiritual-human connections in the world. The European–North American traditions of cognitive-behavioral, existential-humanistic, and psychodynamic helping similarly have developed divination processes based on the individual self—the primary object of value in this culture. Both paradigms have value, and both are deserving of respect.

The parallels between Western and traditional healing paradigms open the way for an understanding of and mutual sharing between these two helping domains. Modern psychotherapy generally upholds the emphasis on community and family inherent in the traditional healing strategies described by Achebe (1995). Increasingly, it is accepted that effective therapy sometimes requires the therapist to work in concert with a traditional healer. However, many professionals may object to doing so. For example, Attneave (1974) quotes a psychiatrist on working with Native American Indian medicine men:

> I'm a careful, hard-working, scientific physician. I don't prescribe medications I don't know about or use therapies that haven't got substantial evidence that they do some good. These medicine men aren't about to tell me what they do or how they did it. No! I can't refer my patients to them. That would be unethical. (p. 53)

Attneave points out that the clients of this psychiatrist seldom returned for additional sessions. She strongly recommends that professionals learn to work within the community and states that it is especially important to develop a respectful relationship with traditional healers such as medicine men and women.

In their edited work describing the relevance of traditional healing practices for counseling and therapy, Moodley and West (2005) recommend that counselors and therapists be aware of the work of shamanistic performances, the aboriginal worldview, herbalists, the Native American Indian practice of the sweat lodge as psychotherapy, Maat and other African-centered approaches to psychological and spiritual wellness, Morita therapy (an Eastern approach to mental health care), Jewish health traditions, and Buddhist psychotherapy, to name a few.

Religious and spiritual systems are particularly important in MCT. This is reflected in the way spiritual and religious images and beliefs are integrated naturally into the helping interview as positive resources for personal development and the promotion of psychological health. Such practices complement the religious and spiritual beliefs of many people in diverse cultural groups. For instance, it is well known that traditional healers in many Islamic countries commonly recite verses from the Koran as part of a healing ritual.

Although MCT encourages awareness and inclusion of traditional healers, it is important to define boundaries. For example, the Native American Indian sweat lodge has become popular in the treatment of posttraumatic stress. This may be an effective addition to treatment if a Native American Indian healer is consulted about the sweat lodge procedure ahead of time. The sweat lodge also has played a part in men's movement gatherings. For many Native Americans, such usage of one of their spiritual traditions is considered disrespectful and insulting. If you plan to use non-traditional approaches in your work, it is important to collaborate with traditional healers and show respect for their traditions by consulting the host culture.

The individual-in-context perspective that MCT embraces not only leads to a greater level of respect for and understanding of the power of traditional health practices, but underlies a psychology of liberation that is a mainstay of this approach to mental health care. The following section explores some aspects of liberation psychology. In doing so it directs particular attention to the liberation of consciousness, which is a key component of the sixth proposition of MCT metatheory.

The Liberation of Consciousness: Self-in-Relation

The sixth MCT proposition directs attention to the importance of fostering clients' liberation of consciousness by stimulating a greater understanding of the notion of self-in-relation. Essentially, counselors and therapists must implement helping strategies that enable clients to become increasingly conscious of the ways in which the broader and multiple social/cultural/environmental/historical contexts of which they are a part impact their psychological development. They also have to become aware of the way they have come to make meaning of themselves and the world in which they live.

> **Proposition VI.** *The liberation of consciousness is a basic goal of MCT. Whereas self-actualization, discovery of how the past affects the present, or behavioral change have been traditional goals of Western psychotherapy and counseling, MCT emphasizes the importance of expanding personal, family, group, and organizational consciousness of self-in-relation, family-in-relation, and organization-in-relation. Thus, MCT is ultimately contextual in orientation. As such it draws from and builds on traditional methods of healing as well as knowledge presented by feminist and relational-cultural theorists (Comstock, 2005). (See also Chapter 11.)*

Paulo Freire, a leading Brazilian educational and political theorist, has had a great impact on helping people develop an understanding of themselves in a social context. Whereas Brazilian peasants had been used to blaming themselves and "fate" (*fatalismo*) for their situation, Freire pointed out that their position in life was "the direct product of a whole situation of economic, social, and political domination—and of the paternalism—of which they were victims" (Shaull, 1970, pp. 10–11). Freire (1972) developed a specific method to help these people identify their situation as resulting from oppression and eventually to act against their oppressors. He was exiled from Brazil for his work in this area, but his writings had an immense influence throughout Central and South America and are considered integral in the democratic movements there.

Freire's theoretical educational processes closely correspond to those of cultural identity development theory as presented in Proposition III. From the perspective of

MCT metatheory, the practical utility of Freire's theoretical framework and cultural identity development theory is that both provide road maps that counselors and therapists can use to foster the consciousness-raising process in counseling and therapy. Both of these theoretical models help clients become more aware of themselves within the broader social/cultural/environmental/historical contexts in which they are situated.

Freire's Five Levels of Consciousness

Freire (1972) notes that dispossessed persons typically create what he refers to as a "culture of silence" (p. 89). This culture of silence routinely results in an abdication of the sort of critical and contextual analysis of one's life situation that is essential in developing a liberated consciousness. For counseling purposes, dispossessed persons can include any group—women, religious groups, ethnic/racial groups, survivors of trauma—that considers itself oppressed and unjustly treated by others.

Essentially, Freire's work was aimed at helping Brazilian peasants become more conscious of their dispossession and learn to act positively for their own futures. The first task in achieving these goals was to address what he called **naive consciousness.** This psychological disposition is similar to the first level of the embedded consciousness that is described in cultural/racial identity development theory. At this level of consciousness, dispossessed persons tend to blame themselves for their condition and do not see themselves in a broader social/historical context.

At a second level, Freire notes that the people often seek to identify with the oppressor. "During the initial stage of their struggle, the oppressed find in their oppressor their model of personhood" (Freire, 1970, p. 30). This identification with the oppressor is similar to some of the later aspects of stage 1 (naiveté) and early dimensions of stage 3 (naming) of the cultural/racial identity development framework described earlier in this chapter.

Freire noted that as the peasants he worked with discovered and named their condition, they often manifested increased anger at their oppressors (the third level of consciousness). Women and African-Americans who develop a greater understanding of their personal and group identity from the self-in-relation perspective are also noted to commonly experience and express a heightened sense of anger as they enter Freire's third level of consciousness (Parham, 2002).

Anger often ensues when those of oppressed groups become more conscious of the ways in which they are adversely impacted by the racism, sexism, and economic oppression that help maintain the privileges and power of the dominant cultural/racial group (hooks, 1995, 2000). The central challenge for counselors/therapists who work with clients at this level of consciousness involves assisting individuals to explore ways that their anger might be directed in positive directions to foster individual, collective, and societal transformation.

The fourth level of Freire's liberation model occurs when the individual begins to reflect on the self as a cultural being. "The insistence that the oppressed engage in reflection on their concrete situation is not a call to armchair revolution. On the contrary, reflection—true reflection—leads to real liberatory and revolutionary action" (Freire, 1970, p. 52).

According to Freire, the fifth level of consciousness results in the realization of more complex and healthier forms of personal identity development. This occurs when individuals develop a perspective of self-in-relation rather than of self-in-opposition.

Freire describes movement to the fifth level of his theoretical framework as the essence of the "human project." Freire (1970) asserts that "there would be no human action if [humankind] were not a 'project,' if he [or she] were not able to transcend him- [or her-] self" (p. 38). Consequently, at the fifth level of consciousness, people not only see themselves in relation to the social/cultural/environmental/historical context, of which they are a part, but as individuals who are ready to move to liberatory action.

Freire's Psychoeducational Method

When Freire worked with the peasants in Brazil who could not read, he developed "culture circles" in which they sat together in a relationship of equality between instructor and student. This approach mirrors the egalitarian structure of both feminist therapy and MCT. Freire wanted his students to develop reading skills in relation to their natural environment. Thus, he used visual, pictorial, graphic, tactile, and auditory images generated by the persons he was working with to elucidate their experience.

As the peasants shared their images of their lives, Freire helped them name their experiences and then write the words in Portuguese. This process resulted in more concrete storytelling so that eventually the peasants could reflect together on what their lives meant.

If the peasants developed, for example, images of the good life of the plantation owner, they would name these images. In turn, these affluent images could be contrasted with their own lives of poverty. This concrete naming frequently resulted in the elicitation of angry reactions, as the peasants began to develop an identity in opposition to the plantation owner.

A distinct group reflective consciousness then emerged as the peasants began to see similarities in their stories and a common action plan to address the injustices that were imposed on them. Thus, although the peasants began instruction with an embedded naive consciousness, Freire's method led them to an increased awareness of alternative perspectives on their situation, the development of a liberated consciousness, and eventually to alternative action planning.

Relating Freire's Educational Method to Counseling and Therapy Practice

Despite being exiled, Freire eventually returned to Brazil. As a result of his steadfast commitment to implement his theoretical model to foster the liberation of the consciousness of the peasants in that South American country, Freire has become an international figure who is influential in many fields.

Freire offers several practical specifics for therapeutic practice. These practical specifics are especially relevant for counselors and psychologists who are committed to using MCT and developmental counseling and therapy (DCT) strategies (Chapter 13) when working with persons from diverse client populations (Ivey, 1994, 1995b). Theoretically, there are significant parallels among many structural developmental theories (Ivey & Ivey, 2001), cultural/racial identity theories (Sue & Sue, 2003), and Freire's notions of liberation consciousness. For example, the techniques and strategies of DCT (Chapter 13) closely parallel Freire's teaching methodology. Like the developmental approach of the DCT model (Ivey & Ivey, 2001), Freire used sensorimotor images to bring out holistic summaries of Brazilian peasants' living conditions and followed up by using concrete naming and storytelling. Freire's reflective consciousness level corresponds to the formal operational aspects of the DCT approach, and his contextual fifth level closely corresponds to the dialectic/systemic analysis of life in general and one's personal/collective development in particular (Ivey, 1995b).

Cultural/racial identity theory also focuses on the cognitive-emotional development of people-in-context, which is the basis of Freire's approach to liberation of consciousness. The following subsections offer examples of how the examination of cultural/racial identity theory can be used in counseling and psychotherapy to facilitate clients' awareness of self-in-relation.

Inviting a Narrative. In this example, a client, traumatized over an incident involving racial or sexual harassment has come for counseling. The following presents two possible client responses:

Therapist: Could you tell me what occurred for you? [*Drawing out the client's story is facilitated by using the basic listening sequence described in Chapter 4: What are the main facts, feelings, and thoughts of the client?*]

Client 1: I don't know, perhaps it was my fault. Maybe I shouldn't have dressed as I did.

Client 2: They called me a _____. I hate that name. I would have liked to kill them.

At this point, the therapist asks for the narrative or story of the event. The discussion can go on at some length, as the client explores issues in depth and as the therapist and client feel appropriate. The second client seems ready for action (albeit inappropriate), whereas the first takes on a great deal of unnecessary personal responsibility. To apply cultural/racial identity development concepts to this exchange, it is evident that a level 1 (naive) or level 2 (identification with oppressor) manifests in client 1 and a level 3 (anger) response is evident in client 2.

Often, counseling and therapy take an issue orientation to clients' narratives and may seek to resolve the client's presenting problem. The psychotherapy-as-liberation perspective maintains an interest in the problem but also seeks to help individuals see their issues from a broader systemic perspective. This approach closely approximates that of Freire, developmental counseling theorists (D'Andrea & Daniels, 2005), and cultural/racial identity theorists (Sue & Sue, 2003). In addition, Freire provides a framework for examining cultural identity.

Reexperiencing the Sensory Dimensions of Cultural Identity Issues. Freire began discussion in his cultural circles with auditory, visual, olfactory, kinesthetic, and even gustatory images. A narrative of a story, valuable and central as it is, can nonetheless separate the client from the direct experience of the event, which originally was experienced in a sensory fashion.

An important part of Freire's naming process was enabling clients to know and learn the sensory elements in their experiences. Similarly, if we are to help clients experience their stories—and eventually the cultural implications of these stories—we need to help them get in touch with their original sensory experiences. Such emotional learning here can help clients move from the naive level to other levels of consciousness. The following lists some of the statements and questions the MCT practitioner might use to help clients explore the sensory dimensions of their narratives:

> Take one dimension of the story that struck you as especially important.
> Focus on that dimension and allow yourself to reexperience the event.
> Can you get a clear image of the event?
> As you focus on that image, what are you seeing, hearing, feeling?

This sequence involves the use of the complex psychodynamic technique of regression, in which clients are encouraged to go back to old events and reexperience them with sensory awareness in the present moment. This helping technique can be powerful and should be used carefully by a supportive helper so that the past negative experience is not repeated in the counseling setting.

The value of moving the narrative to a sensory orientation is that the event is holistically and directly reexperienced in the body rather than solely as an intellectual construct. This technique corresponds to Freire's use of images in teaching reading to Brazilian peasants and is an important part of the psychotherapy of liberation.

Making the Narrative Concrete and Specific. After sensory experiencing, Freire would then have his groups tell concrete stories about how their lives had been affected by the events associated with their situation. These concrete narratives provided a structure and a way to share meaning with one another. As people hear stories from others, they begin to realize that their images, experiences, and stories are at least partially shared and understood by others.

The telling of concrete stories facilitates movement into stage 3 (naming) of cultural/racial identity theory. This stage is often accompanied by expressed anger. Clients are likely to express inconsistencies in their stories as they are encouraged to name the contextual factors that contribute to their problems and express the anger that typically accompanies newly emerging consciousness.

Counselors and therapists need to effectively address such inconsistencies to facilitate the ongoing development of their clients' psychological liberation. MCT practitioners do this by encouraging their clients to continue to express their narratives and by providing gentle confrontations that are aimed at assisting them to examine

Professional Development Extension

Using Network Therapy Concepts for Community Empowerment and Health Interventions

Judy Lewis and her colleagues (2003) have reported numerous ways in which many multicultural counseling and therapy concepts have been incorporated in a broad range of community empowerment and health projects across the United States. Some of the key concepts that have been used in this regard include the implementation of an innovative approach to community mental health care based on collectivistic principles rooted in Carolyn Attneave's (1969) theory of network therapy.

One of the projects that Lewis and colleagues (2003) discuss is the Aunt Martha's Youth Service Center in Park Forest, Illinois. Established in 1972, Aunt Martha's uses a community approach to address the needs of the youths who reside in the Park Forest area, especially those identified as being at high risk for physical, educational, and psychosocial problems. Although traditional individual and small-group counseling services are provided by this agency, the mental health practitioners working there also offer a broad range of other preventive education, life skills training, and personal health services aimed at enabling young people to participate as positive and healthy members of their communities. Since its beginning, Aunt Martha's has grown from a simple counseling center to a complex, highly structured agency serving a wide geographic area through a dozen programs, with a staff of 89 mental health professionals and over 250 community volunteers.

This network of volunteers draws upon the unique perspectives and expertise of many different persons in the greater community. Included in this expansive helping network are parents, extended family members, retired teachers, coaches, members of the various religious groups in the area, business persons, and individuals from other professions who feel a sense of responsibility and connectedness with the youths who represent the next generation of adults in their community.

Another community-based project described by Lewis and her colleagues is the I Have a Future (IHAF) program established in a low-income, African-American neighborhood in Nashville, Tennessee. The counselors who work in this program direct attention to promoting the development of adolescents of African descent who reside in this area by creating a developmental helping context that reflects an Afrocentric worldview. This multicultural venue was built around seven life principles called Nguzo Saba (D'Andrea & Daniels, 1992; Kunjufu, 1986).

One of the other hallmarks of the IHAF program is how the program coordinators solicit help from members of the greater community. This includes calling on parents, extended family members, ministers, coaches, community youth service workers, teachers, law enforcement personnel, and other African-Americans in the community who are recognized for successfully launching new business and economic development ventures.

Evaluation studies indicate that both of these programs are effective in fostering positive developmental changes among the youths they serve (Lewis et al., 2003). One factor that contributes to fostering healthy adolescent development in these projects is that both follow Attneave's concepts of network theory in implementing community-based initiatives that involve the caring assistance and unique input of many concerned members of the neighborhood in which the Aunt Martha's and the IHAF projects were established.

Mental health professionals will increasingly be called upon to develop and implement programs and services that are aimed at addressing the needs of persons in high-risk populations. The rapid cultural/racial/ethnic changes in the demography of the United States suggest that many persons in these high-risk populations will come from diverse cultural/racial/ethnic groups and backgrounds. These two programs demonstrate the significant utility of Attneave's network therapy concepts when developing and implementing such programs.

By using this aspect of MCT metatheory in creating a culturally specific and sensitive helping venue outside of traditional counseling and therapy settings, mental health practitioners are positioned to help advance the dignity and development of larger numbers of persons from diverse backgrounds.

inconsistencies in their story lines. The following statements/questions may be useful in helping clients make their narratives more concrete and clarifying inconsistencies when and if they occur:

Tell me a story of what happened.

What happened first, next, and how did it end?

Tell your story in as much detail as possible.

Can you tell me another story that occurs to you and give me as many details as possible?

Let's talk about some of the differences in these similar stories.

Moving to a Reflective and Liberated Consciousness. When clients tell several concrete and situational stories about their lives, they are better prepared to move to a more reflective and liberated level of consciousness. This is even more likely to occur in group settings, where the sharing of stories almost automatically leads to a more reflective and liberated state of consciousness among different members of the group.

As people share their stories and note similarities with one another, individual stories begin to move from "my story" to "our story," as common cultural and contextual factors are increasingly made apparent. In cultural/racial identity development terms, this process leads to an increasing introspection of the mutiple factors that affect people's psychological development and sense of personal and collective identity.

Through the introspective process, old ideas are taken apart and examined, and new meanings are developed. Counselors and therapists can foster the development of this sort of introspection by using a variety of cognitive techniques that encourage clients to reflect on and reframe the meaning and patterning of their stories. The following statements/questions are helpful in promoting this kind of introspection in individual and group counseling and therapy settings:

Is that a pattern?

Does that happen a lot?

As you reflect on it now, what sense do you make of it?

How are you feeling and thinking right now?

What is common to these stories?

As you look at the story now, old meanings seem to be breaking down.

How is this process of disintegration for you?

How could a new integration be generated?

What common themes do you see in these stories?

As a result of using such formal operational questions and statements, clients are able to think about their life situation and challenges more broadly. This enables many clients to begin to see patterns, whereas before they viewed their lives as being marked by separate and unconnected situations. In doing so, clients start seeing their own behavior in relation to the broader environmental systems of which they are a part. In short, they begin to see themselves in context.

Seeing Self-in-Relation or Self-in-System. Freire was especially concerned that clients see themselves in a broad social context. The sharing and identifying of patterns and themes described above still tend to focus on individual or group perceptions. The following set of questions can be useful in fostering the development of client consciousness in ways that promote a greater understanding and appreciation of the self-in-system (Ivey, 1995b). When working with clients from diverse backgrounds, you may find these questions helpful in loosening old thought patterns, which can then lead to the development of a new belief system.

How might cultural, gender, or racial issues relate to your life story?

Under what rule(s) were you (or the other person or group) operating?

Where did that rule come from?

How might someone else (another family member, a member of the opposition, someone from a different cultural background) describe this situation?

How do these rules relate now?

How might we describe this from the point of view of some other person, theoretical framework, or language system?

How might we put it together using another framework?

How is your experience part of a cultural theme? A family theme?

What do experiences in your family of origin have to say to this?

What shall we do? How shall we do it together?

What is our objective and how can we work together effectively?

In working through these questions, techniques such as the community genogram (Chapter 1) and the microskill of focusing (Chapter 4) can be helpful. Also, various behavioral counseling and therapy techniques (Chapter 7) may be employed to help clients plan specific actions for the future.

Freire, of course, was centrally concerned with generalization, and encouraged the peasants he worked with to take their learnings back to life within the community. From Freire's perspective, words and thoughts need to be enacted in concrete practice. In counseling terms, the issue is finding techniques to encourage "homework" and doing something with the changed narrative. Freire's concept of human projects—helping clients use their newly developed selves in a concrete fashion through action and in relationship with others—is an important consideration here.

Limitations and Practical Implications of MCT

There are many challenges in using the MCT approach. MCT asks the helping practitioner to be highly competent in traditional theory, develop an understanding of MCT metatheory, and become knowledgeable of the specific needs, wishes, and developmental histories of many highly diverse multicultural groups. One of the limitations of MCT is a relatively small research base on which to establish its claims. However, this research base is constantly expanding, and there is increasing evidence that adding multicultural issues to practice improves effectiveness.

In spite of these challenges and limitations, MCT is extremely practical, as it forces us to deal with the realities of difference. Consequently, the complexity and high demands of MCT are a part of developing the multicultural approach necessary in our culturally diverse world. This chapter has provided activities to illustrate some of the interventions that can be applied in multicultural counseling and therapy. Specific helping interventions used by various cultural groups also have been included.

Unfortunately, space limits detailing the contributions and recommended interventions for specific groups. However, the examples discussed above, such as Attneave's network therapy and Freire's work with Brazilian peasants, point to the significant contributions such culturally specific interventions can make to traditional therapy and counseling.

Clearly, MCT provides us with much challenge and much opportunity. It is equally clear that one cannot master its many concepts without extensive time and study. The importance of making a commitment to master various aspects of this important theoretical force is underscored by the recognition that MCT will take a more central place in the mental health profession in the coming years (D'Andrea & Daniels, 2005; U.S. DHHS, 2001). The Professional Development Extension feature explores how an aspect of MCT metatheory—Atteneave's network therapy concepts—can be applied in community settings.

Summary

This chapter has offered a foundational understanding of some of the complex and challenging issues associated with MCT theory. Six central theoretical propositions of MCT have been discussed to help you acquire a foundational understanding of important concepts associated with this approach to counseling and therapy.

Becoming a culturally competent mental health practitioner requires you to become more knowledgeable about new MCT intervention strategies as well as the ways in which traditional helping theories can be modified to more effectively and respectfully meet the needs of persons from diverse groups and backgrounds. Of equal, or perhaps even greater, importance is that counselors and therapists be aware of their own cultural worldview, conditioning, biases, and preferences. Skill-building exercises in the chapter assist you in examining your own level of cultural/racial identity development. Competency-building exercises encourage your development of additional skills aimed at fostering other dimensions of your professional development in becoming a culturally competent professional.

The next chapter provides yet another important theoretical framework for counseling and psychotherapy—developmental counseling and therapy (DCT). This framework provides a means to integrate and use many of the concepts associated with the three traditional forces in ways that reflect a heightened understanding of and respect for feminist and multicultural counseling considerations.

Multimedia Resources for This Chapter

The following online resources offer video and other resources of particular relevance to this chapter of your text.

Companion Website

Go to **www.ablongman.com/Ivey6e** to view the following video clips:

- Video clip 12.1 demonstrates one way to help clients understand some of the assumptions and philosophical tenets commonly manifested in various counseling and psychotherapeutic approaches in the field today. By informing the client of some of these assumptions and philosophical tenets and allowing her to choose the direction she would like to see the helping process take, the therapist helps build the kind of egalitarian relationship that is central to MCT.

- Video clip 12.2 demonstrates one way counselors and therapists can foster an egalitarian relationship with culturally different clients early in the helping process. You will see that the counselor does this by asking the client what she would need to know about him to gain the knowledge and trust that is important for effective counseling and psychotherapy to occur.

- Video clip 12.3 provides an example of one way to build a relationship that reflects the coconstruction and mutuality concepts encouraged in Nwachuku's model and MCT metatheory. By encouraging the client to select how she would prefer therapy to proceed, the counselor fosters the sort of self-determinism and empowerment that are core considerations in these two helping perspectives.

MyHelpingLab

myhelpinglab If a MyHelpingLab passcode was included with your textbook and you have activated your passcode:

- go to **www.ablongman.com/myhelpinglab**
- enter the "Counseling" area of the site by clicking on that tab
- select "Video Lab" from the toolbar to the left of the page
- select "MyHelpingLab Videos by Theoretical Approach"
- select the "Culture-Sensitive Therapy" module to view various video clips of a therapist using this approach with a client

chapter 13

Developmental Counseling and Therapy: Integrative Theory and Practice

This chapter is designed to:

1. Synthesize the many approaches presented in this book in a meaningful way that has direct application to practice.

2. Assess clients' meaning-making styles so that you can match your interventions to their unique needs.

3. Present treatment plans that enable you to provide your clients with holistic, multilevel, and multitheoretical counseling and therapeutic services.

4. Explore some key dimensions of the integrative theory of developmental counseling and therapy.

5. Expand your portfolio of competencies through practice exercises, enabling you to

   - assess client meaning making within four cognitive-emotional developmental styles

   - utilize specific questions to facilitate client conversation and narratives within four cognitive-emotional developmental styles

   - generate comprehensive treatment plans

Introduction

What occurs for you when you focus on the Gestalt image in Figure 13.1? Take a moment and record your perspective. The drawing in the figure is usually described as being both an old woman and a young woman. At first glance, some will see the older woman, while others will see the younger. Take some time until you can see both. Some individuals find it quite difficult to see the second woman, and this form of "stuckness" could be described as a lack of intentionality—an inability to take a new perspective.

There is still more to be found in the drawing. As you look, you will find that the two images alternate; you can see the images move from one to another as if in a motion picture. With further concentration, you can obtain a "still photo" in which you see both women at once.

There are also multicultural implications in our views of the drawing. Why is the woman with the large nose often termed "ugly" or "old," while the woman with a small nose is considered "young and beautiful"? There is no particular reason that a

Figure 13.1 A Figure to Figure: What Is Your Perspective?
Source: From original drawing by W. E. Hill, published in *Puck*, November 6, 1905. First used for psychological purposes by E. G. Boring, "A New Ambiguous Figure," *American Journal of Psychology*, 1930.

person with a large nose is older or less beautiful than one whose nose is smaller. Our perceptions and interpretations often come from our cultural perspective. We think we "see what we see," but we fail to realize that our surrounding environment affects the way data enter our minds.

Chapter 13 is about **multiple seeing**—the ability to hold several perspectives on the counseling and therapy process. Whether you commit yourself to a single theory, become an eclectic, or outline your own metatheoretical integrative approach, the ability to use theories and see clients from multiple perspectives and points of view will be invaluable. This chapter provides yet another important theoretical framework for counseling and psychotherapy—the developmental counseling and therapy (DCT) model. The DCT framework provides an important means to integrate and use many of the concepts associated with the three traditional theoretical forces (psychodynamic, cognitive-behavioral, existential-humanistic theories) in ways that reflect a heightened understanding of and respect for feminist and multicultural counseling considerations.

The Integrative Worldview of Developmental Counseling and Therapy

At one time, those in counseling and psychotherapy would ask each other, "What is your theoretical style?" It was considered important to select one theoretical approach to the field and become an expert in that style.

Fortunately, that day has passed, but a new question focuses on how we integrate multiple approaches to the field. It is apparent from earlier discussions in this book that widely varying worldviews and practical strategies all have merit. But clearly you will not want to use them all at once. How can you make sense of and utilize the many valuable theories and practice strategies? In the concluding chapter of this book you will be asked to generate your own theoretical integration. This chapter will introduce you to an approach that can help integrate various approaches to counseling and therapy.

Developmental counseling and therapy (DCT) is oriented to multiple seeing, to helping us recognize that there are multiple truths in the counseling and psychotherapy process (Ivey, 2000/1986; Ivey, Ivey, Myers, & Sweeney, 2005). DCT can be helpful in organizing these many facets of counseling and psychotherapy into a theoretically coherent and useful set of tools. DCT gives special attention to multicultural considerations in counseling and therapy (see Ivey & Ivey, 2001).

Given that you are likely to work within several theoretical styles during the course of treatment with a single client, it is important to be able to integrate multiple theories and skills. For example, a depressed client might benefit from relaxation techniques to address tension, concrete assertiveness training to enhance personal effectiveness, reflective client-centered methods to increase self-esteem, and feminist therapy to understand the context within which the depression evolved. The task of the integrative counselor and therapist is to combine these varying approaches into a holistic approach.

DCT uses a language system that reinterprets the thinking of the Swiss epistemologist/psychologist/biologist Jean Piaget. Through observation, Piaget (1926/1963, 1965) found that children constructed knowledge at four different levels: sensorimotor, concrete, formal, and postformal. Piaget's observations have been useful in working with children but have had only limited use in adolescent and adult clinical and counseling situations.

DCT's central assumption is that whether child, adolescent, or adult, we metaphorically repeat Piaget's developmental stages of sensorimotor, concrete, formal, and postformal operations again and again. DCT points out that Piaget's tools can be used in working with individuals throughout the life span.

An equally important tenet of DCT is that the multiple strategies of counseling and psychotherapy can be organized into a meaningful holistic presentation, as represented by the developmental sphere (see Figure 13.2). The spiral presents the movement of client meaning-making styles through four types of counseling and

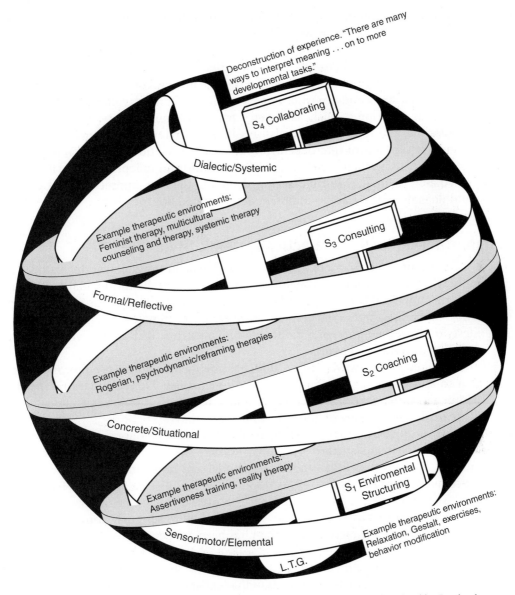

Figure 13.2 The Developmental Sphere: Four Styles of Counseling and Therapy Associated with the Four Cognitive-Emotional Developmental Styles

Source: The developmental sphere was first drawn by Lois T. Grady and is used here with her permission.

psychotherapy environments. The task of the counselor or therapist is to assess where the client is in terms of meaning-making style and then to match language and therapeutic interventions with the client's unique style. In many cases, deliberate mismatching of styles can be beneficial in helping clients learn new ways of thinking and behaving.

This spherical model is important in accomplishing the theoretical and practical integration of counseling theories. As the figure shows, all of us operate at multiple levels of experience. Since experience is interconnected and holistic, a change in one part of the holistic system reverberates and influences the entire developmental sphere.

DCT's holistic frame of reference finds value in views of the helping process that at times may seem antagonistic. For example, DCT finds value in individualistic approaches to helping, such as Freud's psychodynamic theory, Skinner's radical behaviorism, and Rogers's humanism. Native American, Afrocentric, and feminist therapy conceptions of interdependence and self-in-relation are central to the DCT frame. With some clients, the values of autonomy and independence may be more immediately helpful. Multiple seeing demands that we appreciate and consider multiple realities if we are to maintain an integrated holistic view.

The Importance of DCT's Dialectic/Systemic Style

DCT is a contextual theory that considers the person in environmental, historical, and multicultural dimensions. As such it also finds value in the rational-emotive behavioral therapy (REBT) of Albert Ellis (Chapter 8). Ellis was the first psychotherapist who "normalized" gay and lesbian behavior by acknowledging it as a legitimate lifestyle. However, although a pioneer in human rights, REBT has given insufficient attention to contextual issues.

More recently, however, Ellis (2000) has commented on the need for more attention to dialectic/systemic areas of his treatment plan. He recognizes the need for REBT and other theories to consider and integrate cultural, environmental, and contextual issues as part of a holistic approach.

Historically, REBT has not emphasized dialectic/systematic counseling or counselors working to change the sociopolitical system as much as it is heavily encouraged in DCT. It seems that Ellis's theoretical model and most other popular counseling procedures are relatively lax in this respect. The unique element of DCT is its stress on this fourth process. REBT and other practitioners who operate from traditional counseling and therapy frameworks would do well to seriously consider emphasizing dialectic/systemic factors more than has been done in the past and thereby draw from the DCT approach.

Rigazio-DiGilio and her colleagues (1997) note that "theories of counseling and practice that perpetuate the notion of individual and family dysfunction without giving equal attention to societal dysfunction and to the dysfunctional interactions that can occur between individuals, families, and societies (e.g., intentional and unintentional power differentials) may unwittingly reinforce the oppressive paradigm" (p. 241). All systems of counseling need to give serious thought to this warning, though few of them have done so to date.

Truly integrative counseling and psychotherapy, according to DCT, requires attention to cultural, environmental, and contextual factors as they affect clients' psychological development. Without consideration of the social context, any approach to integrative therapy and counseling is incomplete.

Recognizing that cultural, environmental, and contextual factors impact people's development is an important first step in understanding DCT theory. Before you can begin to effectively implement this theory into practice, you must have a solid understanding of the various characteristics associated with the four levels of Jean Piaget's cognitive development theory on which DCT is based.

Piagetian Cognitive Stages

Piaget talks of four major stages of cognitive development. DCT uses Piagetian thinking as a metaphor and speaks of four cognitive-emotional developmental styles that appear and reappear within individuals as they operate in their worlds. Clients function within sensorimotor/elemental, concrete/situational, formal/reflective, and/or dialectic/systemic styles. Although clients may have access to cognitive, emotional, and behavioral resources inherent in several styles, most tend to rely on a primary style in understanding and reacting to their specific issues.

An important task for DCT practitioners is to enter the world of the client—to understand and appreciate how the client makes sense of and operates in that world. Clients make meaning within the four cognitive-emotional developmental styles. Each style involves a different complexity of language that represents the client's meaning-making process. Clients talk about their experiences within these different styles. Some clients will operate within only one style (**rigid access**). Others will randomly or haphazardly present several styles (**diffuse access**). Still others will move in an organized way from style to style throughout an interview or treatment series (**flexible access**).

For example, Kiaka is a client going through a divorce. During the treatment process, he talks about the divorce from several cognitive-emotional styles. As you read the following, keep in mind that it is likely that clients who use several styles will need you to provide therapeutic environments that offer various psychotherapeutic strategies corresponding to each style.

1. *Sensorimotor/elemental.* Tears are present. Kiaka talks in a random, confused fashion and simultaneously denies feelings of hurt and anger. However, there are times when Kiaka is able to directly experience his hurt and confusion.

2. *Concrete/situational.* Kiaka gives many details and tells many stories related to the divorce. He names feelings around situations, but there is an absence of self-reflection as well as considerable blaming and anger toward his spouse.

3. *Formal/reflective.* Kiaka talks more abstractly. He seldom discusses the specifics of what happened between him and his wife. Rather, he defines repeating patterns and is able to reflect on himself and his feelings.

4. *Dialectic/systemic.* Kiaka sees multiple perspectives regarding his pending divorce and can see his wife's frame of reference. He realizes how he learned patterns in his family of origin that are repeated in his relationships. Multicultural issues of gender, ethnicity, and religion become part of his awareness.

It is important that clinicians match their language and treatment techniques with the style primarily influencing a client's feeling, thinking, acting, and response to certain issues. For example, it would not be effective to ask a male client working within a sensorimotor framework to formally analyze how he contributed to a pending divorce. DCT suggests the need to first join clients where they are in their own emotional, cognitive, and behavioral development. The predominant cognitive-emotional developmental style is the style a person primarily uses to make sense of a particular situation or issue.

Table 13.1 illustrates the strengths and weaknesses of each style. Full development of human potential occurs by expanding client awareness and potential within each style. Individuals who work within several styles have access to the strengths inherent in each style. Those who rely on one style can be limited by not having a range of styles and approaches available to them.

Clients usually present their issues within several styles but tend to rely on a predominant style to frame their understanding of their experiences. For example, Susan, a teenager with bulimia, is enmeshed in the sensory world of food and bodily sensations. She also is a gymnast and is able to compete successfully in the world of athletics. She is skilled in formal thinking and is an excellent student, yet she also has low self-esteem. Her family blames her for her negative thoughts and eating patterns while denying that the family and athletic cultures also influence her thoughts, feelings, and behavior. Susan primarily discusses her issues from a sensorimotor/elemental style, usually emphasizing her frustrations and disappointments. The DCT model contains a systematic classification system to help therapists assess the predominant and secondary cognitive, emotional, and behavioral styles a client uses throughout the course of treatment. Research Exhibit 13.1 (p. 411) summarizes research on the DCT model and the importance of multiplicity for mental health. Competency-Building Activity 13.1 (p. 412) provides you with an opportunity to practice assessing cognitive, emotional, and behavioral styles at the different levels of the DCT model.

Things seem very different when viewed from sensorimotor/elemental, concrete/situational, formal/reflective, or dialectic/systemic perspectives. Knowledge of DCT assessment and questioning strategies will likely be helpful as you work with other theoretical approaches. Clinicians who use many approaches and modalities often follow the DCT sequences. For example, cognitive behaviorist Aaron Beck (1976) (see Chapter 7) often asks clients to picture early life images (sensorimotor/elemental). Clients are then encouraged to describe happenings from that time (concrete/situational) and to observe patterns in later life that are derived from these images (formal/reflective). Finally, Beck asks clients to reflect on systems of operations (dialectic/systemic) to reframe their original thinking about their problems in more depth and greater complexity.

Through this process, clients obtain an alternative integration that can lead to new thoughts, feelings, and behaviors. Beck, however, tends not to discuss dialectic/systemic multicultural issues as an inherent part of his systematic procedures. Rogers and Perls have followed similar questioning sequences in their work, but again with the emphasis on an individual focus and not contextual issues.

Table 13.1

Cognitive-Emotional Developmental Styles and Associated Psychotherapy Issues

Cognitive-Emotional Developmental Styles	Emotional Expressions	Psychotherapy Issues	Associated Interventions and Goals
Sensorimotor/Elemental (What are the *elements of experience?*) Clients are able to experience life directly in the immediate here and now. They can become enmeshed in sensory experience and in what they directly see, hear, and feel. They may show randomness in their conversation and behavior. They may lack conscious awareness of environmental issues.	Two types of emotion represent the sensorimotor orientation: (1) emotion is integrated with cognition—"I am my emotions"—with direct access to affective experience; and (2) emotions are split off and unrecognized, as can happen with an adult survivor of child abuse or of an alcoholic family, or a person who is unaware of or denies family/cultural issues.	Counselors and therapists, who are often primarily formal operational, may be weak in skills within this level. They may prefer to talk *about* feelings rather than experience them *directly.* A trainee once said, "I used to think I was good with feelings. Now I know I use formal operational thought and reflect on my feelings rather than experiencing them."	*Interventions:* Focus on the here and now and bring the client to awareness— Gestalt exercises, body work, Freire's (1972) use of images to expand consciousness of cultural issues are all helpful. *Goal:* To help client experience the world directly; remove denial and splitting; accept randomness.
Concrete/Situational (What are the *situational descriptions?*) Clients may describe their life events in great detail— "This happened . . . , then this . . . and so on." They are concerned with action in the world and with objective, observable events. Some clients will be able to establish cause and effect—if/then— thinking.	Clients can name emotions but are unable to reflect on them. In the early phases, naming of emotions will be all that can be done. Later, clients will begin to realize that emotions are related to events in a "causal" fashion. The classic counseling response "You feel . . . because . . ." is a particularly clear example of concrete emotions.	Many formal operational counselors often become bored and frustrated with concrete stories and details. However, Piagetian scholars estimate that from 25 to 40 percent of North American adults do not primarily access full formal operations.	*Interventions:* Focus on action—assertiveness training, decision making on a specific issue, reality therapy, and many behavioral techniques can be useful. *Goal:* To draw out the specifics of a situation and later cultivate if/then thinking and predictable actions.

continued on next page

Table 13.1, continued

Cognitive-Emotional Developmental Styles and Associated Psychotherapy Issues

Cognitive-Emotional Developmental Styles	Emotional Expressions	Psychotherapy Issues	Associated Interventions and Goals
Formal/Reflective			
(What is the nature of *self* and repeating *patterns of self, thought, and action?*) Clients are able to move out of the concrete world and deal with abstractions. They like to think about themselves and their personal patterns of feeling and thinking. They can reflect on their feelings (but may not be able to experience them in the here and now of sensorimotor experience). They are able to analyze and look at their problems with more distance.	Clients working within this orientation can reflect on their feelings and examine patterns of feelings. They may even be able to examine patterns of patterns. But this ability to reflect on self and feelings may make it difficult to experience emotion in the sensorimotor here and now. Also, despite their ability to analyze feelings, the formal client may be unable to act on them.	Much counseling and therapy theory exists primarily within the formal orientation. For example, Rogerian client-centered theory requires one to be able to reflect on feelings, although the microskill of reflection of feelings can be useful within all cognitive orientations. Many therapists and counselors like to work with formal operational clients, as they tend to be verbal and see patterns. The danger is in a client-therapist relationship that is all talk and no action.	*Interventions:* Focus on analysis— Rogerian, psychodynamic, and much of cognitive theory are useful. *Goal:* To help clients look at themselves and their life patterns.
Dialectic/Systemic			
(How did all this develop in a *system* or how is it *integrated?*) Clients are able to reflect on reflections and can work with comfort on systems of operations. They are capable of multiple perspectives and are able to identify how family and cultural pressures affect them and their thinking processes. They may become enmeshed in abstract cognitive processes, with emotion markedly split off from experience.	Clients will see emotions changing with situational context (for example, sadness about death when faced with the immediacy of a loss, but also happiness that a terminally ill parent no longer has to suffer). Emotions are multidimensional and complex. At the same time, this awareness may interfere with an ability to experience feelings directly or to act on these.	More and more counselors and therapists are moving beyond formal thinking to this broader, more contextual, and multiculturally aware frame of reference. The dialectic/systemic frame of reference allows one to take a more metatheoretical, integrative approach to the field. When you generate your own theory or metatheory of helping, you are engaged in dialectic/systemic thought.	*Interventions:* Focus on construction. Consciousness-raising theories, multicultural-feminist-social justice counseling and therapy, and much of family therapy are useful here. *Goal:* To facilitate integrative and multiperspectival thought and awareness of self-in-relation to others and the system.

Research Exhibit 13.1

Cognitive-Emotional Developmental Styles:
Clinical and Research Data on Effectiveness of the DCT Model

Do the constructions of DCT really exist? Can they be identified and measured reliably? Does the claim that clients have the ability to take multiple perspectives hold, and are these styles helpful to clients?

Defining Developmental Styles and Predictability of Client Response

Independent raters classified patient DCT styles with high reliability (0.98 kappa = 0.87). When answering standard questions from the DCT model, both short- and long-term depressed clients responded consistently with the theory by talking at the same level that questions were asked by the interviewer/therapist (99 percent). For example, if you provide a client lead within the formal/reflective style, you can expect the client to respond at the same level. This study found that what you say deeply impacts the style of client verbalization (Rigazio-DiGilio & Ivey, 1990). Heesacker and others (1995) conducted a factor analysis study of DCT constructs with 1,700 subjects, and the four DCT styles were again validated by this research.

Example Research and Clinical Process Work

In multilevel weight treatment, it was found that using DCT constructs resulted in better management of weight and sustained weight loss over time as compared with a control group (Weinstein, 1994). Boyer (1996) found that adolescent substance abusers responded favorably to DCT treatment. Strehorn (1998) applied the framework to learning-disabled college students. Brodhead (1991) found that effective teachers consistently match students' cognitive-emotional style, while ineffective teachers tend to have a mismatch.

The DCT model has proven effective in developing multilevel treatment plans for abused children (Ivey & Ivey, 1998). Kenney and Law (1991) and Mailer (1991) have used the model in rehabilitation and career counseling.

Internationally, Fukuhara (1987) and Tamase (1989, 1991) have applied DCT constructs in empirical and clinical trials in Japan. Treatment of agoraphobia and anxiety disorders has proven useful in Portugal (Goncalves & Ivey, 1992) following this approach.

Narrative Implications

Myers (1998) applied DCT to bibliotherapy and journaling and found that both students and clients gained insight and understanding through the process of multilevel storytelling.

Competency-Building Activity 13.2 can help you exercise your questioning skills as they relate to the DCT framework. As you work through this activity, think about additional questions that would assist clients in reflecting on contextual factors that have impacted their lives and development. Integrating questions about the client's family of origin into the standard series of questions presented in that exercise is particularly valuable in incorporating contextual considerations in the helping process. For example, you could begin Competency-Building Activity 13.2 by asking, "Could you tell me what happens for you when you focus on your family of origin?" Additionally, you could begin the coconstruction segment of the dialectic/systemic style by asking, "How is it that your family of origin may have taught you these rules or assumptions?"

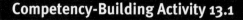

Competency-Building Activity 13.1

Assessing Predominant Cognitive-Emotional Developmental Styles

Integrating multiple theories in working with our clients requires an understanding of how they make meaning of their life experiences. This practice exercise provides a sample of how raters were trained to identify clients' primary cognitive-emotional styles. It provides you with an opportunity to test your own ability to rate a client's statements.

Instructions. Ricardo is a depressed inpatient who is talking about the death of his sister and his current marital problems. The following statements are from varying parts of the interview. Determine what predominant cognitive-emotional developmental style Ricardo is manifesting in each of the responses to his situation. Expect to find dimensions of other levels, but determine if Ricardo talks in a primarily sensorimotor, concrete, formal, or dialectic/systemic fashion in each statement.

1. I'm reacting this time very similarly as I did to my sister's death. I guess everyone saw her as ill but me. I didn't see anything wrong. And when she died I was completely shocked. I fell apart just like I'm falling apart now. Everyone else had to take care of things.

2. I feel paralyzed . . . petrified. I feel like my legs are stiff and still . . . great weights keeping me stuck . . . I feel empty . . . dead inside.

3. What I learned when I was growing up has not prepared me for dealing with loss. My parents did everything to protect me and my sister. . . . We were never taught to look for problems and try to fix them, or that natural things would occur and we would have to adjust. This talk is making it clear that I don't know what to do, so I completely pull into myself and become paralyzed.

4. She came home from work and rather than having dinner on the table, she was sitting at the table looking distraught . . . upset. She said, "We have to talk," and I thought maybe someone died. Then she told me she wanted to leave . . . she was unhappy for five years. I collapsed. I didn't see it coming. I didn't know what to do. That's why I'm here . . . she brought me to the hospital 'cause I didn't know what to do.

Analysis of Statements

Statement 1—formal/reflective. Ricardo is reflecting on himself and is contrasting his reactions with others. A concrete/situational client would have difficulty with this cognitive task.

Statement 2—predominantly sensorimotor/ elemental with some concrete/situational elements. Ricardo usually feels emotions directly ("great weights keeping me stuck," "dead inside") and sometimes names or describes emotions ("I feel paralyzed") instead of experiencing them at a fuller sensorimotor level.

Statement 3—dialectic/systemic. Ricardo is reflecting on his own understanding and response to his sister's death by considering the impact of broad contextual systemic factors ("What I learned from growing up . . .") on his current psychological and emotional functioning. At this developmental stage, emotions are expressed in multidimensional and complex terms.

Statement 4—concrete/situational. Ricardo names his emotional reactions without demonstrating a great deal of reflection about them. Attention is focused on specific and concrete factors associated with responses to his sister's death.

Take a few minutes to write down some of your reactions to assessing Ricardo's statements from a cognitive-developmental perspective on a blank piece of paper and file your responses in your personal/professional development portfolio.

Source: S. A. Rigazio-DiGilio and A. E. Ivey (1990), Developmental therapy and depressive disorders: Measuring cognitive levels through patient natural language, *Professional Psychology: Research and Practice, 21,* 474. Copyright 1990 by American Psychological Association. Reprinted by permission.

Competency-Building Activity 13.2

The DCT Questioning Sequence (abbreviated)

Instructions: A useful practice exercise is to take a volunteer "client" through the four cognitive-emotional developmental styles described above. Begin your exercise by informing your client of what you are planning to do and share the following list of questions with your volunteer. Once you or your client has selected a topic for discussion, ask the first question. Try to assess the client's primary and secondary style; these can be identified in the language used to discuss the selected topic.

Once you have done this, work through each phase of the DCT questioning sequence slowly, giving your client time to experience each style fully. Use particular care within the sensorimotor/elemental style to respect your client's privacy.

Open-Ended Questions for Preliminary Assessment: Assessing the primary cognitive-emotional developmental style

1. Can you tell me what occurs for you when you focus on (the selected topic)? (A useful topic is "your family of origin.")

Goal: To obtain a short story of about one to two hundred words.

Skills: To encourage, paraphrase, and summarize to bring out the story. Try to limit your impact on the story.

Summary: Summarize the client's example, story, or issues. Pay special attention to developmental style(s) presented in client's story.

Cognitive-Developmental Questioning Sequence: Assessing the client's ability to access each style

Sensorimotor/Elemental Explorations (key words: see, hear, feel)

1. What is an image that you come up with when you focus on (the selected topic)? Describe this image for me.

- What are you seeing?
- What are you hearing?
- How are you feeling right now?

Goal: To elicit one image and ask what is seen, heard, and felt. The aim is for here-and-now experiencing; accept randomness.

Skills: Only ask questions that maintain a focus in this style. Do not ask for facts, descriptions, or interpretations; use encouraging, paraphrasing, and summarizing approaches.

Summary: Summarize key elements of the experience. Be sensitive to client's emotional world.

Concrete/Situational Explorations (key words: do, if/then)

1. Choose an example that highlights the selected topic. Give me an illustration of what occurs in relation to (the selected topic), focusing on what I would see if I were there with you. Ask various behavioral tracking questions, such as

- Who was involved?
- What happened first? Next?
- What did he or she do then?
- What did you do? How did you feel?

Goal: To obtain a linear description of the chosen example or story.

Skills: Only ask questions that maintain a focus in this style. Do not ask for feelings, here-and-now experiencing, or interpretations; use an encouraging, paraphrasing, and summarizing approach.

Summary: Summarize key descriptors of the example.

Formal/Reflective Explorations (key words: reflect, patterns, self, relationship)

1. Can you describe other situations in which you take on roles or positions similar to the ones you just described?

2. Can you describe other situations that seem to generate the same set of behaviors, even when you wish it would happen differently?

continued on next page

Competency-Building Activity 13.2, continued

3. Is this a pattern for you?

4. Has anything like this ever happened before? Does it happen a lot?

Goal: To talk about and reflect on repeating patterns of thoughts, feelings, and behaviors as these occur within the self or within different contexts.

Skills: Only ask questions that maintain a focus in this style. Do not ask for feelings, here-and-now experiencing, or descriptive events; use an encouraging, paraphrasing, and summarizing approach.

Summary: Summarize key reflections.

Dialectic/Systemic Explorations (key words: integrate, challenge, change-in-context*)*

Integration

1. Looking back on what we've talked about today, what stands out for you? What central themes do you notice?

Coconstruction

1. How would you define the rules or assumptions that influence how you think, feel, and act in relation to this story or these issues?

2. Where did these rules come from? Where did you learn these rules? Who taught you these rules? For example, did these rules come from your family of origin?

3. What role did/does your wider context (e.g., gender-role socialization, culture, community, religion) play in the development and maintenance of these rules?

Multiple perspectives

1. Are there other ways to look at the rules that you live by?

2. How might someone else see things differently? A friend? Your family?

Deconstruction

1. Can you identify ways that these rules may not be working effectively for you right now?

2. Do you notice any flaws or constraints in these rules—ways that these rules do not get you what you need?

3. How do these rules help or hinder your current way of understanding and acting?

Reconstruction and action

1. If you could add to or change these rules, how would you do it?

2. Based on these possibilities of change, is there anything you could do differently right now to see the issues that brought you here from a different perspective?

3. Based on these possibilities of change, is there anything you could do differently right now to work on the issues that brought you to treatment?

Goal: To obtain an integrated summary of the conversation; facilitate an understanding of coconstruction; obtain different perspectives; note parameters in how one understands, experiences, and operates; and review alternatives for thinking, feeling, and acting.

Skills: Only ask questions that maintain a focus in this style. Use an encouraging, paraphrasing, and summarizing approach.

Summary: Summarize key elements of the experience.

Be sure to take a few minutes to write down your own reactions to doing this activity and file it in your personal/professional development portfolio.

DCT Styles and Cultural Identity Development Theory

The four cognitive, emotional, and behavioral styles can be related to the feminist and cultural identity development theories discussed in Chapters 11 and 12. Feminist and cultural identity theories can be thought of as models that describe the evolution of consciousness. The embedded consciousness of stage 1—naiveté, or passive acceptance of the status quo—is parallel to many of the cognitions and emotions that occur within the sensorimotor/elemental style of the DCT framework. Stages 2 and 3—revelation, encountering, and naming—have parallels to concrete/situational thought, emotion, and action. Stage 4—synthesis and focusing on reflection—has much in common with formal/reflective thought patterns. Finally, the multiple perspective of stage 5—internalization and active commitment—is integrative and simultaneously demands multiperspective thought and action; it is thus similar to the dialectic/systemic frame of reference.

You also can deviate from the sequence of the DCT standard questions. It may be useful with African-American clients, for example, to focus first on dialectic questions and to follow up later with more individually oriented questions. Multicultural counseling and therapy (MCT) (Chapter 12) might go so far as to turn the DCT questioning sequences "upside down," placing the emphasis on cultural and systemic issues (e.g., "How might your gender/ethnicity/sexual style relate to these issues?"). Starting an interview by exploring how individuals are affected by the systems and relationships in their lives is very different from client-centered, cognitive-behavioral, or psychodynamic helping styles.

DCT's Approach to Treatment Planning

DCT believes that "single-shot" treatments (e.g., medication, a specific cognitive-behavioral intervention) may be useful and effective in promoting change in many helping situations. As noted earlier, any change takes place as part of a holistic system and thus affects all other parts of that system. Consequently, single theoretical interventions are by themselves often insufficient to maintain lasting change.

Furthermore, clients are unique and may respond differentially to the same treatment, no matter how efficient it is generally. The DCT framework suggests that we need to have multiple treatment interventions available that may be effective with the varying cognitive-emotional information-processing systems manifested by our clients. Instead of calling the client "resistant" to change when a particular helping approach does not seem to be effective, the task becomes one of working with the client to cogenerate treatment alternatives that are personally meaningful and integrated with the client's needs.

Integrating Treatment at Multiple Developmental Levels

To review the main points presented thus far, DCT theory and research reveal that four primary cognitive-emotional information-processing systems can be identified: sensorimotor, concrete, formal, and dialectic/systemic. The sensorimotor client focuses on here-and-now sensory "reality"—what the client sees, hears, feels, smells, and tastes. Emphasis is on holistic immediate experience. The concrete operational client tends to describe the world in a linear specific fashion and tell concrete, descriptive stories. The formal/operational client is more reflective and is epistemologically removed from the "here and now" to thinking about self and situation. The cognitive-emotional style of the dialectic/systemic client tends to be multidimensional and multiperspective. This last dimension focuses on self-in-system and is particularly important in conceptualizing how internal and external events relate to so-called pathological conditions. Specific therapeutic strategies relate to these systems, as listed in Table 13.2.

None of the cognitive-emotional styles is considered superior. Rather, for full human functioning, development in all areas is to be desired. For our clients, developmental issues will vary; development may be incomplete, or the client may have encountered serious issues or trauma. Beaver (1993) conducted a literature review on incest survivors and categorized their memories and reflections on their trauma.

It is important to note that clients may utilize one or more methods of processing their developmental history and traumatic life experience. At the sensorimotor level, for example, trauma survivors are likely to talk of body memories, play out random images, and make general verbalizations of their trauma. The concrete survivor presents flashbacks, script memories, and specific stories of the events related to her or his trauma. At the formal level, more complete and reflective narratives appear. In the dialectic/systemic style, a multiperspective and contextual discussion may manifest.

Jonathan, a veteran of the war in Iraq, provides an example of a concrete client who is a trauma survivor. Jonathan came to therapy complaining of flashbacks to battle scenes that were so vivid they seemed real. He described these scenes almost as if he were in the middle of a movie. These concrete experiences were accompanied by sensorimotor night sweats and random images playing out in his mind. Part of his therapy involved discussing concrete, linear stories of the war and then reflecting on them through formal/reflective thought. Reflective cognitive therapy (as described by Beck and Ellis in Chapters 7 and 8) was complemented, at times, with sensorimotor imaging strategies. Sensorimotor relaxation training and meditation helped calm Jonathan's vivid flashbacks. Concrete assertiveness training assisted in helping Jonathan take action at work and in the family to follow up on cognitive issues.

Therapy was not complete, however, until the dialectic/systemic style came into play. Jonathan became aware that the total system was involved. His reaction to war was not just his responsibility but was related to larger systemic issues, such as the increasing unpopularity of the war in Iraq, the lack of support he received from friends and family when he returned, and his own feelings of ambivalence about whether or not he should have participated in the war. Jonathan was encouraged to join a group of veterans who shared their experiences about war. As Jonathan came to see his personal issues in a broader social context, he responded more effectively

---

Table 13.2

Illustrative Strategies Corresponding to Each DCT Style

Predominantly Sensorimotor/Elemental Strategies

Body work—acupuncture, acupressure, massage, yoga
Emotional catharsis
Gestalt "hot seat"
Imagery
Medication
Meditation
Relaxation training

Predominantly Concrete/Situational Strategies

Automatic thoughts chart
Assertiveness training
Concrete telling of stories and narratives
Crisis intervention
Decisional counseling
Desensitization therapy
Rational-emotive analysis of a single event
Solution-oriented therapy
Thought stopping

Predominantly Formal/Reflective Strategies

Client-centered therapy
Cognitive therapy
Dream analysis
Logotherapy treatment of hyperreflection
Pattern analysis of stories or narratives
Psychodynamic therapies
Malaysian dream analysis
Rational-emotive therapy

Predominantly Dialectic/Systemic Strategies

Analysis of projective identification
Analysis of transference
Community genogram
Family genogram or chart
Family dream analysis
Introspective developmental counseling
Trauma treatment

Table 13.2, continued

Illustrative Strategies Corresponding to Each DCT Style

Theories and Strategies Applied across Styles

Cognitive-behavioral therapy
DCT and SCDT
Systemic therapies
Feminist-multicultural-social justice counseling and therapy
Self-help groups (e.g., AA, ACOA, Eating Disorders)

to traditional individual techniques such as cognitive therapy, imagery, and assertiveness training. Without providing a social context, integrative therapy would have been incomplete for Jonathan.

In terms of treatment of incest or other trauma survivors, DCT recommends working through these issues at multiple levels. We need to recover our body memories, tell our stories concretely, reflect on them, and discover how they may be systemic in nature, thus enabling us to take multiple perspectives of our clients' unique experiences. Each cognitive-emotional system requires a different theoretical and practical helping strategy that, in turn, must be applied to the specific needs of the client. For example, an incest survivor or war veteran may be embedded in sensorimotor and concrete experience. Using formal/operational treatment strategies will be ineffective. Other trauma survivors, however, may be quite formal and reflective, and the therapist would do best to avoid here-and-now concrete experience. It is vital to meet clients at their operational level of development.

While you need to join clients where they are cognitively and emotionally, you also need to encourage clients to explore their issues at other levels. Sensorimotor and concrete clients must learn to reflect and think about themselves from other perspectives. Formal and dialectic/systemic clients may be using reflective thought to avoid experiencing and taking concrete action on their issues and therefore need to be encouraged to implement more concrete strategies to their life situation. The counselor or therapist must work with clients where they are and help them explore the world from differing vantage points. In the Professional Development Extension, Mary Ivey explains why this is an important need with all clients.

From a narrative perspective, our clients need to experience their stories from the sensorimotor perspective, tell us concrete narratives, reflect on these narratives via formal operations, and view their stories from multiple perspectives and a social-historical context. This multiple perspective storytelling leads to new stories (restorying) as we learn how the self exists in a social environment—the self-in-relation rather than the totally autonomous and separated self.

Professional Development Extension

Using DCT with Children

While the DCT framework was originally developed with and for adults, Mary Ivey points out why the concepts are equally valuable when working with children.

First and foremost, we need to recall that elementary children are primarily concrete in their thinking and conversation, and sometimes a little sensorimotor. However, with careful listening and questioning, many children are capable of formal/reflective thought. And, surprisingly, they are often very aware of how systemic issues affect them personally.

The prevention of bullying is of special interest to me, along with the necessary support and counseling I give those who have been oppressed. Hai, a Cambodian fourth-grader, came running into my office in tears. I knew him well, had been a visitor at his home, and had attended a recent Cambodian celebration where his family was honored. Hai told me his story in random bits and pieces (sensorimotor). It turned out that Carter, a European-American child, had called him racist names and pushed him down. After I had a sense of the story, I repeated what had happened back to him in concrete, specific language, asking him if I had the story right. (Note that concrete storytelling removes the child just a bit from the immediacy of the hurtful experience.)

Our school has a policy against bullying, and so I asked Hai how he could name what had happened to him. (This requires the ability to step back and use formal thinking to reflect on what had happened.)

Hai said, "I guess that's racism and oppression."

These are large concepts for young children, but they also provide protection. Remember that many children take teasing personally, particularly around racist incidents. By reflecting, Hai could see that the problem was not his problem but a problem of the other boy. This takes a lot of pressure off a child.

But what about the dialectic/systemic area? For a child, this is a school responsibility. Our school had an antibullying policy in effect, and the following happened within a week:

1. The other boy was called in and I brought out his story fully and completely. That, coupled with a teacher's playground observation, revealed the accuracy of what Hai had said. I told the boy that I was sorry but there would be consequences for what he had done. I also told him that we would have a few sessions together on bullying and how it would hurt him in the long run.

2. The parents of both children were contacted, and each came in for a parent conference. The conference with Hai's parents was held at their home, as no babysitter was available. We need to be willing to do our work in settings other than the office. Carter's parents were obviously not happy, but they had been informed earlier of the school policy and agreed to work with us and work toward Carter's behaving more responsibly.

3. In counseling with Hai, I asked what would satisfy him. He said that he wanted an apology from Carter, and he decided on a written apology. Working with Carter, I obtained the apology, and Hai seemed satisfied.

4. Further counseling with Hai and Carter separately followed. Hai responded well, but in talking with Carter, I found that he had many friendship problems, so I organized a friendship group with some classmates he chose with the goal of helping him work on how to develop friends more effectively.

5. I also visited the classroom again to talk about the bullying policy, once more stressing that activities that denigrated anyone in any way (race, religion, sexual preference, parental or socioeconomic status, gender, etc.) were not appropriate.

DCT theory reminds me that I need to assess the cognitive-emotional style, whether it be with adults or children. Moreover, it is critical to ensure that multiple orientations to cognitive-emotional style are covered in my sessions. Most theories discussed in this book focus on concrete and reflective styles, giving insufficient attention to sensorimotor direct experience and emotion and certainly little attention to dialectic/systemic issues. DCT offers a way to balance all cognitive-emotional issues.

continued on next page

With adults, be sure to assess the cognitive-emotional style that the client uses to tell the story. Work at first within that style. Then encourage him or her to explore other ways to experience the story. What are the real sensorimotor feelings?

What is the concrete story? How does the client reflect on what happened? And, particularly important, always help the client see the situation and problem in a broader dialectic/systemic perspective.

DCT and the Treatment of Depression

If you develop an integrative view of how to work with and treat depression, you will have a significant advantage in working with many types of client issues. Depression is endemic in society and comes from many causes, ranging from the death of loved ones, to major life failures, to trauma, to biological factors. The fields of counseling and therapy have developed many ways to work with depression. Many of these approaches have been discussed earlier in this book. From the DCT perspective, it is important to look at the ways in which these helping strategies may be integrated in the treatment of depression.

DCT takes an integrated view of depression, considering it to be central to most serious client issues that counselors and therapists encounter (Ivey & Ivey, 1998, 1999b). DCT argues that the personality "disorders" of Axis II of the *Diagnostic and Statistical Manual of Mental Disorders* (DSM-IV-TR) (American Psychiatric Association, 2000) all have some relationship to underlying depression. In fact, most severe diagnoses defined in Axis I have an element of depression. In addition, the normal challenges of life, such as family issues, work, and school, can produce sadness and depressive symptoms among many persons. Most of us suffer at some point from the sense of sadness, discouragement, and helplessness that represents some element of depression.

There is an increasing awareness that depression, like posttraumatic stress, is related to external conditions. Rigazio-DiGilio and Ivey (1990) found that 17 of 20 depressed inpatient clients had severe histories of trauma. Moreover, they found that when clients were interviewed via the systematic DCT assessment approach, virtually all depressed inpatients were able to see their issues in social context rather than blaming themselves alone for their difficulties. Depression is also discussed in terms of multicultural considerations by Ivey and Ivey (2001).

Working with less severe diagnoses, the same pattern of cultural, environmental, and contextual issues needs to be considered for a truly integrative treatment plan. Perhaps you are working with a child who has been bullied or is not getting along well at school. Often such children have elements of depression. Similarly, a person who experiences divorce, the loss of a job, or a major failure in school may have a form of depression. Sadness or depression in these situations can be considered a natural response to external conditions. Once again, a treatment plan that ignores external reality is incomplete. Moreover, it is also potentially damaging, as individuals may blame themselves when, in fact, external systemic issues are the real cause. A reasonable balance of external and internal treatment is likely to be most appropriate.

Table 13.3 presents the multiple treatments that are available for depression and that are appropriate, by extension, to many, perhaps most, client issues, from extremely severe depression to more general depressive symptoms resulting from the concerns of daily life (e.g., divorce, loss of job, etc.). The treatment alternatives are categorized in terms of their predominant DCT cognitive-emotional style. However,

---

Table 13.3

Treatment Interventions for Depression, as Organized around DCT's Cognitive-Emotional Developmental Styles

DCT Cognitive-Emotional Developmental Style	Example Treatment Alternatives
Sensorimotor	Medication, meditation, body work (relaxation, nutrition, exercise, yoga), imagery, Gestalt therapy, holistic work with traditional healers
Concrete	Skills training, drawing out clients' concrete narratives via listening skills, desensitization hierarchies and training, relating positive strengths and stories from the narrative and DCT perspectives, assertiveness training, making an automatic thoughts inventory or REBT A-B-C-D-E-F analysis, thought stopping, ethnic/racial, feminist-multicultural-social justice narratives
Formal	Reflection on any of the above sensorimotor or concrete methods, person-centered theory, psychoanalytic/psychodynamic treatment, cognitive portion of CBT, logotherapy, psychoeducational workshops focusing on self-esteem
Dialectic/systemic	Reflection of how any of the above may have been developed in a family, cultural, or gender system that focuses on how the external world relates to internal experience; feminist-multicultural-social justice counseling and therapy; consciousness-raising groups; examination of countertransference and/or projective identification; psychotherapy as liberation; involvement of traditional healers in the counseling process

it is important to remember that any action taken within any part of the human system reverberates through the total system. For example, medication (a sensorimotor intervention) affects cognitions and emotions throughout other information-processing systems. An example of such a "ripple effect" throughout the intrapersonal system could be the client's self-blame for the "disorder" and consequent failure to deal with external contextual and other developmental issues. For maintenance of change and prevention of relapse, DCT recommends multilevel treatments and particularly stresses the importance of helping the client become aware of how issues are developed in systemic context.

DCT talks about the paradox of the "four-in-one." That is, each cognitive-emotional style contains metaphoric aspects of all the other systems. In its more complex presentation, DCT has specific questions and assessment strategies to identify ways in which a concrete information-processing style contains aspects of sensorimotor, formal, and dialectic/systemic styles. In this sense, DCT is holistic and postmodern (Chapter 1) in recognizing that there are an infinite number of categories for considering human experience.

DCT suggests both an alternative and supplement to differential treatment. If depression underlies many, perhaps most, so-called disorders, then it is possible to generate a unifying treatment plan suitable for conceptualizing treatment for many types of issues. In this sense, DCT's approach to treatment is an extension of Beck's pioneering work with depression and mood disorders (see Chapter 7). Within the DCT framework, it remains important to select specific treatments to meet clients where they are. At the same time, we need to explore alternative treatments from other models that may help clients restore their lives in positive ways.

Many existing therapeutic and counseling interventions are multilevel in intent and practice and involve strategies from several information-processing styles. For example, an effective stress management program will typically use strategies from all cognitive-emotional styles but likely will give less attention to dialectic/systemic issues. Meditation and relaxation training offer effective modes of sensorimotor treatment; skills training and linear analysis of thought patterns provide concrete strategies; and stress management helps clients reflect on their lives through cognitive-emotional self-management and personal reflection. DCT urges counselors to consider how systemic issues, such as intergenerational family patterns, the stress of racism and sexism, and other external factors, relate to internal stress.

The work of Aaron Beck reflects such a multilevel approach. For example, when Beck works with a patient with panic "disorder," we can anticipate that he will

- draw out the client's story, which may be presented primarily at any of the four cognitive-emotional levels or at multiple levels
- ask the client for a sensorimotor image
- develop the story or the image via concrete, linear narrative
- work with the client to reflect on the story or image via formal operations on thoughts, emotions, and behaviors

- construct a treatment plan that will involve a variety of concrete (e.g., automatic thoughts chart), sensorimotor (e.g., relaxation techniques), and formal thinking (e.g., reflecting on information gained through the chart and the interview) capacities

In addition, we can anticipate that concrete strategies for homework and reflective thought after the session will be part of treatment.

Missing from Beck's style, and from most theoretical methods and treatment programs, is the dialectic/systemic style, in which clients examine how their issues were generated in a family and social context. As such, much of cognitive therapy is incomplete and may fail to recognize how cultural, environmental, and contextual issues affect the client. If this style is missing from diagnosis and treatment, the counselor or therapist not only may be offering an incomplete approach but also may be in danger of error.

The psychoeducational approach to treatment and prevention, while often beginning with a focus on concrete issues, soon opens clients to direct experiencing, reflective thought, and dialectic/systemic multiple perspectives. LaFromboise and Jackson (1996) have developed a life skills curriculum for suicide prevention among Native American youth that is consistent with this psychoeducational helping approach.

As such, adolescents are involved in a number of holistic experiential activities and encouraged to share their concrete narratives of their life experiences. Later, they reflect individually and in groups and learn how oppressive systems can be met with personal and cultural pride.

Ivey's (1973, 1993a) work with inpatients in a VA hospital begins with concrete skills training in listening skills, followed by experiential activities to help war veterans get in touch with their bodies. Reflective and systemic thought is encouraged through group work, family interventions, and a review of shared war experiences.

It is also important to consider the place of traditional healers in any treatment program. Achebe's portrayal of traditional healers was described in Chapter 12, where she clearly outlines the relationship of traditional healing to Western systems.

Psychotherapy as liberation, an extension of DCT, is an example of multilevel treatment designed to center on systemic issues (Chapter 12). The word *liberation* is used in this helping framework to emphasize the evolution of consciousness. Clients often start with self-blame, but through effective treatment, they learn how external issues of oppression have shaped their internal beliefs about themselves.

Consciousness evolves through effective therapy and leads to a new balance of external and internal responsibility for problems and concerns. Whereas most theories and practices are focused on individual resolution of issues and thus place the problem in the person, the focus of liberation psychology is on clients' transactions and relationships in the world.

However, psychotherapy as liberation does not deny traditional methods. As appropriate, medication, thought stopping, and formal reflection on the nature of the traditional self would be part of a broad-based treatment plan. What is different in this system is the emphasis on helping the client see self-in-context and self-in-relation. Specific questioning strategies are presented that enable the expansion of client awareness, emotion, cognitions, and behaviors surrounding the issues.

To move toward a culture-centered framework in which diagnostic formulations are balanced between individual and context, the next step may be to raise clients' and therapists' consciousness of how the person and the environment are related. Feminist counseling theories (FCT) and multicultural counseling and therapy (MCT) (Chapters 11 and 12) are part of a new, integrative "fourth force" helping paradigm. DCT complements this new paradigm by also placing contextual considerations (such as cultural, racial, and gender factors) at the center of the helping process.

The Unique Narrative Strategies of DCT

Clients come to us with stories of their lives. These stories be may presented in a confused and disorganized way or they may be clearly stated. Stories may be vague and abstract, or they may be extremely detailed and lengthy. In any case, the counselor initially gets only part of the story. Getting complete and clear stories requires effective listening, which involves considerable patience and use of the microskills discussed in Chapter 4 (Ivey, Pedersen, & Ivey, 2001).

Noting the DCT narrative style of the client is a good way to draw out clients' stories from their perspective. For example, if the client presents a disorganized, emotional, sensorimotor story, you can listen patiently and help her or him gradually move to a more concrete linear perspective. If the client's story is detailed, lengthy, and concrete and you have a more formal, reflective style, you may find yourself impatient and hurrying the client, and both of you may end up frustrated. *If we are to be truly empathic, we need to match the client's style of self and story presentation.*

In addition, having the client tell the story from more than one DCT style is in itself therapeutic. For instance, the client's story may come to you via the sensorimotor/elemental style. You may hear bits and pieces of the client's experience of a sexist or racist incident in a disorganized manner that is heavily influenced by immediate emotional experience. The value of this type of presentation is that you are hearing the client's direct experiencing of the incident. The client may in this way be able to move to a clearer concrete style in which linear, specific, step-by-step details of what happened are presented. The story will have a beginning, middle, and end. You may learn what happened just before the oppressive incident, specifics of the incident itself, and what happened afterward (antecedent, behavior, and consequence; see Chapter 8).

In a formal/reflective story, the client steps back from immediate and concrete experience and begins to analyze what happened. The individual who has experienced an oppressive incident will be able to reflect on the meaning of what happened. With children and less cognitively oriented individuals, this reflective form of storytelling often requires more assistance from the counselor. Accurate paraphrasing and summarizing of patterns of behavior will help less cognitively oriented clients reflect on the incident and examine patterns. Sometimes it will take several interviews before a client is able to reflect on his or her concrete story.

On the other hand, extremely reflective clients may need your assistance in learning how to tell their stories at the sensorimotor or concrete level. Some clients are so involved in reflection and analysis that they miss the immediacy of here-and-now sensorimotor experience. Such clients may be so abstract that you may wonder what happened to the underlying concrete narrative.

An individual who has experienced an oppressive incident may or may not be able to describe what happened at the dialectic/systemic level. Some individuals internalize oppression and think that the problem is their fault rather than viewing it as a systemic issue. If clients experience oppressive incidents, it is not uncommon for them to blame themselves. For example, a woman who is harassed may say that it was her fault that she dressed in such as way to invite the harassment. A Mexican-American may apologize for his Hispanic accent by saying, "If I knew English better, I might have gotten the job." These examples of internal attribution of responsibility fail to recognize that the cultural, environmental, and contextual factors of sexism and racism (external attributions) may be the real cause of what occurred.

Thinking systemically requires clients to examine how family systems, community systems, and cultural background affect our being in the world. The client can then begin to see oneself as a being-in-relationship or a person-in-community. In an individualistic society, this is often a challenge for both the client and the counselor or therapist. Your goal is to help the client balance internal and external responsibility for what occurs in life. The next task for the client is to decide how to act to change oneself and/or external factors in the family, community, or broader culture.

The telling of the story from a different perspective or DCT style is therapeutic in itself. This could be because the individual who presents an upsetting sexist or racist incident at the formal/reflective level may have missed emotional experience at the sensorimotor level, or the client may have left out an important detail that would have been presented at the linear concrete/situational level. Similarly, seeing the relationship of external systemic events to one's individual reactions to such events can be an opportunity for cognitive-emotional growth.

Your style of selective listening and focusing, along with the questions you ask, affects how clients will present their issues and tell their stories. If a woman talks about job-related difficulties and you ask her concrete questions, she will give you specific details. If you focus on formal thoughts, she may reflect and examine patterns in her thoughts, feelings, and behavior. If you focus on issues of job discrimination or sexism, she may operate within the dialectic/systemic style.

DCT uses specific questioning strategies to help clients explore their issues and tell their stories within each developmental style. Your personal style, preferences, and professional competencies will have a major impact on the types of questions and issues you are likely to focus on in the helping setting. Competency-Building Activity 13.3 uses the DCT framework to help you check out how your personal style, preferences, and professional competencies may affect the work you do with clients in the field.

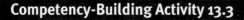

Competency-Building Activity 13.3

Identifying Your Own Personal Style, Present Competencies, and Goals

No one can be fully versed in all helping techniques and theories. This exercise asks you to examine your personal style, preferences, professional understanding, and present counseling and therapy competencies as well as your future goals within the DCT styles.

What is (are) your preferred cognitive-emotional developmental style(s)?

You have been introduced to the importance of direct sensory experience, the usefulness of concrete storytelling, the value of a reflective consciousness, and the significance of balancing all these styles with notions about your self-in-relation and your self-in-systems.

Reflect back on your life experience and identify meaningful events or situations that relate to each of the cognitive-emotional developmental styles. Can you identify a general preferred style? How able are you to operate within each style? Are there some styles that are less comfortable for you?

What is your present knowledge base and skill level in the strategies, techniques, and theories presented in Table 13.1 and Table 13.2?

These two tables cover many skills and strategies used in individual and family counseling and psychotherapy settings. Examine both tables and consider your present level of skills and knowledge. Be sure to register other areas of personal expertise not represented in this list, such as techniques in marriage therapy and group counseling. List areas in which you have some competence and classify these competencies in relation to your current level of expertise. Rank yourself on a five-point scale (1 as low, 5 as high).

Do your areas of expertise match your own preferred cognitive-emotional developmental style? Most counseling and therapy students appear to be most comfortable within the formal/reflective style and often find themselves impatient with the repetition of examples and stories by clients working within a predominantly concrete/situational style. How effective will you be with clients who are different than you?

What are your goals for the future in terms of developing further expertise?

Again, review the listings in Tables 13.1 and 13.2 and consider methods associated with other treatment modalities. What areas do you see as needing further development as you work through this text and plan your professional career?

Briefly make a list of things you think you can and will do in the next year to meet the goals you have for yourself in terms of developing further expertise in counseling or psychotherapy. Be sure to file this list of goals in your personal/professional development portfolio.

Integrative, holistic counseling and psychotherapy often requires helping clients synthesize their thinking through multiple storytelling. Learning how to directly experience the story through sensorimotor narratives and to tell the story in a concrete, linear fashion is an important basis for beginning the therapeutic process. Extending thoughts to formal/reflective stories and analysis is important, as it helps clients recognize the self-in-system in dialectic/systemic thought. Multiple storytelling results in multiple perspectives and a more complete sense of what is occurring with the person. While multiple storytelling is sometimes sufficient in itself for change, it is also important to have integrated a wide variety of helping strategies from the major theoretical forces of counseling and therapy presented in this text.

Limitations and Practical Implications of the DCT Integrative Approach

DCT is a unique and integrative approach to the field. As such, it presents a special challenge, as it asks you to become expert in multiple theories and to match your change strategy to clients' cognitive-emotional styles. If you are not fully expert in a strategy that you think is important for a particular individual you are working with, you may consider referring the client to another professional who has more expertise in that area than yourself. Clients can also benefit from becoming involved in community groups such as Alcoholics Anonymous; cancer support groups; consciousness-raising groups; Parents Without Partners; and churches, mosques, and synagogues. Family therapy or direct action on your (or others') part in working to eliminate oppression in the social context may be important as well. Part of the challenge in using an integrative approach to counseling and psychotherapy is to recognize that you may not be able to provide all the necessary interventions yourself.

A special caution is required as you move toward the sensorimotor style. Clients may become tearful when responding to simple, direct, here-and-now sensorimotor questions. You and your clients may be surprised at the strength of emotion that sensorimotor work elicits. Your own comfort level in this area is an important determinant of how well your clients may cope with expressing their emotions in therapeutic sessions. If you find yourself or your client uncomfortable with emotional experiences, move to a combination of concrete and formal/reflective discussion. Ethics, professional standards, and supervision are essential in situations where you are not comfortable with individuals expressing their emotions from the sensorimotor style. You may also discuss with your client the purpose of varying DCT questions and share the questions with them ahead of time, thus moving toward a more coconstructed helping process.

The major practical implications of developmental counseling and therapy include the following:

1. DCT provides a theoretically coherent way to integrate multiple theories. The assessment of clients' cognitive-emotional styles enables you to match multiple interventions with clients' needs.

2. DCT is holistic, recognizing that a successful intervention from one theoretical perspective may have implications for client change at multiple levels.

3. DCT provides a systematic framework for narrative approaches to counseling and therapy. The emphasis on multiple storytelling from the sensorimotor, concrete, reflective, and dialectic/systemic frames enables clients to examine their lives and situations from many points of view, thus making possible a new, more holistic restorying that leads the client to different actions.

4. DCT is unique among counseling and psychotherapy theories in that it gives special attention to dialectic/systemic issues. It is fully compatible with fourth-force multicultural-feminist-social justice counseling and therapy in that cultural,

environmental, and contextual issues are considered equally important to traditional individualistic concerns.

5. DCT gives special attention to family issues. Chapter 14 on systemic cognitive developmental therapy discusses this dimension of theoretical investigation in greater detail.

Summary

One of the primary purposes of this chapter is to assist you in gaining an understanding of some of the key dimensions of the integrative theory of developmental counseling and therapy (DCT). DCT theory provides a means to synthesize many theoretical concepts presented in the previous chapters. It does so by emphasizing how these theoretical concepts can be directly applied in professional practice.

The competency-building activities included in this chapter are aimed at enhancing your understanding of some of the strategies you can use in assessing clients' meaning-making styles within cognitive-emotional development. By developing these assessment skills, you will be better able to intentionally match different helping strategies to your clients' unique strengths and needs.

Multimedia Resources for This Chapter

The following online resource offers video and other resources of particular relevance to this chapter of your text.

MyHelpingLab

myhelpinglab   If a MyHelpingLab passcode was included with your textbook and you have activated your passcode:

- go to **www.ablongman.com/myhelpinglab**
- enter the "Counseling" area of the site by clicking on that tab
- select "Video Lab" from the toolbar to the left of the page
- select "MyHelpingLab Videos by Theoretical Approach"
- select the "Integrative" module to view various video clips of a therapist using this approach with a client

chapter 14

Family Counseling and Therapy: Theoretical Foundations and Issues of Practice

Sandra Rigazio-DiGilio
University of Connecticut, Storrs

chapter goals

This chapter is designed to:

1. Describe how the systemic worldview undergirds family therapy approaches.

2. Outline the central constructs of family theory and how these principles operate in a specific example of family functioning and life-span events.

3. Apply postmodern, integrative, multicultural, and feminist perspectives in providing counseling and psychotherapy to families.

4. Evaluate the basics of four family therapy models.

5. Identify the underlying conceptual connections between individual counseling, family therapy, and the network therapy model.

6. Explore how principles of family therapy can be applied to solving community problems.

Introduction

Contemporary counseling and psychotherapy emerged from the work of Sigmund Freud (Chapter 5). His individually oriented paradigm provided the model for the main psychodynamic theorists who followed in the first half of the 20th century—namely, Ellis (1958), Frankl (1959), Glasser (1965), Jung (1935), Kelly (1955), Maslow (1971), May (1961), Perls (1969a), Piaget (1963), Rogers (1961), and Skinner (1953). The clinical approaches associated with these theories address various intrapersonal phenomena and tend to minimize the relational, social, and cultural systems that may contribute to and define a presumed disorder and its management (Rigazio-DiGilio, 2000). However, a few theorists did focus on human interaction—namely, Auserwald (1968), Bion (1961), Sullivan (1953), and Yalom, 1995.

In the 1950s, John Bell began seeing families in Worcester, Massachusetts, and the innovative conceptualizations of General Systems (von Bertalanffy, 1968) and Field Theories (Lewin, 1951; Weiner, 1948) were successfully applied to work with families, with promising results. Yet it was still common through the 1970s to provide individually delivered services. The field still has not fully realized the importance of working with the interconnections among individuals, their families, their communities, and the cultural forces that affect them (Brammer, 2004; Kaslow, 1996; McGoldrick, 2002; Sue & Sue, 2003; Sue, Ivey, and Pedersen 1996; Walsh, 2002). The vast majority of current models continue to primarily focus on the individual as the target and agent of change.

Historically and into the present time, the importance of the family has been underestimated when working with clients. As practitioners, our understanding of human development greatly increases when family considerations and the principles of systemic, contextual, and feminist theories are added to the perspective of mental health and disorder. Thus, we must have ways of examining how factors influencing individuals, families, and wider social environments are interconnected. We also need to provide specific recommendations for concrete counseling and therapeutic interventions that are research based and intentionally designed to promote clients' mental health and psychological well-being. A predominant theme of this book is the importance of constructing personal blueprints of the therapeutic territory and designing learning strategies for navigating this territory.

Families often take on the role of mediating internal and external life events and circumstances for their members (Rigazio-DiGilio, 2000). An individual socialized in a family comes to rely on family attitudes and cultural dispositions to understand and cope with life's challenges. Therapists and counselors often work with individuals who are deeply interconnected with their family and multicultural backgrounds. Applying family therapy tools can help practitioners make these various interconnections more coherent.

Family counseling and psychotherapeutic interventions represent powerful strategies for helping clients learn how context and personal history affect who they are and can provide pathways to enhanced mental health. Your clients have many resources and strengths that can be drawn on to cope with their present issues. These personal resources and strengths can be highlighted in the counseling and psychotherapeutic setting by using the community genogram (Chapter 1) and the family genogram (presented later in this chapter).

By using these techniques, counselors and psychologists can gain important insights regarding their clients' strengths as well as the challenges and problems they are encountering in their lives. "Family therapy has been applied to virtually every type of disorder among children, adolescents, and adults, and has demonstrated efficacy with each population studied" (Liddle and Rowe, 2004, p. 395). Competency-Building Activity 14.1 illustrates the benefit of accessing this understanding by using a systemic viewpoint, or "lens," in the counseling process.

Competency-Building Activity 14. 1

The Systemic Perspective and Ethical Treatment

A systemic, family-oriented "lens" can help us address many necessary questions when deciding on an appropriate and ethical treatment plan. The situations in your therapeutic practice will involve complexities about the treatment approach you choose.

For example, consider this scenario. You are counseling an isolated, depressed 14-year-old Italian-American female who is deeply involved with her close-knit family. Should you encourage her to seek out activities that provide some distance from her family of origin, such as spending more time with friends and groups in a wider social and educational community?

At first glance, this may seem a logical plan. But what if your promoting her individuality is seen as disrespectful to and devaluing by her nuclear and extended family networks? What if this move toward more independence induces depressive symptoms in the girl's mother or escalates the already conflicted relationship between her and her father? How would you generate both individual autonomy and traditional connectedness in order to promote this client's psychological health and well-being while also respecting the collective cultural identity of the Italian-American family system, neighborhood, and community?

For other examples, consider the individual, family, and contextual complexities that would need to be addressed in the following scenarios:

1. **Involving parents when treating a child.** A single-parent mother is reluctant to enter treatment with her 10-year-old son, whose behavior is often disruptive enough to require police intervention. Individual counseling may help lessen the negative behavior, but when therapy ends the problems may continue. In fact, individual treatment may stimulate a recycling process that prompts outside intervention when the mother is her most ineffective and the son his most disruptive. Therapy could therefore be just one of many temporary releases for this family at times of escalated stress rather than an intervention that could produce change. Individual treatment could be a wise plan, given the increased disruptive behavior and the ongoing sense of powerlessness created over time. On the other hand, withholding treatment until the mother agrees to participate in services specific to the nature of the problem might be a more responsible course of action to take in this situation. Another factor to consider is the client's right to treatment and the right to refuse treatment.

2. **Timing exposing spousal abuse.** A female client reveals that she is being abused in her home but that she is not yet ready to reveal this situation because she has only begun to secure resources for leaving her marriage and taking her children (who are not being abused). Revealing the secret may endanger her and the children and sabotage her efforts to ensure everyone's safety. Keeping the secret may imply that she has time to get her resources in order and delay a move to safety. Also, keeping the secret may suggest that it is appropriate to keep abuse a secret. On the other hand, exposing the abuse may open the door to supportive resources and services for this client.

3. **Handling complex gender issues.** A family is referred because the female breadwinner's illness has prevented her returning to work. By encouraging a redefinition of roles and rules more in synchrony with the current situation, the male partner may need to find a job. However, this may be inconsistent with the family's collective view as well as the partners' views of themselves. If roles were reversed, societal resources would be more available. However, in this circumstance, there would be an expectation that the husband get work while

continued on next page

Competency-Building Activity 14.1, continued

alternative caregivers for his wife and children were provided. Promoting such a mainstream value could increase individual and family distress, particularly if this family had already tried to counter social oppression they had experienced on such issues as family leave, insurance coverage, and the like.

Instructions: How do you as a therapist determine the focus of treatment? Consider the following scenario:

An 11-year-old Jamaican female, Tia, is brought to therapy by her parents because of her increased lying, centering on her active drug abuse, use of weapons, and sexual escapades. The family has recently moved to a suburban community, where Tia is attending a predominantly White middle-class school. The children constantly tease her, which prompts nightmares and anxiety. The parents have tried to work with the school, but the teasing has not stopped. School officials think it would be better to remove Tia from this environment. Therefore, the parents have decided

to bus Tia to her previous school in the inner city. At this point, Tia begins lying.

1. Assess this case and develop a treatment plan.
2. Examine your plan by answering the following questions: (a) How do you conceptualize this case? (b) What would your treatment plan be?
3. Consider the following questions: (a) Which of the following areas are included in your assessment? (b) Which of the following areas should you consider including in your treatment plan?

Individual Focus   *Family Focus*   *Network Focus*
the lying   the parents' actions the school's actions
the nightmares the family context   the school context

4. Answer these final questions: (a) What does your examination suggest about how you see presenting problems? (b) How do you envision your work as a counselor/therapist?

After you have completed this exercise, take a few minutes to write down your reactions and file them in your personal/professional development portfolio.

Origins of a Family Perspective

Early work in family therapy was based on a systemic conceptualization called cybernetics. The anthropologist Gregory Bateson emerged as a leading theoretician in this area during the 1950s. Cybernetics points out that each action, whether taken by an individual or family, reverberates throughout and influences an entire system of relationships. Using this fundamental cybernetic principle, Bateson and his colleagues promoted a significant breakthrough in the fields of psychology and counseling by describing how severe psychiatric disorders could be accounted for by analyzing family communication patterns (Bateson, Jackson, Haley, & Weakland, 1956). Using their investigative findings as evidence, these researchers explained how family interactions often supported the dysfunctional behavior of the so-called identified patient.

These researchers further noted that therapeutic interventions intended to foster change in individual clients were often met with tremendous resistance from other family members, who were not supportive of such changes. Additionally, these researchers reported that if positive changes were in fact manifested in individual clients, it was not uncommon for another family member to suddenly demonstrate psychological distress.

By using a systemic approach that included the entire family in the helping process, Bateson and colleagues found that clients treated within a family context suffered fewer relapses and improved more quickly than clients treated individually. Bateson's work went on to influence the work of the pioneers in the new field of family counseling and therapy. Virginia Satir (1964), Nathan Ackerman (1958), Murray Bowen (1960), Jay Haley (1963), Salvador Minuchin (1974), Carl Whitaker (1967), and many others throughout the world began writing about family therapy and established community institutes and academic centers for the sole purpose of providing therapeutic services to families.

Since then, the family-oriented approach has been enlarged to encompass contextual conditions of the wider social systems that impact client functioning and recovery. This perspective is viewed as **second-order cybernetics** (Bateson, 1972; Bronowski, 1978; Keeney, 1983). These second-order approaches are intended not only to support symptom reduction but also to enhance healthy psychological development for both individuals and families within a wider framework of psychotherapy as public health discourse (Becvar & Becvar, 2003). Thus, when called on to treat issues such as anxiety, conduct disorders, eating disorders, drug abuse, and many other mental health issues, more and more counselors and psychologists have begun to use family therapeutic approaches in addition to working to foster positive changes in the individual and/or larger group and community systems.

Such approaches include, but are not limited to, working to promote positive change in clients' and their families' neighborhoods, schools, and work settings (Lewis et al., 2002; Murray & Brody, 2004; Rojano, 2004). In these ways, the family counseling and psychotherapy movement has helped the mental health professional move beyond a predominantly individual focus to a recognition of the important role that clients' families play in the helping process and then to an increasing appreciation of the impact of the broader social context in both causing psychological distress and fostering mental health.

Family therapy as a field continues to explore ways "to develop knowledge capable of addressing the most serious problems faced by families and larger systems today—poverty, racism, lack of adequate resources, radical changes in the world of work, coping with life in the information society, addictions, serious illness, abuse, trauma, terror and the critical need for community and helping families not just to survive, but to thrive" (Imber-Black, 2004).

The Systemic Worldview

In understanding the nature of the systemic worldview, it is important to consider the essence of the shift from an individualistic to a family context perspective as well as how the systemic perspective affects the conceptualization of healthy human development, the meaning and impact of a real or presumed disorder, and appropriate therapeutic intervention. The traditional psychological worldview focuses on the individual as the primary actor, with all other persons and environmental factors relegated to supporting, secondary roles.

In contrast, the systemic worldview sees the family as the primary unit and holds that all members of the family are important contributors to clients' psychological functioning and development. In addition to the internal dynamics engendered by relationships, rules, and roles within the family, the systemic worldview acknowledges the impact of dynamics created as family members interact within larger social systems (neighborhoods, schools and universities, workplaces, political institutions, the media, churches, and economic institutions and systems) of which they are a part (Doherty & Carroll, 2003). Consider the relevance of these relationships, rules, and roles to the systemic worldview as you review the following points:

1. *Relationships.* How many people are in your family? If you responded with the number of family members in your nuclear family, you are in the minority. The better question to ask is, "Who is your family?" Many persons from diverse cultural/racial/ethnic groups consider their family to be more expansive and inclusive than do individuals in the dominant cultural group in the United States. This more expansive notion of the family includes, but may not be limited to, a host of other relatives and friends (Speck & Attneave, 1973). Respecting this alternative construction of the family, the systemic worldview concerns itself with relationships that family members have both inside and outside the immediate household setting. From this theoretical perspective, individuals are viewed as integral parts of their households or family subsystems who, at the same time, are identified with other subsystems of larger communities, which in turn are subsystems of the nations, which are subsystems of the human species, and so on. Relationships are evident at, and between, all these levels that reverberate through the crucible of the family, with the family being defined by the member.

2. *Rules.* Families are viewed as subsystems in which intrafamilial patterns of communication are the focal points for understanding family functioning. Family members' use of routinized and regulated communication assists each member in making meaning of life within this human subsystem. Examples of routinized communication include the simple exchanges individuals have with family members when they meet at breakfast or how family members signal that it is time to end conversation when the TV is turned on. By observing and trying to understand repeating patterns of communication that occur within this subsystem, family counselors and therapists are able to learn about some of the unconscious and conscious rules under which a family operates. Attention to whose voice dominates and influences the family conversation and whose voice is silenced or diminished is essential to understanding the family's rule-setting and rule-enforcing process.

3. *Roles.* The roles members are permitted to fulfill within the family system are also communicated to each person. Bateson found that the most vulnerable member of certain families is often given the role of the "identified patient." The roles of "family mascot," "peacemaker," and "gatekeeper" are some of the

ways of behaving expected of individual members in family systems. The identification of roles can help families make informed decisions about how roles come into creation and how they can be modified to promote family members' well-being. Helping families understand the roles family members assume outside and inside the family is an essential goal of all counseling and psychotherapy.

Across all relationships, rules, and roles, the dimension of power is ubiquitous. That is, the sense that one's actions will result in benefits for oneself or others is woven into the type of relationships formed, the severity of punishment for violating family rules, and the flexibility in the roles we acquire across our life span. This concept of power and its related construct of embeddedness are discussed in the section of this chapter describing postmodern models of marriage and family therapy.

Cultural Impact and Extensions of Family Systems

Historically, the cultural influences of society, community, generation, politics, and institutions have been considered noncritical background data when assessing and treating mental health issues. This has also been true for traditional family therapy, where the focus of treatment has been first on assisting individuals and then on helping partners and families to "adapt to" rather than to "understand and influence" the wider contextual forces that significantly and often adversely impact their lives (Falicov, 1995, Imber-Black, 2004).

Since the 1990s, the negative implications of relying solely on theories that emerged within the parameters of a Western, Euro-American, individualistic framework have been acknowledged (Atkinson, Morten, & Sue, 1998; Ivey & Rigazio-DiGilio, 1994; Pedersen, 1991). In response, counseling and therapy approaches that suggest broader and more inclusive ways of understanding human, systemic, and cultural systems and of facilitating change within and across these systems have been developed (Rigazio-DiGilio, 2000). This has led to a broader definition of the family, which includes, among other parameters, living arrangements previously omitted or pathologized, such as same-sex partnerships and single-parent families.

Such alternative familial arrangements have sharply contrasted with the construction of the "healthy and normal family" prevalent during most of the 20th century. During that period, the nuclear family structure dominated American culture. At that time, and often today, the middle-class family system, consisting of a breadwinner, domestic wife, and 2.4 children, was used as the standard of the normal family. This mythologized and idealized standard blinded theorists to historical precedents for various legitimate family arrangements, constricted their perspective of the wide variety of family arrangements that actually existed, and promoted conformity over diversity of viewpoint.

As the idea of what comprised a family was challenged, feminist theorists and clinicians in the 1970s also questioned the narrow interpretation of equity characteristic of family therapy theories. Their claim that women have the same degree of power in the family as men was met with resistance, and the notion that culture bestows privileges to certain members of the community and family persisted in family counseling and therapy theory. "Hare-Mustin (1978), in an earthshaking article, challenged family therapy as an instrument of the status quo that kept women disempowered within patriarchal family systems" (Arnold, 2002, p. 21).

An agent of social change, Kjos (2002) summarizes four values that characterize feminist family therapy:

1. Establish a coequal or nonhierarchical relationship with the client family.
2. Pay attention to the balance of power in the family.
3. Pay attention to the roles and structures (e.g., rules and relationships) within the family.
4. Be aware of the role sexism plays in diagnosis of psychological problems.

Over the last decade, the idea that power and privilege can be found in many levels of healthy and nonhealthy relationships has been integrated into postmodern and multiculturally based methods of family therapy. For example, many cultures (i.e., Asian, African, Latino, and Native American) value the extended family and draw personal, familial, cultural, and community power from a broad network of relationships, including spiritual and ancestral family members.

The concepts of family therapy have been successfully applied in community settings such as college dormitories, group homes, social groups, schools, and businesses. The trend is to include wider and wider networks of family members and community resources to ameliorate dysfunctional forces in our society that may negatively impact individual and family development.

In describing the practice of community family therapy, Rojano (2004) uses Lewinian field theory to explain how individuals and their related social and emotional groups interact and influence each other. From a community level, low-income people can be seen as "trapped in the negative pressures of deprived and oppressive 'life spaces' or 'fields' in which they are 'scheduled' to play the roles of underachievers" (Rojano, 2004, p. 65). Only community-based, profamily interventions that address all the relevant social "fields" the client system brings into treatment can promote an empowering transformation in these situations.

In shifting the emphasis of treatment to the relationship between client and the wider environment, it makes sense that counselors and psychologists deal with issues that exist at the family, cultural, and community levels. Including social and cultural factors in conceptualizing clients' problems and thinking about effective treatment strategies are often overwhelming for many counselors and psychologists. Hence, the inclination is to cast clients in the subordinate position of needing the counselor's help and expertise. For example, treating a poor client for depression is easier and more reinforcing for the therapist than attempting to change the distribution of wealth patterns in society. However, by neglecting to include contextual and familial considerations in analyzing clients' problems and by not developing intervention strategies to promote positive psychological outcomes, counselors and psychologists risk inaccurate and inappropriate interpretations of clients' and their families' behaviors. In writing about this issue, Rigazio-DiGilio et al. (1997) note:

What of the Hispanic children labeled deviant for refusing to go to school? This behavior is often seen as a reflection of the parent's failure to provide proper socialization and guidance. It is less often considered that . . . their deviant behavior may more accurately reflect a legitimate response to a devaluing and dehumanizing society. (p. 79)

Central Constructs of Family Counseling and Theory

A powerful intermediate point between using individual helping approaches and striving to encourage positive changes in larger human systems in an effort to foster clients' psychological health and personal well-being can be to use family counseling and psychotherapy strategies in clinical practice. In family counseling and therapy, the family, rather than the individual, is the primary unit of analysis. As has been noted earlier in this chapter, the word *family* can mean different things to different people. Some corporations consider themselves families, whereas two elderly siblings living together might conceive of their family as only their offspring. The view of family promoted in this text is multicultural and postmodern and therefore open in nature. Specifically, a family is a nexus of people living together or in close contact who take care of and provide support and guidance for one another (Wood, 1995).

The Family Developmental Life Cycle

When counseling individuals and families, it is important to know what is going on in their lives from a developmental perspective. For instance, you may be working with a European-American teenage client just starting to engage in the misuse and/or abuse of drugs. Although from a developmental perspective it may be important to recognize that this teenager may be dealing with issues of identity and intimacy, it is equally important to be knowledgeable as to what is going on in the family. You may find that the parents have just filed for divorce, thus altering the teenager's developmental task of leaving home. Family therapy would promote a treatment plan for this adolescent that includes an awareness of what is occurring in the family.

Family development life cycle models help counselors understand the challenges families may face across the life span. These models provide an explanatory context for the life tasks families must master. Family counseling and psychotherapy stress the value of knowing the key developmental tasks and life stages of the family and of considering the family as a special group of individuals who are experiencing their own individual and collective challenges in life. It is important to approach these models with caution, however, as they are often based on traditional, North American, European frames of reference and do not take into account the nature and impact of the sociopolitical context of the family or the cultural bias of the originators of the models. Therefore, these models do not necessarily describe the unique ways today's families traverse the life cycle. Reliance on these theories can, intentionally or not, constrain families and practitioners within a narrow range of developmental options and treatment avenues. As Skolnick and Skolnick (1994) explain:

> The family theories of the postwar [World War II] era were descriptively correct insofar as they portrayed the *ideal middle-class family* patterns. . . . But they went astray in elevating the status quo to the level of a timeless necessity. In addition, these theories did not acknowledge the great diversity among families that has always existed in America. (p. 4; emphasis added)

While there is some consistency regarding how families develop over the life span, the normative value of most family developmental counseling and psychotherapy theories can be outweighed by the stereotypical application of these theories when working with culturally diverse families. Therefore, as has been reiterated numerous times throughout this book, it is vital that counselors and psychologists view clients through culturally sensitive and respectful "lenses" when working with individuals and families from various cultural groups and backgrounds (McGoldrick, 2002; Lewis et al., 2002).

With this caveat in mind, one model of family development, adapted from the work of Haley (1979) and Carter and McGoldrick (1988), is presented in Table 14.1. This framework suggests that key points in the family life cycle often bring a client into treatment and that general knowledge of these key transition points is helpful to the counselor. For instance, the stages of leaving home or retirement can often create conflict in the family, which may be expressed in the members' relationships with others in the family.

In addition, each of the six transition points listed in Table 14.1 must also be considered within a cultural context to give a full appreciation of the unique stressors families experience at critical life junctures. Adding a contextual lens to the work you do as a family counselor enables you to see, for example, that the launching of children into adulthood is handled very differently in various cultural contexts. Midwestern Swedish-Canadian young adults may be expected to move out on their own directly and quickly, whereas Italian-Canadian or Chinese-Canadian young people may be expected to live in the home until marriage. Each culture's way of handling this important family transition can result in varying types of issues and stressors that are important to address when providing family counseling and psychotherapeutic services among persons from diverse populations.

A personal awareness of the cultural expectations we have regarding these developmental stages must be cultivated. For example, a counselor of Mexican heritage could unintentionally and inappropriately impose values from this culture on clients from Asian or African backgrounds, with problematic results. Again, it is important to realize that healthy family functioning in one culture may be viewed differently, and even as potentially pathological, by another culture (Rohner, in press). Power can also be unequally distributed across gender, age, and mental and physical ability, in addition to ethnic lineage. The clinician must be sensitive to the culturally laden, internal and external power differentials that impede the growth and development of clients.

Theorists and practitioners who value the active role of the perceiver in interpreting and making meaning of one's environment are now repudiating the monocultural perspectives that have been perpetuated by traditional developmental and

Table 14.1

The Stages of the Family Life Cycle

Developmental Stage	Emotional Process of Transition	Separation and Attachment Issues
Young adults	Developing financial, functional, and psychological independence	• Increasing peer attachment • Separating from family of origin • Selecting partners
New couple	Being committed to new partnerships and system formation	• Attaching to partner and new friends • Attaching to partner's parents • Reattaching to parents
Childbirth and childrearing	Accepting into the system new dependents who require guidance and nurturance	• Distancing from partner • Attaching to infant • Renegotiating relationships with parents and peers • Beginning to separate from child as school begins
Middle marriage	Opening boundaries and increasing role responsibilities to include children's independence and grandparents' frailties	• Progressively separating from children • Increasingly reattaching to or distancing from partner • Refocusing on midlife issues • Children beginning to separate from parents
Leaving home	Accepting multiple avenues of entry to and exit from the family system	• Increasing reattachment to partner • Beginning attachment to partners of children • Renegotiation of relationship with family of origin, in-laws, and peers
Families in later life	Accepting the shifting of generational roles	• More movement to attach with mate • Adult children move to reattach as caregivers • Dealing with loss of partner, siblings, or peers • Preparing for own death

Source: Adapted from B. Carter and M. McGoldrick, *The Changing Family Life-Cycle* (1988). Boston: Allyn and Bacon. Copyright 1988. Used by permission.

life-span counseling theories (Sue & Sue, 2003). The meanings that are attached to events, not so much the actual stage of development a person or family is passing through, are what largely determines a client's experience. This experience is filtered through a worldview that was developed as part of the natural, logical consequence of a particular developmental journey within a particular cultural context. Thus, how families and individual members experience, react to, and act on the world will be unique and may or may not fit within the boundaries prescribed by the traditional theories and approaches used by many counselors and family theorists.

Effective Family Functioning

The primary function of families is to provide stability for their members while at the same time changing to manage new life situations. Anderson and Sabatelli (1999) list five family systems characteristics that are thought to positively influence this central function. They suggest that families function most effectively when members (1) have common purposes and tasks, (2) share a sense of family history, (3) experience emotional bonding with one another, (4) devise strategies for meeting the needs of individuals and the collective, and (5) maintain firm yet flexible boundaries within and between family subsystems. They also suggest that effective families recognize the interdependence of their members and strive to provide support for individual as well as family growth.

Such families are capable of making adjustments in their rules, communications, and behavioral patterns to accommodate change while at the same time not disrupting supportive intrafamilial relationships, rules, and roles. Effective families are thought to manifest a strong sense of trust and to avoid manifesting strong oppositional attitudes or taking positions of blame when familial conflicts and stressors occur. Rather, members, individually and collectively, enjoy humor, wit, spontaneity, and lack a preoccupation with themselves.

These characteristics of effective families are necessarily general, because no one type, organizational structure, or relational configuration typifies optimal family functioning. The family unit is the culture bearer, and we need to remember that the nature of the family and the concepts of healthy family functioning vary widely among cultures and family types.

Multicultural Issues in Family Counseling and Therapy

As emphasized in Chapters 11 and 12, a significant component of a person's self-concept is derived from his or her gender socialization and ethnic heritage. Often, when asked to describe themselves, people refer to their gender and/or use their family's nationality as a primary descriptor: "I am an Irish (Jewish, Japanese, African-American, or a mixture of nationalities) woman (or man)." In effect, gender and cultural identity permeate the way people come to see themselves and their relationships, and the family is a central mediator of how they construct these meanings (Rigazio-DiGilio, 2000). While this suggests the need for counselors and therapists to account for gender and cultural variances, McGoldrick, Pearce, and Giordano (1996) note that until recently gender, culture, and ethnicity have been largely ignored by family counseling theorists.

A systems perspective encourages an understanding of how individuals and families experience, understand, and manage their world. You as a counselor or therapist learn to identify the constellation of gender, cultural, and contextual factors that have primarily contributed to these meanings, relational structures, and strategies, as well as those factors that now serve to constrain or enhance effective functioning.

Some family practitioners recommend the use of a "metaperspective" to understand and incorporate family members and considerations into counseling and therapy (Breunlin, Schwartz, & Kune-Karrer, 1992; Rigazio-DiGilio et al., 1997). Such a perspective emphasizes the need to balance our understanding of the predominant beliefs, customs, and practices of families from diverse cultures and contexts with a keen awareness of the common tendency to overgeneralize about the very groups we are attempting to understand (Anderson & Sabatelli, 1999; McGoldrick, 2002). More specifically, Anderson and Sabatelli (1999) suggest:

> We cannot assume that culture, race, and ethnicity have a predictable impact on the structure and experience of family life. Many factors, such as poverty and acculturation, modify or perhaps intensify how cultural factors are integrated into the fabric of family life. Thus, while counselors and psychologists need to be aware of ways in which culture influences different families, it is critical to also keep in mind that family systems are decidedly complex and unique. A truly tolerant perspective on families requires that we be aware of the heterogeneity found within families and the factors that accordingly contribute to the uniqueness found within them. (p. 94)

While knowledge of the gender and cultural values of the larger ethnic groups that clients identify with is critical to effective treatment (McGoldrick 2002; Sue et al., 1996; Walsh, 2002), how the client reflects or rejects these values is also important (Falicov, 1988). In other words, the unique individuality of each client and client system must be accounted for in the development of specific treatment plans.

To work ethically and effectively among culturally diverse families, you must (1) be aware of your own ethnic/racial heritage, (2) be alert to the ways in which sociopolitical factors and scientific norms influence the field and your own theory and therapy approach, (3) demonstrate empathy for members of other cultures, (4) realize that gender and cultural factors may be essential ingredients in a treatment plan, and (5) not assume homogeneity within groups but instead remain keenly alert to the significant variations of each client and family while noting the broad characteristics that differentiate ethnic/racial groups. Rigazio-DiGilio and others (1996) make the following assertion regarding the role of the culturally sensitive therapist:

> We believe that the role of the clinician should be to monitor, support, and encourage the development and use of unique life options for each client. These options flow from a person's actual life experience. In this sense, clinicians take their lead from each particular client, and not from pre-existing, impersonal theory. Interventions and strategies, which may be selected from the various schools of individual, family, or network therapy, are continually evaluated in terms of the reaction of the client. (p. 240)

Attitudes toward Mental Health and Treatment

Research indicates that ethnicity shapes the way families and individuals give meaning to their symptoms and to the causes and implications of the personal difficulties they experience in life (Flores & Carey, 2000; Ingoldsby & Smith, 1995; Okun, 1996). For example, many persons in Italian and Jewish families may use emotional expressiveness to share personal suffering, while those from Scandinavian, Asian, and Native American backgrounds may tend to withdraw and not discuss their feelings with others.

Attitudes toward mental health professionals may also vary depending on cultural influences. For instance, many Italians tend to rely on family members during times of personal distress and to seek professional assistance only as a last resort. Many African-Americans look to the church as the central emotional resource in their lives (Boyd-Franklin, 2003; Cheatham & Stewart, 1990). Research Exhibit 14.1 explores family counseling and therapy issues from an African-American perspective. Many Chinese, Norwegians, and Iranians experiencing stress report physical symptoms and seek medical rather than psychological services during times of heightened stress. Irish, African-American, and Norwegian individuals tend to place blame for their issues on themselves, whereas Greeks, Iranians, and Puerto Ricans tend to blame others (McGoldrick et al., 1996).

Network Therapy

Attneave and colleagues developed an action-oriented form of extended family therapy that allocates a significant degree of attention to the constraints and resources inherent in a client's cultural and contextual environments (Chapter 12). As described by Speck and Attneave (1973), network therapy (NT) stresses the importance of the interdependency of the natural support systems found in families, tribes, clans, and other community groups, such as schools, church congregations, and service organizations.

At first, Attneave's helping model was primarily implemented among Native Americans. However, it was later adapted to inner-city families when she worked with Salvatore Minuchin, Jay Haley, and R. Speck at the Philadelphia Child Guidance Clinic. More recently, many of the basic concepts of network therapy have been used to frame social policy in Great Britain and Scandinavia.

The primary goal of network therapy is to empower people to cope with life crises through the support of their natural social relationships (Rueveni, 1979). This unique form of helping involves convening groups of relatives, friends, neighbors, coworkers, and often those in human service agencies to work on the particular life problem a family member may be experiencing. Network interventions have been proven to offer a better understanding of the issue, foster more open and creative problem-solving discussions, ensure more efficient coordination of community resources, and promote an increased likelihood that the benefits will be experienced by more than just the identified client (LaFromboise & Fleming, 1990).

The primary focus of network therapy (Attneave, 1969) is to enable the group to repeatedly renew itself as new needs and issues emerge. This concept of group

Family Therapy with African-American Families

Cheatham and Stewart (1990) contend that approaches most effective for working with African-American families set aside abstract notions about how to do therapy and instead focus on active interventions that emphasize social functioning over inner feelings. They encourage practitioners to attend to the specifics of African-Americans' historic and cultural experiences, especially the degree to which these experiences have been influenced by racism in North America. Additionally, they guide therapists to recognize the important role that extended family and social institutions like the church play in the lives of these individuals.

Because these external agents and agencies can contribute to stress or can be a support, therapists need to consider their influence in the solution determination process. The following five elements of Cheatham's intervention model address the modifications to family work he suggests as prerequisites to success.

1. *Discussion of Role and Expectations.* What family members and counselors/therapists expect to occur in and because of counseling should be discussed and clarified. Issues of power must also be recognized and carefully negotiated. Therapists can facilitate this process by using surnames until the family invites the use of first names. Then they should use given names rather than nicknames. Changes in the times and location of therapy communicate a therapist's willingness to modify the power quotient. Differences in ethnic backgrounds should be discussed, particularly if the therapist is not African-American.

2. *Identification and Interpretation of the Situation.* The counselor/therapist should be aware of the importance and pride held for cultural norms and values. As the family begins to define and explore the presenting issue, the counselor/therapist should facilitate this exploration in a way that does not compromise the family's sense of cultural propriety. Additionally, Cheatham advocates empowering African-American families to evaluate the situation by promoting treatment within their cultural context.

3. *Resource Inventory.* Cheatham has found it effective to have families conduct a resource inventory. This is similar to the positive asset search associated with microskills (Chapter 4) or to Rogers's positive regard (Chapter 9). Along with such a list, it is important to consider the persons, institutions, and networks available to assist in the resolution process.

4. *Trying Out for Legibility.* In the next stage, the therapist assists the family to enact and own the constructed plan. It is necessary to ensure that the family is able to read and understand the plan. The therapist can facilitate skill transfer and affirm the family's positive expectations by introducing strategies like guided practice and corrective feedback. The therapist must be skilled and conscientious in efforts to provide the family with culture-relevant and culture-specific reinforcers and suggestions that are important to the unique family.

5. *Evaluation.* The final stage is to evaluate the adequacy of the solution with the family. Are the new behaviors working as well as was originally expected? Are there other issues the family now would like to work on? How will the family handle a relapse? As necessary, the process returns to the identification and interpretation stage and then proceeds sensitively through each of the subsequent stages.

renewal is viewed as a six-phase cycle: retribalization (group consensus), polarization (activating conflicting positions within the system), mobilization (channeling energy constructively), depression (working through resistance), breakthrough, and exhaustion/elation. The emphasis on the larger social context has profound implications for family counseling, feminist therapy, and mental health services.

Major Family Counseling and Psychotherapy Theories

During the 1950s and 1960s, the explanation for distress and disorder shifted from individual theories to family systems perspectives (Bateson et al., 1956; Wynne, Ryckoff, Day, & Hirsch, 1958). This change was in part facilitated by industrial and sociological trends that emphasized and idealized the nuclear family as a nomadic, independent unit that could serve the developmental needs of its members as well as the mobility needs of a growing industrial society.

While this shift represented a broader territory of investigation, the emphasis remained on the "subject" (i.e., the family) versus the "subject-in-context" (Anderson, 1993). It is therefore not surprising that family counseling and psychotherapy theories focused mainly on the inner workings of family organization, interactional sequences, and communication patterns (e.g., Haley, 1979; Watzlawick, Beavin, & Jackson, 1967).

More recently, family counseling theories have come to acknowledge that the nature of human and systemic differences and changing contexts leads to the need for multiple perspectives and broader maps. This change has brought forth a surge of ecological, coconstructive (Becvar & Becvar, 1994; Ivey, 2000; Neimeyer & Neimeyer, 1994), cultural (Falicov, 1995), gender-specific (Brown, 2000; Gilligan, 1982; Luepnitz, 1988), relational (Comstock, 2005; Kaslow, 1996), and family composition (Carter & McGoldrick, 1988; Anderson & Sabatelli, 1999) variables, all of which are considered to influence individual and systemic growth and development. Currently, there is a growing movement in the mental health professions that advocates for the existence of the multiple realities derived from interactions occurring between individuals and wider environments that are mediated by these and other individual, social, cultural, and temporal factors.

To deal with the ever-increasing number of theoretical models that continue to emerge within and across disciplines, while at the same time attending to the need to respect the multiple perspectives that clients bring into counseling settings, family systems counselors and therapists are moving toward organizing and synthesizing traditional and alternative approaches within and across individual, systemic, and network domains. Various integrative frameworks have become available that synthesize different elements of our historical roots with conceptual, methodological, and clinical advancements (Breunlin et al., 1992; Pinsof, 1994; Rigazio-DiGilio, Gonçalves, & Ivey, 1996). The current state of research findings related to the different counseling and therapeutic models commonly used by family practitioners is provided in Research Exhibit 14.2.

Research Exhibit 14.2

Research in Family Therapy

In 1986 Gurman, Kniskern, and Pinsof found that when family therapy is rigorously tested, it is noted to be effective without exception. In the mid 1990s, this conclusion was supported by reviews of the outcome literature. In their study of research findings, Pinsof, Wynne, and Hambright (1996) reported that sufficient data exist to support the efficacy of family therapy.

These conclusions were corroborated in two other analytic reviews (Baucom, Shoham, Mueser, Daiuto, & Stickle, 1998; Dunn & Schwebel, 1995). One meta-analysis of randomized clinical trials found that family and marital therapy had a similar impact to other counseling and psychotherapy modalities and was superior to the gains achieved by pharmaceutical, medical, and surgical interventions (Shadish, Ragsdale, Glaser, & Montgomery, 1995).

Pinsof and Wynne (2000) found that when family therapy is used, it has demonstrated efficacy in virtually every type of disorder with each population studied (Liddle & Rowe, 2004). These studies support the effectiveness of family therapy in general. In addition, there are lines of research that have examined the efficacy of different family therapy approaches with different mental health disorders, as follows:

- bipolar depression (Clarkin, Carpenter, Hull, Wilner, & Glick, 1998; Simoneau et al., 1999)
- schizophrenia (Goldstein & Miklowitz, 1995; Barrowclough et al., 2001)
- depression and anxiety (Diamond & Siqueland, 2001; Sexton, Glanville, & Kaslow, 2001)
- alcoholism and substance abuse (Ozechowski & Liddle, 2000; Fals-Stewart & Birchler, 2001; Williams & Chang, 2000)
- couple and marital therapy (Dunn & Schwebel, 1995; Greenberg & Johnson, 1998; Jacobson et al., 2000)
- parental management training (Mabe, Turner, & Josephson, 2001; Sanders, Markie-Dadds, Tully, & Bor, 2000)

- juvenile delinquency (Huey, Henggeler, Brondino & Pickrel, 2000; Robbins, Alexander, & Turner, 2000)
- psychosomatic disorders and physical problems (Campbell & Patterson, 1995; Minuchin & Fishman, 1981; Knutsen & Knutsen, 1991)
- posttrumatic stress disorder (Baucom et al., 1998; Glynn et al., 1999)
- eating disorders (Mazzeo & Espelage, 2002; Scholz & Asen, 2001)
- child and spousal abuse (Estrada & Pinsof, 1995; Lipchik, 1991)
- oppositional, attention-deficit, and conduct disorders (Blechman & Vryan, 2000; Carr, 2000).

Based on family therapy research reviews, Becvar and Becvar (2003, p. 332) report:

- The preferred treatment for alcohol-involved marriages is conjoint couples treatment in groups, which may be superior to individual therapy with the alcoholic spouse.
- Cognitive conjoint marital therapy may be more effective than individual therapy for marital issues.
- Improvement can be expected with about 71 percent of childhood/adolescent behavioral issues when any one of a variety of family therapy methods is used.
- When compared to no treatment, cognitive marital and family counseling therapies are effective in about two-thirds of cases.
- Successful outcomes occur in relatively few (1 to 20) sessions.
- Cotherapy has not been shown to be superior to marital or family therapy by one therapist.
- Higher-level "therapist relationship skills" appear necessary for positive outcomes in therapy. Basic technical skills may prevent worsening, merely maintaining the pretherapy status of the family.

Classifying Systemic Therapies

There are innumerable ways to categorize the various models of family therapy and their key variables. Table 14.2 summarizes a classification system that builds on the work of Grunebaum and Chasin (1982), Hansen and L'Abate (1982), and Pedersen (1991).

The first three categories listed in Table 14.2 represent extensions of the forces inherent in individual therapy. First-force psychodynamic/historical approaches (e.g., Ackerman, 1958; Bowen, 1978), second-force cognitive-behavioral/interactional approaches (e.g., Jacobson, 1981), and third-force existential-humanistic approaches (e.g., Kempler, 1981; Napier & Whitaker, 1972) have origins in this focus on the individual.

Models in the first group emphasize intrapsychic and intergenerational phenomena. Cognitive-behavioral models focus on effective learning processes that expand cognitions and behavioral sequences as well as on the systemic rules and structural indicators related to organizational structures, communication, and interactional processes (e.g., Haley, 1979; Minuchin, 1974). Existential-humanistic models concentrate on current interactional contexts and processes.

The fourth category represents ecological (e.g., Becvar & Becvar, 1994; Imber-Black, 1988) and postmodern (Anderson, 1995; Anderson & Goolishian, 1988; McNamee & Gergen, 2000) perspectives that advance multidimensional, nonpathological, and contextually contingent practices.

Finally, a fifth category, the integrative perspective, presents models that offer alternative ways to organize theories, therapies, and strategies into comprehensive integrative models (Anderson & Bagarozzi, 1983; Breunlin et al., 1992; Pinsof, 1994; Rigazio-DiGilio et al., 1997). For illustrative purposes, one model from each of the first three categories is explained below. Information about the major contributors to the approach, a brief description of the theoretical constructs and treatment goals, and an outline of the therapeutic techniques associated with each model are described.

Following this information, the fourth and fifth categories are explored, and an integrative framework that additionally addresses category four (ecological/postmodern) is presented. The descriptions of these categories are not intended to be exhaustive or to replace the depth of training in each area needed to reach a competent therapeutic level but rather provide a partial conceptual map of the family therapy terrain.

Just as it is recommended that we become conversant with the major theories of individual therapy, family theorists advocate that we gradually become skilled in multiple orientations. Knowing what it is that makes each family counseling and therapy model unique and how each framework is conceptualized allows us to begin the integrative process. As counselors and therapists, we can consider the critical attributes of the following models and how we may begin to use such information to generate broader methods of practice to better address the needs of our ever-changing clientele.

Table 14.2

Classification of Systemic Therapies

Perspective/Orientation	Representative Theorists and Models
Historical	
Historical theories view the family as shaped by past forces and events.	M. Bowen (intergenerational) N. Ackerman (psychoanalytic) J. Framo (psychoanalytic) D. & J. Scharff (object relations)
Interactional/Behavioral	
Interactional theories principally focus on identifying and expanding cognitive understanding, behavioral sequences, and family rules and structures.	S. Minuchin (structural) J. Haley (structural and strategic) G. Patterson (behavioral) R. Stuart (behavioral) R. Liberman (marital) J. Alexander (functional) B. & L. Guerney (relationship enhancement) C. Anderson (psychoeducational)
Existential	
Existential theories focus on understanding and expanding each individual's subjective experience, including family members and the treating therapist.	C. Whitaker (symbolic/experiential) A. Napier (symbolic/experiential) V. Satir (process/communication) R. Levant (client-centered) W. Kempler (Gestalt)
Ecological/Postmodern	

Ecological/postmodern theories focus on how the social context influences the meanings families construct about their systems and members. Believing that meanings and actions are enhanced and constrained by the context within which they are embedded, therapy is meant to extend capabilities beyond disempowering intrapersonal, interactional, and sociocultural constraints.	P. Watzlawick (strategic)
	M. Selvini-Palazzoli (Milan)
	J. Atwood (social constructionism)
	L. Brown (gender-sensitive)
	T. Andersen (reflecting teams)
	H. Anderson & H. Goolishian
	   (problem-determined linguistic systems)
	S. McNamee & K. Gergen
	   (social constructionism)
	D. & R. Becvar (ecological and narrative)
	R. & G. Neimeyer (narrative)

Integrative	
Integrative frameworks are based on the assumption that various therapeutic perspectives and approaches can be organized to provide multiple reference points and options to promote growth.	D. Breunlin (metamodels) W. Pinsof (integrative, problem-centered) S. Anderson & D. Bagarozzi (mythological) S. Rigazio-DiGilio & A. Ivey (systemic cognitive-developmental therapy)

It should be kept in mind, though, that each model has resulted from the clinical wisdom of the major theorists and the empirical findings of the original investigations. These contributing factors were influenced by the general approach to theory building prevalent at the time of their development. As our professional knowledge evolves, some of the fundamental assumptions undergirding each theory may now seem, at best, limited and, at worst, oppressive to some groups.

In the future, therapists and counselors need to continue to use what is most effective about existing theories and approaches and infuse new ideas about culture, human and systemic development, and conceptions of mental health problems to develop more adaptive models. But we must remember that even the most flexible and adaptive models yet to come will be stamped with the temporal and cultural perspectives represented at the time of development and will seem outdated and limited to future generations of therapists and counselors.

Historical Perspective: Intergenerational Family Therapy

Bowen (1960) was a leading proponent of the intergenerational approach. He and his colleagues at Georgetown University articulated a concise theory that explicates the process of individual differentiation within the family context. More than anyone else, this group has shown us how family behaviors, thoughts, and feelings are passed from one generation to the next.

Central Theoretical Constructs. The central concept of Bowenian theory is the emotional system of clients' and their families' lives. This concept refers to the governing dynamics that control the functioning of a system, such as reactions to the environment, relationships, biological needs, and feeling states. All individuals have their own emotional system, and all families have a collective emotional system. This emotional system is similar to the concept of family unconscious, as described by Taub-Bynum in Chapter 5.

Bowen states that two primary opposing forces within this system shape and direct the behaviors of its members. The force within a system that pulls members toward each other is termed *togetherness force*, or *fusion*. The pull to be together can be so extreme in some families that the members cannot function without each other.

The second force in the system propels individuals to seek their own individuality. The term *differentiation* is used to describe the ability of an individual to separate emotions from cognitions, thereby retaining some choice between behavior governed by thinking and behavior governed by emotional reactivity. Mature individuals are able to avoid being overwhelmed by whatever emotions are predominant in the family. Although Bowen did not emphasize cultural context, the level and method of differentiation vary from culture to culture.

Bowenian theory conceives that symptoms currently being manifested by an identified client have their origins in failed differentiation attempts that occurred in previous generations. This multigenerational transmission process influences the interactional patterns of the current family. Parents tend to transmit their level of differentiation to their children, and these children, as adults, continue the transmission process. For example, McGoldrick (2002) suggests that family factors such as family history of suicide attempts and mental disorders are significantly related to individual suicidal ideation and attempts.

The intensity of family disruption due to the multigenerational transmission process is related to two factors: the degree of immaturity or differentiation of the parents and the level of stress or anxiety the family experiences. Research reported by Anderson and Sabatelli (1999) indicates that the emotional patterns of parental and marital functioning do influence an adolescent's ability to appropriately separate from the family. Adolescents reporting the highest level of depression perceived their parents' marital relationship to be dysfunctional.

Bowen also noted that unstable, two-person systems under stress seek to regain balance by bringing in another person. This new triangle is the basic building block in a family's emotional system. Triangles are not limited to three separate individuals. The third side of a triangle can be made up of entities such as work, substance abuse, friends, or children. Triangles allow the couple to project their anxiety onto another, thus relieving the twosome of the unwelcome stress. The role of scapegoat is often the third member of a family triangle, and it is not uncommon to see a parent triangulated by two siblings.

Central Treatment Goals. According to Bowen, the goal of therapy is to assist family members to achieve higher levels of differentiation of self. Specifically, individuals should be able to separate themselves from their families and become more inner directed and autonomous. The family should be able to support both the cognitive and emotional development of each member in a fashion that does not trap that member into only one way of thinking or behaving. Needless to say, this orientation is obviously European-American and would not be culturally appropriate for all clients. Bowen's theories need to be adapted, but nonetheless the general constructs are useful in multicultural situations.

According to this theoretical perspective, the therapist's role is to help families evaluate intergenerational issues. In this regard, Bowenian theory becomes particularly relevant to multicultural counseling. Clients, regardless of cultural background, will enact their cultural history with you in the individual and family counseling/therapy session.

To facilitate multigenerational understanding, the counselor/therapist helps clarify relational boundaries around the spouses and enables the family to identify triangles and family projection processes. The therapist assumes a position outside the family in order to avoid triangulation. The use of "I" statements helps the therapist stay grounded in personal experience and to model differentiation for the family.

Primary Therapeutic Techniques

Genogram. McGoldrick and colleagues (1999) provide a comprehensive description of the use of genograms as a powerful and practical diagnostic and therapeutic tool in family counseling and therapy settings. Genograms are utilized extensively by Bowenian family therapists and increasingly by individual counselors as well.

The family genogram is a graphic representation of the multigenerational family tree. When used effectively, it can make covert family patterns overt. Genograms can help families see the intergenerational transmission process at work and identify existing triangles. By using focusing skills, the therapist can make visible recurring themes and behaviors that flow from one family generation to the next. Genograms can be effectively integrated with individual or family counseling to help clients concentrate on family and cultural influences. Competency-Building Activity 14.2 is presented to encourage you to exercise your own ability to use a family genogram in your professional practices. The Professional Development Extension box will also extend your thinking about family counseling and therapy in general and how practitioners can include the use of community genograms (Chapter 1) to enhance their effectiveness in counseling as well as in promoting organizational changes that reflect greater sensitivity and knowledge of culturally different families in particular.

Other Techniques. In addition to the family genogram, other questions, assignments, and activities are presented to the family to uncover the nature of the family emotional system. These interventions are aimed at assisting family members to work through the differentiation process through cognitive analysis, as opposed to emotional reactions.

In doing so, Bowen encourages clients to "go home again," not for confrontational purposes but to use the knowledge learned in therapy to truly see their family-of-origin members as these members see themselves. Guerin, Fogarty, Fay, and Kautto (1996) provide a useful guide in applying Bowen's ideas to the practice of family therapy.

Interactional Perspective: Structural Family Therapy

Salvador Minuchin is noted for making family therapy popular and legitimate. His book *Families and Family Therapy* (1974) became a handbook for practicing family therapists. It articulated a clear way of diagramming family structure using easily understood maps and symbols.

Central Theoretical Constructs. Structural family theory provides the practitioner with a clear map of what constitutes functional family life. This map can be used to determine the degree of variance presented by any family. With this map, a direction for treatment can be developed. There are obvious cultural and gender limitations inherent in this map that need to be recognized by those who use the model.

Structural family therapy's basic family map reflects the traditional hierarchical structure that Minuchin sees as universal. In the hierarchical organization, parents exercise more power than children, and older children have more responsibilities as well as privileges than younger ones. Most often families seeking therapy are not aligned in such a hierarchical structure and have developed their own idiosyncratic family structure, which is generating symptomatic behavior. In effect, the children sometimes run the family, or a parent may be aligned with a child against another

Competency-Building Activity 14.2

Developing a Family Genogram or Chart

Instructions: Complete the following yourself and with a volunteer "client."

Demographic Data

1. Write out the names of all family members for at least two or three generations.
2. Fill in the dates of birth, marriage, separation, divorce, death, and other significant life events.
3. Make notations regarding ethnicity, occupations, places of residence, and major life events.
4. The symbols used for a genogram should be negotiated with your client. Many clients object to the traditional "X" over those who are deceased, stating that the person "still lives in me." Other clients may prefer a road map, a network of rivers, or other symbolic framework to present their families and community heritage. The traditional model of genograms should not be imposed anymore than we would impose a specific theory or counseling method on an unwilling client.

Basic Relationship Symbols

Close	═══
Enmeshed	≡≡≡
Estranged	─//─
Enmeshed and conflictual	ʌʌʌʌ
Distant	─ ─ ─ ─
Conflictual	ʌʌʌʌ
Separated	─/─

Family Genogram Exercise

As a counselor/therapist, it is important to be aware of your own intergenerational issues, because these issues can affect your life and can be stimulated by your clients. To increase your conscious understanding of your family's legacy, take some time to complete a family genogram yourself before trying this activity out with a volunteer "client."

Begin by talking to your immediate and extended family. Go through family memorabilia. Then, using the above symbols, begin mapping your family genogram. Be sure to include your own perceptions of the relationships with and between family members as well as those of other family members. It's always interesting to see how different family members view each other. Share the genogram with your family and look for patterns and themes. Then share it with a friend or someone who is not a member of your family.

Compare the insights gleaned from the family exploration and the nonfamily description. Which was easier? Which generated more emotions? What themes are important in your family? What personal and professional issues were raised by this exercise?

Now proceed to try to use the family genogram with a volunteer "client" following the same directions. After your "client" has completed the genogram, ask about her or his reactions to completing this activity.

Later, be sure to take time to record your own reactions to completing your genogram as well as in assisting another person to complete this exercise and file them in your personal/professional development portfolio.

parent. Three significant concepts bring meaning to the interpretation of family organization: structure, subsystems, and boundaries.

Structure. All families have many rules that determine the family structure. These rules translate into an invisible set of functional demands that organizes the way family

Professional Development Extension

Using Community Genograms with Families and Community Agencies

Marriage and family therapists can use community genograms (Chapter 1) to better understand families-in-context. This case illustrates how community genograms can be used to emphasize the cultural, community, and institutional strengths and resources essential to culture-centered assessment and treatment planning.

A Jamaican family became involved with protective services after school personnel reported concern about the daughter's bruised upper arm and the son's increasingly poor attendance. Initial exchanges between the caseworker and family were contentious, and the parents obtained a legal advocate to stop "further agency intrusion." A marriage and family therapist was asked to consult with the parents and the caseworker.

The therapist introduced the community genogram as a way to capture cultural and institutional factors that could expand the definition of the problem and identify more options and resources for its resolution (see Figure 14.1). The constellation on the left illustrates the social, political, and institutional influences and significant professionals and clients that contribute to the caseworker's assessment of the family. The right constellation illustrates the cultural, community, institutional, and family influences and significant others identified by the parents. The shaded area highlights the information common to both the family and the caseworker, while the unshaded areas indicate the information that was not shared among them.

Using the diagram, the cultural patterns influencing the family's parent-child relations were reviewed, as were the criteria used by the caseworker to assess the family. The right constellation introduced a range of resources and affiliations beyond the specifics of the referral and served to more holistically identify the family. It became clear that the family's behavior was consistent with family functioning in Jamaica. In Jamaica, it's not unusual for males to turn to the world outside school early in their teens and for girls to be more academically oriented. The son was working with his father in a local gas station and thus missing school. The father noted, "In Jamaica, this happens all the time. It's how we survive." Further, physical discipline is common in Jamaican families. Parents demonstrate love for children by "keeping a firm hand on things." A review of the left constellation made it clear that the information used by the caseworker to assess the family did not address these cultural dimensions of parenting.

The right constellation also highlighted the educational and economic conditions of the Jamaican community. Many Jamaican males do not graduate from the local high school, and those who do seldom secure meaningful employment. These conditions were not part of the caseworker's initial assessment. The left constellation also helped the parents learn more about the institutions and officials they were working with. They were able to see the caseworker in a new light and realized that certain behaviors were less accepted in the United States.

Reviewing the differences between the cultural parenting patterns of Jamaican and American families and the educational and economic realties of the Jamaican community facilitated discussions about ways to address the presenting concerns that were not governed by the concept of deviance. The family was able to understand their cultural situation and to work toward changes in their family patterns. Rather than continuing legal action, they worked with the caseworker and learned to adapt to cultural norms about parent-child interactions expected in the United States.

The caseworker and the agency were able to understand the need to create community supports for this family and for others from the Jamaican community who had been referred under similar circumstances. The agency and the school obtained a state grant to develop educational and vocational training opportunities within the Jamaican community. The parents, with the help of their church, organized a support group for families experiencing the same educational and economic conditions. Finally, school officials contacted a local community college to establish an after-school tutoring program. The son returned to school, and new disciplinary methods were designed to communicate the family's values of respect, hard work, strong effort, and politeness to the children.

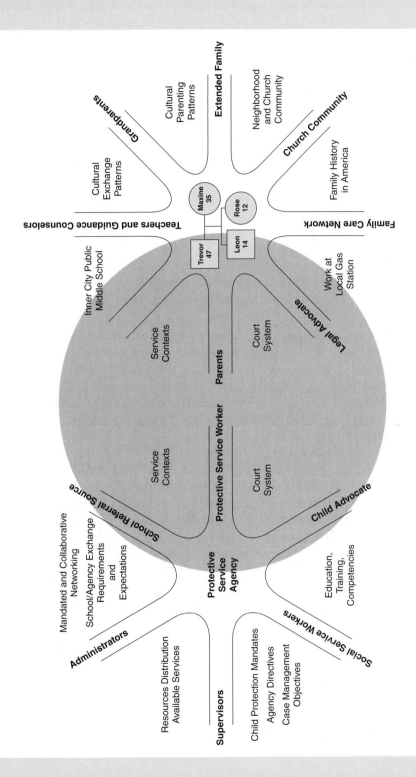

Figure 14.1 Community Genogram

Source: S. A. Rigazio-DiGilio, A. E. Ivey, K. P. Kunkler-Peck, and L. T. Grady (2005) *Community genograms: Using individual, family and cultural narratives with clients.* New York: Teacher's College Press, Columbia University. Reprinted by permission.

members relate to one another. The behavior patterns established by intrafamilial rules position various family members and subsystems into an organized unit and way of being and acting.

Subsystems. There are three types of family subsystems: spouse, parental, and sibling. Subsystems are also organized around other issues, such as gender, generation, common interests, and functions. Any member of the family is a subsystem and is also a member of many other subsystems, such as dyads, triads, or larger groups.

Theoretical groupings of parental, spousal, and sibling subsystems are often less powerful than the real subsystems that have been established over time in the family. Subsystems may cross generational lines and include various combinations of parents and children. Many times families seeking treatment will present themselves with an organization that reinforces a child in the parental subsystem.

Boundaries. According to Minuchin, boundaries delineate individuals and subsystems and define the amount and kind of contact allowed between members of the family. Boundaries can vary in the degree of firmness and flexibility. Some subsystem boundaries are very permeable or diffuse. In this case, the boundaries between individuals are so open that the relationship is described as enmeshed. Children may rule the family. Excessive cohesiveness could lead to a lack of individuation of family members.

Minuchin describes another type of dysfunctional boundary in families as the impermeable or rigid type. Here communication and affect are blocked at the boundary. Parents with rigid boundaries may foster autonomy in their children but not supply or receive affection. In this type of family structure, family members must search elsewhere for support and nurturance.

The final boundary type that Minuchin identified is the healthy or clear boundary, which is firm yet flexible. Clearly defined boundaries between subsystems help maintain separateness while also emphasizing a sense of belongingness. In this situation, the autonomy of members is not sacrificed, and at the same time, care, support, and involvement are available as needed.

Central Treatment Goals. The primary goal of the interactional approach is to restructure the family's system of rules and interactional patterns to improve its flexible adaptation to the environment. Therapeutic change is viewed as the process of releasing family members from rigidly defined positions within the system. The restructuring process frees family members to utilize new resources and enhance their ability to cope with stress and conflict (Simon, 1995). The aim of the therapist is to help the family realign the structural composition of its interactions and work with family members until they are able to maintain this new and more satisfying configuration on their own.

Primary Therapeutic Interventions. Three major structural interventions are as follows:

Relabeling and reframing. Relabeling and reframing are forms of positive connotation that translate symptomatic behavior as adaptive behavior. In this fashion, the family's understanding of the behavior is shifted, thus freeing the members to think and behave differently. This new interpretation releases the potential for a more appropriate solution to the issue. Relabeling can be used to connote specific individual behavior, for example, "Johnny's excessive drinking is a cry for help" or "Your father's anger when you violate the curfew is a sign of his love for you." Reframes can also be used to relabel family behavior.

Straightforward directives and homework assignments. Directives and homework assignments are clear requests for the family to take specific action. Some directives include asking family members to directly discuss the issue or to identify the negative aspects of change. Homework assignments may ask the parents not to make any decisions about the children until all have discussed the issue of concern.

Unbalancing techniques. These are used to create disequilibrium within families to disrupt symptomatic patterns. For example, the therapist may side with one member or subsystem to move the family to a new interpretation of an issue. Specifically, the myth that boys do not show emotion may be unbalanced when a male therapist sides with the mother and tells the son, "It's all right to cry." In this type of unbalancing, the weight of the therapist's authority is used to break a stalemate by supporting one side in a conflict. Unbalancing can explode dysfunctional myths that render the family ineffective (Minuchin & Nichols, 1993).

Existential Perspective: Symbolic/Experiential Family Therapy

Basically a clinical approach, symbolic/experiential family therapy emphasizes the here-and-now phenomena of the encounter of the family and counselor/therapist. Whitaker (1967) and Napier (1977) are the most notable proponents of this approach. Experiential therapists mainly focus on the present experience of the family as opposed to exploring the family's past.

Central Theoretical Constructs and Goals. Whitaker believes the symbolic meaning that family members attach to their intrapersonal and intrafamilial life are the essential structures that influence behavior and emotions. How one feels and thinks about the family is of utmost importance. If a mother believes her daughter is devious, no matter what that daughter does, the mother will always suspect her daughter's motives. Symbolic/experiential therapists consistently attempt to identify and explore these explicit and often implicit images.

Theory does not have a significant role in symbolic/experiential therapy. Unlike Bowen, Whitaker adheres to the belief that therapy should be creative, spontaneous, and authentic. He asserts that rigid theories of how therapists should behave and how families should interact are oversimplifications of reality and do more harm than good.

The primary task of the experiential therapist is to help the family become aware of the underlying symbolism that influences family functioning (Whitaker & Bumberry, 1988). The ultimate purpose of the therapist's work is to assist families in supporting the creative efforts of their members to balance the need for belongingness and the freedom to individuate. Helping family members to examine their symbolic interpretations of family life, to play, and to feel more powerful as a team are all objectives of this approach.

Primary Therapeutic Techniques. Whitaker advocates for a cotherapy or multitherapist team approach to family therapy. He believes this allows for greater creativity, buffers the possibility of becoming enmeshed in the family's pathology, and provides peer support for thinking about the therapeutic situation.

Some additional intervention techniques that experiential family therapists have used to help families become aware of their symbolic structures are described below. Each of these techniques is aimed at helping the family redefine symptoms as efforts on the part of the identified patient to grow and to bring out the family's creative abilities in the service of finding new alternatives for healthy development.

Family sculpture. A family member is asked to position and direct the other members in a typical scene that might be evident when the issue is observable. This technique can help answer such questions as "Where are people in relation to one another?" or "What are they doing?" and also "How do they act?" The family sculpture technique also affords the other family members insight into the perception of the sculptor.

Family art therapy. Utilizing art therapy techniques, experiential therapists ask family members to draw images of their family. Individual or joint drawings can be generated and then explored to gain insight into the family's functioning. One technique, "joint family scribble," requires each member to make a quick scribble. The whole family then incorporates the scribble into a unified picture. The relational implications of this activity are considerable. How does each person feel, as represented by the scribble, and whom do they feel connected to, as represented by the finished picture?

Symbolic drawing of family life space. Using the psychodrama technique of a sociogram, the therapist draws a large circle. The space inside the circle represents the family. All other persons and institutions not considered part of the family are placed outside the circle. Members are directed to draw a small circle that represents where they are in relation to others.

The family floor plan. As with the other experiential techniques mentioned here, the family floor plan is used for two purposes: first, to get the family comfortable with expression, and second, as a diagnostic tool. Members are asked to draw the floor plan for their current family. Sometimes parents are also asked to draw the floor plan of their family of origin as well.

The use of the self. The essential element of a successful intervention, as defined by Whitaker, is the use of the self by the therapist. Whitaker believes that no theory can truly capture the evolution of the therapeutic process. Therapists must move beyond rigid interventions or theories and rely on their own feelings, impulses, and ideas, which are generated in the interactional relationships with the family in counseling and therapy.

Postmodern and Integrative Perspectives: Systemic Cognitive-Developmental Therapy

Systemic cognitive-developmental therapy (SCDT) emphasizes the importance of families as mediators for the culture and the individual. SCDT works to activate and enhance this role by providing suitable therapeutic and consultative environments for facilitating individual, family, and network interaction and growth (Rigazio-DiGilio, 2000). To do so, SCDT provides

- a linguistic system for assessing family cognitive, behavioral, and emotional style
- a framework for action in the interview that is oriented toward family style
- an integration of the diverse theoretical alternatives in the family therapy field

Families always experience pressure to change. These forces may be supportive, disconfirming, or oppressive. Families utilize resources and challenge constraints to maintain a balance of continuity and change. Doing so requires viable worldviews, effective information-processing styles (Anderson et al., 1986; Hoffman, 1990), and the sense of power and influence (Goldner, 1993) to do what is necessary.

Central Theoretical Constructs. Just as with DCT (see Chapter 13), SCDT posits that worldviews evolve in a constant exchange between persons and environments participating in various situational contexts over time. We construct individual worldviews by participating in various contexts (Ivey, 2000; Ivey, Ivey, Myers, & Sweeney, 2005) and collective worldviews by participating in resonating experiences with enduring relationships within these contexts (Rigazio-DiGilio, 1997).

This exchange occurs within parameters inherent in an individual's genetic endowment and worldview, a system's organization and worldview, and a community's social reality. The degree to which individuals and families respond to, influence, or challenge other members of their interactive systems depends on these parameters, current life tasks, and positions held in the organizational structures of the extended system.

SCDT differentiates enabled families from constrained ones by examining their capacity to access varying emotional, cognitive, and behavioral options in response to demands for change. Effective systems optimize a broad range of resources in ways that are in synchrony with the needs of individuals, subsystems, and the collective as influential partners in the systems of which they are a part. Some less effective family, organizational, and community systems may rely on a limited set of resources that are insufficient to effectively understand, adapt to, influence, or challenge demands for change. Others may randomly access less developed resources that often prove ineffective.

Cognitive-developmental resources. Over time, families develop a collective worldview that organizes predictable ways of thinking, feeling, and acting. SCDT focuses on the linguistic representation of these worldviews. The family's worldview can be classified in one of four styles and serves as the primary filter that the family uses to understand its world. It may be a blending of each member's cognitive-developmental style or a combination of some subsystem in the family—for example, a dominant member or the parental subsystem.

Understanding the resources within each style assists clinicians in assessing the capacities families can access at any given time, while understanding representative constraints clarifies the types of distress families may encounter. The supposition is that access to a broad range of orientations leads to capable functioning more than does being constrained within one or two styles.

The systemic translation of cognitive-developmental constructs results in a family therapy model that permits the therapist to identify at any point in the interview the predominant style being used by the family through the natural language of the interview. The four cognitive-developmental styles framed from a systemic perspective come from the developmental counseling and therapy (DCT) framework discussed in Chapter 13 and are summarized briefly below:

1. *Sensorimotor/elemental*—focusing on the elements of immediate experience. The interactions and relationships of families functioning within this style are often guided by direct sensory experience or emotions. If constrained here, they can become overwhelmed by slight variations and may not gain an overall gestalt of the challenges and problems the family faces. The emotional life of families seeking treatment may be out of control, and there may be a loss of family stability and continuity. SCDT suggests that a firm yet flexible structure be a prominent aspect of the therapeutic relationship.

2. *Concrete/situational*—seeking situational descriptions. Families accessing this style can sequentially describe distress and disorder in ways that promote predictable action. If constrained, they develop narrow visions, tending toward linear, contingent, if/then perspectives. These families present in a straightforward, unidimensional fashion characterized by simple cause-and-effect reasoning. They may continue to use "tried-and-true" solutions even though the situation has changed. Although they are "in control" of their emotions, they have great difficulty recognizing patterns of ineffective behavior and thoughts. SCDT recommends a behaviorally oriented coaching style of therapy for these families.

3. *Formal/reflective*—exploring the family-in-context. When accessing this style, families rely on pattern recognition, abstract thinking, and an understanding of self and situation to comprehend distress. Constraint leads to overemphasis on analysis and reflection without change or effect and may promote logic-tight assumptions about functioning, which may impede the family's ability to alter

behavior when necessary. SCDT believes that a client-directed or consultative "we" intervention is useful with these families.

4. *Dialectic/systemic*—integrating the family-in-context. Families accessing this style can interpret the world by viewing the distress as a continual web of interrelated patterns and associations. They realize the powerful influence of the environmental context on their functioning. Intergenerational, intrafamilial, and societal forces can be analyzed and evaluated. Those constrained become overwhelmed by the complexities of this interrelatedness, making challenge more likely than change. This leads to a diffuse abstract sense of family identity that inhibits a collective ability to deal with concrete and sensorimotor reality. SCDT considers a collaborative or mutual therapeutic environment appropriate for these families.

Families repeatedly progress through these styles over the life span and at times may become stuck and immobilized in one style. At such times, the meanings, emotions, and actions a family shares about specific issues tend to be framed by one style. For example, a family faced with a child leaving home may become very concrete and controlling, creating a consequent rebellion from the child. The task is to help the family "move on" by exploring their feelings (sensorimotor) and generating new meanings (formal and dialectic) associated with separation.

By using listening skills as well as a sequential set of questioning strategies, an SCDT therapist can identify which style the family is primarily operating from as well as its ability to use the other styles. In other words, the therapist can identify whether the family can experience (sensorimotor/elemental), act on (concrete/situational), and understand the patterns (formal/reflective) and origins (dialectic/systemic) of the issues that led to counseling and therapy. The degree of organization within a particular style and the range of movement among other styles are labeled as the family's cognitive-developmental structure.

The concept of equilibration, or how a family maintains a balance between its worldview and its changing environment, is also an important element of SCDT. When faced with new situations or emotions, the family must work to either integrate these new data into existing worldviews or modify its own perspectives, thereby altering family members' worldviews. Effective families have demonstrated the capacity to maintain this balance.

For instance, when a healthy, concrete/operational family is faced with the death of a grandparent, the family can feel the sorrow of that loss (sensorimotor) and assist each member to make sense of this experience (formal) while taking care of the necessary legal arrangements (concrete). Less effective families use unproductive methods of integrating data.

On the one hand, families with rigid cognitive-developmental structures hold strongly to one style even in the face of contradictory experience. They do not alter worldviews or consider alternatives for making sense of their experiences. Using the same scenario, the rigid concrete family would attend to funeral and legal details but not to emotions. Some members might repress feelings, which later become resentments that can compromise connectedness.

On the other hand, families with diffuse or underdeveloped structures are highly reactive to changes in their environment and haphazardly move within and between styles, compromising family stability and continuity. They often lack a foundation within any style and so are not able to effectively utilize perspectives or resources within the styles they access. Faced with this same scenario, these families might experience severe mood swings about the death. Tasks would be haphazardly attended to, and members would not be able to assist one another to integrate this experience.

Dealing with issues of power in SCDT. SCDT extends the assessment process beyond the family. The worldviews and styles used by participants of the wider system are identified. How family members are related to the extrafamilial system is classified in terms of power and embeddedness.

Power differentials change the nature of any interaction. Social and economic oppression can compromise the development of individual and family resources. So can the dissonance created when the environment demands interactions outside of a family's physical, psychological, cultural, moral, or spiritual identity. Particularly insidious is oppression created when a family's familiar ways of perceiving and acting are labeled as substandard or deviant.

Knowing who has real or imagined means to exert power and influence, in terms of the definition and management of a presenting issue, is critical if the therapist is to determine if and how families can balance their needs. Social realities that emerge in these systems determine if multiple options for understanding, adapting to, or challenging reified definitions of self, family, network, and culture may be possible or not.

Embeddedness. The concept of embeddedness is used to represent the degree of influence and sense of connectedness exerted by individuals, families, or wider contexts. Influence is generated by the extent to which unanimity and conformity operate across the entire system when defining themes and establishing identities. Individuals whose self-identity and worth are based within their family's worldview are strongly influenced by how their family defines and relates to them. This is often the case for younger children, who depend on family validation to construct a sense of self and self-in-relation. Concomitantly, individuals whose sense of self and others is based in a multitude of environments (e.g., school, community, and peers) will be less connected and therefore less influenced by their family's worldview. The positions of power and embeddedness that individuals and families have in interaction with their environments help to determine how they will understand and operate as members of wider systems. In turn, these same two factors help to determine how wider environments will impact and interact with individuals and families. Rigazio-DiGilio (1997) offers an example:

> To illustrate, consider two different parent systems attending parent-teacher conferences to discuss indicators being used to determine whether or not their sons require evaluative testing for attention-deficit/hyperactivity disorder (ADHD). The parents embedded within the social, political, and

economic realities dominating the local educational community and carrying their own sense of real or perceived power might define themselves as a family that will stand up for the rights of their child. They may bring up the deficiencies of an overpopulated, understaffed school system, note the increased use of Ritalin in the schools, and mention the lack of training for teachers who deal with children requiring more structured learning environments. However, the parents more peripheral to social, political, and economic trends, or carrying less of a sense of real or perceived power, might define themselves and their child as somehow dysfunctional or inadequate. These parents may listen to the steps that school personnel deem necessary to ensure that their child accommodates to the classroom environment. They may not recognize the deficiencies noted by the other parents. In this case, the wider systems of influence could, intentionally or not, neglect the interactional forces at work between the child and his environment, and move toward the ADHD diagnosis. However, in the first case, the systems of influence may in fact be required to reflect upon how social, political, and economic trends have affected the classroom environment, and how these changes are now affecting the child's perception of himself and his educational and behavioral competence. (p. 89)

Central Treatment Goals. SCDT labels distress as a nonpathological response to developmental and contextual stressors that result when discrepancies or oppressive forces emerge between clients and wider contexts. SCDT suggests that the factors influencing how individuals, relationships, and wider collectives relate to the distress should be examined as well as the factors that affect which domains have power and influence in relation to the distress.

The idea is to use such information to coconstruct therapeutic and consultative environments that can generate interaction among individuals, systems, and institutions; advance multiple perspectives regarding treatment issues; and open up alternative ways for participants to understand one another and work together toward the management or dissolution of these issues. The intent is to involve all relevant participants in coconstructing a broader perspective of the possible solutions. To accomplish this, counselors and therapists form partnerships with family members that are intentionally designed to foster changes in the family members' inner thoughts and feelings and in how they participate in their wider contexts.

Primary Therapeutic Techniques. SCDT assessment is linguistically based and uncovers identifiable language patterns in clients and significant others that reflect how they understand and influence presenting issues. This information is used to determine where counselors can most flexibly intervene to relieve unproductive stress.

SCDT begins with a structured interview process that identifies the family members' cognitive developmental structures in general and specifically in relation to the presenting issue. Based on the results of this assessment process, the counselor/therapist creates an environment in the counseling/therapy setting that is intentionally aimed at helping the family and relevant participants use multiple cognitive-emotional styles to explore different perspectives of the issue at hand. In this regard, SCDT does not offer new techniques beyond specific questioning strategies but rather integrates methods from other family approaches within a cognitive-developmental framework.

To illustrate this point, Table 14.3 correlates the four cognitive-emotional styles with representative SCDT questioning strategies and with the primary therapeutic interventions of the three major family therapy models addressed earlier in this chapter. Competency-Building Activity 14.3 provides guidelines that are useful in developing the skills necessary to effectively conduct an SCDT assessment interview.

SCDT believes that change is brought about in one of two directions. The first is helping relevant members of the client system elaborate and explore the most common styles. This type of movement is termed *horizontal change*. The second type of movement is termed *vertical* and involves assisting clients to move to other styles. To illustrate these two concepts, consider a concrete family that has been asked to complete a family genogram. At first, as the family is directed to gather more and more specific information about the intergenerational family network, the therapist utilizes the family's natural descriptive skills. In this fashion, the therapist makes a horizontal intervention aimed at helping the family use and extend its descriptive abilities. The completed genogram then becomes the focus of therapy as the family is encouraged to search for patterns of interactions. This enables the family to move to a more formal/operational skill, which is an example of vertical movement in the SCDT approach to family counseling and therapy.

Many strategies lend themselves to multiple styles. The intentionality of their use will determine the impact on the family. For instance, the family sculpture activity can be used to help a family identify interpersonal closeness (sensorimotor), describe a typical family scene (concrete/operational), analyze a recurrent pattern (formal/operational), or consider the impact of contextual forces (dialectic/systemic) on family functioning. By using this SCDT conceptualization system, a therapist is empowered to use a variety of therapeutic interventions in a horizontal or vertical direction, depending on the specific developmental needs of the family.

SCDT is an emerging theory of family therapy that presents practical methods to unite concepts of family development with the strategies of clinical practice. Additionally, SCDT provides a framework for family counselors and therapists to integrate the approaches of various other helping models using a developmental perspective. In this way, SCDT offers an alternative paradigm for the assessment, treatment, and conception of family issues.

Limitations and Practical Implications of Family Counseling and Therapy

Family therapy has left its mark on the counseling field. With a cadre of charismatic leaders, new forms of family treatment have emerged and found a wide audience of practitioners. One reason these methods caught on so quickly is because they appear

Table 14.3

Therapeutic Environments, Corresponding SCDT Questions, and Associated Family Therapy Interventions

Orientation and Therapeutic Environment	Sample SCDT Questioning Strategies	Sample Family Therapy Interventions
Sensorimotor/elemental Environmental structuring	1. How do the two of you feel right now as you see your son and wife act this way? 2. Tell your daughter what happens inside you when she talks about her pain. 3. What is happening for you now, at this moment?	*Structural approach:* heightening intensity; crisis induction *Transgenerational approach:* directing core affective exchanges; contextual holding *Experiential approach:* fantasy alternatives; highlighting covert conflict
Concrete/situational Coaching	1. Would you two discuss what happens just before your daughter has a temper tantrum? 2. Who stepped in afterward? 3. Given the way these facts emerged, what do you think causes or triggers what?	*Structural approach:* enactment; boundary making *Transgenerational approach:* constructing therapeutic triangles; facilitating direct communication *Experiential approach:* teaching stories; sculpting
Formal/reflective Consulting	1. Has anything like this ever happened before? 2. What else in the family seems related to or influenced by this problem? 3. Can you describe other things that happen that seem to require each of you to take similar positions?	*Structural approach:* reframing/enhancing; search for strengths *Transgenerational approach:* genogram pattern analysis; enlarging field of participation *Experiential approach:* relational symptom expansion; metaphor
Dialectic/systemic Collaborating	1. How would you define the rule(s) that influence how your family thinks, feels, and acts? 2. What role does your religion, ethnicity, family background, and wider context play in the way you have developed and held to these rules? 3. Could you describe your family from another point of view?	*Structural approach:* reframing/transforming; challenging worldview *Transgenerational approach:* community genogram; exploring transgenerational legacies and loyalties *Experiential approach:* transgenerational symptom expansion; family reconstruction

Competency-Building Activity 14.3

The SCDT Assessment Interview

Instructions: The SCDT assessment interview is easy to learn and apply. To practice, have at least two people who have an issue they would like to address and some history together that they can draw on during your interview with them.

Pose the open-ended questions first to your volunteer clients. Let the clients talk about the issues of interest to them without interference. Listen and try to classify which cognitive-emotional style from the SCDT model most dominates the discussion, in terms of how the volunteers perceive the issue and the patterns of communication they rely on.

Watch for the particular cues and see if you can name which style seems to bring forth the dominant communication patterns.

- Sensorimotor cues include random and disorganized thoughts and emotions about the issue, with an inability to form a consensual understanding.
- Concrete cues include specific linear descriptions about events, persons, and interaction, with if/then causal thinking.
- Formal cues include reflections and analyses of self, relationship, and situation, with less focus on challenging what is believed or on experiencing the real situation in thoughts and feelings.
- Dialectic/systemic cues include examinations of the wider context and its influence and the system of rules and beliefs that governs us, removed from actual experience.

Now go to the questioning sequence that is provided below. Using these questions, facilitate communication that explores the issue from within each of the four styles or frames of reference. As an assessment tool, you simply ask the questions and take note of competencies and constraints in the volunteer's ability to respond from each style. In research and as you practice, you will see that if

you stay directly in a style, using the questions offered, the lens from each style will be used. Basically, the questions create the environments that hold a particular vantage point long enough for successful exploration of the client's issue or concern from that particular style.

Be advised, though, when encountering a foreign way to perceive, clients easily drift to more familiar ways of thinking and interacting. When this occurs, it is the careful and patient rewording of particular questions that promotes change.

At the end of this assessment process, you will have a good understanding of the styles most accessed and those most discarded. At the end of conducting the more structured interview described below, it is often the case that the issue of interest will be seen from broader perspectives.

Open-Ended Questions for Initial Assessment (assessing the preferred style)

1. Please *talk together and reach consensus* regarding the issues of mutual concern.
2. Please *talk together and reach consensus* about what you envision will happen here.

Cognitive-Developmental Questioning Sequence (assessing the family's ability to communicate from within each style)

Sensorimotor/Elemental Processing Style

1. When you all focus together on the issues that brought you here, *what image* can you generate all together?
2. Once the image is generated, ask questions about it, the feelings associated with it, and how they saw themselves come up with it. Ask such questions as

- Can you describe the image generated?
- Are any sounds connected with it?
- What feelings came up as you generated this image?

continued on next page

Competency-Building Activity 14.3, continued

3. Summation question: What does this image and the feelings it generates say about your family?

Concrete/Situational Processing Style

1. You know the issues that brought you here. Can you all help put together an example that highlights what occurs between you when the issue is really visible?

2. Use the example to ask a list of behavioral tracking questions such as

- Who is involved?
- What happened first, second, next, etc.?
- Who steps in at that point?
- What happens afterward?
- Who else is watching the process?
- What do they do?

3. Summation question: As you describe this example, what are you learning about how you influence one another?

Formal/Reflective Processing Style

1. Please identify *other episodes* where you act sort of the same way, where you take on similar roles.

2. Are there *other situations* that trigger similar reactions?

3. Summation question: As you describe these similar ways of acting across many different situations, what are you learning about the patterns operating in your family?

Dialectic/Systemic Processing Style

Integration
1. Is there a central theme(s) that emerges when we talk about things like this?

Coconstruction
1. What are some of the *rules* that seem to influence how each of you thinks, feels, and acts in relation to these themes?

2. What are the origins of these rules? Where did you learn these rules? Who taught you these rules?

3. What role did/does the wider context play in the development and maintenance of these rules?

Multiple Perspectives
1. Are there other ways to look at these *rules*?

2. How might another family see things differently?

Deconstruction
1. How are these *rules* at the present time not working for you and your family?

2. Are you aware of any flaws or constraints in these rules—ways that these rules interfere with the family attempting to get what it needs at this time?

3. How are these rules helping or hindering your current way of understanding and acting?

Reconstruction and Action
1. How might you change or modify these rules? How might you do that?

2. Given the possibilities of change, is there anything you could change immediately to view the issues that brought you here from a different perspective?

3. Using these possibilities of change, is there anything you could do right now to work on the issues that brought you to treatment?

4. Summation question: Based on all of this, what could your family do differently—right now, in this room—to address the issues that have prompted treatment?

After you have completed this competency-building activity, take a few minutes to write down your reactions and file them in your personal/professional development portfolio.

to work and research supports family therapy's importance and usefulness. Therapists who do not consider family issues miss an important dimension of their clients' development. The systemic focus on the family as a context of a person's development and behavior is one method of integrating family counseling strategies within an individual treatment setting.

Some limitations of family therapy models include issues of philosophical orientation and larger sociocultural concerns. It is difficult for some therapists to consider the family as a system when they are focused on the intrapsychic world of the individuals who make up the families they work with. Further, many counselors and therapists feel overwhelmed when confronted with the depth and intensity of a family in trouble. (Remember the layers of ethical complexity explored in Competency-Building Activity 14.1.) Training and supervision in family systems theory are important aids in developing a systemic worldview.

Several contextual limitations related to the first three family counseling and therapy categories (historical, interactional/behavioral, existential) discussed in this chapter are also noted. First, cultural sensitivity is not an important element of the foundations of these models. Second, these models tend to replicate the male-privileged status quo of our culture. The third criticism concerns the epistemological ground of theory building and professional practice on which these three approaches to family counseling and therapy are based.

Traditional approaches to family counseling and therapy have been based on a positivistic belief system that minimizes the role of the subject (family members) and the observer (the counselor/therapist) and concentrated primarily on defining the object (the presenting issues) in reliable and valid ways. Sometimes that object was the intrapsychic world of the client, sometimes the dynamic communication patterns of the family.

In these decontextualized approaches, the goal was to provide a cure for the client. These drawbacks are most evident when mental health professionals naively assume that the values and dispositions inherent in their current psychotherapeutic theories are universally held and seek to impose these beliefs on clients who may differ in terms of racial/ethnic, gender, socioeconomic, and other characteristics (Sue et al., 1996). It also has been noted that family counseling and therapy will only be capable of bringing about real change for families when the larger social and cultural forces as well as the power distribution within the family and the community are addressed (Avis, 1988; D'Andrea & Daniels, 2005; Falicov, 1995; Hoffman, 1990; Luepnitz, 1988; Olson, 2002; Romney, 2000; Walsh, 2002).

Ecological and postmodern theories of family counseling and therapy also have limitations. First, most of these theories still primarily deal with the thought and action processes of clients but omit action with and reflection on the wider social systems that may have contributed to or labeled the distress that families experience. Second, the process of theory advancement is not yet distributed across all levels of the profession. New methods of knowledge advancement must be applied in order to directly link theory, research, and practice so that credible, broad-based models of ecological and postmodern family counseling and therapy theories can be developed.

Integrative family counseling models are not without their problems as well. A primary caution about these helping models is that counselors and therapists may apply any of a variety of techniques they only superficially understand, increasing the potential for ineffective treatment. Another concern is that the link between treatment and outcome becomes harder to define. Third, integrative family counseling and therapy models can be presented in dogmatic fashion, suggesting a recurrent emphasis on competition and superiority and a continuing distance between theoretical knowledge and craft knowledge.

Finally, integrative models have emerged within the parameters of a Western, Euro-American, individualistic framework. As a result, it is rarely the case that integrative counselors and therapists extend beyond the borders of their profession to examine alternative theories of counseling and therapy from other mental health fields (e.g., counseling psychology, social work, clinical psychology and psychiatry). Basically, these models may simply attach a wide range of skills to deeply rooted principles that are known to pathologize and decontextualize persons from diverse groups and backgrounds.

Practitioners espousing a particular perspective need "to clearly specify the parameters of their approaches, and to be clear about their limitations" (Rigazio-DiGilio et al., 1997, p. 246). Only through this expanded discussion can the tacit biases inherent in ecological, postmodern, and integrative models come to the surface and be addressed.

Summary

The discussion of the numerous family counseling and therapy models presented in this chapter is designed to increase your understanding of other helping strategies that many counselors and therapists commonly implement in their professional practices. The various limitations and challenges practitioners face in effectively implementing these theories among persons from diverse groups and backgrounds propel family counselors/therapists to reevaluate their worldview in order to reduce cultural, gender, and problem-solving bias.

It will be a long struggle, but in the future the quality of effective counseling and therapy will be measured not merely by the removal of family symptomatic behavior but also by demonstrating a consideration of cultural diversity and gender equity and the ability to liberate our clients from the personal, familial, and contextual boundaries that create and maintain distress and disorder. Sampson (1990) squarely places the responsibility on mental health professionals to continue to challenge the outdated assumptions of our prevailing models:

In the long run, psychology's legitimacy resides in the hands of the people. These people have become both more diverse and more restless. Their differences are showing and will not be silenced by appeals to the ideas that continue to speak in the voice of the dominators. Either psychology will listen and change, or it will lose its thrust as an important contributor to the tasks of our time. (p. 1228)

The final chapter in this book assists you in thinking in greater depth about your own personal style of counseling and psychotherapy. It provides guidelines that are useful in helping you to synthesize many of the theoretical ideas that are discussed in all of the preceding chapters in ways that will enable you to integrate your own personal style and preferences for counseling and therapy.

Multimedia Resources for This Chapter

The following online resource offers video and other resources of particular relevance to this chapter of your text.

MyHelpingLab

If a MyHelpingLab passcode was included with your textbook and you have activated your passcode:

- go to **www.ablongman.com/myhelpinglab**
- enter the "Counseling" area of the site by clicking on that tab
- select "Video Lab" from the toolbar to the left of the page
- select "MyHelpingLab Videos by Theoretical Approach"
- select any of these modules—"Family Systems," "Reality," or "Person-Centered"— to view various video clips of therapists using these approaches with clients

chapter 15

Identifying Your Own Integrated Approach to Counseling and Therapy

---

chapter goals

This chapter is designed to:

1. Review the major concepts of this book.

2. Encourage you to start generating your own personal view and integration of the helping process in a more concrete fashion through

   - examining and defining your own counseling and therapy worldview
   - developing your own construction of the counseling and psychotherapeutic process

---

Introduction

Now that you have read about the many theoretical models, skills, and intervention strategies discussed in this book, you are challenged to answer this critical question: How will you integrate the concepts of this book into your own daily practice? Theory remains only theory unless it is translated into direct practice.

All too often, excellent theories remain "on the shelf" because insufficient attention has been given to practicing the skills and strategies of the theory. This book has brought a host of counseling and psychotherapy theories to your attention, and we believe that we have more than covered the most critical points related to each. But the really vital issue is: *Can you use what you have learned in this book in your daily practice of counseling and interviewing?* To help you answer this question, we invite you to reflect on the metaphor of the Japanese samurai.

The samurai, Japanese champions of sword handling, learn their skills through a complex training program. The special movements and philosophy of sword work are broken down into specific components that are studied carefully, one at a time. In learning the precise handling of the sword, even the naturally gifted sword handler can find that there is a temporary decrease in dexterity and performance. Awareness of the many components involved in learning a skill can interfere with coordination. Nonetheless, skills and concepts are learned thoroughly and practiced again and again.

Once the skills reach close to virtuoso level, the samurai retire to a mountaintop to meditate. There they deliberately forget what they have learned. When they return to the valley, they find that the discrete skills they have learned have been naturally integrated into their style or way of being. They seldom have to think about skills at all; they have become samurai.

Consider the samurai and your own experience. You may be naturally talented as a musician, dancer, writer, or athlete. You likely also have found that practicing the fundamentals of your art or sport made a large difference in your performance.

Now, apply this metaphor to you and your future. Like the samurai, you may be a naturally gifted helper. The theory is helpful, but the rehearsal and practice of the skills and concepts contained in this book can enable you to become even more accomplished as a counselor or therapist. That is why we have stressed the importance of competency-building exercises in each chapter. Practice and mastering these basics can build a deeper understanding that later will be integrated into your personal style and approach to helping.

The Search for the "Best" Theory

The field of therapy and counseling has changed dramatically since its beginning with Freud. As former Yankee and Hall of Fame baseball player Yogi Berra aptly put it, "If Sigmund Freud was alive today, he'd be turning over in his grave" (cited in Cummings, 1988). In many ways it was simpler during much of Freud's lifetime. Then there was really only one major theory, and all one had to do to train for therapy work was learn the Freudian approach. Next, cognitive-behavioral theory and existential-humanistic theory were added to the picture, but still one only had to decide which was the "best" theory. The task for new counselors and therapists as recently as twenty years ago remained simply deciding on a single theoretical approach.

Historically, the field tends to talk about first-, second-, and third-force theories of helping, and these categories reflect the major theories in the historical order in which they appeared. Psychodynamic is considered the first force, due to Freud's vast original influence. Later, Adlerian, Jungian, object relations, and attachment theories brought new life to Freud's at times outdated constructs.

Cognitive-behavioral psychology is considered the second force, being connected to the work of early behavioral theorists such as Watson and Skinner. With the advent of cognitive approaches and the influence of Beck, Meichenbaum, Ellis, and Glasser, the second force broadened its scope and became metatheoretical and integrative. It remains the dominant force today, and to ignore it would be a major mistake.

Rogers's person-centered therapy brought a more humanistic view to the field—the third force. The work of Rogers and of Maslow focused the attention of a generation of therapists on the importance of the person and relationship in therapy. The ideas of Rogers, Frankl, and Perls are now part of the approach and practice of most counselors and therapists, even if they claim to adhere to another theoretical orientation. *Relationship is central regardless of your theoretical approach.*

Feminist theory (FCT) and multicultural counseling and therapy (MCT) have become recognized as a distinct fourth force in the field. Traditional theories gave minimal attention to the gender and cultural base of helping until FCT and MCT developed. In a short period of time, these theoretical orientations began to reshape the fields of counseling and psychology.

MCT is different than the other three forces in that it does not discount the importance of any theoretical orientation. Rather, MCT recognizes, adapts, and supports all approaches to therapy. However, MCT also requires developing increased awareness and sensitivity to multicultural issues. MCT is becoming perhaps the central metatheory of helping owing to its recognition that all helping stems from a cultural base (D'Andrea & Daniels, 2005; Sue, Ivey, & Pedersen, 1996; Ivey, Ivey, Myers, & Sweeney, 2005).

The Foundational Chapters: Basic to All Theories

The first four chapters of this book explored concepts that can be useful in understanding the four major theoretical orientations described above as well as an emerging field in the mental health profession referred to as positive psychology and wellness counseling. In going through these chapters, you have learned much about the relevance of many concepts as they relate to the practice of counseling and psychotherapy. This includes concepts related to cultural intentionality and community, social justice, empathy and family understanding, and microskills. If you are skilled in these concepts, you have a solid foundation for mastering the many complexities of theory and practice in counseling and psychotherapy.

The empathic conditions, particularly as they integrate community and family concepts, are important in all theoretical orientations. Positive regard and the positive asset search of the microskills approach have been stressed throughout this book. Helping clients identify and build on strengths is increasingly recognized as a basic foundation for change and growth in counseling and therapy in general and particularly relevant for the positive psychology and wellness counseling movement discussed in Chapter 3.

The basic listening sequence of the microskills framework is used by virtually all theories to draw out client stories and narratives. The five-stage structure of the interview not only is useful in decisional counseling, but also is a way to structure your work in existential-humanistic, cognitive-behavioral, and other frames of reference (see Chapter 4).

The developmental counseling and therapy (DCT) model (see Chapter 13) is an integrative framework that enables you to "mix and match" varying models and strategies of helping (first, second, third, and fourth forces) in a theoretically coherent and practical manner. DCT is also oriented to encouraging you to adapt and extend theoretical integration in your own fashion.

Family work is another integrative model. Many in the field argue that family work is as important as, or even more important than, individual counseling and therapy. Chapter 14 explores how family counseling and therapy complements DCT and relates to individual theory. Once again, however, you are the one who will integrate the theories of therapy into your own approach.

As you move toward your own theory of choice, you may also want to consider what issues you think are most foundational and basic to all other theories. On what substructure will you develop your own construction of the world of helping theory and practice?

Searching for Theoretical Integration

Over time, research and clinical practice have revealed that traditional theories have considerable value. However, a key concern has been how to integrate these concepts in a meaningful fashion.

In 1967, Gordon Paul made the classic statement "What treatment, by whom, is most effective for this individual with that specific problem, and under which set of circumstances?" Thereafter, drawing the best from many theories, as opposed to working within only one approach, became respectable. Nonetheless, eclecticism has still been criticized as lacking a central theoretical rationale for therapeutic action—changing theories or methods with clients other than the intuitive preference and clinical experience of the practitioner (D'Andrea & Daniels, 1994, 2005).

Lazarus's multimodal therapy (1981, 1995) is an attempt to organize eclecticism into a more coherent and organized way of thinking, primarily from a behavioral frame of reference. Lazarus divides treatment into seven parts, the BASIC-ID (*B*ehavior, *A*ffective response, *S*ensations, *I*mages, *C*ognitions, *I*nterpersonal relationships, and *D*rugs). The goal is to draw from each dimension in counseling and therapy to create a holistic treatment plan.

Integrative theories are currently becoming more numerous and influential. Meichenbaum's construction of cognitive-behavioral theory brings diverse theories together in a coherent fashion and thus offers a broader scope than traditional behavioral frames of reference. Developmental counseling and therapy (DCT) integrates theory and practice in a different format and provides an overall rationale for moving from sensory to behavioral to cognitive to systemic approaches. DCT, perhaps more than other theories, emphasizes sensorimotor and systemic/cultural foundations of experience, arguing that a network approach is essential if change is to be maintained over time (see Chapter 13).

In this book, you have been exposed to many alternatives that have stood the test of time or, if new, show some promise of influencing future change. As a professional, you will be part of the process of moving the field toward new approaches. How can you continually add new dimensions of helping while retaining the best of the past?

Multicultural Counseling and Therapy as the Theoretical Fourth Force

Multicultural counseling and therapy (MCT) recognizes the value of traditional methods of helping *as long as they are employed in a culturally meaningful and culturally sensitive fashion.* Furthermore, MCT starts from a different place than traditional theory, beginning with client assessment of individual, family, and cultural experience. Rather than impose a theory on a client, MCT seeks to find how the client constructs meaning in the world. MCT stresses an egalitarian, non-hierarchical therapist-client relationship. MCT suggests that counselors and clients together can draw from and integrate other theories to meet individual, family, and cultural needs.

In seeking a major new direction, the multicultural orientation works to turn the history of counseling and therapy "on its head." The issue is not imposing a theory on a client, but rather working *with* the client in a culturally sensitive fashion to find a technique, strategy, theory, or set of theories that meets the client's needs. *Self-in-relation* becomes the focus rather than individually oriented self-actualization.

MCT stresses the importance of using traditional first-, second-, and third-force theories in practice. Working together, client and therapist first identify the goal and then match the goal with the culturally and individually appropriate approach. For example, if a European-American client seeks self-understanding, perhaps a Rogerian or psychodynamic approach may be appropriate. However, if the goal is to feel less anxious in social situations, the approach may be cognitive-behavioral. If the client is a woman, gender-aware CBT assertiveness training may be undertaken. If the client is a Latina, culturally sensitive assertiveness training that acknowledges the complexities of changing a woman's role and behavior may be an appropriate action.

MCT might expand Gordon Paul's earlier statement by adding the following:

> What set of treatments, by whom, is most effective for this individual or family with what specific problem, with what specific culturally and individually appropriate goal, and under which set of circumstances? Additionally, how can relapse of treatment be prevented, and how can we involve this client (and her or his family) in treatment planning in an egalitarian culturally sensitive fashion?

How might you rephrase the above comments? How will you personally organize this exciting, but extremely complex, field? What sense do you make of the integrative approaches such as those of Meichenbaum, Lazarus, and Ivey's DCT framework? Would you place multicultural issues at the core of your theory, or would they be more peripheral? These are important questions that will define you as a professional. Not only will you be making these decisions, you will be asked to define the rationale for what you decide. Competency-Building Activity 15.1 asks you to start the process of generating your own integrated helping style by carefully reflecting on your own counseling and psychotherapy worldview.

The following summary of major theories is designed to help you work toward your own integration of counseling and psychotherapy theories.

Competency-Building Activity 15.1

What Is Your Counseling and Therapy Worldview?

Instructions: The purpose of this exercise is to have you consider your own construction of counseling and therapy. Take time to consider these questions: What is important to you? Where do you stand? Where are you heading? How does your family and cultural history relate to these issues? Then write your responses to the following questions on a piece of paper that you can file in your personal/professional development portfolio.

1. *How do you view the goals of counseling and therapy?* Client-centered theory focuses on self-actualization; behavioral theory, on behavioral change; psychodynamic theory, on awareness of unconscious forces; family theory, on an adequate family organization; feminist theory, on awareness of one's gender; multicultural theory, on becoming aware of how individual and family have been shaped and affected by the environment and history. These are only a few of the types of goals offered by different theoretical orientations.

   Consider these and other personal goals and values of your own. What do you want to have happen for your clients in your work as a counselor and therapist? Write a statement of your values and convictions regarding the key goals and values you have for the helping process.

2. *Where do your values and convictions come from? How were they derived? Do they come from reading this book? Or are they influenced by your own life-span developmental process? How does your family, gender, and multicultural background affect your values?* The key constructs in your worldview are generated in a gender, family, and multicultural context. Write a statement in which you discuss how your own life-span development relates to your selection of worldview and goals.

3. *Where might your worldview be limited with some of your clients? Given the vast array of multicultural experiences you will encounter, what types of groups do you need to learn more about? What types of values and behaviors might give you difficulty?* No one can relate equally well with all clients. Write a statement describing areas where you need to learn more, and indicate some specific steps you plan to take to reach an expanded awareness.

4. *Moral issues inform your counseling and therapy practice. What do you see as your moral framework for counseling and psychotherapy action?*

5. *What additional questions would you ask of yourself and others that would be helpful in becoming more conscious of your counseling and therapy worldview?* The questions here are only the beginning of serious questioning on the nature of counseling and psychotherapy practice.

A Summary of the Four Major Theoretical Forces of Counseling and Psychotherapy

There are many ways to consider the field of counseling and psychotherapy, and no one perspective has all the answers. This book is about multiple perspectives on reality. Clients often can get "stuck" in a single perspective. The theories and practice presented in this book and summarized in this section offer a range of ways of thinking that may be helpful with clients from diverse groups and backgrounds who are experiencing a broad range of challenges and problems in their lives.

The four broad orientations to counseling and therapy stressed in this book are summarized in Table 15.1. As you review these theories, think about how you personally would integrate them. What are your own preferences at this moment? What theoretical concepts appeal to you personally? And what can you find in your own developmental history, family history, and multicultural background that might help explain your answers?

Qualitative Research—Multicultural Issues

Many people might agree that an ethical practice of multicultural counseling and therapy is one that, among other things, constantly examines and evaluates effectiveness. Furthermore, the importance of reading and conducting one's own research is often stressed. Research and reading keep us all alive and aware of new developments.

Too often, counselors and therapists think about research as something that is "elsewhere"—something found in professional journals and not part of "real life." The busy practitioner sometimes finds journals boring and irrelevant and often cannot find the time to read. However, reading, research, and writing can be important and even vital to avoiding burnout and staying alive in the profession. It is unfortunate that some therapists choose not to read or conduct research and thus often continue to provide therapy that research data and new theory clearly show to be irrelevant, time consuming, expensive, and perhaps even damaging to the client.

How can you surmount this challenge? Research Exhibit 15.1 demonstrates how individual qualitative research can be used in the active practice of counseling and psychotherapy. Qualitative research has been especially popular in the MCT movement, as it has the flexibility required for work with complex multicultural issues.

Constructing Your Own View or Theory of Counseling and Therapy

It is the task of the professional counselor and therapist to know as many theories and techniques as possible—their similarities and differences—and to select from each theory that which is most helpful to the client. At the same time, the counselor seeks to enter and understand clients' worlds and to learn how clients construct and make sense of the world—what their meaning-making system is. The suggestion in this book is that rather than impose a theory of your choice on the client, you may want to engage clients as coparticipants in finding a therapeutic approach that fits.

The theories in this book are only "views"—constructions about how the world works. It is helpful to remember that *theories are simply descriptions—ways to examine reality.* If we become wrapped up in the belief that our theory of counseling and therapy is reality, we risk operating under an illusion. Although a particular illusory view of the world may work for you, it will not work for everyone.

In the practice of counseling and therapy, you likely will encounter many persons in the mental health professions who claim to have found the "truth," the "final answer,"

Table 15.1

Overview of Four Major Forces in Counseling and Psychotherapy Theory

Theoretical System	Worldview	Major Concepts and Strategies
Psychodynamic (1st force) (Freud, Bowlby, Taub-Bynum, Adler, Jung)	The past is prelude to the present. We cannot really understand humanity without awareness of human history. Our early attachments to family in a multicultural situation form our lives.	In traditional Freudian theory, the emphasis is on psychosexual development with minimal attention to family and cultural constraints. Bowlby expands this view through attachment theory and the nature of the parent-child relationship. Taub-Bynum shows that the family unconscious can be a broader and more useful multiculturally sensitive model. Adler brings awareness of context and positive social development. Jung's mystical emphasis allows attention to spirituality. Strategies include free association, dream analysis, review of situation from theoretical perspectives. All strategies seek to help the client understand how here-and-now life is impacted by the past.
Cognitive-behavioral (2nd force) (Pavlov, Watson, Skinner, Meichenbaum, Beck, Ellis, Glasser, Cheek)	This approach is rooted in scientific method and research, but enhanced by Cheek's multicultural emphasis and reinforced by Meichenbaum. Early behavioral work focused on humanity as a machinelike organism but has expanded over time to become humanistic as well as scientific. The cognitive revolution of Ellis and Beck focuses on humankind as rational and emphasized the stoic philosophy "We are not disturbed by events, but by our thoughts about them."	Functional analysis is particularly important as a foundation so that we understand the antecedents and consequences of behavior. Operant conditioning (reward-punishment) concepts can be helpful. On the cognitive side, analysis of thought patterns and their consequences is critical. Cheek reminds us that cultural issues underlie functional analysis, operant conditioning, and cognitive issues. Strategies include functional analysis to help clients understand the situation, thought stopping, stress management, assertiveness and social skills training, automatic thoughts analysis, REBT ABCDEF analysis.

Table 15.1, continued

Overview of Four Major Forces in Counseling and Psychotherapy Theory

Theoretical System	Worldview	Major Concepts and Strategies
Existential-humanistic (3rd force) (Rogers, Perls, Frankl, Vontress)	The human task is to find meaning in a sometimes meaningless world. Rogers stresses the ability of the person to find his or her own direction; Vontress, our spiritual and multicultural roots; Frankl, the importance of positive meanings; and Perls, that people are wholes, not parts, and that our task is to help people see themselves fully in relation to self and other.	Each individual constructs the world uniquely and thus reflects the modern constructivist and postmodern movements. Rogers stresses self-actualization; Vontress is attuned to connectedness. Frankl emphasizes spirituality and meaning; Perls focuses on actions. Strategies include active listening, focus on meaning, finding positives even in negative experiences, and active strategies within Gestalt therapy.
Multicultural counseling and therapy (4th force) (Draws on the first three forces in a culturally sensitive fashion, plus many cooperating authorities within the multicultural movement. Feminist theory is a major part of the 4th force.)	Counseling and therapy need to move away from encapsulations to fuller awareness of the human person in the social and cultural context. We need to draw on context to develop an understanding of each client's uniqueness.	This approach focuses on issues of race/ethnicity, gender, sexual orientation, spirituality/religion, family background, history of trauma, socio-economic background, and other factors that need to be considered, as well as traditional individual issues. The client becomes unique as we begin to see her or him in socio- and multicultural context. Strategies include all of the above, if cultural awareness becomes part of the treatment. Feminist therapy, Morita therapy, indigenous therapies, social justice issues, and many other approaches enrich the multicultural approach.

Research Exhibit 15.1

Using Qualitative Research in Counseling and Clinical Practice

Ponterotto and Casas (1991) identified four key characteristics of qualitative research methodology.

1. Use an inductive approach based on observation of client needs and wishes. Imagine you are working with a client who presents you with issues of anxiety and tension. Rather than deciding beforehand what to evaluate or measure, focus on your observations of this particular client and generate hypotheses about what issues might be important in therapy. In addition, think about ways in which you might evaluate whether or not therapy is helpful to this client.

2. Take a holistic stance and set joint client-counselor objectives for evaluation of therapy. Much of quantitative research focuses on single dimensions of human experience. You are working with a whole person who comes from a family and cultural background. As part of a holistic stance, you may want to consider the whole life of the client, not just single dimensions. Obviously, you cannot measure everything in your client's life, but with your client you can set goals for therapy that can be validated by both you and the client.

   At Flinders University in Australia, Kapelis (personal communication, 1991) has built on the concept of joint goals and, with the client, selects concrete thought, feeling, and behavioral changes based on jointly agreed-on criteria for success. In some cases, standardized tests are used, but in these cases, the client is always a participant in the selection. With a client struggling with anxiety, you might jointly decide that feeling relaxed and easy in interpersonal contacts is one objective of therapy. Another objective might be sleeping through the night. These objectives lead to certain specific types of treatment plans (e.g., assertiveness training, relaxation training).

3. Be flexible and change objectives and evaluation design as therapy progresses. Establishing joint goals for counseling is important, because therapy does not always proceed as you and the client predict. You and your client may find new objectives as therapy progresses. For instance, the client may discover an abusive family history in the process of stress management training. If your qualitative research approach is open ended, with a joint commitment for exploration, you will be better positioned to evolve a new evaluation design as therapy enters new areas. A short-term evaluative research agreement, for example, may be client satisfaction with the counseling/therapy process. At the same time, you must work to concretize other goals more precisely at the next stage of counseling or therapy.

4. Emphasize clinical significance. This point is vital to the qualitative researcher. The change and evaluation design must be important to the client and to the therapist. Ponterotto and Casas (1991) list a variety of possibilities for qualitative research, including journal entries, case studies, structured interviews, reports by the client's family members or friends, asking the client's permission to audio- or videotape certain types of interactions, and so on. When conducting qualitative research, it is essential that your client be involved in the process throughout.

Competency-Building Activity 15.2

Eleven Questions to Ask Yourself about Your Own Construction of the Counseling and Psychotherapy Process

Instructions: The following questions aim to help you come to a clearer understanding of your own theoretical construction of counseling and therapy. This activity will take about 30 minutes to complete. Find a quiet place where you can reflect on and write down your responses to the following questions.

1. What is your overall worldview, and how does it relate to multicultural issues? Have you carefully elaborated your worldview and its implications for your future practice?

2. What are the central dimensions of your definition of ethical practice? (These dimensions were introduced in Chapter 1. The effective professional is constantly examining ethical and moral issues.)

3. As you think about each of the empathic concepts, what is your personal construction of their meaning? What sense do you make of them?

4. With which microskills and concepts do you feel particularly comfortable? Which have you already mastered, and which need further work so that they can actually be used in the clinical session?

5. How do you make sense of the focusing concept? How might you choose to focus your interventions? Can you focus on individuals, family context, and the multicultural dimensions of your clients' development and environmental context?

6. What is to be your position on research and keeping up with new ideas that are published in the professional literature?

7. What is your understanding of the challenge of multicultural-feminist-social justice counseling and therapy? What place will this fourth force have in your mind and in your practice? What place will social justice and community action have?

8. At several points in this book, issues of spirituality have been raised. What has been your reaction to these ideas? Would you avoid them or carry them further in your professional practices?

9. What theories of counseling and therapy appeal to you? What type of integration of these diverse theories are you moving toward? (This book has attempted to stress that all theories are potentially valuable to some clients, but you are not expected to be immediately skilled in all. Learning theories in more depth is a lifelong practice.) From what approach do you personally plan to start practice, and what type of professional curriculum for further learning do you see for yourself in the future?

10. Have you examined how your personal developmental history in family and culture affects your answers to the above questions? (It is critical that you constantly be able to reflect on yourself and how your personal history and present life issues affect your performance as a counselor or therapist.)

11. Return to Competency-Building Activity 13.3, Identifying Your Own Personal Style, Present Competencies, and Goals. Repeat this exercise. What changes do you note since your first response to the activity? In completing other competency-building activities in this book, you undoubtedly have a better sense of where you stand personally and professionally. Taking theory into practice—and then returning to theory for reflection and possible change in your work—is the route toward competence.

"the one way" to conduct counseling and therapy. These people are likely false prophets. But, as the authors of this book have learned, even false prophets often speak important truths.

For example, there was a time when meditation was considered irrelevant to the practice of counseling and psychotherapy. Now meditation is a standard technique in many stress management programs. Similarly, issues of women's development and multicultural understanding, now considered to be increasingly important, were once considered to be outside the field. Thus, it seems important that we all listen, learn, and be willing to accommodate an alternative perspective or a challenging new theory. The advice in the following maxim seems worth considering: Beware of prophets proclaiming a new truth—they just may be right! Competency-Building Activity 15.2 provides a final exercise in which you are asked to review your own thinking about this book and organize its meaning in your own way.

The general or metatheoretical position requires that each counselor or therapist develop her or his own conception of the counseling process and remain constantly open to change and examination. A student working through the draft of this book commented, "I think I've got the point. I find myself rewriting the book in my own way. I use some of it, but ultimately the book I am rewriting in my head is mine, my own general theory that is similar in some ways to the book, but in other ways very different."

We hope that you will rewrite this book and use it authentically in your own way. At the same time, we hope that you will extend that same privilege to your clients. How might they help you rewrite and reconstrue your constructions of counseling and therapy? Counseling and therapy are very much about listening and learning—for all of us as therapists and for our clients as well.

References

Aboriginal Educational Foundation. (1992). *Aboriginals respond to the Royal Commission into Aboriginal deaths in custody*. Bedford Park, Australia: Flinders Press.

Achebe, C. (1986). *The world of the Ogbanje*. Enugu, Nigeria: Fourth Dimension.

Achebe, C. (1995). *Things fall apart*. New York: Random House.

Ackerman, N. W. (1958). *The psychodymanics of family life*. New York: Basic Books.

Adler, A. (1959). *Individual psychology*. Paterson, NJ: Littlefield, Adams, & Company.

Adler, A. (1963). *The problem child*. New York: Putnam.

Ainsworth, M. (1967). *Infancy in Uganda: Infant care and the growth of love*. Baltimore: Johns Hopkins University Press.

Ainsworth, M. (1977). Social development in the first year of life. In J. Tanner (Ed.), *Developments in psychiatric research*. London: Hodder & Stoughton.

Ainsworth, M. (1985). I. Patterns of infant-mother attachment; II. Attachments across the life-span. *Bulletin of the New York Academy of Medicine, 61*, 771–812.

Ainsworth, M., & Bowlby, J. (1991). An ethological approach to personality development. *American Psychologist, 46*, 333–341.

Akbar, N. (1994). *Light from ancient Africa*. Tallahassee, FL: Mind Productions.

Alberti, R., & Emmons, M. (1995). *Your perfect right: A guide to assertive living* (7th ed.). San Luis Obispo, CA: Impact Books.

American Counseling Association. (1992). ACA professional standards. *Journal of Counseling and Development, 20*, 64–88.

American Counseling Association. (1995a). *Ethical standards* (rev. ed.). Alexandria, VA: Author.

American Counseling Association. (1995b). Summit results in formation of spiritual competencies. *Counseling Today*, p. 30.

American Counseling Association. (2003). *Multicultural counseling competencies*. Alexandria, VA: Author.

American Counseling Association. (2005). *Code of ethics and standards of practice*. Alexandria, VA: Author.

American Psychiatric Association. (1994). *Diagnostic and statistical manual of mental disorders* (4th ed.). Washington, DC: Author.

American Psychological Association. (2003). *Guidelines on multicultural education, training, research, practice, and organizational change for psychologists*. Washington, DC: Author.

American Psychological Association. (1987). *General guidelines for providers of psychological services*. Washington, DC: Author.

Andersen, T. (1993). See and hear: And be seen and heard. In S. Friedman (Ed.), *The new language of change* (pp. 54–68). New York: Guilford.

Anderson, C. (1995). *Flying solo*. New York: Norton.

Anderson, H., & Goolishian, H. (1988). Human systems as linguistic systems: Preliminary and evolving ideas about the implications for clinical theory. *Family Process, 27*, 371–393.

Anderson, H., Goolishian, H. A., & Winderman, L. (1986). Problem determined systems: Toward transformation in family therapy. *Journal of Strategic and Systemic Therapies, 5*, 1–14.

Anderson, S., & Bagarozzi, D. (1983). The use of family myths as an aid to strategic therapy. *Journal of Family Therapy, 5*, 145–164.

Anderson, S. A., & Sabatelli, R. M. (1999). *Family interaction: A multigenerational developmental perspective* (2nd ed.). Boston: Allyn and Bacon.

Anthony, W., & Carkhuff, R. (1977). The functional professional therapeutic agent. In A. Gurman & A. Razin (Eds.), *Effective psychotherapy* (pp. 103–119). Elmsford, NY: Pergamon Press.

APA Monitor. (1984, November). Rogers calls peace results "surprising," p. 15.

Arnold, M. S. (2002). Culture-sensitive family therapy. In Carlson, J. and D. Kjos (Eds.), *Theories and strategies of family therapy* (pp. 19–40). Needham Heights, MA: Allyn and Bacon.

Arredondo, P., & D'Andrea, M. (1995, September). AMCD approved multicultural counseling competency standards. *Counseling Today,* pp. 28–32.

Arredondo, P., & D'Andrea, M. (1998). Defining the term "multicultural counseling." *Counseling Today,* p. 48.

Arredondo, P., & D'Andrea, M. (1999, November). How do Jews fit into the multicultural counseling movement? *Counseling Today, 42,* 16, 36.

Arredondo, P., Toporek, R., Brown, S. P., Jones, J., Locke, D.C., Sanchez, J., & Stadler, H. (1996). Operationalization of the multicultural counseling competencies. *Journal of Multicultural Counseling and Development, 24,* 42–78.

Asante, M. (1987). *The Afrocentric idea.* Philadelphia: Temple University Press.

Ascher, L. M., & Turner, R. M. (1979). Controlled comparison of progressive relaxation, stimulus control, and paradoxical intention therapies for insomnia. *Journal of Consulting and Clinical Psychology, 47* (3), 500–508.

Atkinson, D. R., Morton, G., & Sue, D. W. (1998). *Counseling American minorities* (5th ed.). Boston: McGraw-Hill.

Attneave, C. (1969). Therapy in tribal settings and urban network interventions. *Family Process, 8,* 192–210.

Attneave, C. (1974). Medicine men and psychiatrists in the Indian health service. *Psychiatric Annals, 4*(9), 49–55.

Attneave, C. (1982). American Indian and Alaskan native families: Emigrants in their own homeland. In M. McGoldrick, J. Pearce, &

J. Giordano (Eds.), *Ethnicity and family therapy* (pp. 55–83). New York: Guilford.

Auerbach, A., & Johnson, M. (1977). Research on the therapist's level of experience. In A. Gurman & A. Razin (Eds.), *Effective psychotherapy* (pp. 84–102). Elmsford, NY: Pergamon.

Auerswald, E. (1968). Interdisciplinary versus ecologicial approach. *Family Process, 2,* 202–216.

Avis, J. (1988). Deepening awareness: A private study guide to feminism and family therapy. In L. Braverman (Ed.), *A guide to feminist family therapy.* New York: Harrington Park Press.

Bailey, B., Good, M., & McGrady, A. (1990). Clinical observations on behavioral treatment of a patient with insulin-dependent diabetes mellitus. *Biofeedback and Self Regulation, 15,* 7–13.

Baker Miller, J. (1986). *Toward a new psychology of women* (2nd ed.). Boston: Beacon.

Baker Miller, J. (1991). The development of a woman's sense of self. In J. Jordan, A. Kaplan, J. B. Miller, I. Striver, & J. Surrey (Eds.), *Women's growth in connection* (pp. 11–26). New York: Guilford.

Baker, S., & Daniels, T. (1989). Integrating research on the microcounseling program: A meta-analysis. *Journal of Counseling Psychology, 35,* 213–22.

Baker, S., Daniels, T., & Greenley, A. (1990). Systematic training of graduate-level counselors: Narrative and meta-analytic reviews of three major programs. *Counseling Psychologist, 18,* 355–421.

Ballou, M. (1996a). Interview transcript (Manuscript). Boston: Northeastern University.

Ballou, M. (1996b). MCT theory and women. In D. W. Sue, A. E. Ivey, & P. B. Pedersen (Eds.), *A theory of multicultural counseling and therapy* (pp. 236–46). Pacific Grove, CA: Brooks/Cole.

Ballou, M., & Brown, L. (Eds.). (2002). *Rethinking mental health and disorder: Feminist perspectives.* New York: Guilford.

Ballou, M., & Gabalac, N. (1984). *A feminist position on mental health.* Springfield, IL: Thomas.

Ballou, M., & West, C. (2000). Feminist therapy approaches. In M. Biaggio & M. Hersen (Eds.), *Issues in the psychology of women* (pp. 273–97). New York: Kluwer Academic/Plenum Publishers.

Bandler, R., & Grinder, J. (1982). *Reframing: neurolinguistic programming and the transformation of meaning.* Moab, UT: Real People Press.

Bandura, A. (1959). *Adolescent aggression.* New York: Ronald.

Bandura, A. (1962). *Social learning and imitation.* Lincoln: University of Nebraska Press.

Bandura, A. (1975). *Social learning and personality development.* Newark, NJ: Holt, Rinehart & Winston.

Bandura, A. (1976). Effecting change through participant modeling. In J. Krumboltz & C. Thoresen (Eds.), *Counseling methods* (pp. 248–64). Troy, MO: Holt, Rinehart & Winston.

Bandura, A. (1982). Self-efficacy: Mechanism in human agency. *American Psychologist, 37,* 122–47.

Bandura, A. (1989). Human agency in social cognitive theory. *American Psychologist, 44,* 1175–85.

Bandura, A. (1997). *Self-efficacy: The exercise of control.* New York: Cambridge University Press.

Bankart, C. P. (1997). *Talking cures: A history of Western and Eastern psychotherapies.* Pacific Grove, CA: Brooks/Cole.

Barlow, D. H. (1996). Health care policy, psychotherapy research, and the future of psychotherapy. *American Psychologist, 51,* 1050–58.

Barlow, D. H., & Craske, M. G. (1994). *Mastery of your anxiety and panic: II.* Albany, NY: Graywind.

Barrett, P. M., Dadds, M. R., & Rapee, R. M. (1996). Family treatment of childhood anxiety: A controlled trial. *Journal of Consulting and Clinical Psychology, 64,* 333–342.

Barrett, S. E. (2005). Multicultural feminist therapy: Theory in context. In M. Hill & M. Ballou (Eds.), *The foundation and future of feminist therapy* (pp. 122–147). New York: Haworth.

Barrett-Lennard, G. (1962). Dimensions of therapist response as causal factors in therapeutic change. *Psychological Monographs, 76,* 43. (Ms. No. 562)

Barrowclough, C., Haddock, G., Tarrier, N., Lewis, S. W., Moring, J., O'Brien, R., Schonfield, N., & McGovern, J. (2001). Randomized controlled trial of motivational interviewing, cognitive behavior therapy, and family intervention for patients with co-morbid schizophrenia and substance use disorders. *American Journal of Psychiatry, 158,* 1706–1713.

Baruth, L. G., & Manning, M. L. (2003). *Multicultural counseling and psychotherapy: A lifespan approach* (3rd ed.). Upper Saddle River, NJ: Merrill Prentice-Hall.

Bateson, G. (1972). *Steps to an ecology of mind.* New York: Ballantine.

Bateson, G., Jackson, D., Haley, J., & Weakland, J. (1956). Towards a theory of schizophrenia. *Behavioral Science, 1,* 251–64.

Baucom, D., Shoham, V., Mueser, K. T., Daiuto, A. D., & Stickle, T. R. (1998). Empirically supported couple and family interventions for marital distress and adult mental health problems. *Journal of Consulting and Clinical Psychology, 66,* 53–88.

Beaver, A. (1991, September). *Some potential issues of unconscious sexist behavior in counseling and therapy.* Paper presented at the University of Massachusetts, Amherst.

Beaver, A. (1993). *Delayed memory of childhood trauma: Models of memory and therapeutic practice.* Unpublished comprehensive examination, University of Massachusetts, Amherst.

Beck, A. (1976). *Cognitive therapy and the emotional disorders.* New York: International Universities Press.

Beck, A. (1991). Cognitive therapy: A 30-year retrospective. *American Psychologist, 46,* 368–75.

Beck, A. (1996). Beyond belief: A theory of modes, personality, and psychopathology. In P. Salkovskis (Ed.), *Frontiers of cognitive therapy* (pp. 1–25). New York: Guilford.

Beck, A., Freeman, A., & Associates. (1990). *Cognitive therapy of personality disorders.* New York: Guilford.

Beck, J. G., & Zebb, B. J. (1994). Behavioral assessment and treatment of panic disorder:

Current status, future directions. *Behavior Therapy, 25,* 581–611.

Beck, J. S., & Beck, A. T. (1995). *Cognitive therapy: Basics and beyond.* New York: Guilford.

Becvar, D., & Becvar, R. (2003). *Family therapy: A systemic integration* (5th ed.). Needham Heights, MA: Allyn and Bacon.

Becvar, R. J., & Becvar, D. S. (1994). The ecosystemic story: A story about stories. *Journal of Mental Health Counseling, 16,* 22–32.

Berg, I. (1994). *Family-based services: A solution-based approach.* New York: Norton.

Berman, J. (1979). Counseling skills used by Black and White male and female counselors. *Journal of Counseling Psychology, 26,* 81–84.

Berne, E. (1996). *Games people play: The psychology of human relationships* (reissue ed.). New York: Ballantine Books.

Beutler, L. E. (2000). David and Goliath: When empirical and clinical standards of practice meet. *American Psychologist, 55,* 997–1007.

Binswanger, L. (1958). The existential analysis school of thought. In R. May, E. Angel, & H. Ellenberger (Eds.), *Existence* (pp. 191–213). New York: Basic Books.

Binswanger, L. (1963). *Being-in-the-world: Selected papers of Ludwig Binswanger.* New York: Basic Books.

Bion, W. R. (1961). *Experience in groups.* New York: Tavistock.

Blassingame, J. (1972). *The slave community.* New York: Oxford University Press.

Blechman, E. A., & Vryan, K. D. (2000). Prosocial family therapy: A manualized preventive intervention for juvenile offenders. *Aggression and Violent Behavior, 5*(4), 343–378.

Blocksma, D., & Porter, E. (1947). A short-term training program in client-centered counseling. *Journal of Consulting Psychology, 11,* 55–60.

Boeree, C. G. (2004). *Alfred Adler.* Retrieved December 12, 2004, from http://www.ship.edu/~cgboeree/adler.html.

Bohart, A. (1991). The missing 249 words: In search of objectivity. *Psychotherapy, 28,* 497–503.

Boss, M. (1958). *The analysis of dreams.* New York: Philosophical Library.

Boss, M. (1963). *Psychoanalysis and daseinanalysis.* New York: Basic Books.

Bowen, M. (1960). A family concept of schizophrenia. In D. D. Jackson (Ed.), *The etiology of schizophrenia.* New York: Basic Books.

Bowen, M. (1978). *Family therapy in clinical practice.* New York: Jason Aronson.

Bowlby, J. (1940). The influence of early environment in the development of neurosis and neurotic character. *International Journal of Psycho-Analysis, 21,* 154–178.

Bowlby, J. (1951). *Maternal care and mental health.* Geneva: World Health Organization.

Bowlby, J. (1969). *Attachment.* New York: Basic Books.

Bowlby, J. (1973). *Separation.* New York: Basic Books.

Bowlby, J. (1988). *A secure base: Parent-child attachment and healthy human development.* New York: Basic Books.

Bowman, S. L., Rasheed, S., Ferris, J., Thompson, D. A., McRae, M., & Weitzman, L. (2001). Interface of feminism and multiculturalism: Where are the women of color? In J. G. Ponterotto, J. M. Casas, L. A. Suzuki, & C. M. Alexander (Eds.), *Handbook of multicultural counseling* (2nd ed.) (pp. 779–798). Thousand Oaks, CA: Sage.

Boyd-Franklin, N. (2003). *Black families in therapy* (2nd ed.). New York: Guilford.

Boyer, D. (1996). *DCT and adolescent drug abuse.* Unpublished doctoral dissertation, University of Massachusetts, Amherst.

Bozarth, J. (1999). *Person-centered therapy: A revolutionary paradigm.* Ross-on-Wye, UK: PCCS Books.

Brabeck, M. (Ed.). (1999). *Practicing feminist ethics in psychology.* Washington, DC: American Psychological Association.

Brammer, L. (1990). *The helping relationship.* Englewood Cliffs, NJ: Prentice-Hall.

Brammer, R. (2004). *Diversity in counseling.* Belmont, CA: Brooks/Cole–Thomson Learning.

Brassard, M., Germain, R., & Hart, S. (1987). *Psychological maltreatment of children and youth.* New York: Pergamon Press.

Bray, J. H., & Jouriles, E. N. (1995). Treatment of marital conflict and prevention of divorce.

Journal of Marital and Family Therapy, 21, 461–474.

Breunlin, D., Schwartz, R., & MacKune-Karrer, B. (1992). *Metaframeworks: Transcending the models of family therapy.* San Francisco: Jossey-Bass.

Brodhead, M. (1991). *Training teachers to use the developmental assessment paradigm.* Unpublished doctoral dissertation, University of Massachusetts, Amherst.

Bronowski, J. (1978). *The origins of knowledge and imagination.* New Haven, CT: Yale University Press.

Brown, L. S. (1994). *Subversive dialogues: Theory in feminist therapy.* New York: Basic Books.

Brown, L. S. (1995). Cultural diversity in feminist therapy: Theory and practice. In H. Landrine (Ed.), *Bringing cultural diversity to feminist psychology: Theory, research, and practice* (pp. 143–161). Washington, DC: American Psychological Association.

Brown, L. S. (2000). Discomforts of the powerless: Feminist constructions of distress. In R. Neimeyer & J. Raskin (Eds.), *Constructions of disorder* (pp. 287–308). Washington, DC: American Psychological Association.

Brown, L. S., & Ballou, M. (1992). *Personality and psychopathology feminist reappraisals.* New York: Guilford.

Brown, L. S., & Root, M. P. P. (Eds.). (1990). *Diversity and complexity in feminist theory.* New York: Harrington Park.

Buber, M. (1970). *I and thou.* New York: Scribner's.

Bumpus, G. (1991, October 25). Skin color doesn't determine culture. *Amherst Record,* p. 4.

Butler, A. C., & Beck, J. S. (in press). Cognitive therapy outcomes: A review of meta-analyses. *Journal of the Norwegian Psychological Association.*

Campbell, T. J., & Patterson, J. M. (1995). The effectiveness of family interventions in the treatment of physical illness. *Journal of Marital and Family Therapy, 21,* 545–84.

Camus, A. (1942). *The stranger.* New York: Random House.

Camus, A. (1958). *The myth of Sisyphus.* New York: Knopf.

Capuzzi, D., & Gross, D. R. (1999). *Counseling and psychotherapy: Theories and interventions* (2nd ed.). Upper Saddle River, NJ: Merrill.

Carkhuff, R. (1969). *Helping and human relations* (Vols. 1 & 2). Troy, MO: Holt, Rinehart & Winston.

Carkhuff, R. (1987). *The art of helping VI.* Amherst, MA: Human Resource Development Press.

Carlson, J., & Sperry, L. (2001). Adlerian counseling theory and practice. In D.C. Locke, J. E. Myers, & E. L. Herr (Eds.), *The handbook of counseling* (pp. 171–179). Thousand Oaks, CA: Sage.

Carr, A. (2000). Evidence-based practice in family therapy and systemic consultation 1. Child-focused problems. *Journal of Family Therapy, 22,* 29–60.

Carter, B., & McGoldrick, M. (1988). *The changing family life-cycle.* Boston: Allyn and Bacon.

Cartwright, B., & D'Andrea, M. (2004). Counseling for diversity. In T. F. Riggar & D. R. Maki (Eds.), *Handbook of rehabilitation counseling.* New York: Springer.

Cartwright, B., D'Andrea, M., & Daniels, J. (2003). *Confronting racial and gender differences: Three approaches to multicultural counseling and therapy.* [Video]. Framingham, MA: Microtraining and Multicultural Development.

Casas, M., & Pytluk, S. (1995). Hispanic identity development: Implications for research and practice. In J. Ponterotto, M. Casas, L. Suzuki, & C. Alexander (Eds.), *Handbook of multicultural counseling.* Thousand Oaks, CA: Sage.

Cassidy, J., & Shaver, P. (1999). *Handbook of attachment theory and research.* New York: Guilford.

Centers for Disease Control and Prevention. (1998). *Trends in the HIV and AIDS epidemic.* Atlanta, GA: Author.

Chamberlain, P., & Rosicky, J. G. (1995). The effectiveness of family therapy in the treatment of adolescents with conduct disorders and delinquency. *Journal of Marital and Family Therapy, 21,* 441–460.

Cheatham, H. (1990). Empowering Black families. In H. Cheatham and J. Stewart (Eds.), *Black families* (pp. 373–93). New Brunswick, NJ: Transaction Press.

Cheatham, H., & Stewart, J. (Eds.). (1990). *Black families*. New Brunswick, NJ: Transaction Press.

Cheek, D. (1976). *Assertive Black . . . puzzled White*. San Luis Obispo, CA: Impact.

Chen, C. (1995). Counseling applications of RET in a Chinese cultural context. *Journal of Rational-Emotive and Cognitive-Behavior Therapy, 13*, 117–129.

Chen-Hayes, S. F., Chen, M., & Athar, N. (2000). Challenging linguicism: Action strategies for counselors and client-colleagues. In J. Lewis & L. Bradley (Eds.), *Advocacy in counseling: Counselors, clients, and community* (pp. 25–36). Alexandria, VA: American Counseling Association.

Chissell, J. T. (2000). *Pyramids of power: An ancient African American centered approach to optimal health*. Baltimore, MD: Positive Perceptions Publications.

Chodorow, N. (1978). *The reproduction of mothering: Psychoanalysis and the reproduction of gender*. Berkeley: University of California Press.

Chopra, D., & Simon, D. (2001). *Grow younger, live longer*. New York: Three Rivers.

Chung, M. (1994). Can reality therapy help juvenile delinquents in Hong Kong? *Journal of Reality Therapy, 14*, 68–80.

Chung, R. C-Y., & Bemak, F. (2002). The relationship of culture and empathy in cross-cultural counseling. *Journal of Counseling and Development, 80*, 154–159.

Chunn, J. C. (Ed.). (2002). *The health behavioral change imperative: Theory, education, and practice in diverse populations*. New York: Kluwer Academic/Plenum.

Clark, D. A., Beck, A. T., & Alford, B. A. (1999). *Scientific foundations of cognitive theory and therapy of depression*. Philadelphia, PA: Wiley.

Clark, R., Anderson, N. B., Clark, V. R., & Williams, D. R. (1999). Racism as a stressor for African Americans: A biopsychosocial model. *American Psychologist, 54*, 805–16.

Clarkin, J. F., Carpenter, D., Hull, J., Wilner, P., & Glick, I. (1998). Effects of psychoeducational intervention for married patients with bipolar disorder and their spouses. *Psychiatric Services, 49*, 531–533.

Comstock, D. (Ed.). (2005). *Diversity and development: Critical contexts that shape our lives and relationships*. Belmont, CA: Brooks/Cole–Thomson Learning.

Comstock, D. L., & Qin, D. (2005). Relational-cultural theory: A framework for relational development across the lifespan. In D. L. Comstock (Ed.), *Diversity and development: Critical contexts that shape our lives and relationships* (pp. 25–46). Belmont, CA: Brooks/Cole–Thomson Learning.

Comstock, D. L., Duffey, T. H., & St. George, H. (2002). The relational-cultural model: A framework for group process. *Journal for Specialists in Group Work, 23*, 254–272.

Consumer Reports. (1995, November). Mental health: Does therapy help? pp. 734–739.

Contratto, S., & Rossier, J. (2005). Early trends in feminist theory and practice. In M. Hill & M. Ballou (Eds.), *The foundation and future of feminist therapy* (pp. 78–101). New York: Haworth.

Corey, G. (1995). *Theory and practice of group counseling* (4th ed.). Pacific Grove, CA: Brooks/Cole.

Cox, R. H. (1998). *Sport psychology: Concepts and applications*. Boston, MA: McGraw-Hill.

Cross, W. (1971). The Negro to Black conversion experience. *Black World, 20*, 13–25.

Cross, W. (1991). *Shades of Black*. Philadelphia: Temple University Press.

Cross, W. (1995). The psychology of Nigrescence: Revising the Cross model. In J. Ponterotto, M. Casas, L. Suzuki, & C. Alexander (Eds.), *Handbook of multicultural counseling*. Thousand Oaks, CA: Sage.

Cummings, N. (1988). Emergence of the mental health complex: Adaptive and maladaptive responses. *Professional Psychology, 19*, 308–315.

D'Andrea, M. (1999, May). Alternative needed for the DSM-IV in a multicultural-postmodern society. *Counseling Today, 41*, 44, 46.

D'Andrea, M. (2000). Postmodernism, social constructionism, and multiculturalism: Three forces that are shaping and expanding our thoughts about counseling. *Journal of Mental Health Counseling, 22*, 1–16.

D'Andrea, M. (2001, January). Dealing with gender and multiculturalism: Beyond intellectual parochialism and political paralysis. Keynote address presented at the National Multicultural Conference and Summit II, Santa Barbara, CA.

D'Andrea, M. (2003, October). Examining the links between White racial identity development and White racism. Paper presented at the Diversity Challenge Conference sponsored by the Institute for the Study and Promotion of Race and Culture, Boston, MA.

D'Andrea, M. (2004a). Using racial-cultural identity theories in group counseling. In J. L. DeLucia-Waak, D. Gerrity, C. Kalodner, & M. Riva (Eds.), *The handbook of group work* (pp. 265–282). Thousand Oaks, CA: Sage.

D'Andrea, M. (2004b). *Using attachment theory to explain common adult behaviors.* Unpublished paper presented to students in the Department of Counselor Education, University of Hawaii, Honolulu.

D'Andrea, M. (2005a). *Promoting multicultural competence and social justice.* Workshop presented to students, faculty members, and administrators at George Mason University as part of a national tour sponsored by the National Institute for Multicultural Competence (NIMC).

D'Andrea, M. (2005b, January). *Reclaiming "positive psychology" from a multicultural perspective: Combating new forms of ethnocentrism and racism in psychology.* Unpublished paper presented at the national Multicultural Summit, Hollywood, CA.

D'Andrea, M. (2006a). In liberty and justice for all: A comprehensive approach to ameliorating the complex problems of White racism and White superiority in the United States. In M. Constantine and D. W. Sue (Eds.), *Addressing racism: Facilitating cultural competence in mental health and educational settings* (pp. 251–270). Hoboken, NJ: Wiley.

D'Andrea, M. (2006b). *Using attachment theory to expand graduate students' thinking about psychoanalytic defense mechanisms.* Honolulu: Department of Counselor Education, University of Hawaii.

D'Andrea, M., & Arredondo, P. (1998, April). Defining the term "multicultural counseling." *Counseling Today,* p. 40.

D'Andrea, M., & Daniels, J. (1994). Group pacing: A developmental eclectic approach to group counseling. *Journal of Counseling and Development, 72* (6), 585–90.

D'Andrea, M., & Daniels, J. (2001a). Facing the changing demographic structure of our society. In D.C. Locke, J. Meyers, & E. Herr (Eds.), *Handbook of counseling* (pp. 529–539). Thousand Oaks, CA: Sage.

D'Andrea, M., & Daniels, J. (2001b). Respectful counseling. In D. B. Pope-Davis & H. L. K. Coleman (Eds.), *The intersection of race, class, and gender in multicultural counseling* (pp. 417–466). Thousand Oaks, CA: Sage.

D'Andrea, M., & Daniels, J. (2005). *Multicultural counseling: Empowerment strategies for a diverse society.* Honolulu: Department of Counselor Education, University of Hawaii.

D'Andrea, M., & Daniels, J. (2006). *The peace project.* Unpublished manuscript, Department of Counselor Education. University of Hawaii, Honolulu.

D'Andrea, M., Arredondo, P., & Daniels, J. (2005, March). Multicultural advocacy and community service. *Counseling Today, 47,* 40–41.

D'Andrea, M., Daniels, J., Arredondo, P., Ivey, A. E., Ivey, M. B., Locke, D.C., O'Bryant, B., Parham, T. A., & Sue, D. W. (2001). Fostering organizational changes to realize the revolutionary potential of the multicultural movement: An updated case study. In J. G. Ponterotto, J. M. Casas, L. A. Suzuki, & C. M. Alexander (Eds.), *Handbook of multicultural counseling* (2nd ed.) (pp. 222–253). Thousand Oaks, CA: Sage.

D'Zurilla, T. (1996). *Problem-solving therapy.* New York: Springer.

Dacey, J., & Travers, J. (2004). *Human development across the lifespan* (5th ed.). New York: McGraw-Hill.

Daniels, J., & D'Andrea, M. (1996). Implications for ameliorating ethnocentrism in counseling. In D. W. Sue, A. E., Ivey, & P. D. Pedersen (Eds.), *A theory of multicultural counseling and therapy* (157–173). Pacific Grove, CA: Brooks/Cole.

Daniels, J., Arredondo, P., D'Andrea, M., Locke, D.C., O'Bryant, B., Parham, T., & Sue, D. W. (2000, March). *Social justice counseling, research, and training: Our responsibility and potential.* Paper presented at the annual meeting of the American Counseling Association, Washington, DC.

Daniels, J., Arredondo, P., D'Andrea, M., Ivey, M. B., Ivey, A. E., Locke, D.C., Parham, T., & Sue, D. W. (2002, March). *Culturally competent social justice counseling: Promoting unity through diversity.* Paper presented at the annual meeting of the American Counseling Association, New Orleans, LA.

Daniels, T. (2001). *Microcounseling: A summary of research.* Unpublished manuscript, Memorial University of Newfoundland, Cronerbrook.

Daniels, T., and Ivey, A. E. (2007). *Microcounseling* (3rd ed.). Springfield, IL: Thomas.

Dare, C., Eisler, I., Russell, G., & Szmukler, G. (1990). The clinical and theoretical impact of a controlled trial of family therapy in anorexia nervosa. *Journal of Marital and Family Therapy, 16,* 39–57.

Davis, M., Eshelman, E., & McKay, M. (1995). *The relaxation and stress reduction workbook* (4th ed.). Oakland, CA: New Harbinger.

Davis, M., Robbins, E., & McKay, M. (1995). *The relaxation and stress management workbook* (4th ed.). Oakland, CA: New Harbinger.

Davison, G. (1991). Constructionism and morality in therapy for homosexuality. In J. Gonsiorek & J. Weinrach (Eds.), *Homosexuality: Research implications for public policy.* Newbury Park, CA: Sage.

de Shazer, S. (1985). *Keys to solution in brief therapy.* New York: Norton.

Diamond, G. S., & Siqueland, L. (2001). Current status of family intervention science. *Child and Adolescent Psychiatric Clinics of North America, 10* (3), 641–661.

Diffily, A. (1984). Aaron Beck: A profile. *Brown Alumni Monthly.* Providence, RI, pp. 39–46.

Dinkmeyer, D., & Dinkmeyer, D., Jr. (1995). *Client change through strength assessment.* Paper presented at the annual meeting of the American Counseling Association, Denver, CO.

Dinkmeyer, D.C., & Dinkmeyer, D.C., Jr. (1982). *Developing understanding of self and others (DUSO).* Circle Pines, MN: American Guidance Service.

Dinkmeyer, D.C., Dinkmeyer, D.C., Jr., & Sperry, L. (1987). *Adlerian counseling and psychotherapy* (2nd ed.). Columbus, OH: Merrill.

Dinkmeyer, D.C., McKay, G. D., & Dinkmeyer, D.C., Jr. (1998). *STEP: Parent's handbook.* Circle Pines, MN: American Guidance Service.

Dobson, K. (1989). A meta-analysis of the efficacy of cognitive therapy for depression. *Journal of Consulting and Clinical Psychology, 57,* 414–419.

Doherty W., & Carroll, J. (2003). The citizen therapist and family centered community building. Introduction to a new section of the journal. *Family Process, 41*(4), 561–568.

Donk, L. (1972). Attending behavior in mental patients. *Dissertation Abstracts International, 33* (Ord. No. 72–22, 569).

Douglas, C. (2005). Analytical psychotherapy. In R. J. Corsini & D. Wedding (Eds.), *Current psychotherapies* (pp. 96–129). Belmont, CA: Brooks/Cole–Thomson Learning.

Dowd, T., & Tierney, J. (2005). *Teaching social skills to youths* (2nd ed.). Boys Town, NE: Boys Town Press.

Downing, N. E., & Roush, K. L. (1985). From passive-acceptance to active commitment: A model of feminist identity development for women. *Counseling Psychologist, 13,* 695–709.

Dreikurs, R. (1981). The three life tasks. In L. Baruth & D. Eckstein (Eds.), *Lifestyle: Theory, practice, and research* (2nd ed.) (pp. 34–41). Dubuque, IA: Kendall/Hunt.

Dunn, R. I., & Schwebel, A. I. (1995). Meta-analytic review of marital therapy outcome research. *Journal of Family Psychology, 9,* 58–68.

Duran, E. (2006). *Healing the soul wound: Counseling with American Indians and other native peoples.* New York: Teachers College Press.

Duran, E., & Duran, B. (1995). *Native American postcolonial psychology.* Albany, NY: State University of New York.

Edwards, M. E., & Steinglass, P. (1995). Family therapy treatment outcomes for alcoholism.

Journal of Marital and Family Therapy, 21, 475–510.

Egan, G. (1994). *The skilled helper.* Pacific Grove, CA: Brooks/Cole.

Eisenberger, N. I., Lieberman, M. D., & Williams, K. D. (2003). Does rejection hurt? A FMRI study of social exclusion. *Science, 302,* 290–292.

Elias, M. J., & Tobias, S. E. (1996). *Social problem solving: Interventions in the schools.* New York: Guilford.

Ellis, A. (1958). *Sex without guilt.* Secaucus, NJ: Lyle Stuart.

Ellis, A. (1971). *Growth through reason.* Palo Alto, CA: Science and Behavior Books.

Ellis, A. (1983). The origins of rational-emotive therapy (RET). *Voices, 18,* 29–33.

Ellis, A. (1994). *Reason and emotion in psychotherapy.* New York: Birch Lane.

Ellis, A. (1995). Changing rational-emotive therapy to rational-emotive behavior therapy. *Journal of Rational-Emotive and Cognitive-Behavior Therapy, 13,* 85–90.

Ellis, A. (1996). Postmodernity or reality? A response to Allen E. Ivey, Don C. Locke, and Sandra Rigazio-DiGilio. *Counseling Today, 39,* 26–27.

Ellis, A. (1997). Postmodern ethics for active-directive counseling and psychotherapy. *Journal of Mental Health Counseling, 19,* 211–225.

Ellis, A. (1998). *How to make yourself happy and remarkably less disturbable.* San Luis Obispo, CA: Impact.

Ellis, A. (1999). Rational emotive behavior therapy as an internal control psychology. *International Journal of Reality Therapy, 19,* 4–11.

Ellis, A. (2000). A continuation of the dialogue on issues in counseling in the postmodern era. *Journal of Mental Health Counseling, 22,* 97–106.

Ellis, A., & Dryden, W. (1997). *The practice of rational emotive behavior therapy: A therapist's guide.* San Luis Obispo, CA: Impact.

Ellis, A., Abrams, M., & Abrams, L. (2005). *A brief biography of Albert Ellis.* Retrieved from http://www.rebt.ws/albertellisbiography.html.

Enns, C. (1987). Gestalt therapy and feminist therapy: A proposed integration. *Journal of Counseling and Development, 66,* 93–95.

Enns, C. (1993). Twenty years of feminist counseling and therapy: From naming biases to implementing multifaceted practice. *Counseling Psychologist, 21,* 83–87.

Erikson, E. (1963). *Childhood and society* (2nd ed.). New York: Norton. (Original work published 1950)

Esman, A. (1985). Kleinian theory revisited. *Contemporary Psychology, 30,* 303–304.

Estrada, A. U., & Pinsof, W. M. (1995). The effectiveness of family therapies for selected behavioral disorders of childhood. *Journal of Marital and Family Therapy, 21,* 403–404.

Evans, K., & Sullivan, M. (1990). *Dual diagnosis: Counseling the mentally ill substance abuser.* New York: Guilford.

Eysenck, H. J. (1966). *The effects of psychotherapy.* New York: International Science.

Fabry, J. (1984). Personal communication. *International Forum for Logotherapy.*

Fagan, J., & Shepherd, I. (1970). *Gestalt therapy now.* Palo Alto, CA: Science and Behavior Books.

Falicov, C. (1988). *Cultural perspectives in family therapy.* Rockville, MD: Aspen.

Falicov, C. (1995). Training to think culturally. *Family Process, 34,* 373–388.

Fals-Stewart, W., & Birchler, G. R. (2001). A national survey of the use of couples therapy in substance abuse treatment. *Journal of Substance Abuse Treatment, 20,* 277–283.

Fals-Stewart, W., Birchler, G. R., & O'Farrell, T. J. (1996). Behavioral couples therapy for male substance-abusing patients: Effects on relationship adjustment and drug-using behavior. *Journal of Consulting and Clinical Psychology, 64,* 959–972.

Fay, A., & Lazarus, A. (1993). On necessity and sufficiency in psychotherapy. *Psychotherapy in Private Practice, 12,* 33–39.

Feeney, J. A., & Noller, P. (1996). *Adult attachment.* London: Sage.

Fiedler, F. (1950a). A comparison of therapeutic relationships in psychoanalytic, nondirective, and Adlerian therapy. *Journal of Consulting Psychology, 14,* 435–36.

Fiedler, F. (1950b). The concept of an ideal therapeutic relationship. *Journal of Consulting Psychology, 14,* 239–245.

Fiedler, F. (1951). Factor analysis of psychoanalytic, nondirective, and Adlerian therapeutic relationships. *Journal of Consulting Psychology, 15,* 32–38.

Fisher, H. (2004). *Why we love: The nature and chemistry of romantic love.* New York: Holt.

Flaherty, M. (1989). *Perceived differences in early family relationship and parent/child relations between adults diagnosed as borderline personality or bipolar disorder.* Unpublished doctoral dissertation. School of Education, University of Massachusetts, Amherst.

Flores, M. T., & Carey, G. (2000). *Family therapy with Hispanics.* Boston: Allyn and Bacon.

Foa, E., Hearst-Ikeda, D., & Perry, K. (1995). Evaluation of a brief cognitive-behavioral program for prevention of chronic PTSD and recent assault victims. *Journal of Consulting and Clinical Psychology, 63,* 948–55.

Foa, E., Rothbaum, B., Riggs, D., & Murdock, T. (1991). Treatment of post-traumatic stress disorder in rape victims: A comparison between cognitive-behavior procedures and counseling. *Journal of Clinical and Consulting Psychology, 99,* 715–23.

Foerster, F. (1990). *Refinement and verification of a model of the resolution of unfinished business.* Unpublished master's thesis, York University, Toronto, Canada.

Frankl, V. E. (1959). *Man's search for meaning.* New York: Pocket Books. (Original work published 1946.)

Frankl, V. E. (1969). *The will to meaning.* New York: New American Library.

Frankl, V. E. (1970). Fore-runner of existential psychiatry. *Journal of Individual Psychology, 26,* 38.

Frankl, V. E. (1984). *Man's search for meaning* (rev. ed.). New York: Washington Square Press/Pocket Books.

Frankl, V. E. (1985a). Logos, paradox, and the search for meaning. In M. J. Mahoney & A. Freeman (Eds.), *Cognition and psychotherapy* (pp. 259–75). New York: Plenum.

Frankl, V. E. (1985b). *The unheard cry for meaning: Psychotherapy and humanism.* New York: Simon & Schuster.

Frankl, V. E. (1996). *Viktor Frankl—recollections: An autobiography.* (J. and J. Fabray Trans.) New York: Plenum. (Originally published in 1995 as *Was nicht in meinen Buchern steht.*)

Frankl, V. E. (2000). *Man's search for meaning: An introduction to logotherapy.* New York: Beacon.

Freeman, A., & Simon, K. (1989). Cognitive therapy of anxiety. In A. Freeman, K. Simon, L. Beutler, & H. Arkowitz (Eds.), *Comprehensive handbook of cognitive therapy* (pp. 346–66). New York: Plenum.

Freire, P. (1970). *Pedagogy of the oppressed.* New York: Continuum.

Freire, P. (1972). *Pedagogy of the oppressed.* New York: Herder & Herder.

Freud, A. (1982). *Psychoanalytic psychology of normal development: 1970–80.* London: Hogarth.

Freud, S. (1964). Negation. In S. Freud, *On metapsychology* (pp. 435–42). London: Penguin. (Original work published 1925.)

Freud, S. (1966). *A general introduction to psychoanalysis.* New York: Norton. (Original work published 1920.)

Fukuhara, M. (1987). *Adolescent cognitive development from the viewpoint of developmental therapy.* Paper presented at the meeting of the ninth International Society for the Study of Behavioral Development, Washington, DC.

Fukuyama, M. (1990). Taking a universal approach to multicultural counseling. *Counselor Education and Supervision, 30,* 6–17.

Fukuyama, M., & Sevig, T. D. (1999). *Integrating spirituality into multicultural counseling.* Thousand Oaks, CA: Sage.

Gaines, J. (2000). *Fritz Perls, here and now.* Tiburon, CA: Integrated Press.

Garfield, A., & Bergin, A. (1986). *Handbook of psychotherapy and behavior change.* New York: Wiley.

Gendlin, E. (1970). A short summary and some long predictions. In J. Hart & T. Tomlinson (Eds.), *New directions in client-centered therapy.* Boston: Houghton-Mifflin.

Gendlin, E. (1988). Carl Rogers. *American Psychologist, 43*, 127–28.

Gendlin, E., & Hendricks, M. (1978). Changes. In E. Gendlin, *Focusing* (pp. 659–88). Palo Alto, CA: Annual Reviews.

Gergen, K. (1991). *The saturated self: Dilemmas of identity in contemporary life*. New York: Basic Books.

Gergen, K. (1994). Warranting voice and the elaboration of the self. In J. Shotter & K. Gergen, *Texts of identity* (pp. 221–242). Newbury Park, CA: Sage.

Gilligan, C. (1982). *In a different voice*. Cambridge, MA: Harvard University Press.

Gilliland, B. E., & James, R. K. (1998). *Theories and strategies in counseling and psychotherapy* (4th ed.). Needham Heights, MA: Allyn and Bacon.

Gladding, S. T. (2000). *Counseling: A comprehensive profession* (4th ed.). Upper Saddle River, NJ: Merrill.

Glasser, W. (1965). *Reality therapy*. New York: HarperCollins.

Glasser, W. (1998). *Choice theory: A new psychology of personal freedom*. New York: HarperPerennial.

Glasser, W. (1999). Schoolwork won't improve until schools demand competence. *International Journal of Reality Therapy, 19*, 17–20.

Glasser, W. (2001). *Counseling with choice theory, the new reality therapy* (5th ed.). New York: HarperCollins.

Glynn, S. M. Eth, S., Randolph, E. T., Foy, D. W., Urbaitis, M., Boxer, L., Paz, G., Leong, G., Firman, G., Salk, J., Katzman, J., & Crothers, J. (1999). A test of behavioral family therapy to augment exposure for combat-related posttraumatic stress disorder. *Journal of Consulting and Clinical Psychology, 67*(2), 243–251.

Goldberg, S., Muir, R., & Kerr, J. (1995). *Attachment theory: Social, developmental, and clinical perspectives*. Hillsdale, NJ: Analytic Press.

Goldner, V. (1993). Power and hierarchy: Let's talk about it! *Family Process, 32*, 157–162.

Goldstein, M. J., & Miklowitz, D. J. (1995). The effectiveness of psychoeducational family therapy in the treatment of schizophrenic disorders. *Journal of Marital and Family Therapy, 21*, 361–376.

Goncalves, O., & Ivey, A. E. (1992). Developmental therapy: Clinical applications. In K. Kuehlwein and H. Rosen (Eds.), *Cognitive therapy in action* (pp. 221–254). San Francisco: Jossey-Bass.

Graham, M. (2005). Maat: An African-centered paradigm for psychological and spiritual healing. In R. Moodley and W. West (Eds.), *Integrating traditional healing practices into counseling and psychotherapy* (pp. 210–220). Thousand Oaks, CA: Sage.

Greenberg, L. S., & Johnson, S. M. (1998). *Emotionally focused therapy for couples*. New York: Guilford.

Greenberg, L., & Saffran, J. (1987). *Emotion in psychotherapy*. New York: Guilford.

Greene, B. (Ed.). (1997). *Ethnic and cultural diversity among lesbians and gay men*. Thousand Oaks, CA: Sage.

Greenspan, M. (1983). *A new approach to women and therapy*. New York: McGraw Hill.

Greenspoon, J. (1955). The reinforcing effect of two spoken sounds on the frequency of two responses. *American Journal of Psychology, 68*, 409–416.

Griffith, M., & Jones, E. (1978). Race and psychotherapy: Changing perspectives. In J. Masserman (Ed.), *Current psychiatric therapies* (Vol. 18) (pp. 225–235). Orlando, FL: Grune & Stratton.

Grunebaum, H., & Chasin, R. (1982). Thinking like a family therapist: A model for integrating the theories and methods of family therapy. *Journal of Marital and Family Therapy, 8*, 403–416.

Guerin, P. J., Fogarty, T. F., Fay, L. F., & Kautto, J. G. (1996). *Working with relationship triangles: The one-two-three of psychotherapy*. New York: Guilford.

Gunner, M., & Sroufe, A. (Eds.). (1991). Self-processes and development. In *The Minnesota Symposia on Child Development* (Vol. 23). Hillsdale, NY: Erlbaum.

Guntrip, H. (1968). *Schizoid phenomena, object relations, and the self*. New York: International Universities Press.

Gurman, A. S., Kniskern, D. P., & Pinsof, W. M. (1986). Research on the process and outcome of marital and family therapy. In S. Garfield & A. Bergin (Eds.), *Handbook of psychotherapy and behavior change* (3rd ed.) (pp. 525–623). New York: Wiley.

Guterman, J. T. (1994). A social constructionist position for mental health counseling. *Journal of Mental Health Counseling, 16,* 226–244.

Guterman, J. T. (1996). Reconstructing social constructionism: A response to Albert Ellis. *Journal of Mental Health Counseling, 18,* 29–40.

Guterman, J. T. (1997). Tales of mental health counseling. *Journal of Mental Health Counseling, 19,* 211–225.

Guterman, J. T., Ellis, A., Rigazio-DiGilio, S. A., & D'Andrea, M. (1999). *Counseling in the postmodern era.* Debate held at the annual meeting of the American Counseling Association, San Diego, CA.

Gutman, H. (1976). *The Black family in slavery and freedom: 1750–1925.* New York: HarperCollins.

Hackney, R., Ivey, A., & Oetting, E. (1970). Attending, island, and hiatus behavior: A process conception of counselor and client interaction. *Journal of Counseling Psychology, 17,* 342–346.

Haley, A. (1977). *Roots: Saga of an American family.* New York: Doubleday.

Haley, J. (1963). *Strategies of psychotherapy.* New York: Grune & Stratton.

Haley, J. (1973). *Uncommon therapy: The psychiatric techniques of Milton H. Erikson.* New York: Norton.

Haley, J. (1979). *Leaving home.* New York: McGraw-Hill.

Hamilton, C. E. (2000). Continuity and discontinuity of attachment from infancy through adolescence. *Child Development, 71,* 219–228.

Hansen, J. C., Rossberg, R. H., & Cramer, S. H. (1994). *Counseling: Theory and process.* Needham Heights, MA: Allyn and Bacon.

Hansen, J., & L'Abate, L. (1982). *Approaches to family therapy.* New York: Macmillan.

Hansen, L. S. (2000). Integrative life planning: A new worldview for career professionals. In J. Kummerow (Ed.), *New directions in career planning and the workplace* (2nd ed.; pp. 123–159). Palo Alto, CA: Davies-Black.

Hansen, S. (1990, July). *Work and family roles: An integrated context for career planning.* Paper presented at the International Round Table for the Advancement of Counseling, Helsinki, Finland.

Hansen, S. (1991). Integrative life planning: Work, family, community. *Futurics, 15,* 80–86.

Hardy, K., & Laszloffy, T. (1995). The cultural genogram: Key to training culturally competent family therapists. *Journal of Marital and Family Therapy, 21,* 227–237.

Hare-Mustin, R. T. (1978). A feminist approach to family therapy. *Family Process, 17,* 181–194.

Hawkins, D. R. (2002). *Power vs. force: The hidden determinants of human behavior.* Carlsbad, CA: Hay House.

Hayashi, S., Kuno, T., Osawa, M., Shimizu, M., & Suetake, Y. (1992). The client-centered therapy and person-centered approach in Japan: Historical development, current status, and perspectives. *Journal of Humanistic Psychology, 32,* 115–36.

Heesacker, M., Prichard, S., Rigazio-DiGilio, S., & Ivey, A. (1995). *Development of a paper and pencil measure on cognitive-developmental orientation.* Unpublished paper, Department of Psychology, University of Florida, Gainesville.

Heidegger, M. (1962). *Being and time.* New York: HarperCollins.

Helms, J. E. (1985). Toward a theoretical explanation of the effects of race on counseling: A Black and White model. *Counseling Psychologist, 12,* 153–165.

Helms, J. E. (1990). *Black and White racial identity.* Westport, CT: Greenwood.

Helms, J. E. (1995). An update of Helms's White and People of Color identity models. In J. Ponterotto, M. Casas, L. Suzuki, & C. Alexander (Eds.), *Handbook of multicultural counseling.* Thousand Oaks, CA: Sage.

Helms, J. E., & Cook, D. A. (1999). *Using race and culture in counseling and psychotherapy: Theory and process.* Boston: Allyn and Bacon.

Henggeler, S., Borduin, C., & Mann, B. (1992). Advances in family therapy: Empirical foundations. In T. Ollendick & R. Prinz (Eds.),

Advances in clinical child psychology (Vol. 15). New York: Plenum.

Henry, W., Strupp, H. H., Butler, S., Schacht, T., & Binder, J. (1993). Effects of training in time-limited dynamic therapy: Changes in therapist behavior. *Journal of Consulting and Clinical Psychology, 63*, 434–40.

Hill, M., & Ballou, M. (2005). *The foundation and future of feminist therapy*. New York: Haworth Press.

Hilliard, R. B., Henry, W. P., & Strupp, H. H. (2000). An interpersonal model of psychotherapy: Linking patient and therapist developmental history, therapeutic process, and types of outcome. *Journal of Consulting and Clinical Psychology, 68*, 125–133.

Hines, P., & Boyd-Franklin, N. (1982). Black families. In M. McGoldrick, J. Pearce, & J. Giordano (Eds.), *Ethnicity and family therapy*. New York: Guilford.

Hoffman, L. (1990). Constructing realities: An art of lenses. *Family Process, 29*, 1–12.

Hollan, S., & Najavits, L. (1988). Review of empirical studies of cognitive therapy. In A. Frances & R. Hales (Eds.), *American Psychiatric Press review of psychiatry* (Vol. 7; pp. 643–666). Washington, DC: American Psychiatric Press.

Hollon, S. D. (1996). The efficacy and effectiveness of psychotherapy: Relative to medications. *American Psychologist, 51*, 1025–1030.

hooks, b. (2000). *Feminist theory: From margin to center* (2nd ed.). Cambridge, MA: South End Press.

Huey, S. J., Henggeler, S. W., Brondino, M. J., & Pickrel, S. G. (2000). Mechanisms of change in multisystemic therapy: Reducing delinquent behavior through therapist adherence and improved family and peer functioning. *Journal of Consulting and Clinical Psychology, 68*(3), 451–467.

Husserl, E. (1931). *Ideas: General introduction to pure phenomenology*. London: Allen & Unwin.

Hwang, P. O. (2000). *Other-esteem: Meaningful life in a multicultural society*. Philadelphia, PA: Accelerated Development.

Imber-Black, E. (1988). *Families and larger systems: A family therapist's guide through the labyrinth*. New York: Guilford.

Imber-Black, E. (2004). Of continuities, beginnings and generativities. *Family Process, 43(1)*, 1–5.

Inbar, D., Aviram, U., Spiro, S., & Kotler, M. (1989). Officers' attitude toward combat stress reaction: Responsibility, treatment, return to unit, and personal distance. *Military Medicine, 154*, 480–489.

Ingoldsby, B., & Smith, S. (1995). *Families in multicultural perspectives*. New York: Guilford.

Ivey, A. E. (1971a). Media therapy: Educational change planning for psychiatric patients. *Journal of Counseling Psychology, 20*, 338–343.

Ivey, A. E. (1971b). *Microcounseling: Innovations in interviewing training*. Springfield, IL: Thomas.

Ivey, A. E. (1986). *Developmental therapy: Theory into practice*. San Francisco: Jossey-Bass.

Ivey, A. E. (1988). *Managing face-to-face communication*. Lund, Sweden: Studentlitteratur, Chartwell Bratt.

Ivey, A. E. (1989). *Object relations: An introduction*. Unpublished manuscript, University of Massachusetts, Amherst.

Ivey, A. E. (1991a, September). *Developmental therapy and media therapy: An update*. Presentation to Veterans Administration Conference, Orlando, FL.

Ivey, A. E. (1991b, October). *Media therapy reconsidered*. Paper presented at Veterans Administration Conference, Orlando, FL.

Ivey, A. E. (1993a). *Developmental counseling and therapy: A review of the 1971–73 microtraining/media therapy psychoeducational project with psychiatric inpatients*. Paper presented at the Veterans Administration Conference, Orlando, FL.

Ivey, A. E. (1993b). *Developmental strategies for helpers: Individual, family and network interventions*. Pacific Grove, CA: Brooks/Cole.

Ivey, A. E. (1994, Fall). *Multicultural counseling and therapy: A contextual approach*. Paper presented at Wing Memorial Hospital, Palmer, MA.

Ivey, A. E. (1995a, April). *The community genogram: A strategy to assess culture and community resources*. Paper presented at the annual meeting of the American Counseling Association, Denver, CO.

Ivey, A. E. (1995b). Psychotherapy as liberation: Toward specific skills and strategies in multicultural counseling and therapy. In J. G. Ponterotto, J. M. Casas, J. Suzuki, & C. M. Alexander (Eds.), *Handbook of multicultural counseling* (pp. 53–72). Thousand Oaks, CA: Sage.

Ivey, A. E. (2000). *Developmental therapy: Theory into practice.* North Amherst, MA: Microtraining Associates. (Original work published 1986.)

Ivey, A. E., & Gluckstern, N. (1974). *Basic attending skills.* North Amherst, MA: Microtraining.

Ivey, A. E., & Ivey, M. B. (1990). Assessing and facilitating children's cognitive development: Developmental counseling and therapy in a case of child abuse. *Journal of Counseling and Development, 68,* 299–306.

Ivey, A. E., & Ivey, M. B. (1998). Reframing DSM-IV: Positive strategies from developmental counseling and therapy. *Journal of Counseling and Development, 76,* 334–50.

Ivey, A. E., & Ivey, M. B. (1999a). *Intentional interviewing and counseling* (4th ed.). Pacific Grove, CA: Brooks/Cole.

Ivey, A. E., & Ivey, M. B. (1999b). Toward a developmental *Diagnostic and Statistical Manual*—The vitality of a contextual framework. *Journal of Counseling and Development, 77,* 484–490.

Ivey, A. E., & Ivey, M. B. (2001). Developmental counseling and therapy and multicultural counseling and therapy: Metatheory, contextual consciousness, and action. In D.C. Locke, J. Myers, & E. Herr (Eds.), *The handbook of counseling* (pp. 219–238). Newbury Park, CA: Sage.

Ivey, A. E., & Ivey, M. B. (2007). *Intentional interviewing and counseling: Facilitating client development in a multicultural society* (7th ed.). Pacific Grove, CA: Brooks/Cole–Thomson Learning.

Ivey, A. E., & Matthews, W. (1984). A meta-model for structuring the clinical interview. *Journal of Counseling and Development, 63,* 237–243.

Ivey, A. E., & Rigazio-DiGilio, S. A. (1993). The standard cognitive-developmental classification system. In A. E. Ivey, *Developmental strategies for helpers: Individual, family and network interventions.* North Amherst, MA: Microtraining Associates.

Ivey, A. E., & Rigazio-DiGilio, S. A. (1994). Developmental counseling and therapy: Can still another theory be useful to you? *Journal for the Professional Counselor, 9,* 23–48.

Ivey, A. E., & Simek-Downing, L. (1980). *Counseling and psychotherapy: Skills, theories, and practice.* Englewood Cliffs, NJ: Prentice Hall.

Ivey, A. E., D'Andrea, M., Ivey, M. B., & Simek-Morgan, L. (2002). *Counseling and psychotherapy: A multicultural perspective* (5th ed.). Needham Heights, MA: Allyn and Bacon.

Ivey, A. E., Gluckstern, N., & Ivey, M. (1992). *Basic attending skills* (3rd ed.). North Amherst, MA: Microtraining.

Ivey, A. E., Ivey, M. B., D'Andrea, M., Daniels, J., Arredondo, P., Parham, T., & Sue, D. W. (2005, January). *A vital necessity for multicultural competence: Changing our training programs.* Paper presented at the National Multicultural Conference and Summit, Hollywood, CA.

Ivey, A. E., Ivey, M. B., Myers, J., & Sweeney, T. (2005). *Developmental counseling and therapy: Promoting wellness over the lifespan.* Boston: Lahaska Press.

Ivey, A. E., Locke, D.C., & Rigazio-DiGilio, S. A. (1996). The spirit and the challenge: Postmodernity or reality? *Counseling Today, 36,* 33.

Ivey, A. E., Normington, C., Miller, C., Morrill, W., & Haase, R. (1968). Microcounseling and attending behavior: An approach to pre-practicum counselor training. *Journal of Counseling Psychology, 15,* 1–12.

Ivey, A. E., Pedersen, P. B., & Ivey, M. B. (2001). *Intentional group counseling: A microskills approach.* Belmont, CA: Brooks/Cole.

Ivey, M. B. (1984). Reflection of feeling [Videotape]. In A. Ivey, N. Gluckstern, & M. Ivey, *Basic attending skills.* North Amherst, MA: Microtraining.

Ivey, M. B. (1994, April). *Developmental counseling and therapy: Feminist issues.* Paper presented at Hong Kong Polytechnic University.

Jackson, B. (1975). Black identity development. *Journal of Educational Diversity and Innovation, 2,* 19–25.

Jackson, B. (1990, September). *Building a multicultural school.* Paper presented to the Amherst Regional School System, Amherst, MA.

Jackson, B., & Hardiman R. (1983). Racial identity development: Implications for managing the multiracial work force. In R. Vitvo & A. Sargent (Eds.), *The NTL managers' handbook* (pp. 107–19). Arlington, VA: NTL Institute.

Jackson, L. C., & Greene, B. (Eds.). (2000). *Psychotherapy with African American women: Innovations in psychodynamic perspectives and practice.* New York: Guilford.

Jackson, M. L. (1995). Multicultural counseling: Historical perspectives. In J. G. Ponterotto, J. M. Casas, L. A. Suzuki, & C. M. Alexander (Eds.), *Handbook of multicultural counseling.* (pp. 3–16). Thousand Oaks, CA: Sage.

Jacobson, N. (1981). Behavioral marital therapy. In A. S. Gurman & D. P. Kniskern (Eds.), *Handbook of family therapy* (pp. 556–91). New York: Brunner/Mazel.

Jacobson, N., & Addis, M. E. (1993). Research on couples and couple therapy: What do we know? Where are we going? *Journal of Consulting and Clinical Psychology, 61,* 85–93.

Jacobson, N., & Christensen, A. (1996). *Integrative couple therapy: Promoting acceptance and change.* New York: Norton.

Jacobson, N. S., Christensen, A., Prince, S. E., Cordova, J., & Eldridge, K. (2000). Integrative behavior couple therapy: An acceptance-based, promising new treatment for couple discord. *Journal of Consulting and Clinical Psychology, 68*(2), 351–55.

James, R. K., & Gilliland, B. E. (2003). *Theories and strategies in counseling and psychotherapy* (5th ed.). Needham Heights, MA: Allyn and Bacon.

Johnson, S. L., & Jacob, T. (2000). Sequential interactions in the marital communication of depressed men and women. *Journal of Consulting and Clinical Psychology, 69,* 1–12.

Jones, E. (1978). Effects of race on psychotherapy process and outcome. *Psychotherapy Theory, Research, and Practice, 15,* 226–236.

Jones, E. (1985). Psychotherapy and counseling with Black clients. In P. Pedersen (Ed.), *Handbook of cross-cultural counseling and therapy* (pp. 173–79). Westport, CT: Greenwood.

Jones, J. M. (1997). *Prejudice and racism* (2nd ed.). New York: McGraw-Hill.

Jordan, J. V. (1992). Relational resilience. *Work in Progress,* No. 57. Wellesley, MA: Stone Center Working Paper Series.

Jordan, J. V. (2001). A relational-cultural model: Healing through mutual empathy. *Bulletin of the Menninger Clinic, 65*(1), 92–103.

Jordan, J. V., & Dooley, C. (2000). *Relational practice in action: A group manual.* Wellesley, MA: Stone Center Publications.

Jung, C. (1935). The personal and collective unconscious. In C. Jung, *Collected works* (Vol. 7, pp. 87–110). New York: Pantheon.

Jung, C. (1958). *Psychology and religion.* New York: Pantheon.

Jung, C. G. (1954). The development of personality. *Collected works* (Vol. 11), Bollongen series XX (G. Adler, M. Fordham, & H. Read, Eds.). (R. F. C. Hull, Trans.). New York: Pantheon Books.

Jung, C. G. (1960). The structure and dynamics of the psyche. *Collected works* (Vol. 8), Bollongen series XX (G. Adler, M. Fordham, & H. Read, Eds.). (R. F. C. Hull, Trans.). New York: Pantheon Books.

Jung, C. G. (1964). *Man and his symbols.* New York: Doubleday.

Jung, C. G. (1971). *The portable Jung.* New York: Penguin Books.

Kabat-Zinn, J. (1990). *Full catastrophe living.* New York: Delta.

Kantrowitz, R., & Ballou, M. (1992). A feminist critique of cognitive-behavioral therapy. In L. Brown & M. Ballou (Eds.), *Theories of personality and psychopathology: Feminist reappraisals* (pp. 70–87). New York: Guilford.

Kapelis, L. (1991). Personal communication. Adelaide, Australia: Department of Psychology, Flinders University.

Kaslow, F. (Ed.). (1996). *Handbook of relational diagnosis and dysfunctional family patterns.* New York: Wiley.

Kaufmann, Y. (1989). Analytical psychotherapy. In R. J. Corsini & D. Wedding (Eds.), *Current psychotherapies* (4th ed.) (pp. 118–125). Itasca, IL: Peacock.

Kazdin, A. E., & Weisz, J. R. (1998). Identifying and developing empirically supported child and adolescent treatments. *Journal of Consulting and Clinical Psychology, 66,* 37–52.

Keeney, B. P. (1983). *Aesthetics of change.* New York: Guilford.

Kelly, E. W. (1995). *Spirituality and religion in counseling and psychotherapy: Diversity in theory and practice.* Alexandria, VA: American Counseling Association.

Kelly, G. (1955). *The psychology of personal constructs* (Vols. 1 and 2). New York: W. W. Norton.

Kelly, W. L. (1990). *Psychology of the unconscious: Mesmer, Janet, Freud, Jung, and current issues.* New York: Prometheus.

Kempler, W. (1981). *Experiential psychotherapy with families.* New York: Brunner/Mazel.

Kenney, D., & Law, J. (1991). Developmental counseling and therapy with involuntary midlife career changers. *Journal of Young Adulthood and Middle Age, 3,* 25–39.

Kerwin, C., & Ponterotto, J. (1995). Biracial identity development. In J. Ponterotto, M. Casas, L. Suzuki, & C. Alexander (Eds.), *Handbook of multicultural counseling* (pp. 199–217). Thousand Oaks, CA: Sage.

Kikoski, K. (1980). *A study of cross-cultural communication, Arabs and Americans: Paradigms and skills.* Unpublished doctoral dissertation, University of Massachusetts, Amherst.

Kim, K. I., & Hwang, M. G. (2001). The effects of internal control and achievement motivation in group counseling based on reality therapy. *International Journal of Reality Therapy, 20,* 12–15.

King, M. L., Jr. (1986). The drum major instinct. In James M. Washington (Ed.), *A testament of hope: The essential writing of Martin Luther King, Jr.* (pp. 259–267). San Francisco: HarperCollins.

Kjos, D. (2002). Feminist family therapy. In J. Carlson and D. Kjos (Eds.), *Theories and strategies of family therapy.* Needham Heights, MA: Allyn and Bacon.

Klein, M. (1975). *Envy and gratitude and other works, 1946/1963.* London: Hogarth.

Knutsen, S. P., & Knutsen, R. (1991). The Tromso survey: The family intervention study—the effect of intervention on some coronary risk factors and dietary habits, a 6-year follow-up. *Preventive Medicine, 20,* 197–212.

Korman, M. (1973). *Levels and patterns of professional training in psychology.* Washington, DC: American Psychological Association.

Krech, G. (2002). *Naikan: Gratitude, grace, and the Japanese art of self-reflection.* Berkeley, CA: Stone Bridge Press.

Kuehl, B. (1995). The solution-oriented genogram: A collaborative approach. *Journal of Marital and Family Therapy, 21,* 239–250.

Kunjufu, J. (1986). *Motivating and preparing black youth to work.* Chicago: African American Images.

Lacan, J. (1977). *Ecrits: A selection.* New York: Norton. (Original work published 1966)

LaFromboise, T. (1996a). *American Indian life skills curriculum.* Madison: University of Wisconsin Press.

LaFromboise, T. (1996b). On multicultural issues. *Microtraining Newsletter,* p. 5.

LaFromboise, T., & Fleming, C. (1990). Keeper of the fire: A profile of Carolyn Attneave. *Journal of Counseling and Development, 68,* 537–47.

LaFromboise, T., & Jackson, M. (1996). MCT theory and Native American populations. In D. W. Sue, A. E. Ivey, & P. B. Pedersen (Eds.), *A theory of multicultural counseling and therapy* (pp. 192–203). Pacific Grove, CA: Brooks/Cole.

LaFromboise, T., & Low, K. (1989). American Indian adolescents. In J. Gibbs & L. Hwang (Eds.), *Children of color* (pp. 114–147). San Francisco: Jossey-Bass.

LaFromboise, T., Foster, S., & James, A. (1996). Ethics in multicultural counseling. In P. B. Pedersen, J. G. Draguns, W. J. Lonner, & J. E. Trimble (Eds.), *Counseling across cultures* (4th ed.) (pp. 47–72). Thousand Oaks, CA: Sage.

Lago, C., & MacMillan, M. (Eds.). (1999). *Experiences in relatedness: Groupwork and* the person-centered approach. Ross-on-Wye, UK: PCCS Books.

Laing, R. (1967). *The politics of experience.* New York: Ballantine.

Lambert, M., & Bergin, A. (1994). The effectiveness of psychotherapy. In A. Bergin & S. Garfield, *Handbook of psychotherapy and behavior change* (4th ed.) (pp. 144–168). New York: Wiley.

Lambert, M., DeJulio, S., & Stein, D. (1978). Therapist interpersonal skills. *Psychological Bulletin, 85,* 467–489.

Landrine, H. (1995). *Bringing cultural diversity to feminist psychology: Theory, research, and practice.* Washington, DC: American Psychological Association.

Lanier, J. (1991). Personal communication, Sangamon State University, Springfield, IL.

Lankton, S. (1980). *Practical magic.* Cupertino, CA: Meta.

Laplanche, J., & Pontalis, J. (1973). *The language of psychoanalysis.* New York: Norton.

Lark, S. M., & Richards, J. A. (2000). *The chemistry of success: Secrets of peak performance.* San Francisco, CA: Bay Books.

Lazarus, A. (1971). Behavior therapy and beyond. New York: McGraw-Hill.

Lazarus, A. (1981). *The practice of multimodal psychotherapy.* New York: McGraw-Hill.

Lazarus, A. (1986). Multimodal psychotherapy. *International Journal of Eclectic Psychotherapy, 5,* 95–103.

Lazarus, A. (1992). *I can if I want to.* New York: Morrow.

Lazarus, A. (1995). Adjusting the carburetor: Pivotal interventions in marital and sex therapy. In R. Rosen & S. Leiblum (Eds.), *Case studies in sex therapy* (pp. 81–95). New York: Guilford.

Lazarus, A. A., & Fay, A. (2000). *I can if I want to.* New York: FMC Books.

Lazarus, A. A., & Lazarus, C. N. (1997). *The 60-second shrink: 101 strategies for staying sane in a crazy world.* New York: Impact.

Lee, C. (1994). Pioneers of multicultural counseling: A conversation with Clemmont E. Vontress. *Journal of Multicultural Counseling and Development, 22,* 66–78.

Lee, C. (1996). Implications for indigenous healing systems. In D. Sue, A. Ivey, & P. Pederson (Eds.), *Toward a theory of multicultural counseling and therapy* (pp. 86–97). Pacific Grove, CA: Brooks/Cole.

Lee, C. C., & Armstrong, K. L. (1995). Indigenous models of mental health intervention: Lessons from traditional healers. In J. G. Ponterotto, J. M. Casas, L. A. Suzuki, & C. M. Alexander (Eds.), *Handbook of multicultural counseling* (pp. 441–56). Thousand Oaks, CA: Sage.

Leong, F. T. L., Wagner, N. S., & Tata, S. P. (1995). Racial and ethnic variations in help-seeking attitudes. In J. G. Ponterotto, J. M. Casas, L. A. Suzuki, & C. M. Alexander (Eds.), *Handbook of multicultural counseling* (pp. 415–38). Thousand Oaks, CA: Sage.

Lerner, H. (1992). The limits of phenomenology: A feminist critique of the humanistic personality theories. In L. Brown & M. Ballou (Eds.), *Theories of personality and psychopathology* (pp. 8–19). New York: Guilford.

Levine, M. (2000). *The positive psychology of Buddhism and yoga.* Mahwah, NJ: Erlbaum.

Lewin, K. (1951). *Field theory in social science.* New York: Harper.

Lewis, J. A., Arnold, M. S., House, R., & Toporek, R. (2003). *Advocacy competencies.* Alexandria, VA: American Counseling Association.

Lewis, J. A., Lewis, M. D., Daniels, J. A., & D'Andrea, M. J. (2003). *Community counseling: Empowerment strategies for a diverse society* (3rd ed.). Pacific Grove, CA: Brooks/Cole–Thomson Learning.

Lewis, J., & Bradley, L. (Eds.). (2002). *Advocacy in counseling: Counselors, clients, and community.* Greensboro, NC: Caps Publications.

Liddle, H. A., & Dakof, G. A. (1995). Efficacy of family therapy for drug abuse: Promising but not definitive. *Journal of Marital and Family Therapy, 21,* 511–44.

Liddle, H. A., & Rowe, C. L. (2004). Advances in family therapy research. In M. Nichols & R. Schwartz (Eds.), *Family therapy: Concepts and methods* (6th ed.). Needham Heights, MA: Allyn and Bacon.

Lieberman, M., Yalom, I., & Miles, E. (1972). *Encounter groups: First facts.* New York: Basic Books.

Lipchik, E. (1991, May/June). Spouse abuse: Challenging the party line. *Family Therapy Networker*, pp. 59–63.

Liu, W. M. (2001). Expanding our understanding of multiculturalism: Developing a social class worldview model. In D. B. Pope-Davis & H. L. K. Coleman (Eds.), *The intersection of race, class and gender in multicultural counseling* (pp. 101–122). Thousand Oaks, CA: Sage.

Loevinger, J. (1986). *Paradigms of personality.* New York: Freeman.

Lojk, L. (1986). My experiences using reality therapy. *Journal of Reality Therapy, 5,* 28–35.

Lombardi, D. N. (1996). Antisocial personality disorder and addictions. In L. Sperry & J. Carlson (Eds.), *Psychopathology and psychotherapy* (pp. 371–390). Washington, DC: Accelerated Development.

Luepnitz, D. (1988). *The family interpreted: Feminist theory in clinical practice.* New York: Basic Books.

Lukas, E. (1984). *Meaningful living.* Cambridge, MA: Schenkman.

Lukas, E. (1989, June). *From self-actualization to global responsibility.* Paper presented at the seventh World Congress of Logotherapy, Kansas City.

Lundin, R. W. (1989). *Alfred Adler's basic concepts and implications.* Muncie, IN: Accelerated Development.

Lyons, L., & Woods, P. (1992). The efficacy of rational-emotive therapy: A quantitative review of the outcome literature. *Clinical Psychology Review.*

Mabe, P. A., Turner, K., & Josephson, A. M. (2001). Parent management training. *Child and Adolescent Psychiatric Clinics of North America, 10*(3), 451–474.

MacFarlane, K., & Feldmeth, J. (1988). *Child sexual abuse: The clinical interview.* New York: Guilford.

Mahler, M. S., Pine, F., & Bergman, A. (2000). *The psychological birth of the human infant: Symbiosis and individuation.* New York: Basic Books.

Mahoney, M., & Freeman, A. (Eds.). (1985). *Cognition and psychotherapy.* New York: Plenum.

Mailer, W. (1991). *Preparing students for the workplace: Personal growth and organizational change.* Paper presented at the North Atlantic Regional Association for Counselor Education and Supervision, Albany, NY.

Malcolm, J. (1985). *In the Freud archives.* New York: Vintage.

Mann, L., Beswick, G., Allouache, P., & Ivey, M. (1982). *Decision workshops for the improvement of decision making skills.* Adelaide, Australia: Flinders University.

Maples, M. F., & Sieber, C. (1999). Gestalt theory. In D. Capuzzi, & D. R. Gross (Eds.), *Counseling and psychotherapy: Theories and interventions* (2nd ed.) (pp. 231–260). Upper Saddle River, NJ: Merrill.

Marcos, L. (1979). Effects of interpreters on the evaluation of psychopathology in non-English-speaking persons. *American Journal of Psychiatry, 136,* 171–174.

Marlatt, G., & Donovan, D. (2005). *Relapse prevention: Maintenance strategies in the treatment of addictive behaviors* (2nd ed.). New York: Guilford.

Marlatt, G., & Gordon, J. (1985). *Relapse prevention: Maintenance strategies in the treatment of addictive behaviors.* New York: Guilford.

Martin-Baro, I. (1994). *Writings for a liberation psychology.* Cambridge, MA: Harvard University Press.

Maslow, A. (1971). *The farther reaches of human nature.* New York: Viking.

Maslow, A. H. (1970). Holistic emphasis. *Journal of Individual Psychology, 26,* 39.

Masson, J. (Ed.). (1985). *The complete letters of Sigmund Freud to Wilhelm Fliess: 1887–1904.* Cambridge, MA: Harvard University Press.

May, R. (1958). The origins and significance of the existential movement in psychology. In R. May, E. Angel, & H. Ellenberger (Eds.), *Existence* (pp. 3–36). New York: Basic Books.

May, R. (1969). *Love and will.* New York: Norton.

May, R. (1970). Myth and guiding fiction. *Journal of Individual Psychology, 36,* 42.

May, R. (Ed.). (1961). *Existential psychology.* New York: Random House.

Mazzeo, S. E., & Espelage, D. L. (2002). Association between childhood physical and emotional abuse and disordered eating behaviors in female undergraduates: An investigation of the mediated role of alexithymia and depression. *Journal of Counseling Psychology, 49*(1), 86–100.

McAdoo, H. P. (Ed.). (1997). *Black families* (3rd ed.). Thousand Oaks, CA: Sage.

McAdoo, H. P. (Ed.). (1999). *Family ethnicity: Strength in diversity* (2nd ed.). Thousand Oaks, CA: Sage.

McFadden, J. (Ed.). (1999). *Transcultural counseling* (2nd ed.). Alexandria, VA: American Counseling Association.

McGinnis, E., & Goldstein, A. P. (1997). *Skillstreaming the elementary school child: New strategies and perspectives for teaching prosocial skills.* New York: Research Press.

McGoldrick, M. (2002). *Re-visioning family therapy: Race, culture, and gender in clincial practice.* New York: Guilford.

McGoldrick, M., Gerson, R., & Shellenberger, S. (1999). *Genograms: Assessment and intervention* (2nd ed.). New York: Norton.

McGoldrick, M., Giordano, G., & Pearce, J. K. (Eds.). (1996). *Ethnicity and family therapy* (2nd ed.). New York: Guilford.

McGrath, W. (1986). *Freud's discovery of psychoanalysis: The politics of hysteria.* Ithaca, NY: Cornell University Press.

McIntosh, P. (1989, July/August). White privilege: Unpacking the invisible knapsack. *Peace and Freedom,* pp. 8–10.

McMullin, R. E. (2000). *The new handbook of cognitive therapy techniques.* New York: Norton.

McNamee, S., & Gergen, K. (2000). *Social construction and the therapeutic process* (2nd. ed.). Newbury Park, CA: Sage.

McNeilly, M. (1996, March 18). Stress of racism may kill, study finds. *Honolulu Advertiser,* p. A7.

McWhirter, E. H. (1994). *Counseling for empowerment.* Alexandria, VA: American Counseling Association.

Mearns, D., & Thorne, B. (1999). *Person-centered counseling in action.* Thousand Oaks, CA: Sage.

Meichenbaum, D. (1985). *Stress inoculation training.* New York: Pergamon Press.

Meichenbaum, D. (1991). Evolution of cognitive behavior therapy. In J. Zeig (Ed.), *The evolution of psychology, II.* New York: Brunner/Mazel.

Meichenbaum, D. (1993). Stress inoculation training: A twenty-year update. In R. Wolfolk & P. Lehrer (Eds.), *Principles and practices of stress management.* New York: Guilford.

Meichenbaum, D. (1994). *A clinical handbook/practical therapy manual for assessing and treating adults with post-traumatic stress disorder (PTSD).* Waterloo, Ontario: Institute Press.

Meichenbaum, D. (2003). *Treatment with individuals with anger-control problems and aggressive behavior.* New York: Crown House.

Mencher, J. (1990). Intimacy in lesbian relationships: A critical reexamination of fusion. *Work in Progress.* Stone Center Series No. 42. Wellesley College, Wellesley, MA.

Miller, A. (1981). *The drama of the gifted child.* New York: Basic Books.

Miller, A. (1984). *Thou shalt not be aware.* New York: Signet.

Miller, A. (1990). *The untouched key: Tracing childhood trauma in creativity and destructiveness.* New York: Doubleday.

Miller, J. B. (1986). *Toward a new psychology of women* (2nd ed.). Boston: Beacon.

Miller, J. B. (1991). The development of women's sense of self. In J. Jordan, A. Kaplan, J. Baker Miller, I. Stiver, & J. Surry (Eds.), *Women's growth in connection* (pp. 11–26). New York: Guilford.

Miller, J. B., & Stiver, I. P. (1997). *The healing connection: How women form relationships in therapy and in life.* Boston: Beacon.

Miller, J. B., Stiver, I. P., & Hooks, T. (Eds.). (1998). *The healing connection: Women in relationships in therapy and life.* Boston: Beacon.

Miller, W., & Thoresen, C. (2003). Spirituality, religion, and health: An emerging research field. *American Psychologist, 58,* 24–35.

Minuchin, S. (1974). *Families and family therapy.* Cambridge, MA: Harvard University Press.

Minuchin, S., & Fishman, H. C. (1981). *Family therapy techniques.* Cambridge, MA: Harvard University Press.

Minuchin, S., & Nichols, M. P. (1993). *Family healing: Tales of hope and renewal from family therapy.* New York: Free Press.

Mitchell, K., Bozarth, J., & Krauft, C. (1977). A reappraisal of the therapeutic effectiveness of accurate empathy, nonpossessive warmth and genuineness. In A. Gurman & A. Razin (Eds.), *Effective psychotherapy* (pp. 482–502). Elmsford, NY: Pergamon.

Montgomery, M., & Kottler, J. (2005). The developing counselor. In D. Comstock (Ed.), *Diversity and development: Critical contexts that shape our lives and relationship* (pp. 91–110). Belmont, CA: Brooks/Cole–Thomson Learning.

Moodley, R., & West, W. (Eds.). (2005). *Integrating traditional healing practices into counseling and psychotherapy.* Thousand Oaks, CA: Sage.

Morris, L. A. (1997). *The male heterosexual.* Thousand Oaks, CA: Sage.

Mosak, H. H. (1989). Adlerian psychotherapy. In R. J. Corsini & D. Wedding (Eds.), *Current psychotherapies* (4th ed.) (pp. 65–116). Itasca, IL: F. E. Peacock.

Mosak, H. H., & Goldman, S. E. (1995). An alternative view of the purpose of psychosis. *Individual Psychology: Journal of Adlerian Theory, Research, and Practice, 51,* 46–49.

Murray, V. M., & Brody, G. H. (2004). Partnering with community stakeholders: Engaging rural African American families in basic research and the Strong African American Families Preventive Intervention Program. *Journal of Marital and Family Therapy, 30*(3), 271–284.

Myers, J. E. (1998). Bibliotherapy and DCT: Coconstructing the therapeutic metaphor. *Journal of Counseling and Development, 76,* 243–250.

Myers, J. E., & Sweeney, T. J. (2005a) The indivisible self: An evidence-based model of wellness. *Journal of Individual Psychology, 61*(3), 269–279.

Myers, J. E., & Sweeney, T. J. (Eds.). (2005b). *Counseling for wellness: Theory, research, and practice.* Alexandria, VA: American Counseling Association.

Myers, J. E., Sweeney, T. J., & Witmer, J. M. (2000). Counseling for wellness: A holistic model for treatment planning. *Journal of Counseling and Development, 78,* 251–266.

Myers, L. (1988). *Understanding an Afrocentric world view: Introduction to an optimal psychology.* Dubuque, IA: Kendall/Hunt.

Myers, L. (1992). Transpersonal psychology: The role of the Afrocentric paradigm.

Myers, L., Speight, S., Highlen, P., Cox, C., Reynolds, A., Adams, E., & Hanley, P. (1991). Identity development and worldview: Toward an optimal conceptualization. *Journal of Counseling and Development, 54,* 54–55.

Nakayama, T. K., & Martin, J. (Eds.). (1999). *Whiteness: The communication of social identity.* Thousand Oaks, CA: Sage.

Napier, A. Y. (1977). Follow-up to divorce labyrinth. In P. Papp (Ed.), *Family therapy: Full-length case studies.* New York: Gardner Press.

Napier, A. Y., & Whitaker, C. A. (1972). *The family crucible.* New York: Harper & Row.

National Child Abuse and Neglect Data System (NCANDS). (2000). *Child maltreatment: Victimization rates.* [Online] http://www.acf.dhhs.gov/programs/cb/stats/ncands.

National Institute of Mental Health. (2000). *Panic disorder: A real illness.* Publication No. 00–4679. Bethesda, MD: Author.

Neimeyer, G., & Neimeyer, R. A. (1994, January 11). Constructivist methods of marital and family therapy: A practical precis. *Journal of Mental Health Counseling,* pp. 85–104.

Nobles, W. W. (1997). African American family life: An instrument of culture. In H. P. McAdoo (Ed.), *Black families* (3rd ed.) (pp. 83–93). Thousand Oaks, CA: Sage.

Nobles, W. W. (1998). To be African or not to be: The question of identity or authenticity—Some preliminary thoughts. In R. L. Jones (Ed.), *African American identity development* (pp. 32–49). Hampton, VA: Cobb & Henry.

Nugent, F. A. (2000). *Introduction to the counseling profession* (3rd ed.). Upper Saddle River, NJ: Merrill.

Nwachuku, U. (1989). *Culture-specific counseling: The Igbo case.* Unpublished doctoral dissertation, University of Massachusetts, Amherst.

Nwachuku, U. (1990, July). *Translating multicultural theory into direct action: Culture-specific counseling.* Paper presented at the International Roundtable for the Advancement of Counseling, Helsinki, Finland.

Nwachuku, U., & Ivey, A. (1991). Culture specific counseling: An alternative approach. *Journal of Counseling and Development, 70,* 106–111.

O'Hanlon, W., & Weiner-Davis, M. (1989). *In search of solutions.* New York: Norton.

Obasi, E. M. (2002). Reconceptualizing the notion of self from the African deep structure. In T. Parham (Ed.), *Counseling persons of African descent: Raising the bar of practitioner competence.* (pp. 52–74). Thousand Oaks, CA: Sage.

Obholzer, K. (1982). *The Wolf-Man: Sixty years later: Conversations with Freud's controversial patient.* New York: Continuum.

Oetting, E. (1992). Planning programs for prevention of deviant behavior: A psychosocial model. In J. Trimble, C. Bolek, & S. Niemcryk (Eds.), *Ethnic and multicultural drug abuse: Perspectives on current research* (pp. 211–28). New York: Harworth.

Ogbonnaya, O. (1994). Person as community: An African understanding of the person as an intrapsychic community. *Journal of Black Psychology, 20,* 75–87.

Okonji, J. (1995). Counseling style preference and perception of counselors by African American male students. *Dissertation Abstracts,* B 55/09, 3811.

Okun, B. (1992). Object relations and self-psychology: Overview and feminist perspective. In L. Brown & M. Ballou (Eds.), *Theories of personality and psychopathology: Feminist reappraisals* (pp. 20–45). New York: Guilford.

Okun, B. (1996). *Understanding diverse families.* New York: Guilford.

Olson, M. (Ed.). (2002). *Feminism, community, and communication.* New York: Hawthorn.

Ornish, D. (1990). *Dr. Dean Ornish's program for reversing heart disease.* New York: Ballantine.

Ortiz, V. (1978). *Let me speak! Testimony of Domitila, a woman of the Bolivian mines.* New York: Monthly Review Press.

Ozechowski, T., & Liddle, H. A. (2000). Family-based therapy for adolescent drug abuse: Knowns and unknowns. *Clinical Child and Family Psychology Review, 3*(4), 269–298.

Paivio, S., & Greenberg, L. (1995). Resolving "unfinished business": Efficacy of experiential therapy using empty-chair dialogue. *Journal of Consulting and Clinical Psychology, 73,* 419–25.

Paniagua, F. A. (2001). *Diagnosis in multicultural context.* Thousand Oaks, CA: Sage.

Paniagua, F. A. (2005). *Assessing and treating culturally diverse clients: A practical guide* (3rd ed.). Thousand Oaks, CA: Sage.

Parham, T. (1989). Cycles of psychological Nigrescense. *Counseling Psychologist, 17*(2), 187–226.

Parham, T. (Ed.). (2002). *Counseling persons of African descent: Raising the bar of practitioner competence* (pp. 52–74). Thousand Oaks, CA: Sage.

Parham, T. A., & Parham, W. D. (2002). Understanding African American mental health. In T. A. Parham, *Counseling persons of African descent* (pp. 25–51). Thousand Oaks, CA: Sage.

Parham, T. A., Daniels, J., & D'Andrea, M. (2006). *Promoting optimal health from an African-centered perspective.* [Video]. Honolulu: Department of Counselor Education, University of Hawaii.

Parham, T. A., White, J. L., & Ajamu, A. (1999). *The psychology of Blacks: An African centered perspective* (3rd ed.). Upper Saddle River, NJ: Prentice Hall.

Parkes, C. M., Stevenson-Hinde, J., & Morris, P. (Eds.). (1991). *Attachment across the life cycle.* New York: Routledge.

Parsons, F. (1967). *Choosing a vocation.* New York: Agathon. (Original work published 1909.)

Patterson, C. H. (1999). Outcomes in counselor education. *Asian Journal of Counseling, 2,* 81–07.

Paul, G. (1967). Strategy of outcome research in psychotherapy. *Journal of Consulting Psychology, 31,* 109–118.

Pavlov, I. P. (1927). *Conditioned reflexes.* (G. V. Anrep, Trans.). London: Oxford University Press.

Pedersen, C., & Seligman, M. (2004). *Character, strengths, and virtues: A handbook and classification.* Oxford: Oxford University Press.

Pedersen, P. B. (Ed.). (1991). Multiculturalism as a fourth force in counseling. *Journal of Counseling and Development, 70* [special issue].

Pedersen, P. B., & Carey, J. C. (2003). *Multicultural counseling in schools: A practical handbook.* Needham Heights, MA: Allyn and Bacon.

Pedersen, P. B., Draguns, J. G., Lonner, W. J., & Trimble, J. E. (Eds.). (2002). *Counseling across cultures* (5th ed.). Thousand Oaks, CA: Sage.

Pedersen, P., & Ivey, A. (1993). *Culture-centered counseling.* New York: Greenwood.

Pedersen, P., & Marsella, T. (1982). The ethical crisis for cross-cultural counseling and therapy. *Professional Psychology, 13,* 492–500.

Peluso, P. R., Pelsuo, J. P., White, J. F., & Kern, R. M. (2004). A comparison of attachment theory and individual psychology: A review of the literature. *Journal of Counseling and Development, 82,* 139–145.

Perls, F. S. (1969). *Gestalt therapy verbatim.* Moab, UT: Real People Press.

Perls, F. S. (1992a). *Gestalt therapy verbatim* (rev. ed.). San Francisco: Gestalt Journal Press.

Perls, F. S. (1992b). *In and out of the garbage pail* (reprint ed.). San Francisco: Gestalt Journal Press.

Perls, F. S., Hefferline, R., & Goodman, P. (1951). *Gestalt therapy: Excitement and growth in human personality.* New York: Dell.

Peterson, C., & Seligman, M. E. P. (2004). *Character strengths and virtues: A handbook and classification.* New York: Oxford University Press.

Phelps, S. (1987). *The assertive woman.* San Luis Obispo, CA: Impact.

Piaget, J. (1963). *The origins of intelligence in children.* New York: Norton. (Originally published 1926.)

Piaget, J. (1965). *The moral judgment of the child.* New York: Free Press.

Piaget, J. (1985). *The equilibration of cognitive structures.* Chicago: University of Chicago Press.

Pinsof, W. (1994). An overview of integrative problem-centered therapy: A synthesis of family and individual psychotherapies. *Journal of Family Therapy, 16,* 103–120.

Pinsof, W., Wynne, L., & Hambright, A. (1996). The outcomes of couples and family therapy: Findings, conclusions, and recommendations. *Psychotherapy, 33,* 321–31.

Ponterotto, J., & Casas, M. (1991). *Handbook of racial/ethnic minority counseling research.* Springfield, IL: Thomas.

Ponterotto, J. G., & Pedersen, P. B. (1993). *Preventing prejudice: A guide for counselors and educators.* Newbury Park, CA: Sage.

Ponterotto, J. G., Casas, J. M., Suzuki, L. A., & Alexander, C. M. (Eds.). (2001). *Handbook of multicultural counseling.* Thousand Oaks, CA: Sage.

Ponterotto, J. G., Utsey, S. O., & Pedersen, P. B. (2006). *Preventing prejudice: A guide for counselors, educators, and parents* (2nd ed.). Thousand Oaks, CA: Sage.

Pope-Davis, D. B., Coleman, H. L. K., Liu, W., & Toporek, R. L. (2003). *Handbook of multicultural competencies in counseling and psychology.* Thousand Oaks, CA: Sage.

Powell, L. Shahabi, L., & Thoresen, C. (2003). Religion and spirituality: Linkages to mental health. *American Psychologist, 58,* 36–52.

Prince, S. E., & Jacobson, N. S. (1995). A review and evaluation of marital and family therapies for affective disorders. *Journal of Marital and Family Therapy, 21,* 377–401.

Ram Dass, Baba. (1971). *Be here now.* New York: Crown.

Rape, Abuse, and Incest National Network (2000). *RAINN statistics: A national shame.* [Online] http://www.rainn.org/stats.html.

Rawlings, E. I., & Carter, D. K. (Eds.). (1977). *Psychotherapy for women: Treatment toward equality.* Springfield, IL: Thomas.

Reed, H. J. (1964). Guidance and counseling. *Journal of Negro Education, 33,* 282–289.

Reicherzer, S. (2005). Coming out and living out across the lifespan. In D. Comstock (Ed.), *Diversity and development: Critical contexts that shape our lives and relationships* (pp. 161–184). Belmont, CA: Brooks/Cole–Thomson Learning.

Reynolds, D. (1990). Morita and Naikan therapies—Similarities. *Journal of Morita Therapy, 1,* 159–63.

Ridley, C. R. (1995). *Overcoming unintentional racism in counseling and therapy: A practi-*

tioner's guide to intentional intervention. Thousand Oaks, CA: Sage.

Rigazio-DiGilio, S. A. (1989). *Developmental theory and therapy: A preliminary investigation of reliability and predictive validity using an inpatient depressive population sample.* Unpublished doctoral dissertation, University of Massachusetts, Amherst.

Rigazio-DiGilio, S. A. (1994). A coconstructive-developmental integration of treatment for individuals, families, and networks. *Journal of Mental Health Counseling, 16,* 43–73.

Rigazio-DiGilio, S. A. (1997). From microscopes to holographs: Client development within a constructivist paradigm. In T. Sexton & B. Griffin (Eds.), *Constructivist thinking in counseling practice, research, and training* (pp. 74–100). New York: Teachers College Press.

Rigazio-DiGilio, S. A. (2000). Reconstructing psychological distress and disorder from a relational perspective: A systemic coconstructive-developmental framework. In R. Neimeyer & J. Raskin (Eds.), *Constructions of disorder* (pp. 309–32). Washington, DC: American Psychological Association.

Rigazio-DiGilio, S. A. (2001). Postmodern theories of counseling. In D.C. Locke, J. E. Myers, & E. L. Herr (Eds.), *The handbook of counseling* (pp. 219–236). Thousand Oaks, CA: Sage.

Rigazio-DiGilio, S. A., & Ivey, A. (1990). Developmental therapy and depressive disorders: Measuring cognitive levels through patient natural language. *Professional Psychology: Research and Practice, 21,* 470–75.

Rigazio-DiGilio, S. A., Gonçalves, O. F., & Ivey, A. E. (1996). From cultural to existential diversity: The impossibility of an integrative psychotherapy within a traditional framework. *Applied and Preventative Psychology: Current Scientific Perspectives, 5,* 235–48.

Rigazio-DiGilio, S. A., Ivey, A. E., & Locke, D.C. (1997). Continuing the postmodern dialogue: Enhancing and contextualizing multiple voices. *Journal of Mental Health Counseling, 19,* 233–55.

Rigazio-DiGilio, S., Ellis, A., D'Andrea, M., Ivey, A. E., & Gutterman, J. (1999, April). *Counseling in the postmodern era.* Paper presented at the annual meeting of the American Counseling Association, San Diego, CA.

Rigazio-DiGilio, S., Ivey, A., Kunkler, K., & Grady, L. (2005). *Community genograms: Using individual, family and cultural narratives with clients.* New York: Teacher's College Press.

Rigney, M. (1981, April). *A critique of Maslow's self-actualization theory: The "highest good" for the Aboriginal is relationship* [Videotape]. Aboriginal Open College, Adelaide, Australia.

Robb, C. (2006). *This changes everything: The relational revolution in psychology.* New York: Farrar, Straus, & Giroux.

Robbins, M. S., Alexander, J. F., & Turner, C. W. (2000). Disrupting defensive family interactions in family therapy with delinquent adolescents. *Journal of Family Psychology, 14*(4), 688–701.

Roberts, W. (1982). *Black and White managers in helping: Interaction effects of managers in responding to culturally varied subordinate vignettes.* Unpublished doctoral dissertation, University of Massachusetts, Amherst.

Robinson, T. L., & Howard-Hamilton, M. F. (2000). *The convergence of race, ethnicity, and gender: Multiple identities in counseling.* Upper Saddle River, NJ: Prentice Hall.

Rogers calls peace results "surprising." (1984, November). *APA Monitor,* p. 15.

Rogers, C. (1957). The necessary and sufficient conditions of therapeutic personality change. *Journal of Consulting Psychology, 21,* 95–103.

Rogers, C. (1961). *On becoming a person.* Boston: Houghton Mifflin.

Rogers, C. (1969). *Freedom to learn.* Columbus, OH: Merrill.

Rogers, C. (1970). *On encounter groups.* New York: HarperCollins.

Rogers, C. (1972). *Becoming partners.* New York: Delta.

Rogers, C. (1977). *On personal power.* New York: Delacourt.

Rogers, C. (1995). *On becoming a person: A therapist's view of psychotherapy.* Boston: Houghton Mifflin.

Rogers, C., & Wallen, J. (1946). *Counseling with returned servicemen.* New York: McGraw-Hill.

Rogers, C., Gendlin, G., Kiesler, D., & Truax, C. (1967). *The therapeutic relationship and its impact: A study of psychotherapy with schizophrenics.* Madison: University of Wisconsin Press.

Rohner, R. P. (in press). The parental acceptance-rejection syndrome: Universal correlates of perceived rejection. *American Psychologist.*

Rojano, R. (2004). The practice of community family therapy. *Family Process, 43*(1), 59–78.

Romney, P. (2000). Can you love them enough? Organizational consulting as a spiriatual quest. In M. Olson (Ed.), *Feminism, community, and communication* (pp. 65–82). New York: Hawthorn.

Root, B. A. (2000). *Understanding panic and other anxiety disorders.* Jackson, MS: University Press of Mississippi.

Rosenthal, P., & Rosenthal, S. (1980). Holocaust effect in the third generation. *American Journal of Psychotherapy, 34,* 572–579.

Rosenthall, R. (1990). How are we doing in soft psychology? *American Psychologist, 45,* 775–76.

Rueveni, U. (1979). *Networking families in crisis.* New York: Human Services Press.

Rychlak, J. F. (1973). *Introduction to personality and psychotherapy: A theory construction approach.* Boston: Houghton Mifflin.

Salzman, M. (2001). Cultural trauma and recovery: Perspectives from terror management theory. *Trauma, Violence, & Abuse, 2,* 172–191.

Sampson, J. (1990). Psychology in the modern world. *American Psychologist, 79,* 1225–29.

Sanders, M. R., Markie-Dadds, C., Tully, L. A., & Bor, W. (2000). The Triple P-Positive Parenting Program: A comparison of enhanced, standard, and self-directed behavioral family intervention for parents of children with early onset of conduct problems. *Journal of Consulting and Clinical Psychology, 68*(4), 624–640.

Sartre, J. (1946). *No exit.* New York: Knopf.

Sartre, J. (1956). *Being and nothingness.* London: Methuen.

Satir, V. (1964) *Conjoint family therapy.* Palo Alto, CA: Science and Behavior Books.

Sayers, J. (1995). Consuming male fantasy: Feminist psychoanalysis retold. In A. Elliott & S.

Frosh (Eds.), *Psychoanalysis in contexts.* New York: Routledge & Kegan Paul.

Scheurich, J. J. (1993). Toward a discourse on white racism. *Educational Researcher, 22,* 5–10.

Scheurich, J. J., & Young, M. D. (1997). Coloring epistemologies: Are our research epistemologies racially biased? *Educational Researcher, 26,* 4–16.

Schmidt, N. B., & Woolaway-Bickel, K. (2000). The effects of treatment compliance on outcome in cognitive-behavioral therapy for panic disorder: Quality versus quantity. *Journal of Consulting and Clinical Psychology, 68,* 13–18.

Scholz, M., & Asen, E. (2001). Multiple family therapy with eating disordered adolescents: Concepts and preliminary results. *European Eating Disorders Review, 9,* 33–42.

Schwartz, M. S., & Andrasik, F. (1998). *Biofeedback: A practitioner's guide.* New York: Guilford.

Schwartz, S. E. (1999). Jungian analytical theory. In D. Capuzzi & D. R. Gross (Eds.), *Counseling and psychotherapy: Theories and interventions* (2nd ed.) (pp. 91–112). Upper Saddle River, NJ: Merrill.

Scorzelli, J., & Reineke-Scorzelli, M. (1994). Cultural sensitivity and cognitive therapy in India. *Counseling Psychologist, 22,* 603–610.

Seligman, L. (2001). *Systems, strategies, and skills of counseling and psychotherapy.* Upper Saddle River, NJ: Merrill–Prentice Hall.

Seligman, M. E. P. (2002a). *Authentic happiness: Using the new positive psychology to realize your potential for lasting fulfillment.* New York: Free Press.

Seligman, M. E. P. (2002b). *Positive psychology.* Washington, DC: American Psychological Association. Available online at http://www.apa.org/releases/positivepsy.html

Seligman, M. E. P., & Csikszentmihalyi, M. (2000). Positive psychology: An introduction. *American Psychologist, 55,* 5–14.

Sexton, S. B., Glanville, D. N., & Kaslow, N. J. (2001). Attachment and depression: Implications for family therapy. *Child and Adolescent Psychiatric Clinics of North America, 10*(3), 465–486.

Sexton, T. L., & Griffin, B. L. (Eds.). (1997). *Constructivist thinking in counseling, practice, research, and training.* New York: Teachers College Press.

Shadish, W. R., Ragsdale, K., Glaser, R. R., & Montgomery, L. M. (1995). The efficacy and effectiveness of marital and family therapy: A perspective from meta-analysis. *Journal of Marital and Family Therapy, 21,* 345–60.

Shaull, R. (1970). Foreword. In P. Freire, *Pedagogy of the oppressed.* New York: Continuum.

Shea, M., Elkin, I., Imber, S., Stosky, S., Watkins, J., Collins, J., Pilkonis, P., Leber, W., Krupnick, J., Donan, R., & Parloff, M. (1990). *Course of depressive symptoms over follow-up: Findings from the National Institute of Mental Health Treatment of Depression Collaborative Research Program.* Manuscript submitted for publication, cited in A. Beck, Cognitive therapy: A 30-year retrospective. *American Psychologist,* 1991, *46,* 368–375.

Shostrum, E. (Prod.). (1965). *Three approaches to psychotherapy* [Film]. Santa Ana, CA: Psychological Films.

Shulman, B. H. (1973). *Contributions to individual psychology.* Chicago: Alfred Adler Institute.

Simon, G. M. (1995). A revisionist rendering of structural family therapy. *Journal of Marital and Family Therapy, 21,* 17–26.

Simoneau, T. L., Milkowitz, D. J., Richards, J. A., Saleem, R., & George, E. I. (1999). Bipolar disorder and family communication: Effects of a psychoeducational treatment program. *Journal of Abnormal Psychology, 108*(4), 588–597.

Simpkins, C. A., & Simpkins, A. (1999). *Simple Taoism: A guide to living in balance.* Boston: Tuttle.

Skinner, B. F. (1953). *Science and human behavior.* New York: Free Press.

Skinner, B. F. (1969). *Contingencies of reinforcement: A theoretical analysis.* New York: Appleton-Century-Crofts.

Sklare, G. (2004). *Brief counseling that works: A solution-focused approach for school counselors and administrators.* Beverly Hills, CA: Corwin.

Skolnick, A., & Skolnick, J. (Eds.). (1994). *Family in transition.* New York: HarperCollins.

Sloane, R., & Staples, F. (1984). Psychotherapy versus behavior therapy: Implications for future psychotherapy research. In J. Williams & R. Spitzer (Eds.), *Psychotherapy research: Where are we and where should we go?* (pp. 203–15). New York: Guilford.

Sloane, R., Staples, F., Cristol, A., Yorkston, N., & Whipple, K. (1975). *Psychotherapy versus behavior therapy.* Cambridge, MA: Harvard University Press.

Smith, D. P. (2005). The sweat lodge as psychotherapy: Congruence between traditional and modern healing. In R. Moodley & W. West (Eds.), *Integrating traditional healing practices into counseling and psychotherapy* (pp. 196–209). Thousand Oaks, CA: Sage.

Snyder, C., & Lopez, S. (2001). *Handbook of positive psychology.* Oxford: Oxford University Press.

Solyom, L., Garza-Perez, J., Ledwidge, B. L., & Solyom, C. (1972). Paradoxical intention in the treatment of obsessive thoughts: A pilot study. *Comprehensive Psychiatry, 13* (3), 291–297.

Speck, R. V., & Attneave, C. L. (1973). *Family networks.* New York: Pantheon.

Speck, R., & Attneave, C. (1973). *Family process.* New York: Pantheon.

Sprinthall, N. A., Peace, S. D., & Kennington, P. A. D. (2001). Cognitive-developmental stage theories for counseling. In D.C. Locke, J. E. Myers, & E. L. Herr (Eds.), *The handbook of counseling* (pp. 109–130). Thousand Oaks, CA: Sage.

Stevens-Smith, P. (1998). Maintaining behavior change: Relapse prevention strategies. In P. Stevens-Smith & R. L. Smith (Eds.), *Substance abuse counseling: Theory and practice* (pp. 1–24). Upper Saddle River, NJ: Merrill/Prentice Hall.

Stewart, K. (1951). Dream theory in Malaya. *Complex, 6,* 21–34.

Stiver, I. (1991). The meanings of "dependency" in female-male relationships. In J. Jordan, A. Kaplan, J. Baker Miller, I. Stiver, & J. Surry (Eds.), *Women's growth in connection* (pp. 143–161). New York: Guilford.

Strehorn, K. (1998). *Examining services to post-secondary students with learning disabilities through the use of Ivey's developmental counseling and therapy (DCT) model.* Unpublished dissertation, University of Massachusetts, Amherst.

Strong, S., & Schmidt, L. (1970). Expertness and influence in counseling. *Journal of Counseling Psychology, 17,* 81–87.

Strupp, H. (1977). A reformulation of the dynamics of the therapist's contribution. In A. Gurman & A. Razin (Eds.), *Effective psychotherapy* (pp. 1–22). Elmsford, NY: Pergamon.

Strupp, H. (1989). Psychotherapy: Can the practitioner learn from the researcher? *American Psychologist, 44,* 717–24.

Strupp, H. H. (1993). The Vanderbilt psychotherapy studies: Synopsis. *Journal of Consulting and Clinical Psychology, 61,* 431–33.

Strupp, H., & Hadley, S. (1976). Contemporary view on negative effects in psychotherapy. *Archives of General Psychiatry, 33,* 1291–1302.

Strupp, H., & Hadley, S. W. (1979). Specific versus nonspecific factors in psychotherapy: A controlled study of outcome. *Archives of General Psychiatry, 36,* 1125–1136.

Strupp, H. H., Horowitz, L. M., & Lambert, M. J. (Eds.). (1997). *Measuring patient changes in mood, anxiety, and personality disorders.* Washington, DC: American Psychological Association.

Stuart, G. L., Treat, T. A., & Wade, W. A. (2000). Effectiveness of an empirically based treatment for panic disorder delivered in a service clinic setting: One-year follow-up. *Journal of Consulting and Clinical Psychology, 68,* 506–512.

Sue, D. (1990). Culture-specific strategies in counseling: A conceptual framework. *Professional Psychology, 21,* 424–33.

Sue, D. W. (1995). Toward a theory of multicultural counseling and therapy. In J. Banks & C. Banks (Eds.), *Handbook of research on multicultural education* (pp. 5–29). New York: Macmillan.

Sue, D. W., & Sue, D. R. (1990). *Counseling the culturally different* (2nd ed.). New York: Wiley.

Sue, D. W., & Sue, D. R. (1999). *Counseling the culturally different: Theory and practice* (3rd ed.). New York: Wiley.

Sue, D. W., & Sue, D. R. (2003). *Counseling the culturally diverse: Theory and practice* (4th ed.). New York: Wiley.

Sue, D. W., Arredondo, P., & McDavis, R. J. (1992). Multicultural counseling competencies and standards: A call to the profession. *Journal of Counseling and Development, 70,* 477–86.

Sue, D. W., Carter, R. T., Casas, J. M., Fouad, N. A., Ivey, A. E., Jensen, M., LaFromboise, T., Manese, J. E., Ponterotto, J. G., & Vasquez-Nuttal, E. (1998). *Multicultural counseling competencies: Individual and organizational development.* Thousand Oaks, CA: Sage.

Sue, D. W., Ivey, A., & Pedersen, P. (1996). *A theory of multicultural counseling and therapy.* Pacific Grove, CA: Brooks/Cole.

Sue, D. W., Ivey, A. E., & Pedersen, P. B. (1997). *A theory of multicultural counseling and therapy.* Pacific Grove, CA: Brooks/Cole.

Sue, D. W., Ivey, A. E., & Pedersen, P. B. (Eds.). (1996). *A theory of multicultural counseling and therapy.* Pacific Grove, CA: Brooks/Cole.

Sue, S. (1988). Psychotherapeutic services for ethnic minorities: Two decades of research findings. *American Psychologist, 43,* 301–8.

Sue, S., & Zane, N. (1987). The role of culture and cultural techniques in psychotherapy: A reformation. *American Psychologist, 42,* 37–45.

Sullivan, H. S. (1953). *The interpersonal theory of psychiatry.* New York: Norton.

Sweeney, T. J. (1989). *Adlerian counseling: A practical approach for a new decade* (3rd ed.). Muncie, IN: Accelerated Development.

Sweeney, T. J., & Myers, J. (2005). Optimizing human development over the lifespan: A new paradigm for helping. In A. E. Ivey, M. B. Ivey, J. Myers, & T. Sweeney (Eds.), *Developmental strategies for helpers* (2nd ed.) (pp. 39–68). Amherst, MA: Microtraining.

Sweeney, T. J., & Witmer, J. M. (1991). Beyond social interest: Striving toward optimum health and wellness. *Individual Psychology, 47,* 527–540.

Tamase, K. (1989). Introspective developmental counseling. *Bulletin of Nara University of Education, 38,* 161–77.

Tamase, K. (1991, April). *The effects of introspective-developmental counseling*. Paper presented at the American Association of Counseling and Development, Reno, Nevada.

Tamase, K. (1998). *Kaunselingu gihou nyumon* (Introduction to counseling skills). Tokyo: Kyoiku-Shuppan.

Tamase, K., & Hirano, K. (1997). The effect of restriction of preliminary remarks prior to open question upon response contents. *Bulletin of the Institute of Educational Research at Nara University of Education, 36*, 275–87. (In Japanese with English abstract.)

Tamase, K., & Inui, S. (2000). The effect of counselor's directivity on advice acceptability rating. *Bulletin of the Institute for Educational Research at Nara University of Education, 46*, 77–85.

Tamase, K., & Kato M. (1990). Effect of questions about factual and affective aspects of life events in an introspective interview. *Bulletin of Nara University of Education, 24*, 153–63.

Tamase, K., & Rigazio-DiGilio, S. A. (1997). Expanding client worldviews: Investigating developmental counseling and therapy assumptions. *Journal for the Advancement of Counseling, 19*, 229–47.

Taub-Bynum, E. B. (1980). The use of dreams in family therapy. *Psychotherapy: Theory, Research, and Practice, 17*, 227–31.

Taub-Bynum, E. B. (1984). *The family unconscious*. Wheaton, IL: Quest.

Taub-Bynum, E. B. (1992). *Family dreams: The intricate web*. Ithaca, NY: Haworth Press.

Taub-Bynum, E. B. (1999). *The African unconscious: Roots of ancient mysticism and modern psychology*. New York: Teachers College Press.

Taylor, S. E. (2002). *The tending instinct: How nurturing is essential to who we are and how we live*. New York: Times Books.

Thomas, C. (1971). *Boys no more*. Beverly Hills, CA: Glencoe.

Tillich, P. (1961). Existentialism and psychotherapy. *Review of Existential Psychology and Psychiatry, 1*, 8–16.

Toporek, R. L., Gerstein, L. H., Fouad, N. A., Roysircar, G., & Israel, T. (2006). *Handbook for social justice counseling in counseling psychology: Leadership, vision, and action*. Thousand Oaks, CA: Sage.

Trepper, T., & Barrett, M. (1989). *Systemic treatment of incest: A therapeutic handbook*. New York: Brunner/ Mazel.

Tyler, L. (1961). *The work of the counselor* (2nd ed.). East Norwalk, CT: Appleton & Lange.

U.S. Department of Health and Human Services (DHHS), Surgeon General's Report. (2001). *Mental health: Culture, race, and ethnicity*. Washington, DC: U.S. Government Printing Office.

Van Pelt, I. (1993). Logotherapy: Mission for the future. *International Forum for Logotherapy, 16*, 105–8.

Van Pelt, I. (1995). Spirituality and logotherapy. Personal communication, Amherst, MA.

Van Pelt, I. (2000, October). *Logotherapy, headaches, and psychological practice*. Paper presented to the Mental Health Center, University of Massachusetts.

Vazquez, L., Santiago-Rivera, A., & Orjuela, E. (2000). *Innovative approaches to counseling Latina/o people* [Video]. (Available from Microtraining Associates, Inc., Box 9641, North Amherst, MA 01059–9641.)

von Bertalanffy, L. (1968). *General systems theory*. New York: Braziller.

Vontress, C. (1979). Cross-cultural counseling: An existential approach. *Personnel and Guidance Journal, 58*, 117–22.

Vontress, C. (1986). Social and cultural foundations. In M. Lewis, R. Hayes, & J. Lewis (Eds.), *An introduction to the counseling profession*. Itasca, IL: Peacock.

Vontress, C. (1995a). Existentialism: My view. Personal communication, George Washington University.

Vontress, C. (1995b). The breakdown of authority: Implications for counseling young African-American males. In J. Ponterotto, J. Casas, L. Suzuki, & C. Alexander (Eds.), *Handbook of multicultural counseling* (Vol. 1). Thousand Oaks, CA: Sage.

Vontress, C. (1995c). The philosophical foundations of the existential-humanistic perspective: A personal statement. Washington, DC: George Washington University.

Vontress, C. E. (1969). Counseling the culturally different in our society. *Journal of Employment Counseling, 6,* 9–16.

Vontress, C. E. (1971). *Counseling Negroes: Series 6. Minority groups and guidance.* Boston: Houghton Mifflin.

Vontress, C. E., Johnson, J. A., & Epp, L. R. (1999). *Cross-cultural counseling: A casebook.* Alexandria, VA: American Counseling Association.

Walker, J. B., Johnson, S., Manion, I., & Cloutier, P. (1996). Emotionally focused marital intervention for couples with chronically ill children. *Journal of Consulting and Clinical Psychology, 64,* 1029–36.

Wallace, R., D'Andrea, M., & Daniels, J. (2001). *The rainbow circle of excellence: Lessons from a championship season.* Honolulu, HI: Watermark.

Wallerstein, R. (1989). The psychotherapy research project of the Menninger Foundation: An overview. *Journal of Consulting and Clinical Psychology, 57,* 195–205.

Walsh, F. (2002). Normal family processes (3rd ed.). New York: Guilford.

Wampold, B. E., Lichenberg, J. W., & Waehler, C. A. (2002). Principles of empirically supported interventions in counseling psychology. *Counseling Psychologist, 30,* 197–217.

Waters, E., Merrick, S., Treboux, D., Crowell, J., & Albersheim, L. (2000). Attachment security in infancy and early adulthood: A 20-year longitudinal study. *Child Development, 71,* 211–18.

Watson, D., Clarke, L. A., & Tellegen, A. (1988). Development and validation of brief measures of positive and negative affect: The PANAS scales. *Journal of Personality and Social Psychology, 54,* 1063–1070.

Watson, J. B. (1925). *Behaviorism.* New York: Norton.

Watzlawick, P., Beavin, J., & Jackson, D. (1967). *Pragmatics of human communication.* New York: Norton.

Wehrly, B., Kenney, K. R., & Kenney, M. E. (1999). *Counseling multiracial families.* Thousand Oaks, CA: Sage.

Weiner, N. (1948) *Cybernectics or control and communication in the animal and machine.* Cambridge, MA: Technology Press.

Weinrach, S. (1990a). Anecdotes. In D. DiMattia & L. Lega (Eds.), *Will the real Albert Ellis please stand up?* (pp. 42–43, 108–109, 124–125). New York: Institute for Rational Emotive Therapy.

Weinrach, S. (1990b). Rogers and Gloria: The controversial film and the enduring relationship. *Psychotherapy, 27,* 282–290.

Weinstein, T. (1994). *The application of developmental counseling and therapy (DCT) theory to group treatment of binge eating and weight management.* Unpublished doctoral dissertation, University of Massachusetts, Amherst.

Welsing, F. C. (1991). *The Isis papers: The key to the colors.* Chicago: Third World Press.

West, C. (1999). *The Cornel West reader.* New York: Basic Books.

Whitaker, C. A. (1967). The growing edge. In J. Haley & L. Hoffman (Eds.), *Techniques of family therapy.* New York: Basic Books.

Whitaker, C. A., & Bumberry, W. M. (1988). *Dancing with the family: A symbolic experiential approach.* New York: Brunner/Mazel.

White, M., & Epston, D. (1992). *Narrative means to therapeutic ends.* New York: Norton.

Williams, R. J., & Chang, S. Y. (2000). A comprehensive and comparative review of adolescent substance abuse treatment outcome. *Clinical Psychology: Science and Practice, 7,* 138–166.

Winnicott, D. (1988). *Human nature.* New York: Schocken.

Witmer, J. M. (1985). *Pathways to personal growth.* Muncie, IN: Accelerated Development.

Witmer, J. M., & Sweeney, T. J. (1992). Wellness throughout the life span. *Journal of Counseling and Development, 71*(2), 140–148.

Wolfe, B. E., & Maser, J. D. (1994). *Treatment of panic disorder: A consensus development conference.* Washington, DC: American Psychiatric Press.

Wolpe, J. (1958). *Psychotherapy by reciprocal inhibition.* Stanford, CA: Stanford University Press.

Wolpe, J. (1982). *The practice of behavior therapy* (3rd ed.). New York: Pergamon.

Wolpe, J., & Lazarus, A. (1966). *Behavior therapy techniques.* Elmsford, NY: Pergamon.

Wong, P. T. P., & Fry, P. (1998). *The human quest for meaning: A handbook of psychological research and clinical applications.* Mahwah, NJ: Lawrence Erlbaum.

Wood, B. L. (1995). A developmental biopsychosocial approach to the treatment of chronic illness in children and adolescents. In R. Mikesell, D. D. Lusterman, & S. McDaniel (Eds.), *Integrating family therapy* (pp. 37–55). Washington, DC: American Psychological Association.

Woolfolk, R., & Richardson, F. (1984). Behavior therapy and the ideology of modernity. *American Psychologist, 39,* 777–86.

Worrell, J., & Remer, P. (2003). *Feminist perspectives in therapy: Empowering diverse women* (2nd ed.). Hoboken, NJ: Wiley.

Wubbolding, R. E., Brickell, J., Imhof, L., Kim, R. I., Lojk, L., & Al-Rashidi, B. (2004). Reality therapy: A global perspective. *International Journal for the Advancement of Counseling, 26,* 219–228.

Wynne, L., Ryckoff, I., Day, J., & Hirsch, S. (1958). Pseudo-mutuality in the family relations of schizophrenics. *Psychiatry, 21,* 205–220.

Wynne, L., Shields, C., & Sirkin, M. (1992). Illness, family theory, and family therapy: I. Conceptual issues. *Family Process, 31,* 3–18.

Yalom, I. (1995). *The theory and practice of group psychotherapy* (4th ed.). New York: Basic Books.

Yontef, G., & Simkin, J. (1989). Gestalt therapy. In R. Corsini & D. Wedding (Eds.), *Current psychotherapies* (4th ed.) (pp. 323–361). Itasca, IL: Peacock.

Name Index

Subject Index

Page numbers followed by an *f* or *t* indicate figures and tables.